Boys 'n' Bikes

Behind the scenes of professional cycling heroes

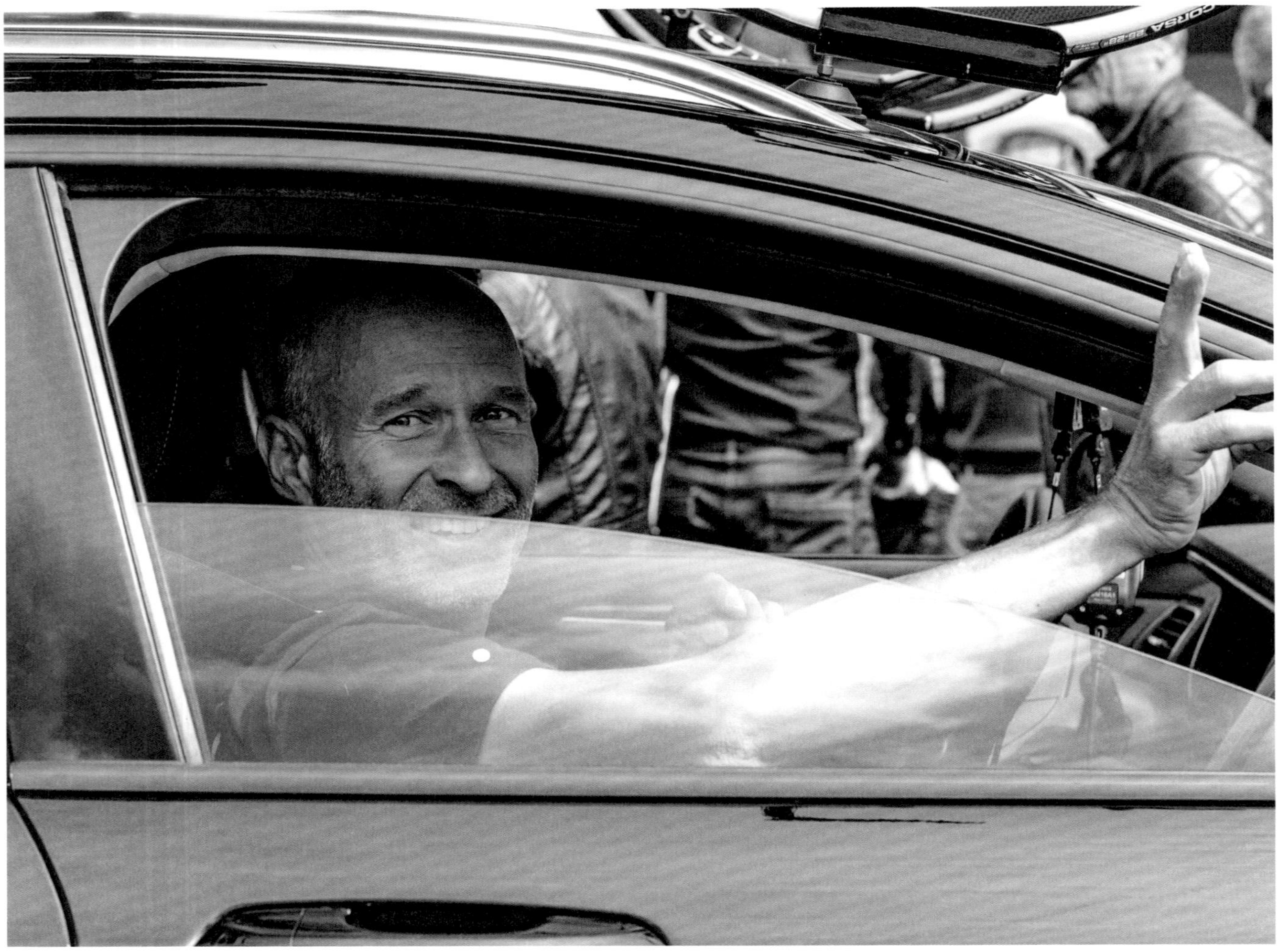

Welcome

Regennasse Straßen, huckelige Kopfsteinpflaster, kurvige Pässe, die sich schier endlos schlängeln, und Berg-Etappen, die alles abfordern: Das sind die Bedingungen, denen sich Profi-Radsportler stellen. Immer und immer wieder. Weil sie eine Passion und Willenskraft in sich tragen, die täglich wieder aufs Neue erstaunen und die Hingabe für die schönste Sportart der Welt erahnen lassen. Dieses Buch nimmt Sie mit hinter die Kulissen einiger der spannendsten Rennen, die wir im Jahr 2016 begleitet haben. Was wir erlebt haben - die atemberaubende Schönheit der Landschaften, die unterschiedlichsten Rennanforderungen, die Highlights und die Magie der Tour de France mit ihren Spektakeln in Paris -, all das wollen wir mit Ihnen teilen. Unsere Begeisterung, unsere Leidenschaft und das Privileg, die Fahrer hautnah erleben zu dürfen. Ihren Rennalltag mit ihren Familien und ihren Fans, deren Begeisterung und Applaus nur so mitreißen. Ihre Verletzungen, die bei den immensen Herausforderungen schonungslos dazugehören. Ihre Manager und Mechaniker, ihre Physiotherapeuten und Köche. Ein ganzes Team steht hinter jedem Team. Es war mir ein persönliches Anliegen, den Radsport in seiner ganzen Breite allen Interessierten so nahezubringen, dass sie einen tiefen, beinahe intimen Einblick in diese faszinierende Welt bekommen. Blättern Sie durch dieses Bilderbuch und lassen Sie sich mitreißen von der Kraft und dem Speed, den wir für Sie eingefangen haben. BORA sponsert seit Jahren mit großem Engagement und Elan ein Radteam, das nun in der WorldTour fährt – nach diesen Fotografien werden Sie unsere Faszination verstehen und teilen.

Rain-drenched streets, bumpy cobblestones, curvy passes that seem to meander endlessly and mountain stages that demand everything: these are the conditions that professional cyclists crave. Again and again. Because they embrace a passion and willpower rejuvenated by every daybreak with new amazement and devotion for the most beautiful sport in the world. This book takes you behind the scenes of some of the most exciting races that we accompanied in 2016. What we have experienced – the breathtaking beauty of the landscapes, the most distinguished racing challenges, the highlights and the magic of the Tour de France with its spectacular showdowns in Paris – all of this we want to share with you. Our enthusiasm, our passion and the privilege to have experienced the cyclists so closely. The race routine every day with family and fans and being carried away by their enthusiasm and applause. Their injuries are part and parcel of the challenges. Their managers and mechanics, their physiotherapists and cooks. An entire team stands behind every team. It has become my personal calling to to bring all of cycling, its highs and lows, so close to all who are interested that they experience a deep, intimate insight into this fascinating world. Browse through this picture book and allow yourself to be carried away by the power and the speed that we have captured for you. For years now, BORA has shown great commitment and zeal in sponsoring a cycling team that now participates on the WorldTour – after seeing these photographs you will understand and share our fascination.

Rues trempées par la pluie et pavés inégaux, étapes de montagne et cols sinueux sans fin, les conditions rencontrées au quotidien par les cyclistes professionnels sont impitoyables. L'effort est continu. La passion et la volonté qui les animent, laissant entrevoir la dimension de leur engagement dans le plus beau sport du monde, ne cessent de nous impressionner. Ce livre dévoile les coulisses de quelques-unes des courses les plus palpitantes que nous avons eu le privilège d'accompagner au cours de l'année 2016. Beauté éblouissante des paysages traversés, diversité des conditions de course, moments forts et magie du Tour de France et de son spectacle final à Paris, nous avons eu à cœur de vous faire partager toutes ces expériences enivrantes. Notre émerveillement, notre passion et le privilège de vivre au plus près le quotidien des coureurs. Un quotidien partagé entre leur famille et leurs fans, porté par leur engouement et leurs applaudissements. Leurs blessures, lot indissociable de leur profession et de ses contraintes prométhéennes. Leurs directeurs sportifs, mécaniciens, soigneurs et cuisiniers. Derrière chaque équipe se tient une véritable écurie de course. Mon souhait était de présenter à tous les passionnés ce sport dans toute son étendue afin de les amener au plus proche de ce monde fascinant. Laissez-vous griser au fil de ces pages par les images de puissance et de vitesse que nous avons réussi à capturer. C'est avec engagement et dynamisme que BORA sponsorise, depuis plusieurs années, une équipe participant aujourd'hui au WorldTour. Ces photographies ont pour objectif de vous faire découvrir et partager notre fascination.

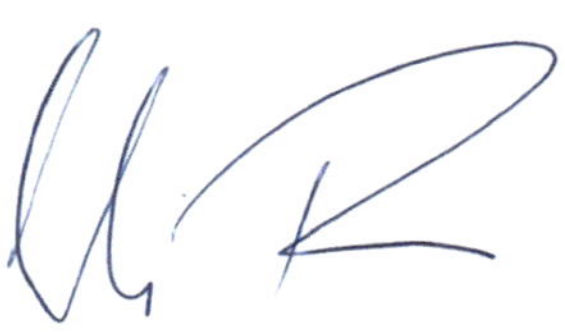

Willi Bruckbauer

Herausgeber und Gründer der BORA Lüftungstechnik
Editor and founder of BORA Lüftungstechnik
Gérant et fondateur de BORA Lüftungstechnik

Paris Roubaix

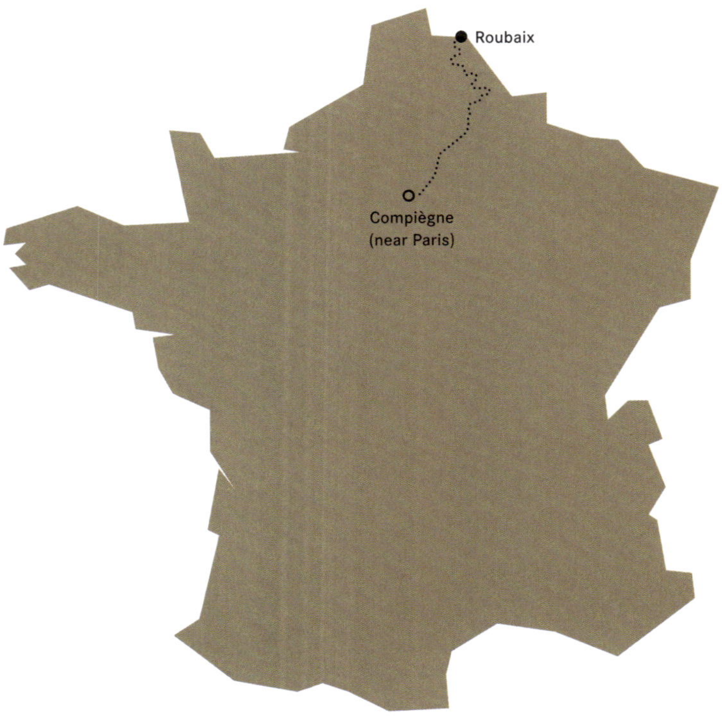

Die Königin der Klassiker wird nicht umsonst die „Hölle des Nordens“ genannt, ihre Kopfsteinpflasterpassagen stehen für Blut, Schweiß und Tränen. Das Rennen endet traditionell im Vélodrome von Roubaix. **The queen of classic races is not called the 'hell of the north' for nothing. Its cobbled sections represent blood, sweat and tears. The race traditionally ends in the velodrome at Roubaix.** *La reine des classiques n'est pas appelée par hasard « l'enfer du Nord », car ses passages de pavés sont là pour le sang, la sueur et les larmes. La course finit traditionnellement au vélodrome de Roubaix.*

257.5

KILOMETRE

DATE: 10.04.2016

FIRST TOUR: 1896

DURATION: 05:51:53

43.907

KM/H AVG. SPEED WINNER

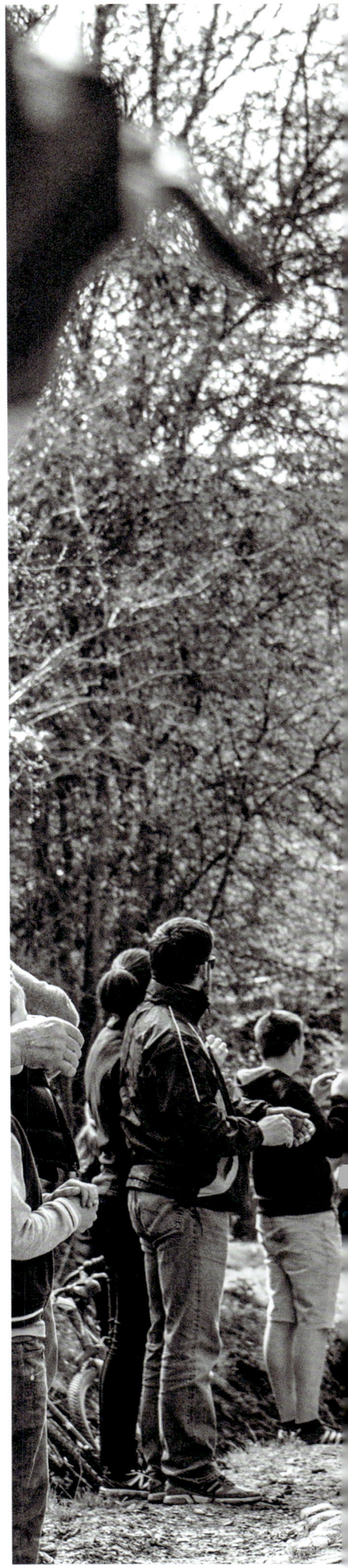

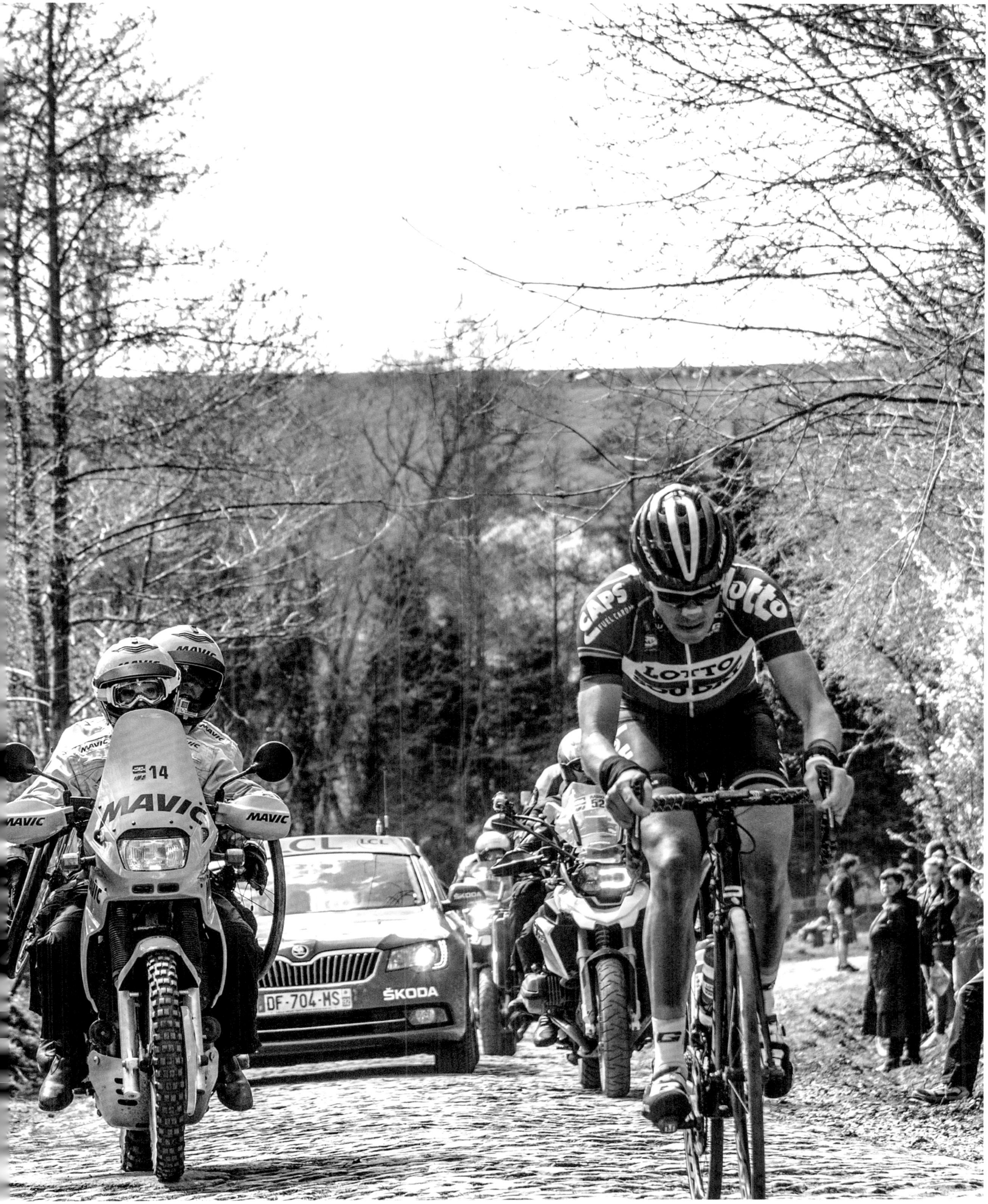

Lars Bak (Lotto Soudal), „alter Hase“ im Rennen. **Lars Bak (Lotto Soudal), an ‘old hand’ at racing.** *Lars Bak (Lotto Soudal), « vieux briscard » de ce tour.*

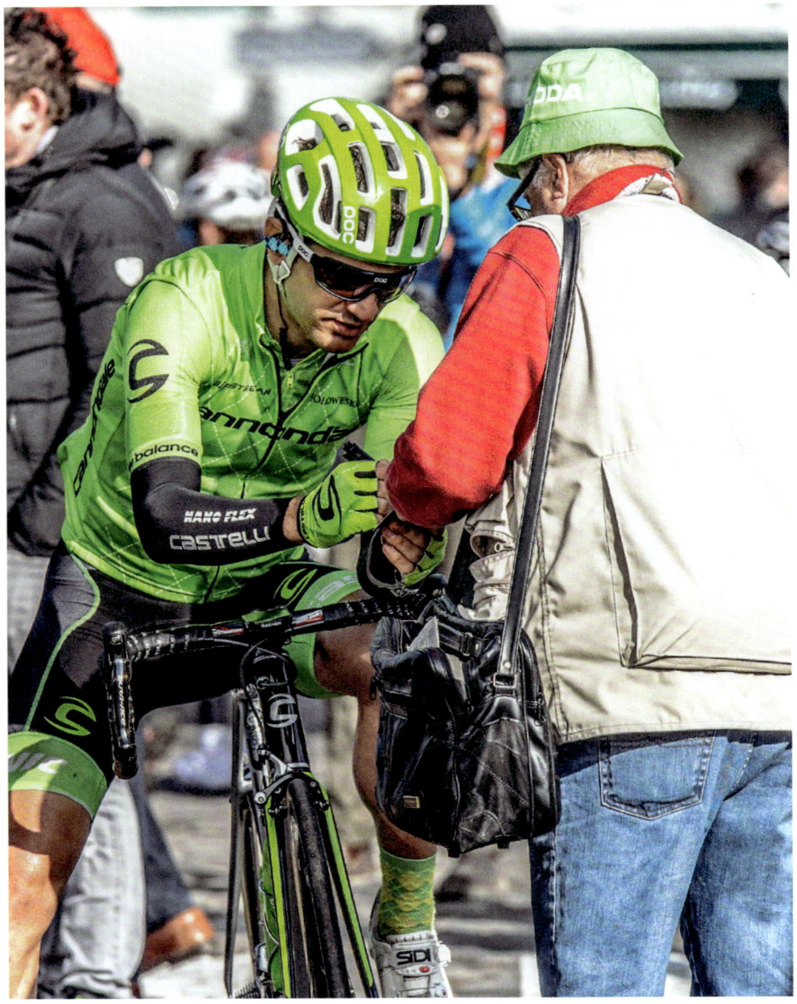
NANO FLEX
castelli
SIDI

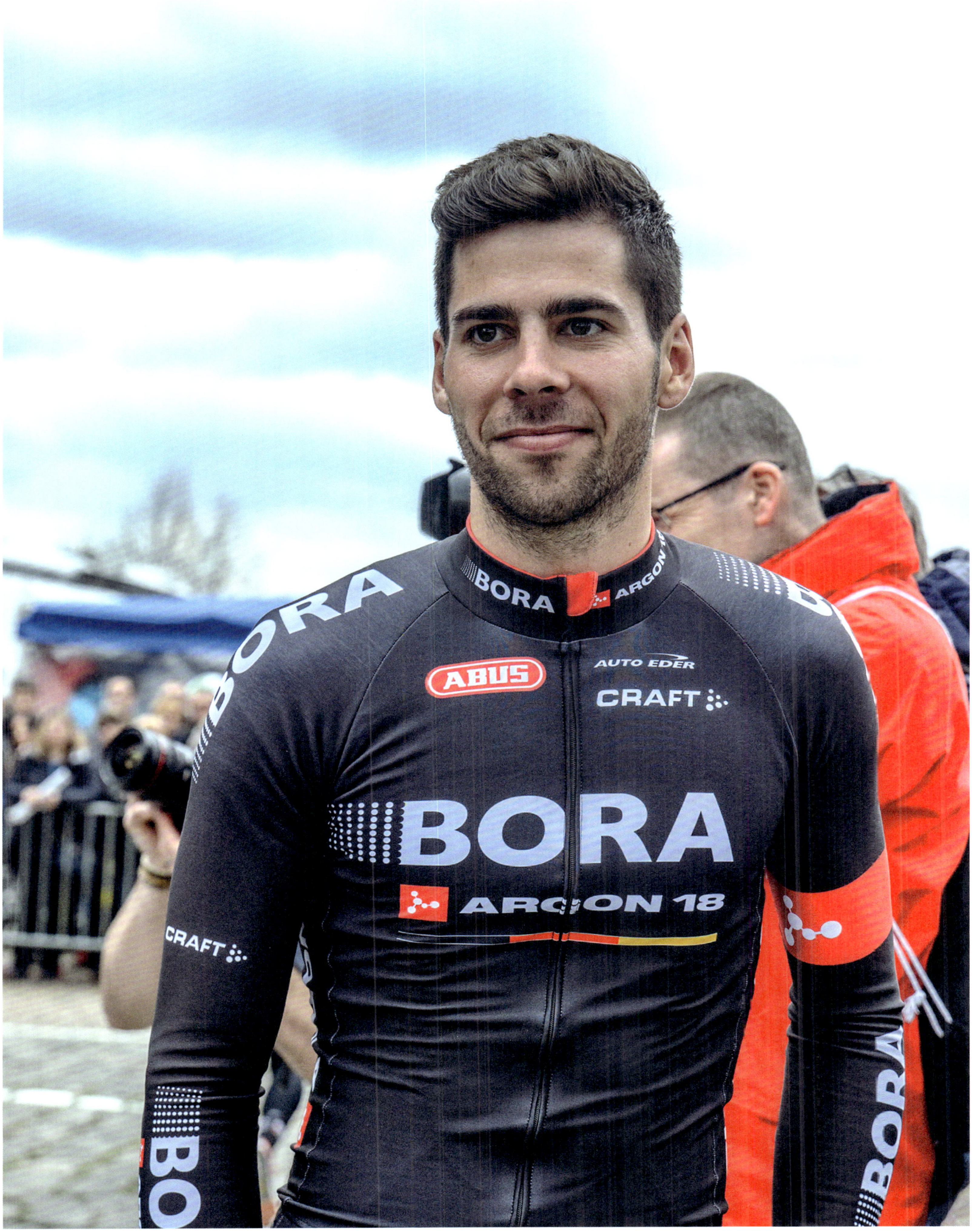

↑ Vor dem Start in Compiègne: Michael Schwarzmann (BORA - ARGON 18). **Before the start in Compiègne: Michael Schwarzmann (BORA - ARGON 18).**
Avant le départ de Compiègne : Michael Schwarzmann (BORA - ARGON 18).

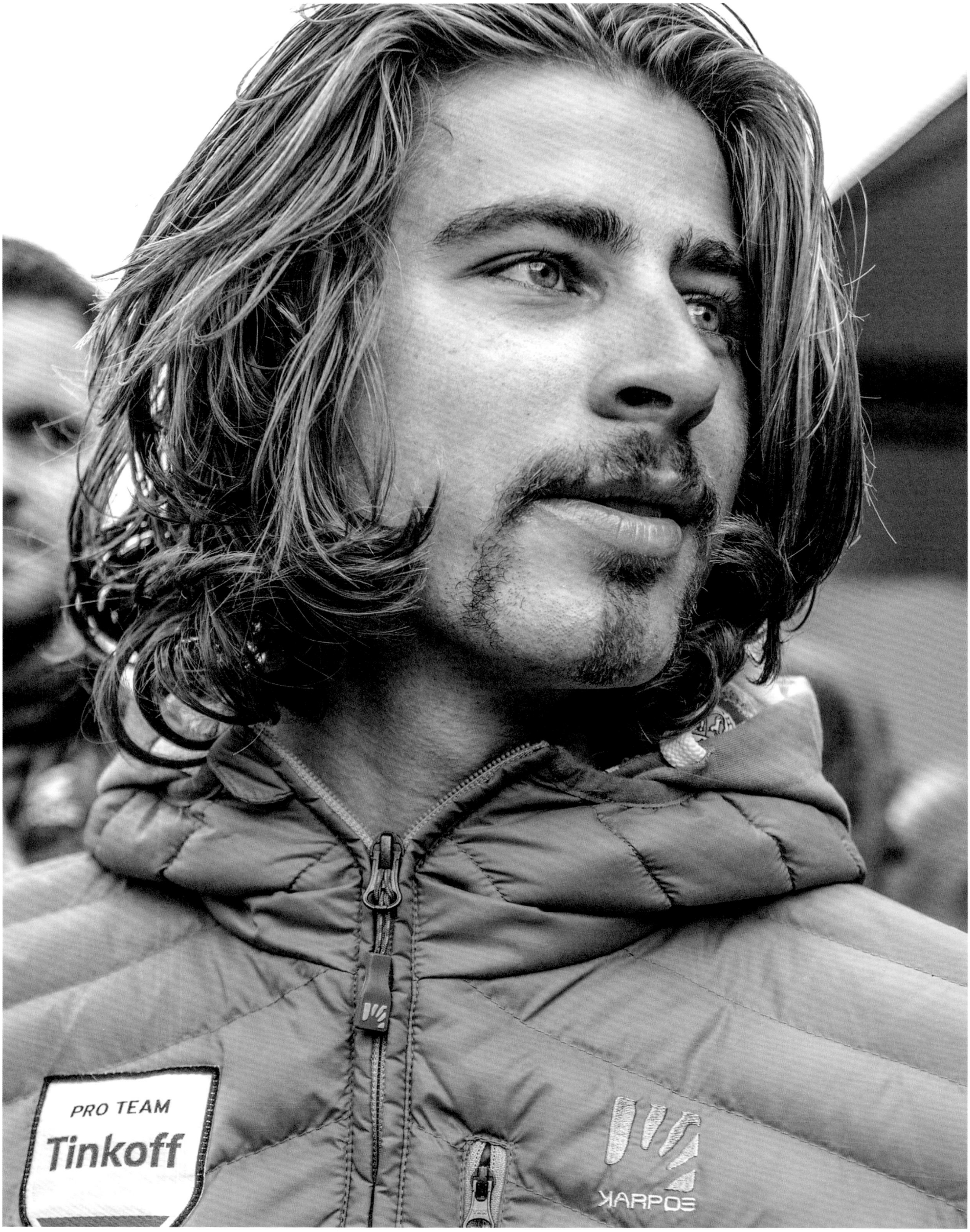

↑ Mehr als nur ein Radfahrer: Peter Sagan (Tinkoff). **More than just a cyclist: Peter Sagan (Tinkoff).** *Plus qu'un simple coureur : Peter Sagan (Tinkoff).*

↘ Mark Cavendish (Dimension Data) bei der Team-Präsentation. **Mark Cavendish (Dimension Data) at the team presentation.** *Mark Cavendish (Dimension Data) lors de la présentation des équipes.*

↗ Taylor Phinney (BMC Racing Team). **Taylor Phinney (BMC Racing Team).** *Taylor Phinney (BMC Racing Team).*

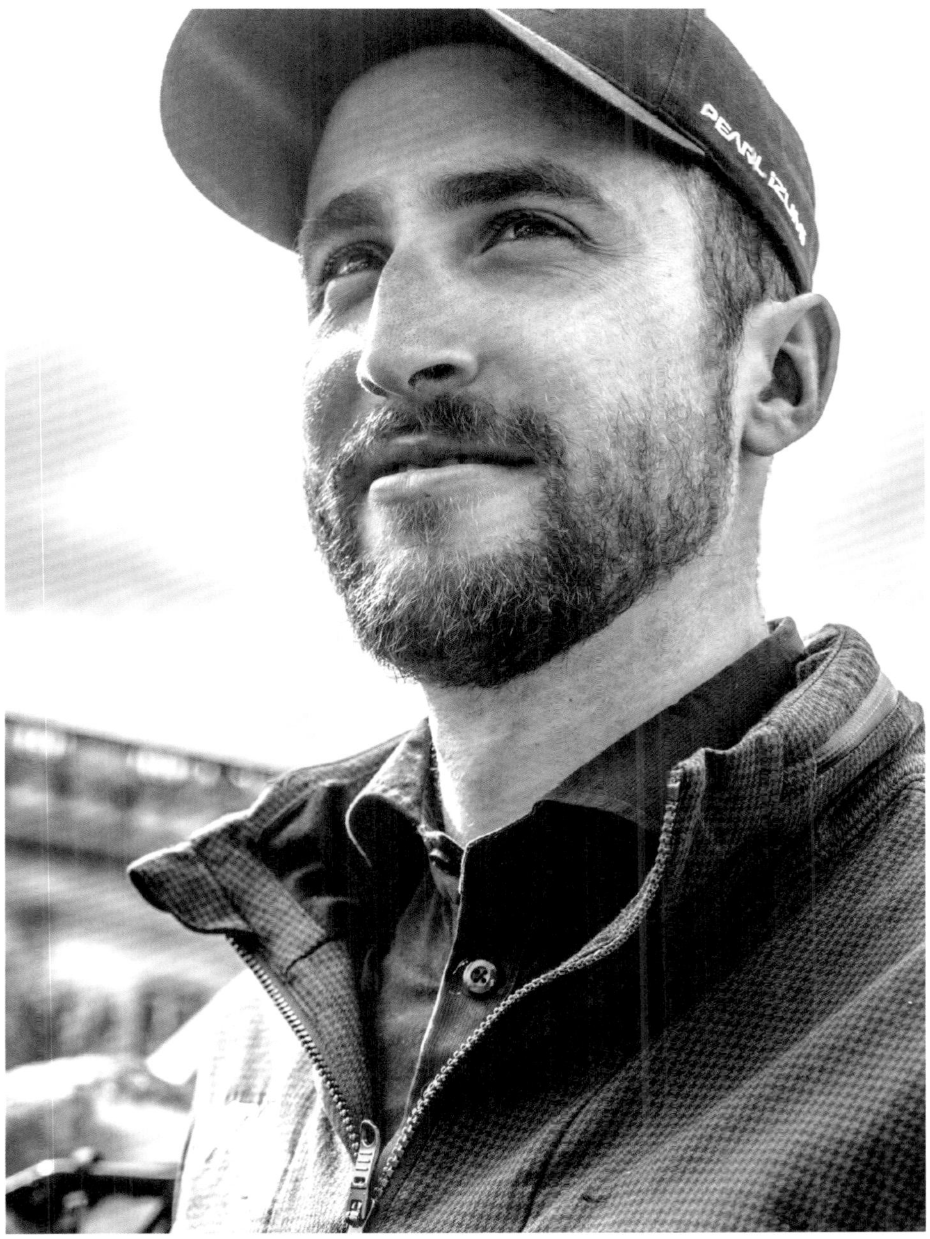

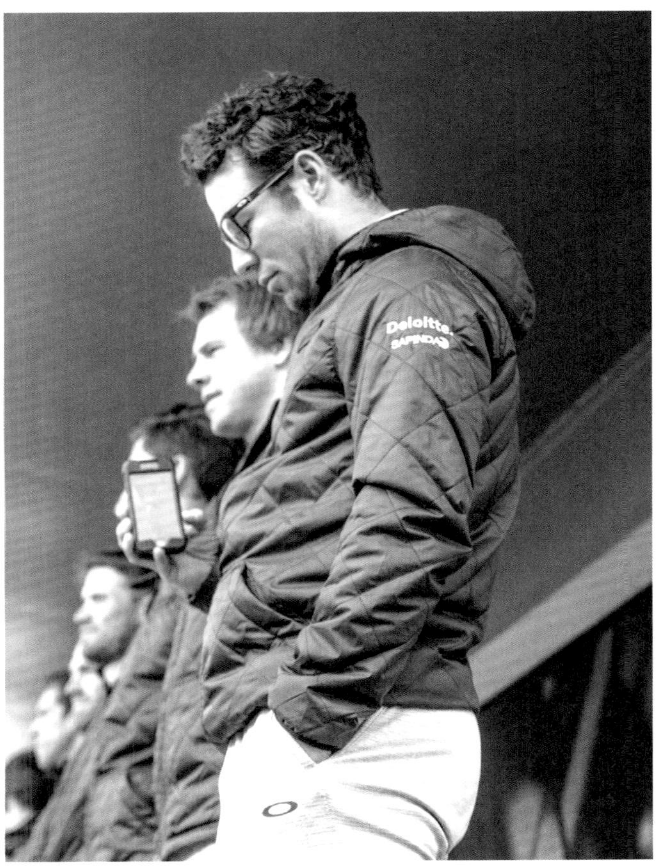
Deloitte.

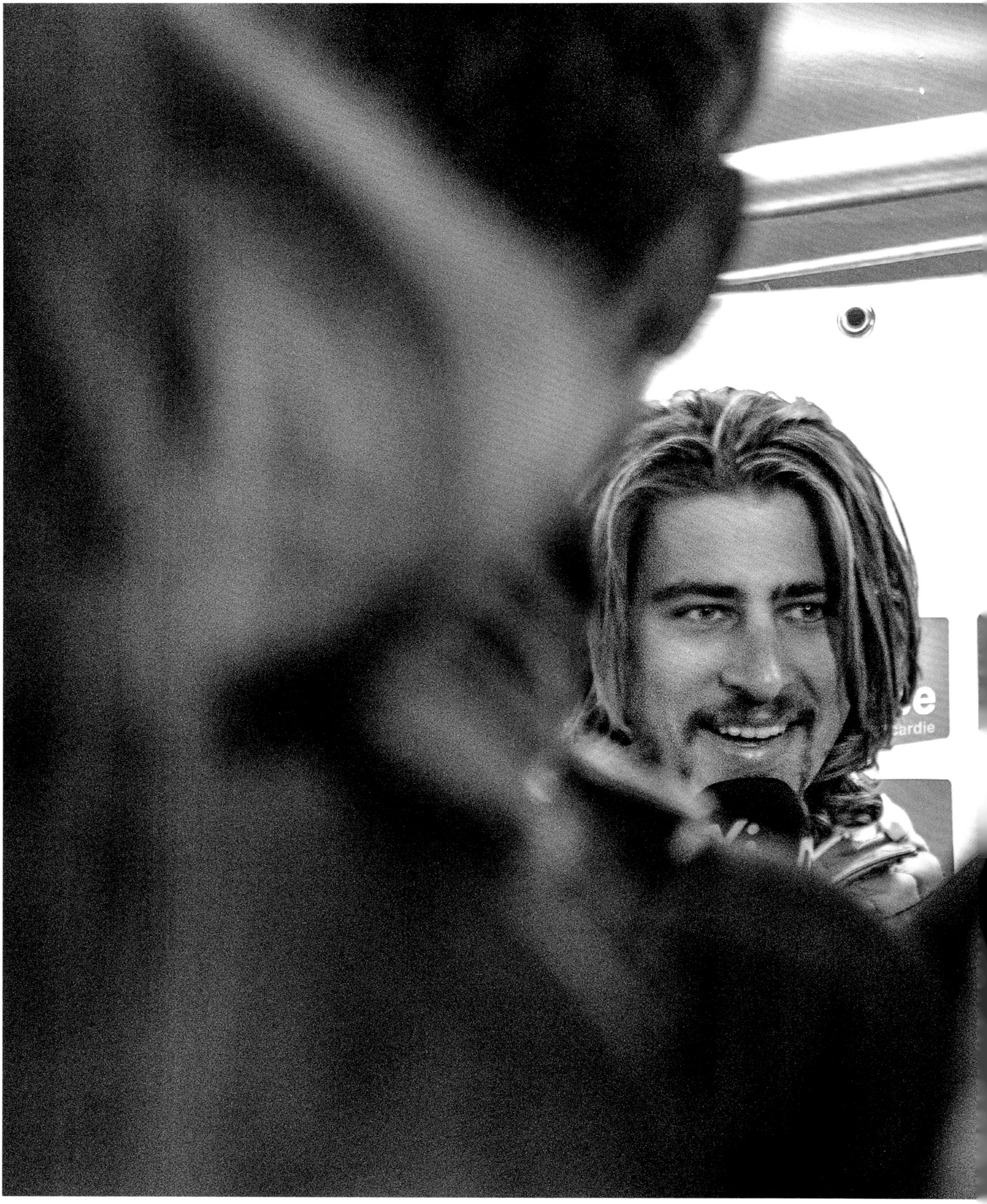

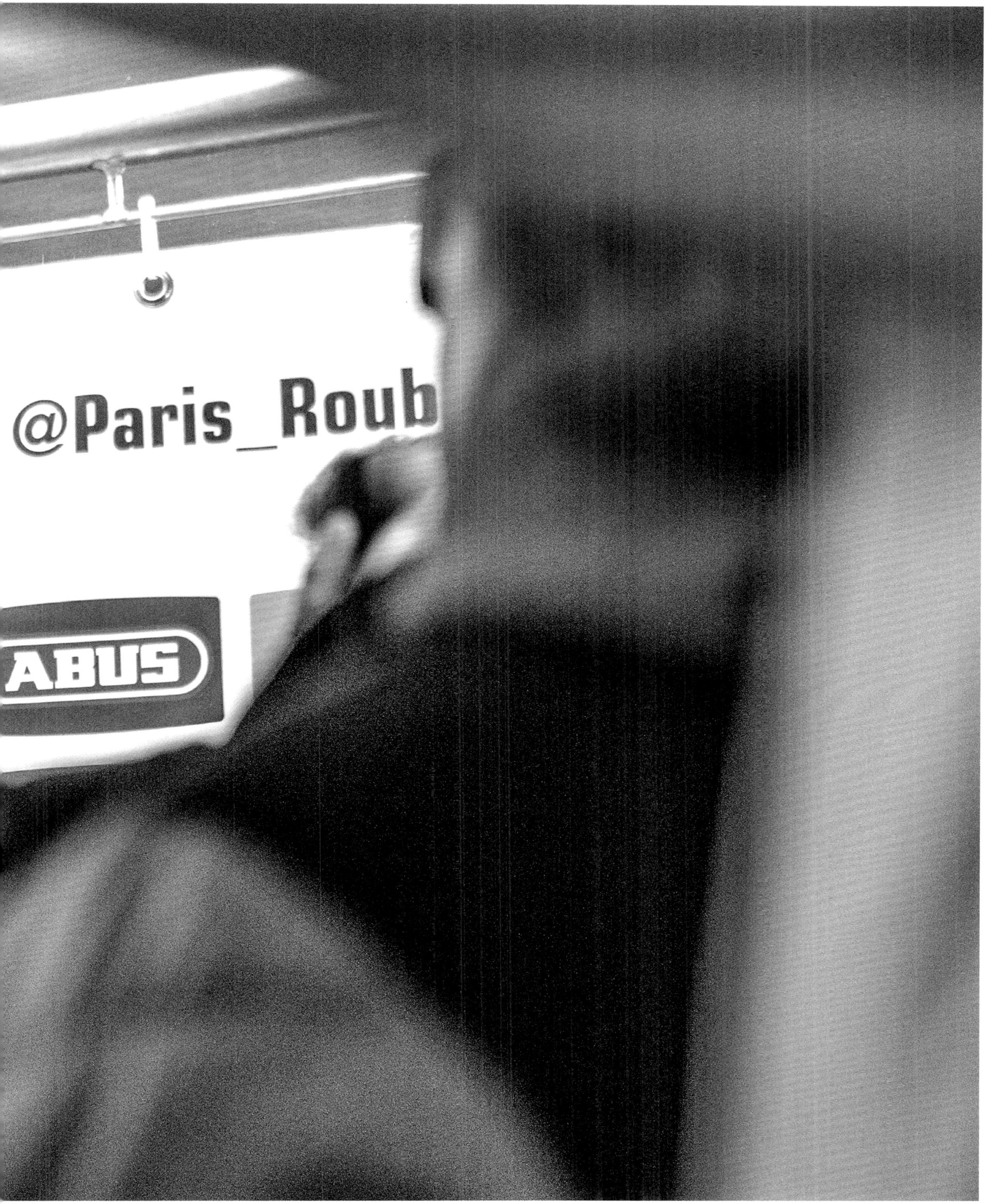

Immer im Mittelpunkt des Interesses: Peter Sagan (Tinkoff). **Always stealing the limelight: Peter Sagan (Tinkoff).** *Comme toujours sous les feux des projecteurs : Peter Sagan (Tinkoff).*

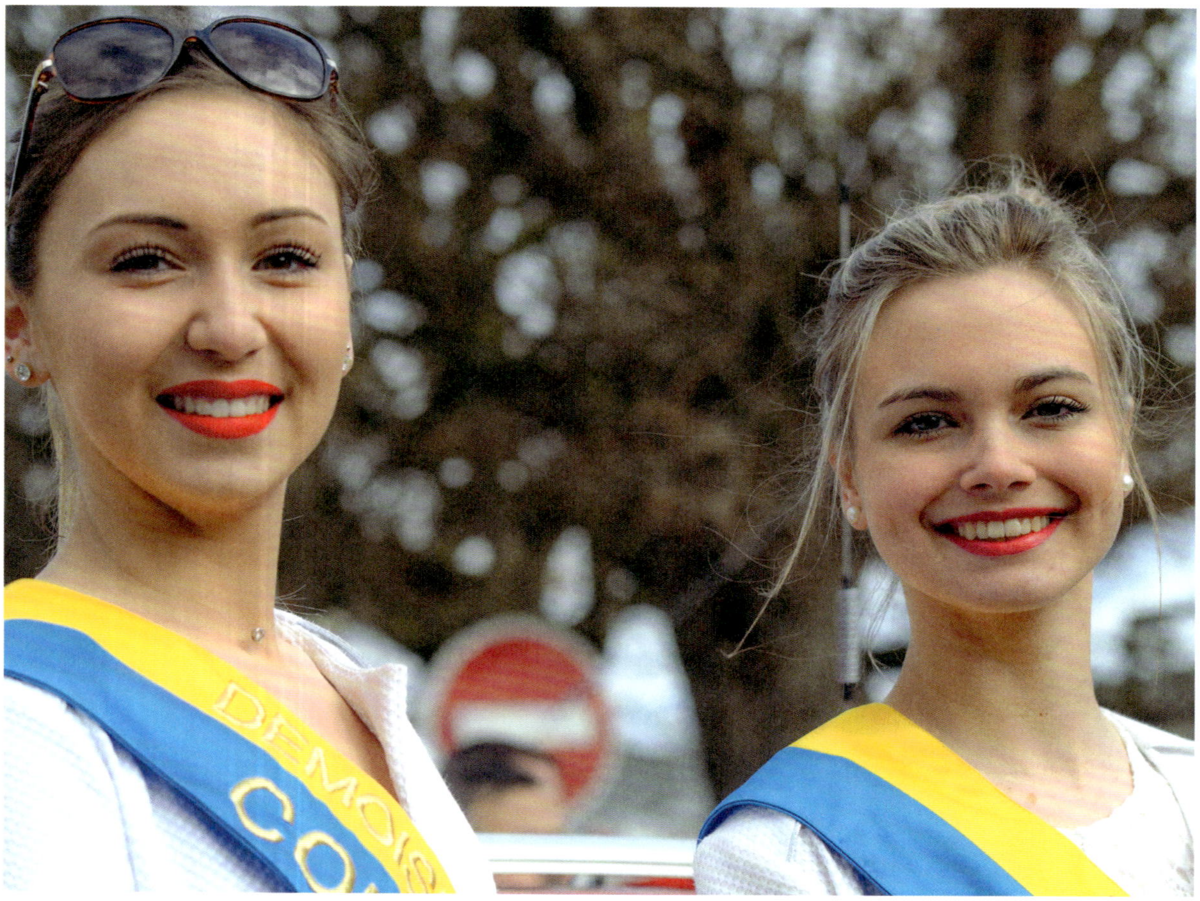

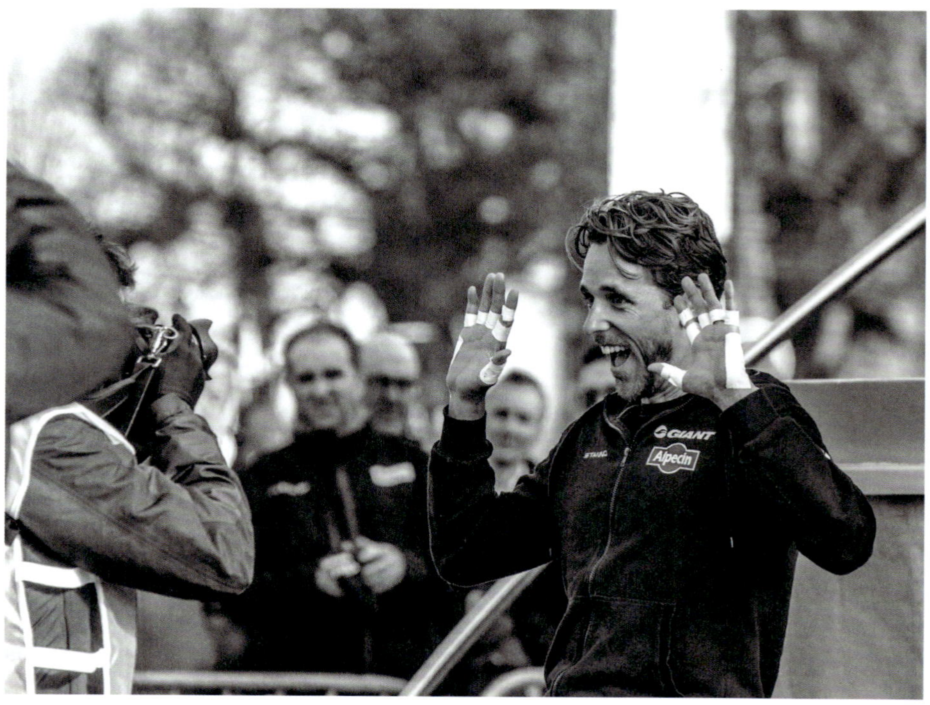
GIANT
Alpecin

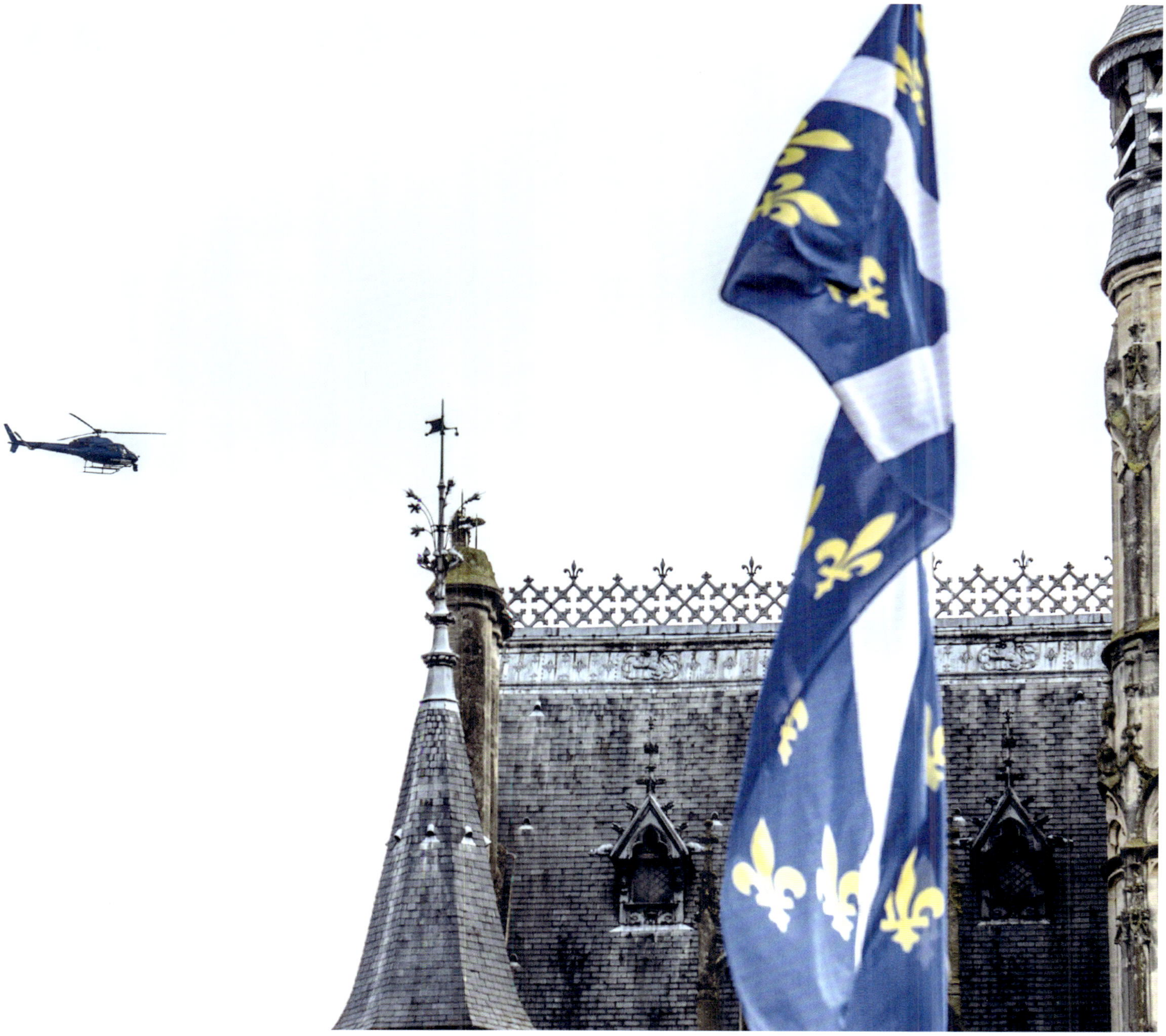

← Ein Lächeln für die Kameras: kasachische Fans und Koen de Kort (Team Giant-Alpecin). **A smile for the cameras: Kazakh fans and Koen de Kort (Team Giant-Alpecin).** *Un sourire pour la photo : des fans kazakhes et Koen de Kort (Team Giant-Alpecin).*

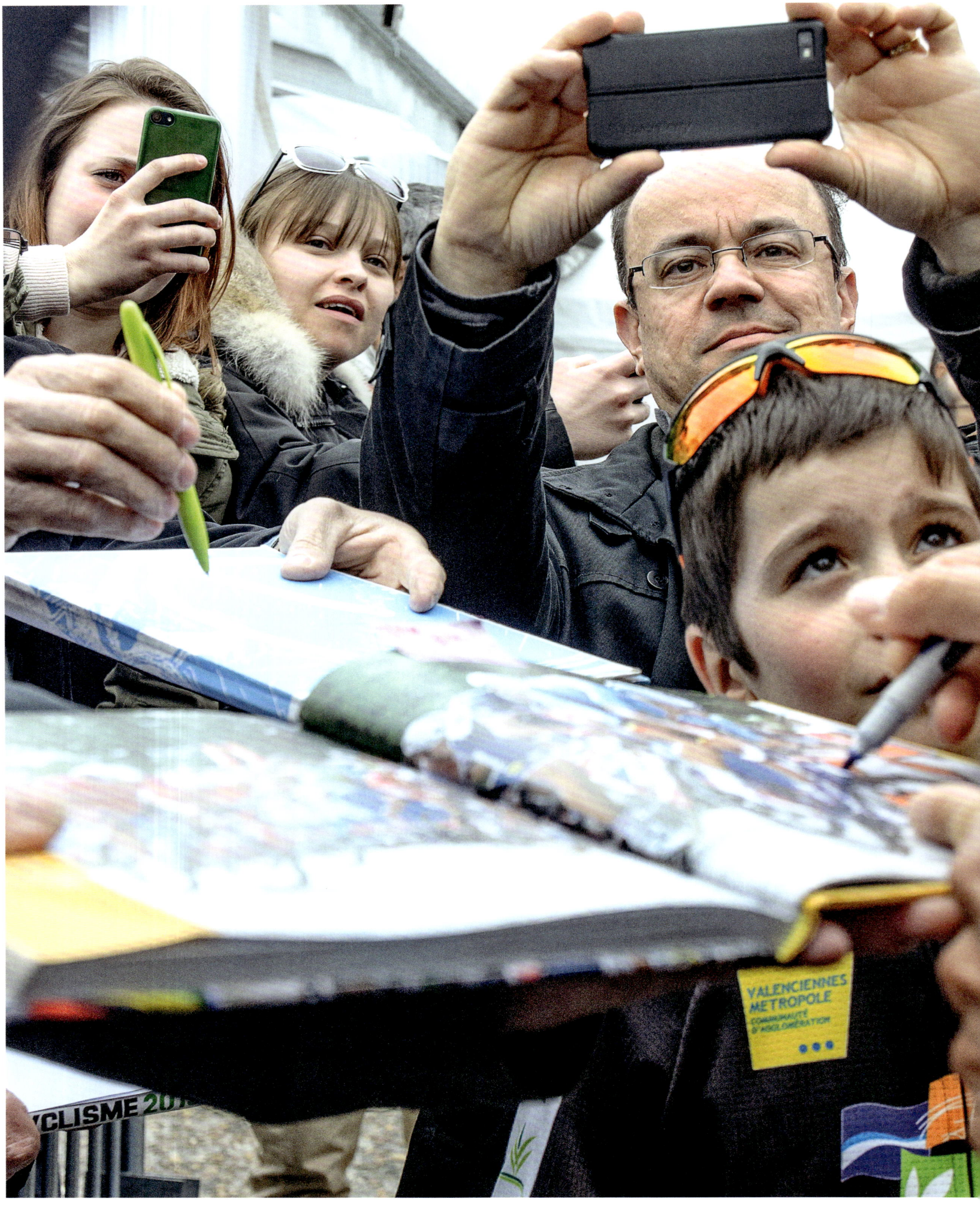
VALENCIENNES
METROPOLE
COMMUNAUTÉ D'AGGLOMÉRATION

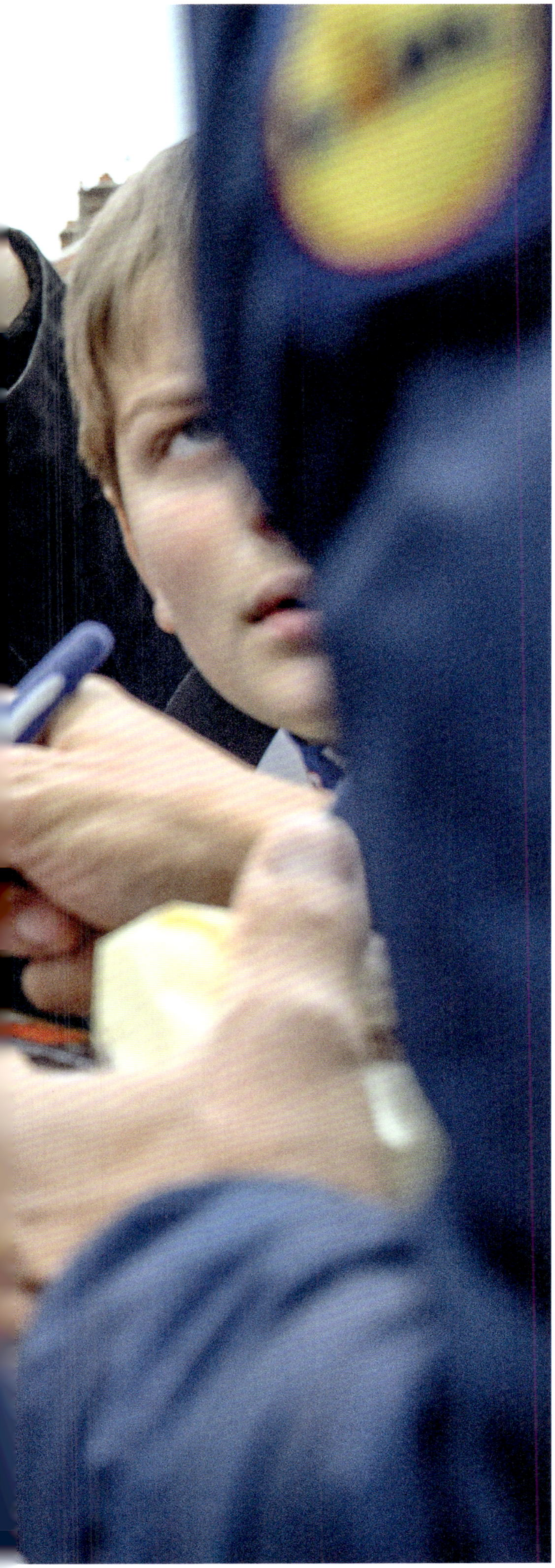

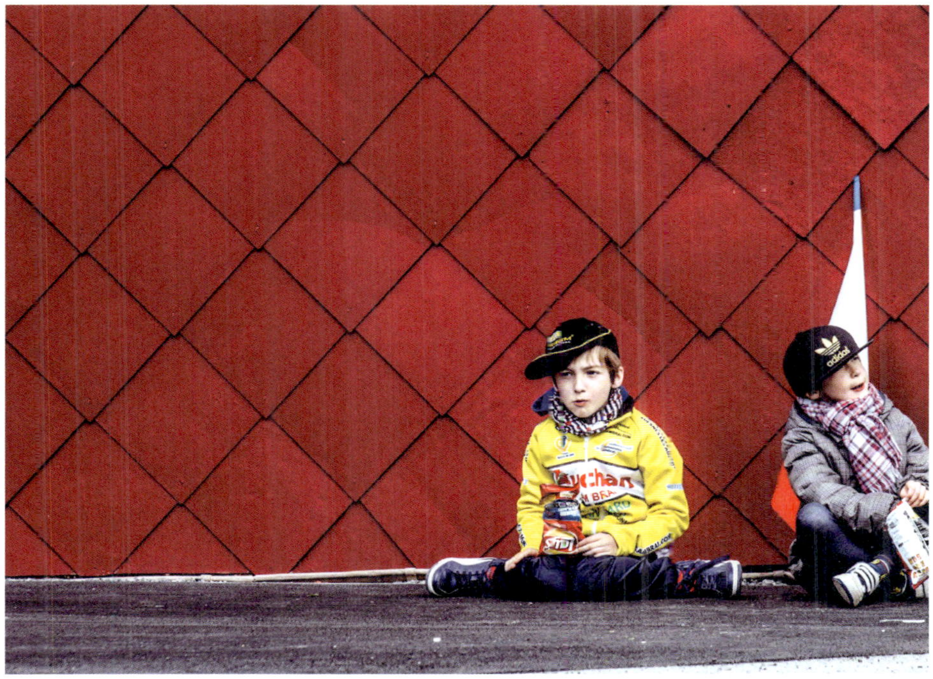

Autogrammstunde für Jung und Alt. **Autographs for young and old.** *L'instant des autographes pour jeunes et moins jeunes.*

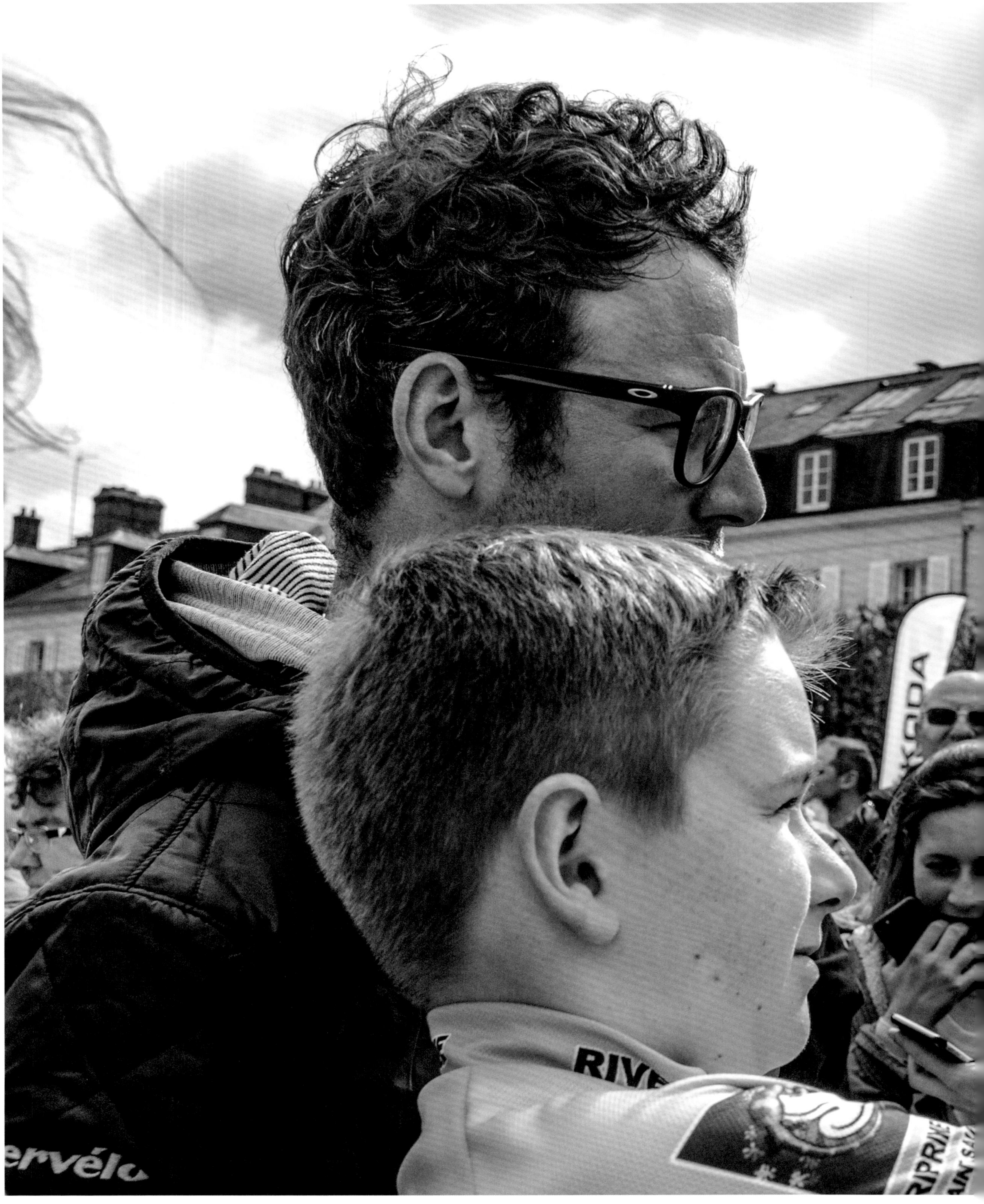

Selfie mit dem Star Mark Cavendish (Dimension Data). **Selfie with the star, Mark Cavendish (Dimension Data).**
Selfie avec la star Mark Cavendish (Dimension Data).

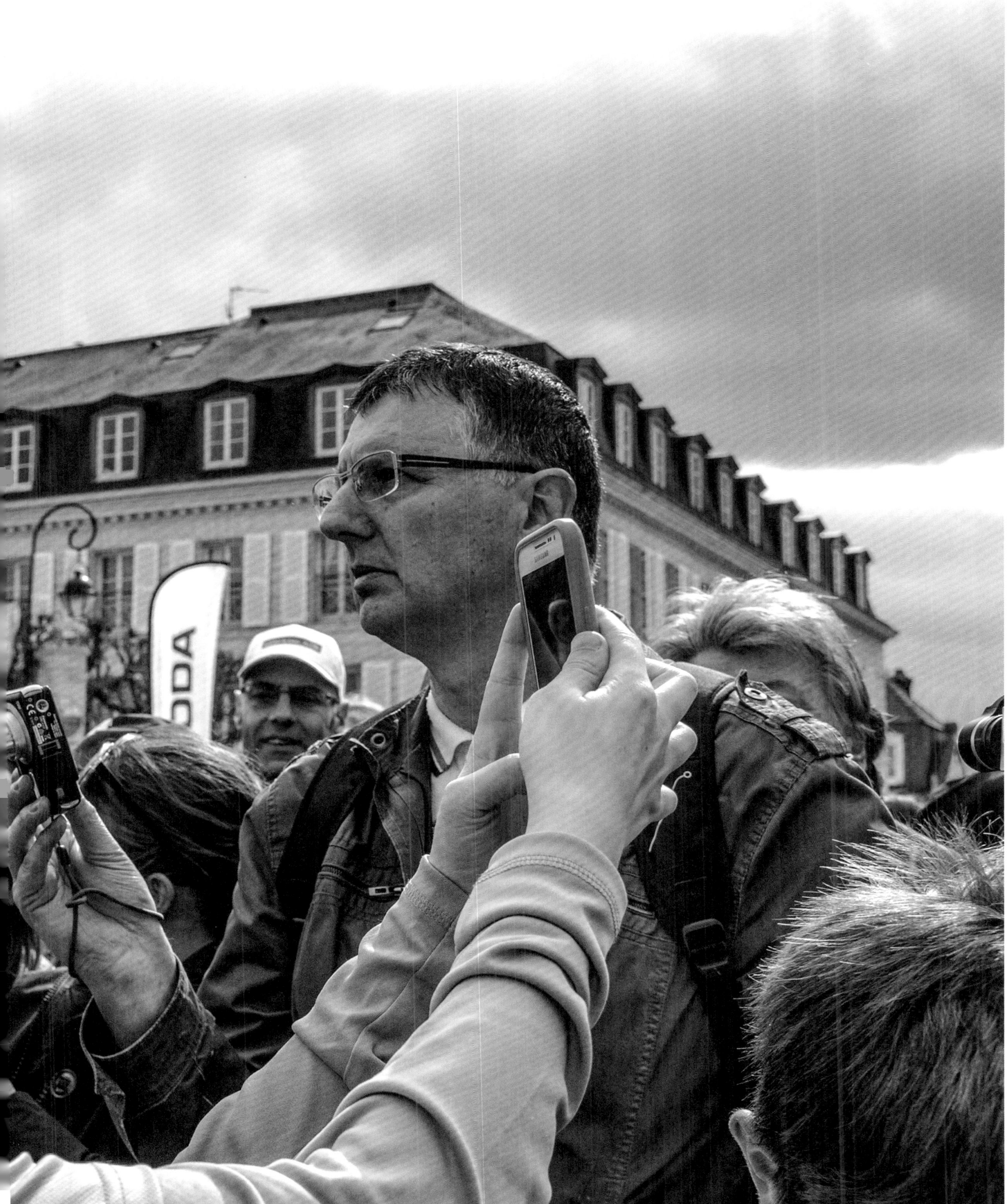
ODA

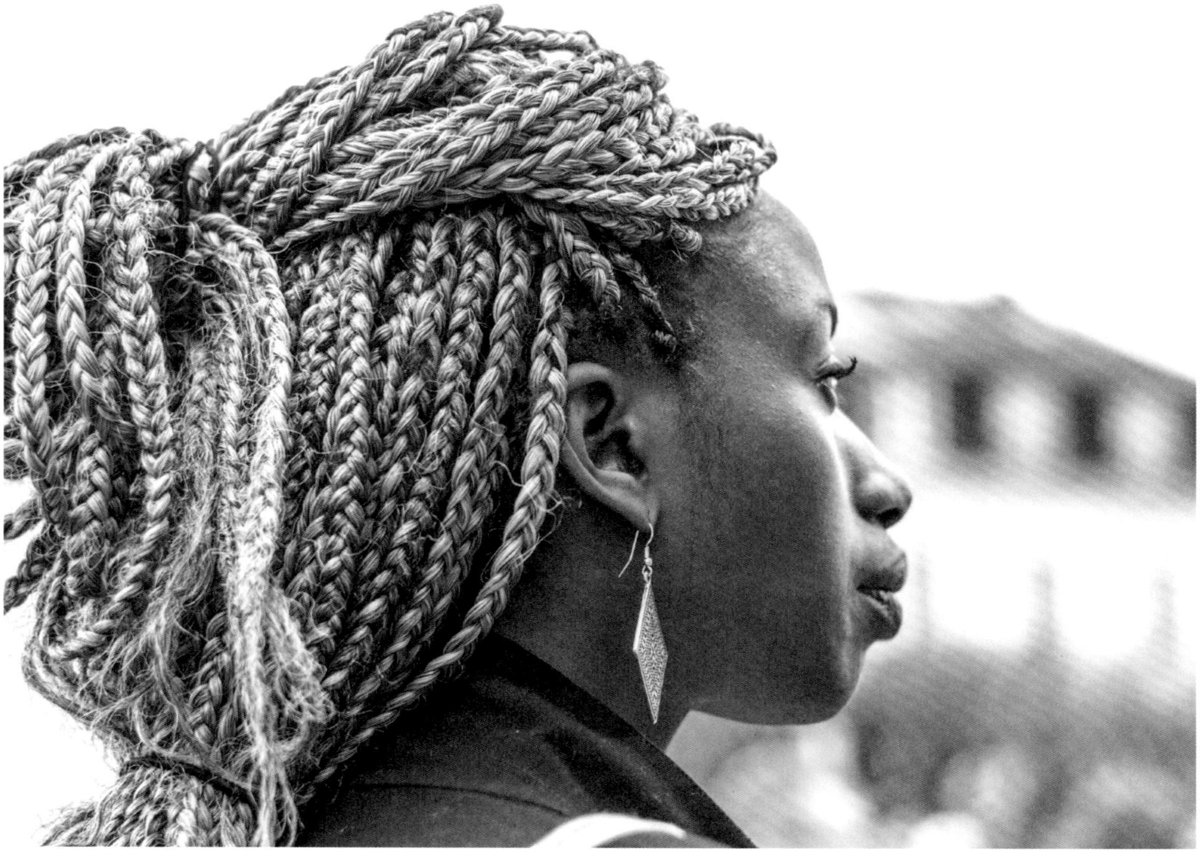

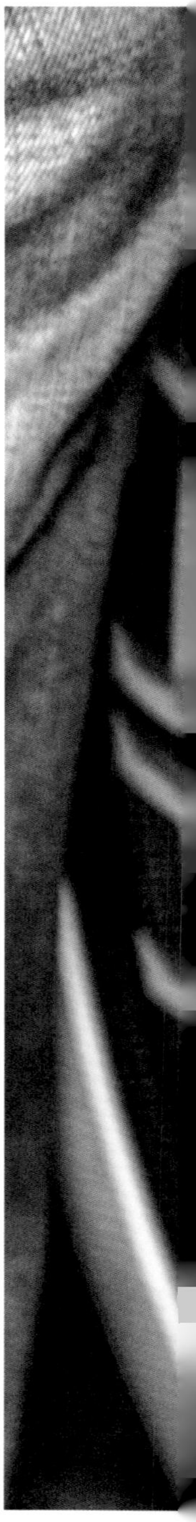

Konzentration, Anspannung, Vorbereitung: Sam Bennett (BORA - ARGON 18, oben rechts). **Concentration, tension, preparation: Sam Bennett (BORA - ARGON 18, top right).** *Concentration, tension et préparation : Sam Bennett (BORA - ARGON 18, en haut à droite).*

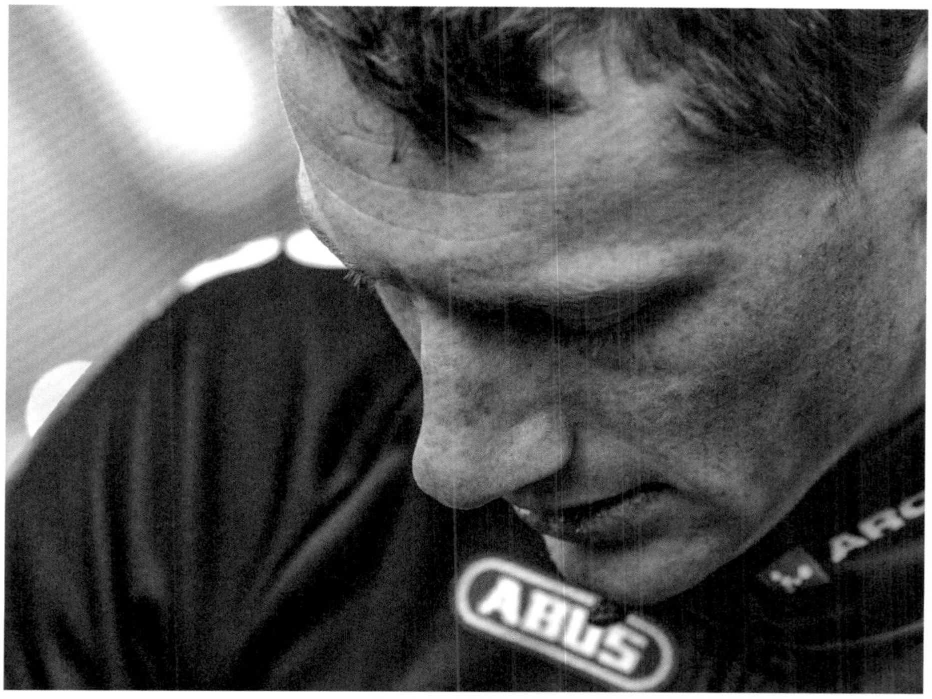
ABUS

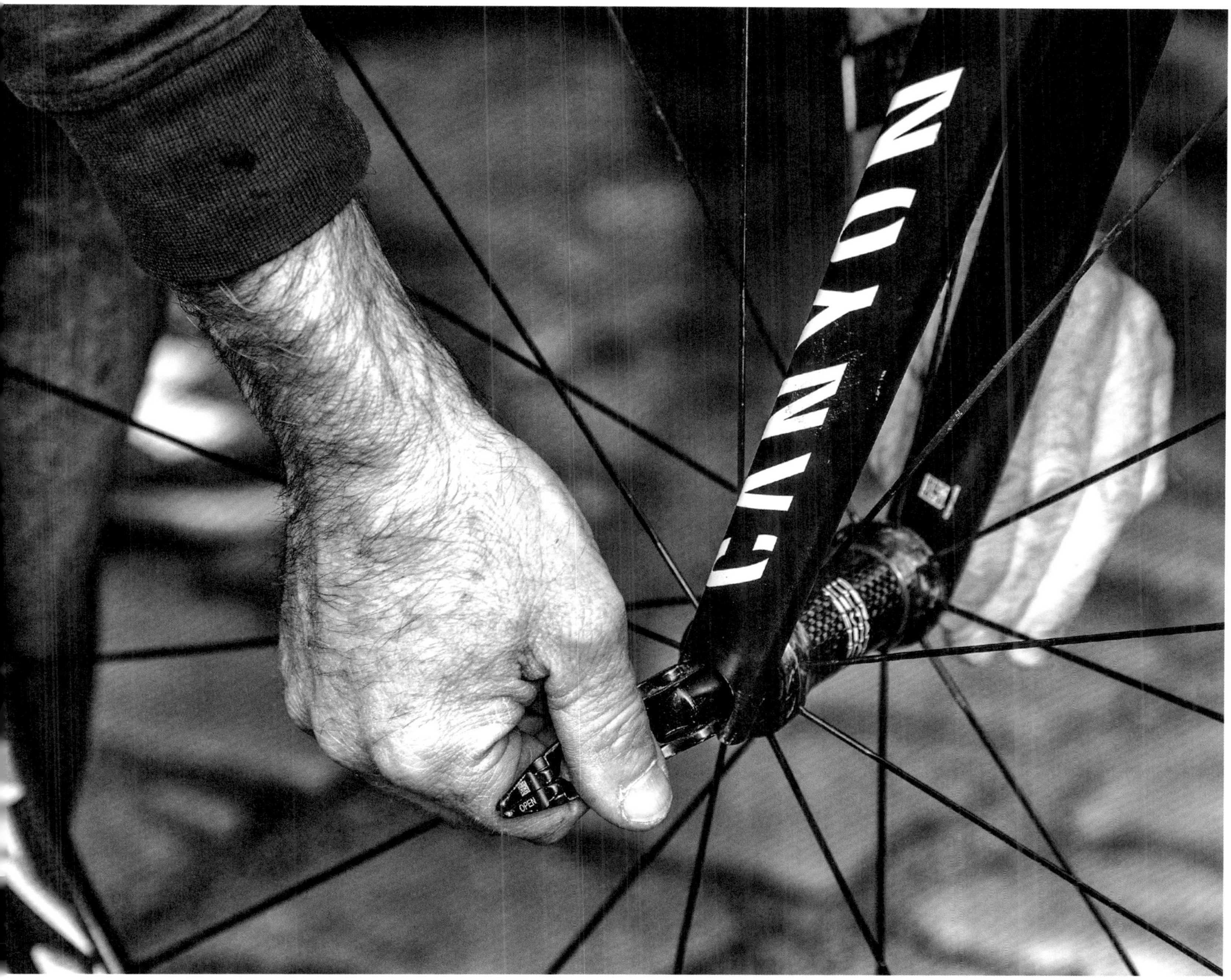
CANYON
OPEN

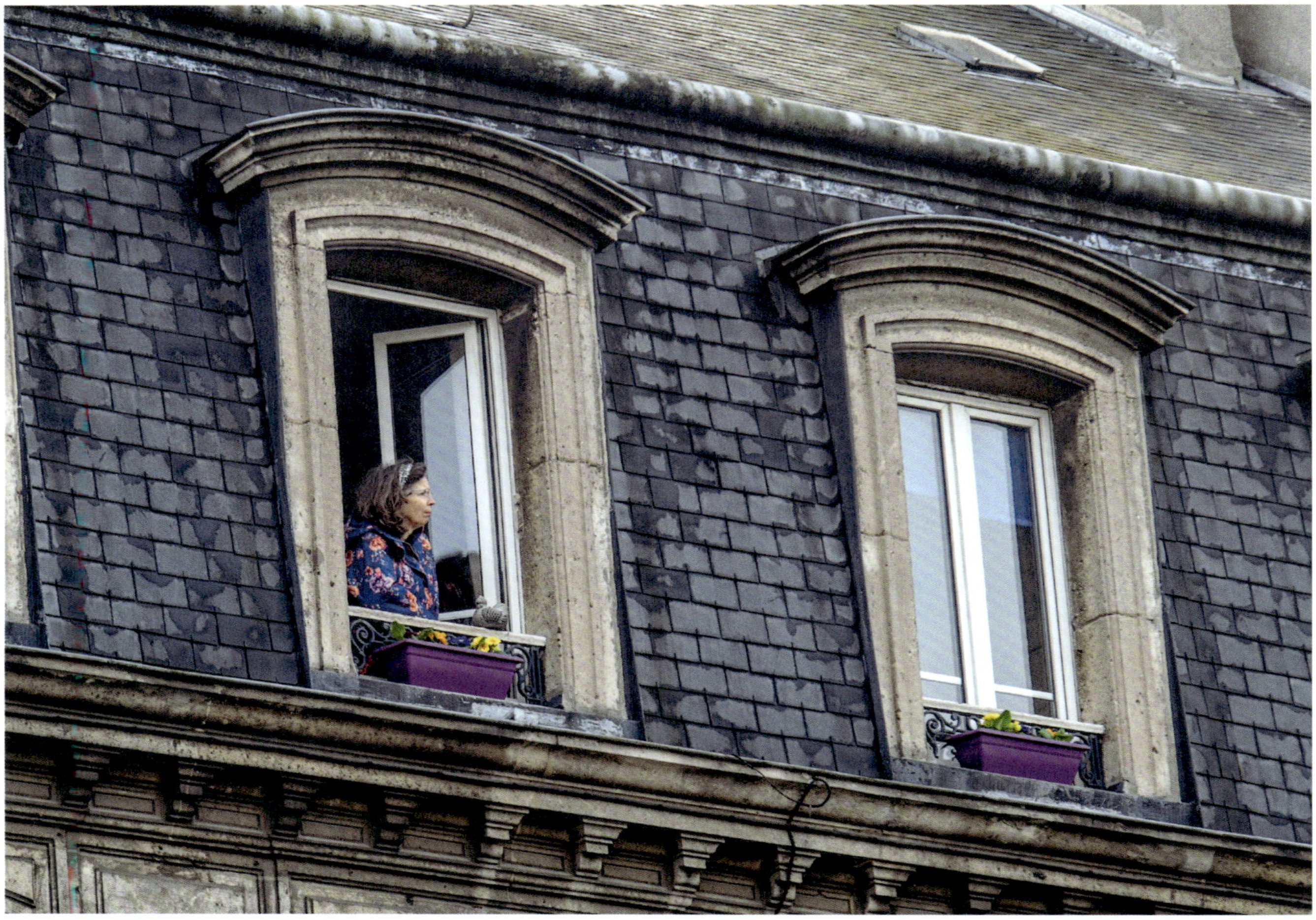

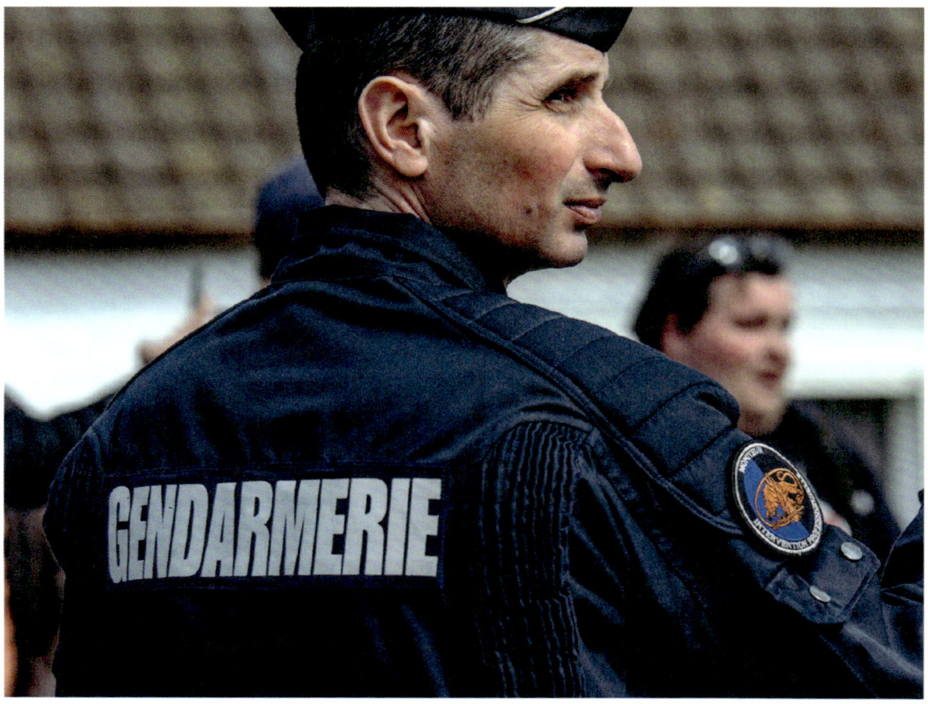

Und los geht's. Compiègne/Frankreich. **And they're off. Compiègne/France.** *Et c'est parti! Compiègne.*

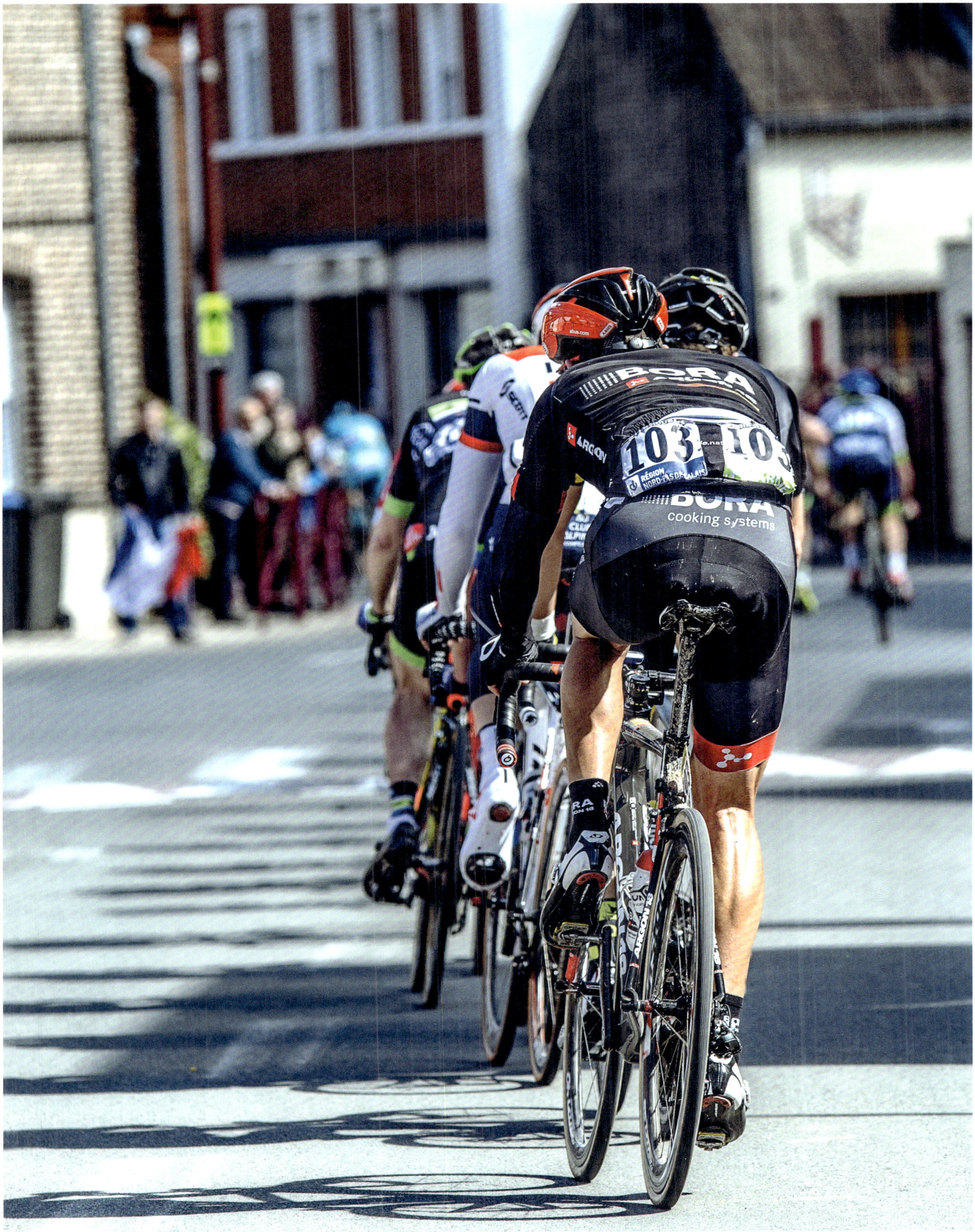
BORA
103
BORA
cooking systems

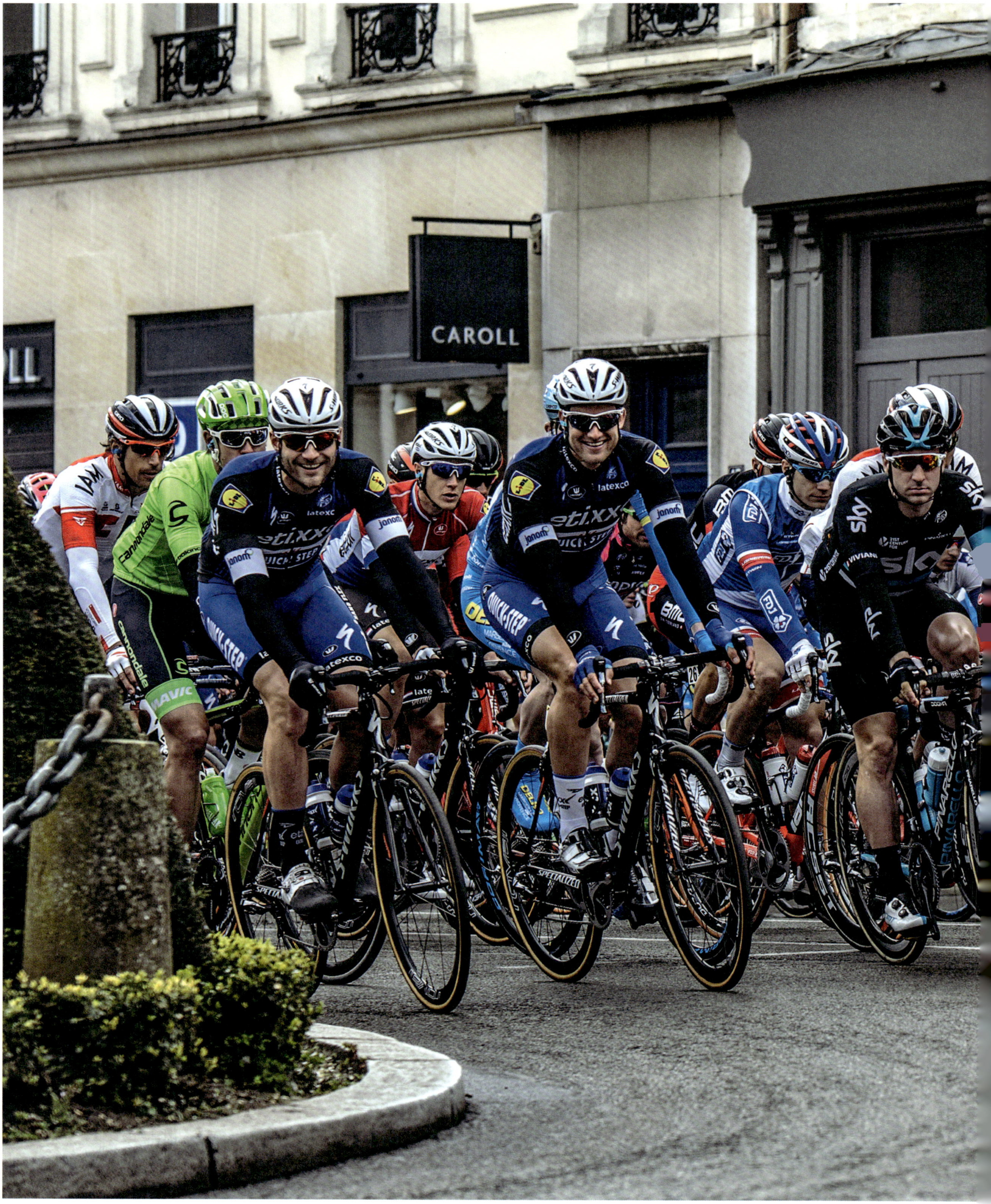
CAROLL

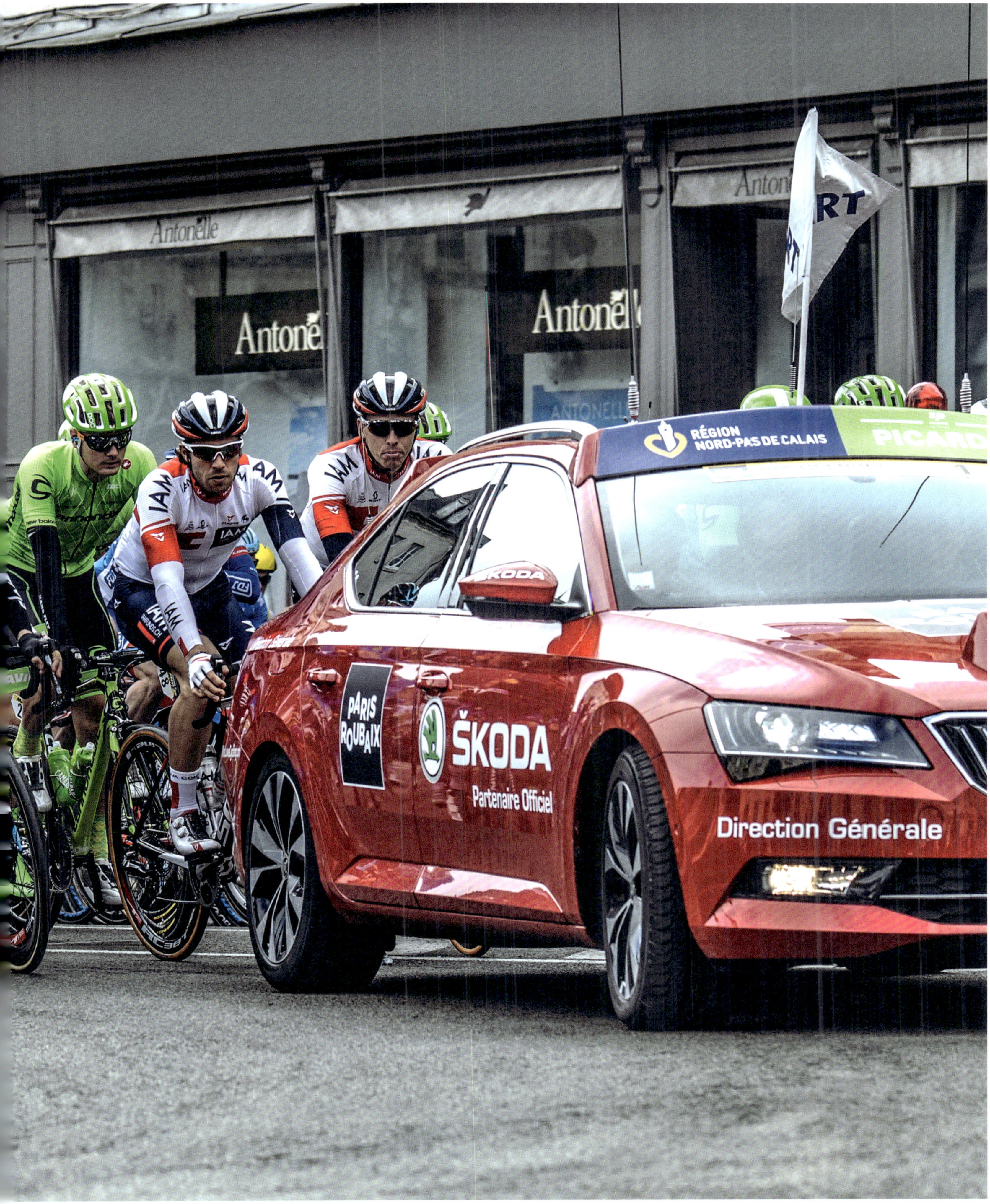

Tom Boonen (Etixx – Quick Step) am Start in Compiègne vorne. **Tom Boonen (Etixx – Quick Step) in front at the start in Compiègne.**
Tom Boonen (Etixx – Quick Step) devant, au départ de Compiègne.

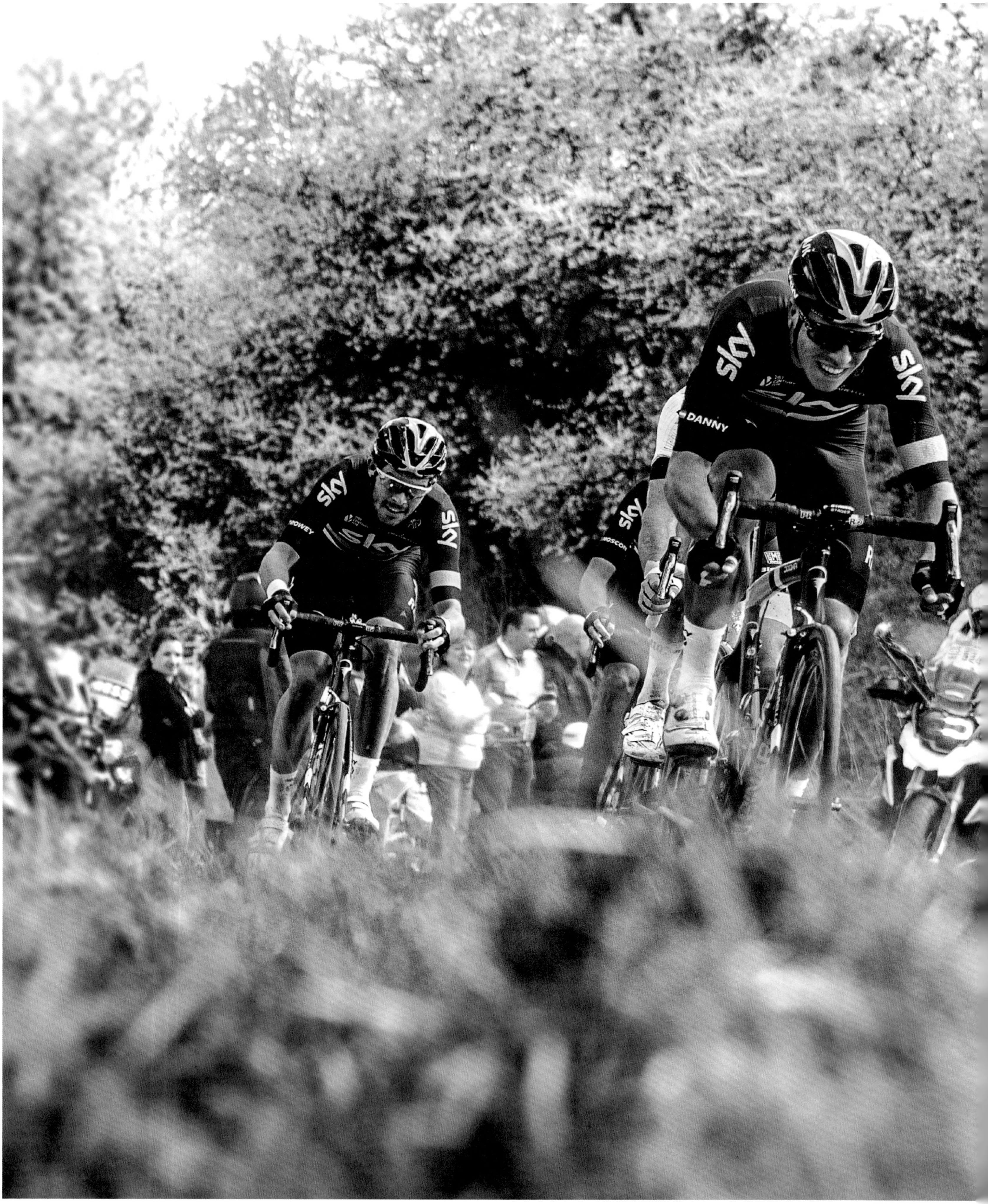
sky
DANNY

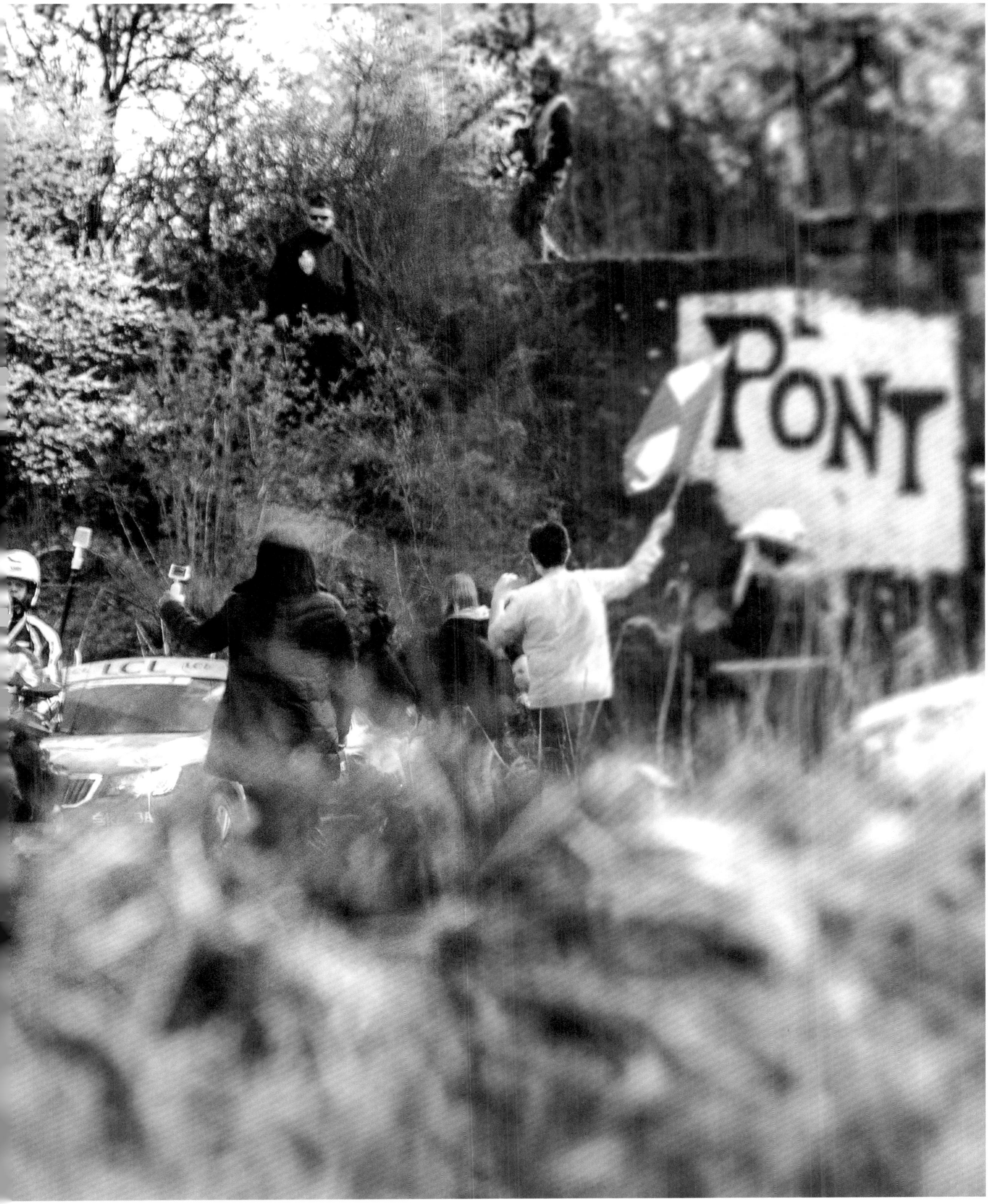

Team Sky macht Tempo: Danny van Poppel und Luke Rowe. **Team Sky dashes for position: Danny van Poppel and Luke Rowe.** *La Team Sky impose le rythme : Danny van Poppel et Luke Rowe.*

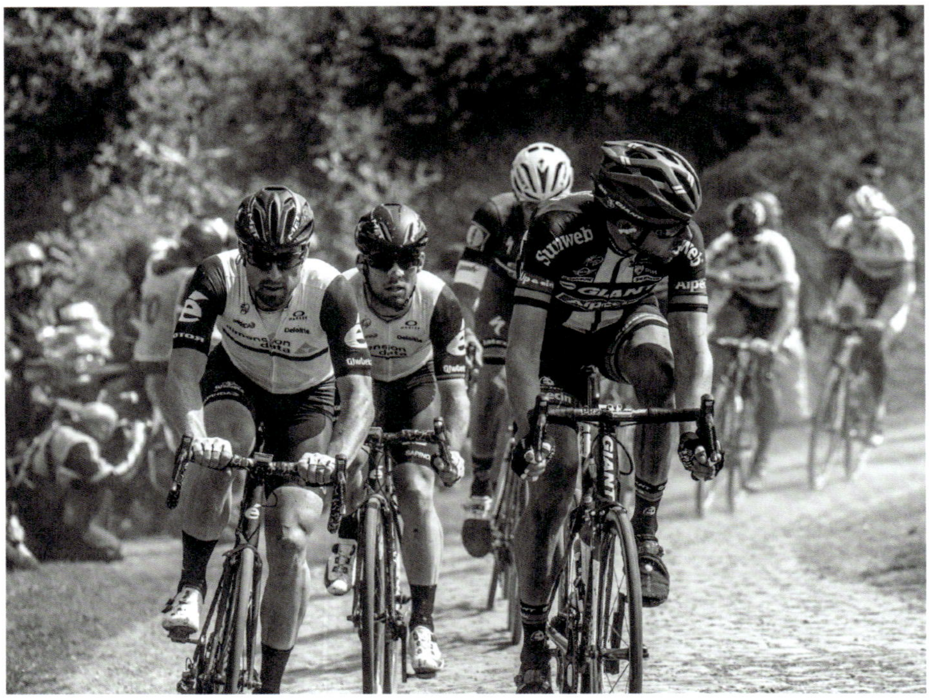

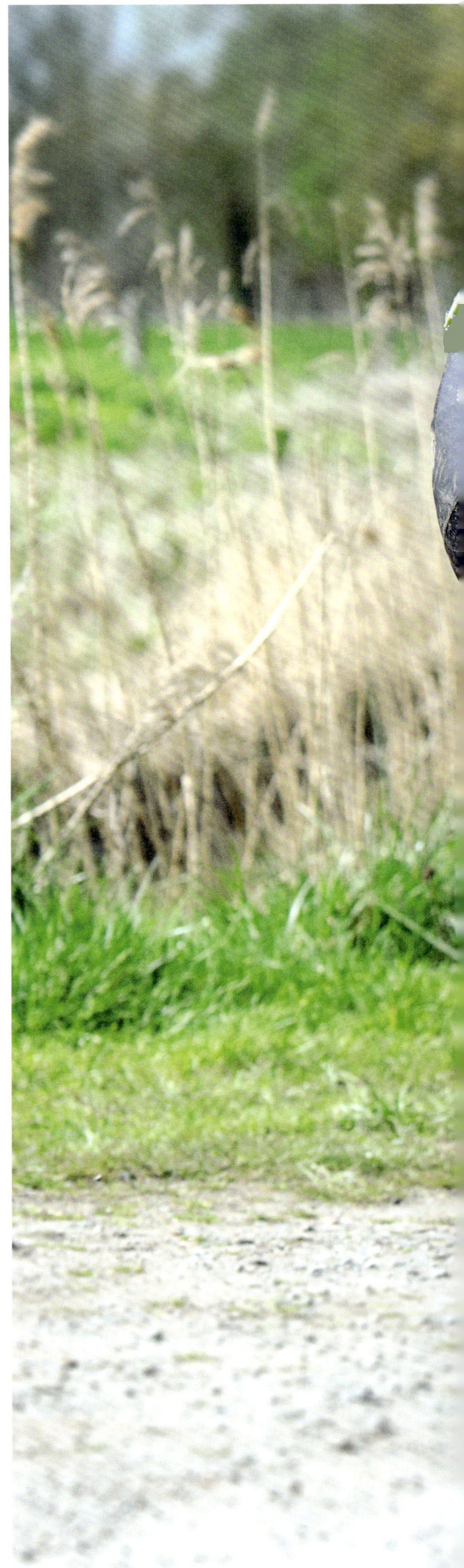

Herausforderung Kopfsteinpflaster. **Challenging cobbles.** *Les routes pavées : un vrai challenge.*

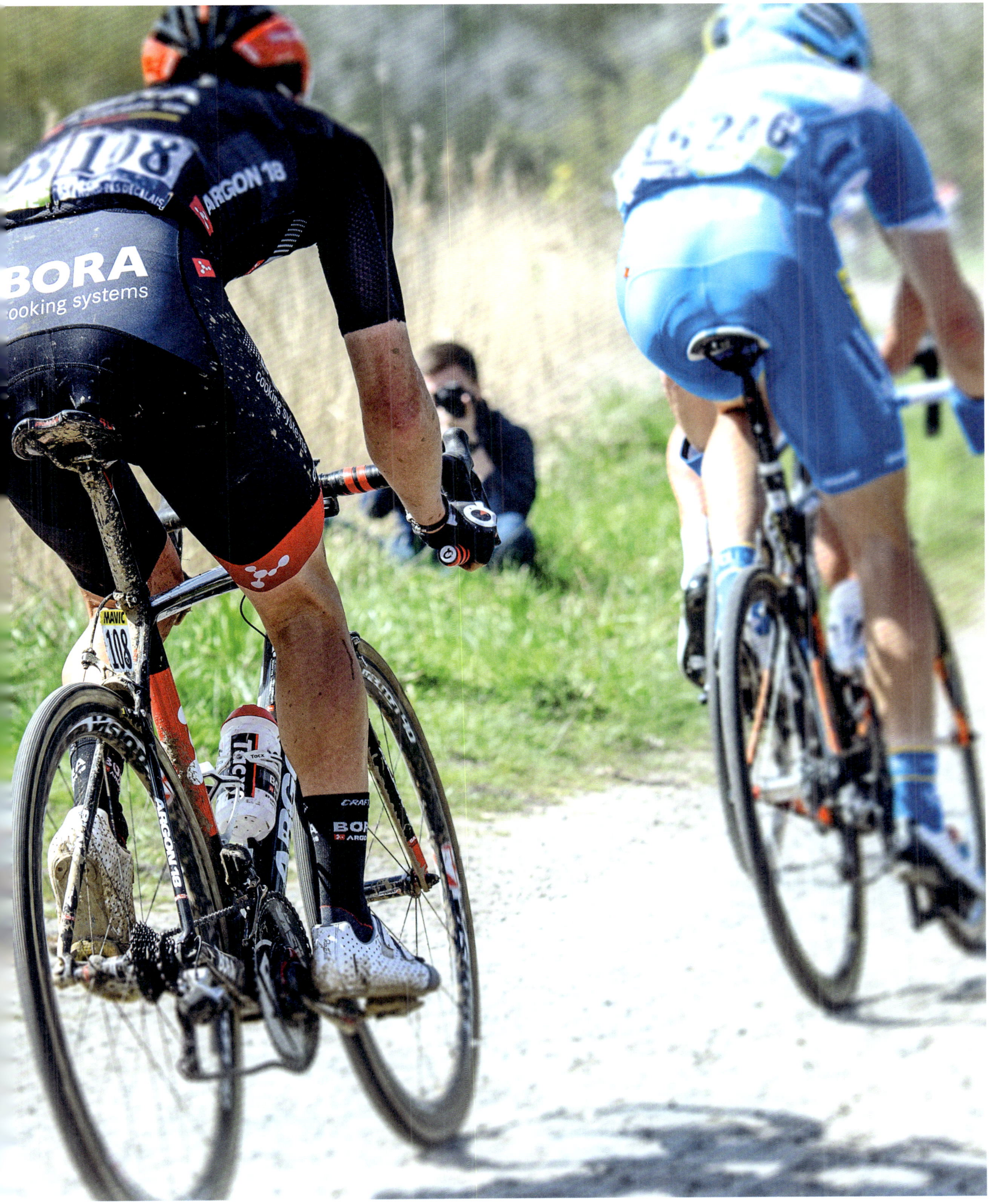
BORA
ARGON 18
MAVIC
108

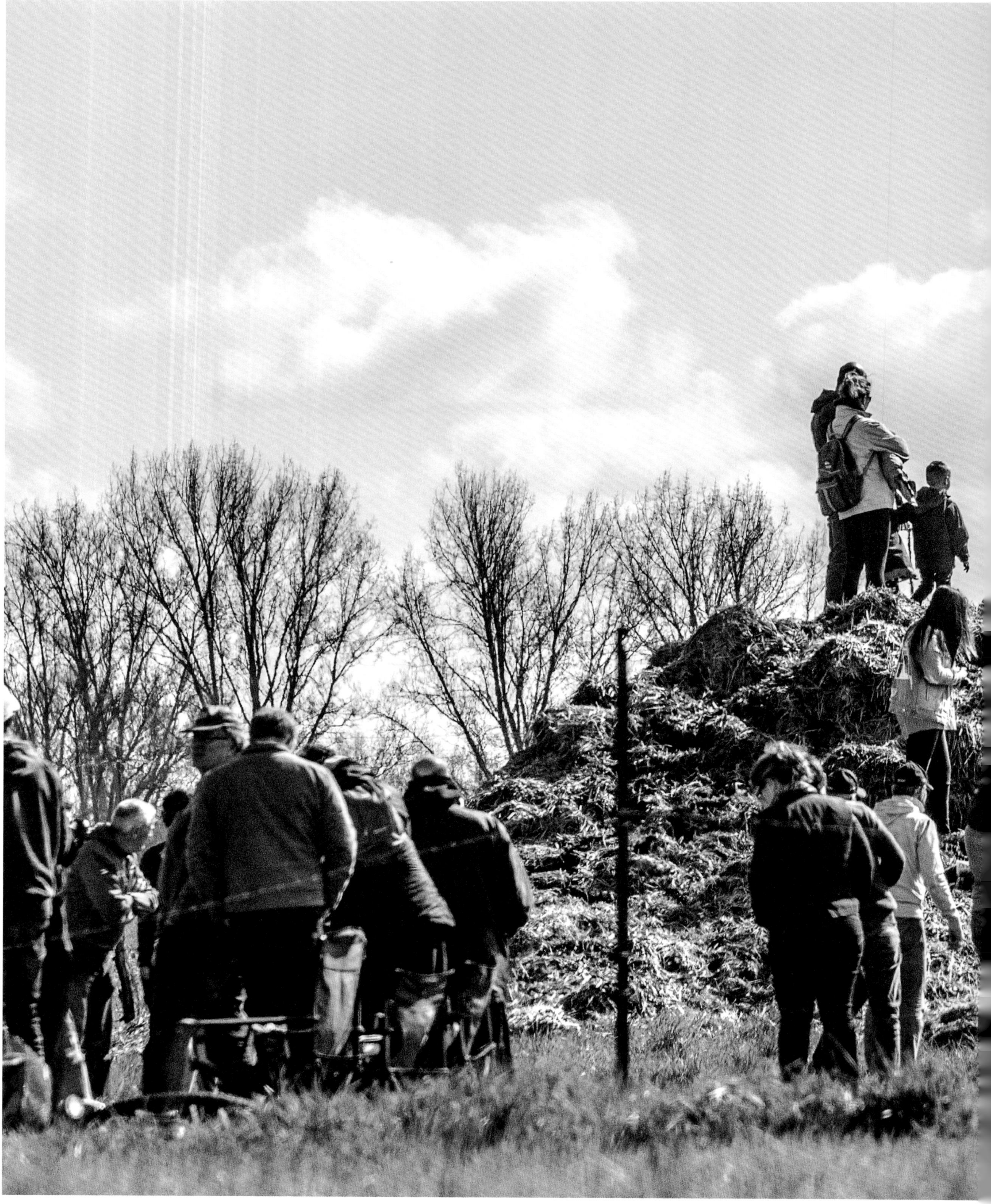

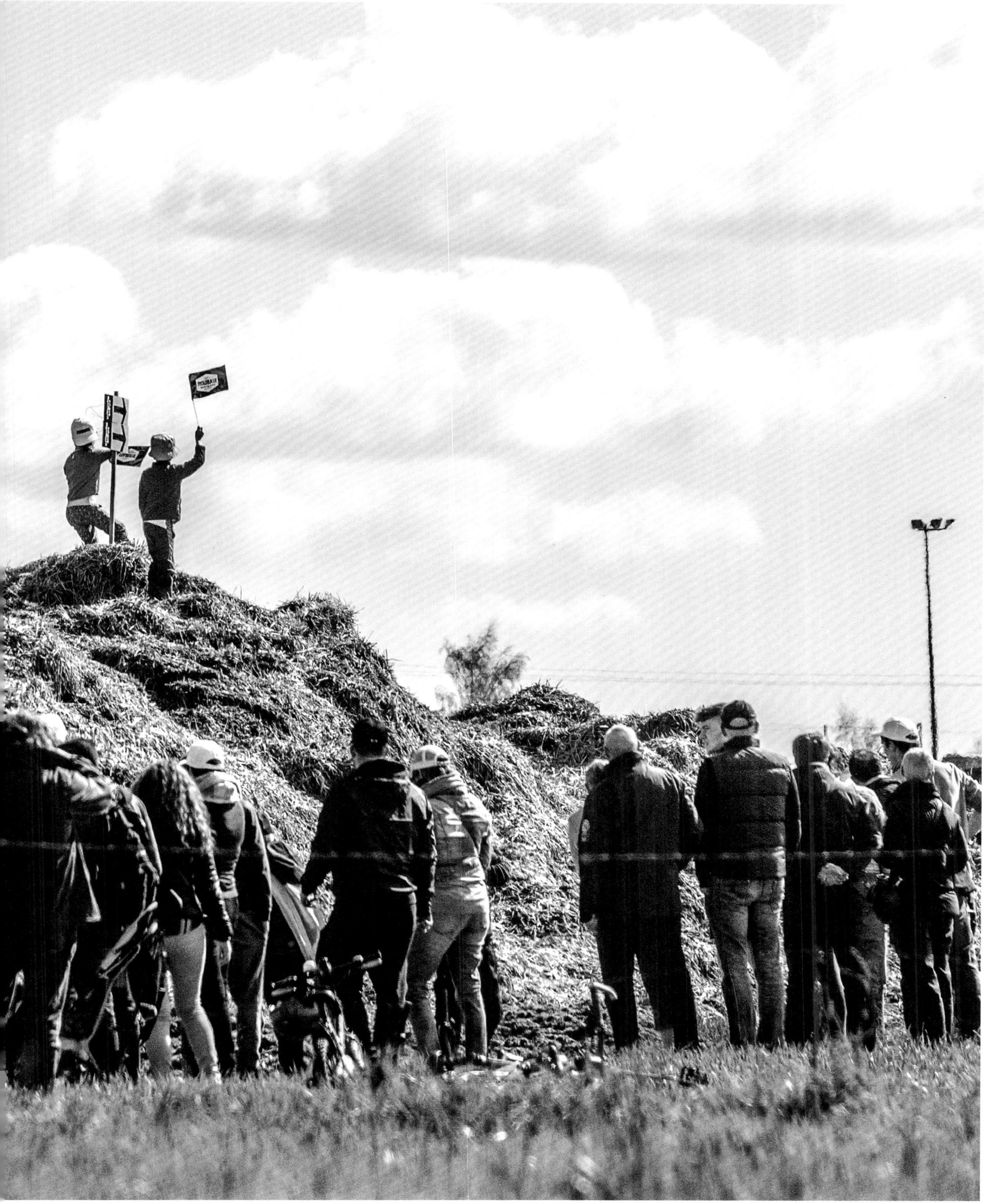

Wartende Fans. **Waiting fans.** *En attendant les coureurs.*

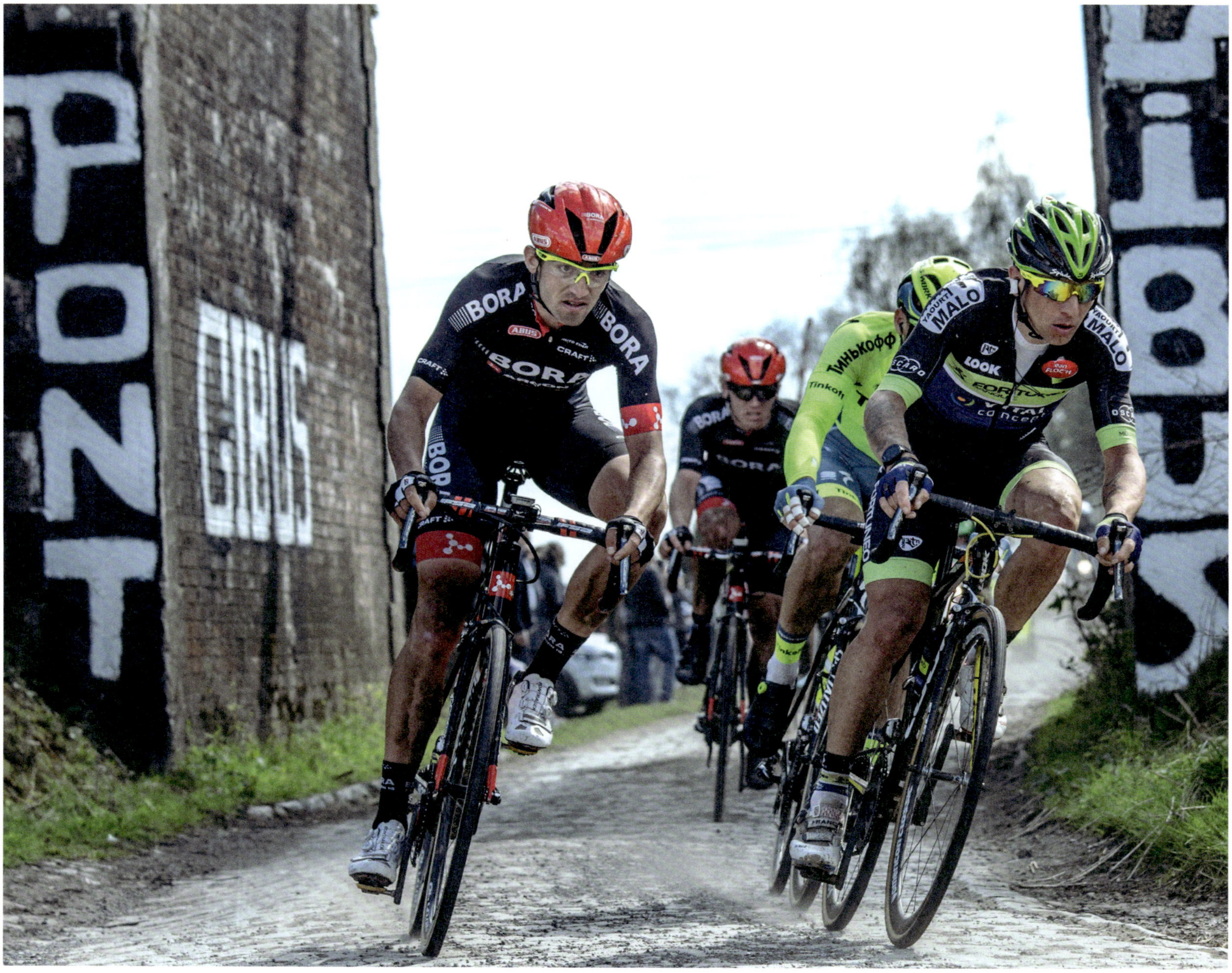

Immer 100 % fokussiert. **Always 100 % focussed.** *Concentrés toujours à 100 %.*

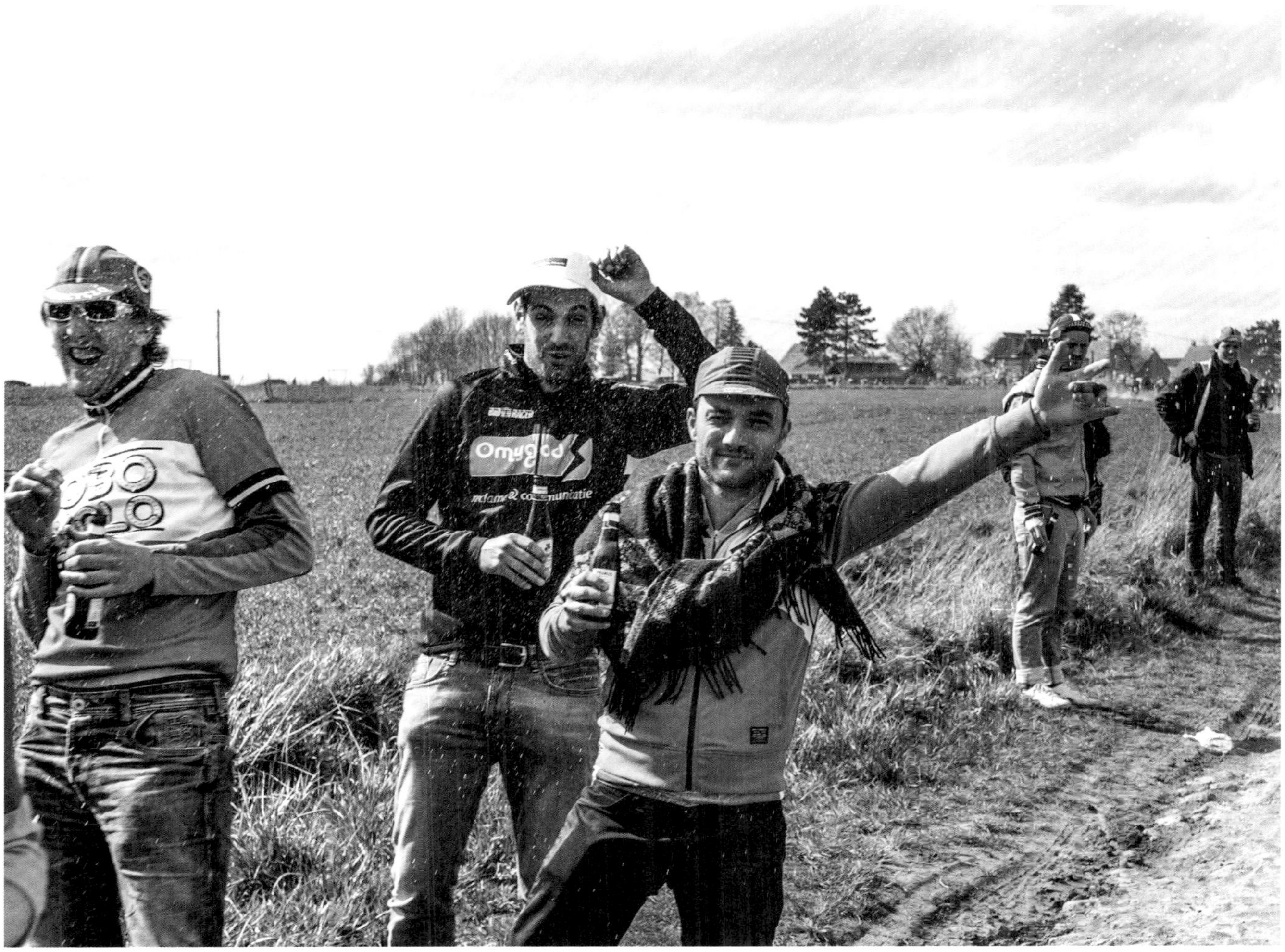

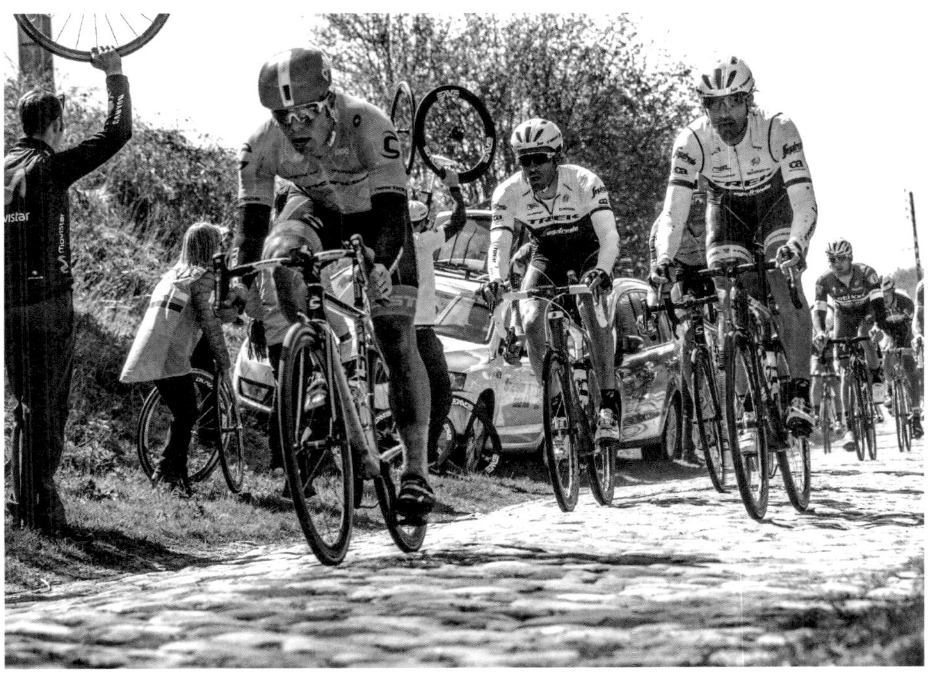

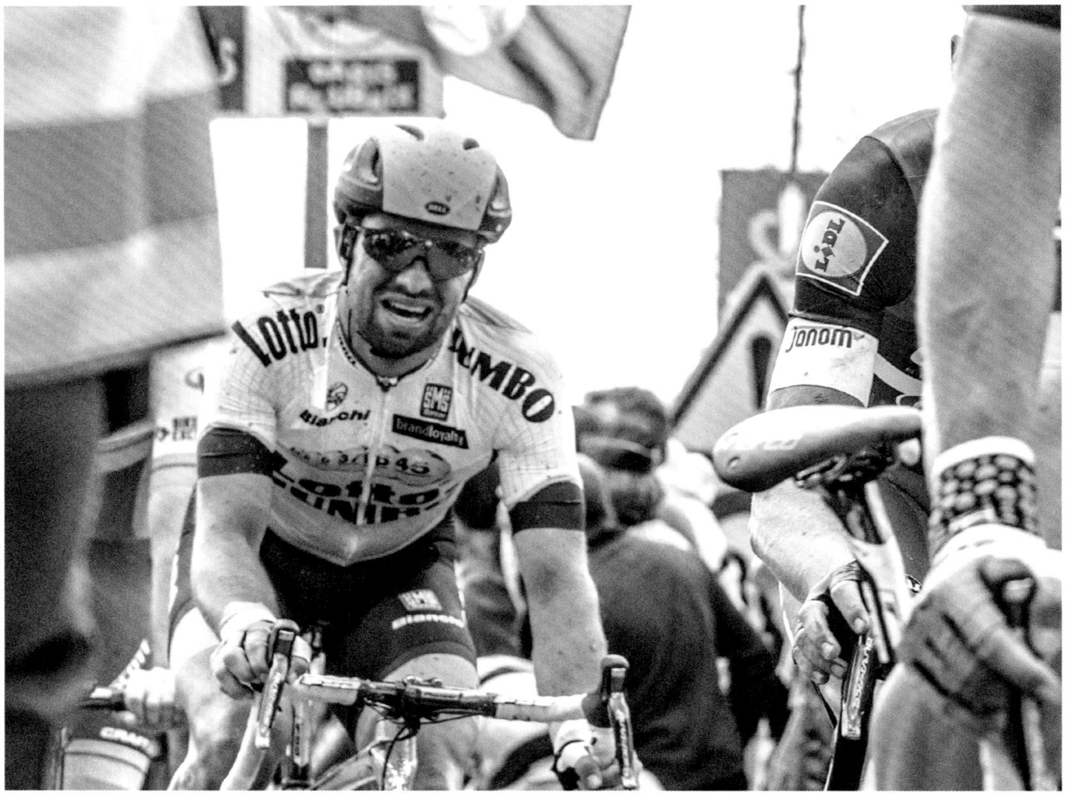
Lotto
brandloyalty
LIDL

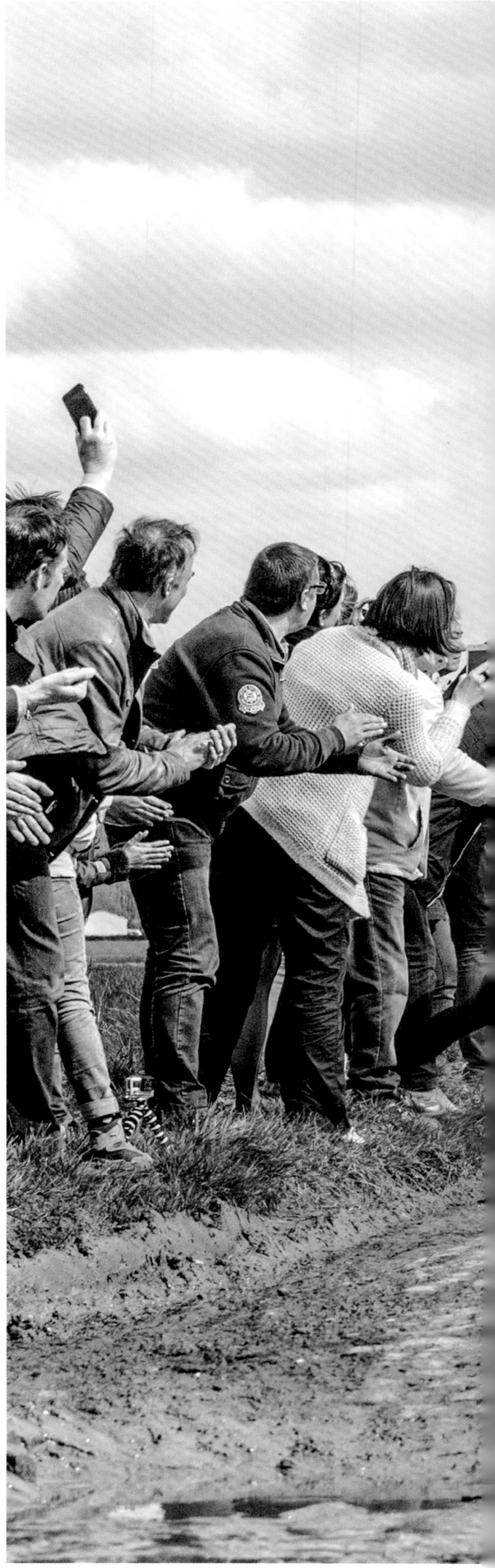

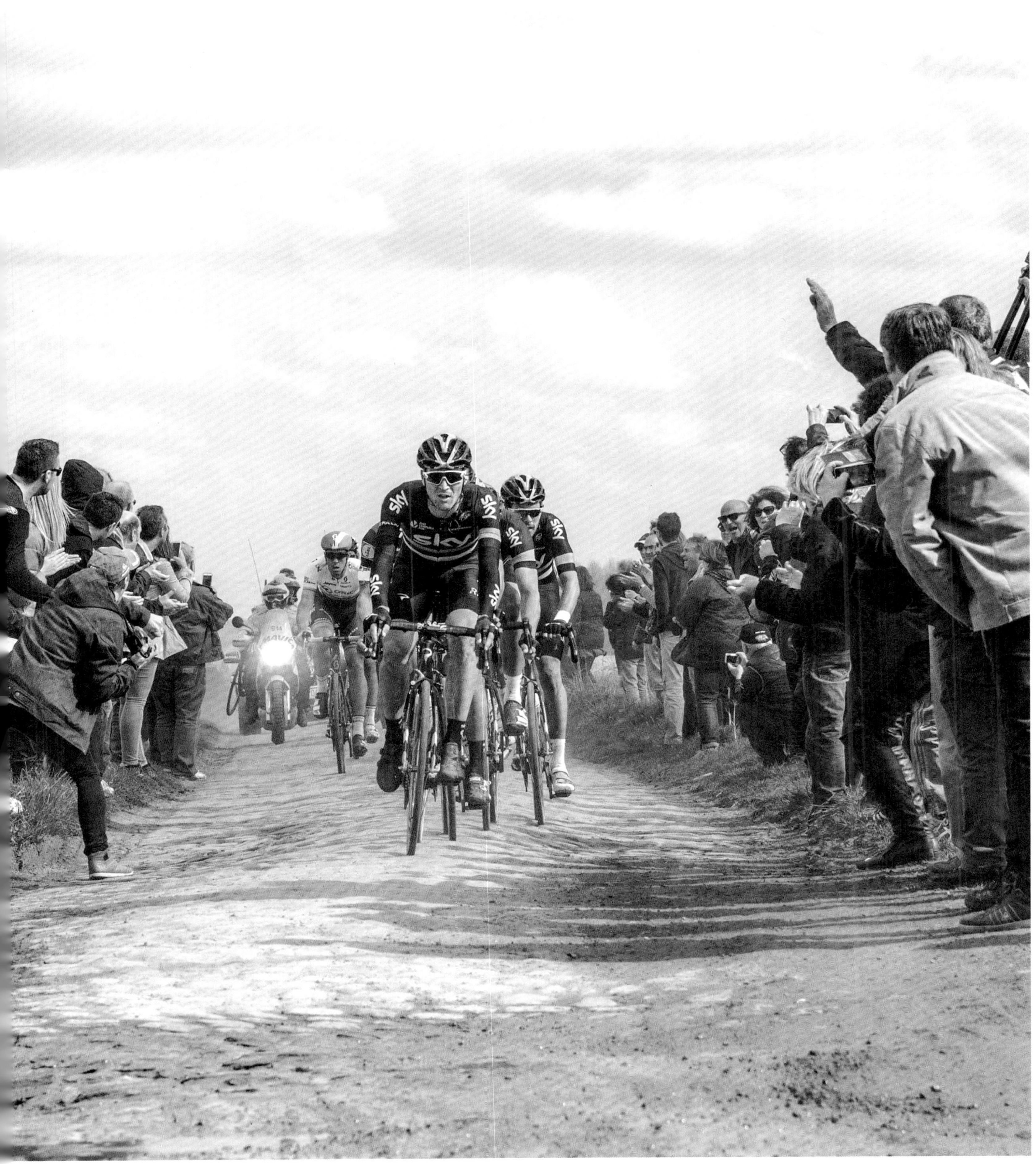

Hölle des Nordens. **The hell of the north.** *L'enfer du Nord.*

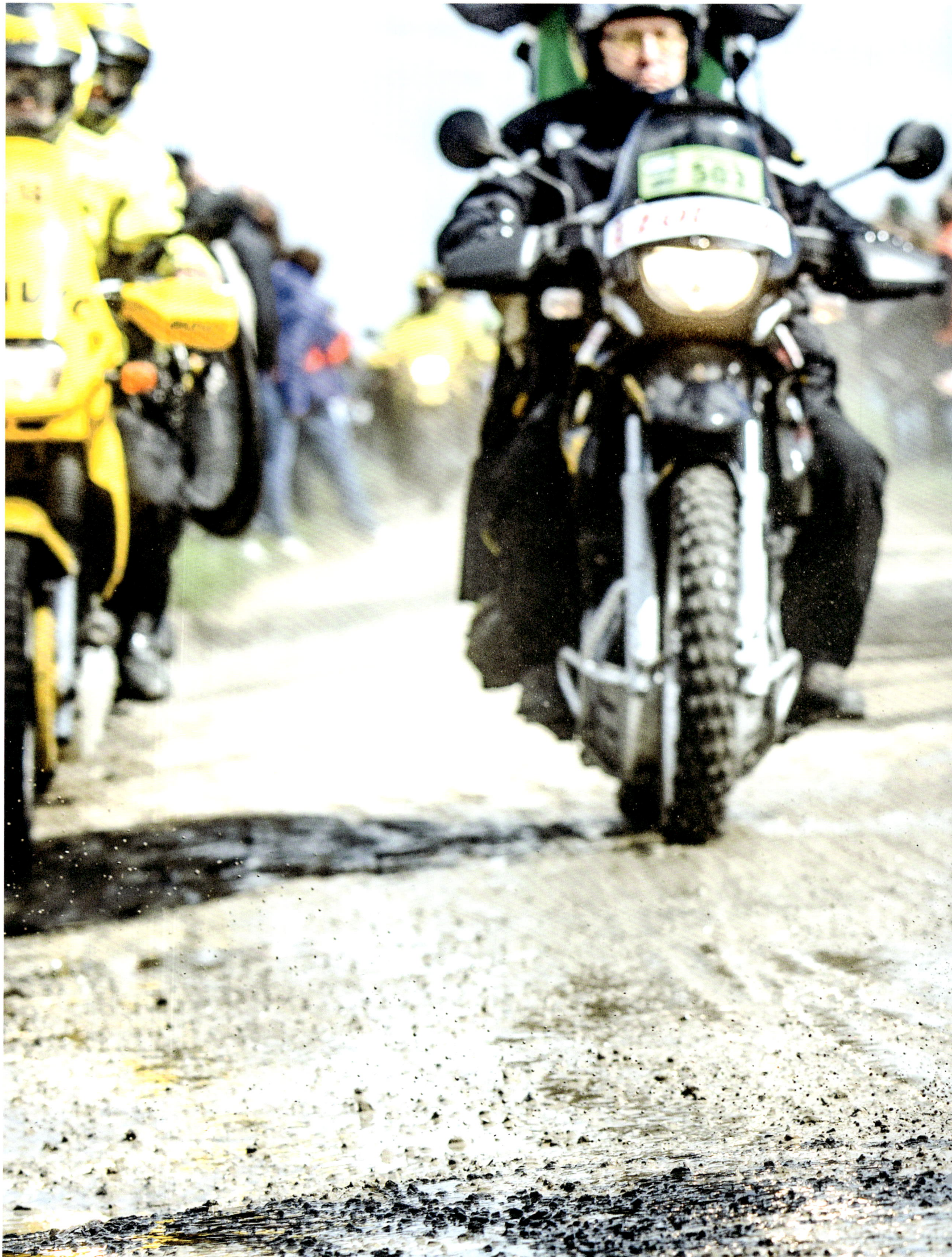

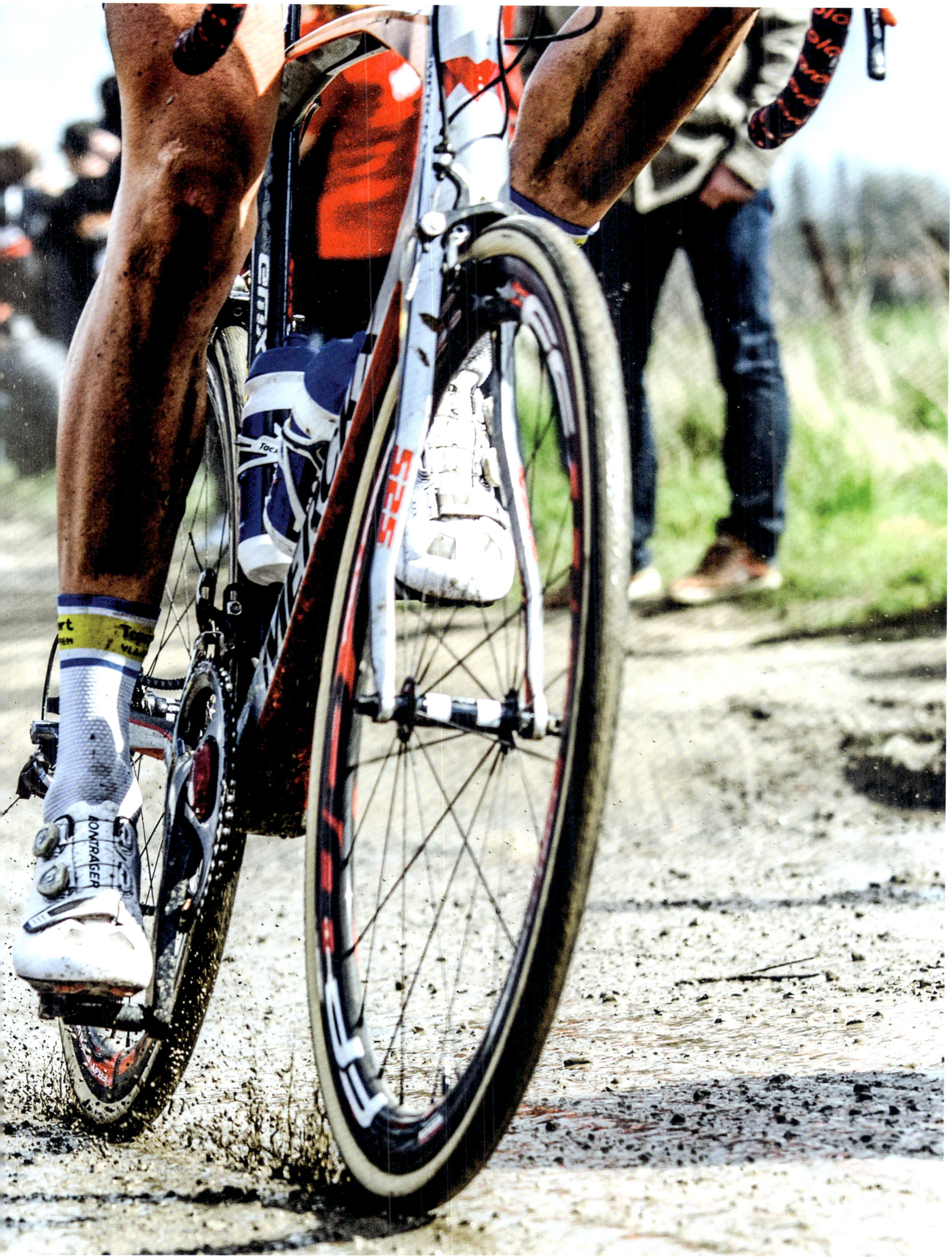

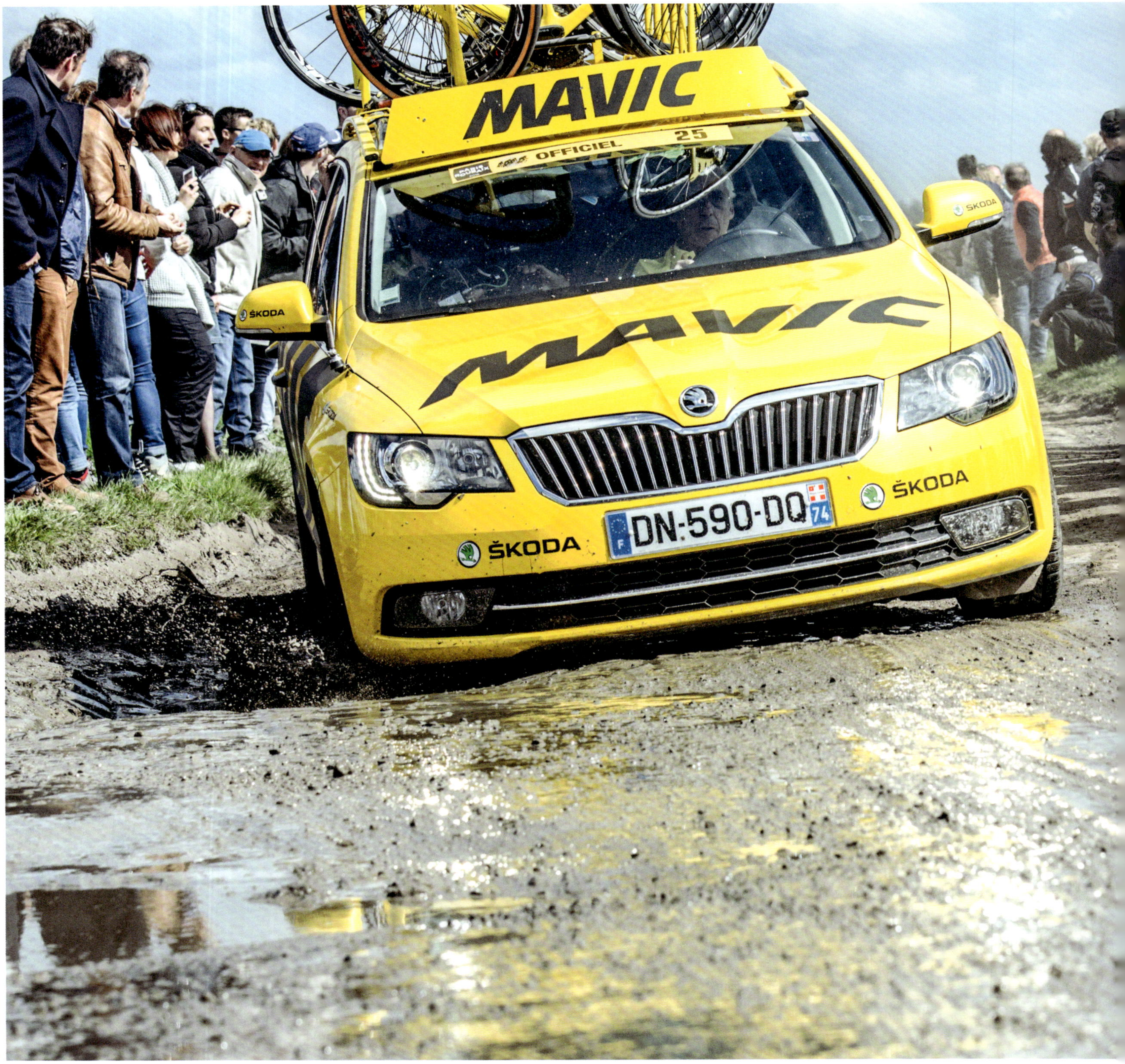

↑ Test für Mensch und Material. **Test for man and material.** *Hommes et matériel à rude épreuve.*

→ Salvatore Puccio (Team Sky). **Salvatore Puccio (Team Sky).** *Salvatore Puccio (Team Sky).*

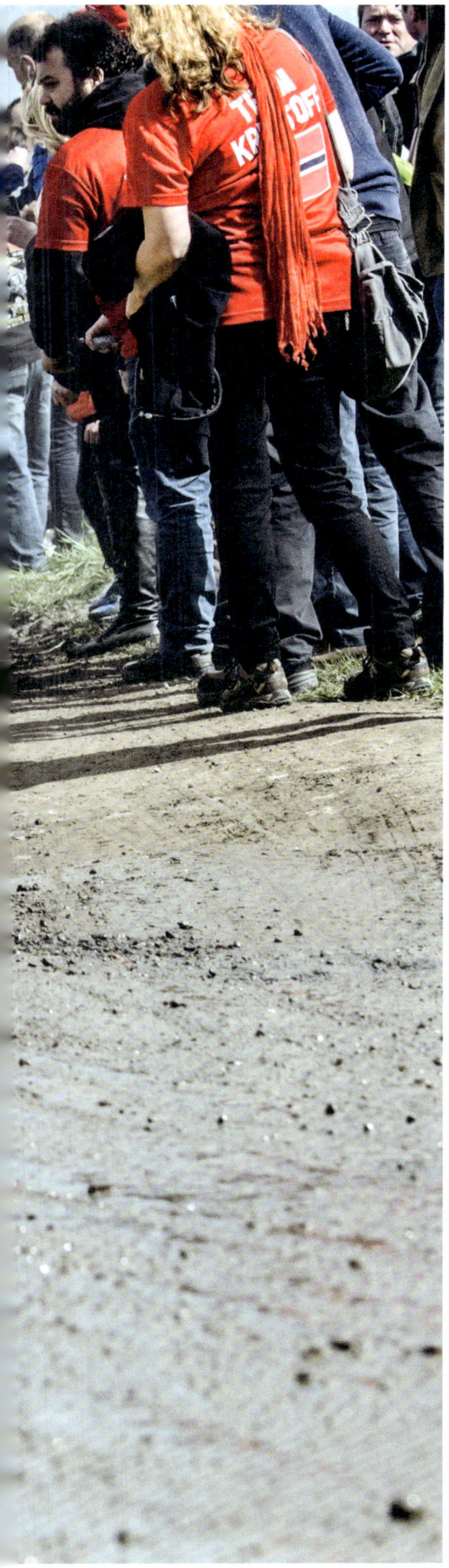

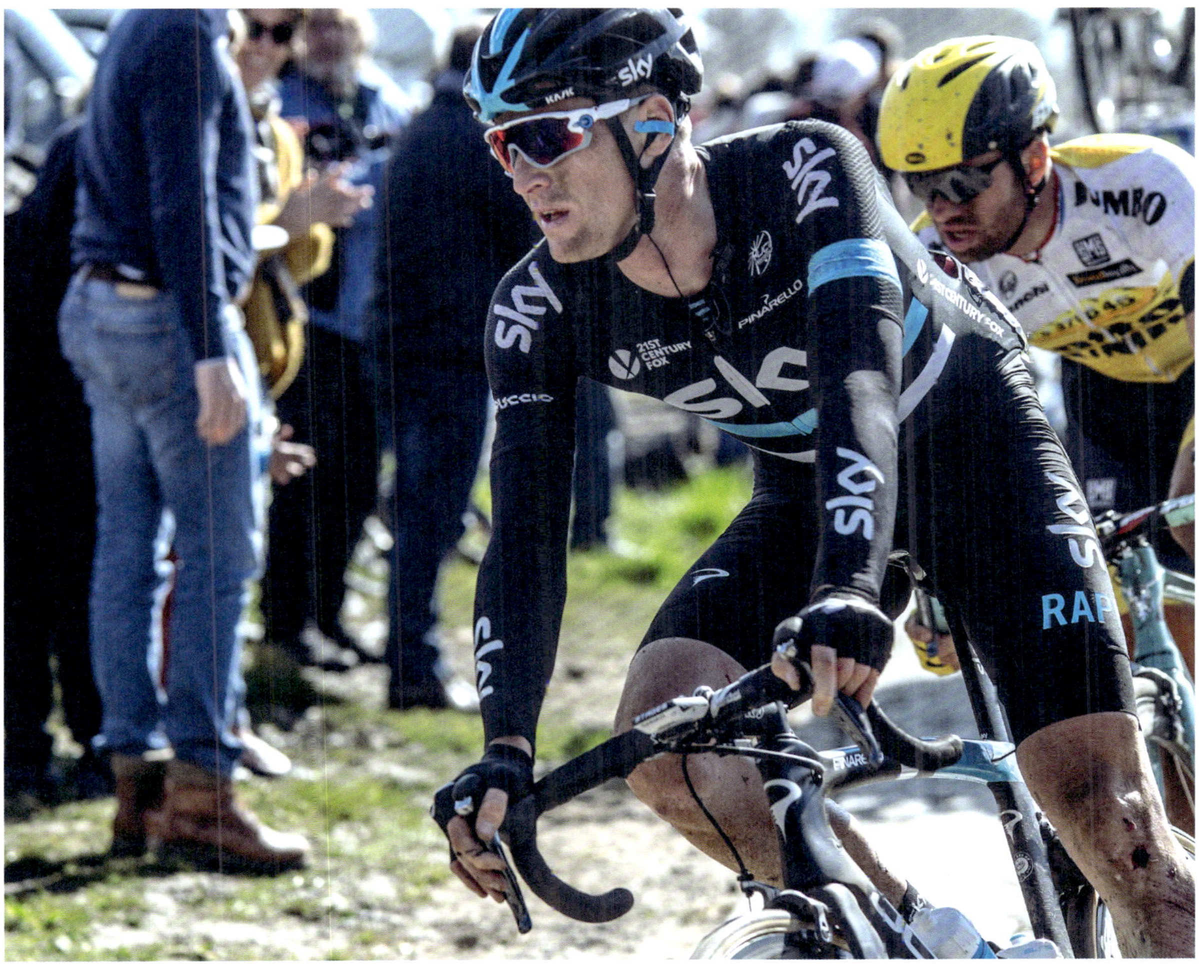
sky
PINARELLO
21ST CENTURY FOX

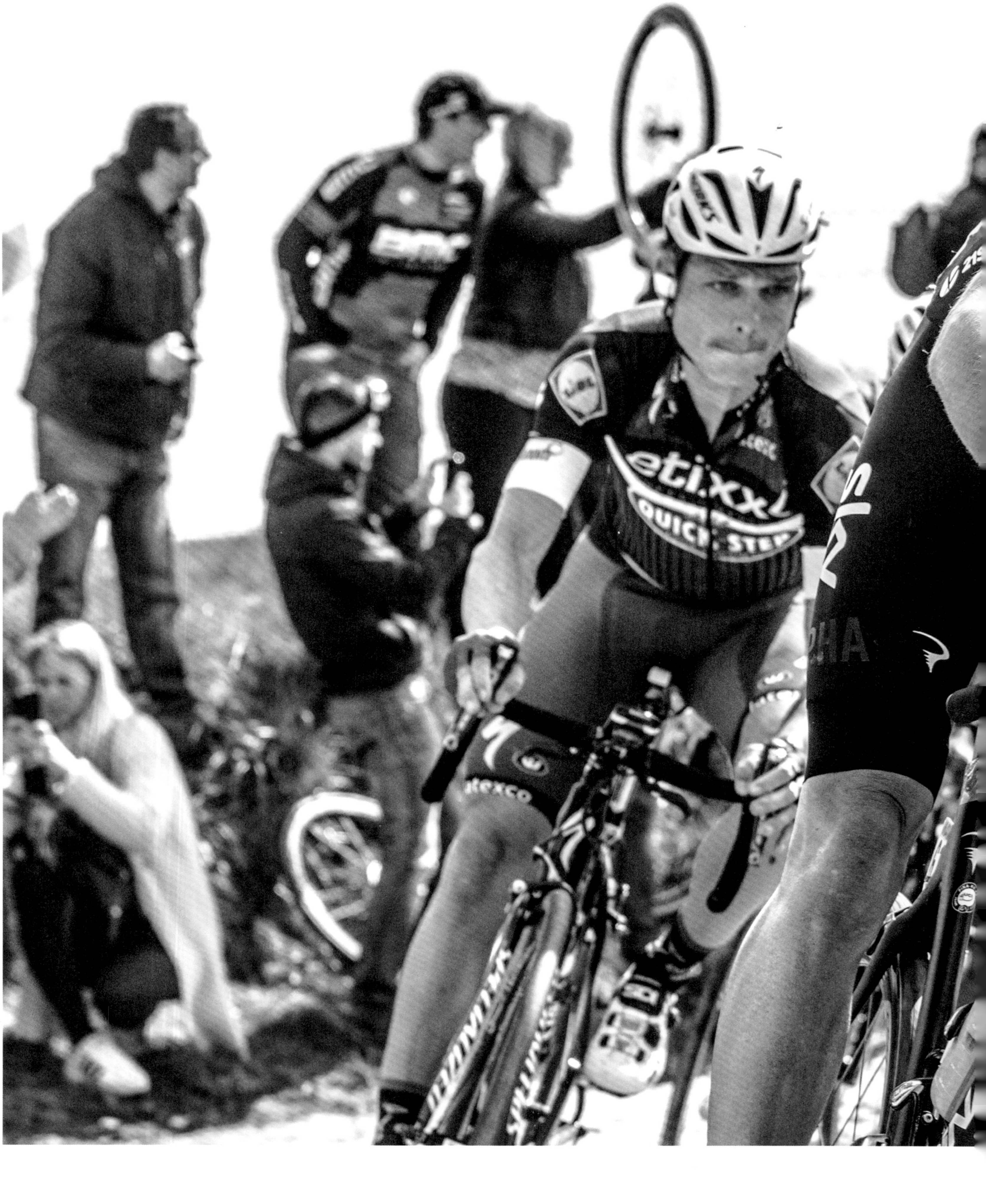
etixx

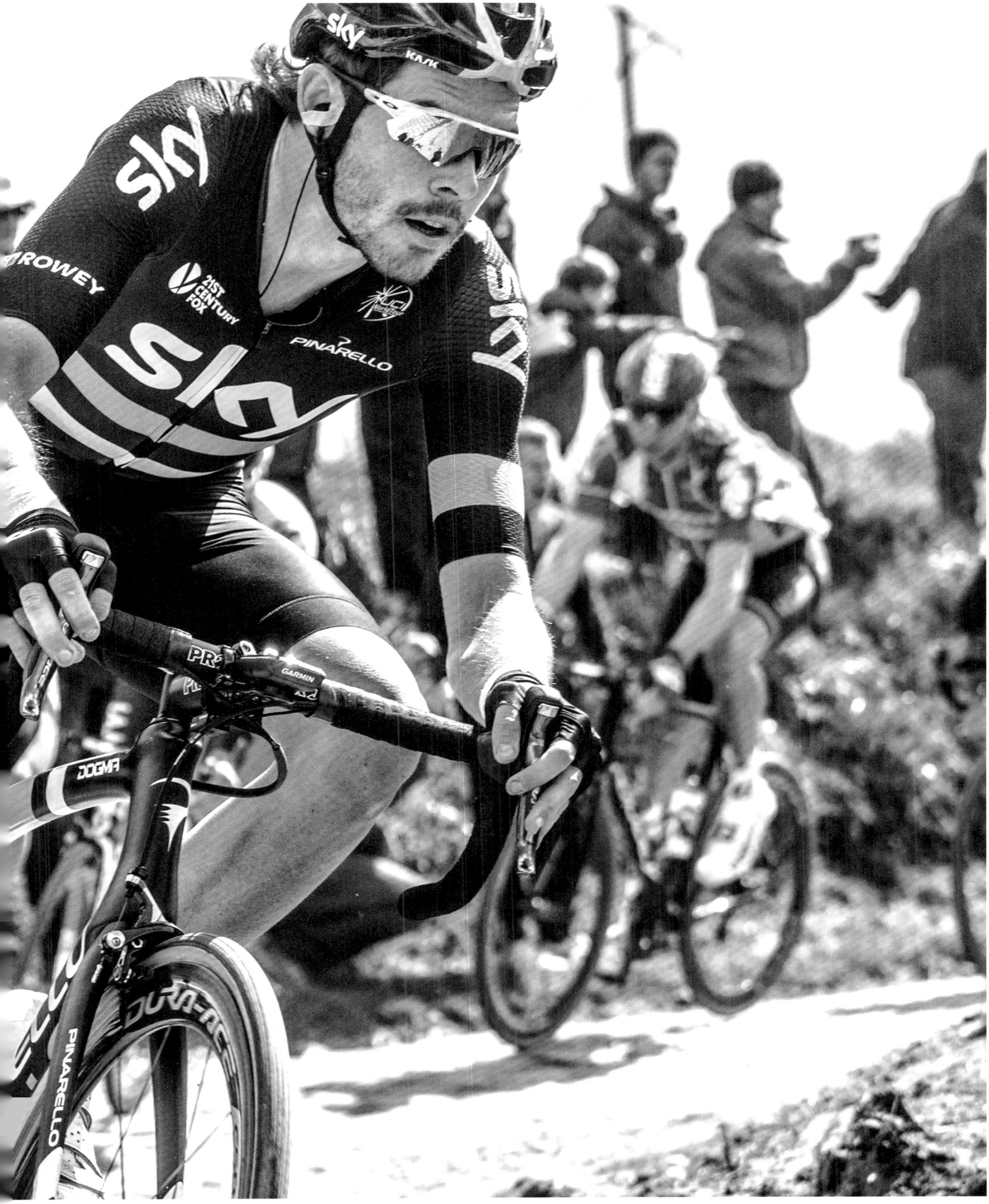

Konzentriert in die Kurve: Tony Martin (Etixx – Quick Step), Luke Rowe (Team Sky). **Taking the bend with concentration: Tony Martin (Etixx – Quick Step), Luke Rowe (Team Sky).** *Concentrés dans le virage : Tony Martin (Etixx – Quick Step), Luke Rowe (Team Sky).*

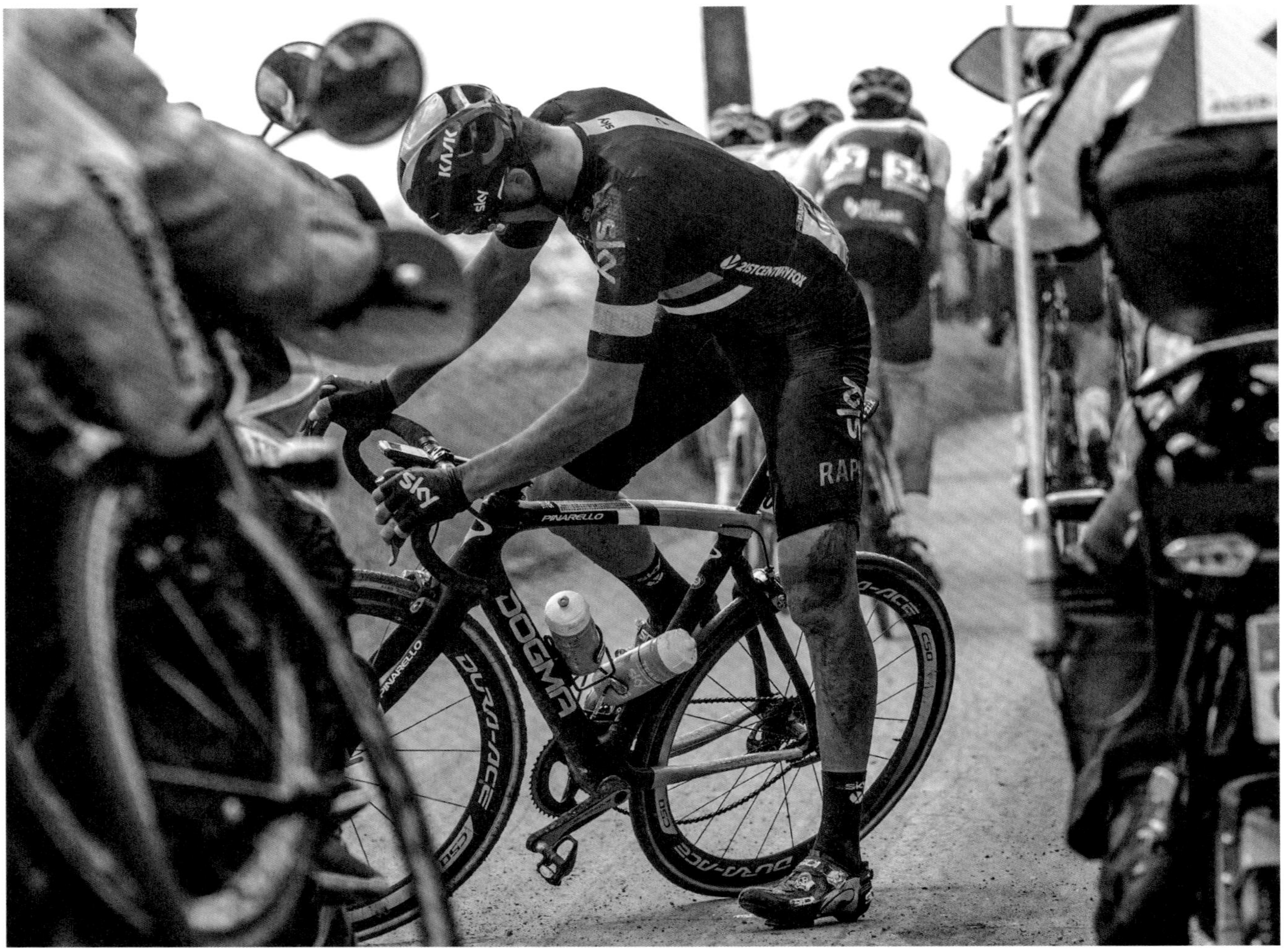
KASK
sky
21ST CENTURY FOX
PINARELLO
DOGMA
DURA-ACE

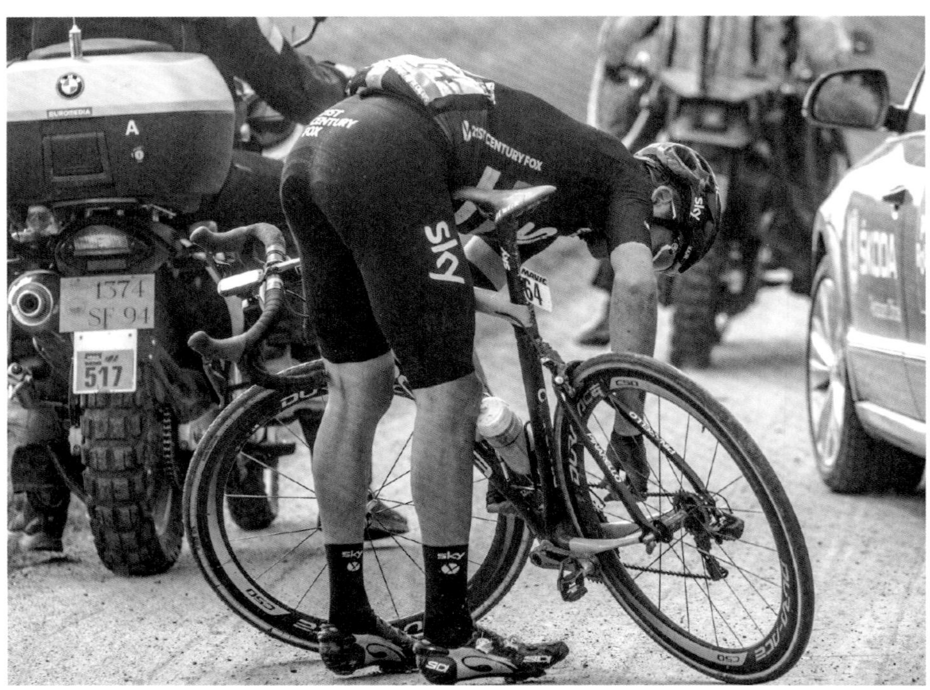
1374
SF 94
517
21ST CENTURY FOX
sky
ŠKODA

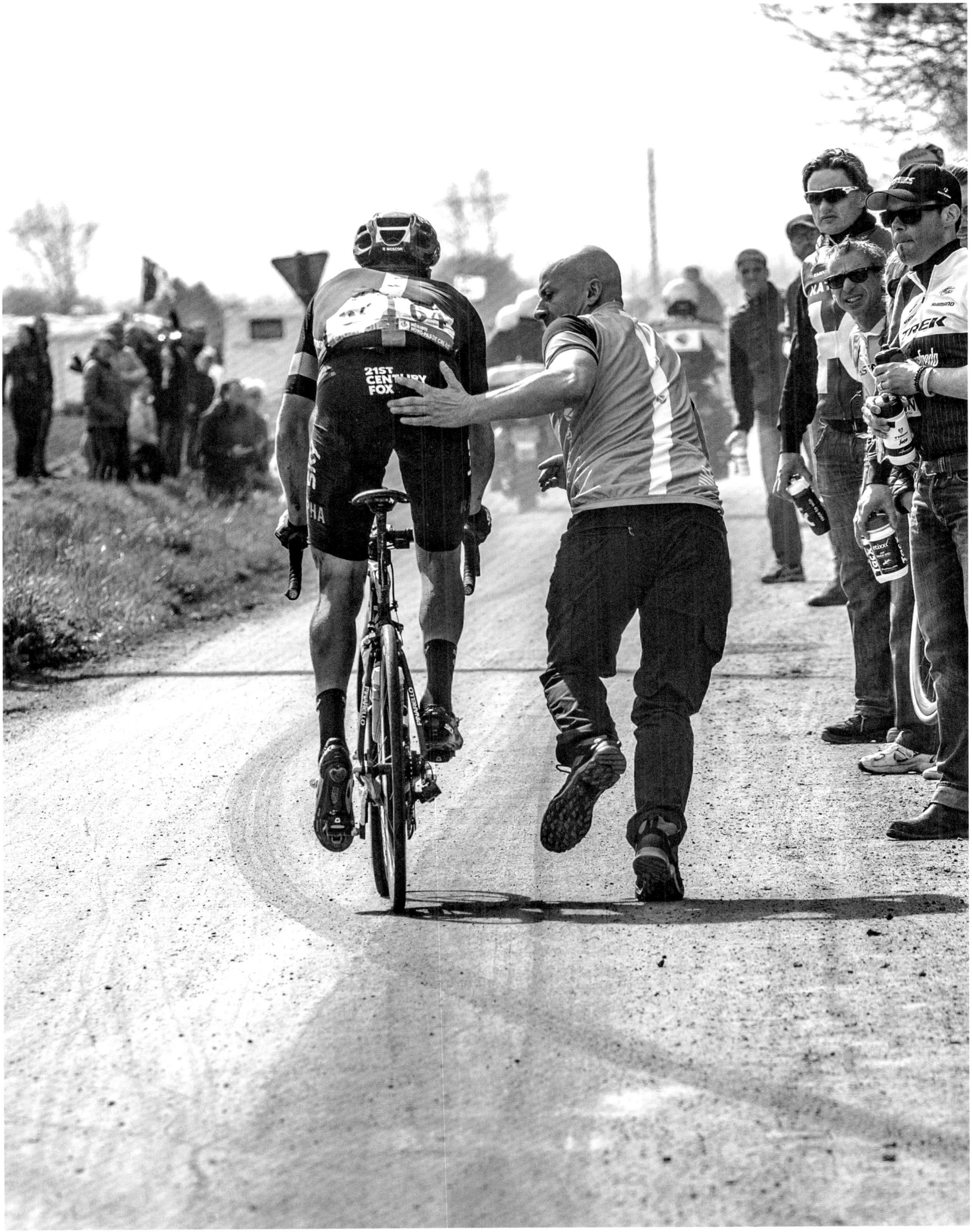

Sturz für Gianni Moscon (Team Sky). **Crash for Gianni Moscon (Team Sky).** *Chute pour Gianni Moscon (Team Sky).*

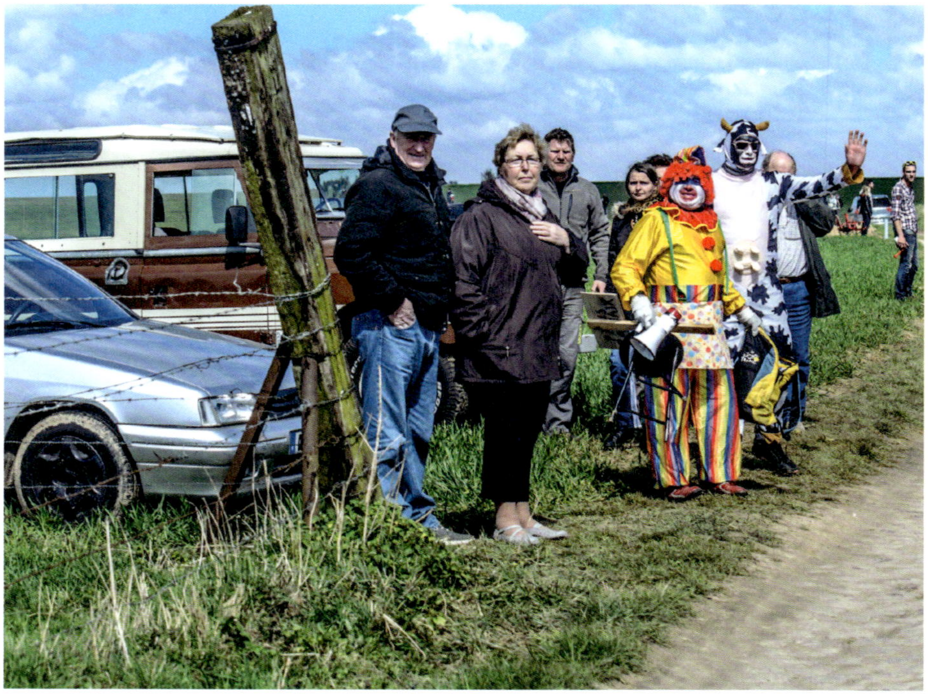

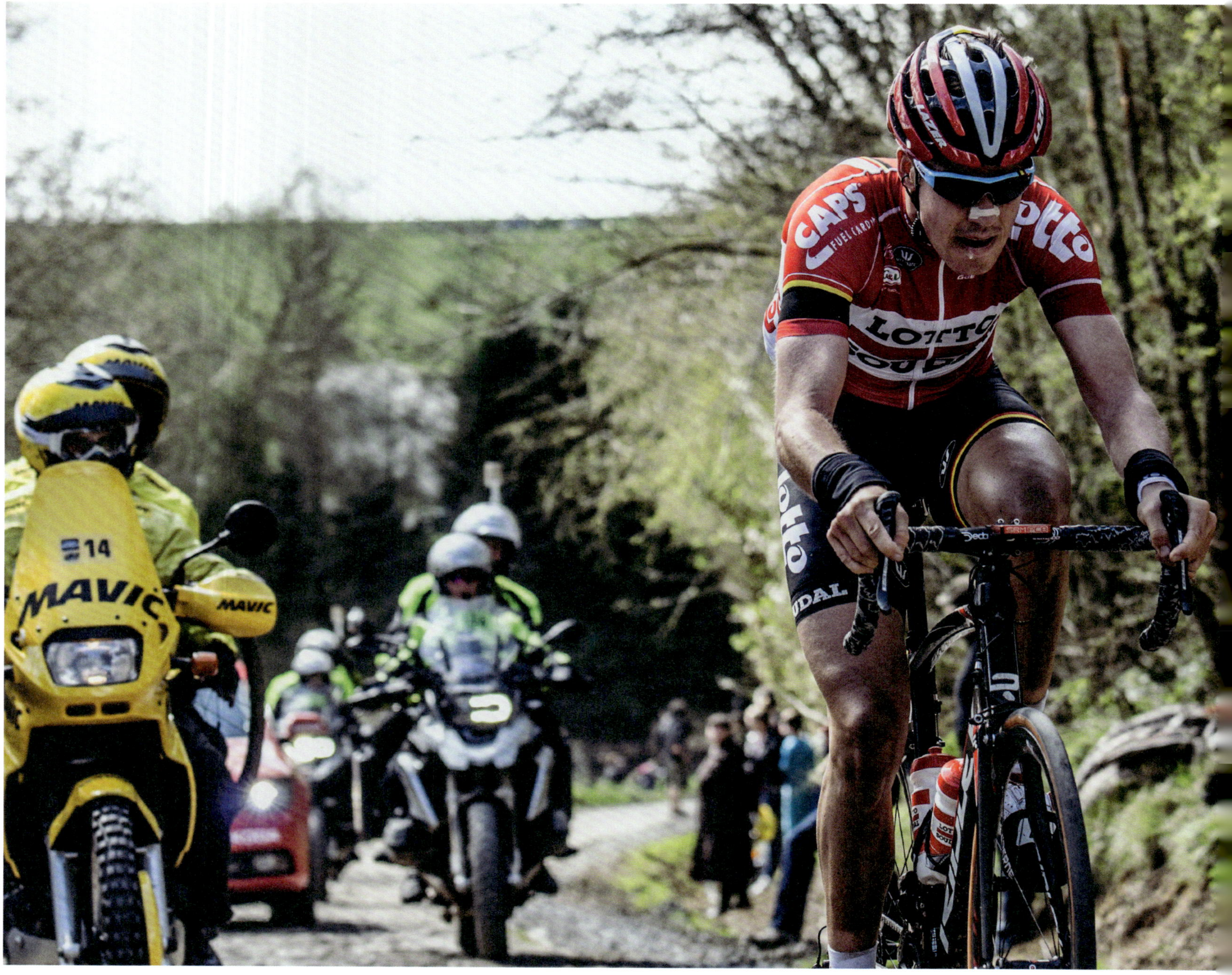
14
MAVIC
MAVIC
CAPS
LOTTO

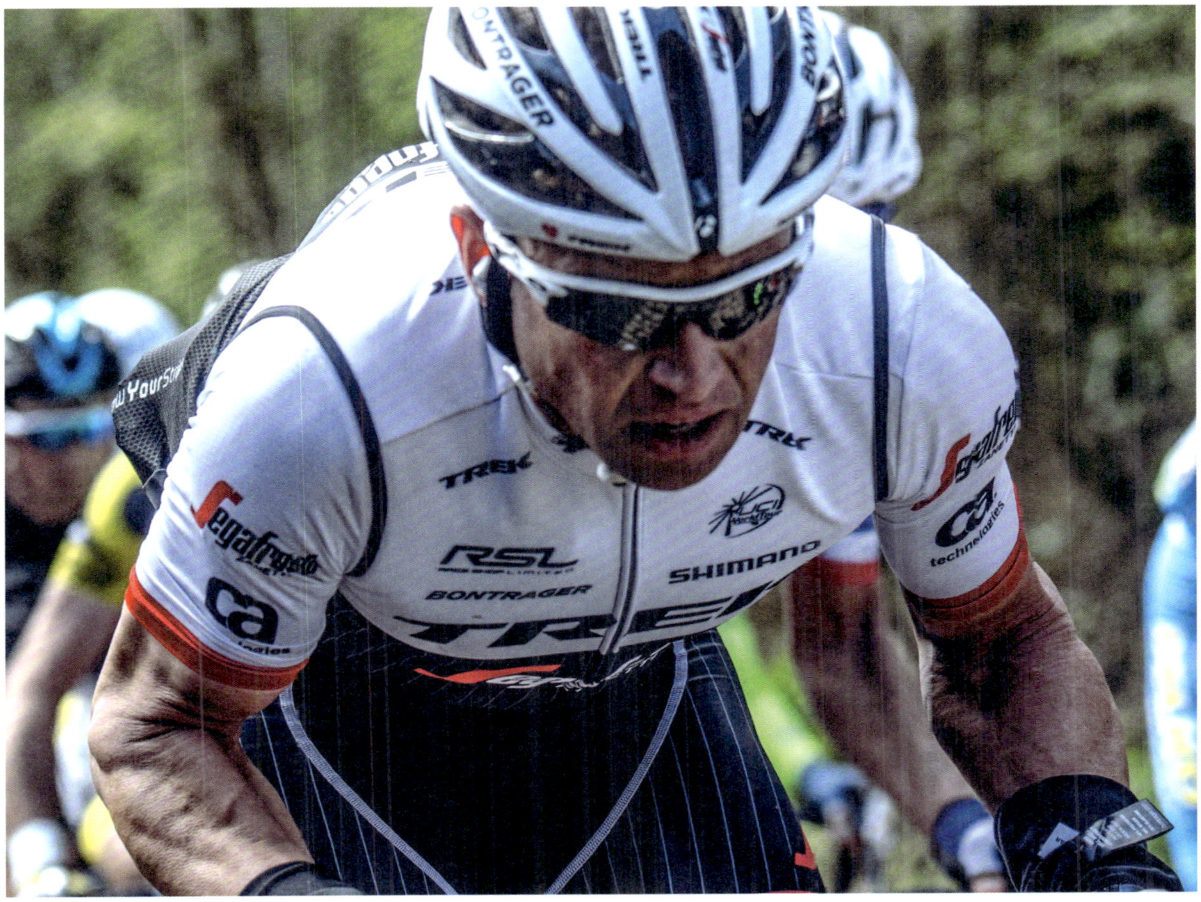

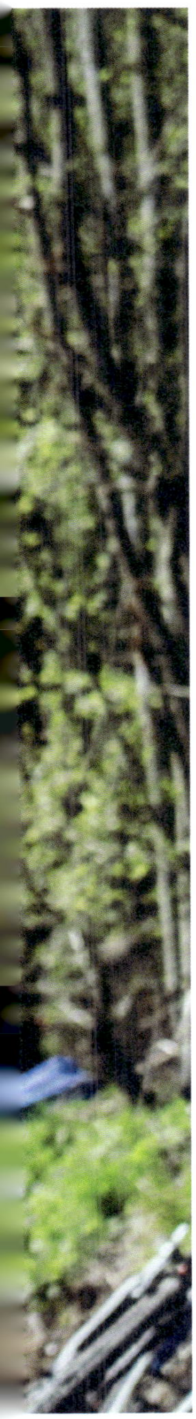

↖ Lars Bak (Lotto Soudal) im Kampf gegen das Kopfsteinpflaster. **Lars Bak (Lotto Soudal) fighting the cobbles.** *Lars Bak (Lotto Soudal) au combat contre les pavés.*
↗ Fabian Cancellaras Helfer Yaroslav Popovych (Trek – Segafredo). **Fabian Cancellara's domestique Yaroslav Popovych (Trek – Segafredo).** *Yaroslav Popovych (Trek – Segafredo), assistant de Fabian Cancellara.*

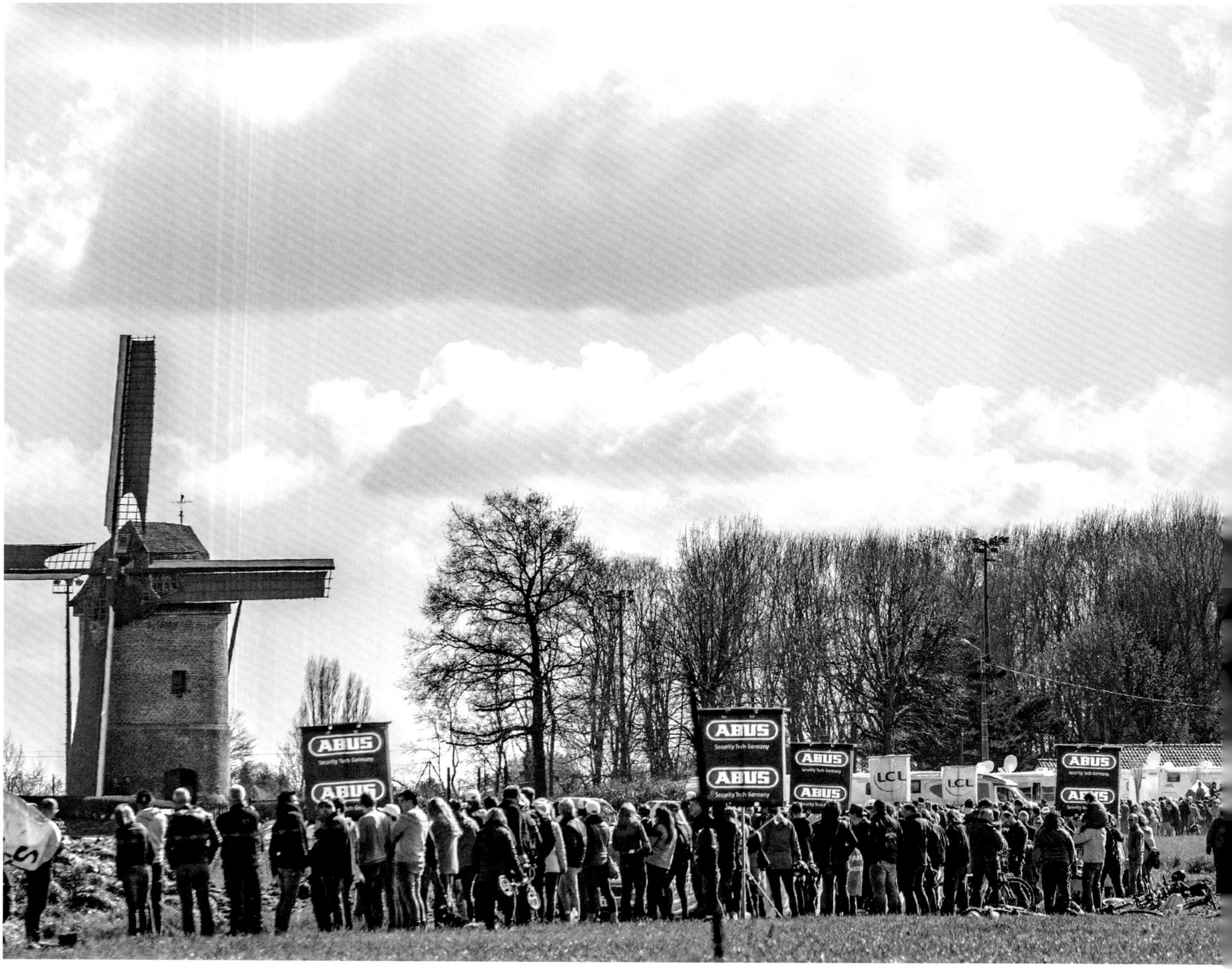

Trügerische Idylle. **Treacherous idyll.** *Idylle trompeuse.*

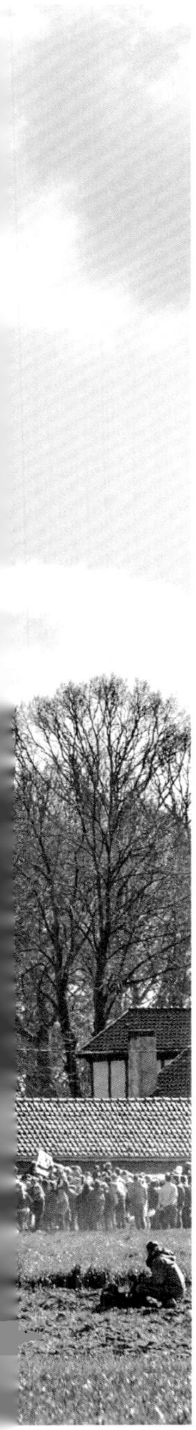

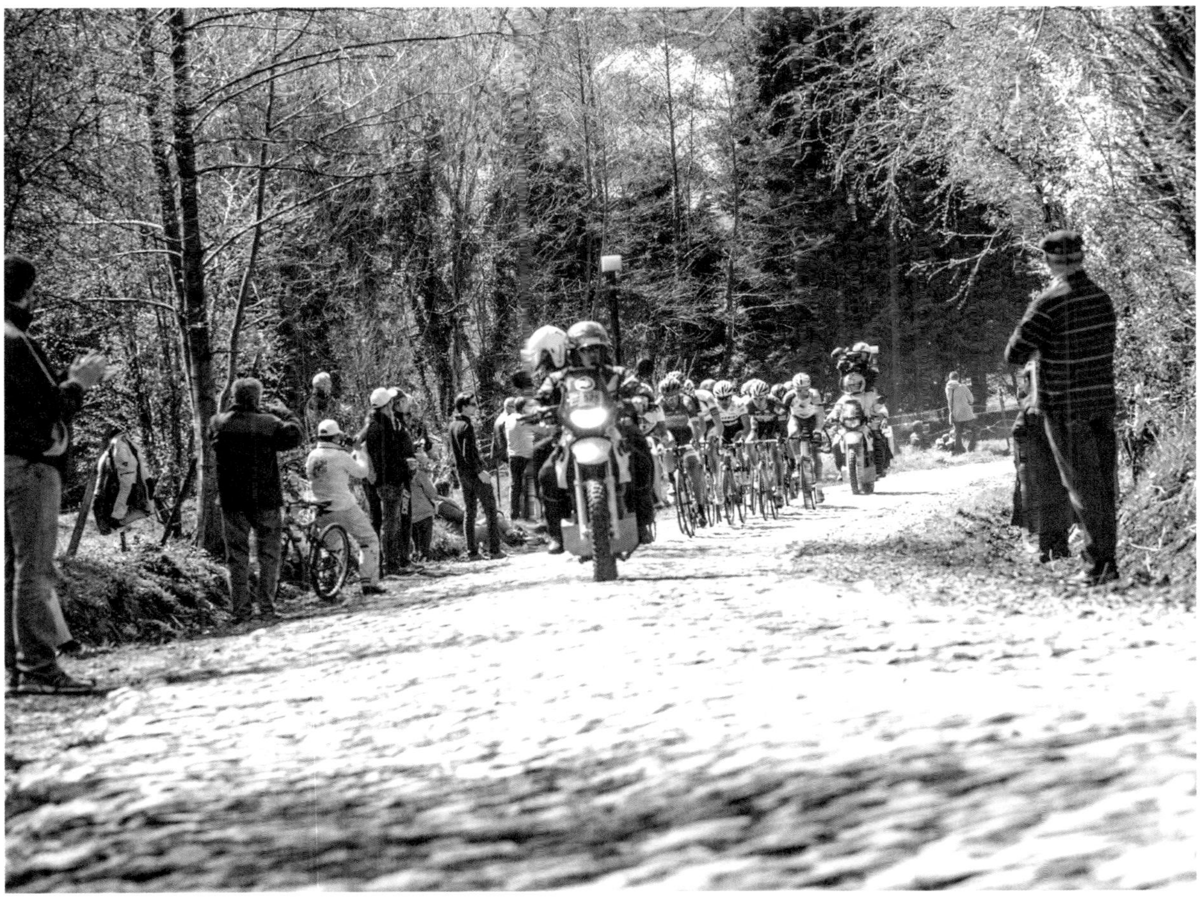

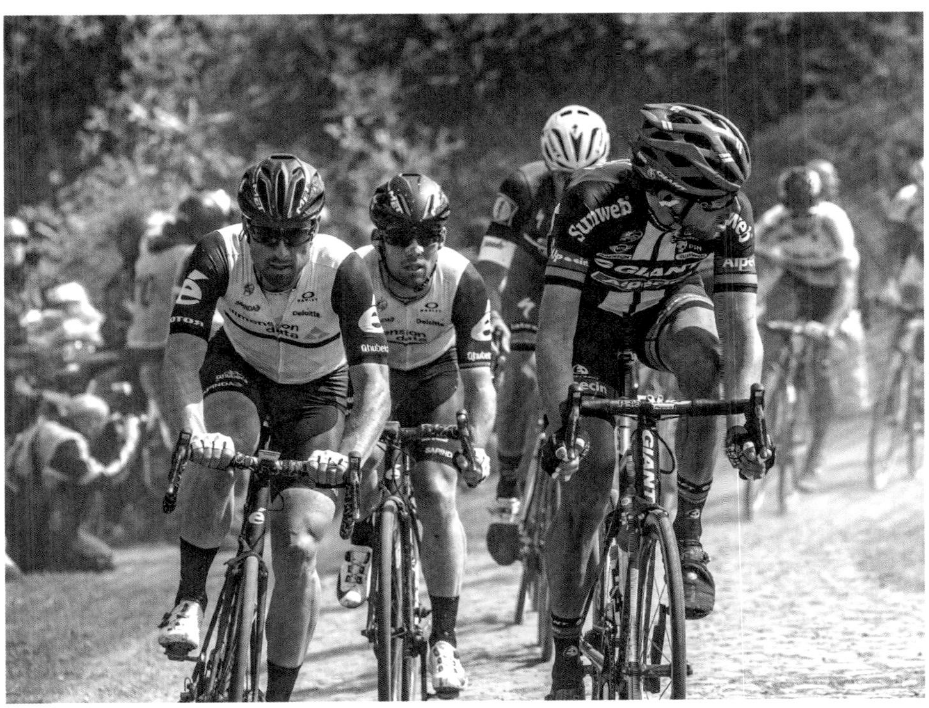

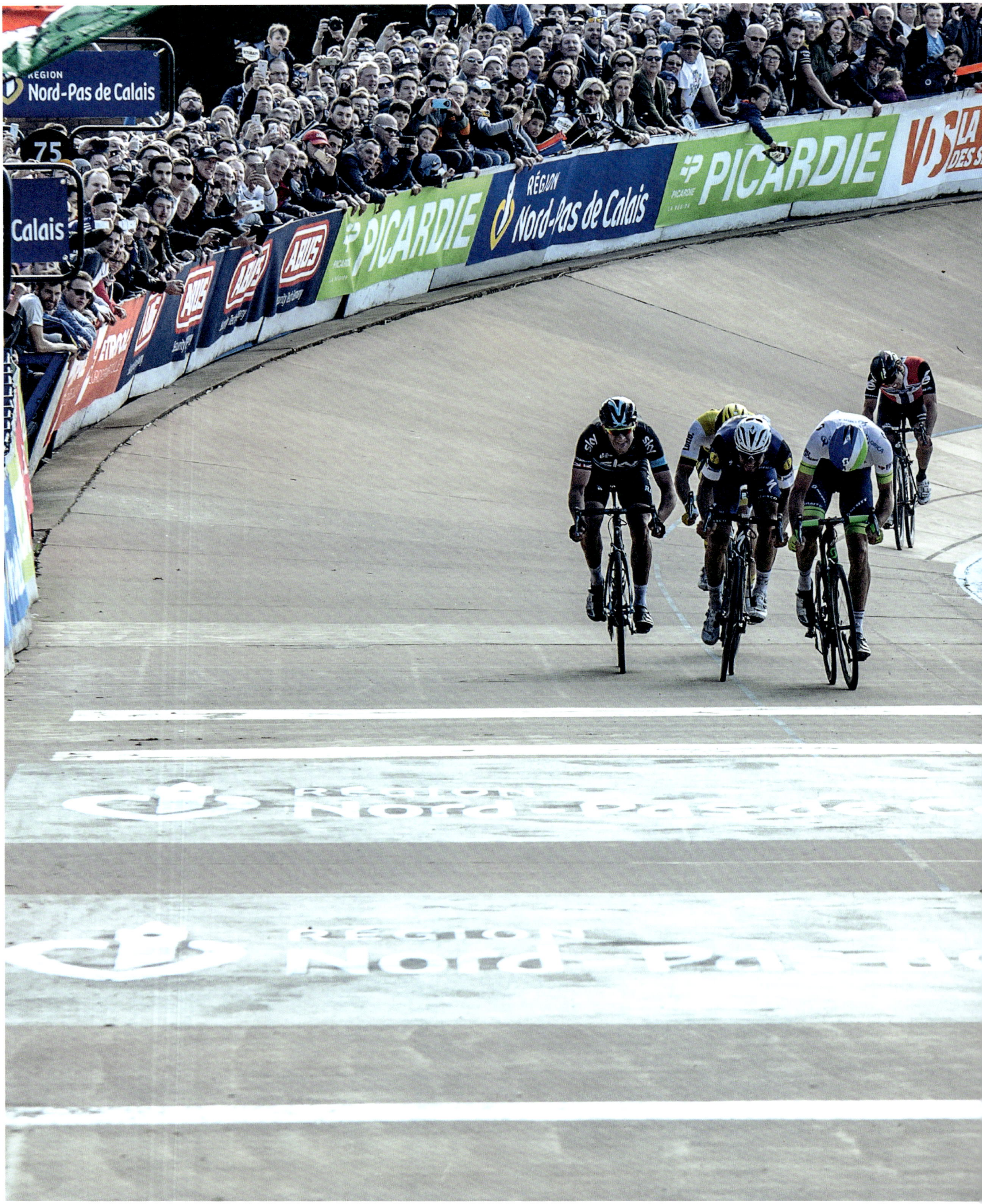
RÉGION
Nord-Pas de Calais
75
Calais
ABUS
PICARDIE
RÉGION
Nord-Pas de Calais
PICARDIE

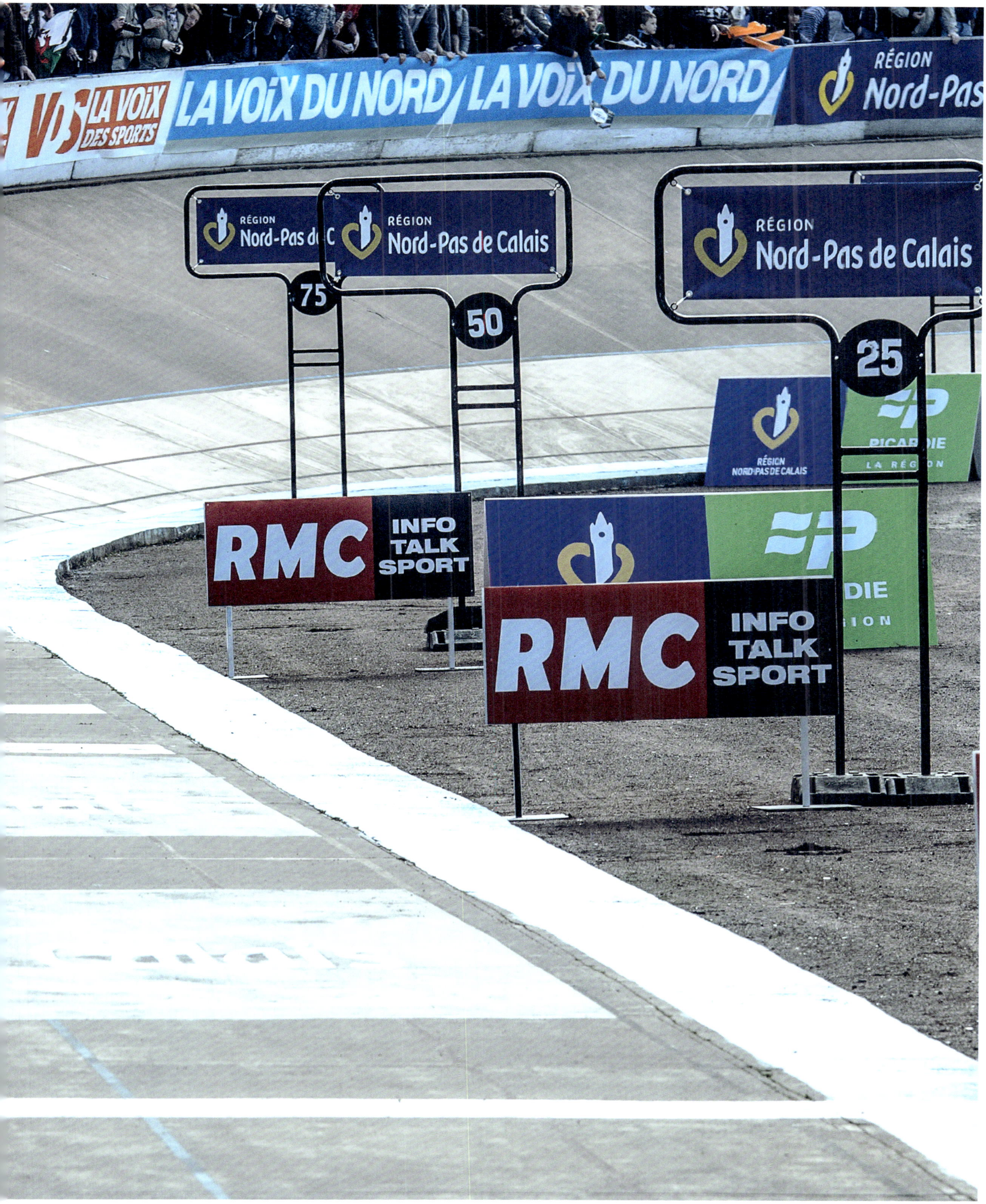

Entscheidung im Vélodrome: Mathew Hayman (ORICA-GreenEDGE) erfüllt sich einen Traum und gewinnt knapp vor Tom Boonen (Etixx – Quick Step) und Ian Stannard (Team Sky). **Decider in the Vélodrome: a dream comes true for Mathew Hayman (ORICA-GreenEDGE) as he just beats Tom Boonen (Etixx – Quick Step) and Ian Stannard (Team Sky).** *Le final au vélodrome : Mathew Hayman (ORICA-GreenEDGE) réalise son rêve en remportant la course de justesse devant Tom Boonen (Etixx – Quick Step) et Ian Stannard (Team Sky).*

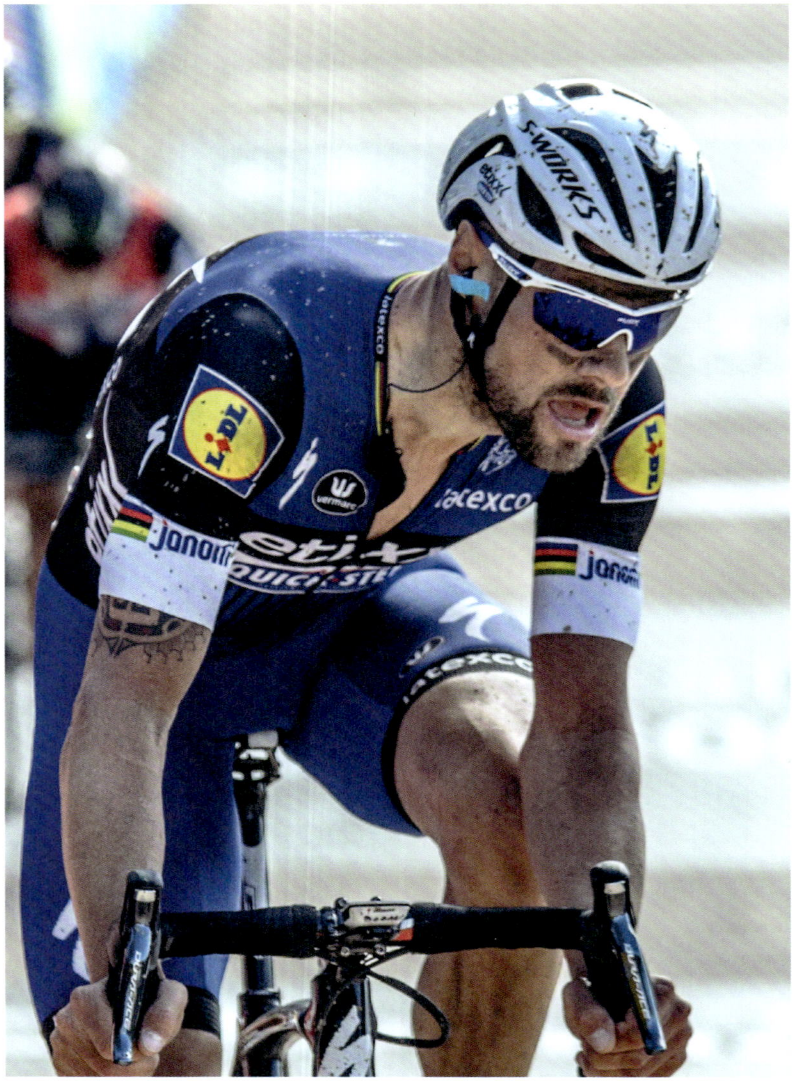

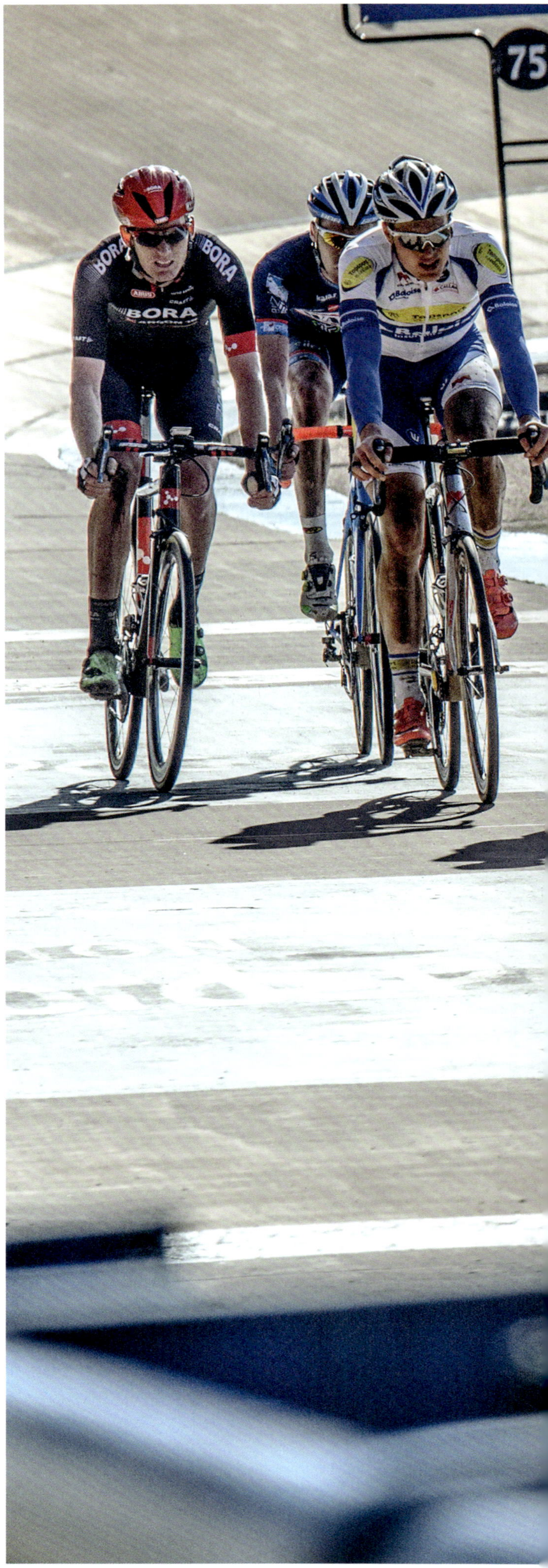

Abgekämpft: Tom Boonen (Etixx – Quick Step, links). **Exhausted: Tom Boonen (Etixx – Quick Step, left).** *Épuisé par la bataille : Tom Boonen (Etixx – Quick Step, à gauche).*

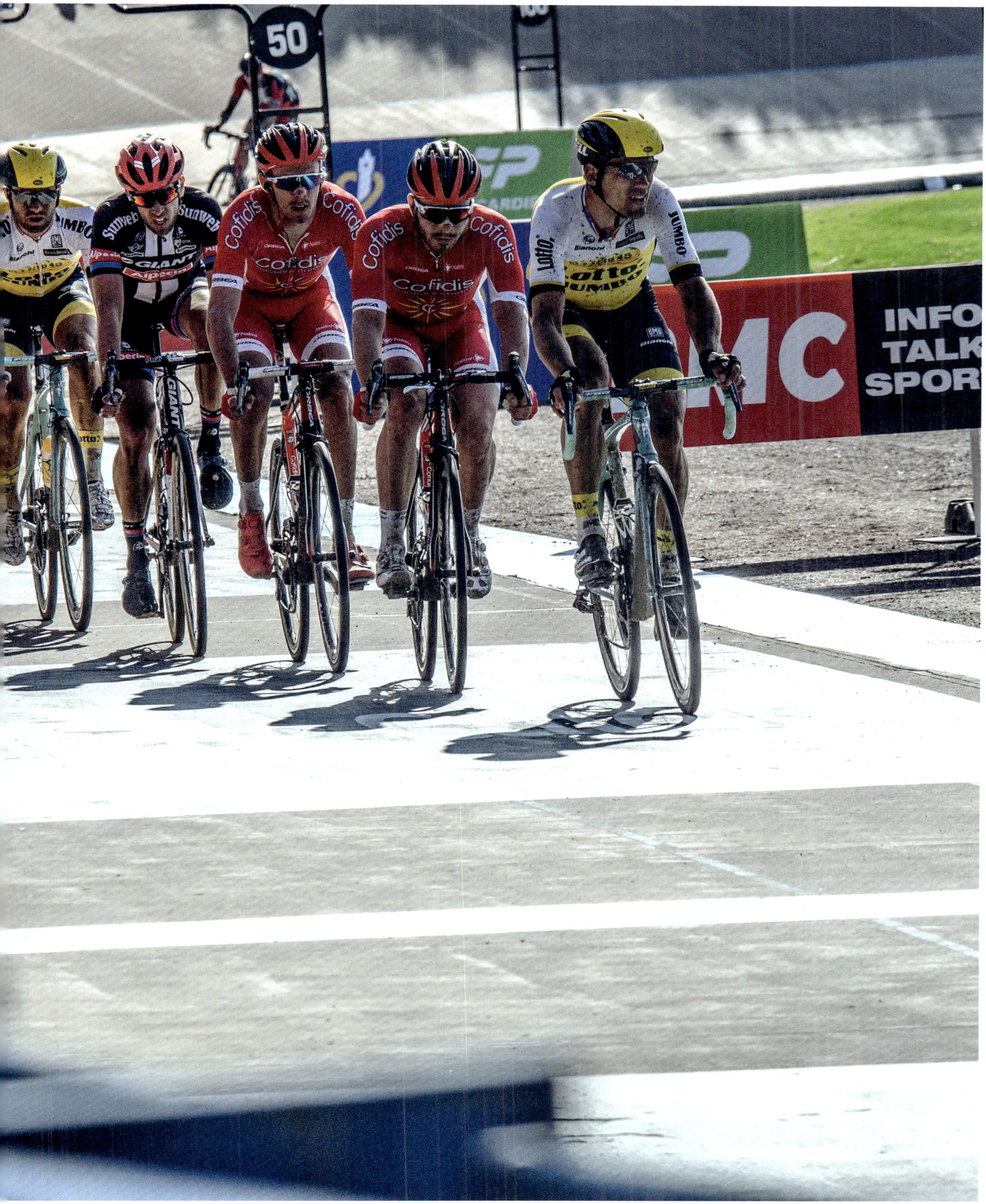
50
Cofidis
Cofidis
GIANT
JUMBO
INFO

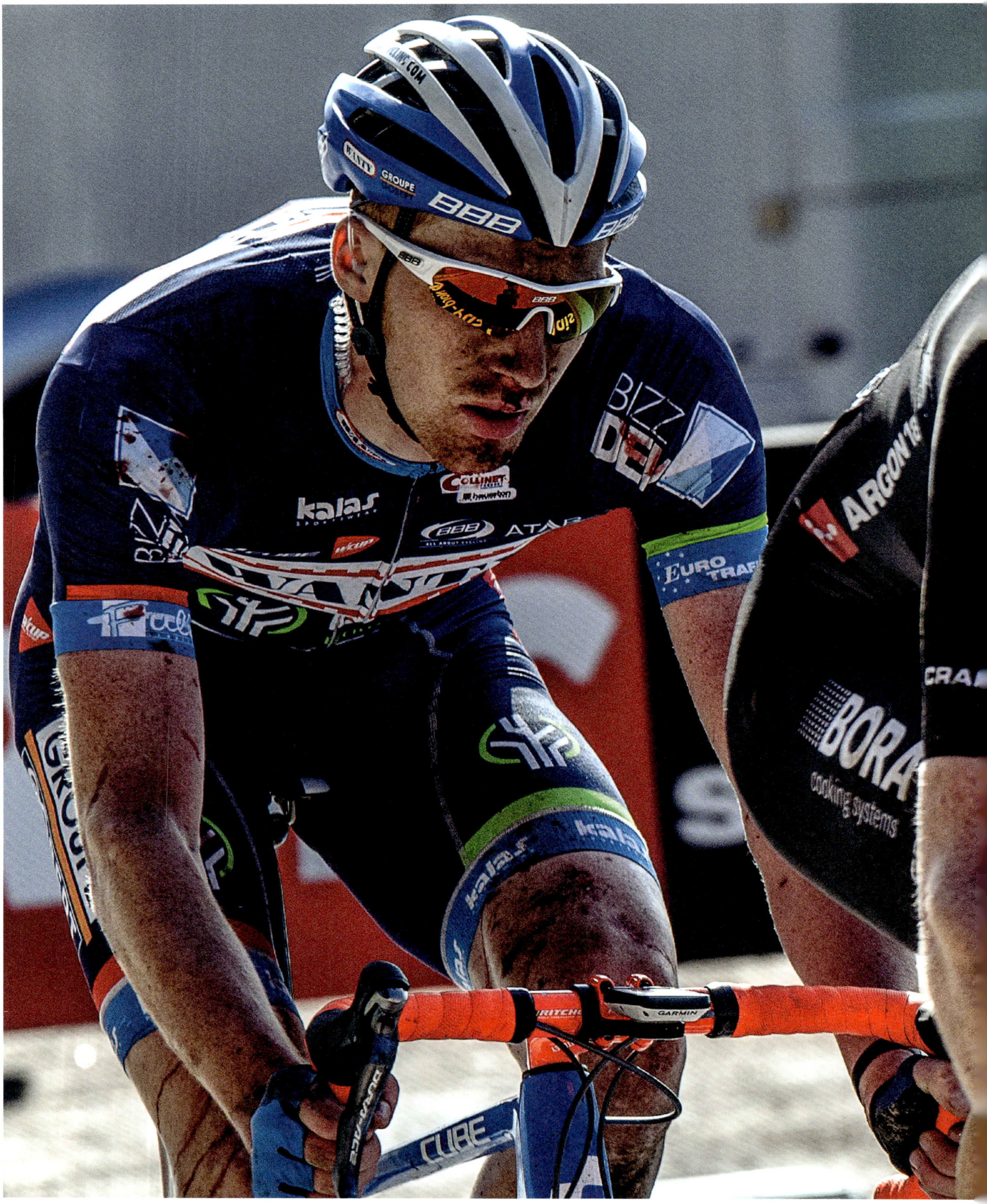
BBB
GROUPE
kalas
ATAR
EURO
ARGON 18
BORA
cooking systems
GARMIN
CUBE

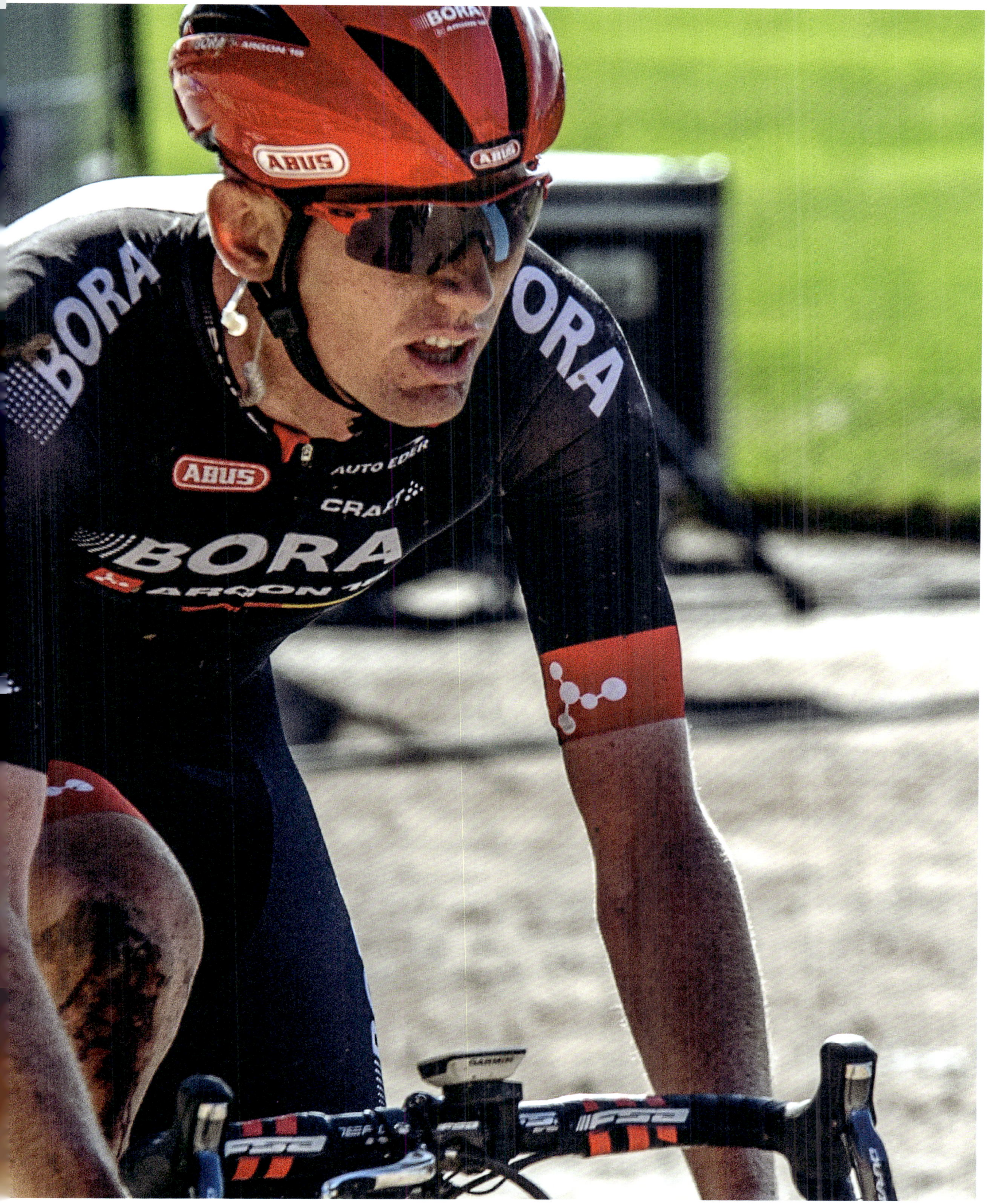

Die Hölle des Nordens überlebt: Frederik Backaert (Wanty-Groupe Gobert, Platz 22) und Zak Dempster (BORA - ARGON 18, Platz 24). **Surviving the hell of the north: Frederik Backaert (Wanty-Groupe Gobert, 22nd) and Zak Dempster (BORA - ARGON 18, 24th).** *Après la traversée de l'enfer du Nord : Frederik Backaert (Wanty-Groupe Gobert, 22e place) et Zak Dempster (BORA - ARGON 18, 24e place).*

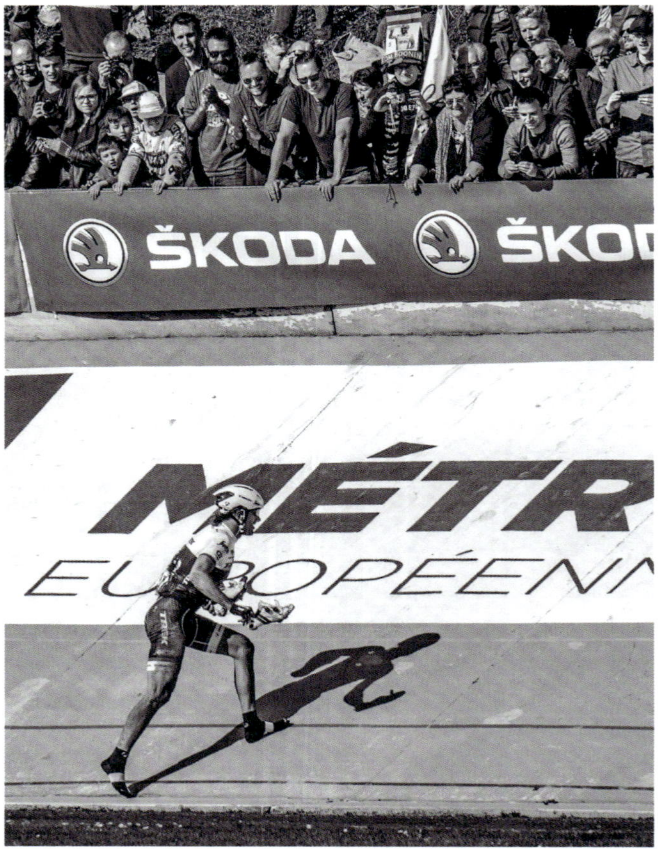
ŠKODA ŠKOD
MÉTR
EUROPÉENN

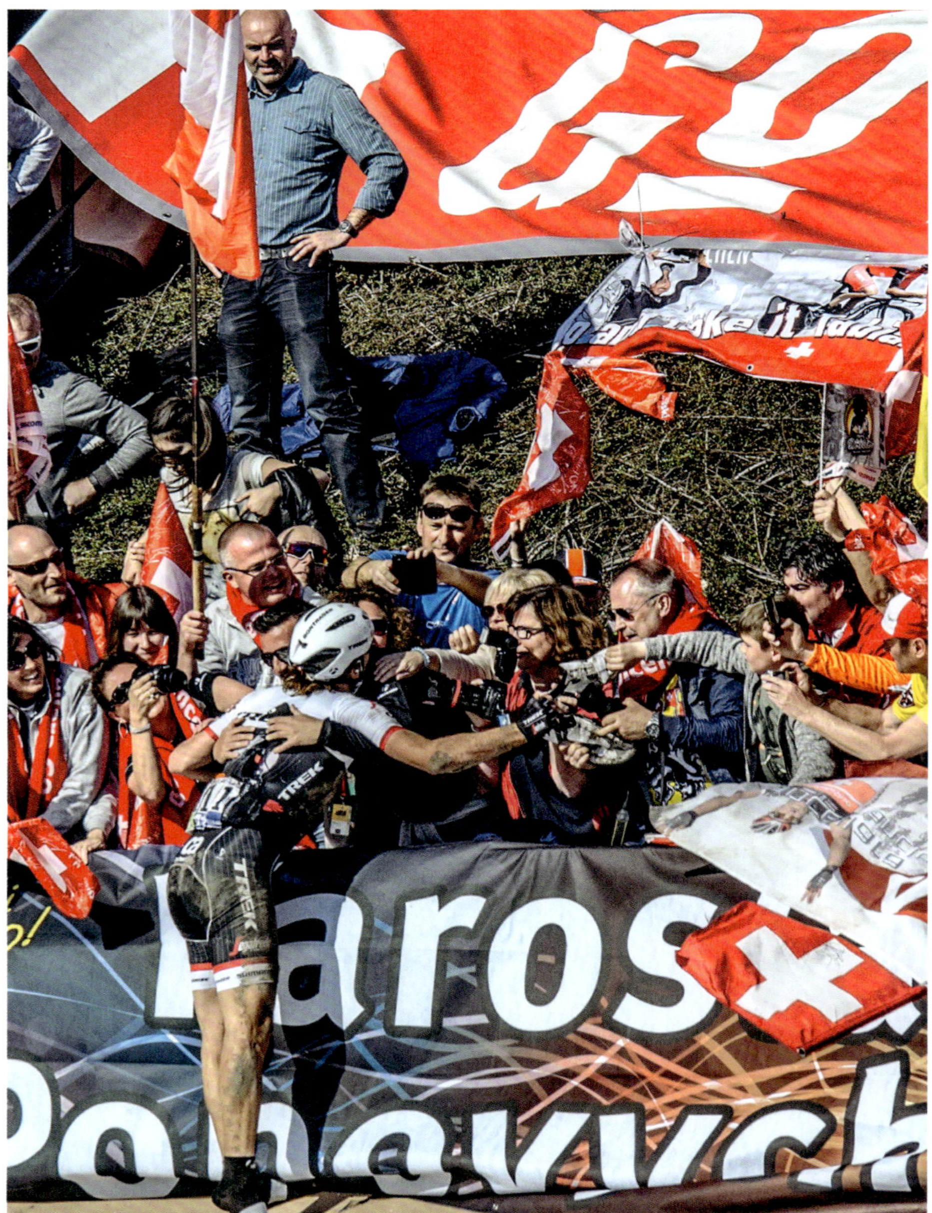
TREK

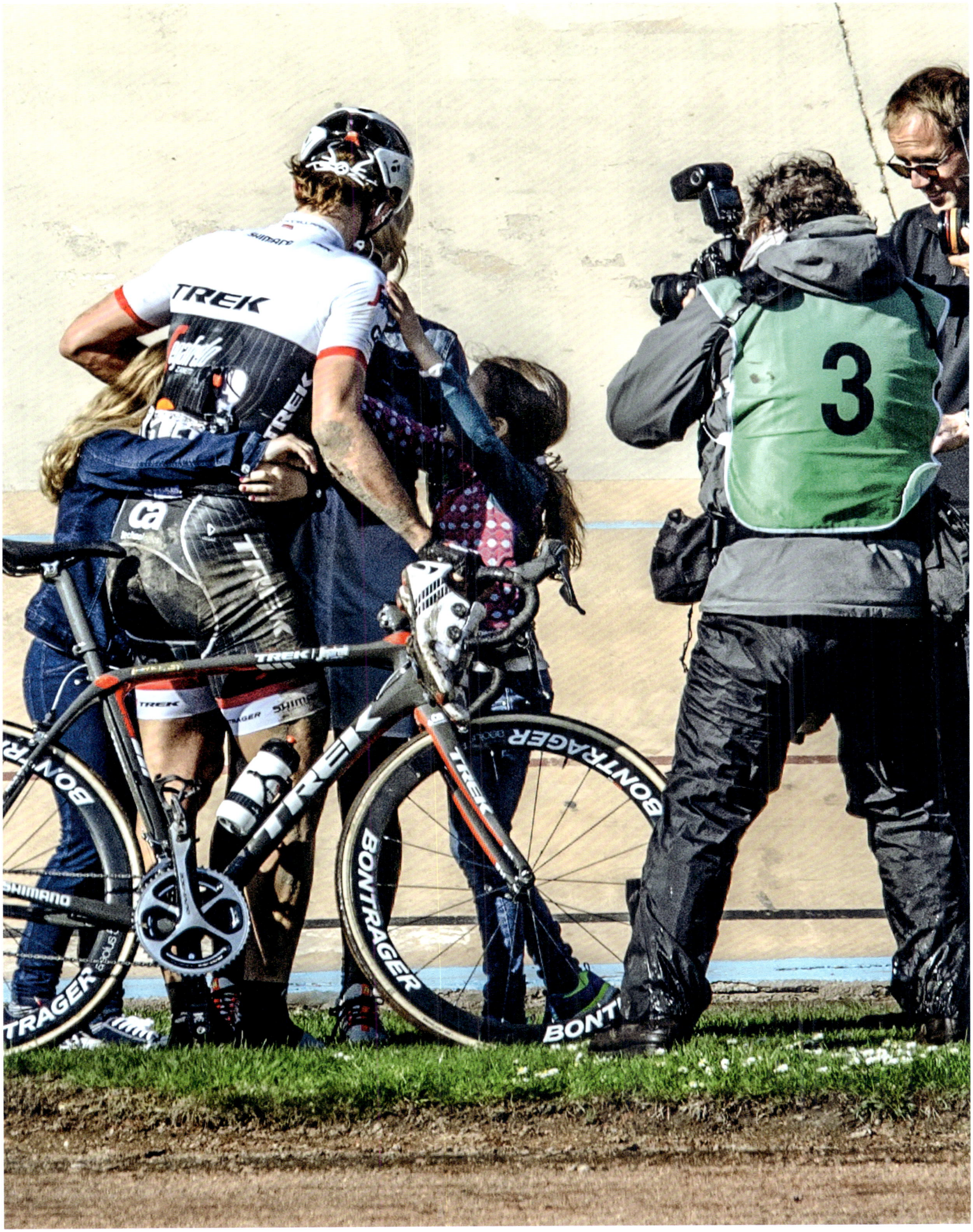

Sein letztes Paris – Roubaix: Fabian Cancellara (Trek – Segafredo) lässt sich von Freunden, Familie und Fans im Vélodrome feiern. **His final Paris – Roubaix: Fabian Cancellara (Trek – Segafredo) celebrates with friends, family and fans in the Vélodrome.** *Son dernier Paris – Roubaix : Fabian Cancellara (Trek – Segafredo) félicité par ses amis, sa famille et ses fans au vélodrome.*

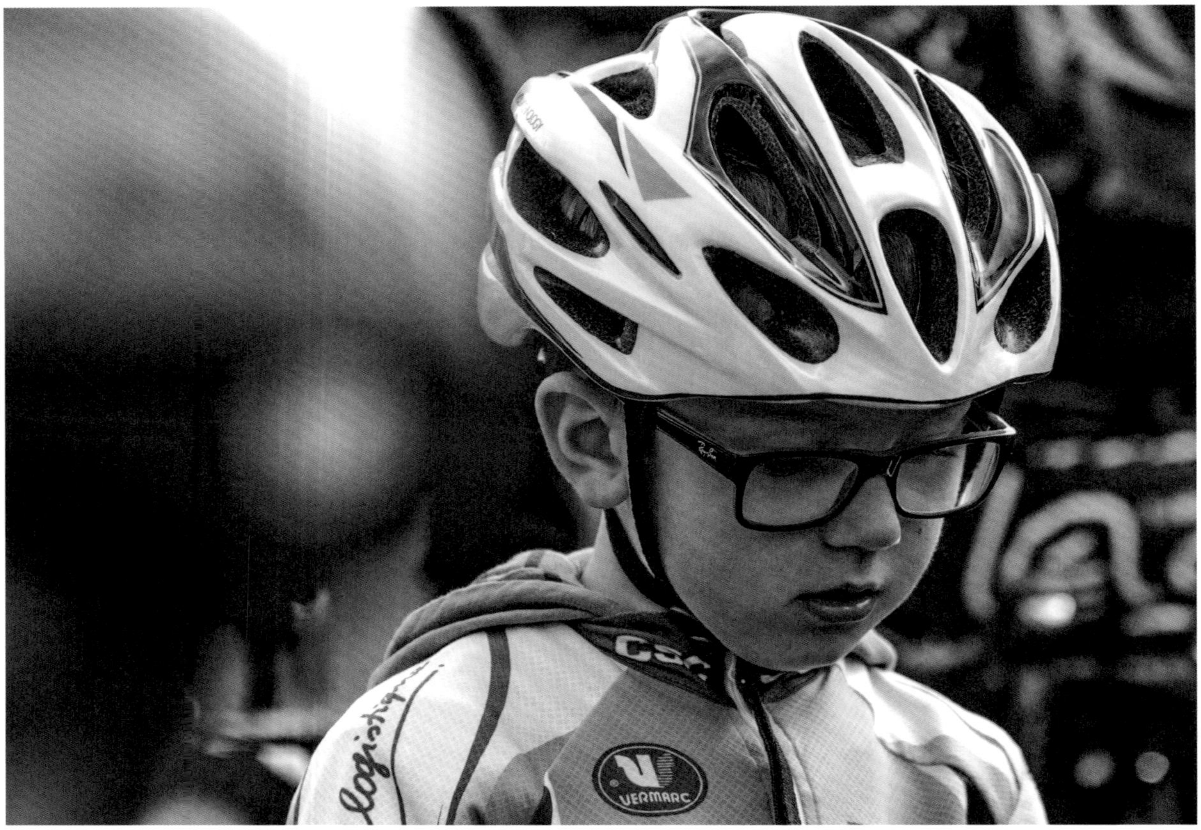
VERMARC

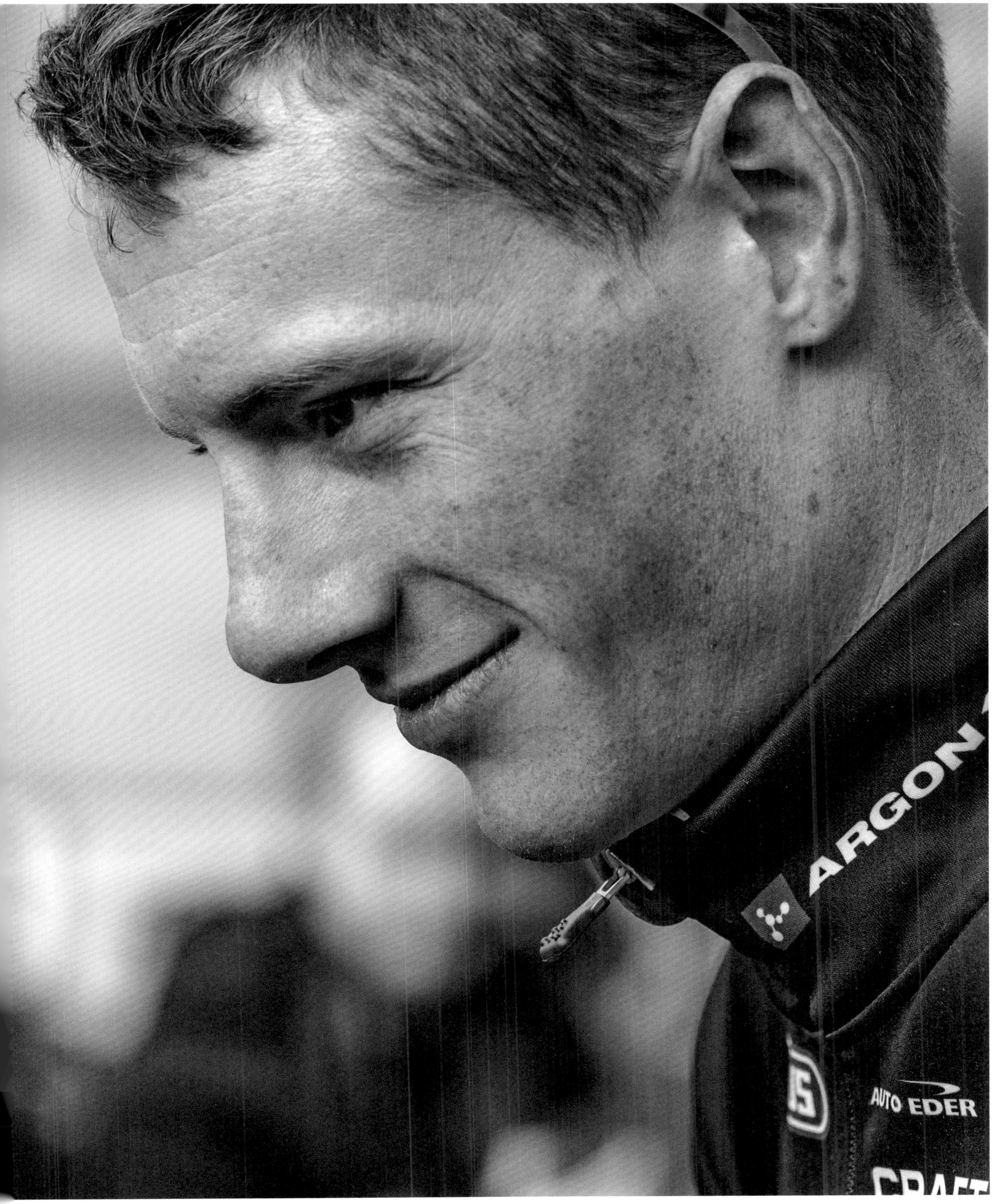

Sam Bennett (BORA - ARGON 18). **Sam Bennett (BORA - ARGON 18).** *Sam Bennett (BORA - ARGON 18).*

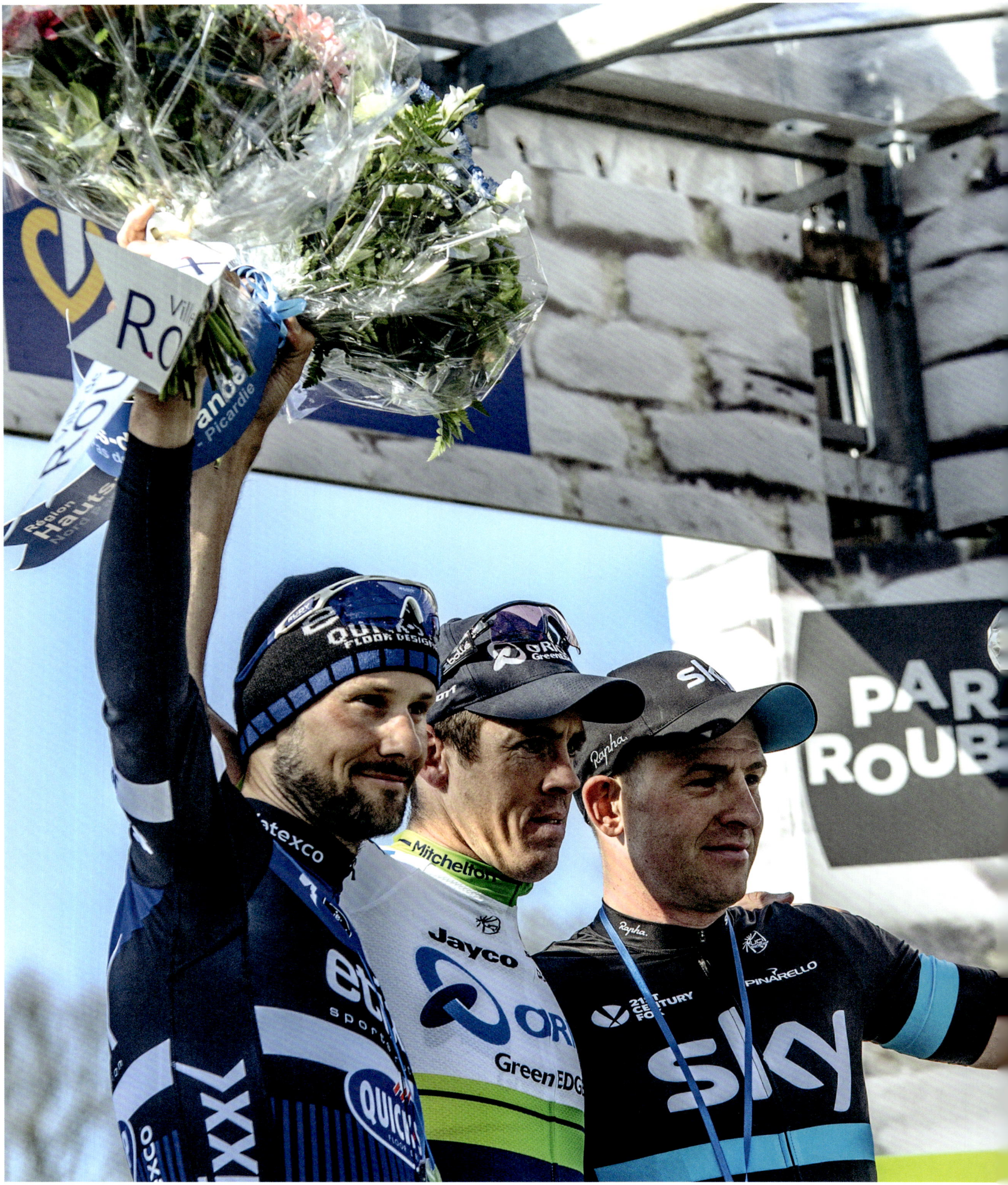

↑ Das Podium 2016: Sieger Mathew Hayman (ORICA-GreenEDGE) vor Tom Boonen (Etixx – Quick Step) und Ian Stannard (Team Sky). **The 2016 podium: winner Mathew Hayman (ORICA-GreenEDGE) followed by Tom Boonen (Etixx – Quick Step) and Ian Stannard (Team Sky).** *Le podium 2016 : Mathew Hayman (ORICA-GreenEDGE), vainqueur devant Tom Boonen (Etixx – Quick Step) et Ian Stannard (Team Sky).*

↗ Wouter Wippert (Cannondale-Drapac Pro Cycling Team). **Wouter Wippert (Cannondale-Drapac Pro Cycling Team).** *Wouter Wippert (Cannondale-Drapac Pro Cycling Team).*

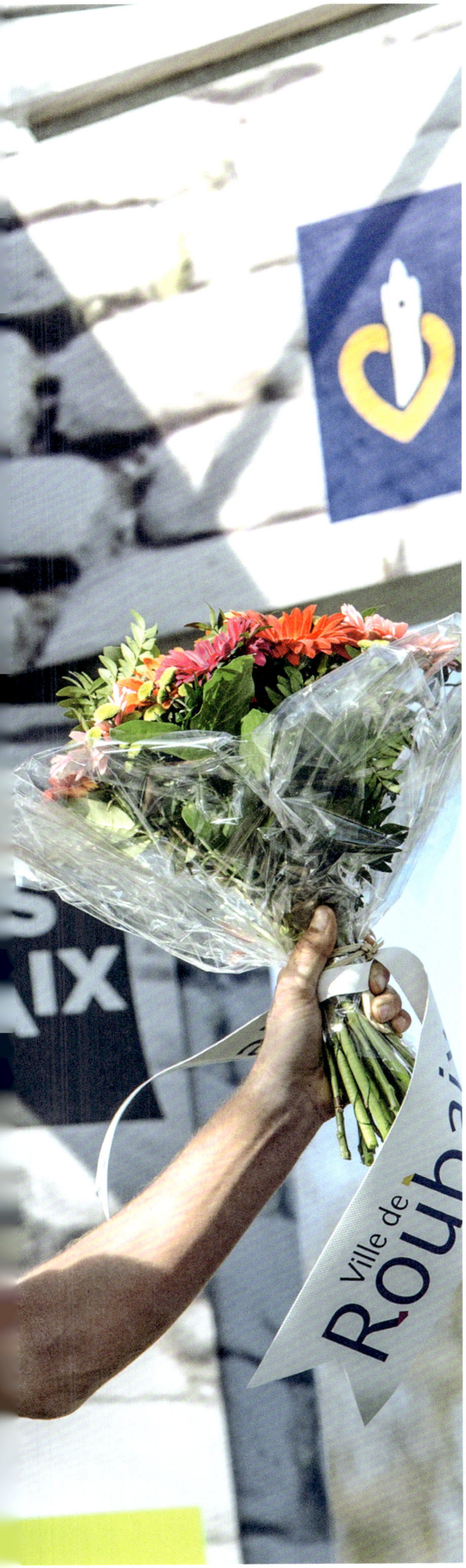
Ville de
Roubai

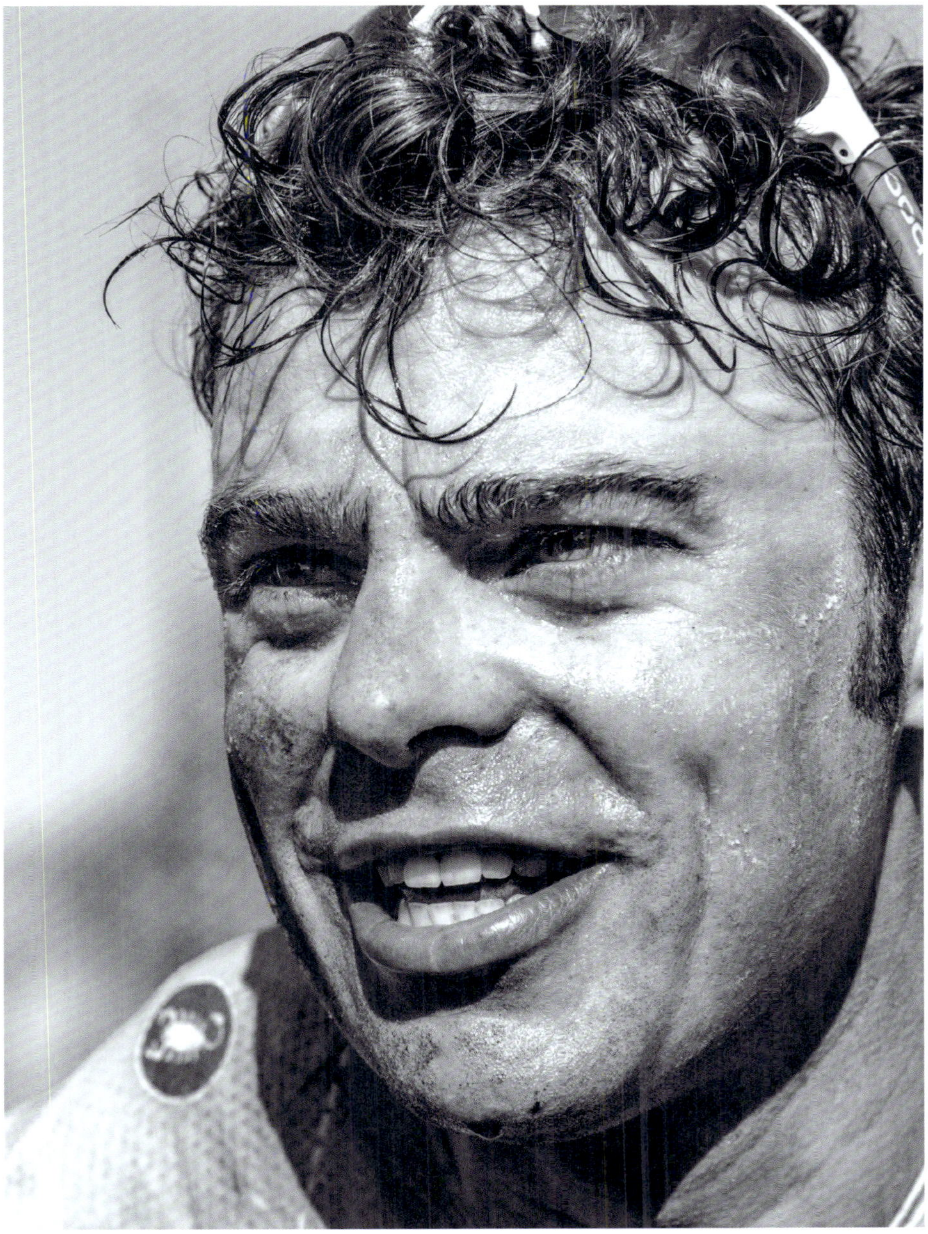

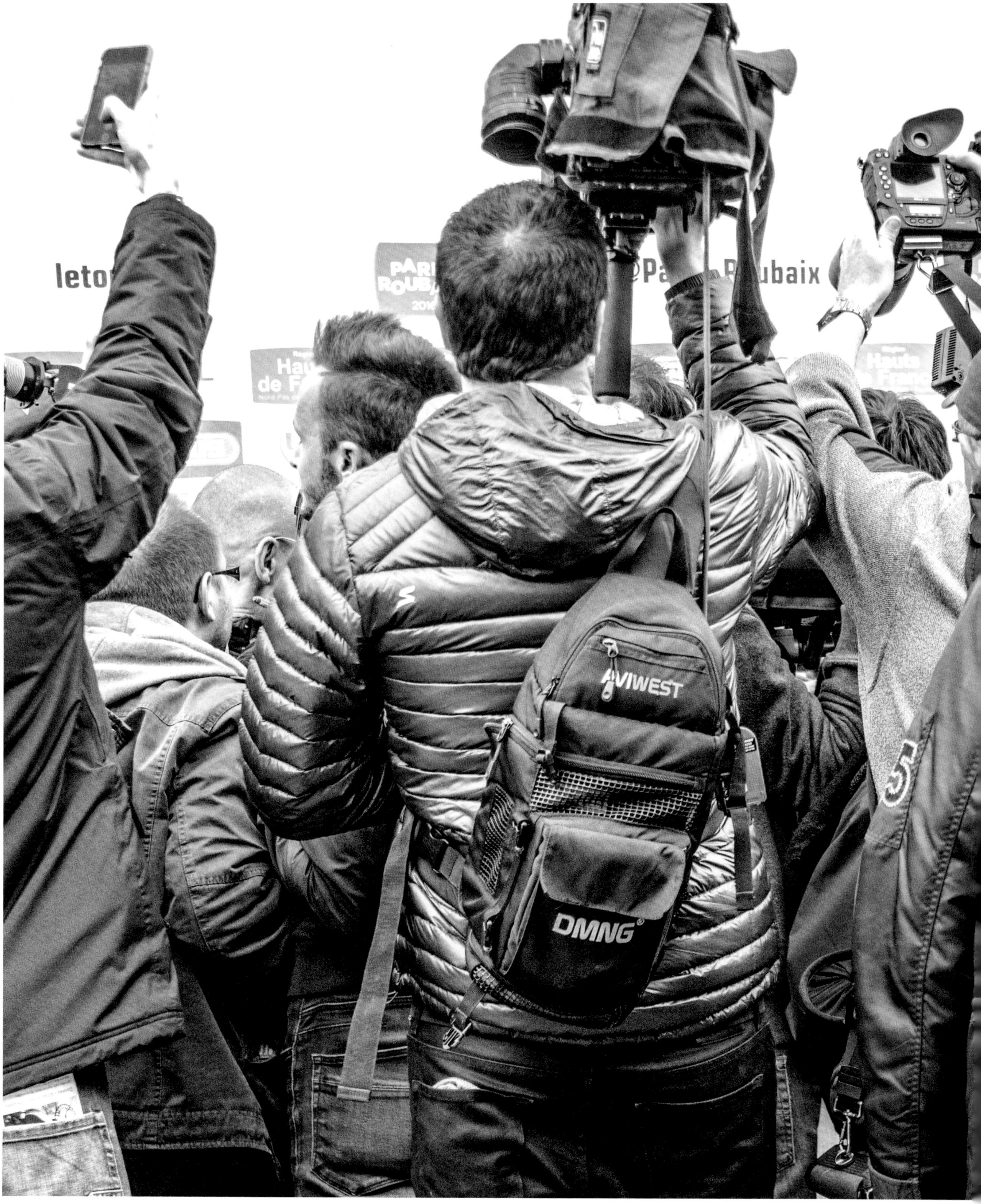
AVIWEST
DMNG

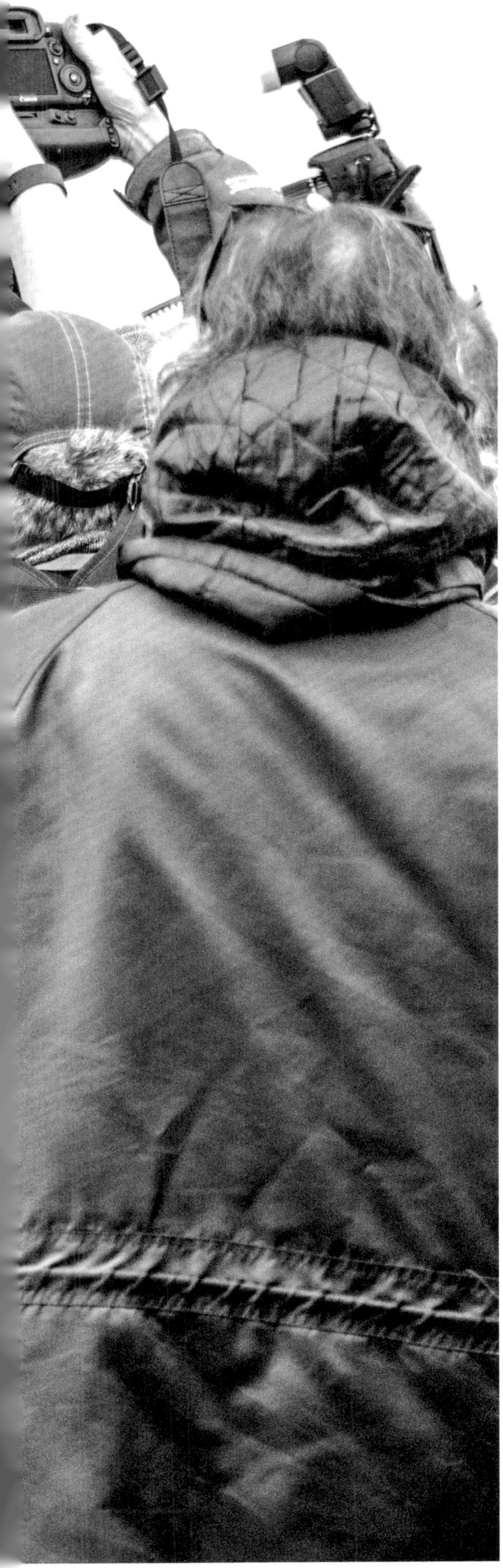

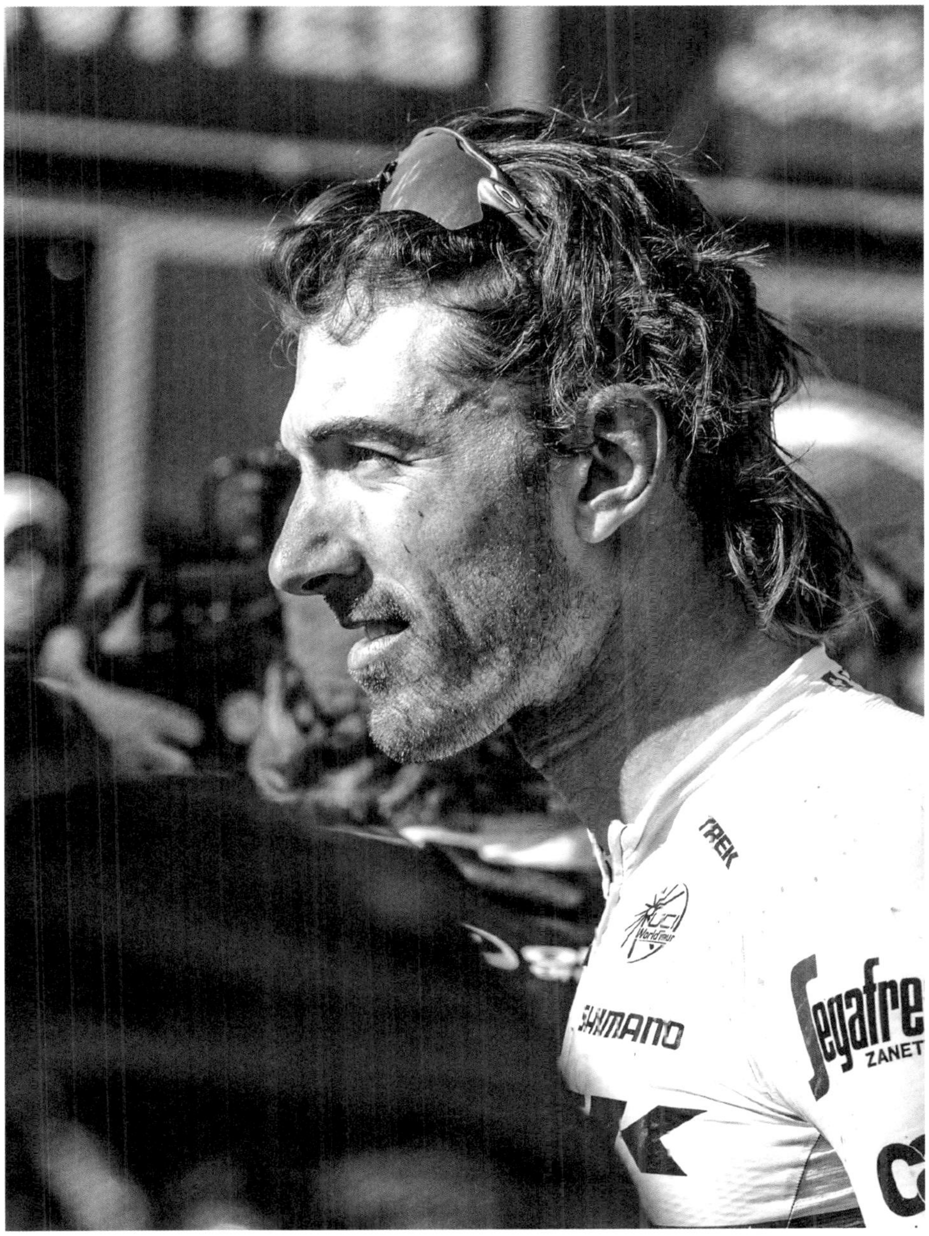

Im Fokus der Medien: Fabian Cancellara (Trek – Segafredo). **The focus of the media: Fabian Cancellara (Trek – Segafredo).** *Les journalistes se pressent autour de Fabian Cancellara (Trek – Segafredo).*

Liège Bastogne Liège

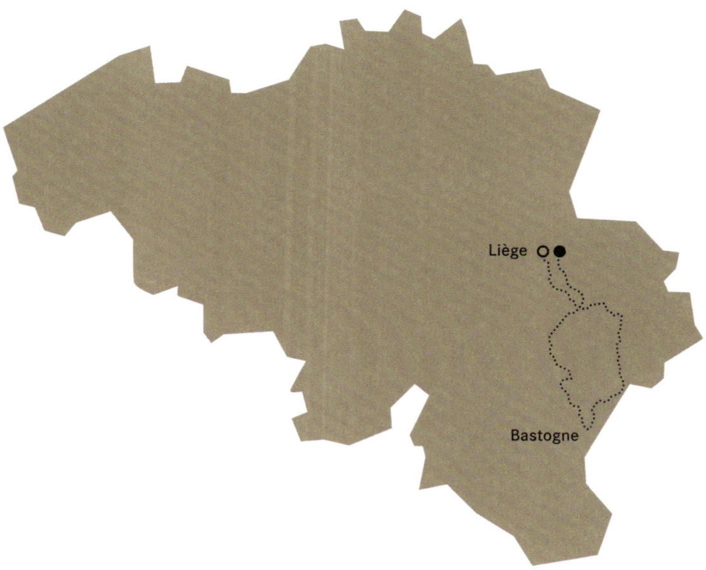

248

KILOMETRE

DATE: 24.04.2016

FIRST TOUR: 1892

DURATION: 06:24:29

ALTIMETRE: 4,470 m

38.70

KM/H AVG. SPEED WINNER

„La Doyenne" („Die Älteste") ist das älteste Eintagesrennen und eins der fünf Monumente des Radsports. Zahlreiche steile Anstiege mit teilweise über 12 % machen es zu einem der anspruchsvollsten Rennen, das Radsportlegende Eddy Merckx insgesamt fünf Mal gewann. **'La Doyenne' ('The Oldest') is the oldest one-day race and one of the five monuments of cycling. Numerous steep climbs, some with an incline of over 12 %, make it one of the most demanding races which cycling legend Eddy Merckx won a total of five times.** *La « doyenne » est la plus ancienne des classiques et l'un des cinq monuments du cyclisme. De nombreuses pentes raides à plus de 12 % en font l'une des courses les plus exigeantes, la légende du cyclisme Eddy Merckx l'a gagnée cinq fois.*

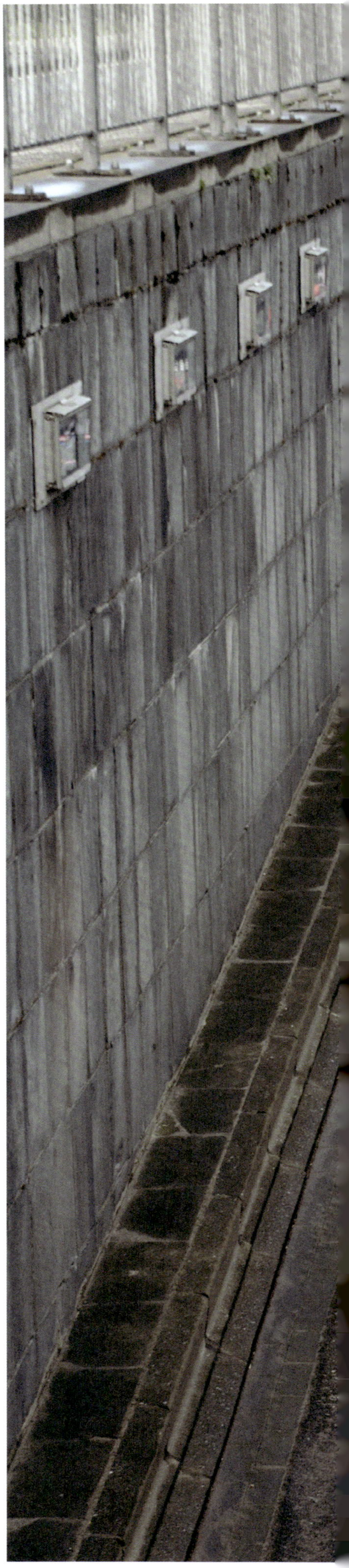

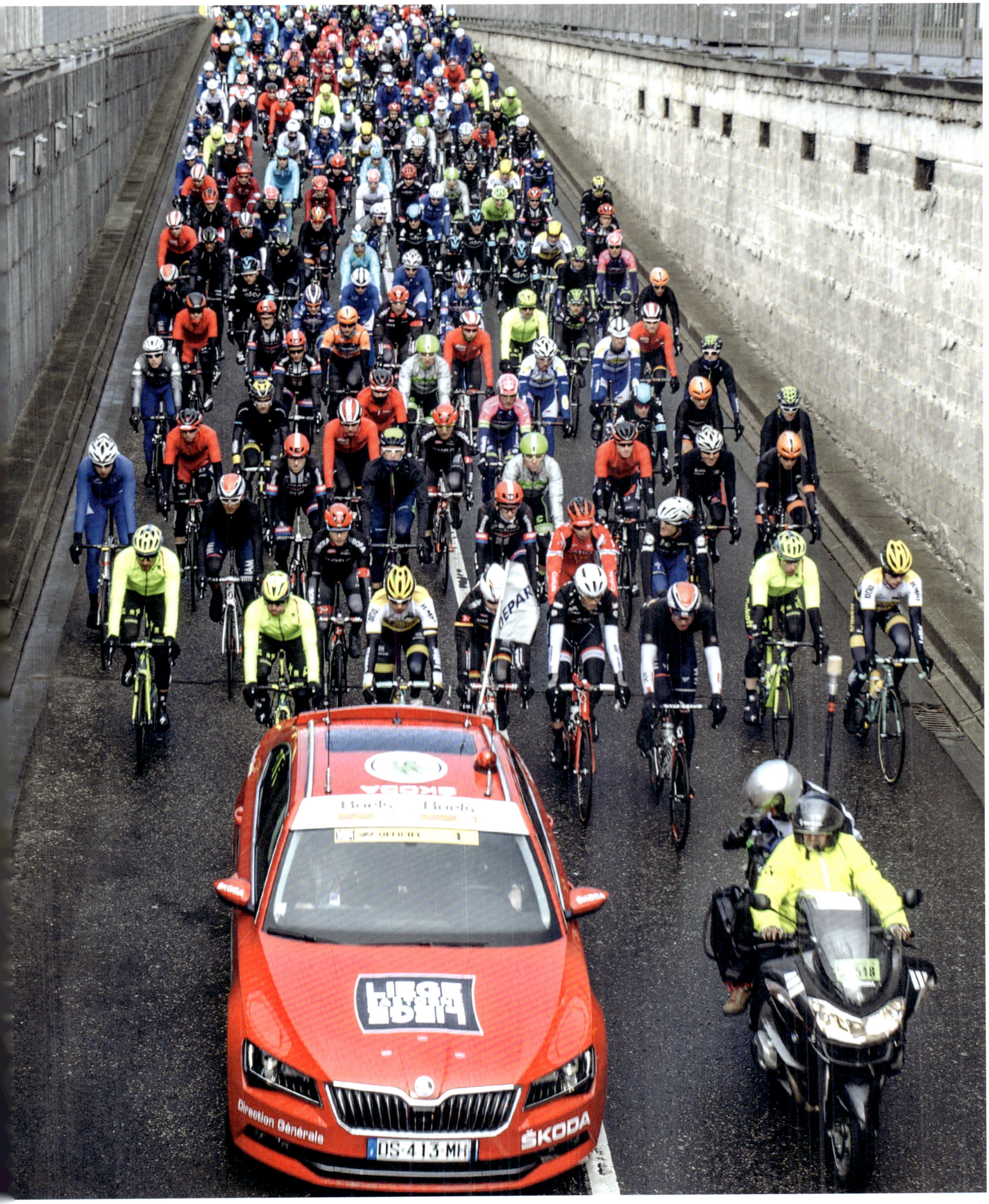

Start von „La Doyenne", des ältesten Eintagesrennen der Welt und eins der fünf Monumente des Radsports. The start of 'La Doyenne', the world's oldest one-day race and one of the five momuments of cycling. *Au départ de « La Doyenne » : la plus ancienne classique du monde et l'un des cinque monuments du cyclisme.*

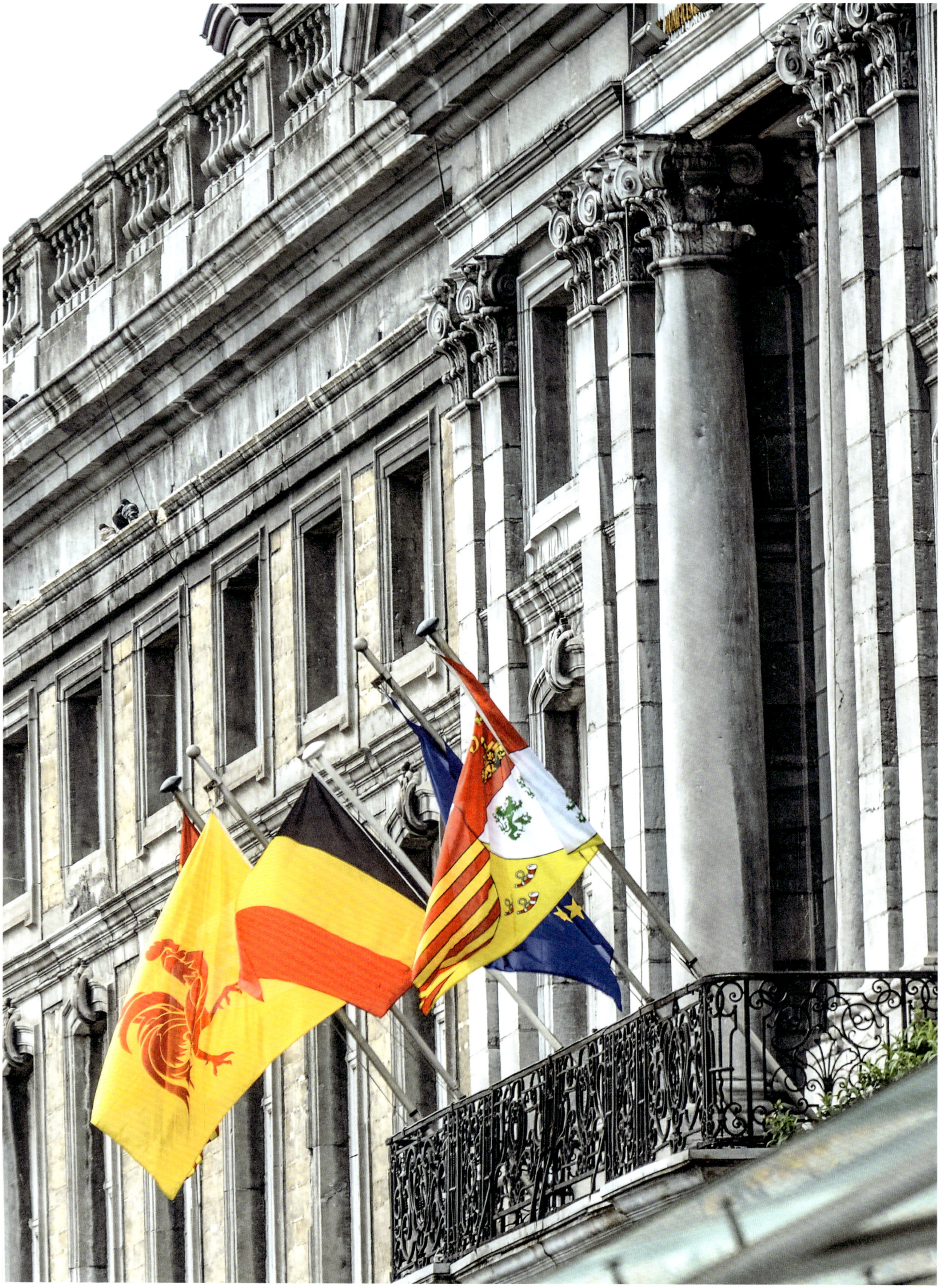

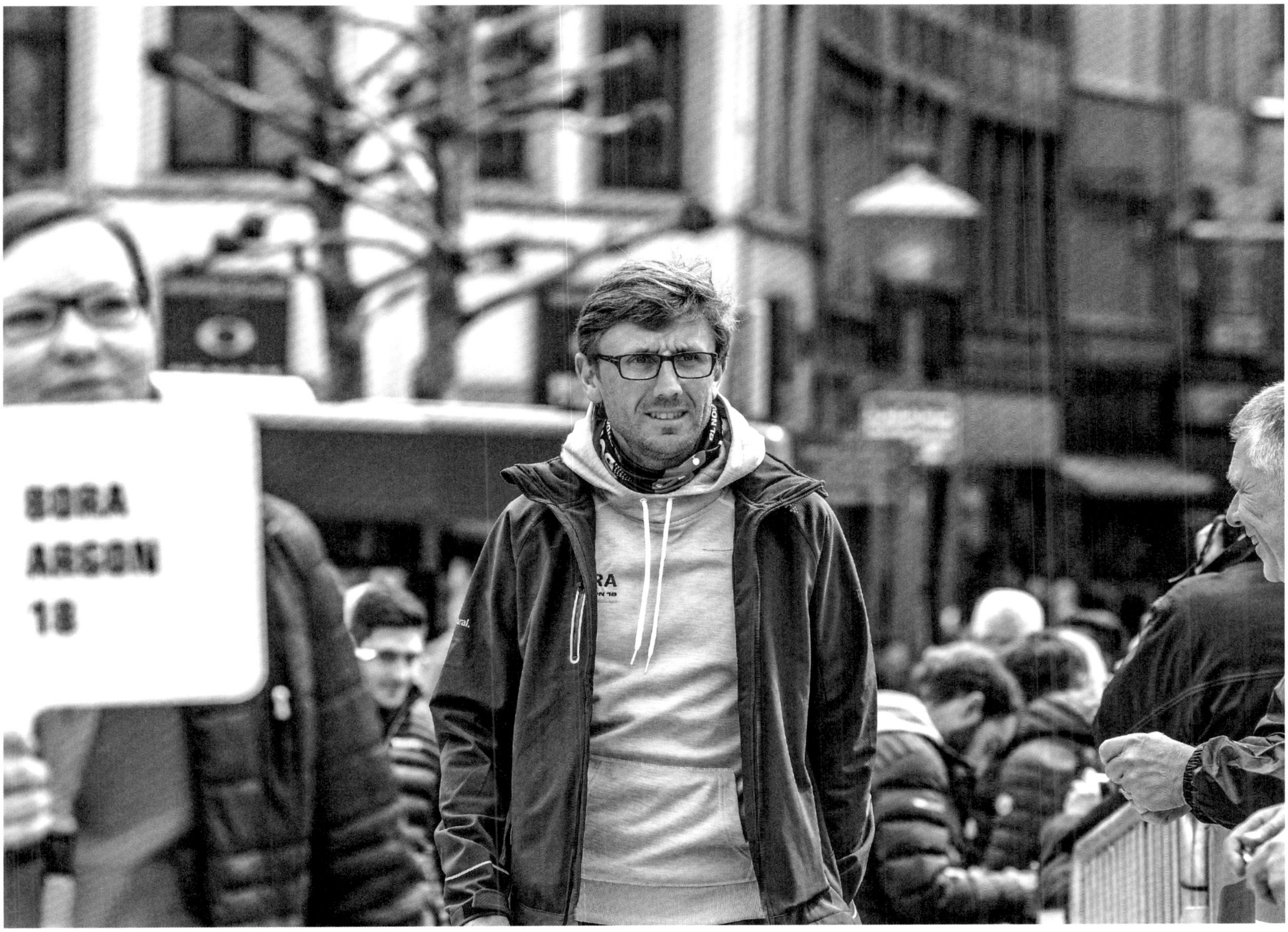

Bartosz Huzarski (BORA - ARGON 18) auf dem Weg zur Team-Präsentation. **Bartosz Huzarski (BORA - ARGON 18) on his way to the team presentation.**
Bartosz Huzarski (BORA - ARGON 18) se dirige vers la présentation des équipes.

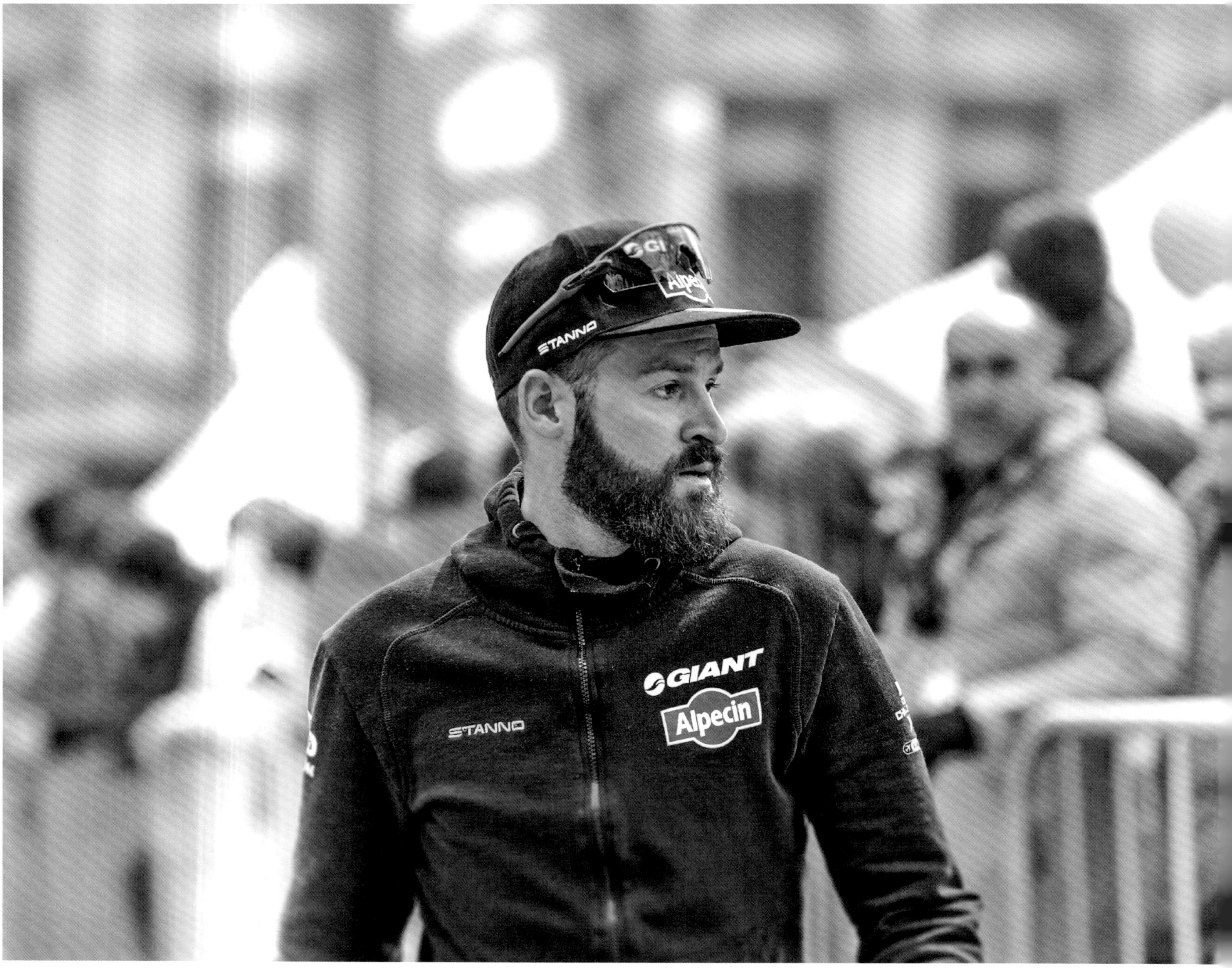

↑ Simon Geschke (Team Giant-Alpecin). **Simon Geschke (Team Giant-Alpecin).** *Simon Geschke (Team Giant-Alpecin).*
↗ Cesare Benedetti (BORA - ARGON 18). **Cesare Benedetti (BORA - ARGON 18).** *Cesare Benedetti (BORA - ARGON 18).*

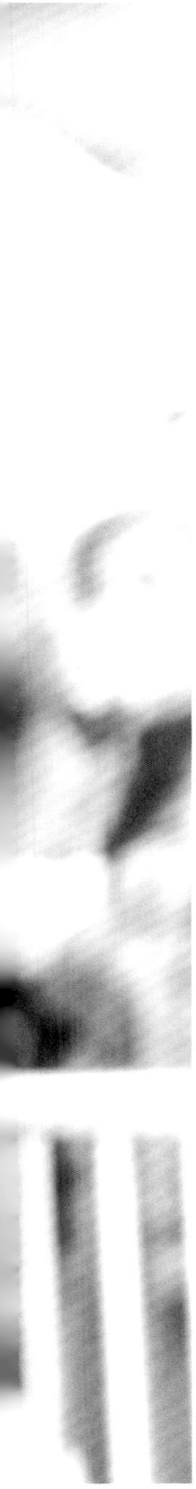

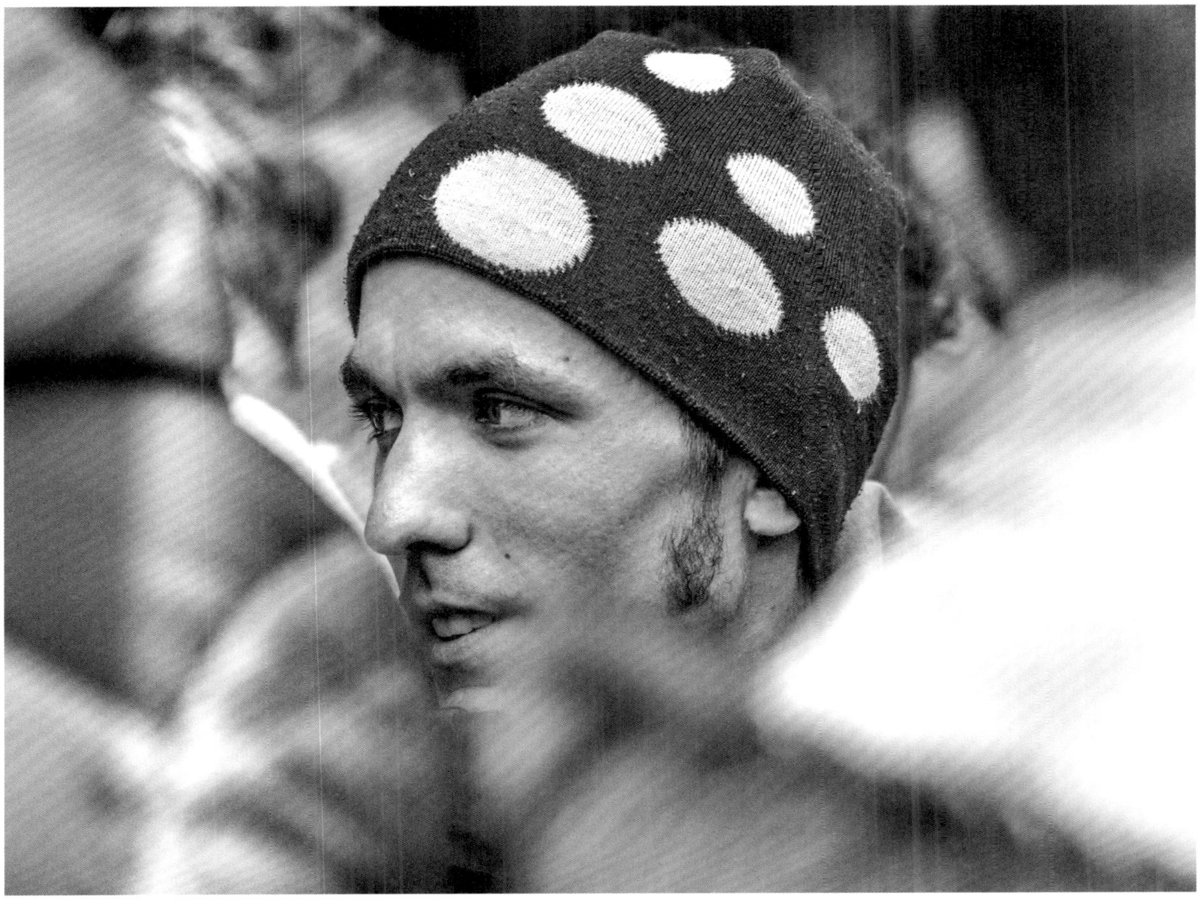

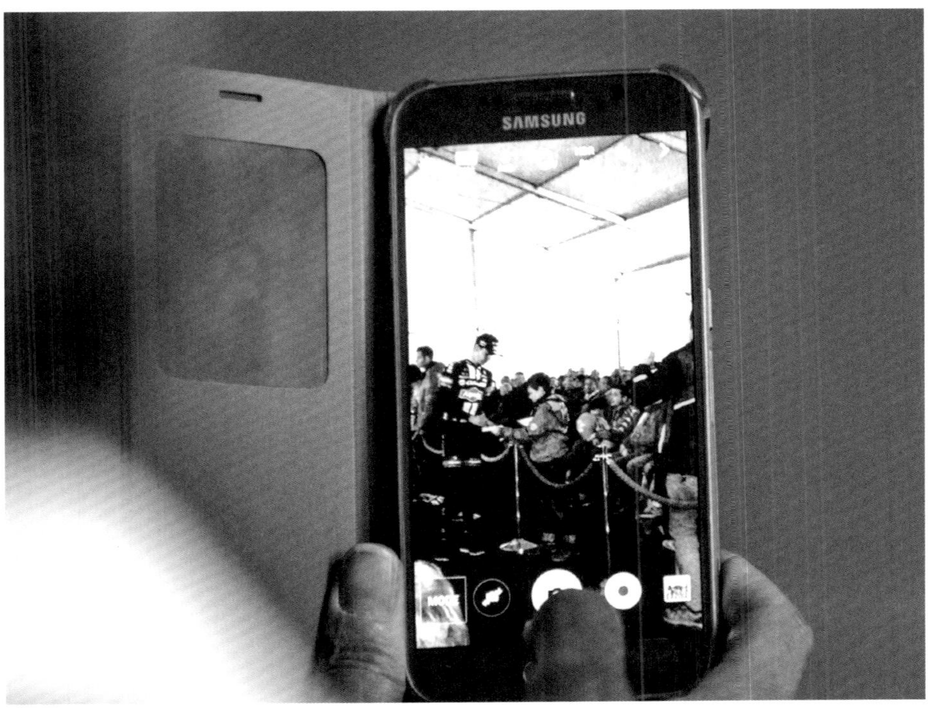
SAMSUNG

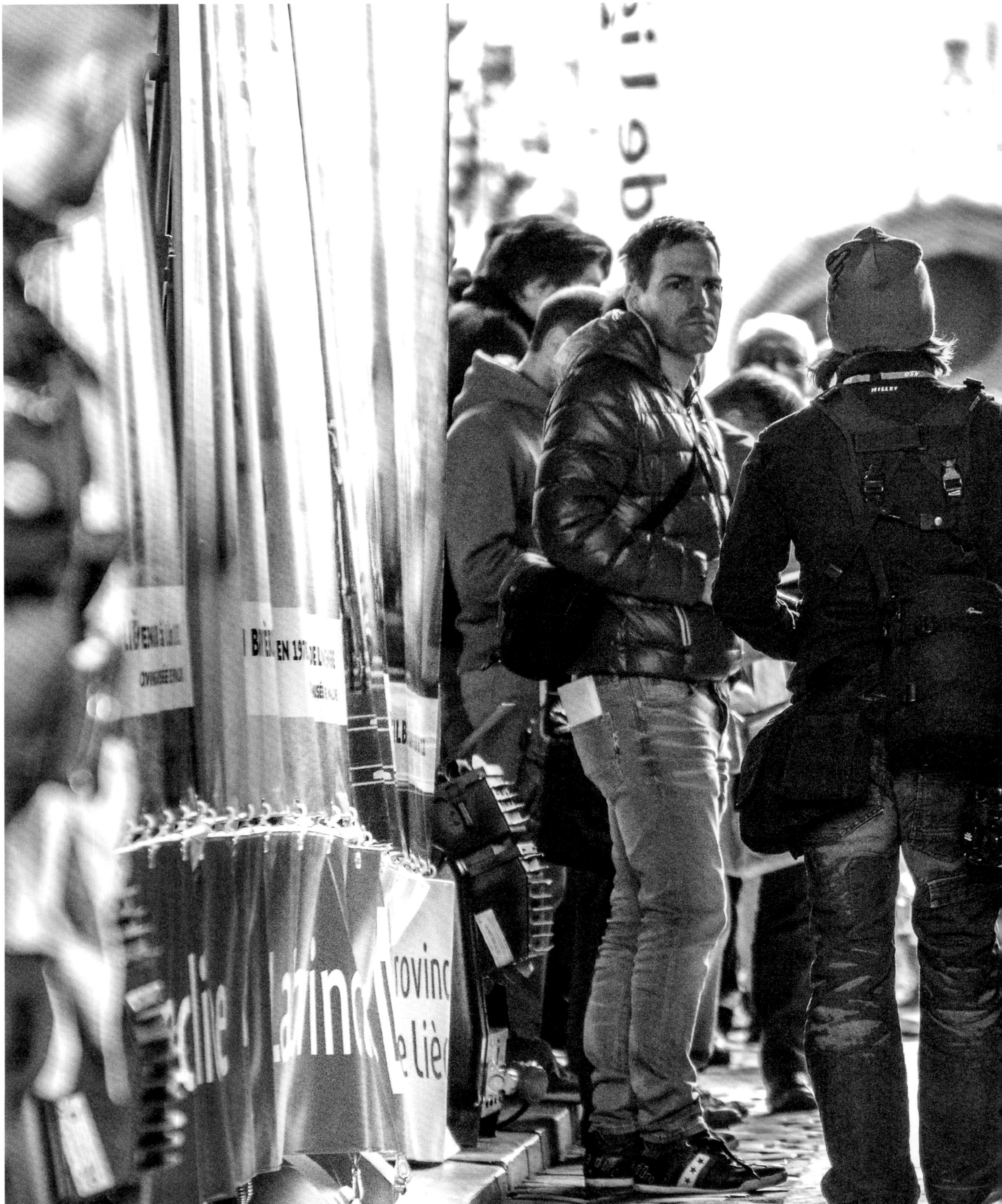

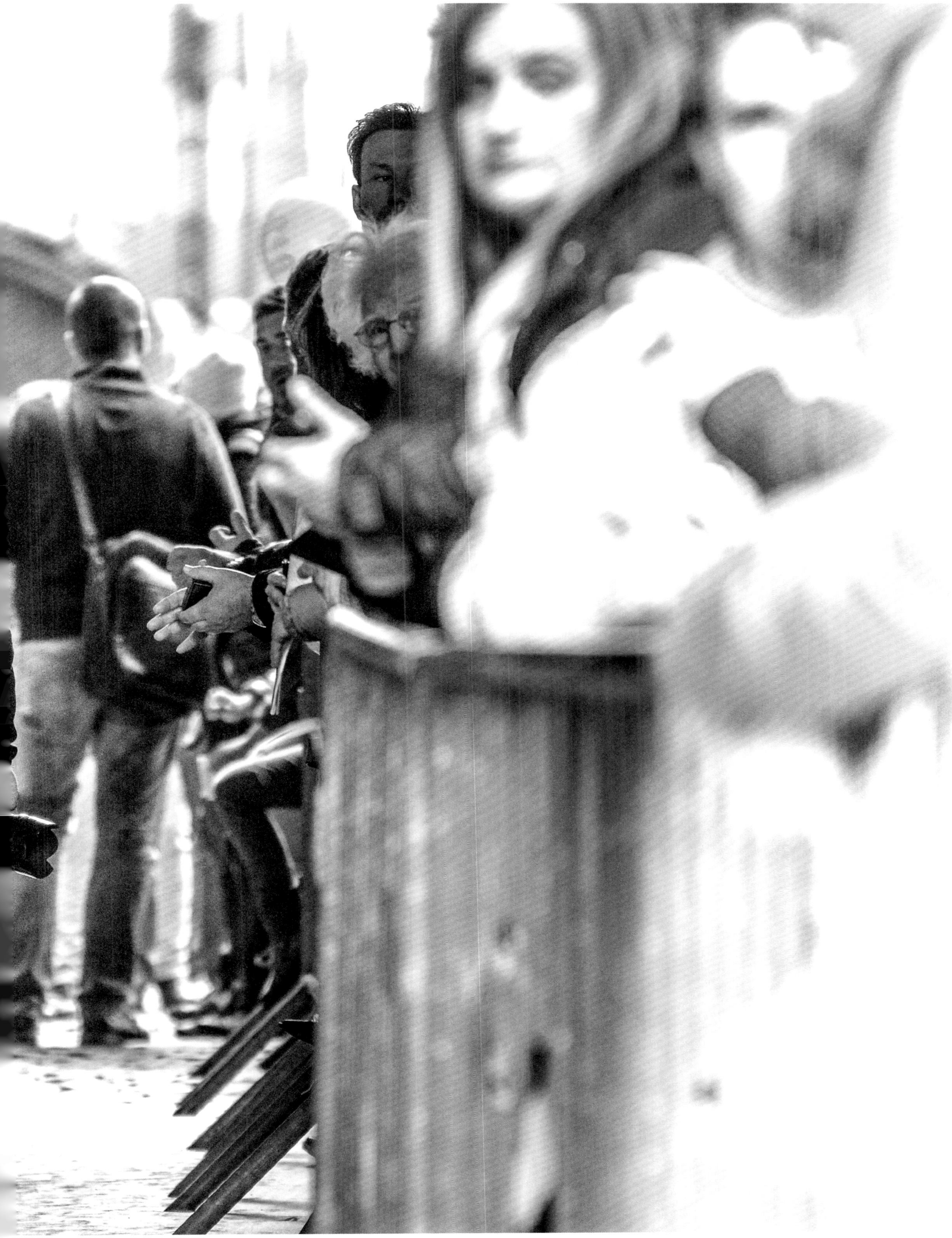

Angespanntes Warten auf den Start der 102. Edition des Rennens. **Nervous waiting for the start of the 102nd edition of the race.** *Dans l'expectative au départ de la 102e édition de la course.*

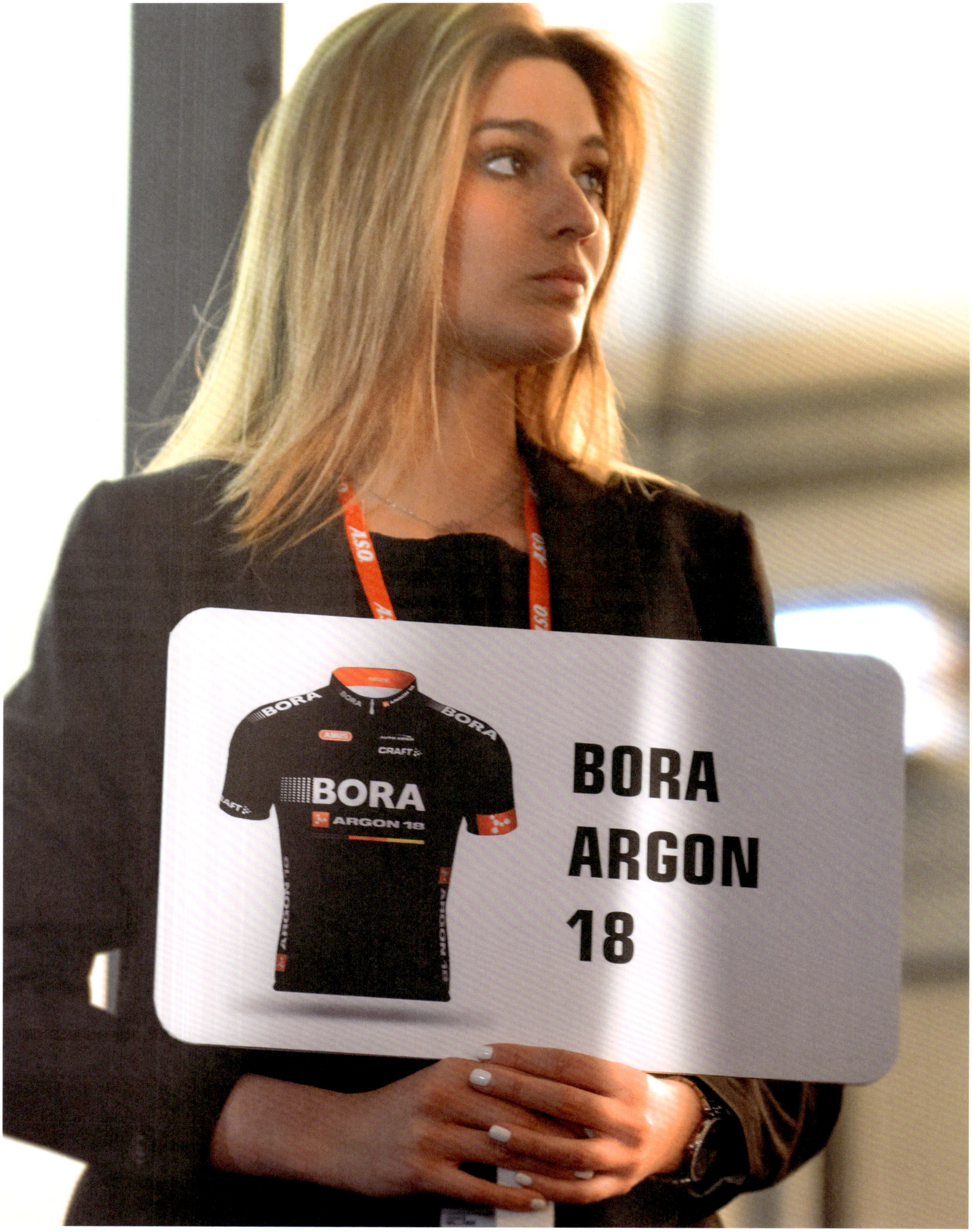

Vor der Teampräsentation. **Before the team presentation.** *Avant la présentation des équipes.*

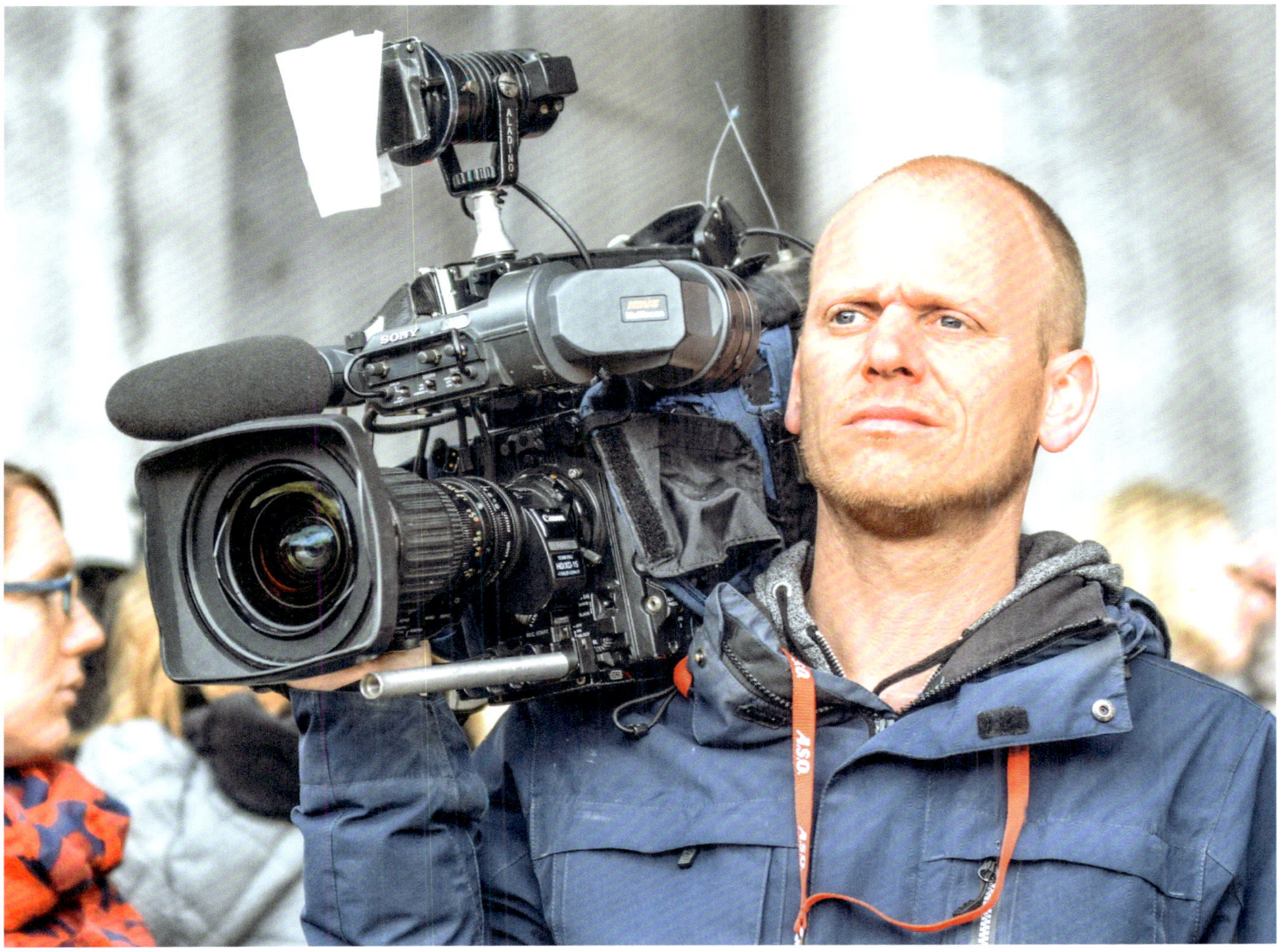
SONY

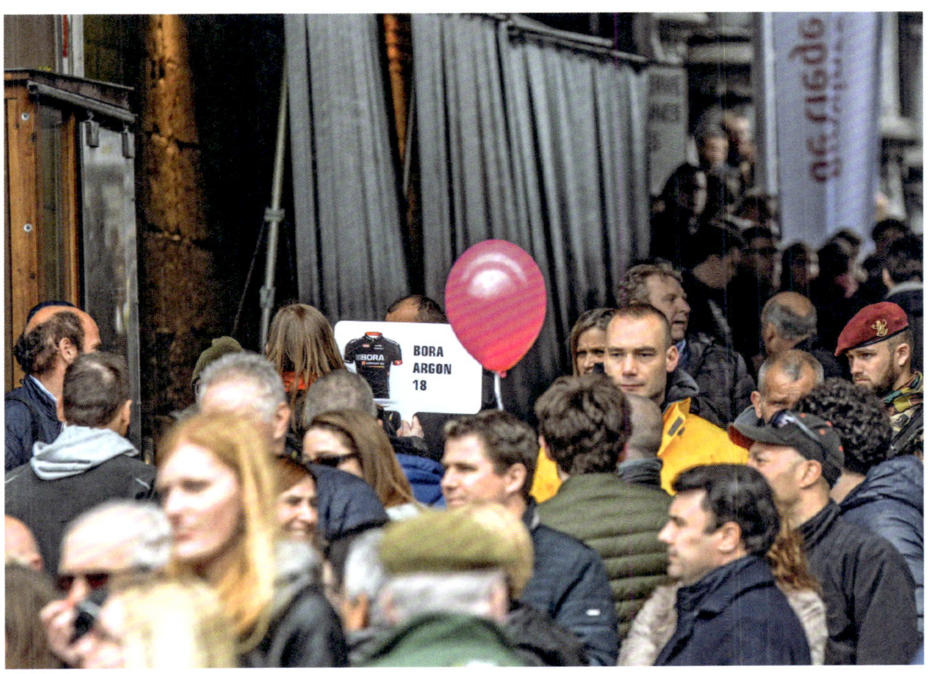
BORA
ARGON
18

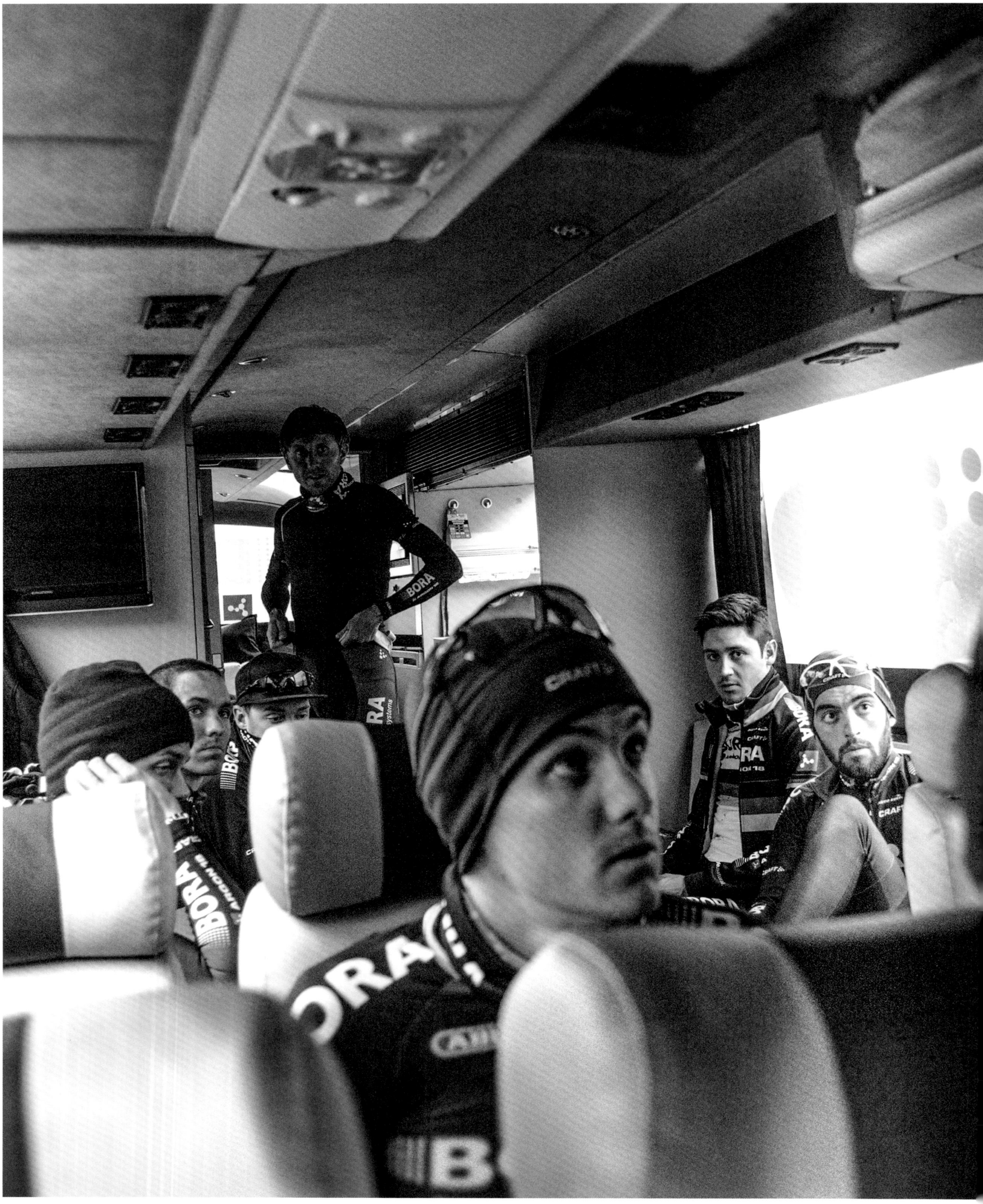

Auf dem Weg zum Rennen: Der Teambus von BORA - ARGON 18. **On the way to the race: in the BORA - ARGON 18 team bus.**
En route pour la course : le bus de l'équipe BORA - ARGON 18.

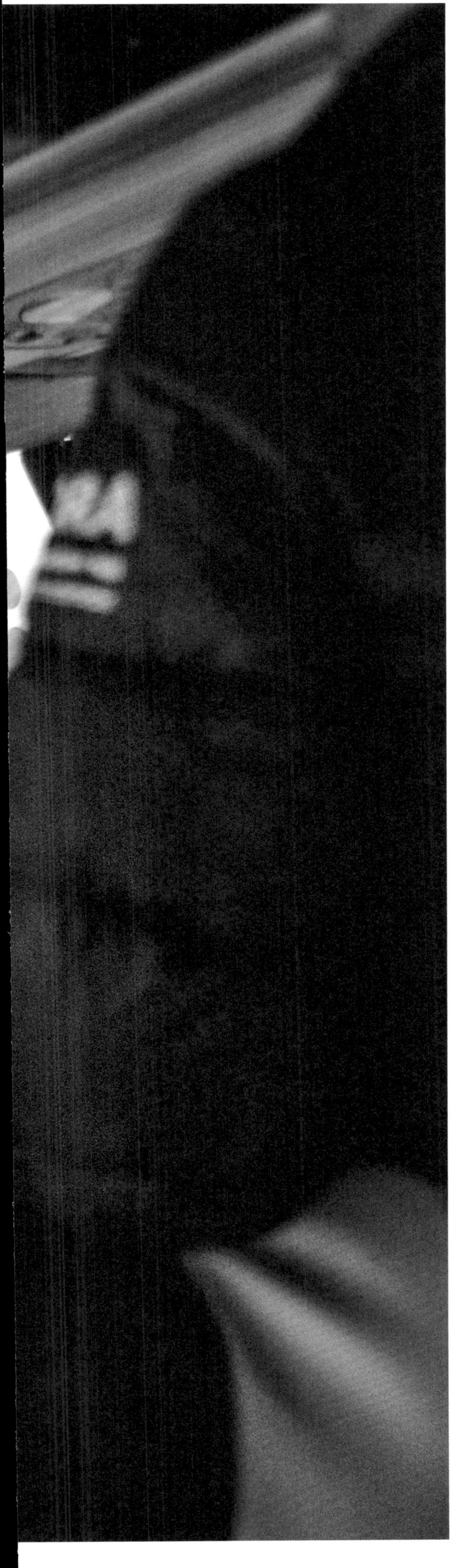

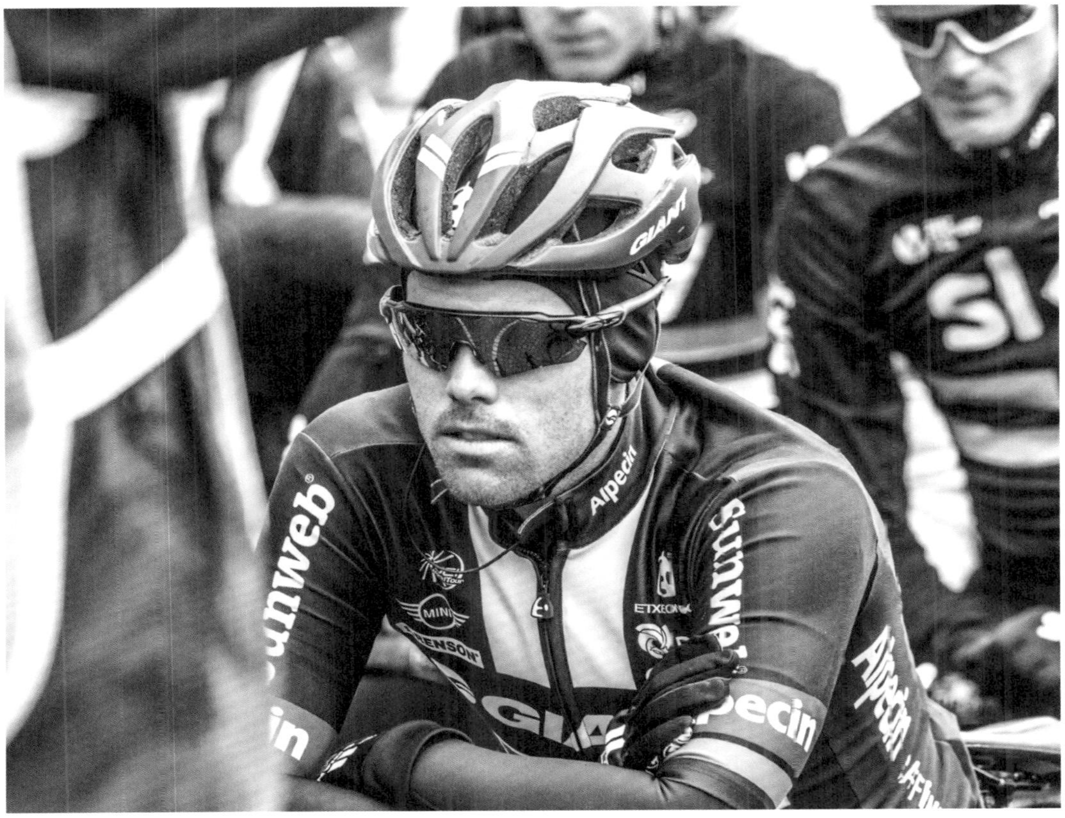
GIANT
Alpecin
sunweb
ETXEONDO
Alpecin
MINI
Alpecin
Sky

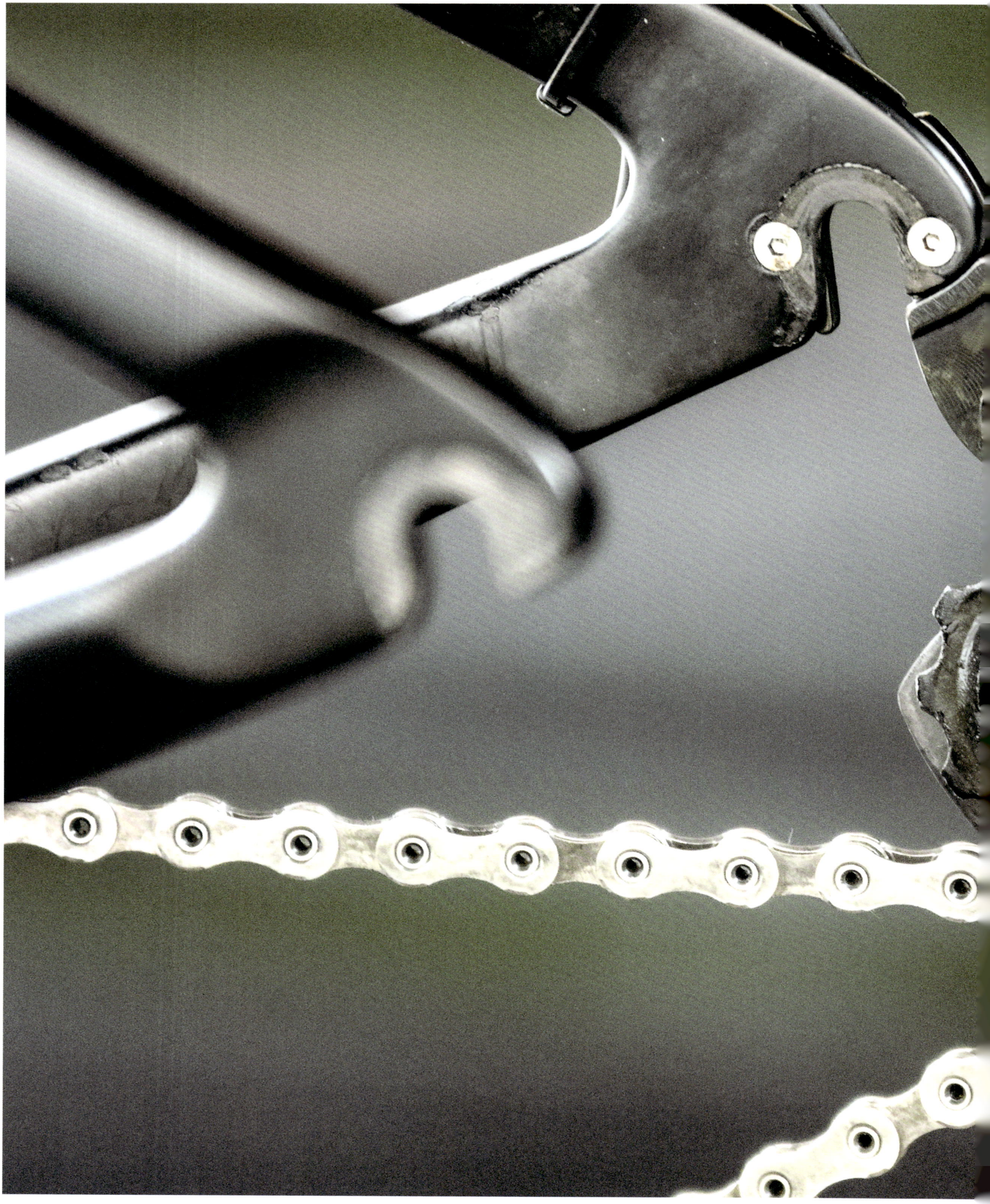

Alles muss perfekt vorbereitet sein. **Everything must be in perfect working order.** *Toute la préparation doit être impeccable.*

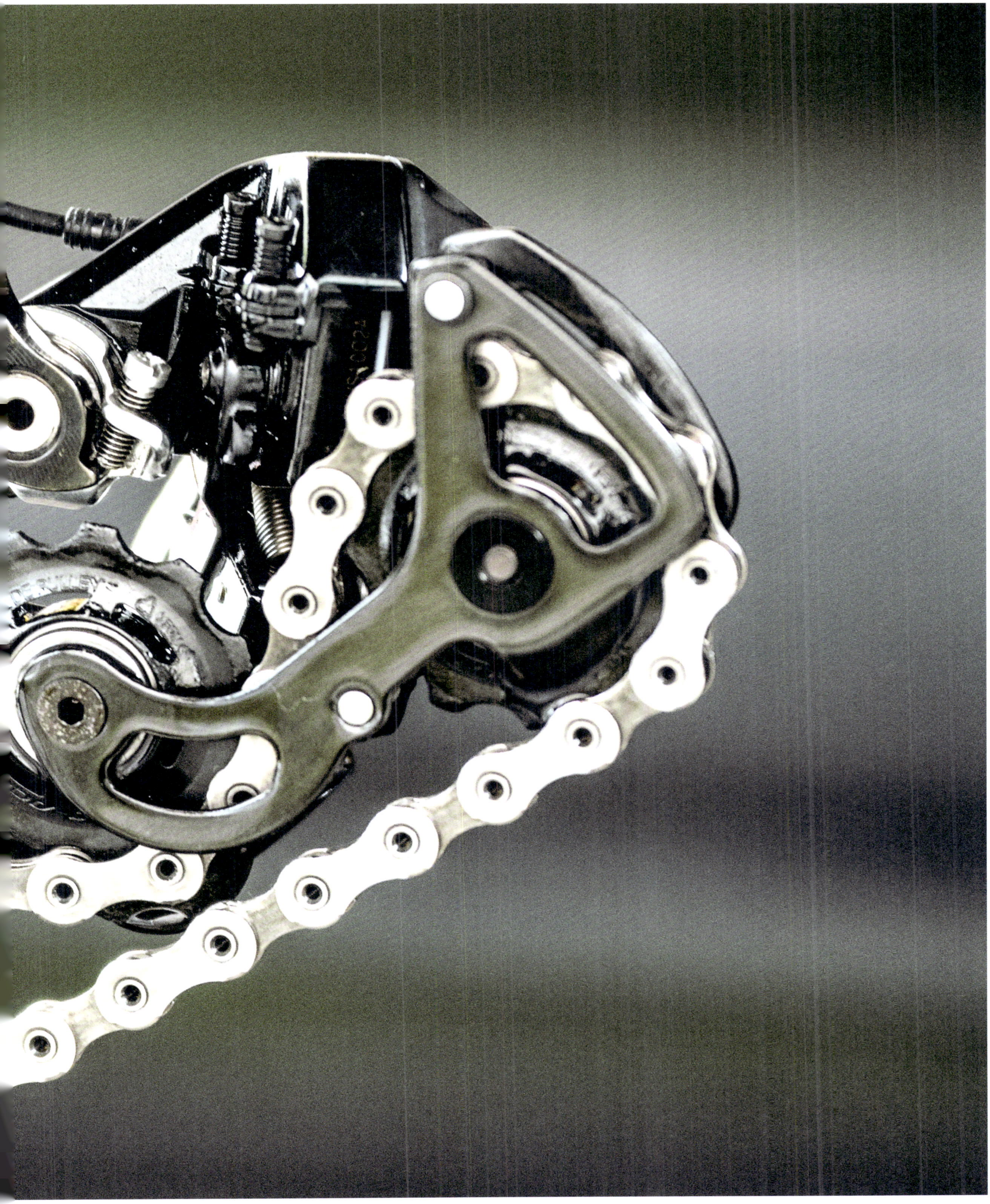

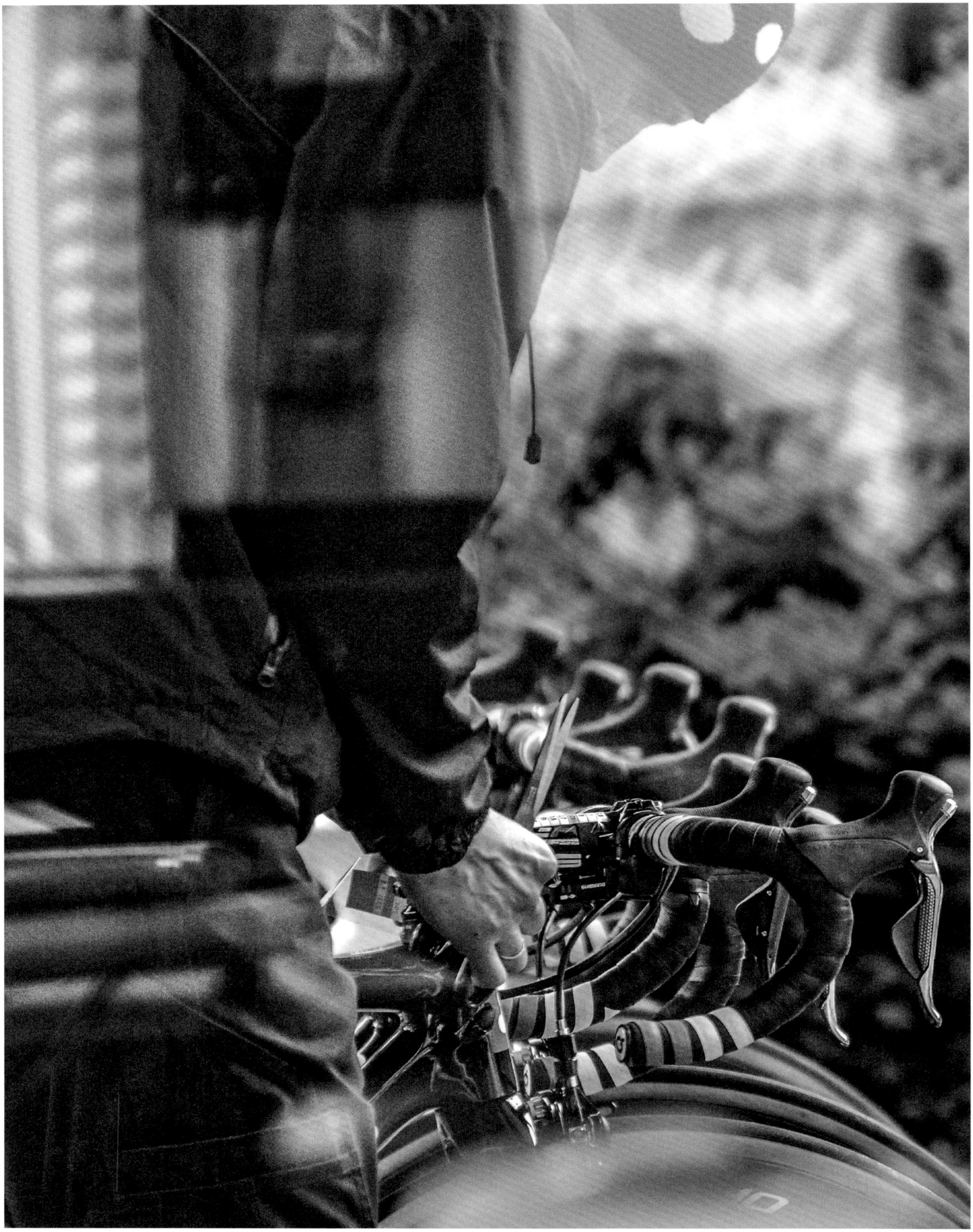

Mit Liebe zum Detail. Die Mechaniker Andrei und Gerd von BORA - ARGON 18. **With attention to detail. Andrei and Gerd, mechanics of BORA - ARGON 18.**
L'amour pour le détail: les mécaniciens Andrei et Gerd de BORA - ARGON 18.

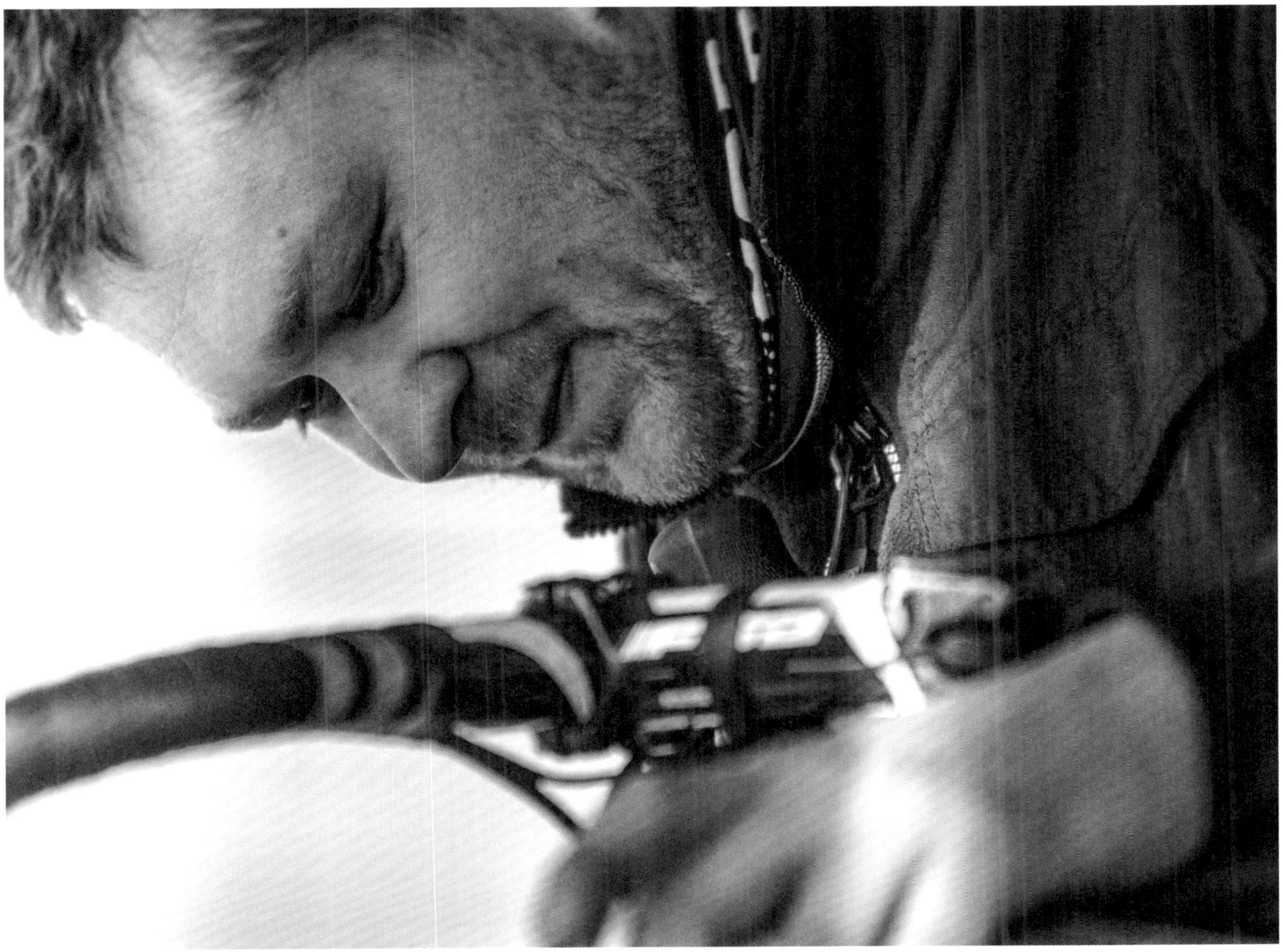

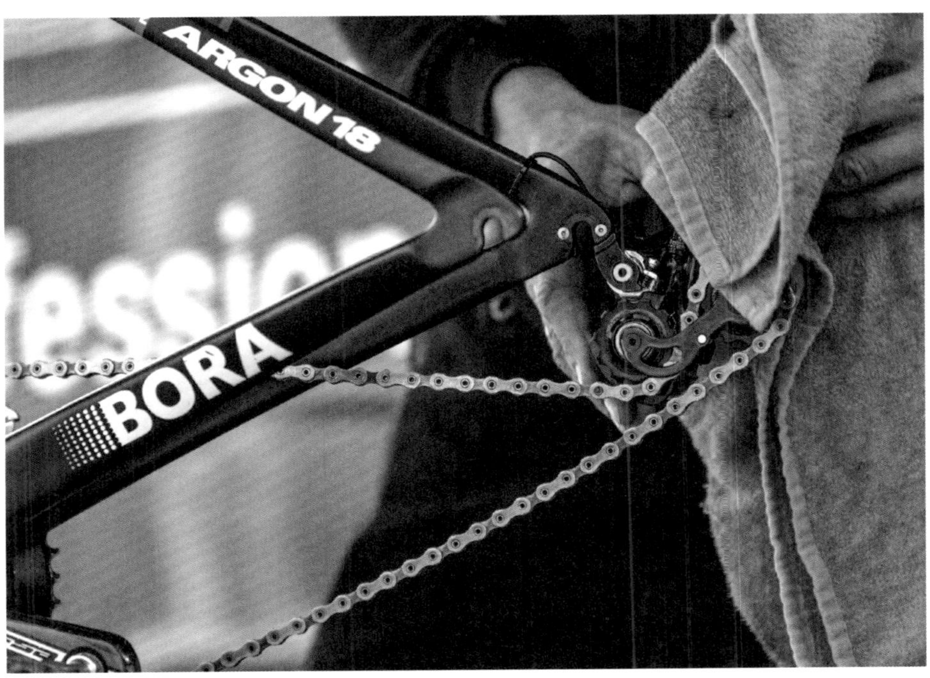
ARGON 18
BORA

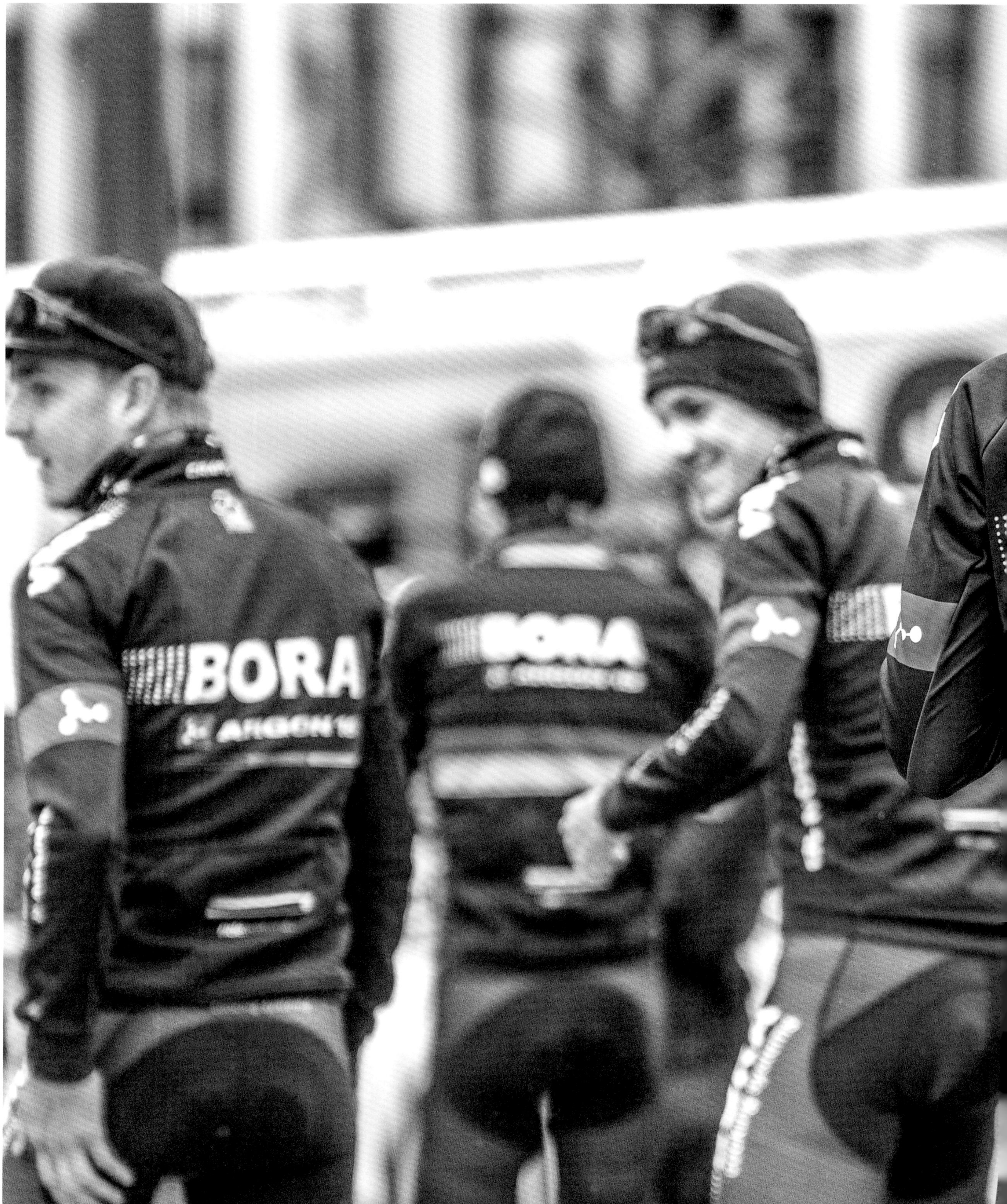

Startklar: BORA - ARGON 18. **All set: BORA - ARGON 18.** *Prête à partir : l'équipe BORA - ARGON 18.*

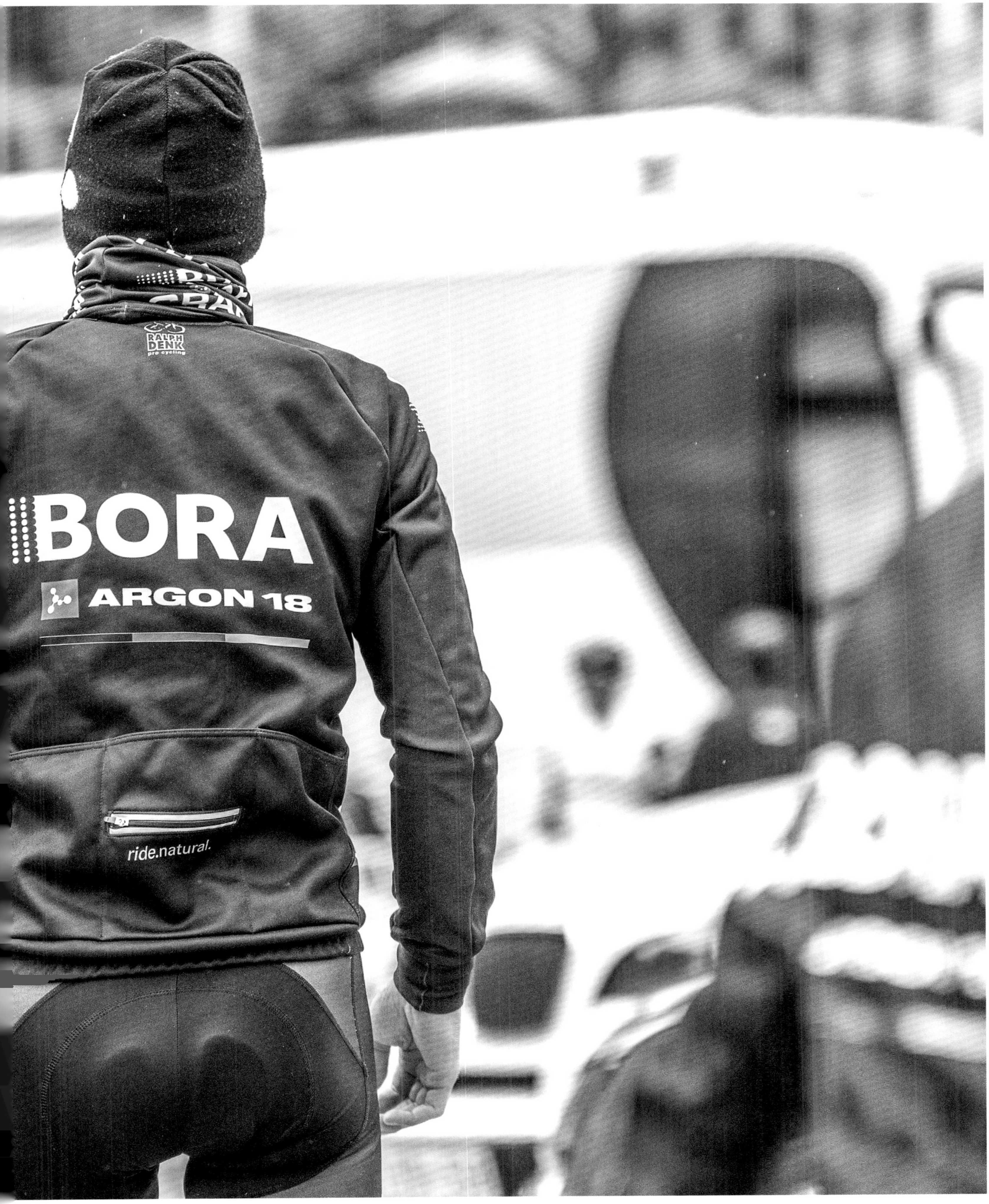
BORA
ARGON 18
RALPH DENK
pro cycling
ride.natural.

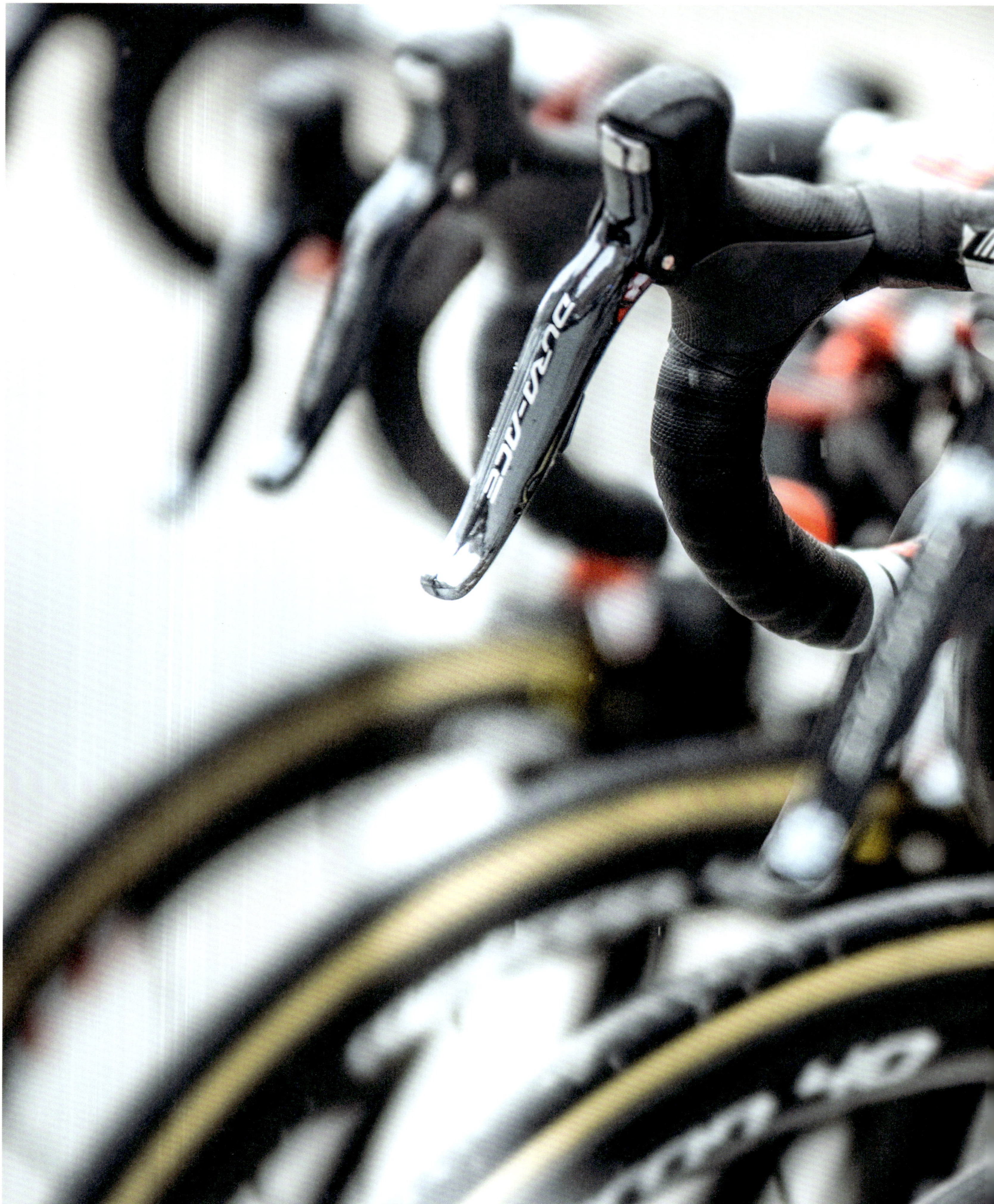

Bereit für den Härtetest für Mensch und Material. **Ready to test the endurance of man and material.** *L'endurance des hommes et du matériel sera mise à rude épreuve.*

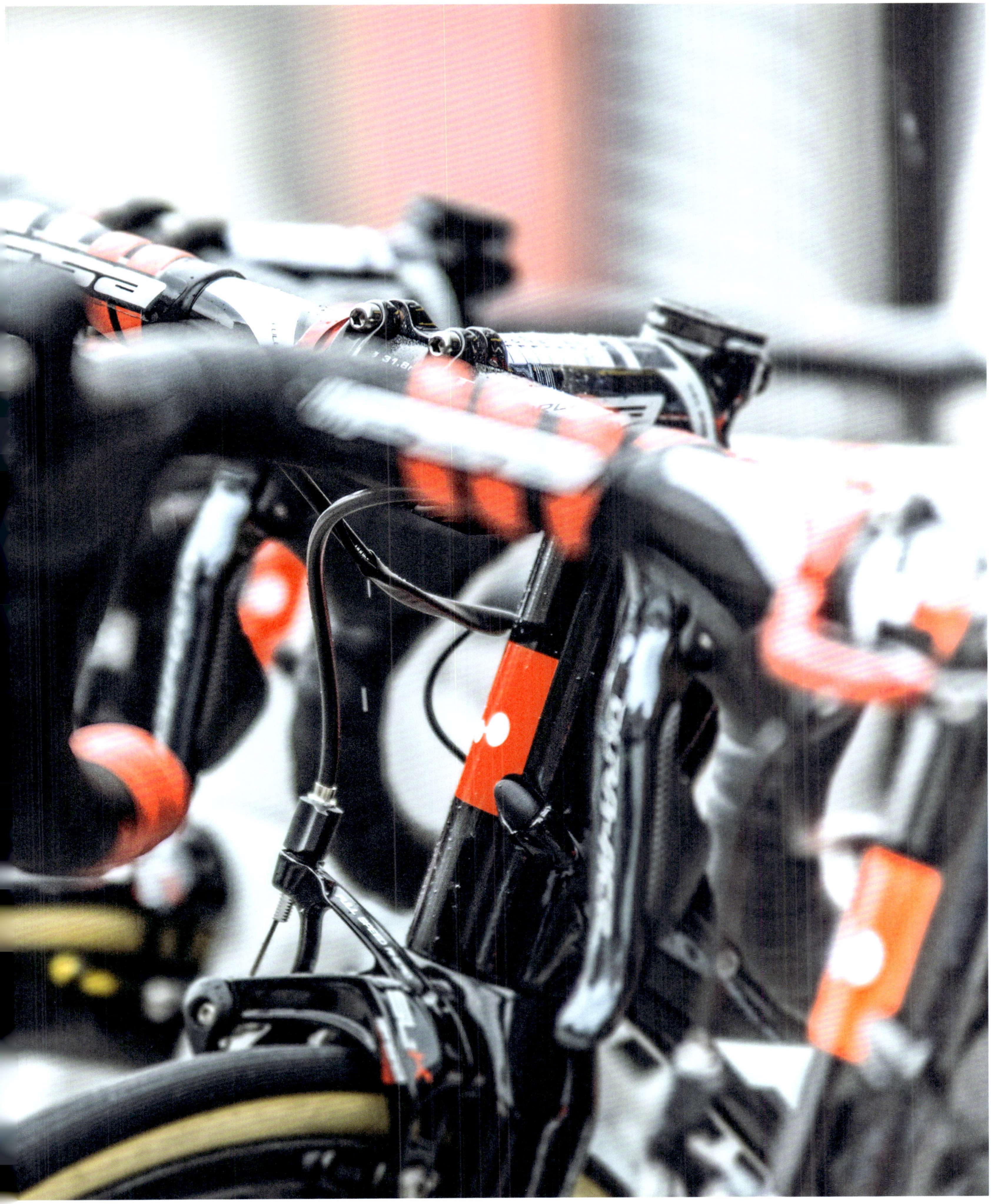

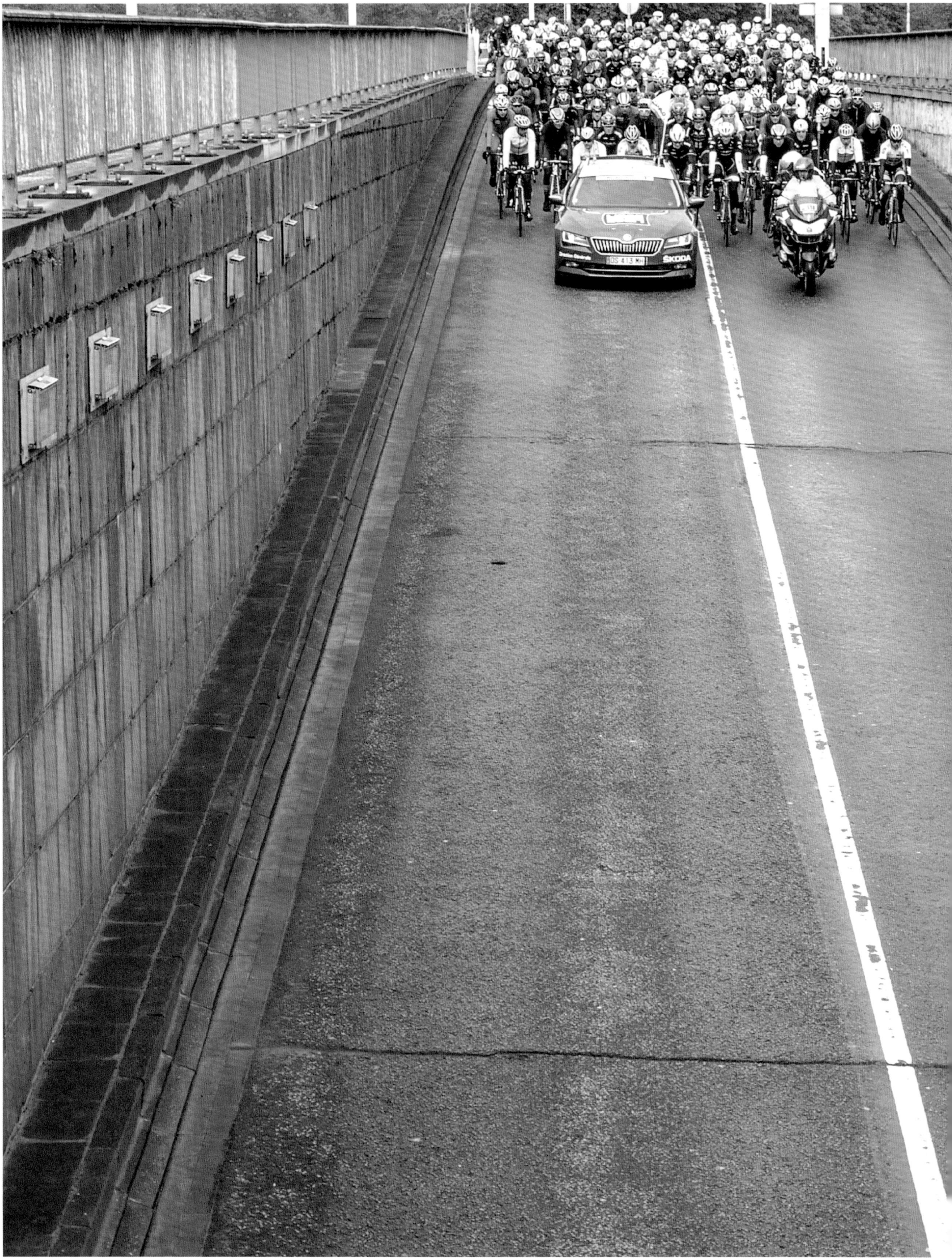
DS 413 MH
ŠKODA

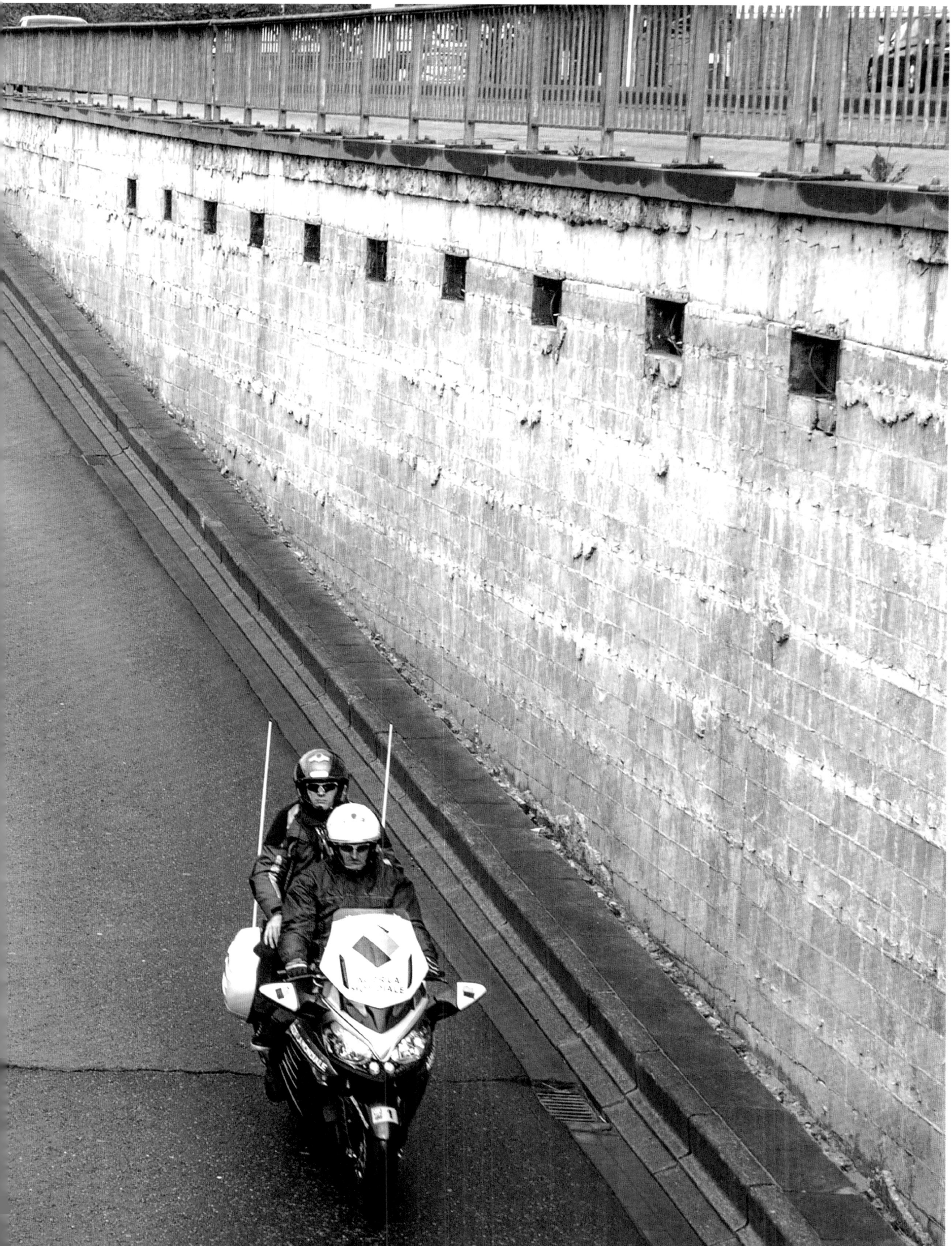

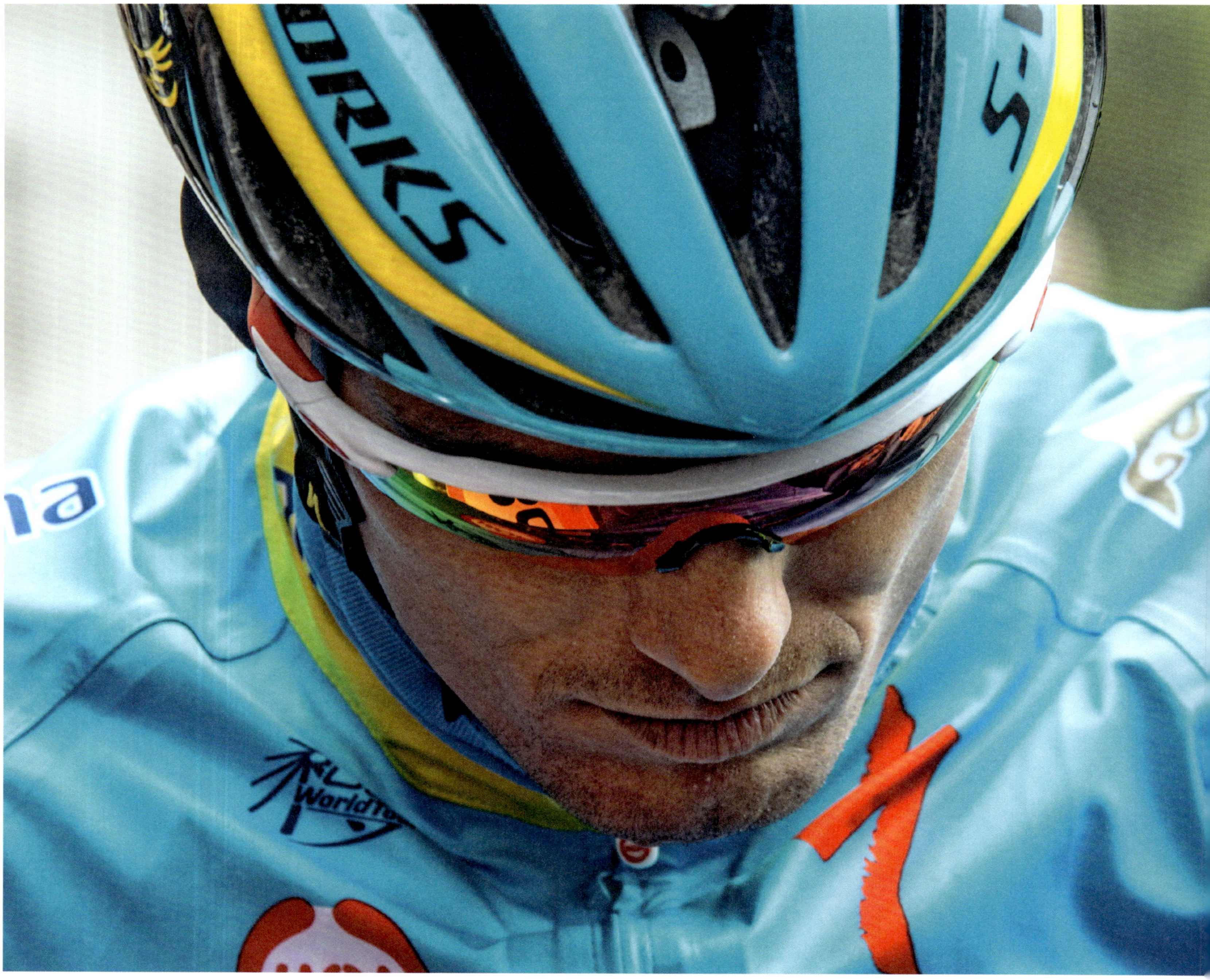

Keine Angst vor Wind und Wetter. **Who cares about wind and rain?** *Sans crainte du vent et des intempéries.*

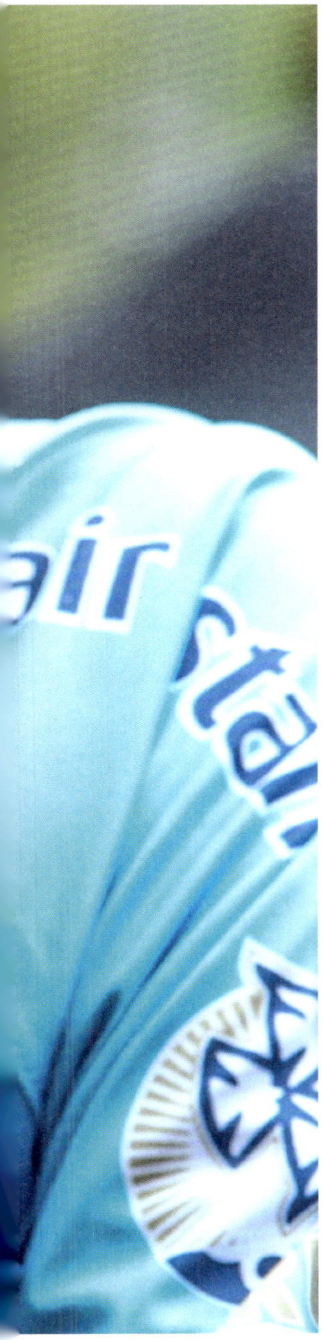

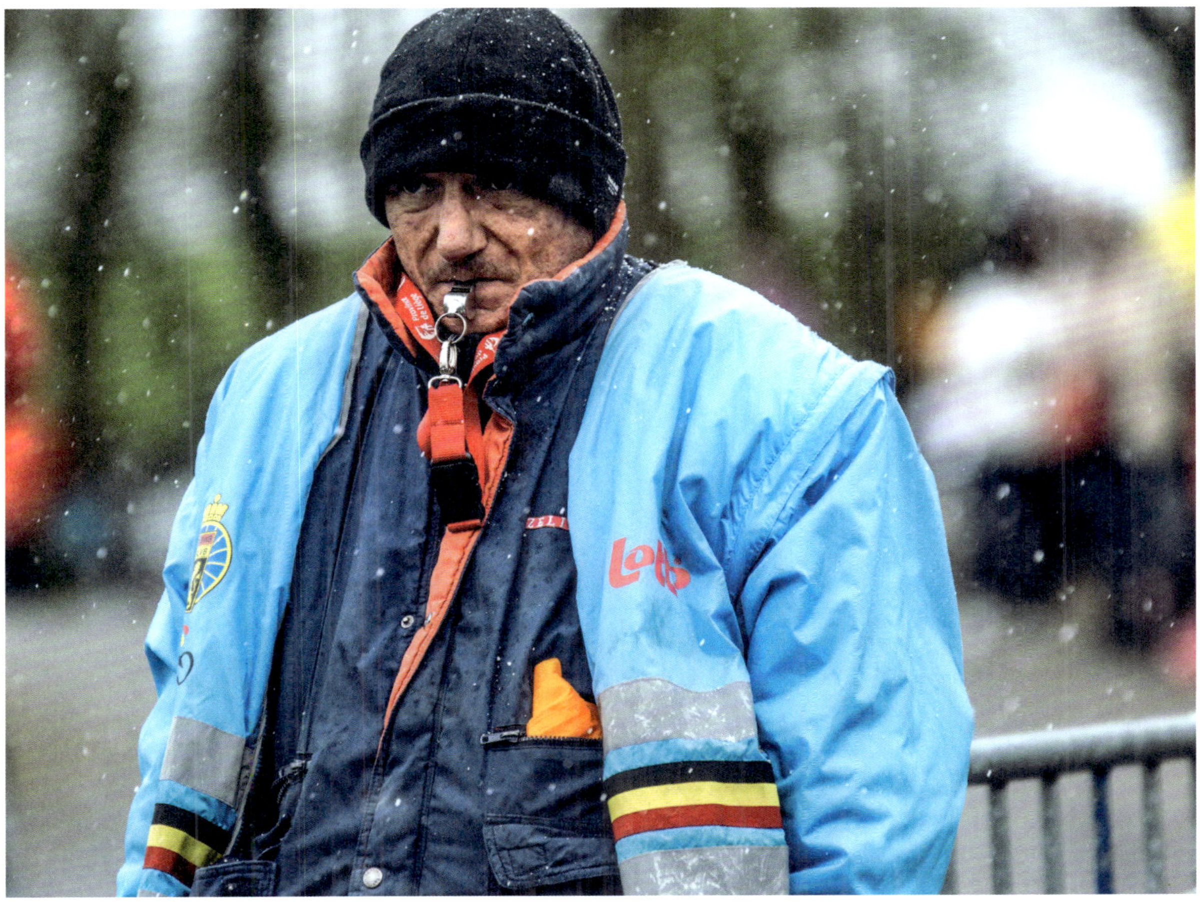

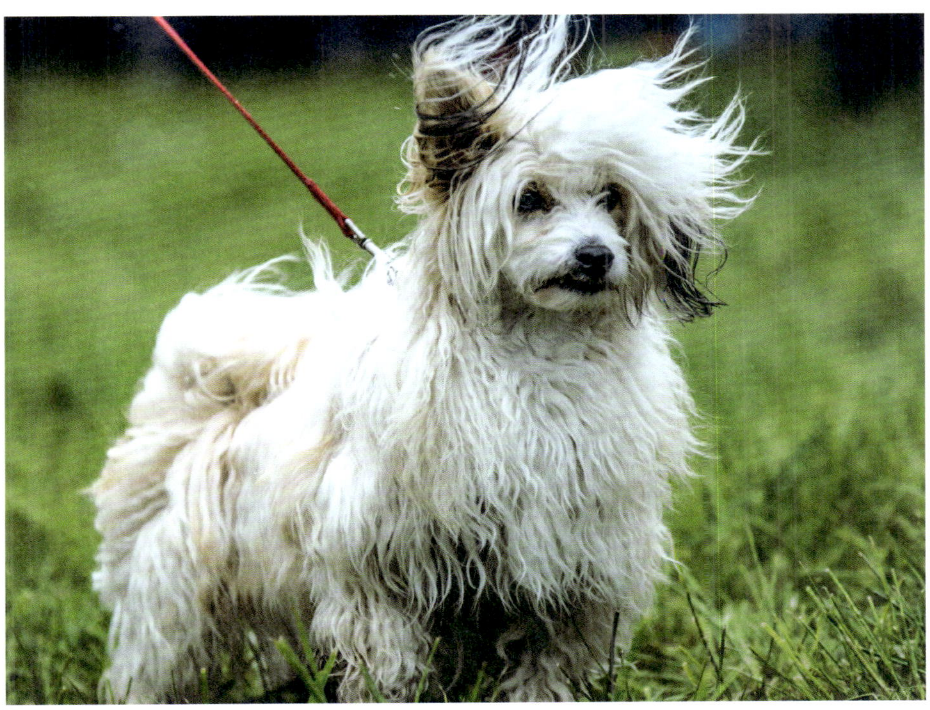

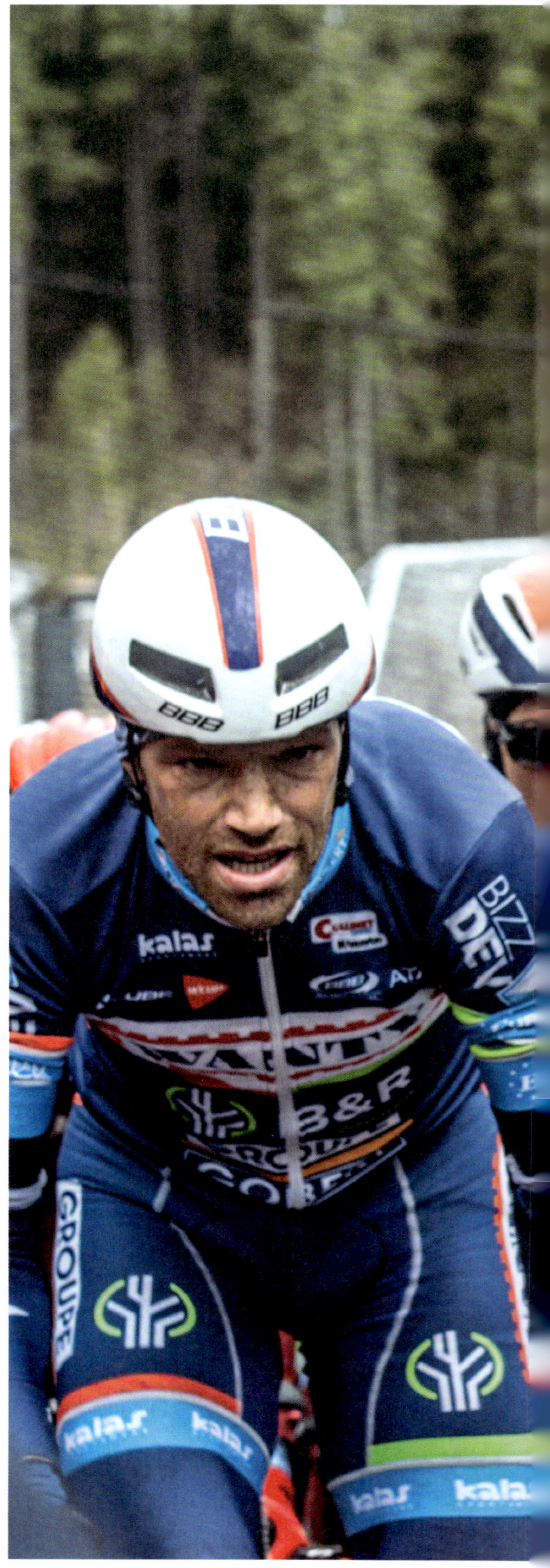
BBB
BBB
kalas
B&R

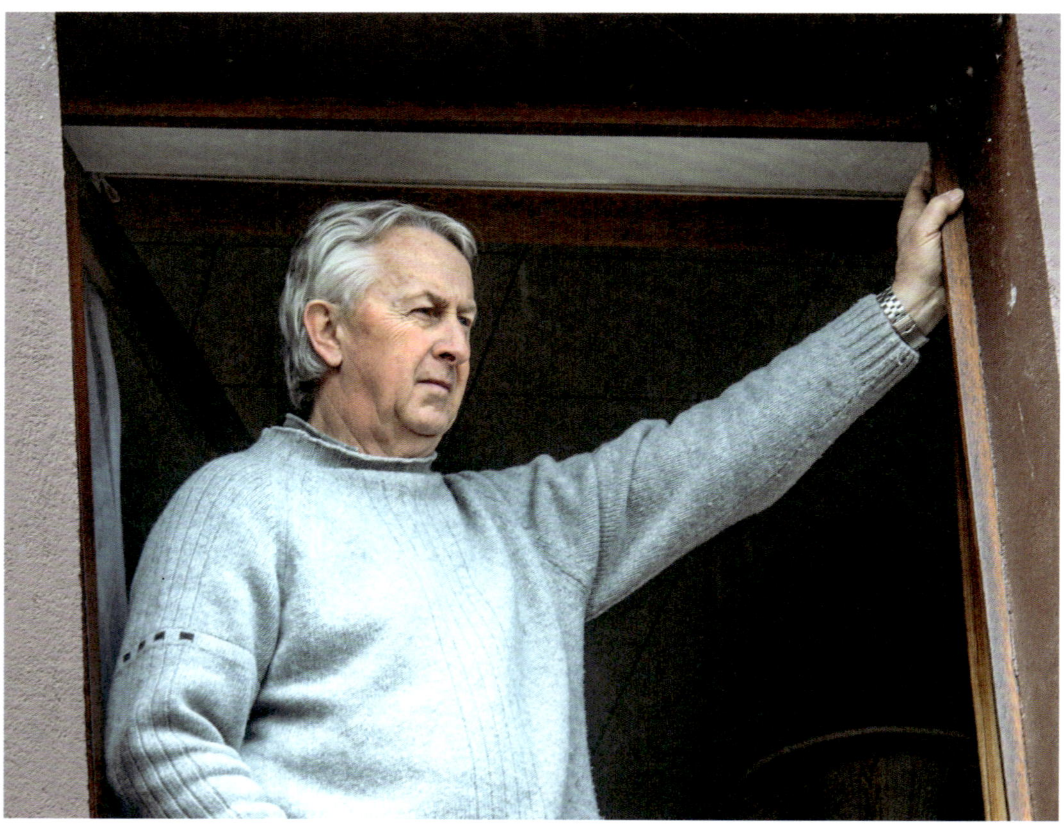

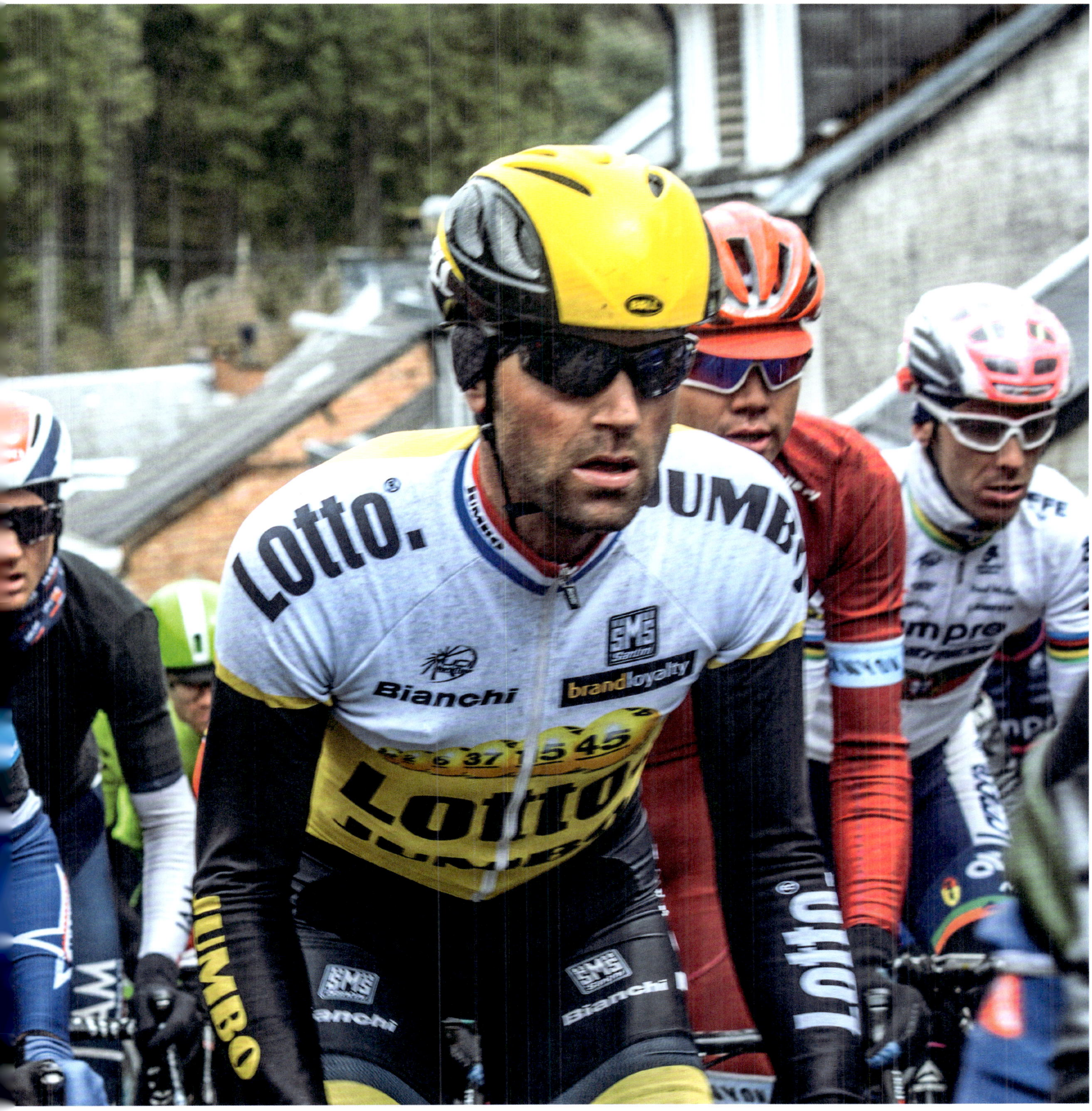

Fokussiert. V. l. n. r. Frederik Veuchelen (Wanty-Groupe Gobert), Paul Martens (Team LottoNL-Jumbo), Joaquim Rodríguez (Team Katusha), Rui Costa (Lampre-Merida). **Focussed. From left to right: Frederik Veuchelen (Wanty-Groupe Gobert), Paul Martens (Team LottoNL-Jumbo), Joaquim Rodríguez (Team Katusha), Rui Costa (Lampre-Merida).** *Concentrés. De g. à dr. : Frederik Veuchelen (Wanty-Groupe Gobert), Paul Martens (Team LottoNL-Jumbo), Joaquim Rodríguez (Team Katusha), Rui Costa (Lampre-Merida).*

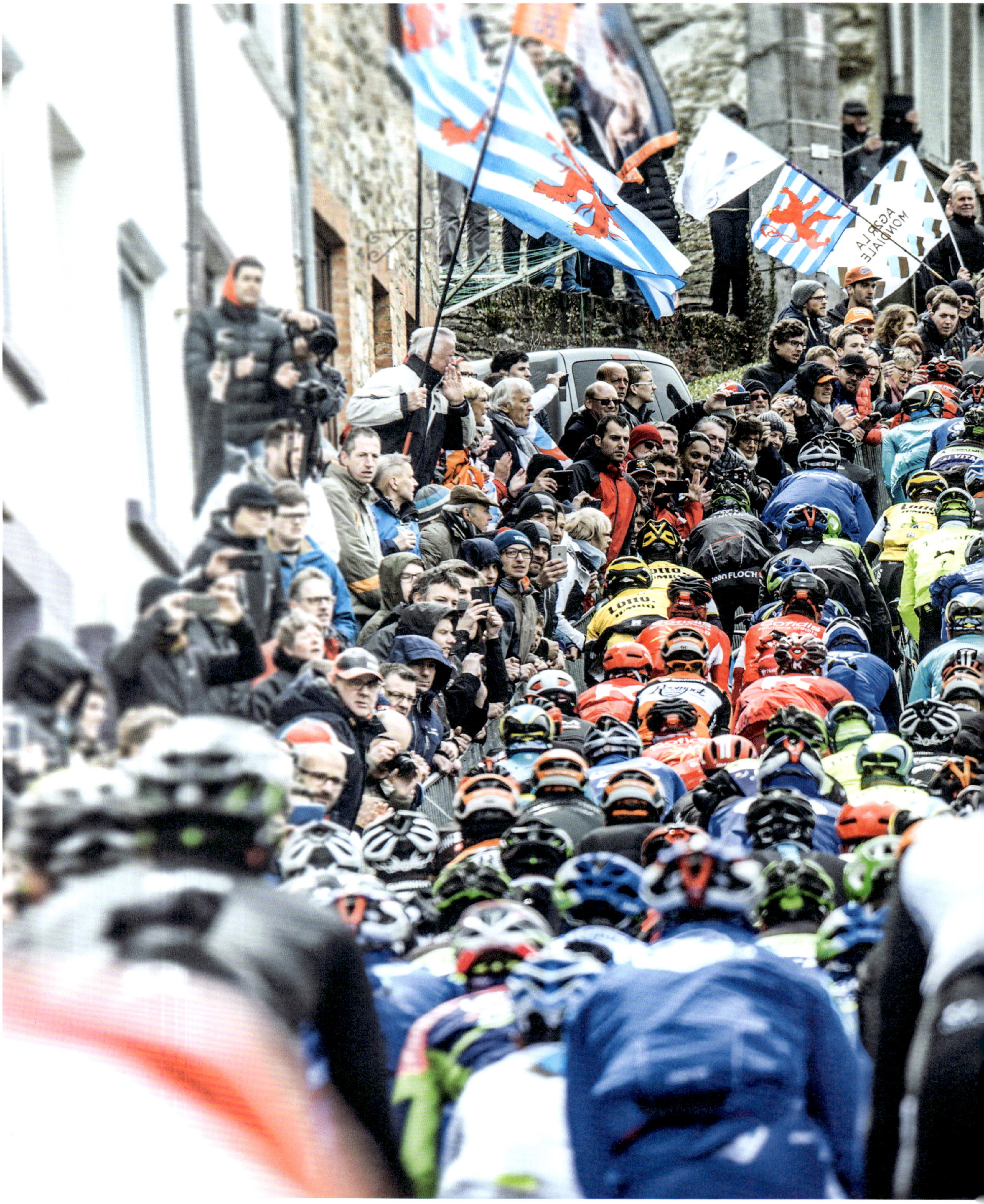

Das Peloton kämpft sich die Côte de Saint-Roch, den legendären Anstieg in Houffalize, hoch. **The peloton tackling the Côte de Saint-Roch, the legendary climb in Houffalize.** *Le peloton dans l'abrupte côte de Saint-Roch, montée légendaire de Houffalize.*

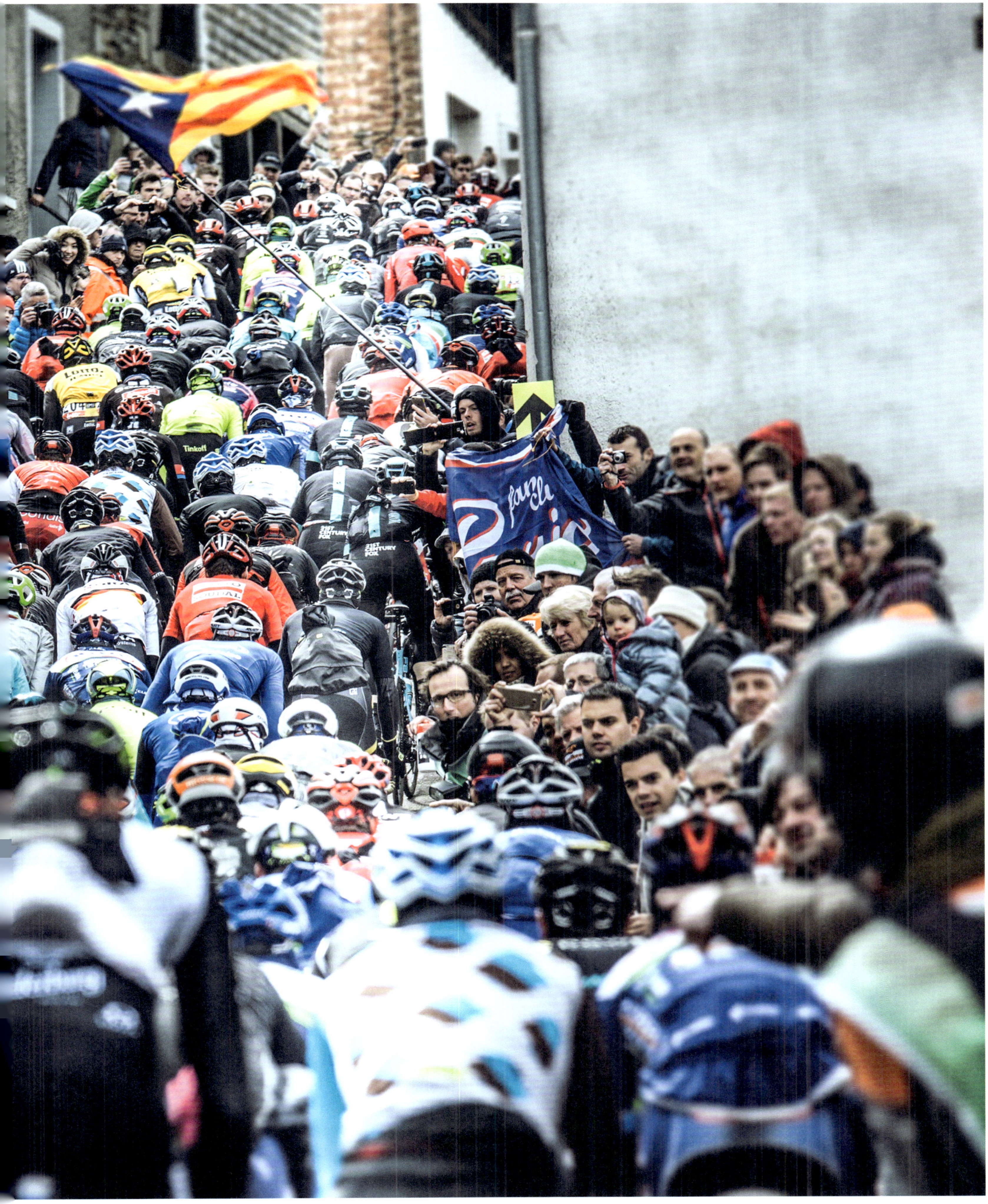
Tinkoff

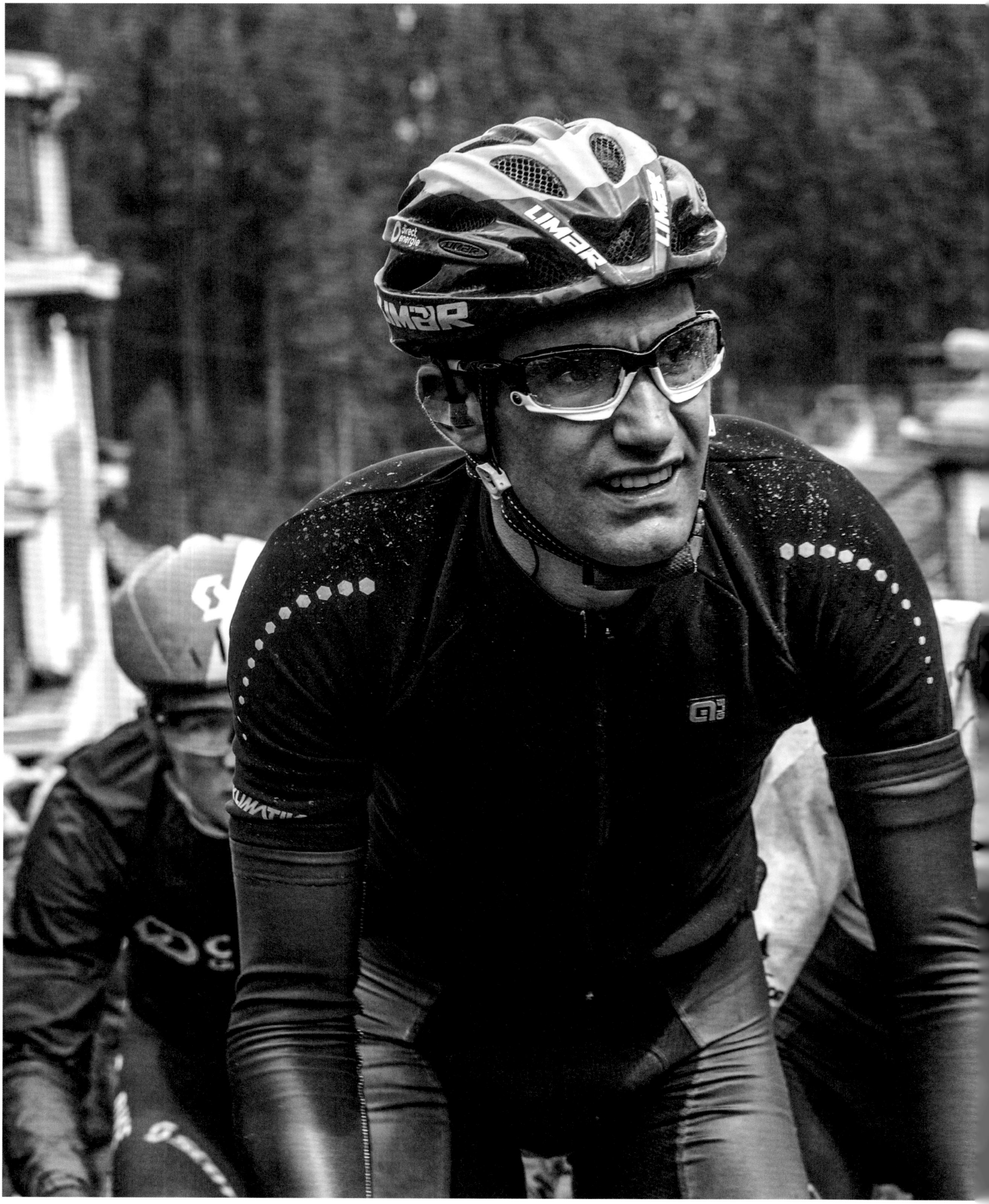

Fabien Grellier (Direct Énergie). **Fabien Grellier (Direct Énergie).** *Fabien Grellier (Direct Énergie).*

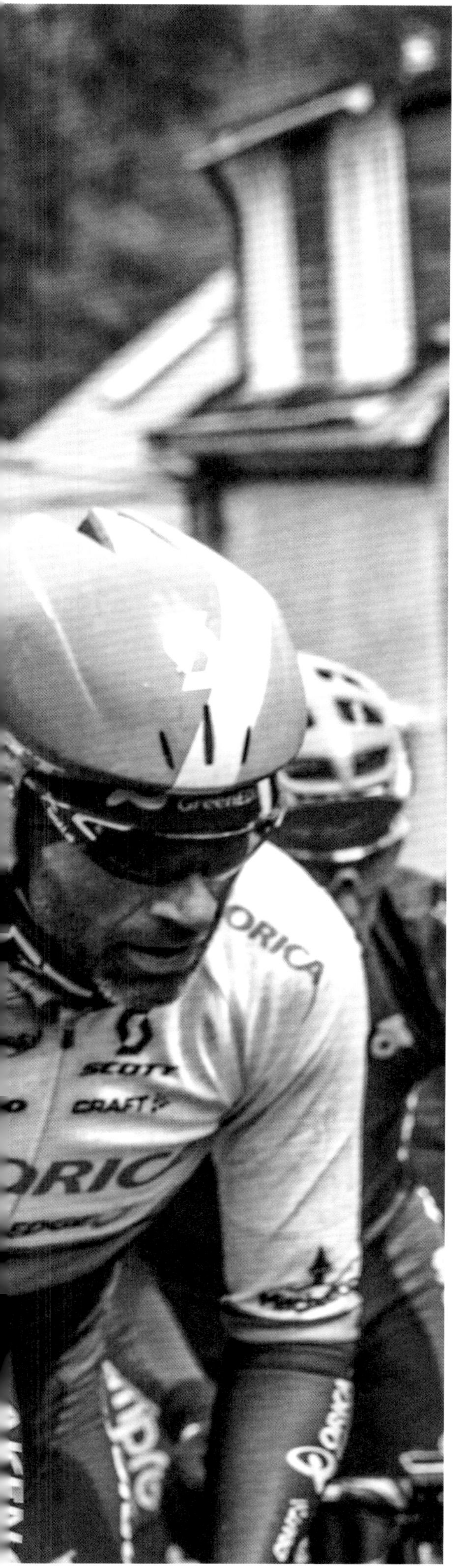
ORICA
SCOTT
CRAFT

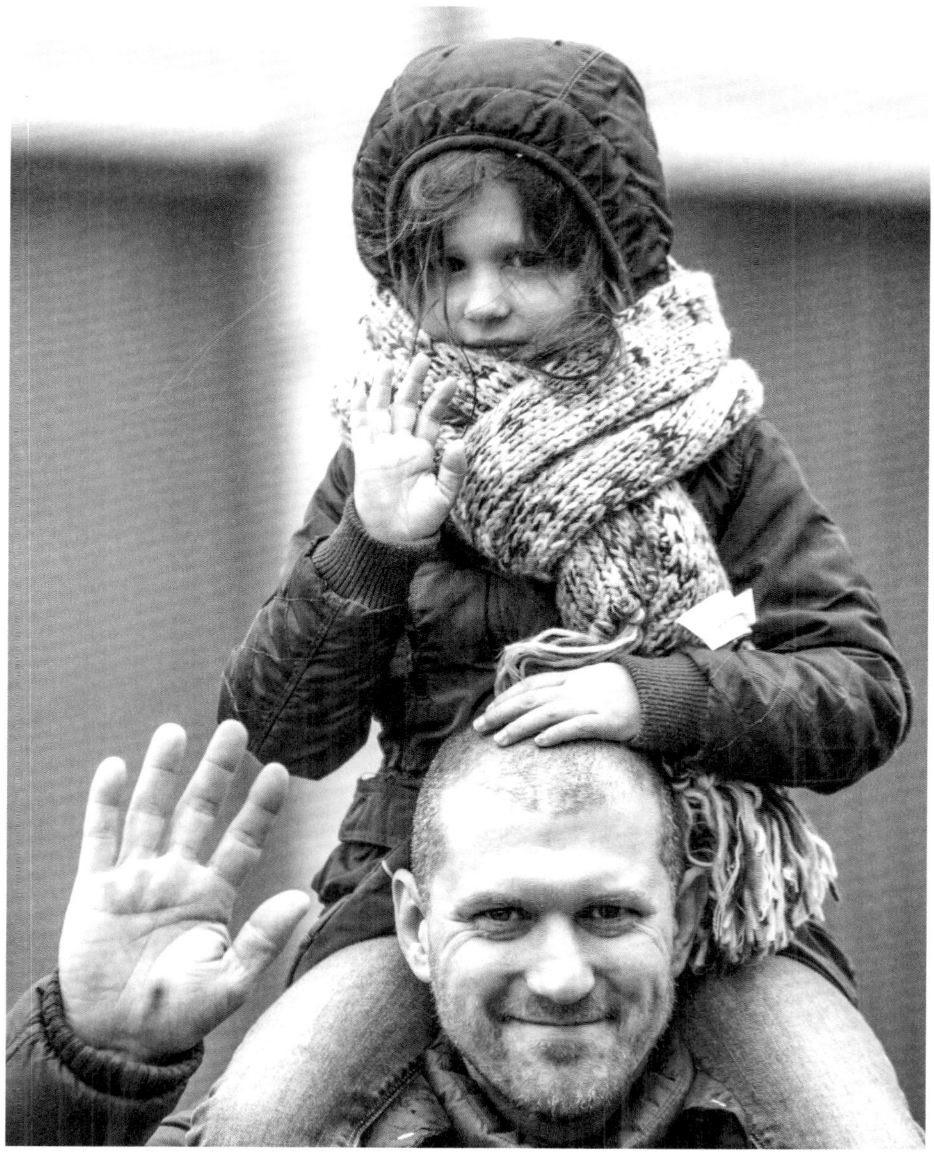

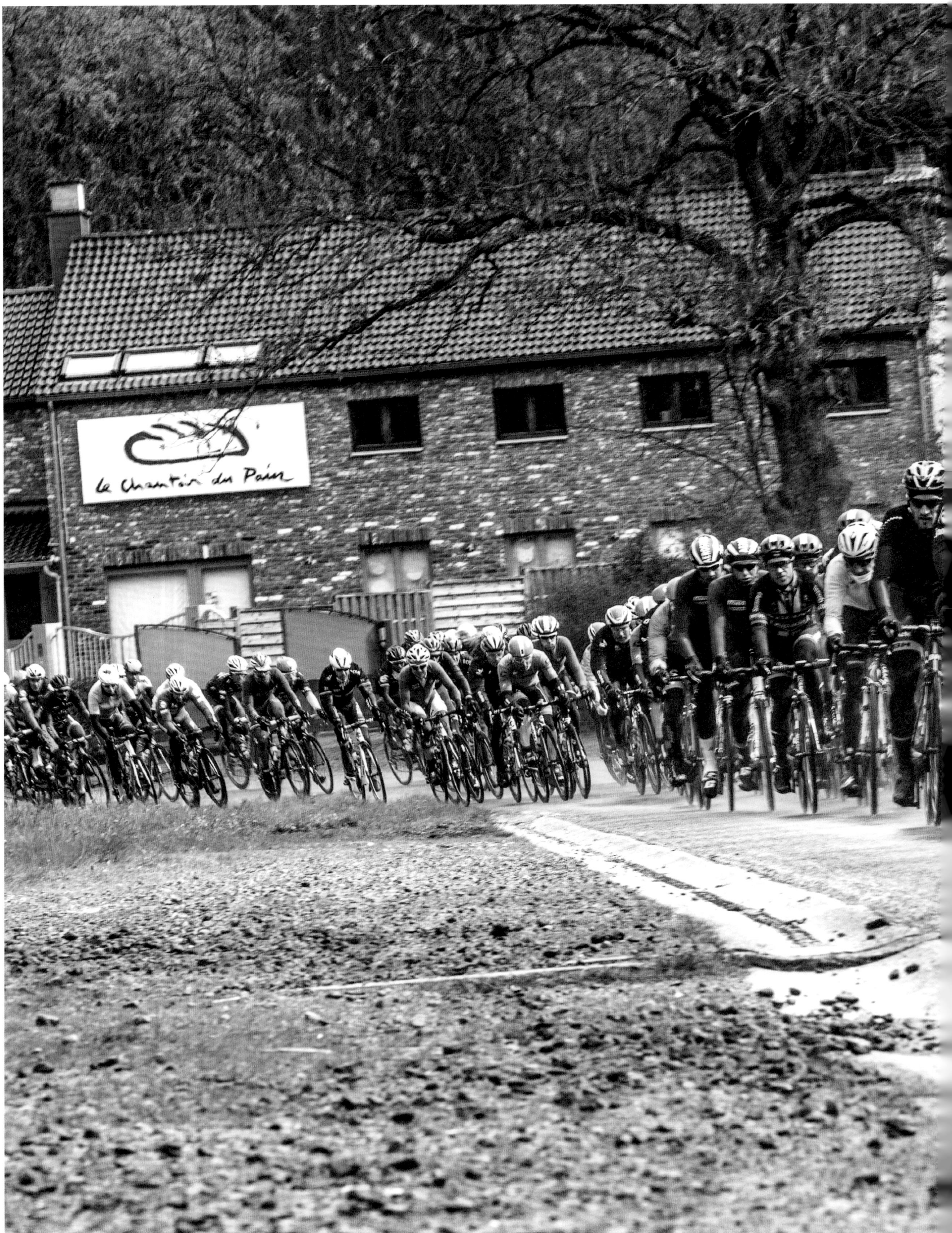
Le Chantoir du Pain

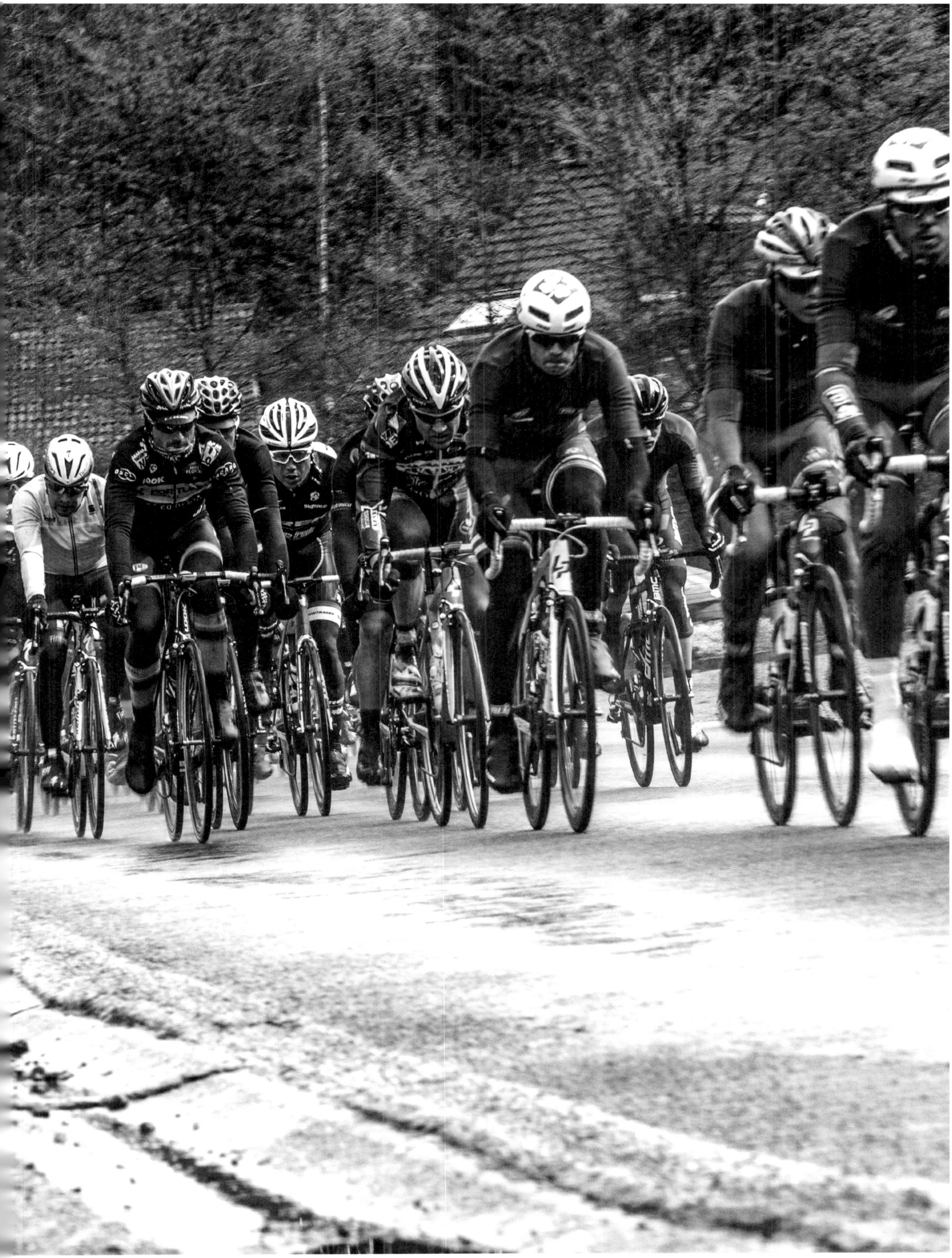

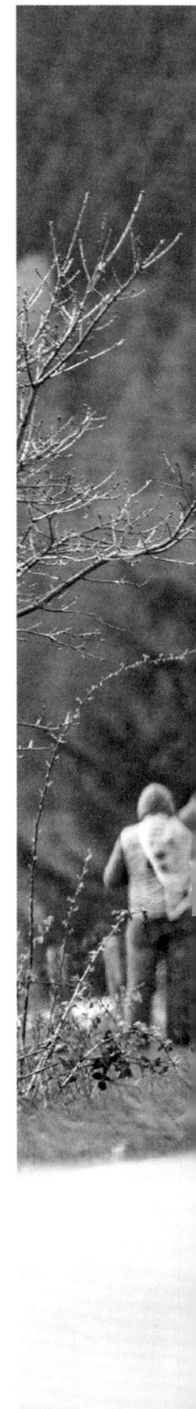

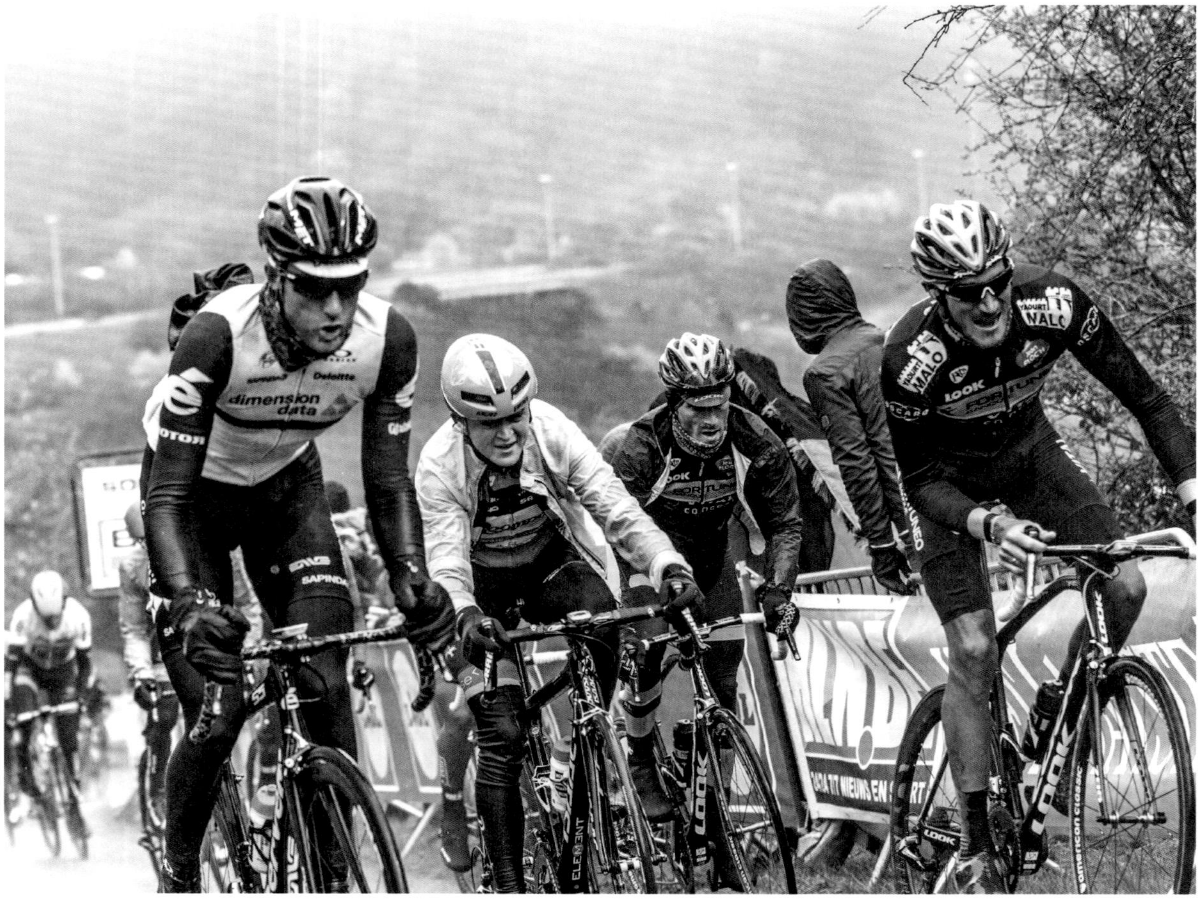
dimension
data

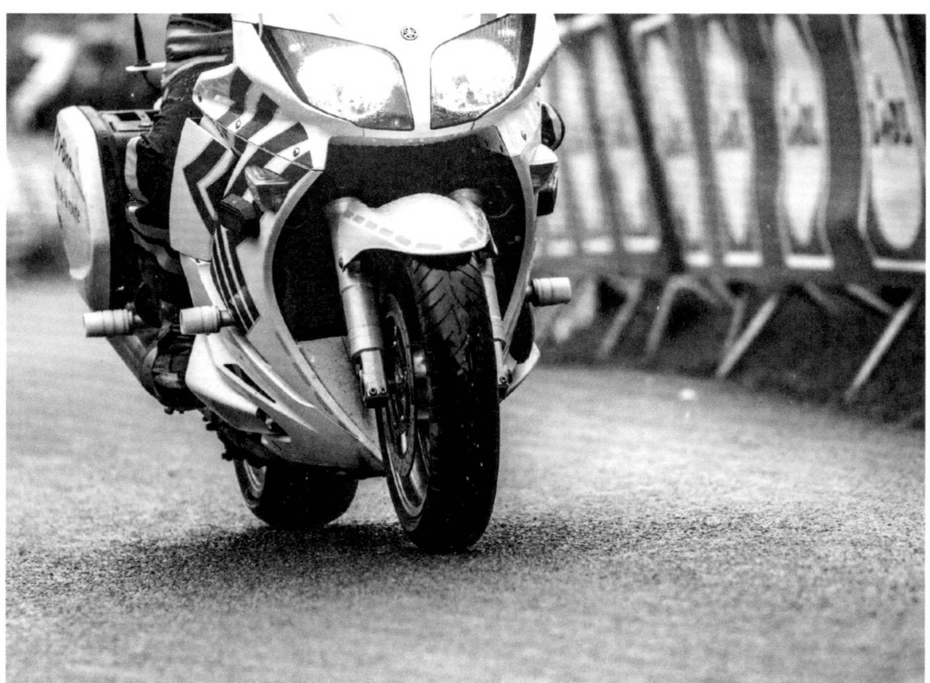

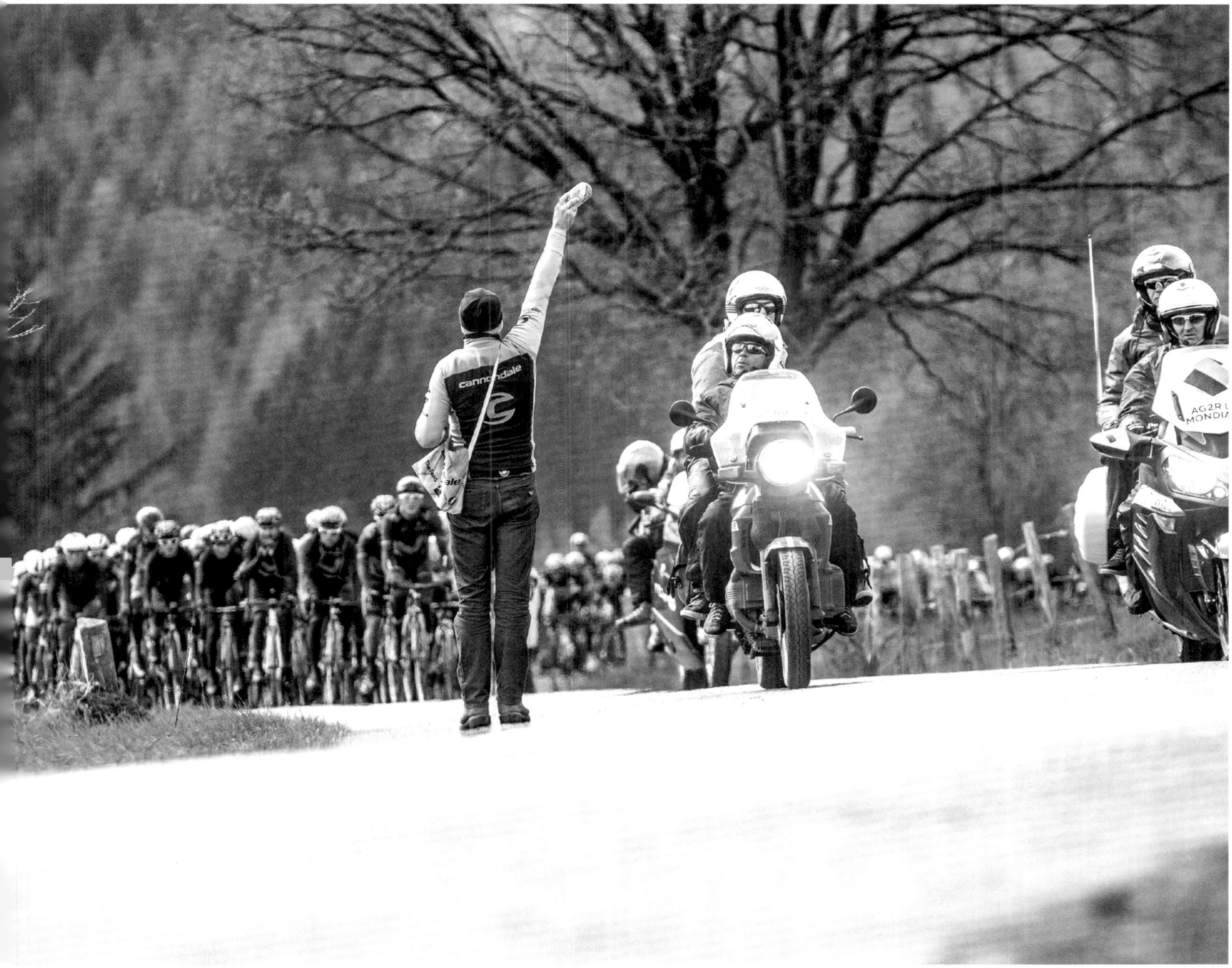

Zweite Verpflegungsstation bei Kilometer 180. **The second feed zone at the 180 kilometre point.**
Second zone de ravitaillement au kilomètre 180.

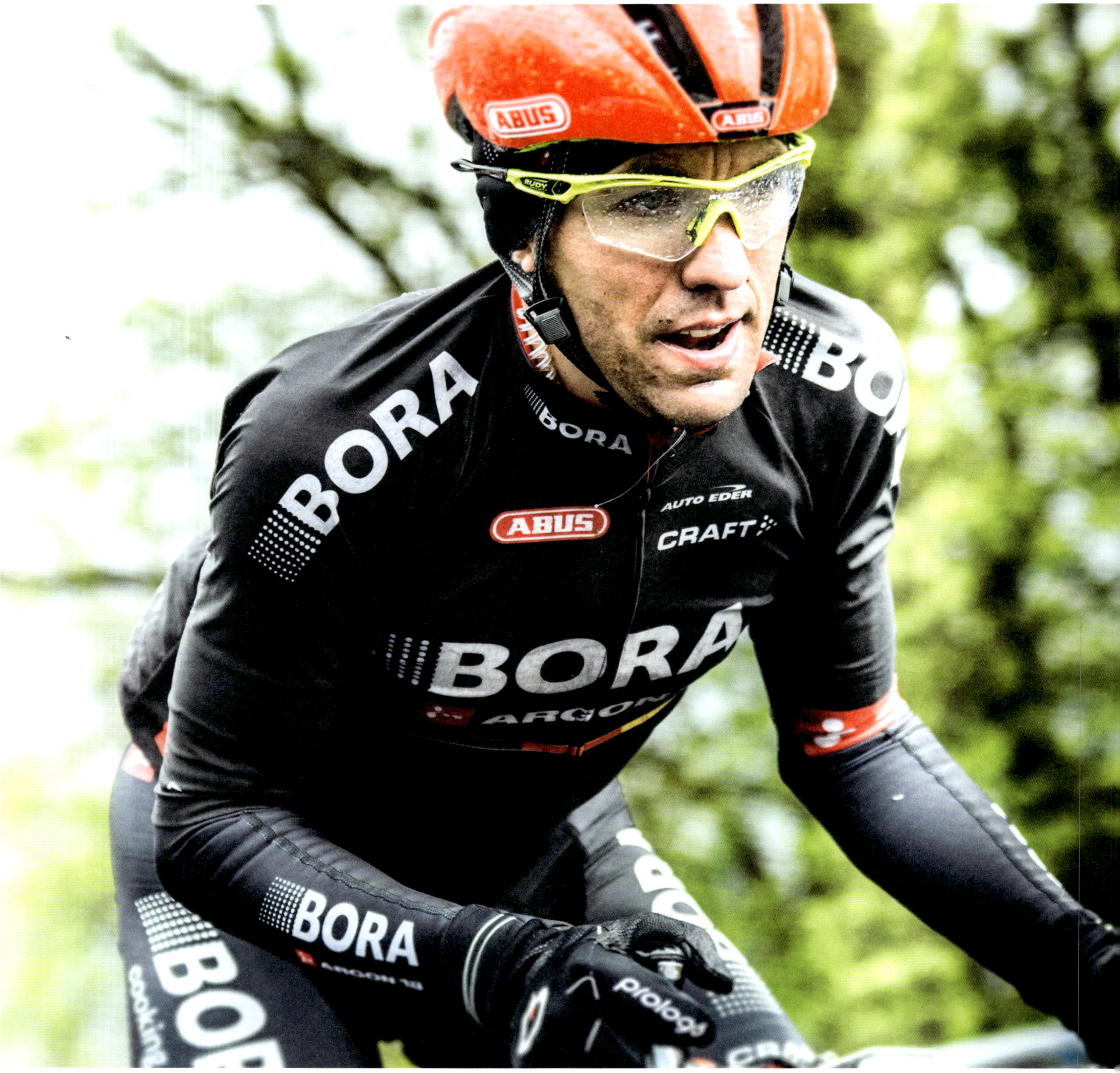

↑ Cesare Benedetti (BORA - ARGON 18). **Cesare Benedetti (BORA - ARGON 18).** *Cesare Benedetti (BORA - ARGON 18).*
→ Oliver Zaugg (IAM Cycling). **Oliver Zaugg (IAM Cycling).** *Oliver Zaugg (IAM Cycling).*

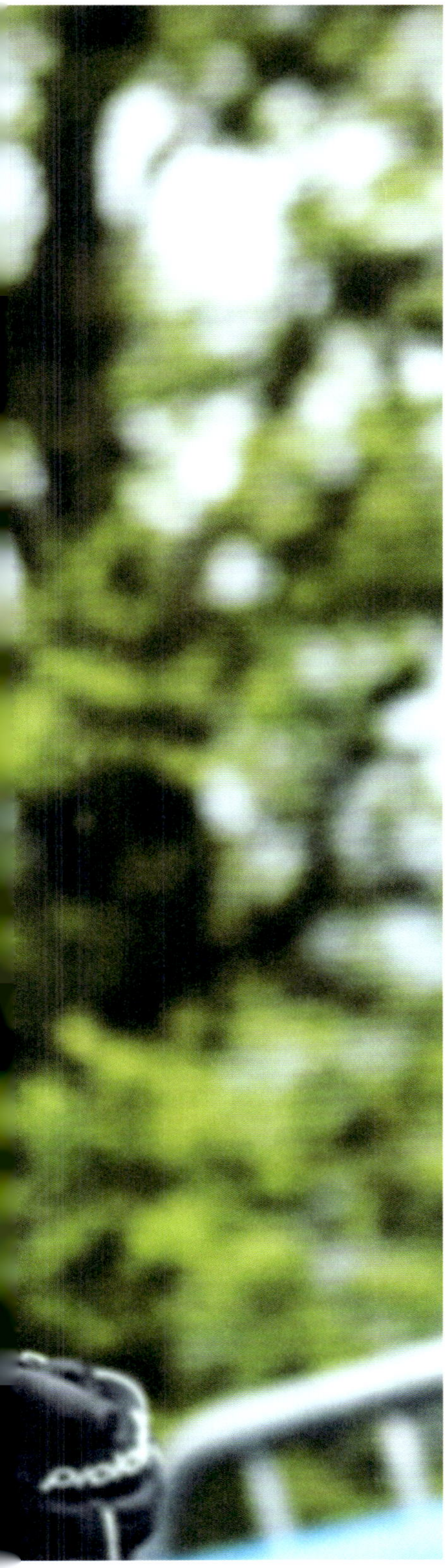

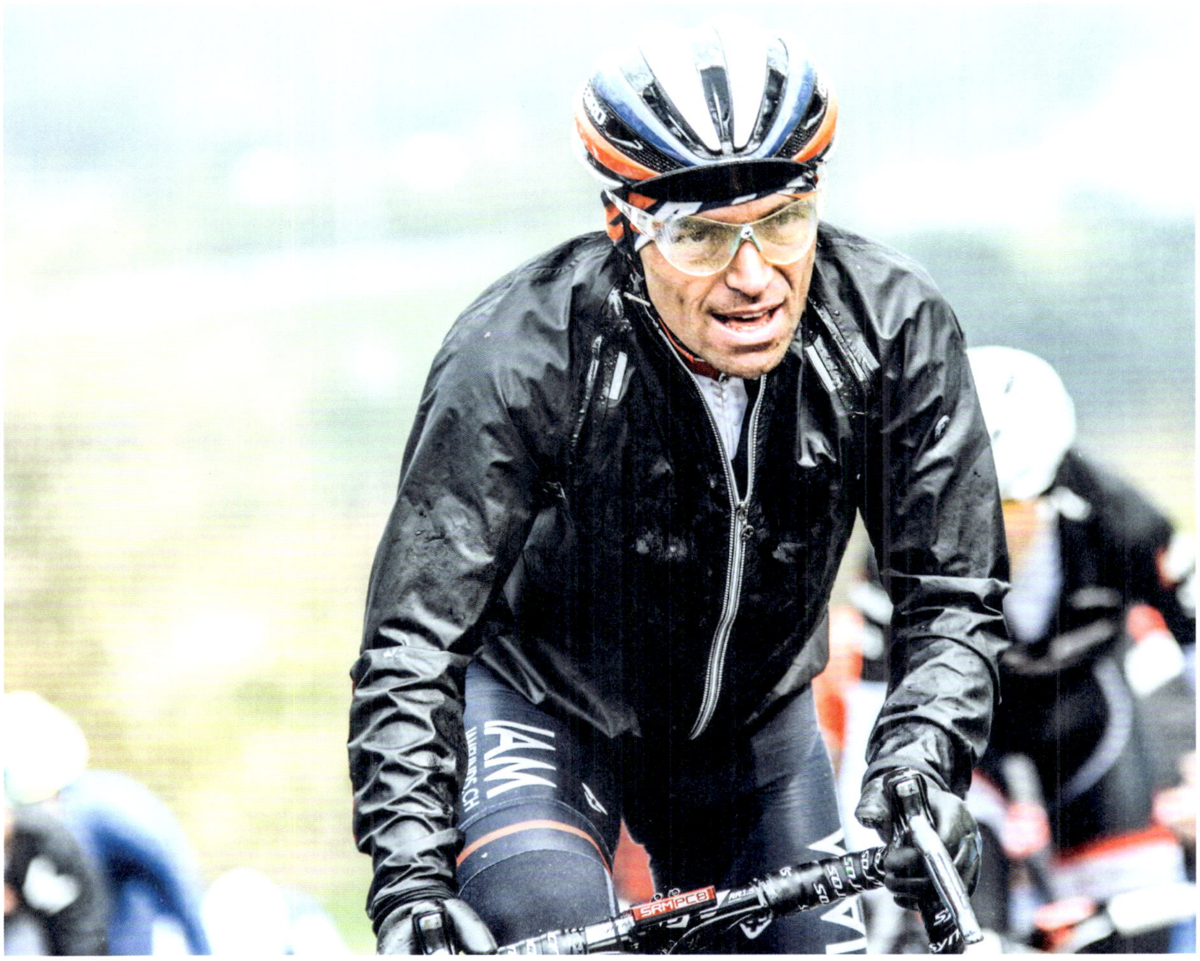
IAM

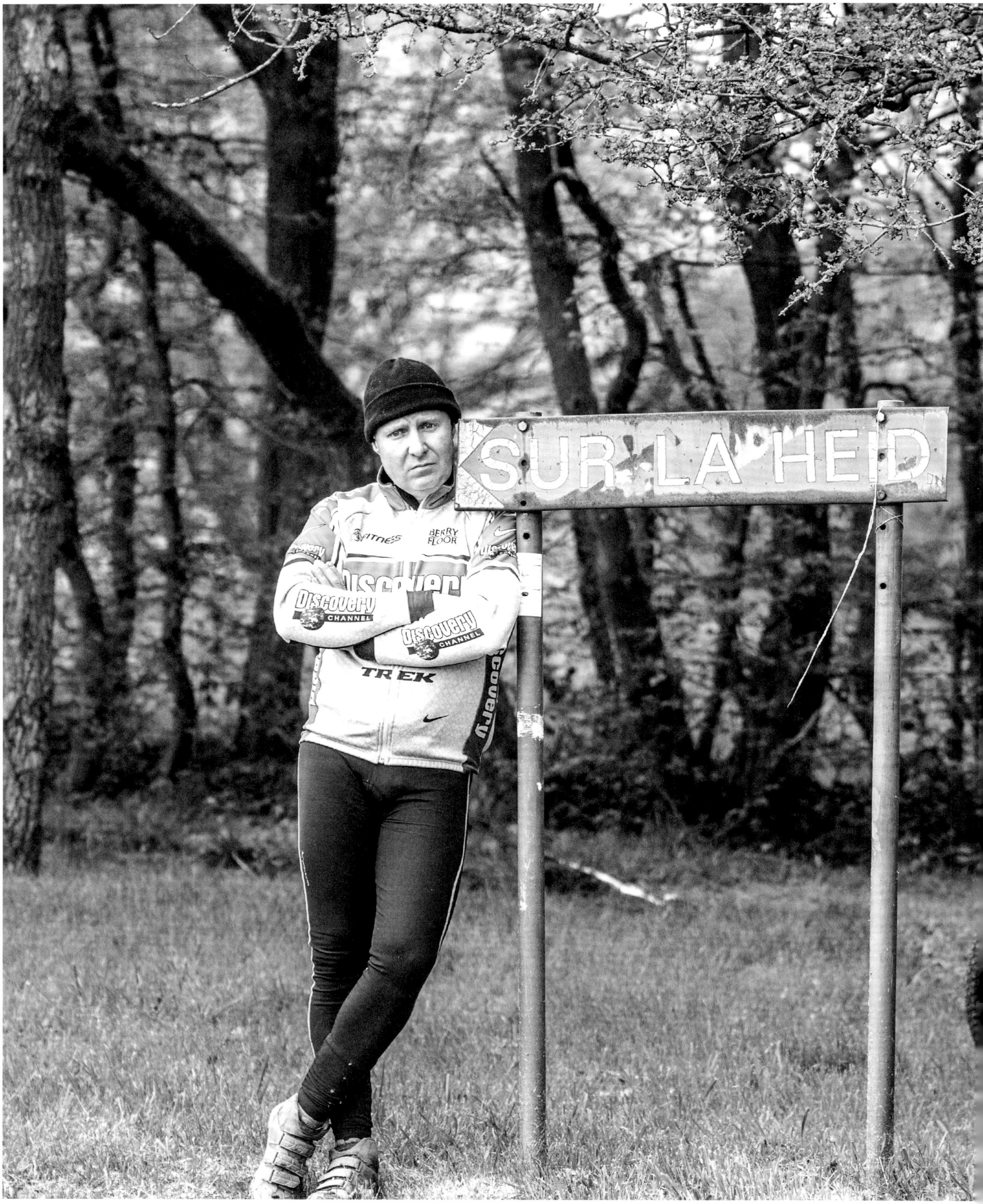
SUR LA HEID
BERRY FLOOR
Discovery
CHANNEL
TREK

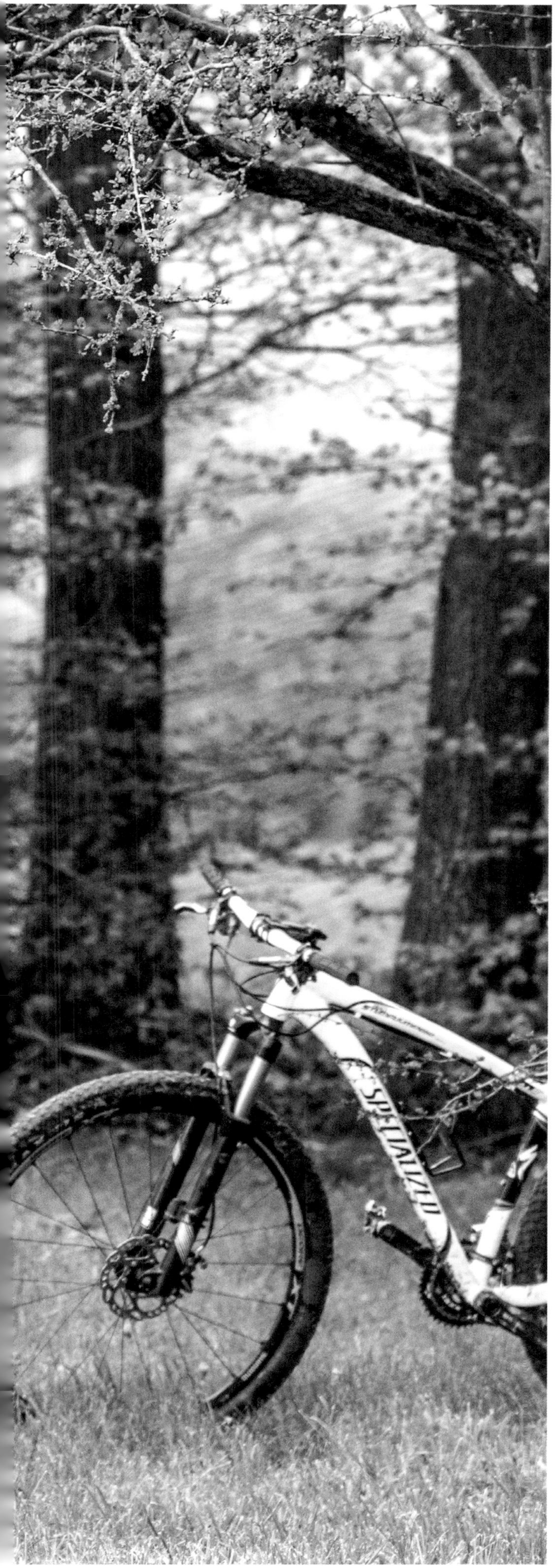

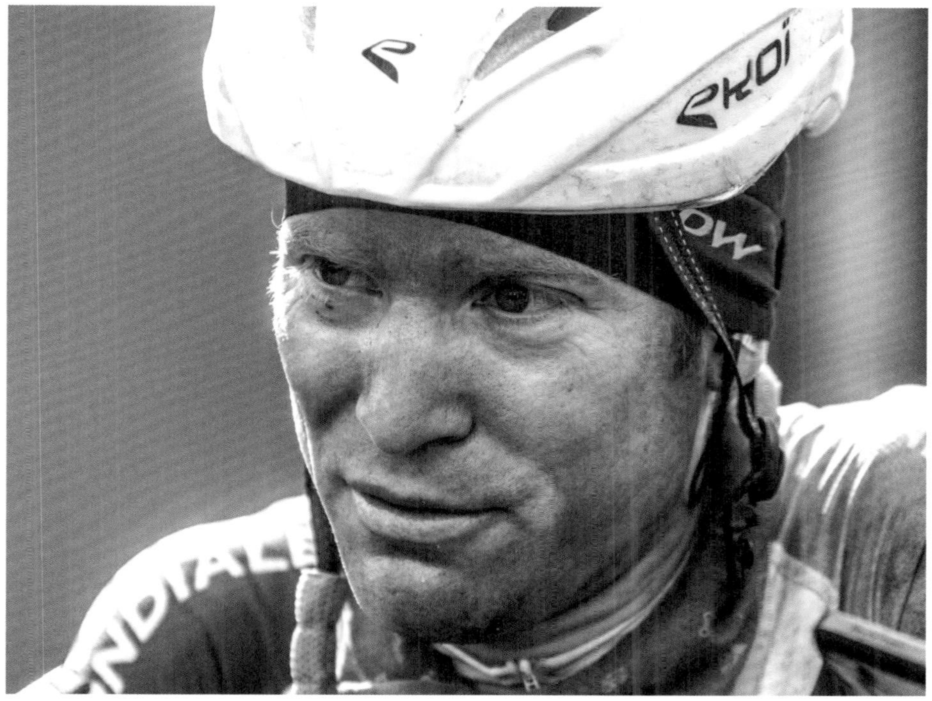

↖ Warten. **Waiting.** *L'attente.*
↗ Jan Bakelants (AG2R La Mondiale). **Jan Bakelants (AG2R La Mondiale).** *Jan Bakelants (AG2R La Mondiale).*

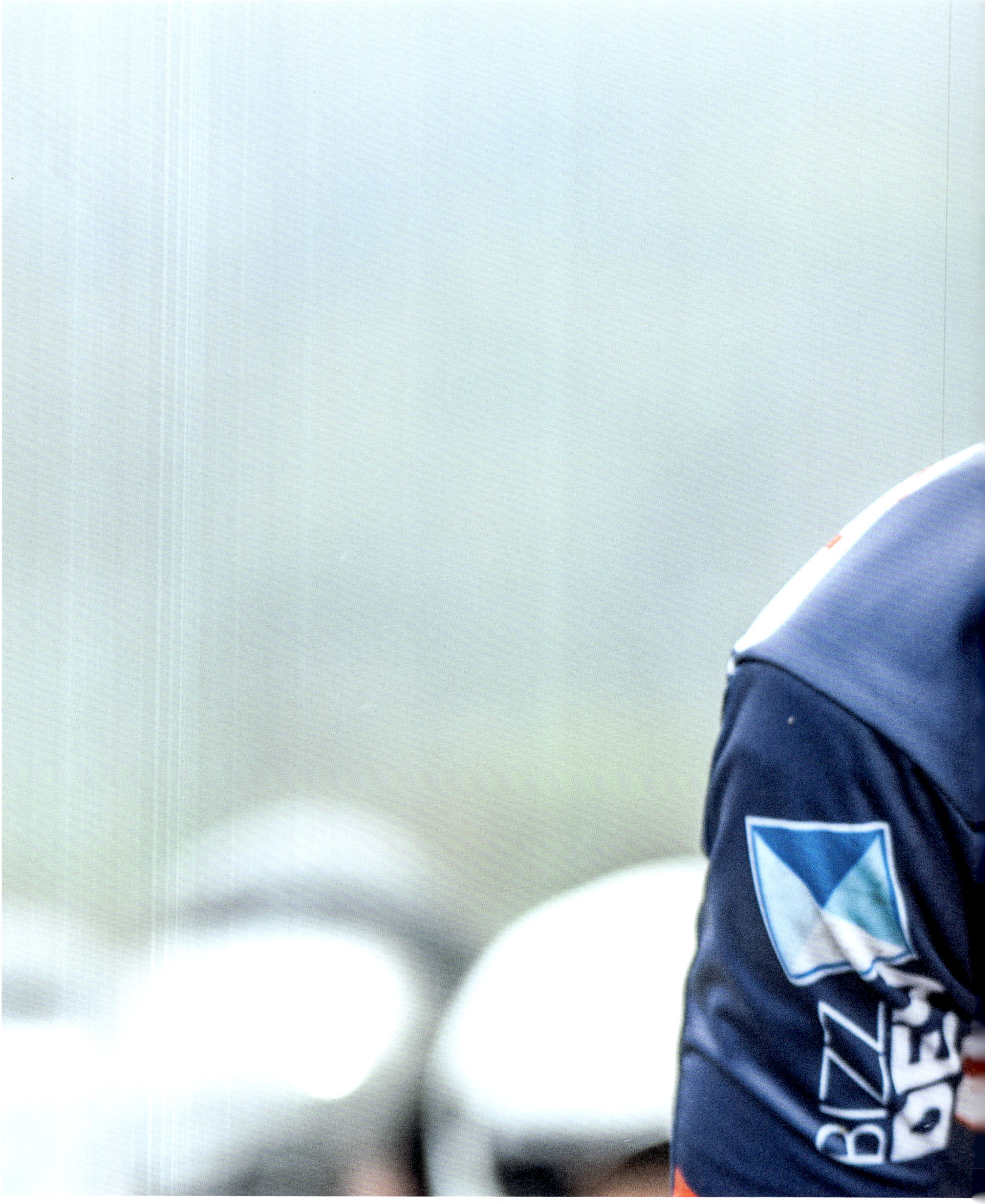

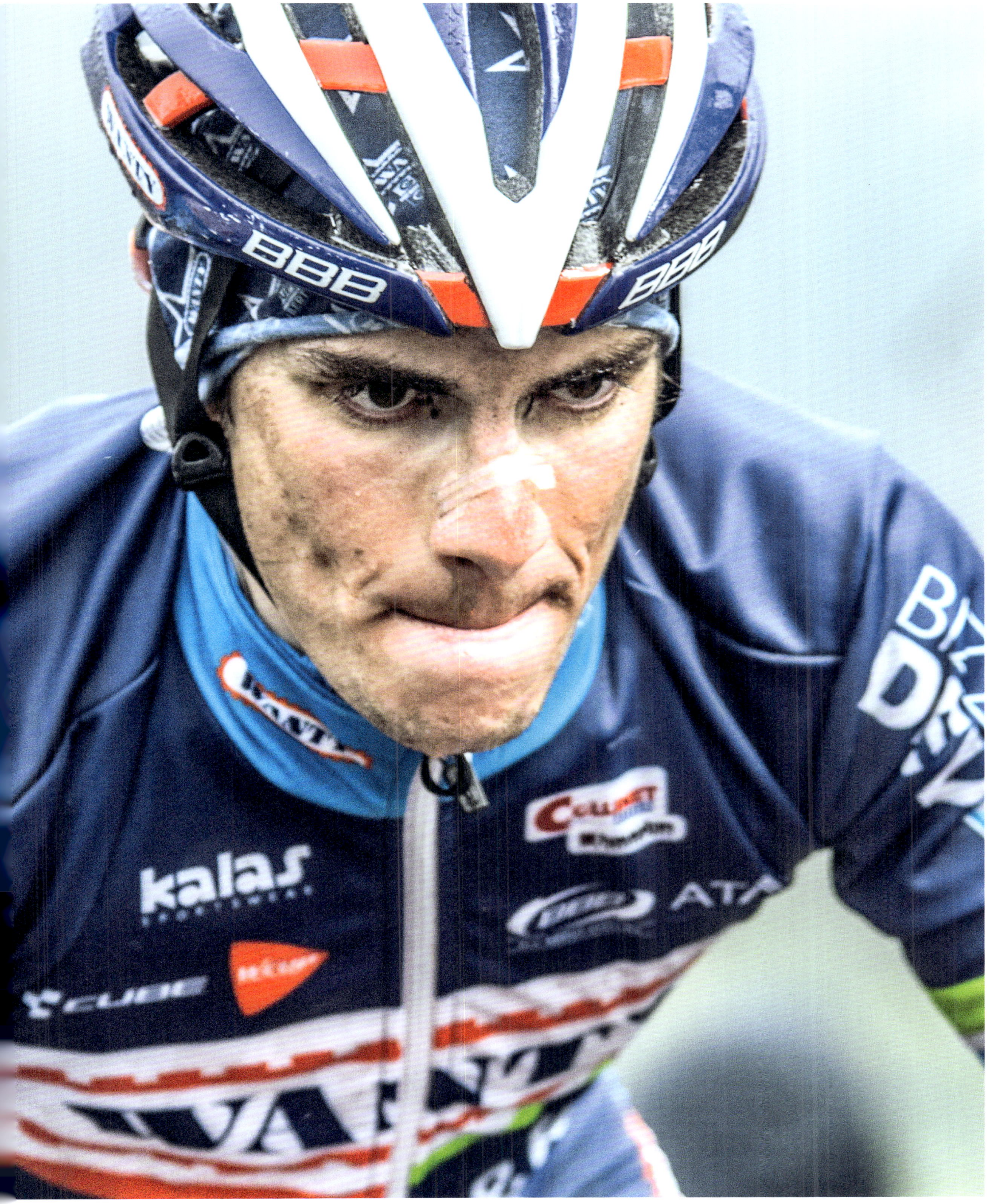

Gaëtan Bille (Wanty-Groupe Gobert). **Gaëtan Bille (Wanty-Groupe Gobert).** *Gaëtan Bille (Wanty-Groupe Gobert).*

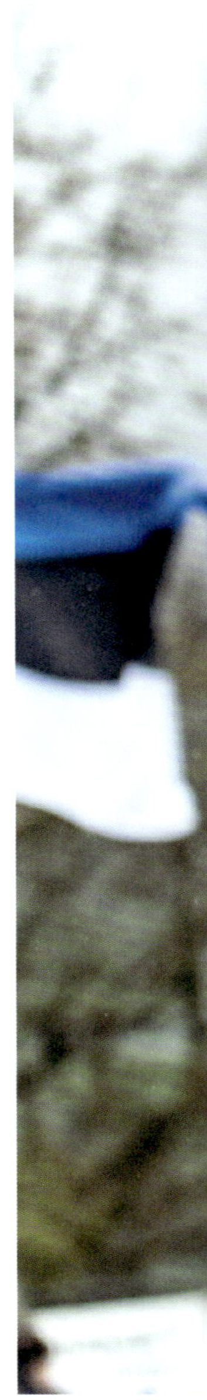

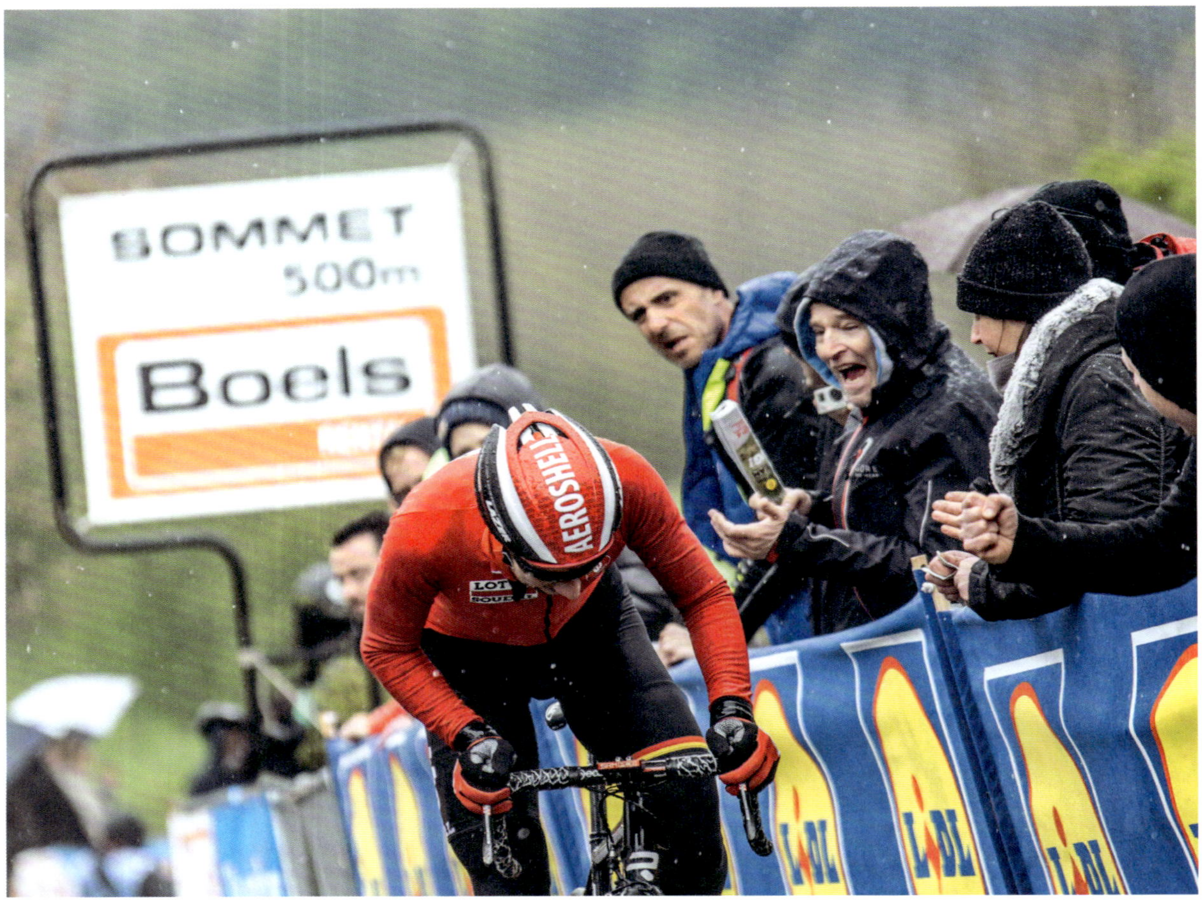
SOMMET
500m
Boels
AEROSHELL

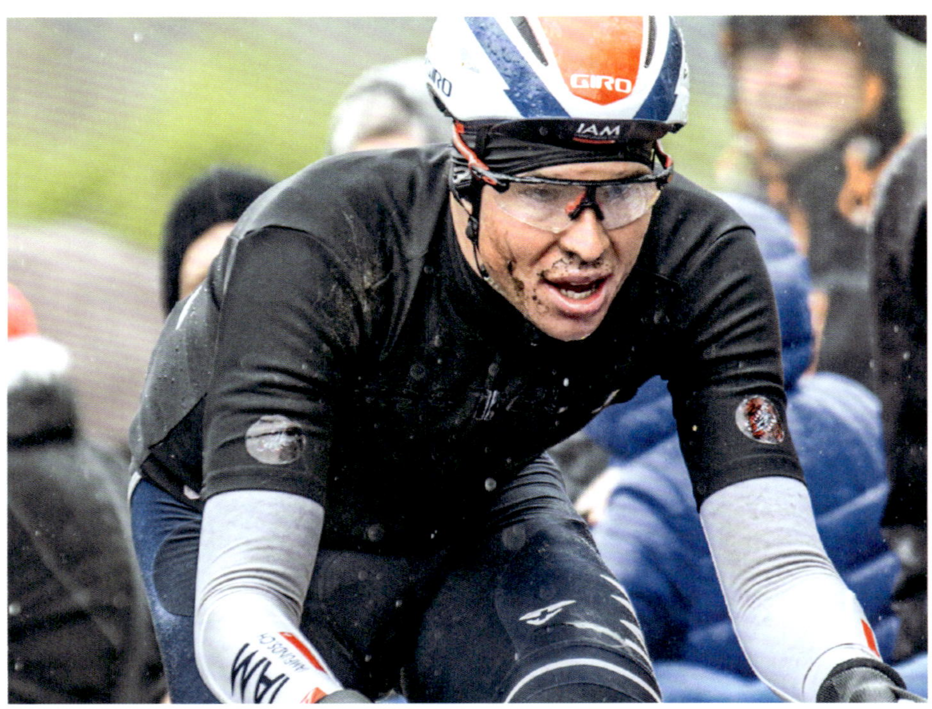
GIRO
IAM

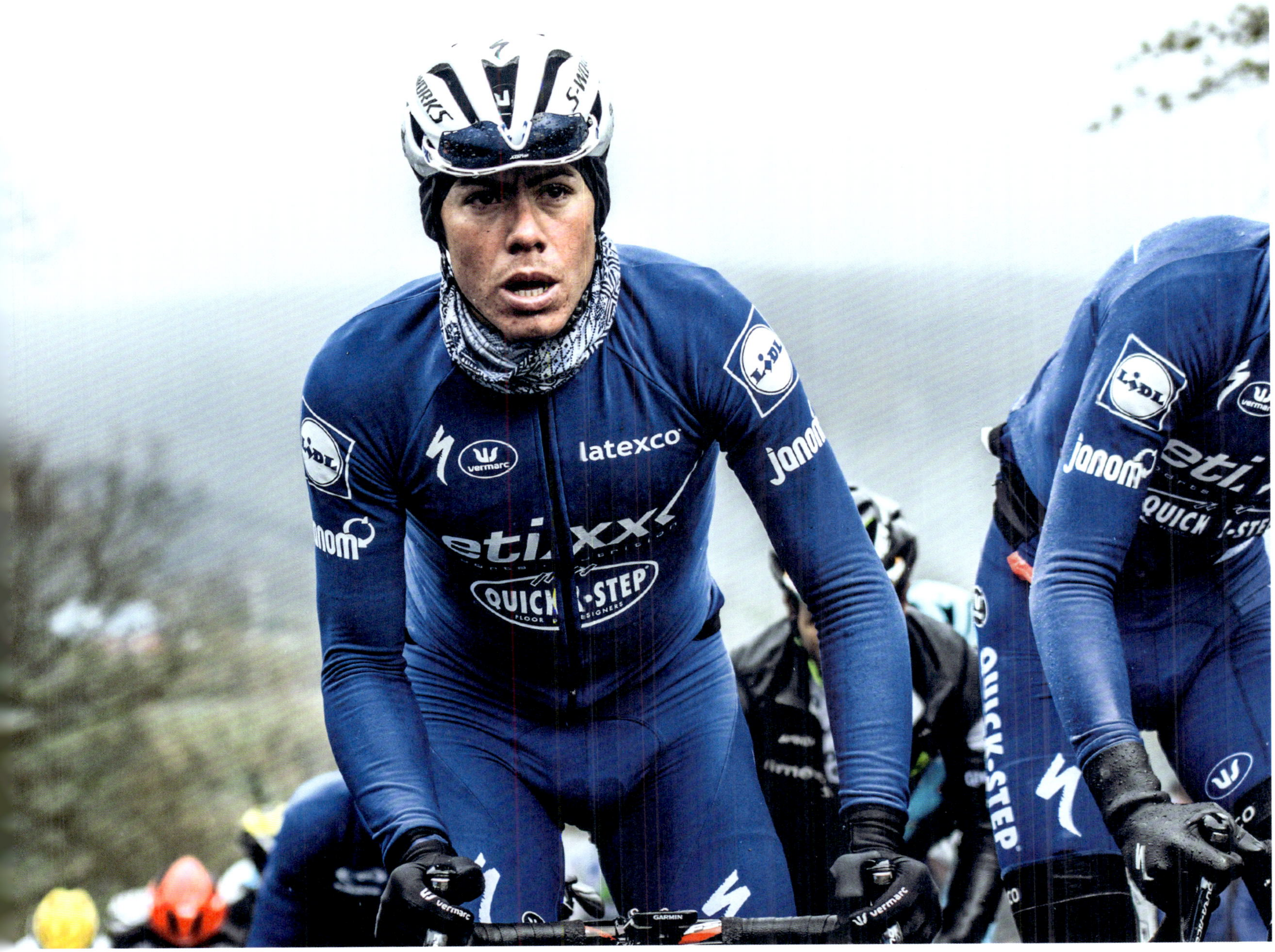
latexco
QUICK-STEP

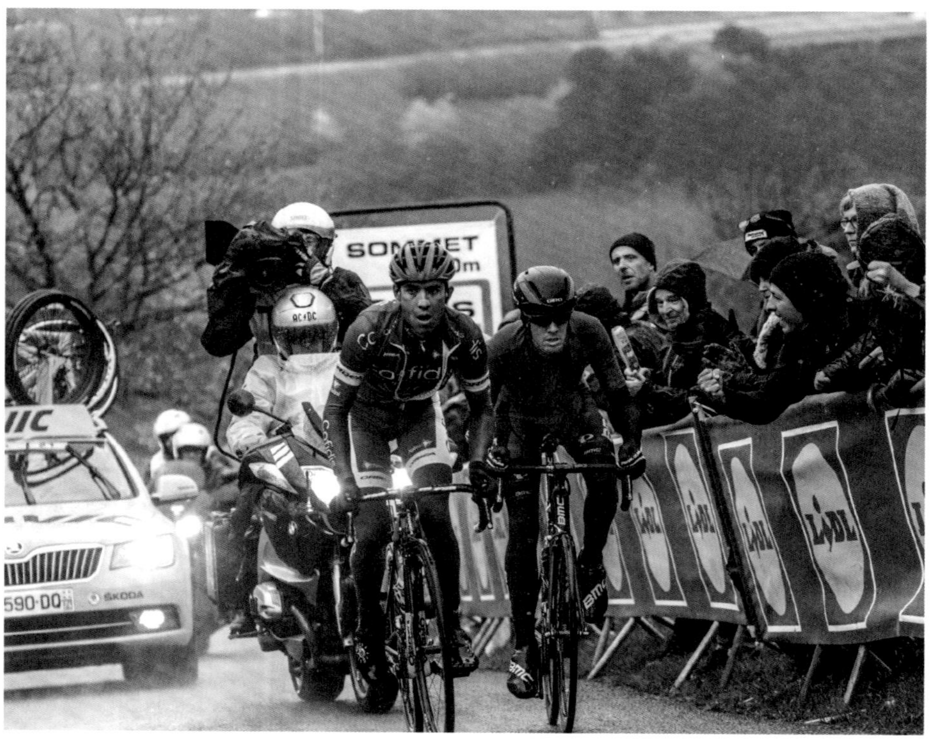

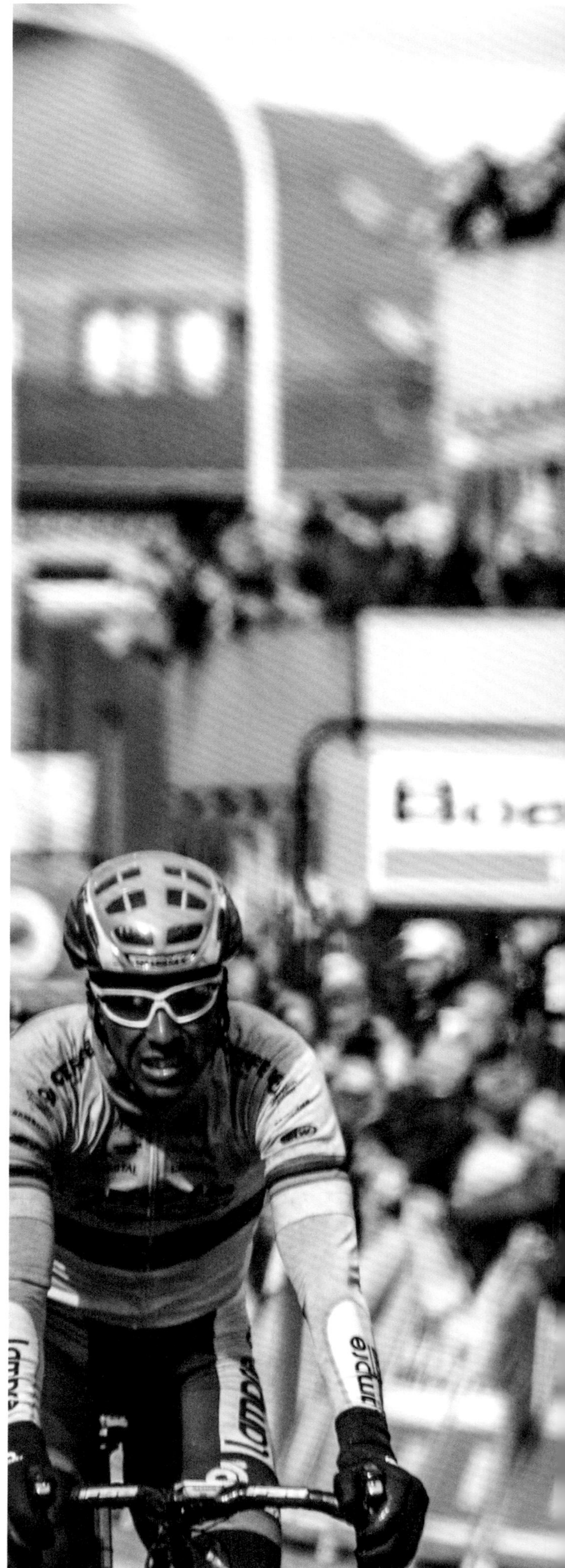

Wout Poels (Team Sky) gewinnt vor Michael Albasini (ORICA-GreenEDGE, nicht im Bild) und Rui Costa (Lampre-Merida). **Wout Poels (Team Sky) beats Michael Albasini (ORICA-GreenEDGE, not in the picture) and Rui Costa (Lampre-Merida).** *Wout Poels (Team Sky) remporte la course devant Michael Albasini (ORICA-GreenEDGE, absent de la photo) et Rui Costa (Lampre-Merida).*

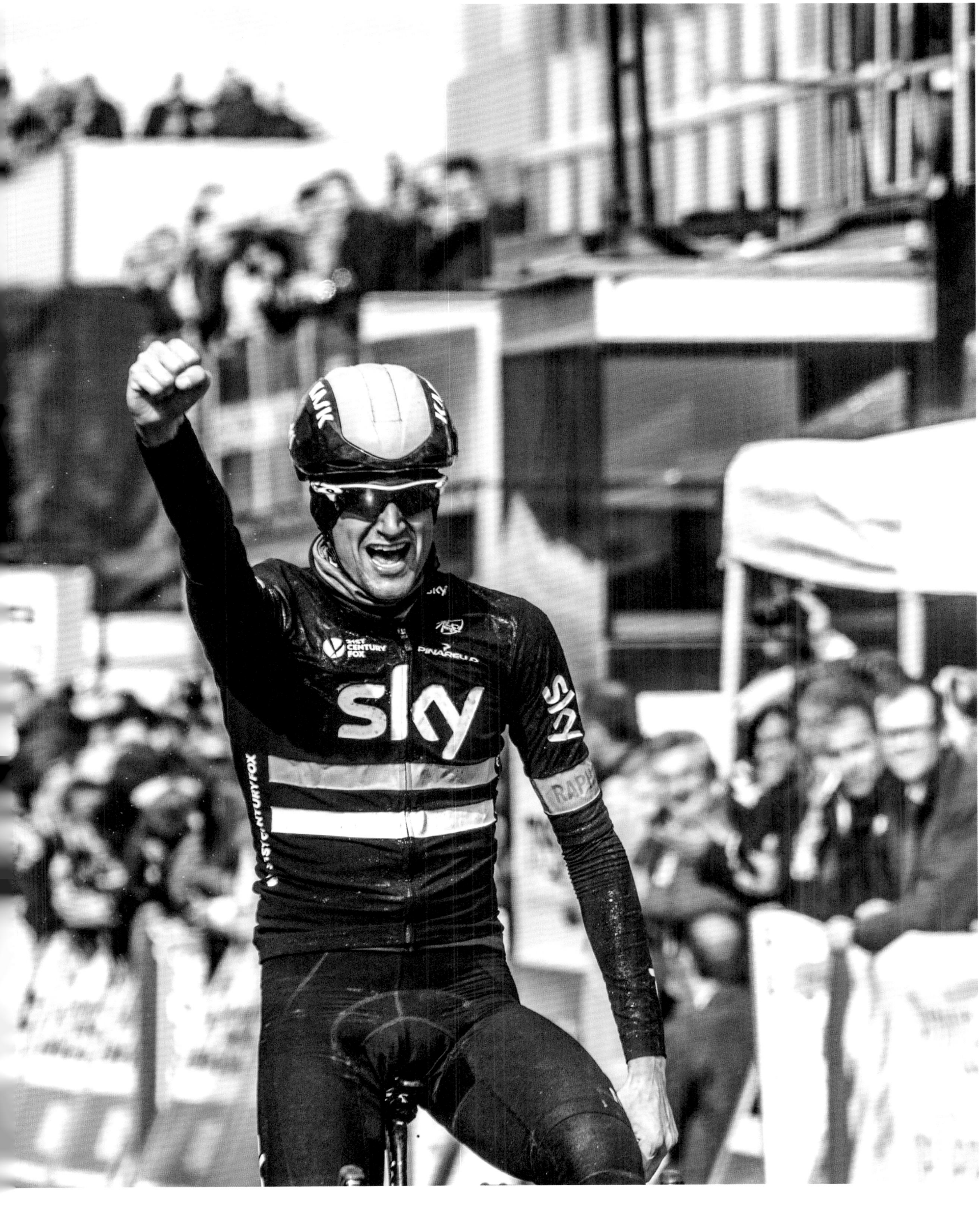
sky

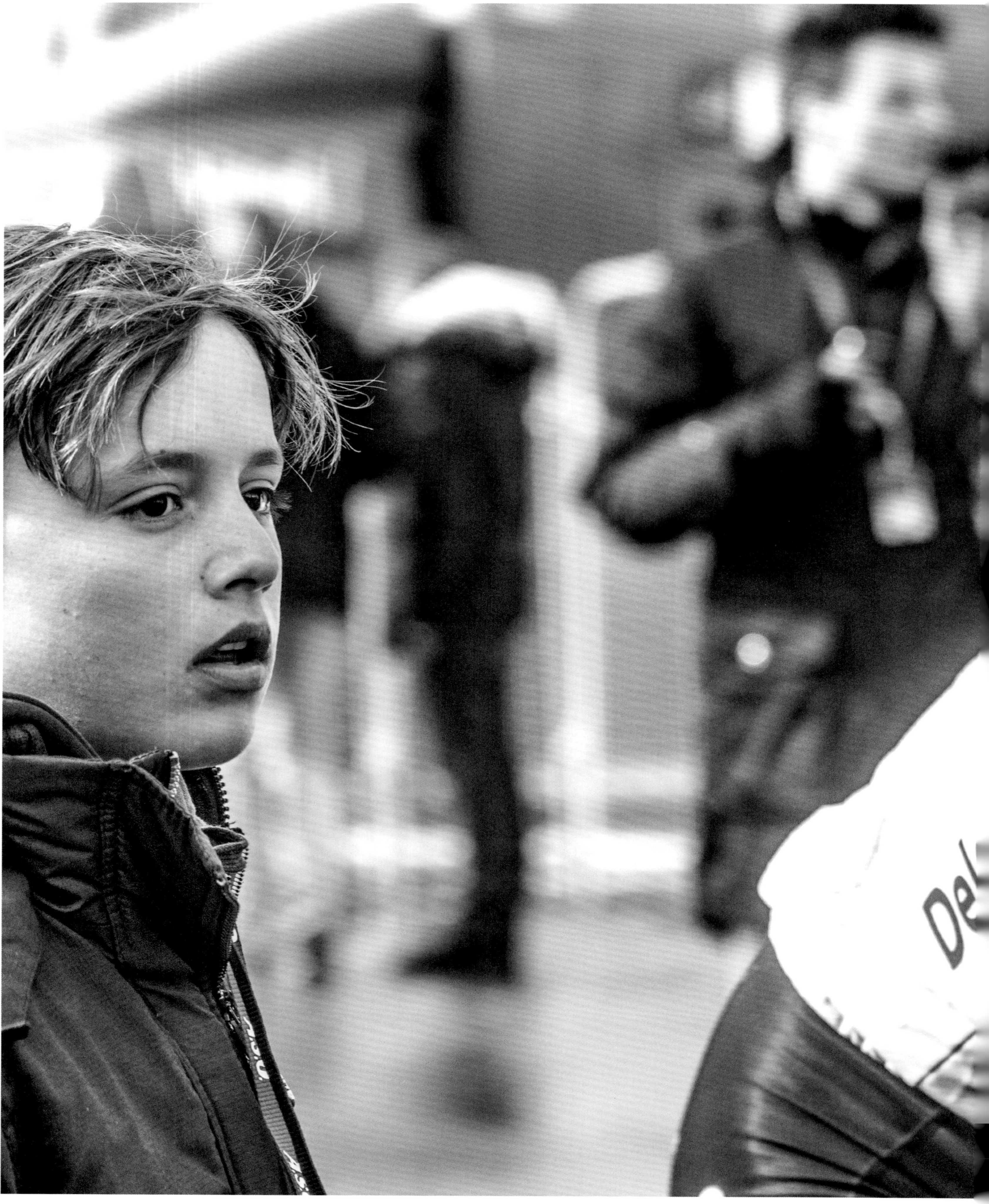

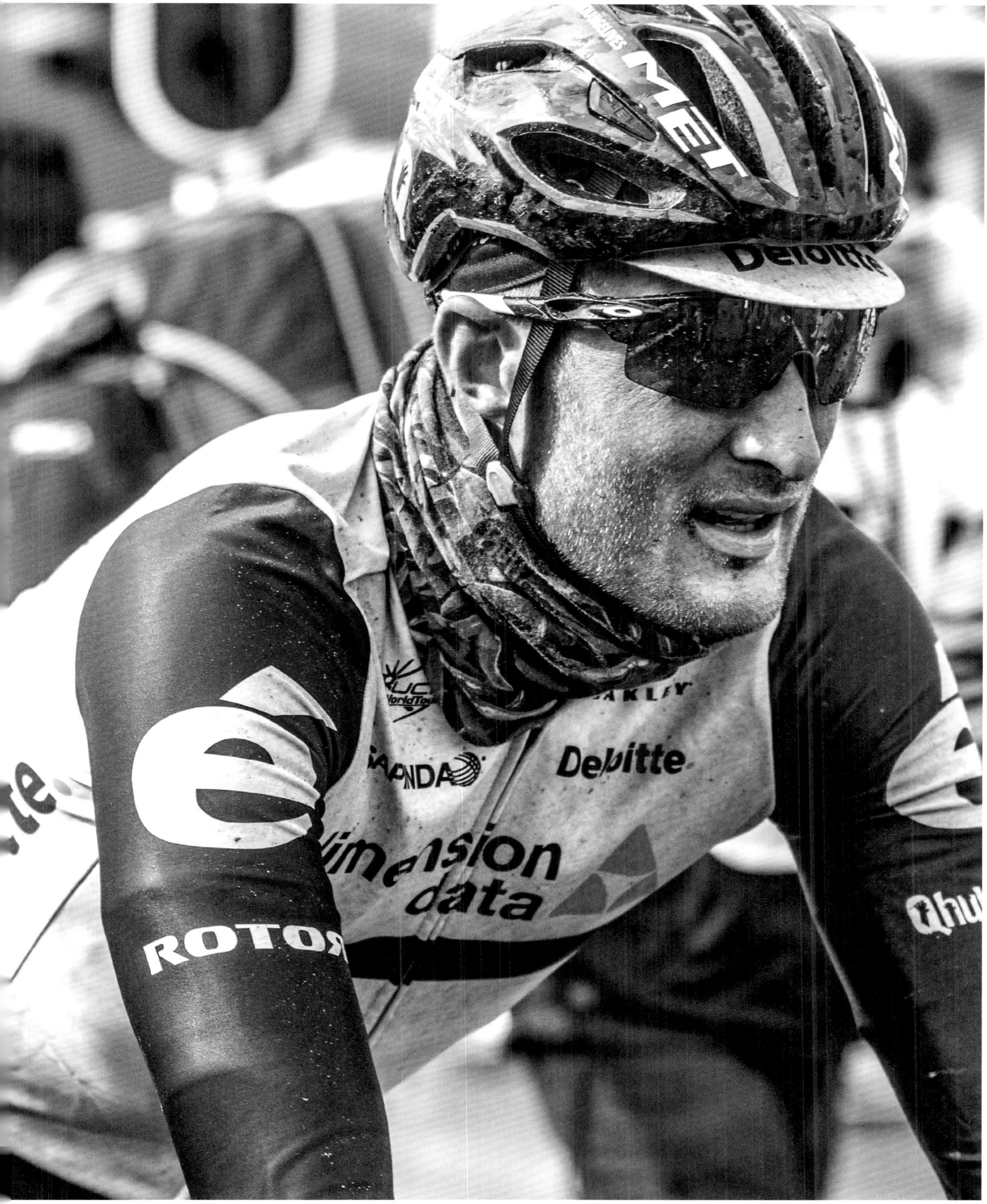

Done and dusted: Stephen Cummings (Dimension Data). **Done and dusted: Stephen Cummings (Dimension Data).**
Fourbu et couvert de boue : Stephen Cummings (Dimension Data).

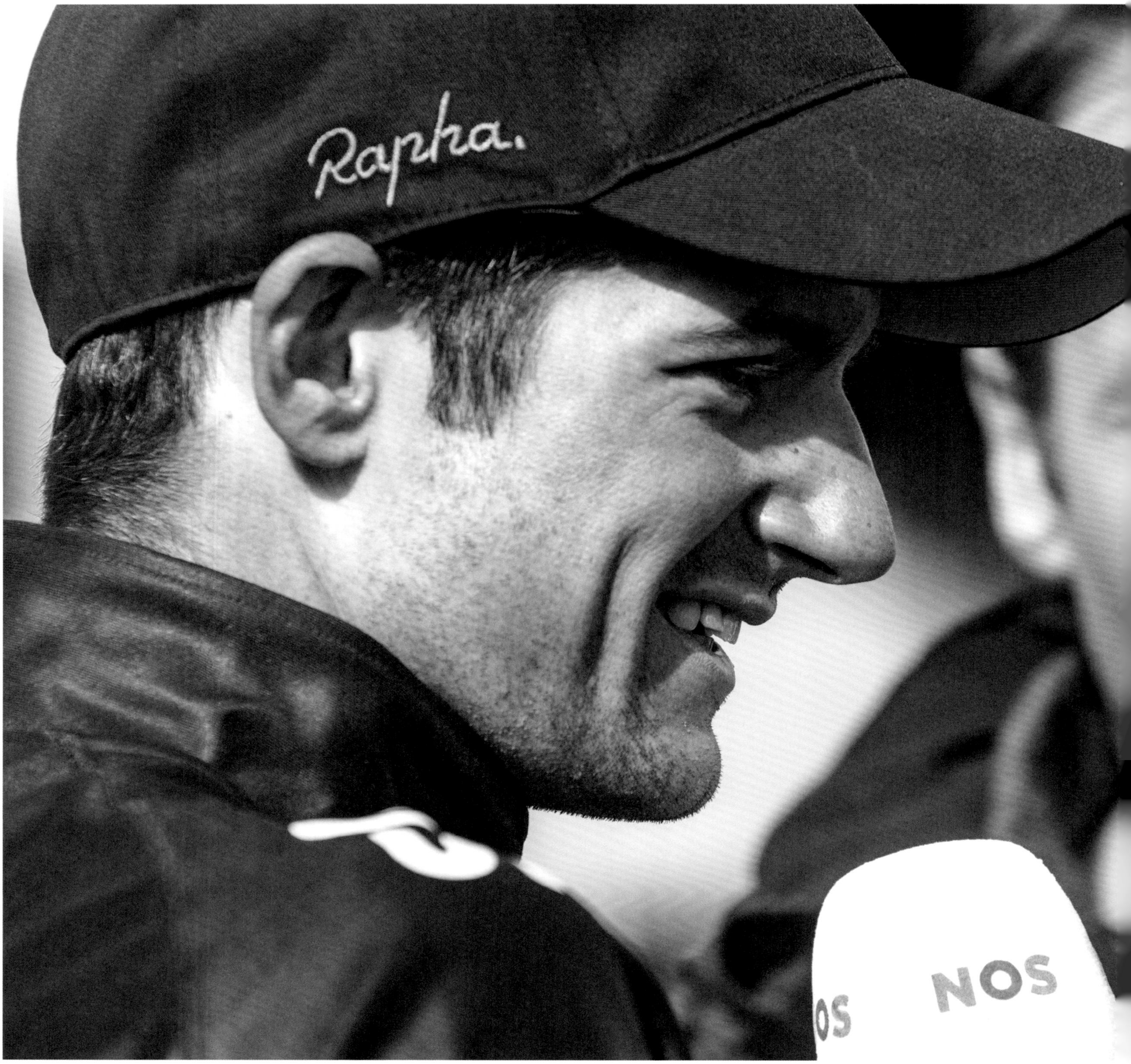

↑ Wout Poels (Team Sky). **Wout Poels (Team Sky).** *Wout Poels (Team Sky).*

↗ V. l. n. r. Rui Costa (Lampre-Merida), Wout Poels (Team Sky), Michael Albasini (ORICA-GreenEDGE). **From left to right: Rui Costa Rui Costa (Lampre-Merida), Wout Poels (Team Sky), Michael Albasini (ORICA-GreenEDGE).** *De g. à dr. : Rui Costa (Lampre-Merida), Wout Poels (Team Sky), Michael Albasini (ORICA-GreenEDGE).*

→ Dylan Teuns (BMC Racing Team). **Dylan Teuns (BMC Racing Team).** *Dylan Teuns (BMC Racing Team).*

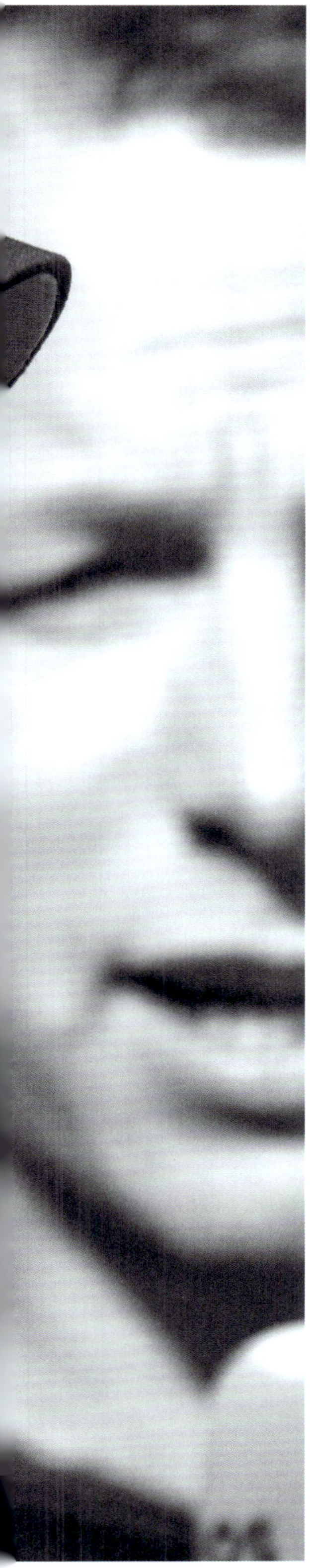

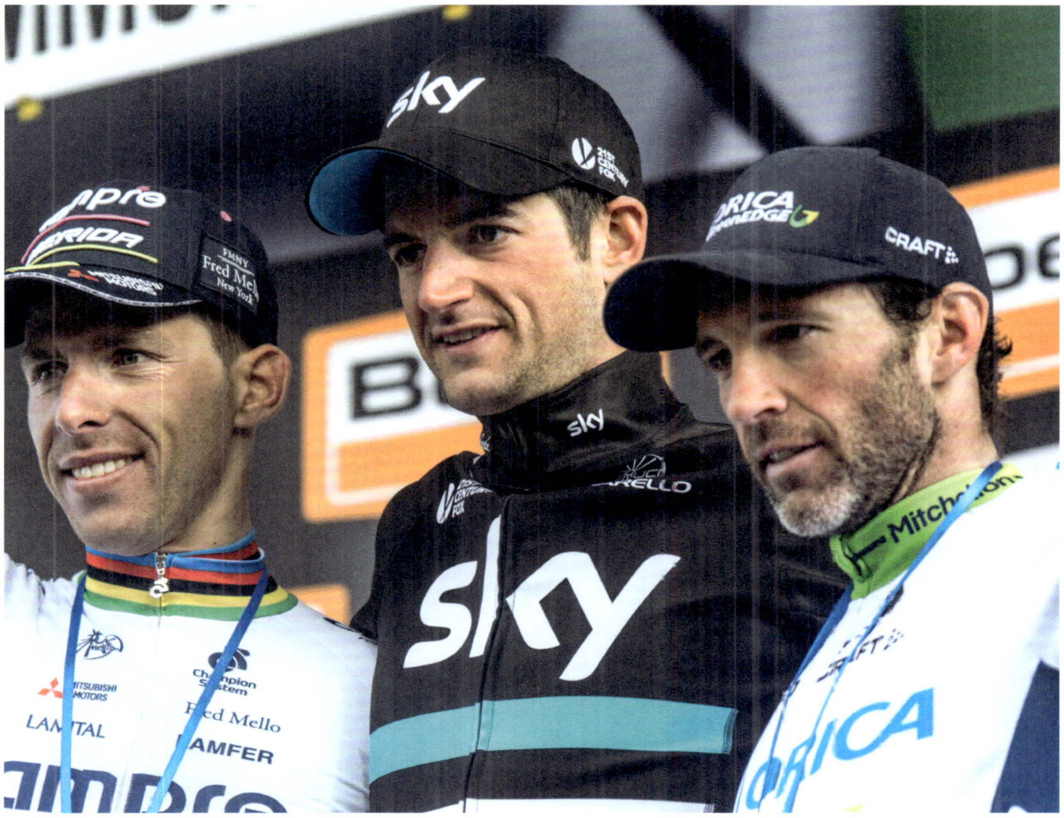
sky
CRAFT
Fred Mello
sky

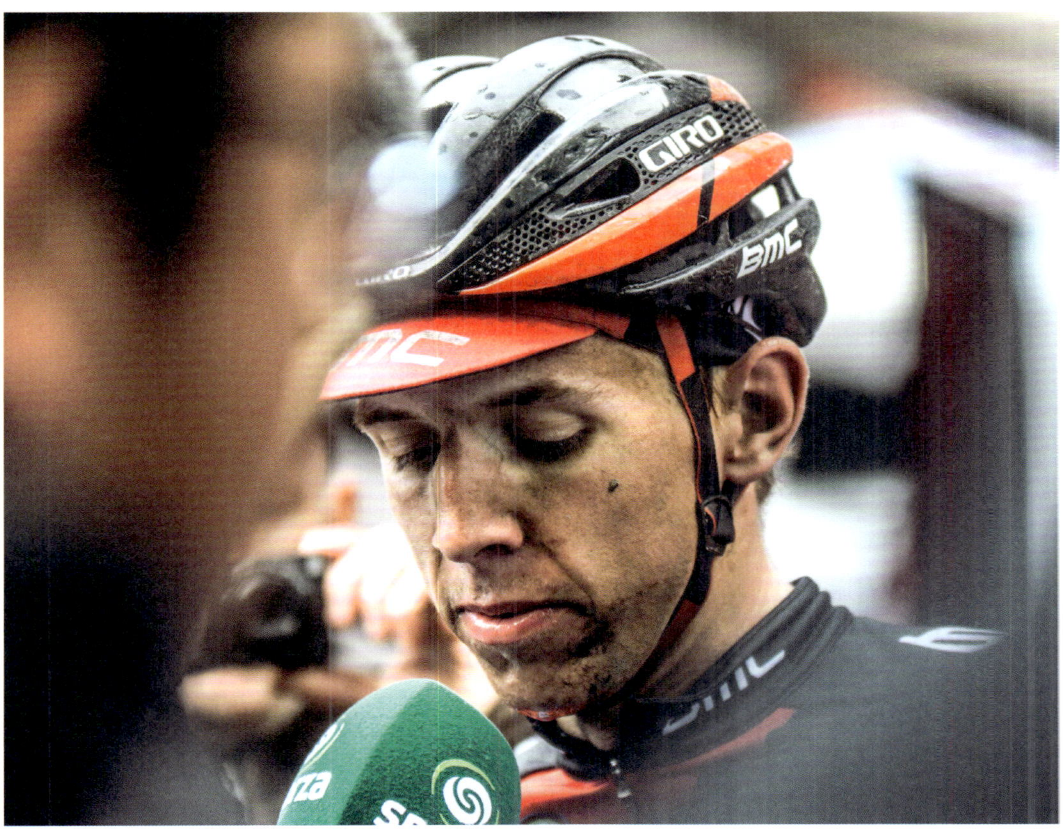
GIRO
bmc

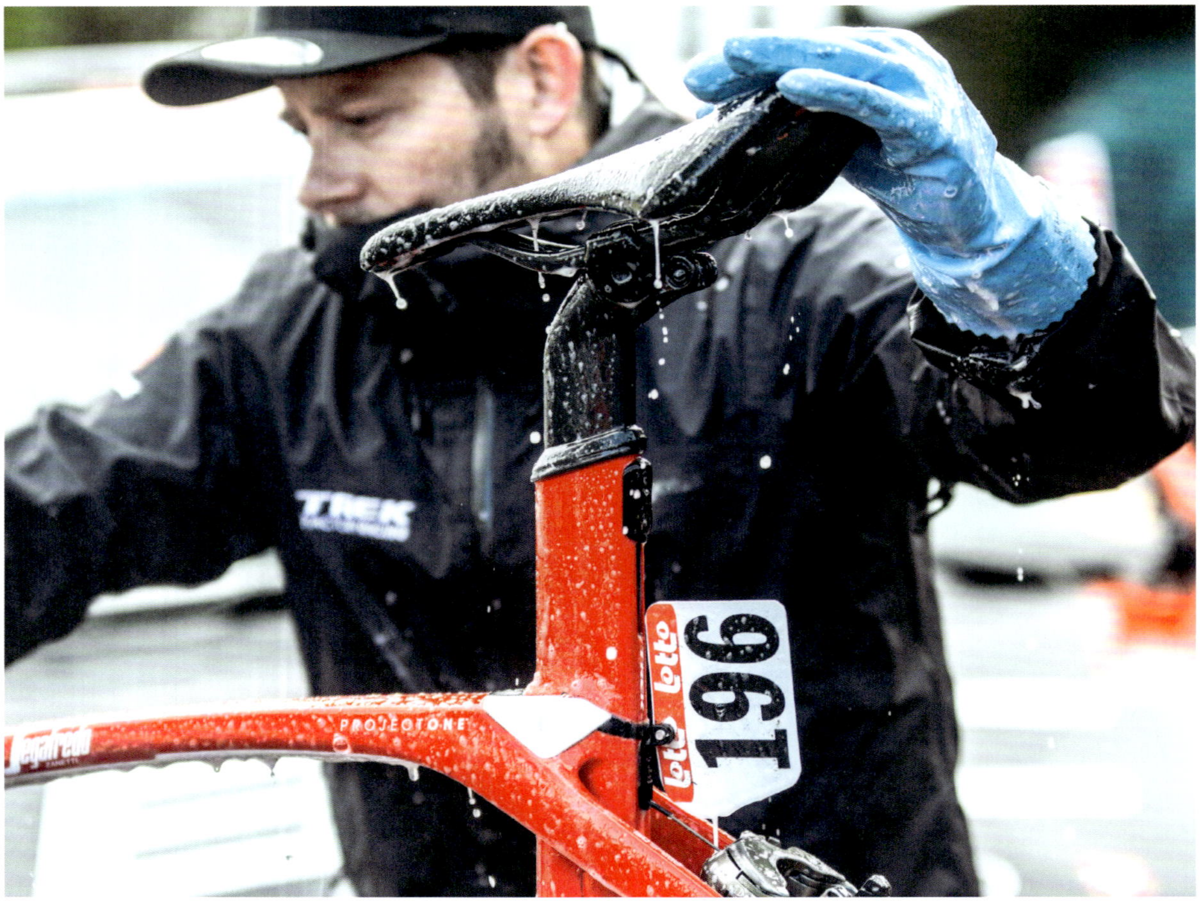
TREK
lotto
196

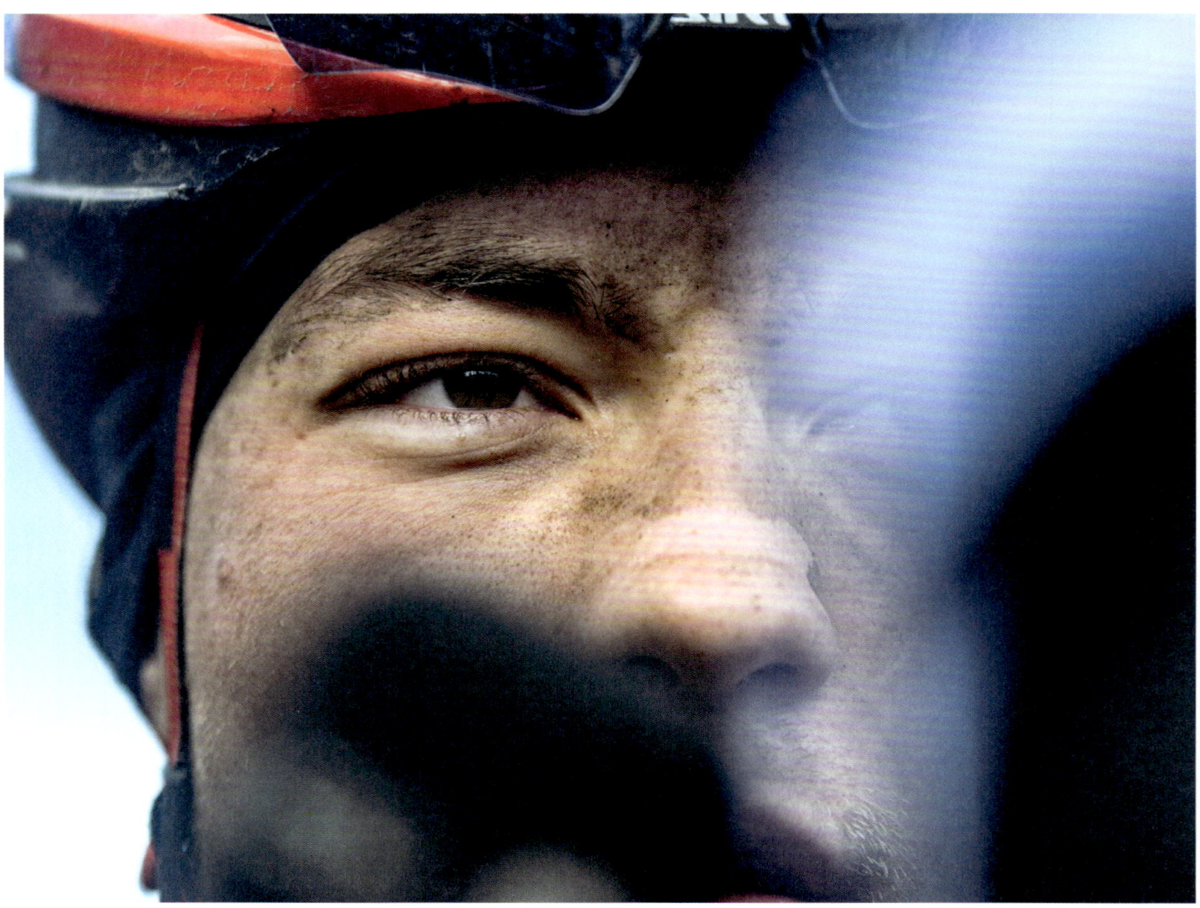

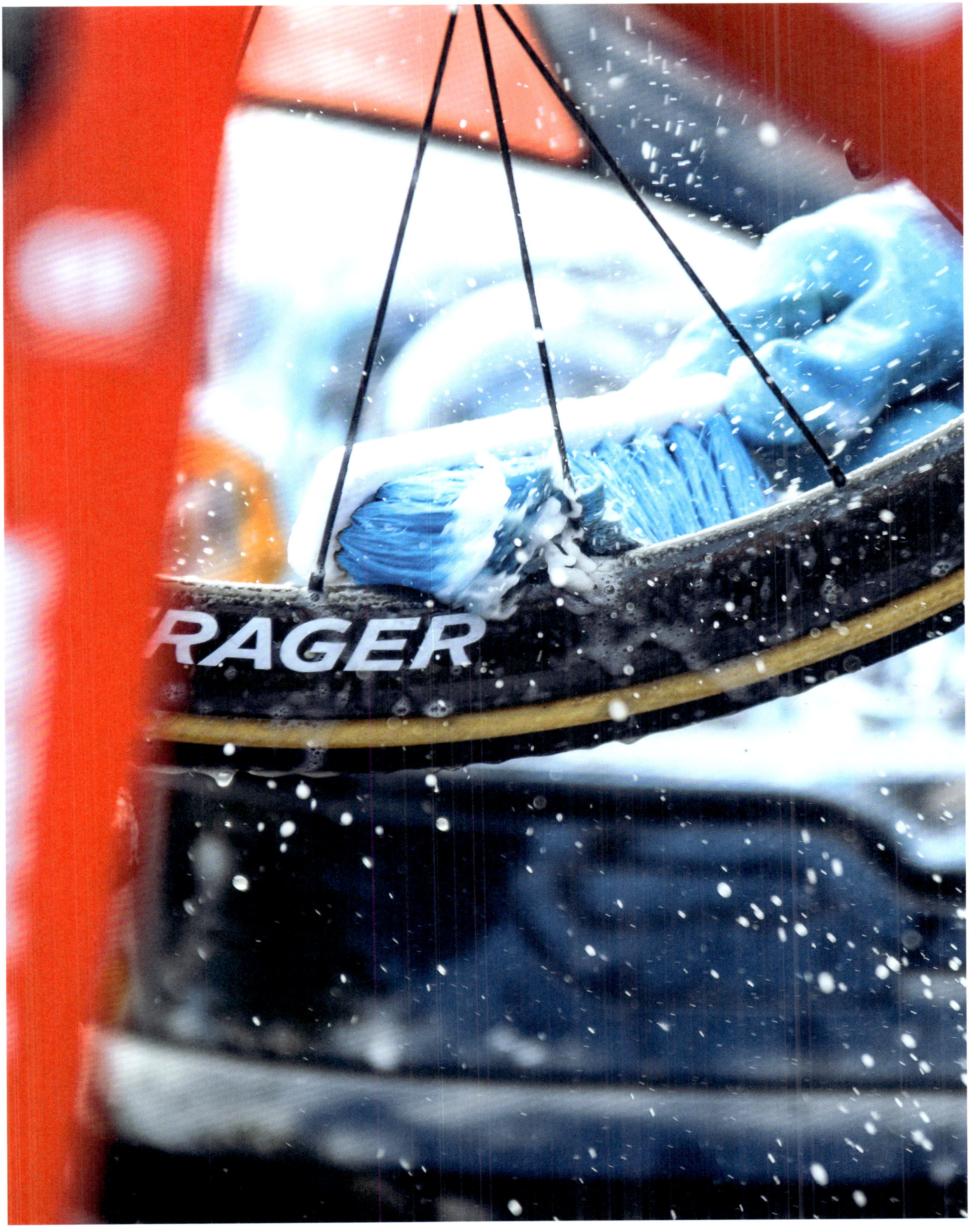

Nach dem Rennen ist vor dem Rennen für die Mechaniker. **After the race is before the race for the mechanics.**
À l'épreuve des coureurs succède celle des mécaniciens.

Critérium du Dauphiné

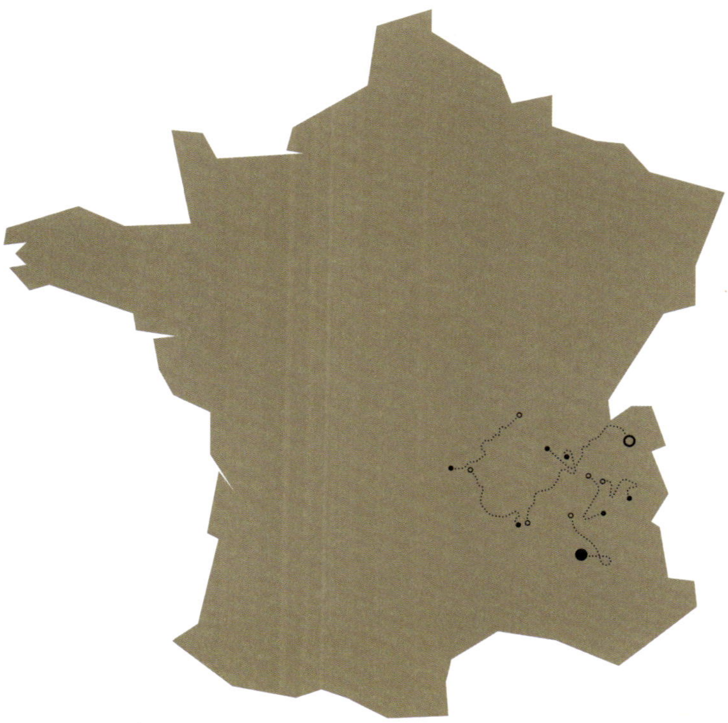

1,153.5

KILOMETRE

DATE: 5. – 12. 06. 2016

FIRST TOUR: 1947

DURATION: 29:59:31

38.460

KM/H AVG. SPEED WINNER

Seit 1947 ausgetragen, ist das Etappenrennen in der Dauphiné eines der wichtigsten in der Vorbereitung zur Tour de France. **Held since 1947, the Dauphiné stage race is one of the most important preparations for the Tour de France.** *Organisée depuis 1947, cette course par étapes dans le Dauphiné est l'un des plus importants préparatifs au Tour de France.*

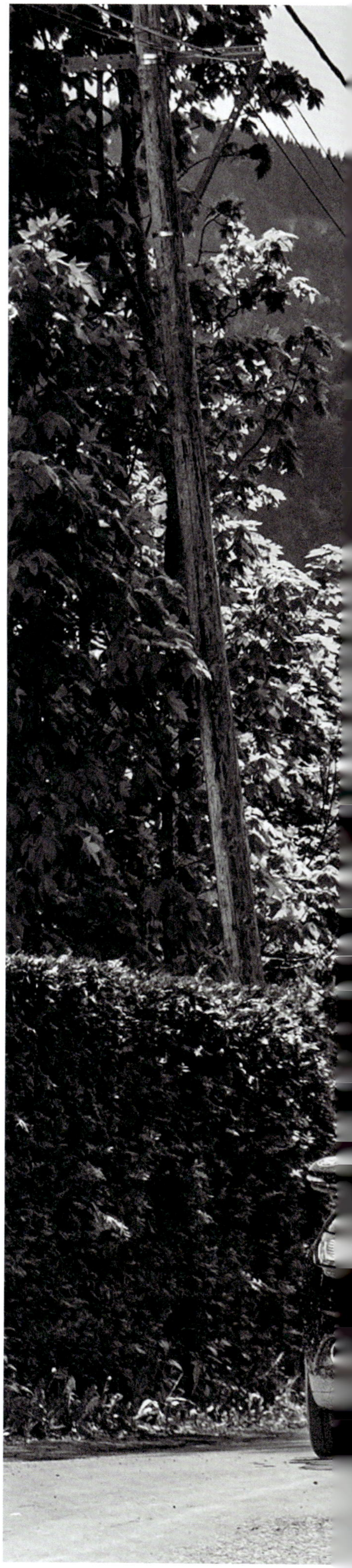

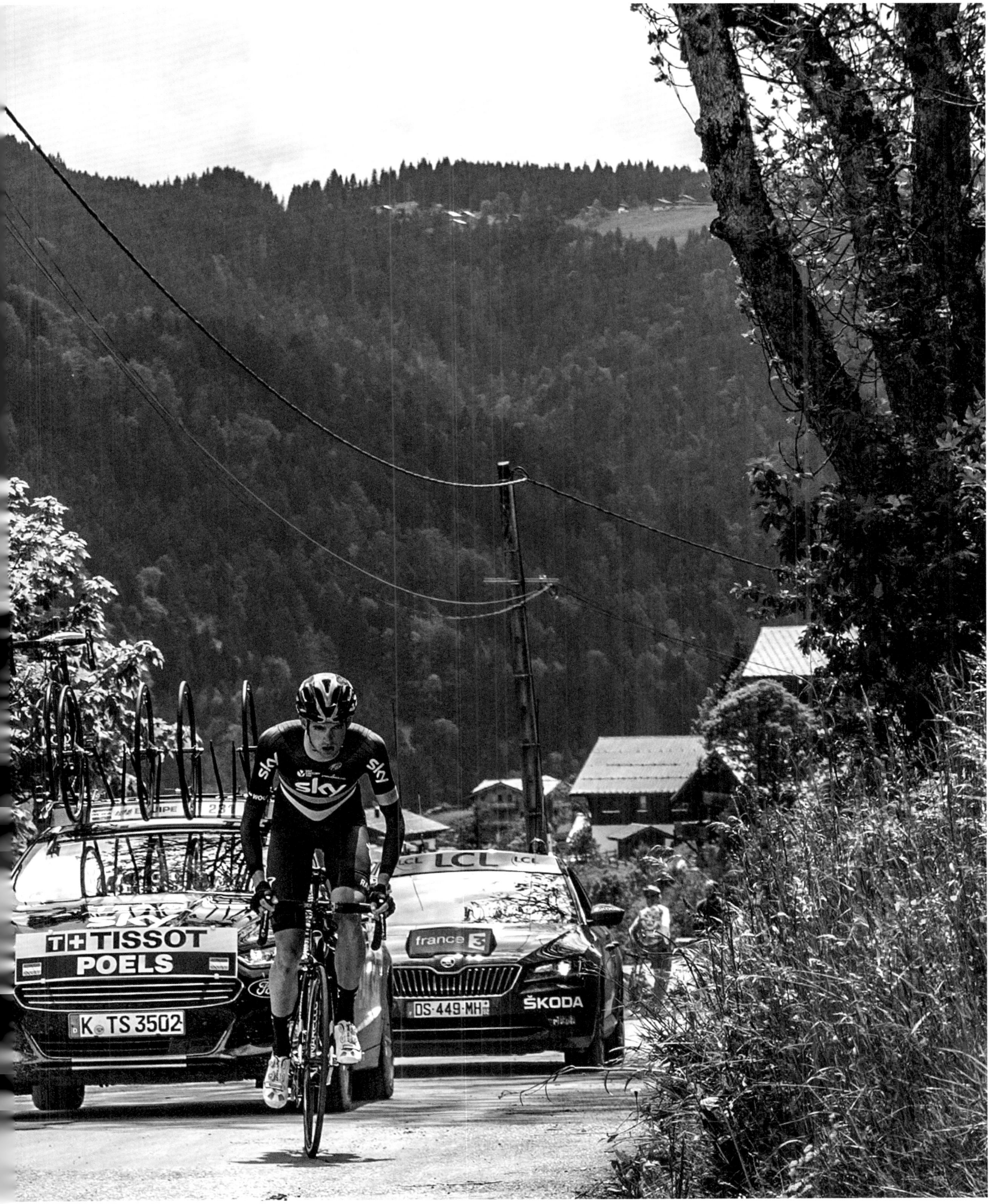

Wout Poels (Team Sky) auf dem Weg zum Gipfel des Mont Chéry – und zum 6. Platz bei diesem Bergzeitfahren. **Wout Poels (Team Sky) en route to the summit of Mont Chéry – and to 6th place in this mountain time trial.** *Wout Poels (Team Sky) en route vers le sommet du mont Chéry, et la 6e place de cette course de montagne.*

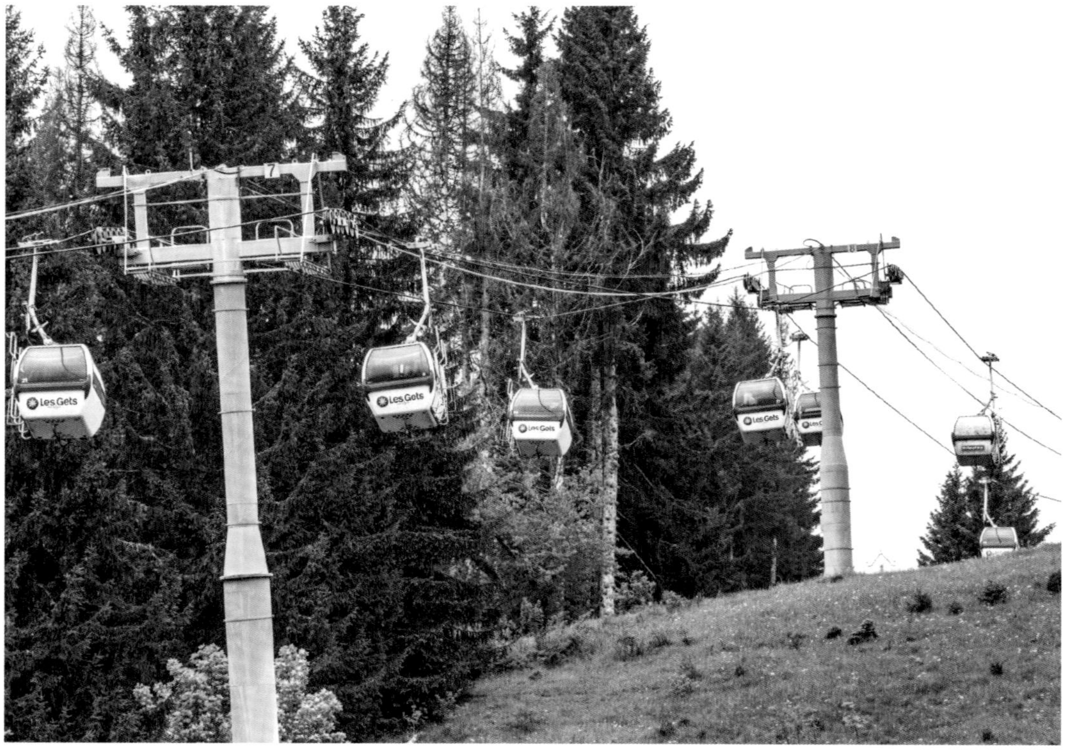
Les Gets

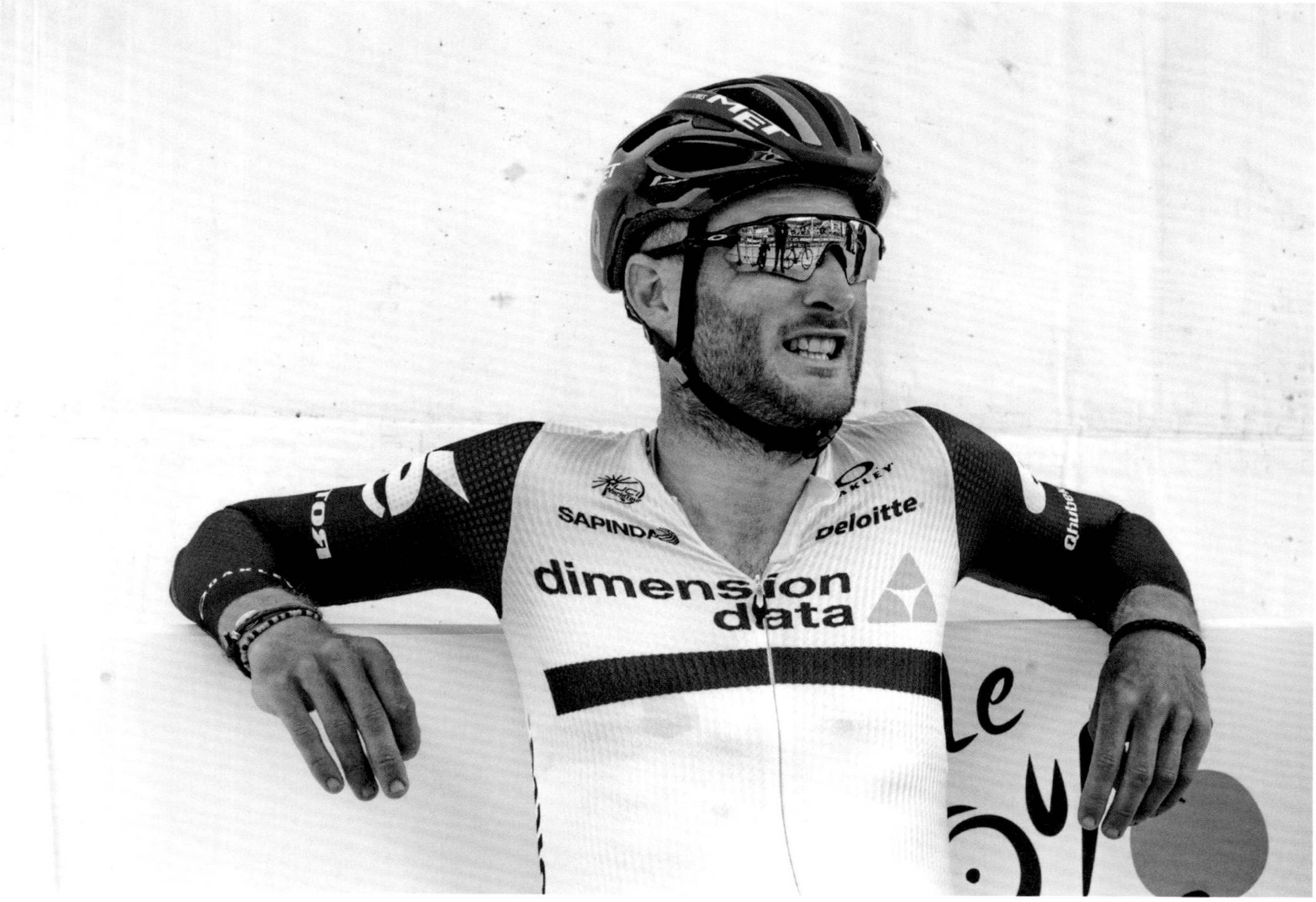
SAPINDA
Deloitte
dimension data

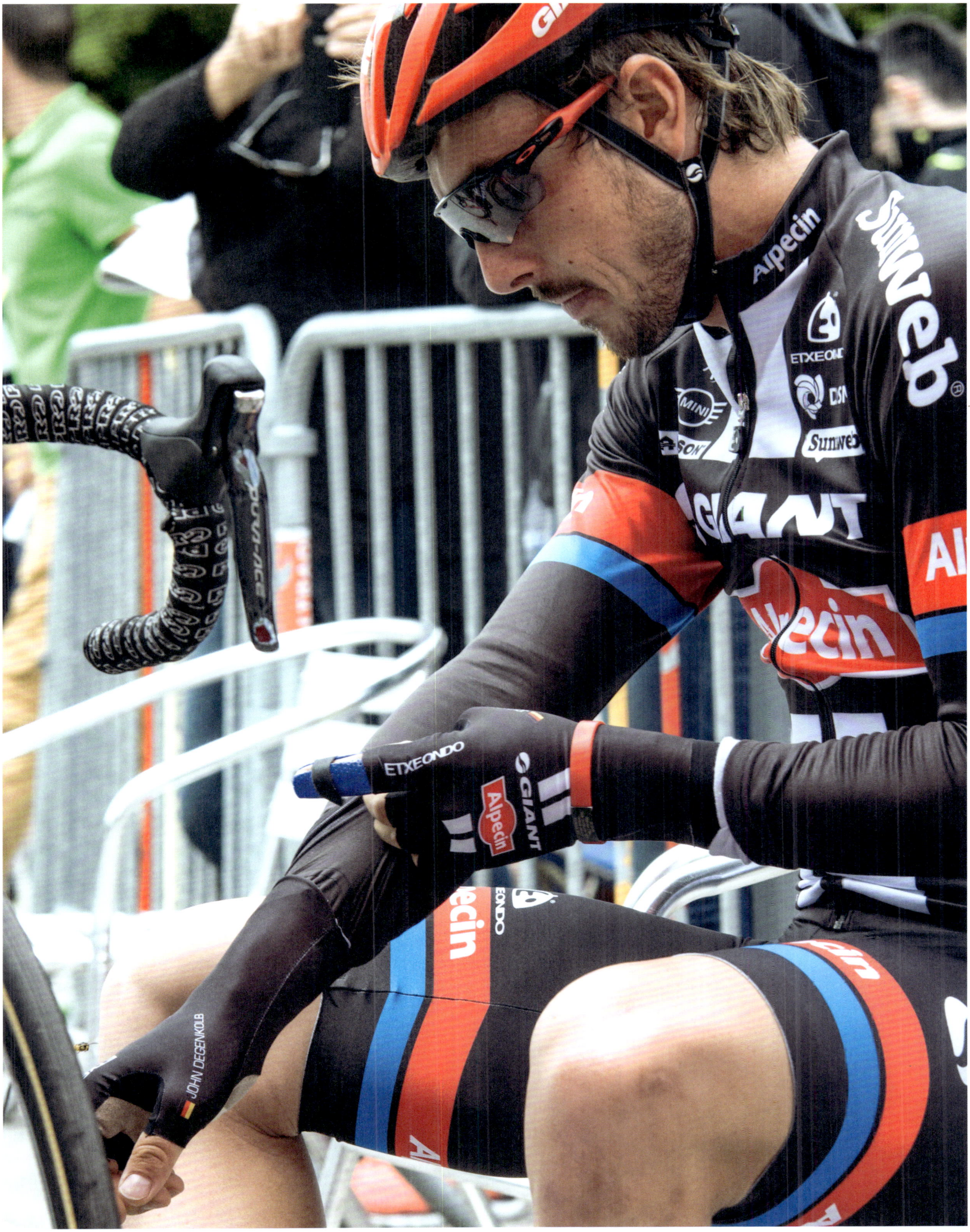

Stephen Cummings (Dimension Data, links) beim Warm-down und John Degenkolb (Team Giant-Alpecin) in der Vorbereitung zum Zeitfahren.
Stephen Cummings (Dimension Data, left) warming down and John Degenkolb (Team Giant-Alpecin) preparing for the time trial. *Stephen Cummings (Dimension Data, à gauche) lors de « warm-down » et John Degenkolb (Team Giant-Alpecin) lors de la préparation au contre-la-montre.*

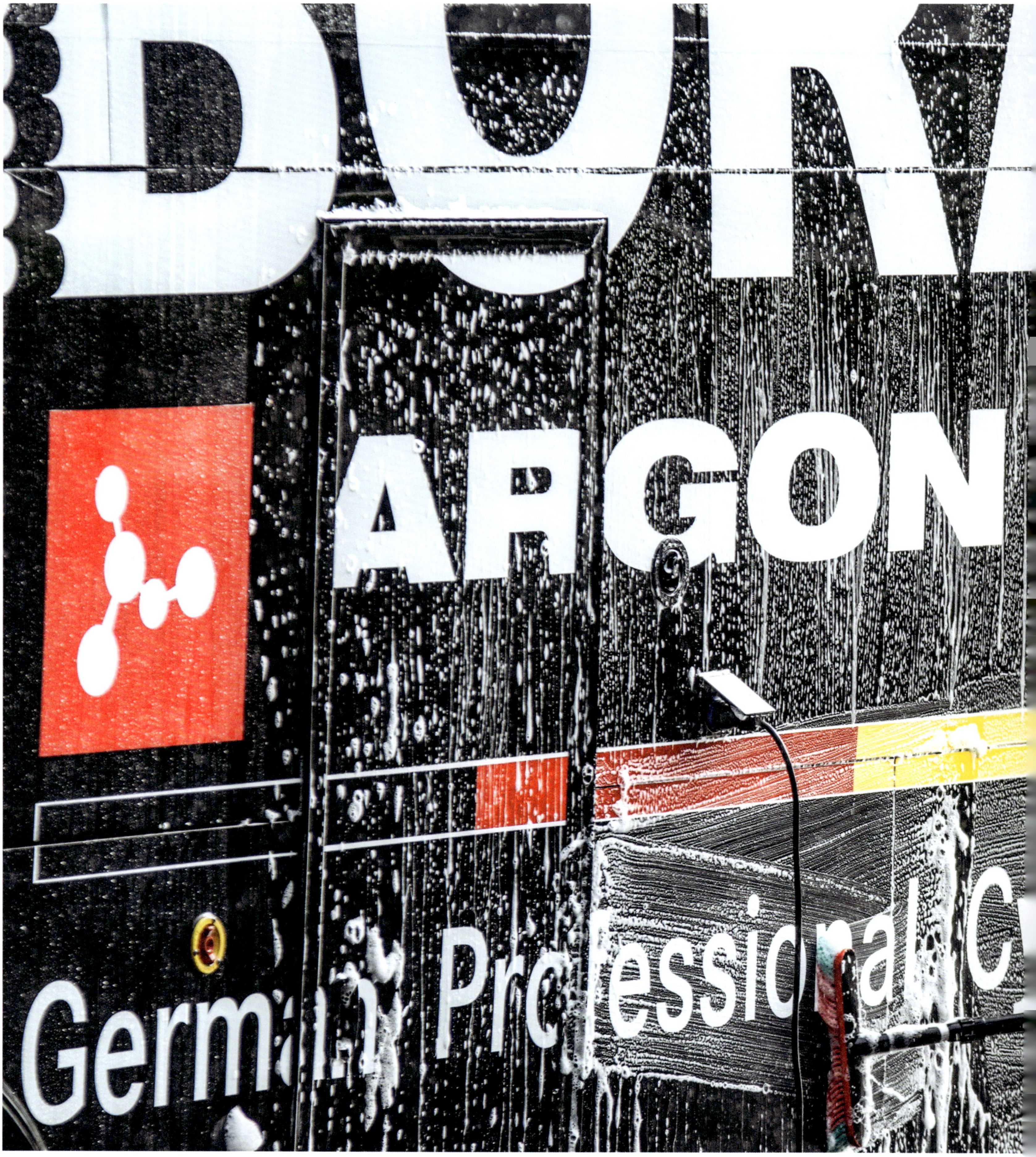
ARGON

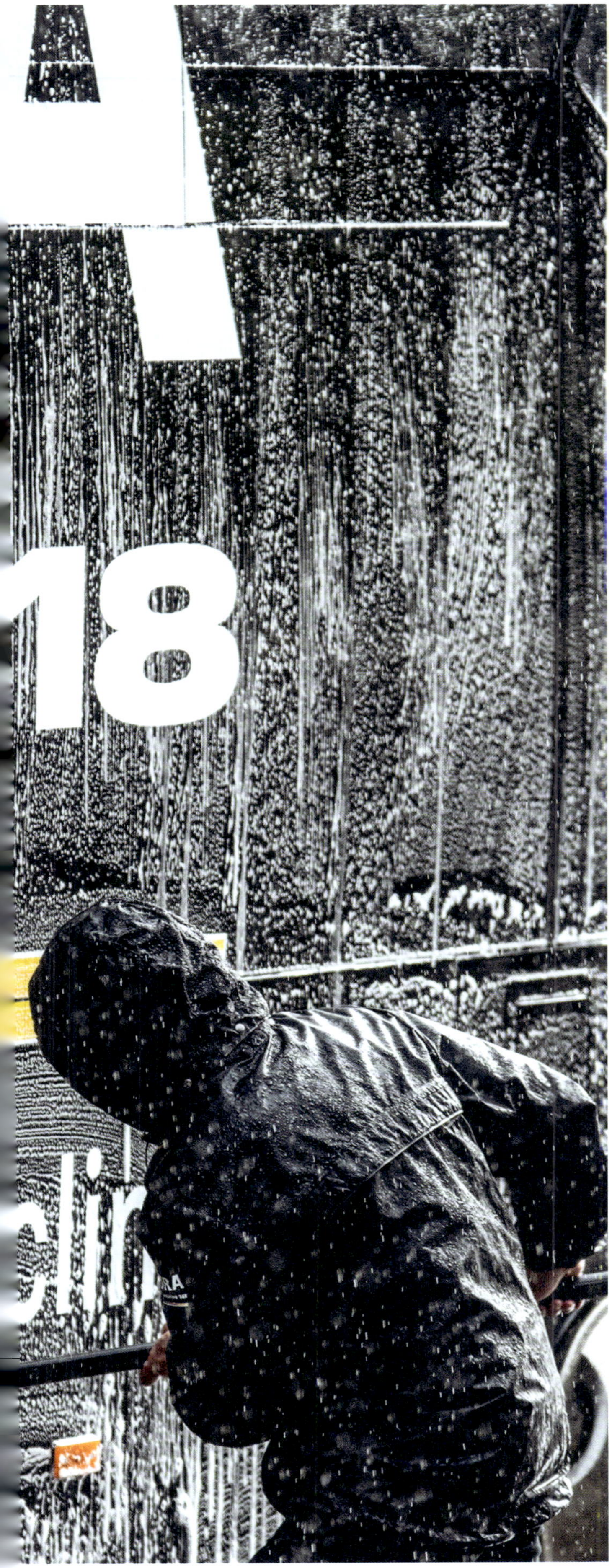

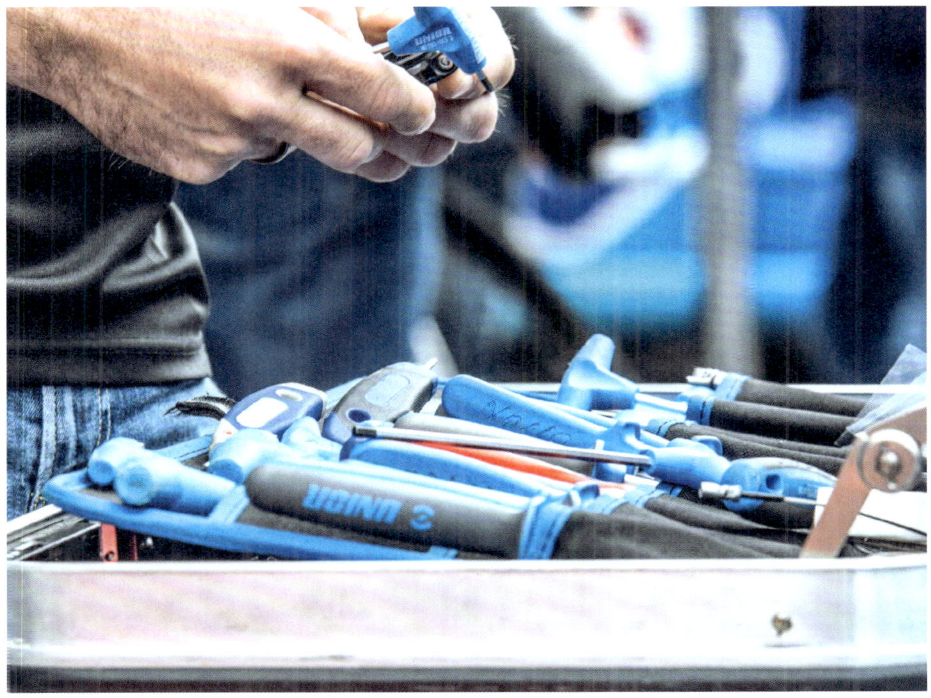

Materialpflege. **Material maintenance.** *Entretien des équipements.*

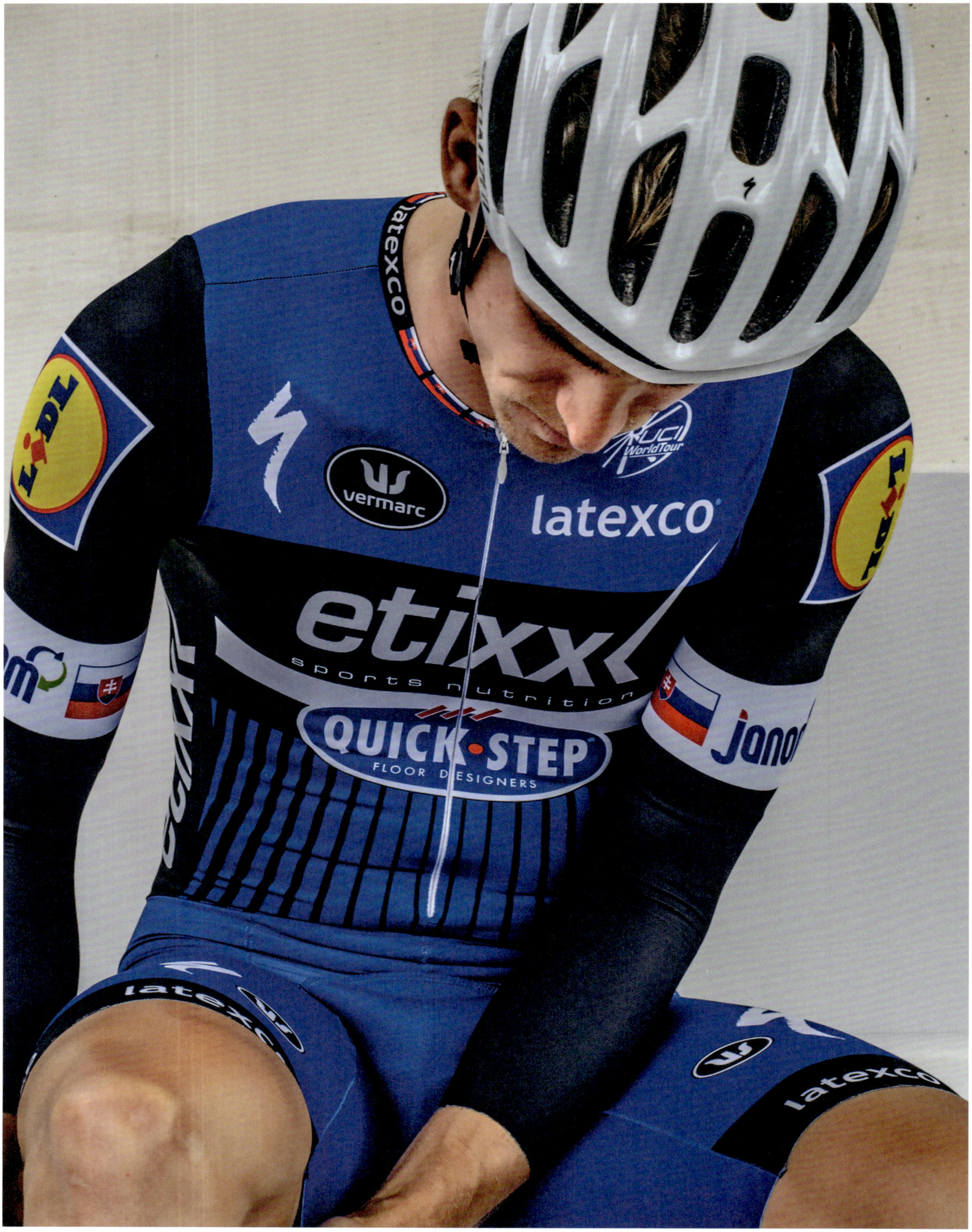

Martin Velits (Etixx – Quick Step) und Alexander Kristoff (Team Katusha) vor dem Start. **Martin Velits (Etixx – Quick Step) and Alexander Kristoff (Team Katusha) before the start.** *Martin Velits (Etixx – Quick Step) et Alexander Kristoff (Team Katusha) avant le départ.*

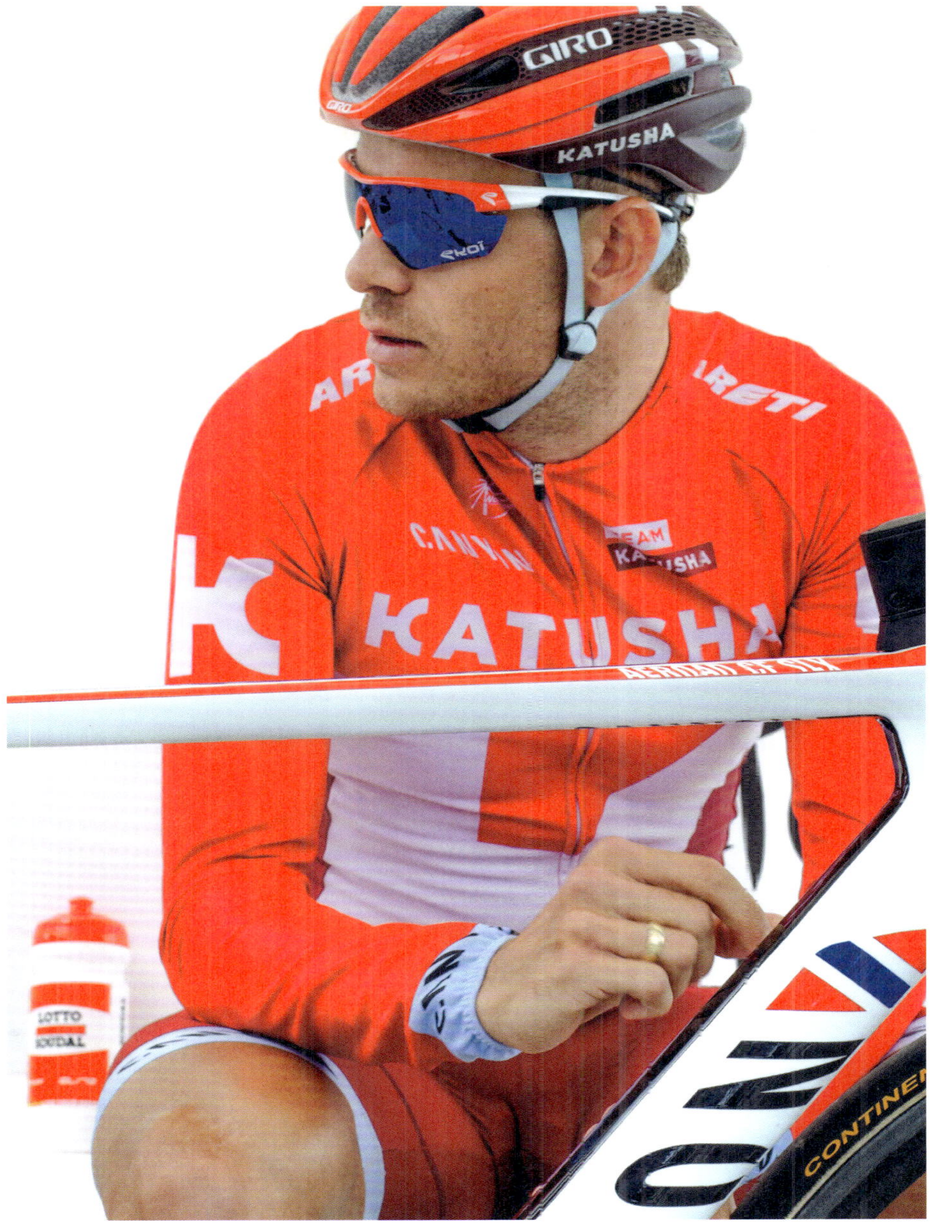
GIRO
KATUSHA
TEAM KATUSHA
KATUSHA
LOTTO
SOUDAL

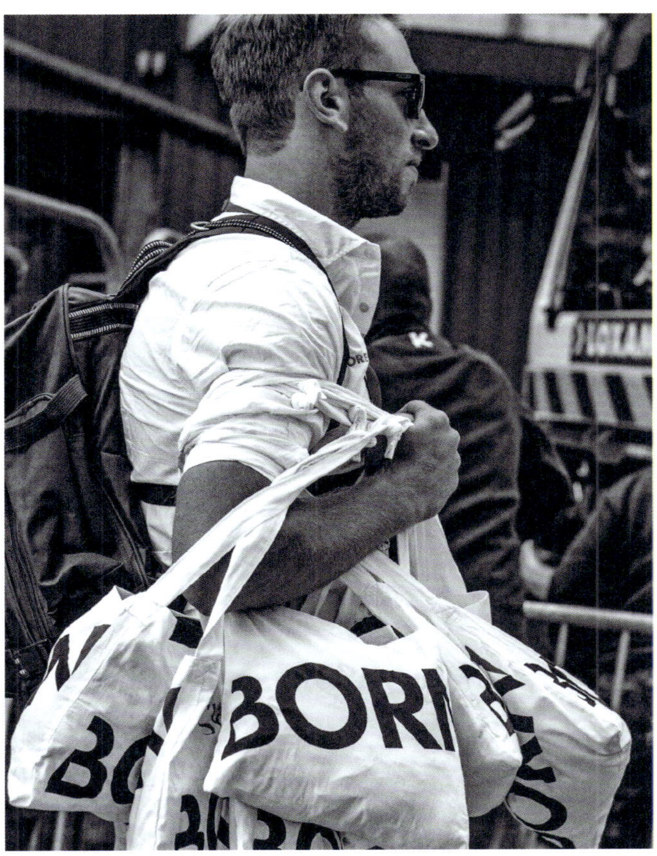

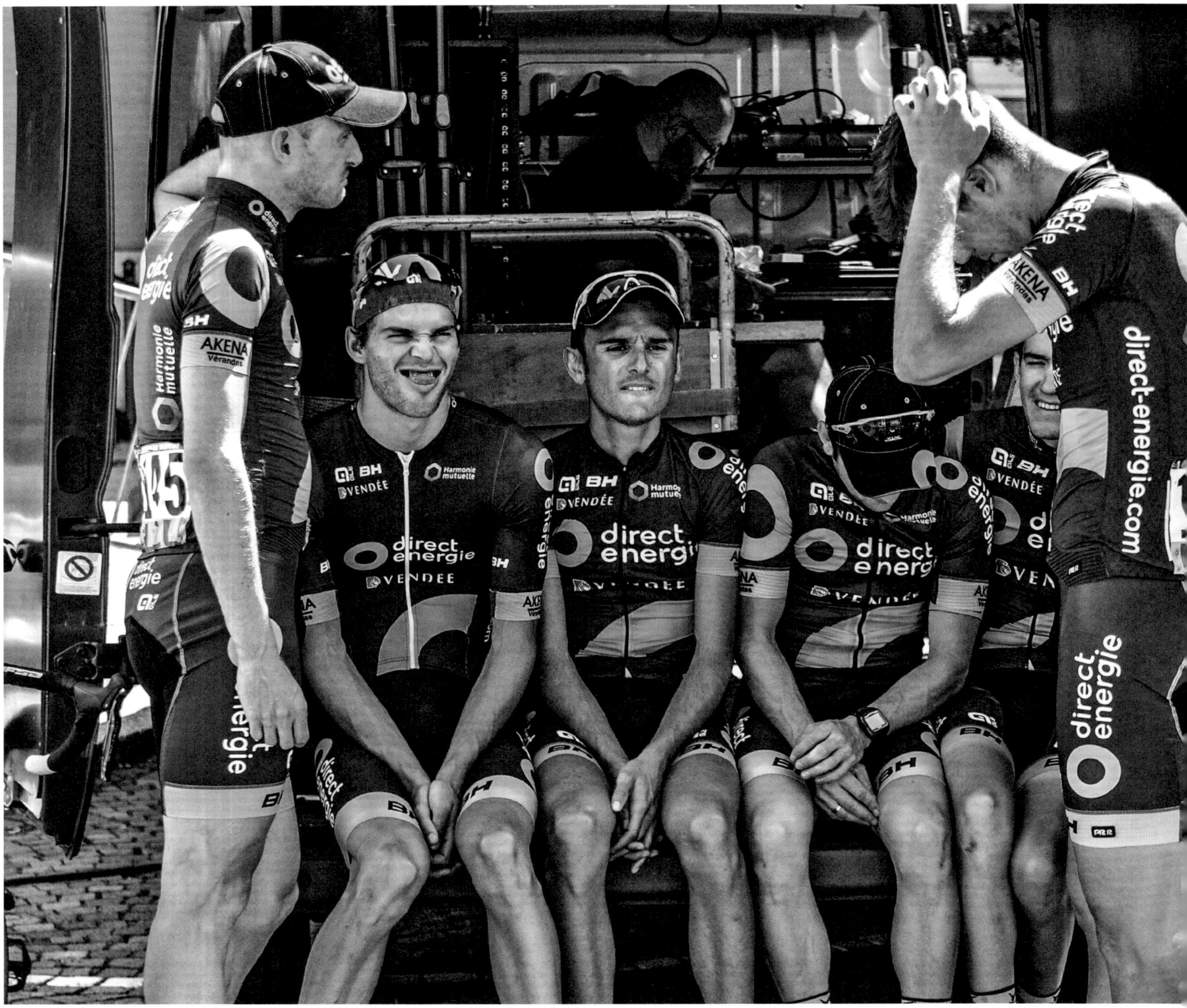

↑ Stressabbau beim Team Direct Énergie. **Exhaustion at Team Direct Énergie.** *Épuisement chez l'équipe Direct Énergie.*

→ Nacer Bouhanni und seine Teamkollegen von Cofidis. **Nacer Bouhanni and his teammates of Team Cofidis.** *Nacer Bouhanni et les coureurs de l'équipe Cofidis.*

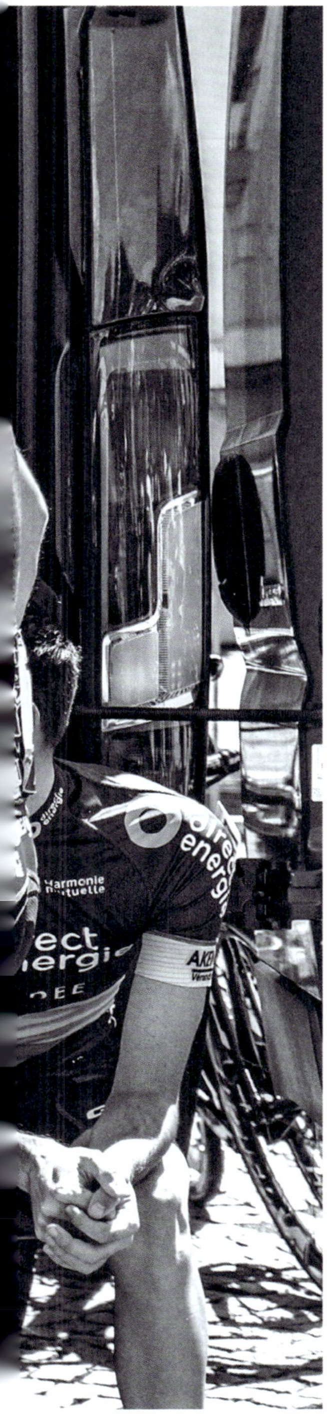

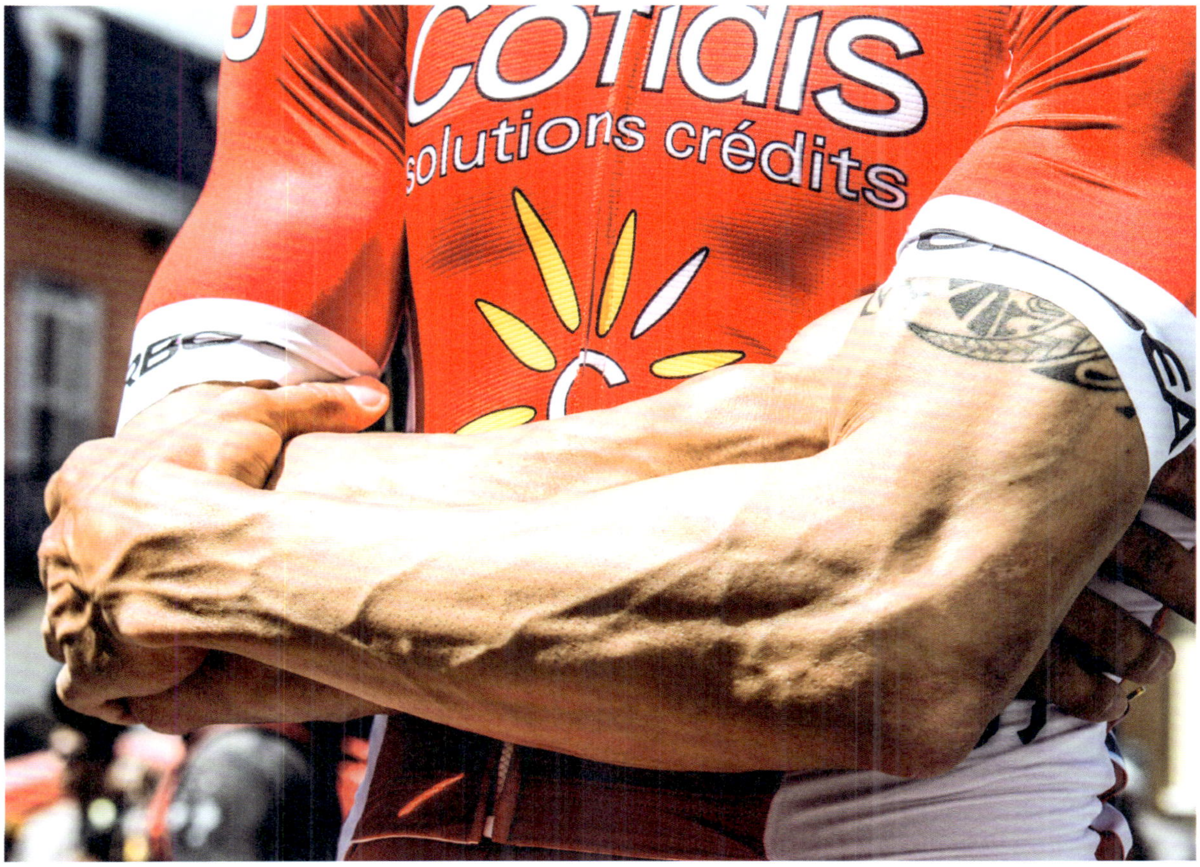
Cofidis
solutions crédits

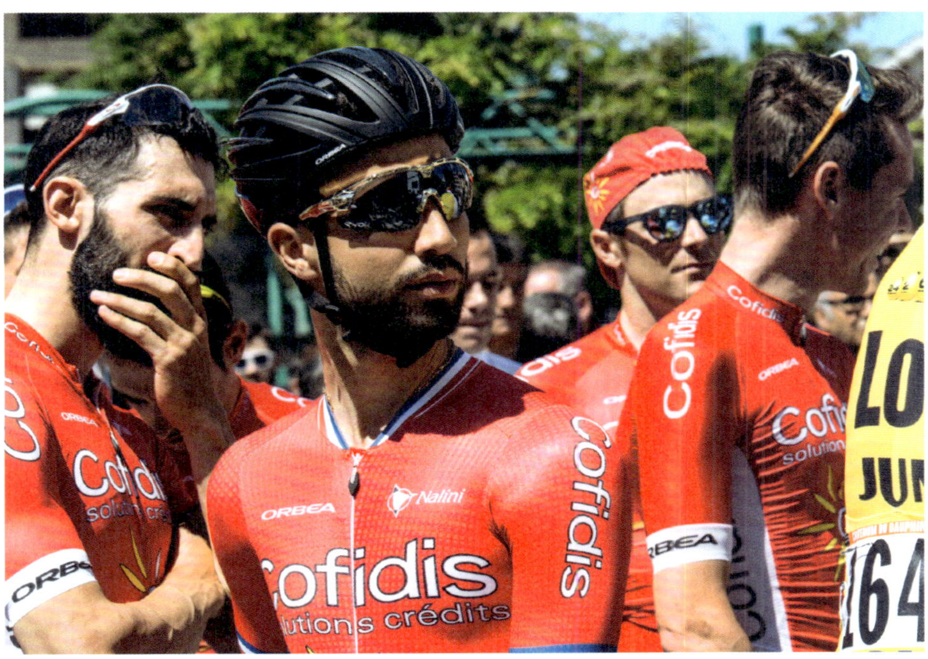
ORBEA
Nalini
cofidis
solutions crédits

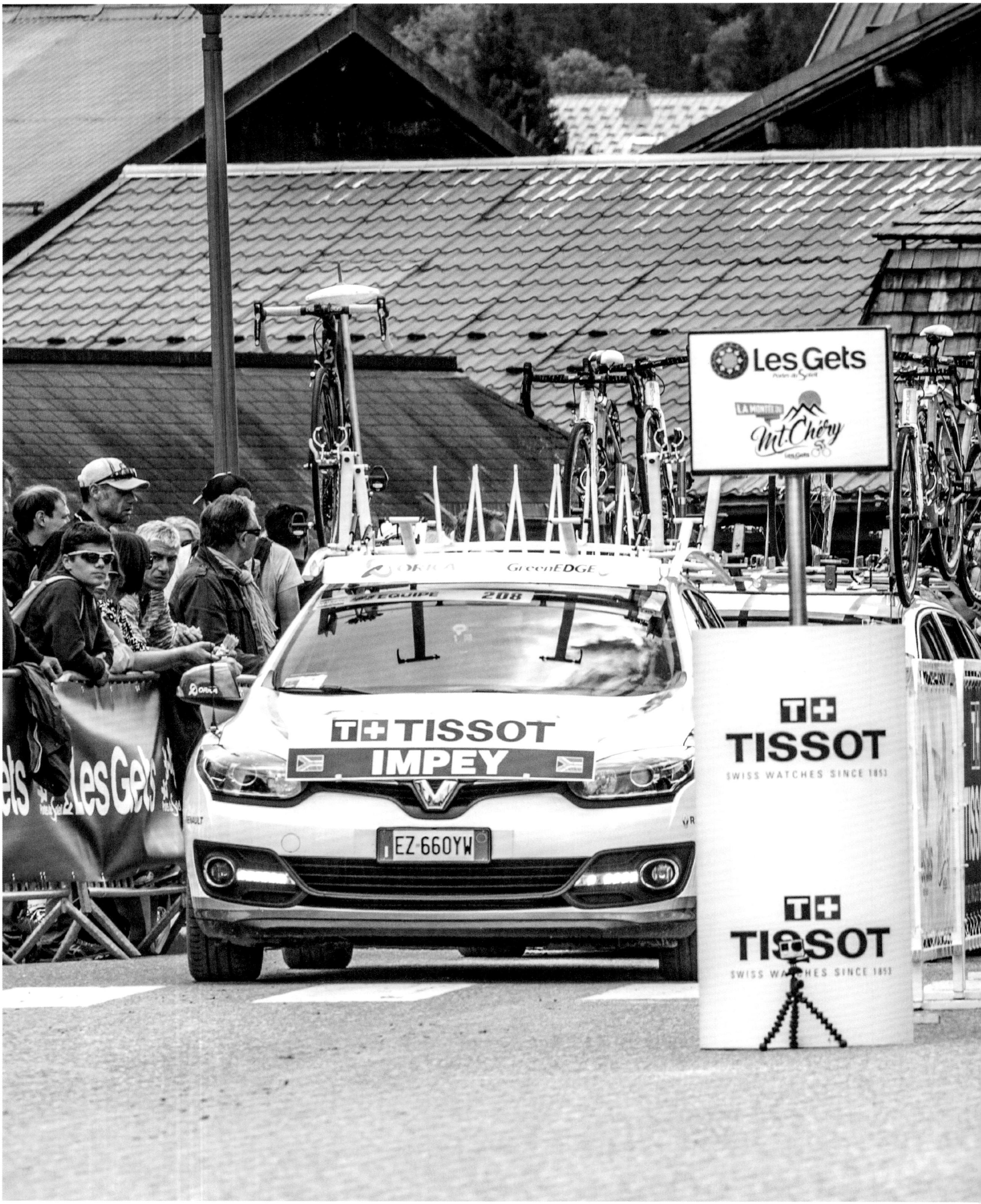
Les Gets
GreenEDGE
208
TISSOT
IMPEY
EZ 660YW
TISSOT
SWISS WATCHES SINCE 1853
TISSOT
SWISS WATCHES SINCE 1853
Les Gets

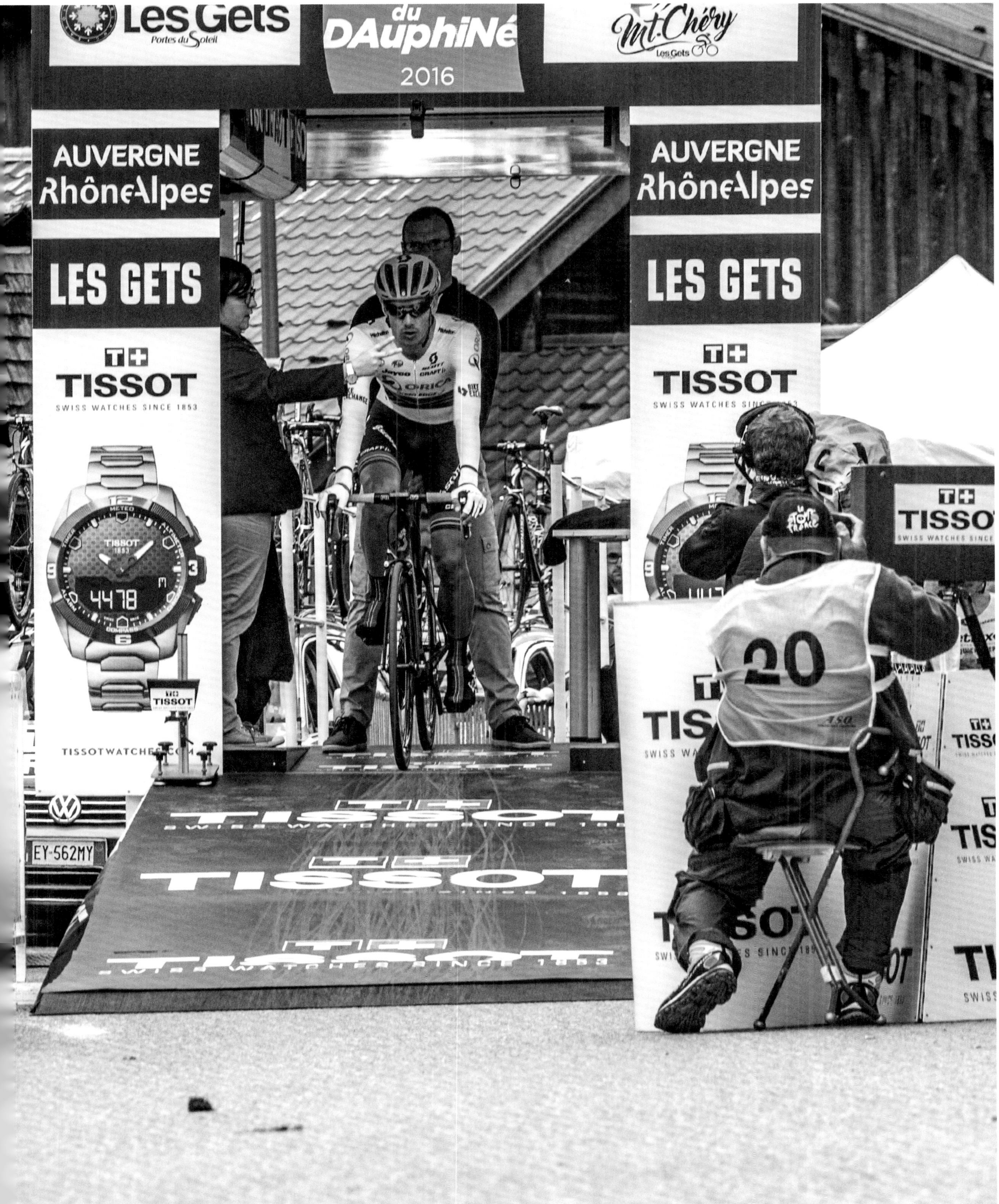

Daryl Impey (ORICA-GreenEDGE) auf der Startrampe in Les Gets. **Daryl Impey (ORICA-GreenEDGE) on the start ramp in Les Gets.**
Daryl Impey (ORICA-GreenEDGE) sur la rampe de départ dans la commune des Gets.

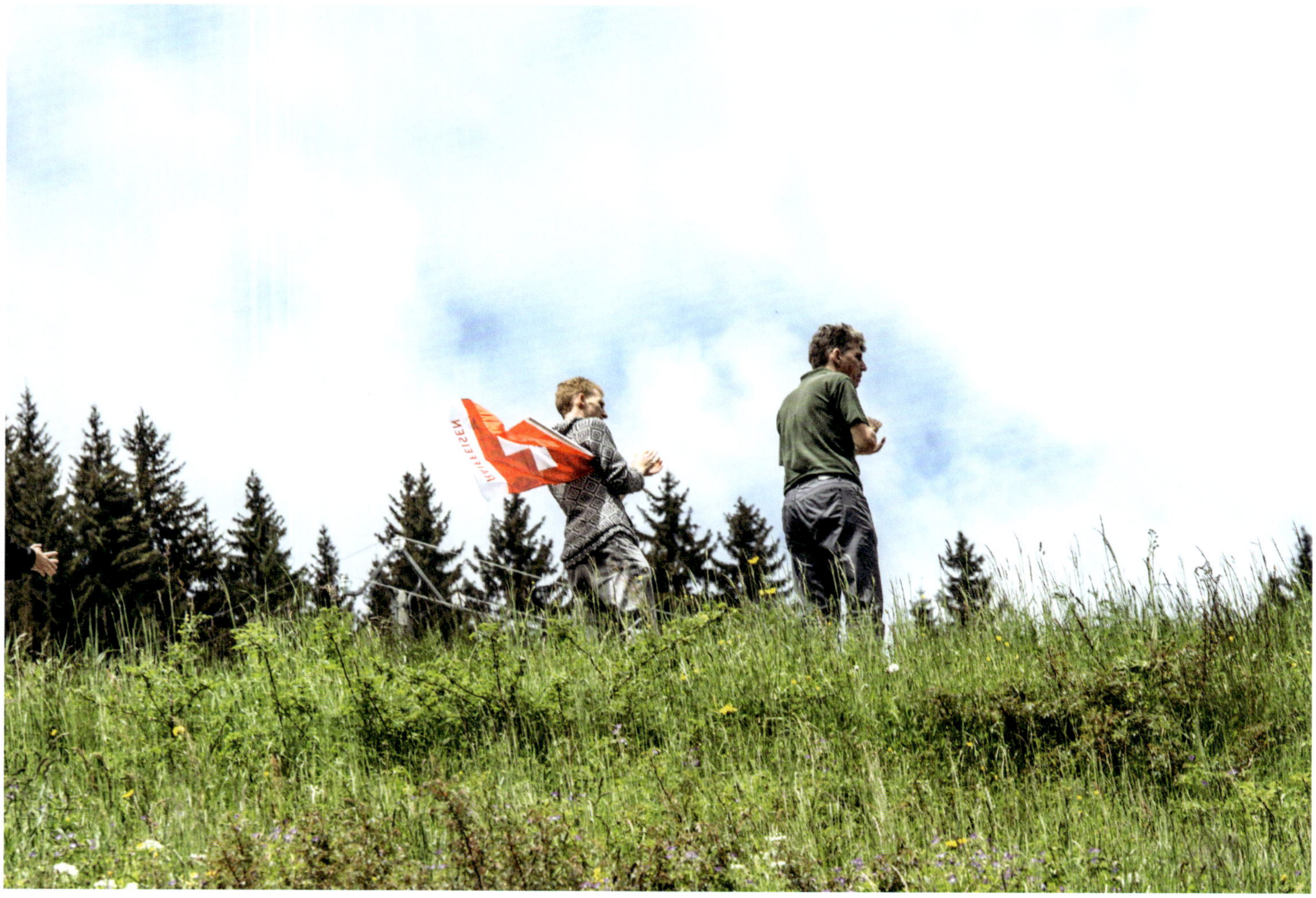

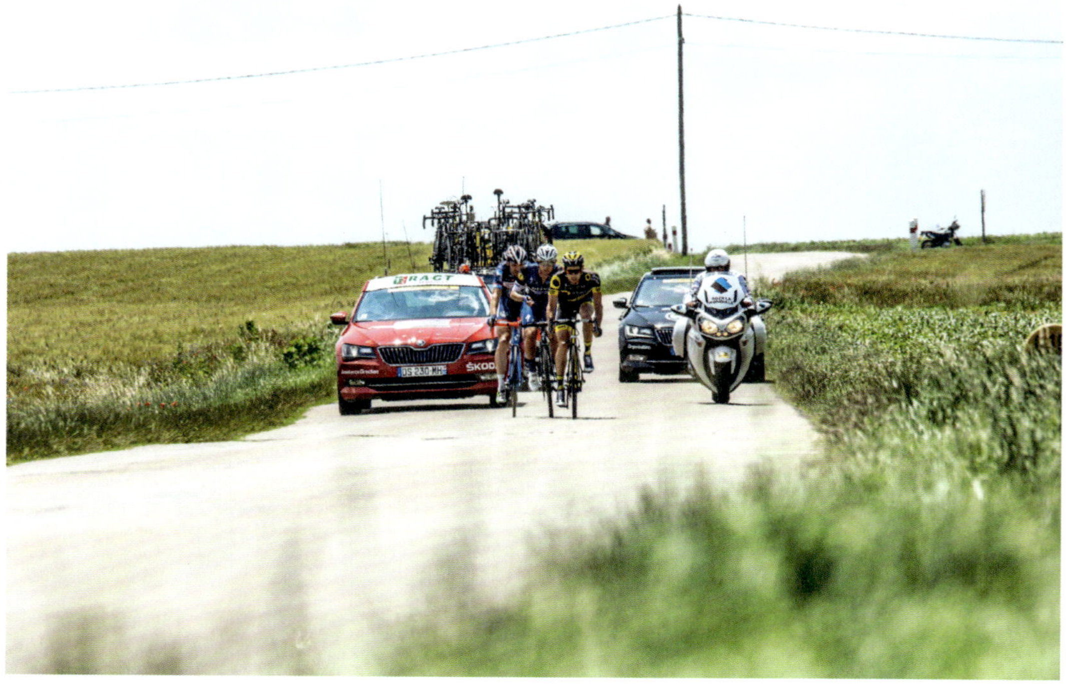

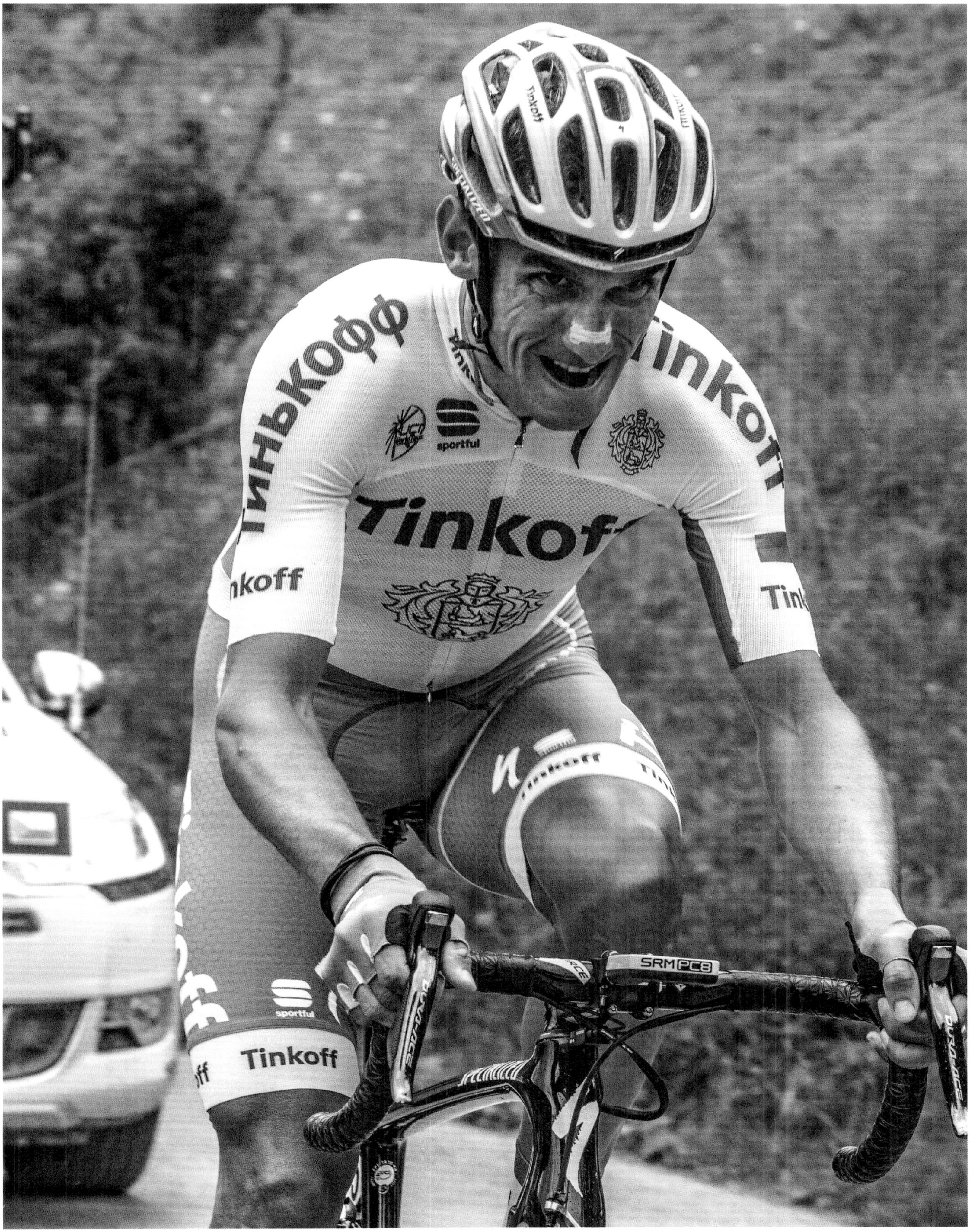

Roman Kreuziger (Tinkoff) kämpft sich hinauf zum Mont Chéry. **Roman Kreuziger (Tinkoff) fights his way up Mont Chéry.** *Roman Kreuziger (Tinkoff) lutte courageusement pour atteindre le mont Chéry.*

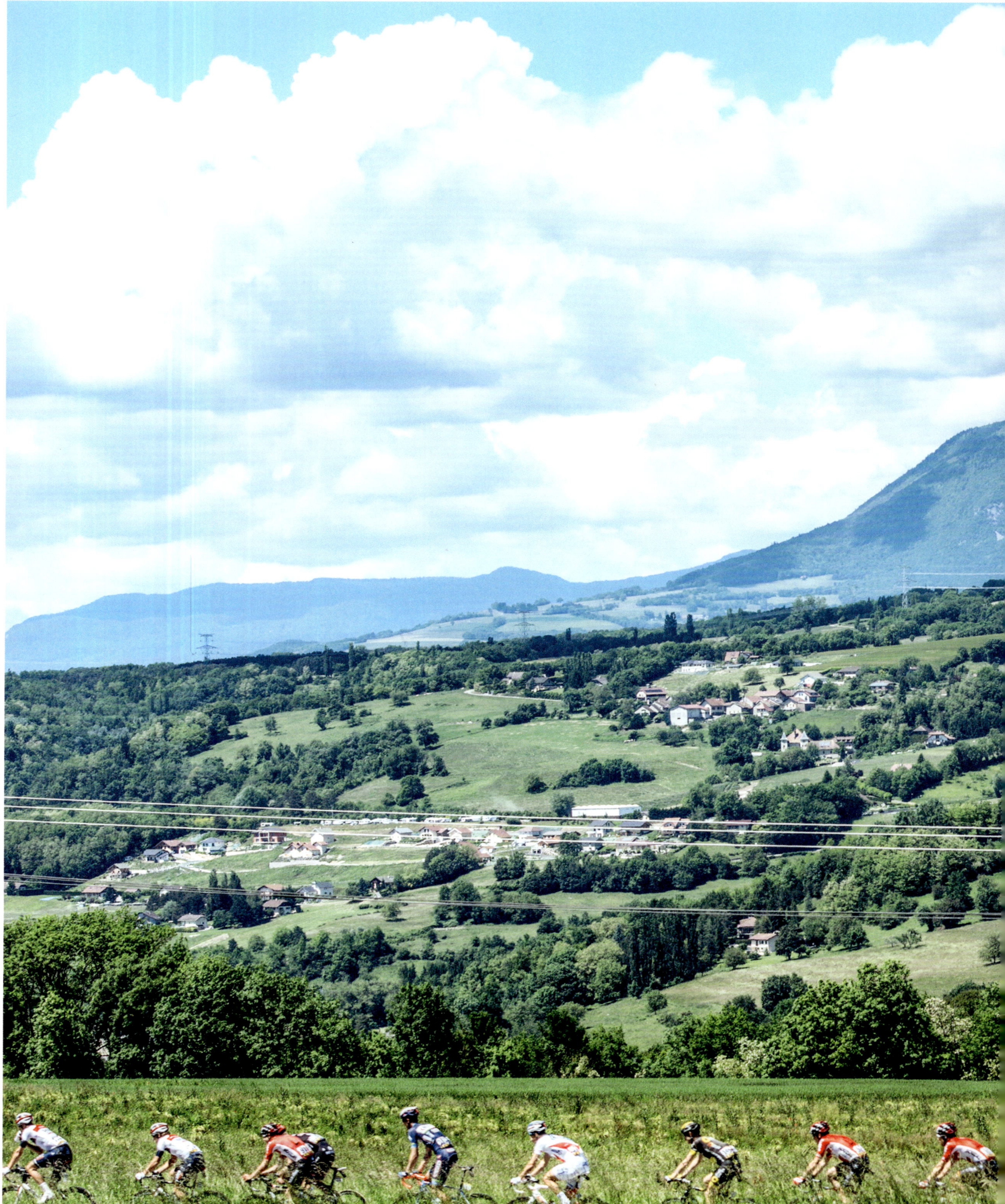

1. Etappe der Dauphiné. **1st stage of the Dauphiné.** *1re étape du Dauphiné.*

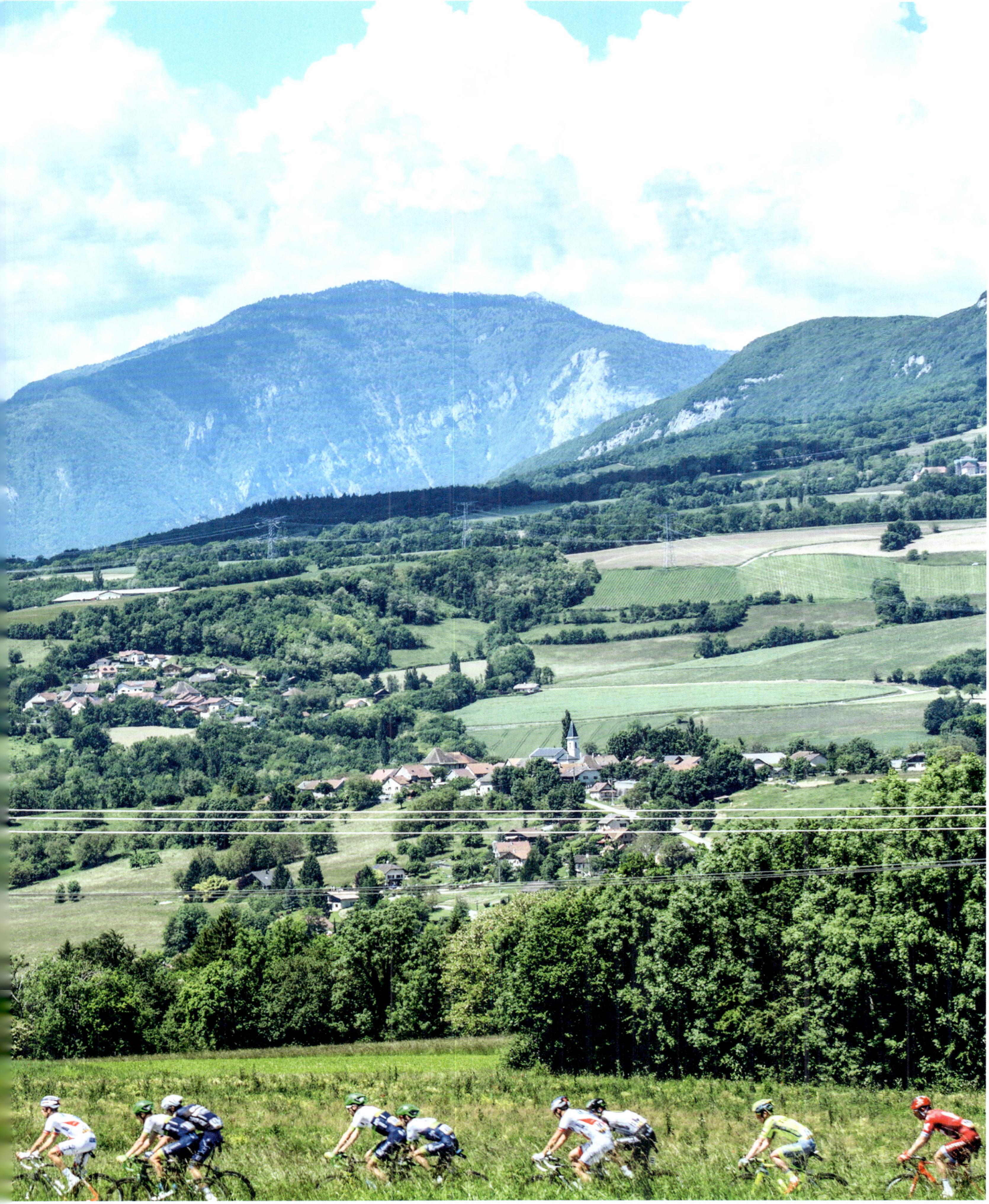

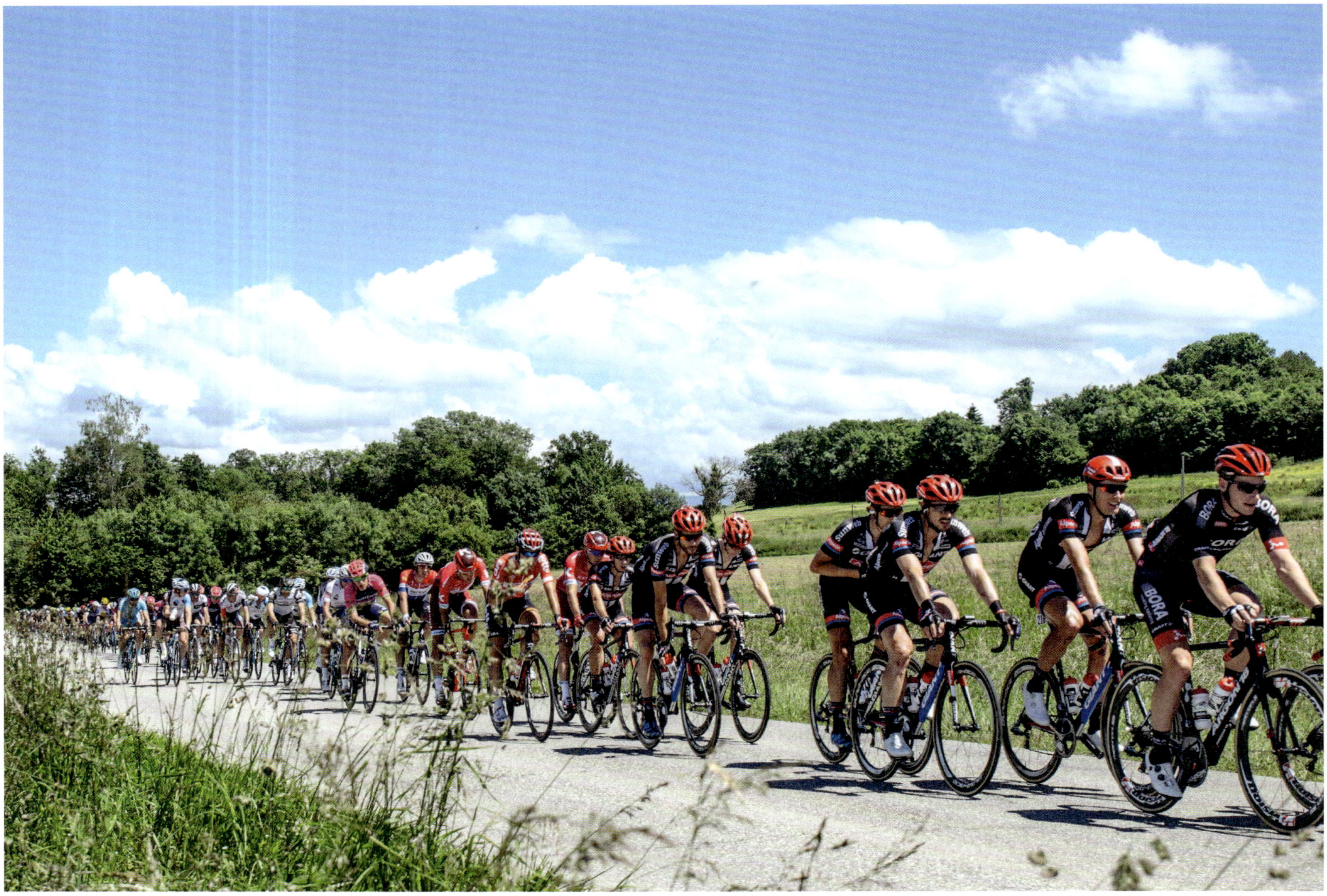

Am Anfang noch im Bummeltempo. **Starting at a leisurely pace.** *Au départ, le rythme n'est pas encore très soutenu.*

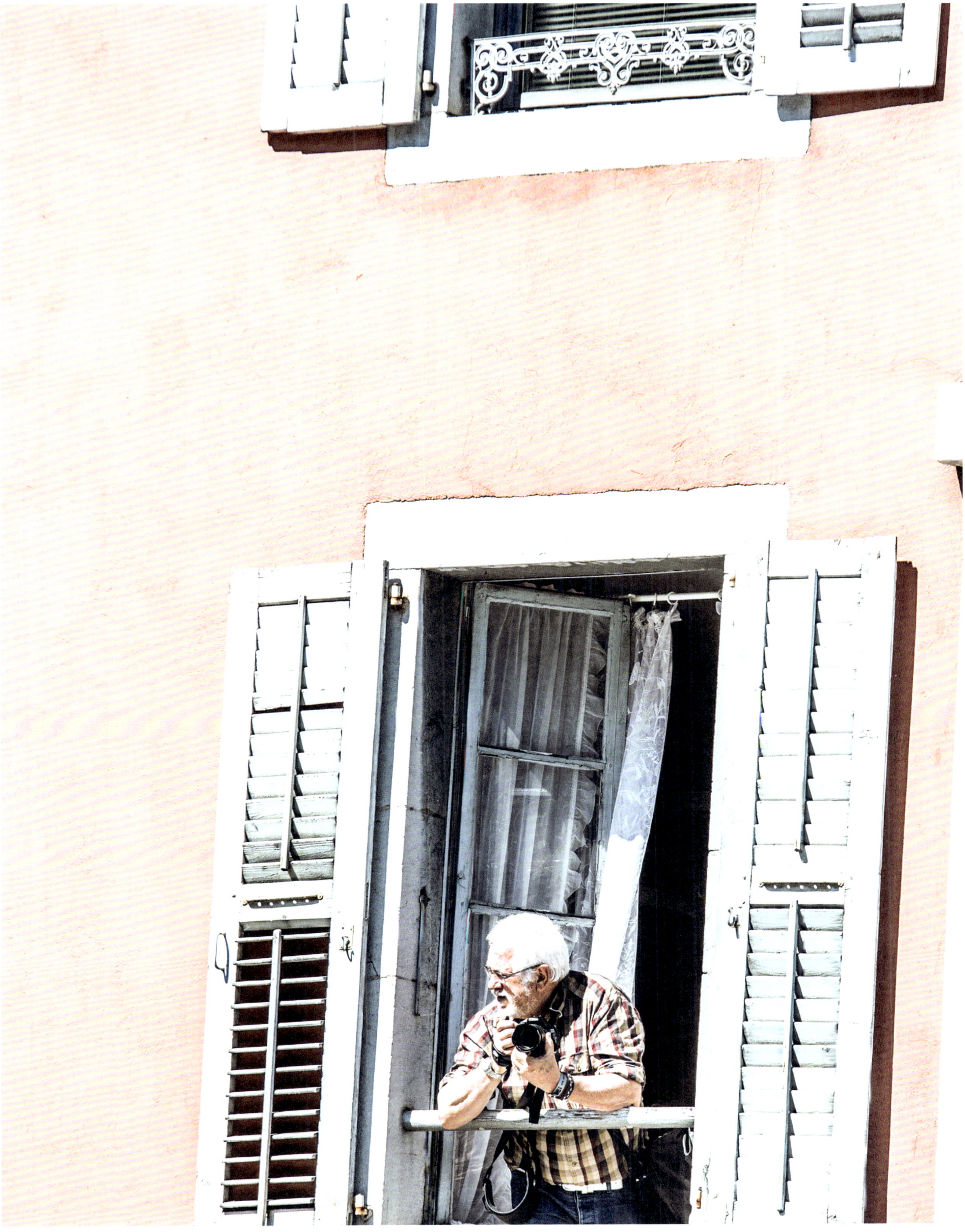

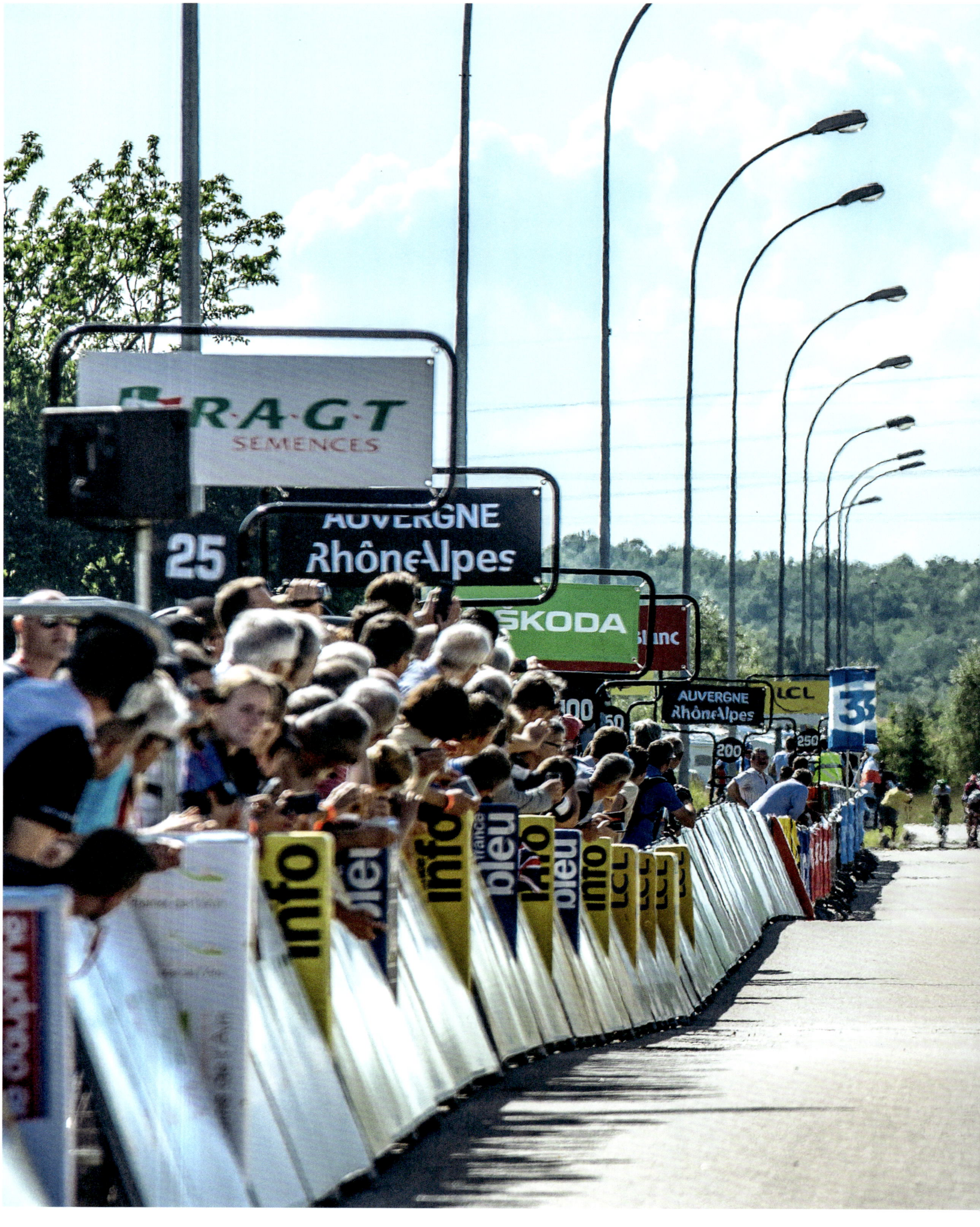

Das Peloton an der 300-Meter-Marke in Saint-Vulbas. **The peloton at the 300 metre marker in Saint-Vulbas.** *Le peloton au repère des 300 mètres à Saint-Vulbas.*

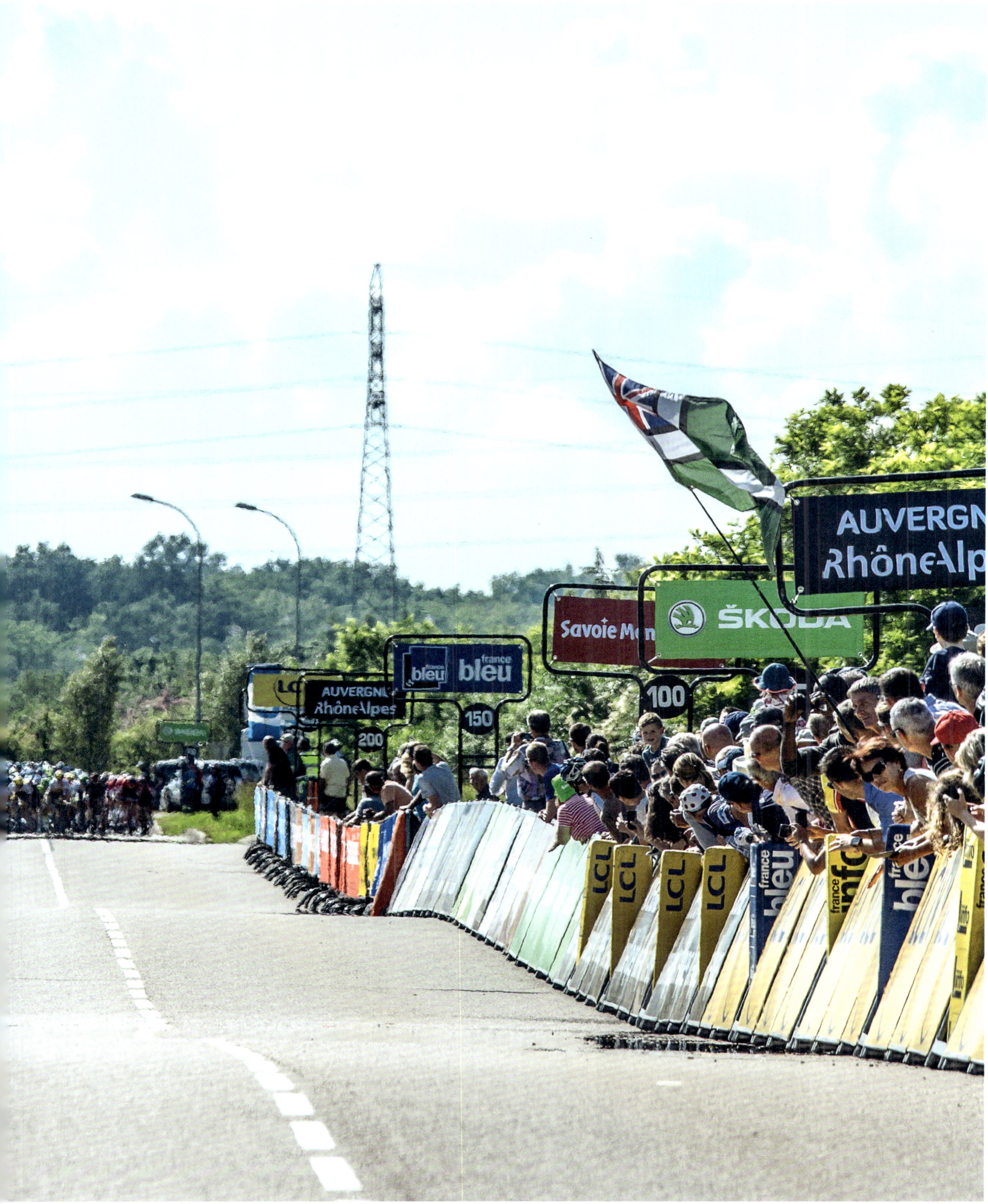
AUVERGN
RhôneAlp
ŠKODA
Savoie Mon
france bleu
AUVERGNE
RhôneAlpes
100
150
200
LCL
LCL
LCL
LCL
france bleu
france bleu

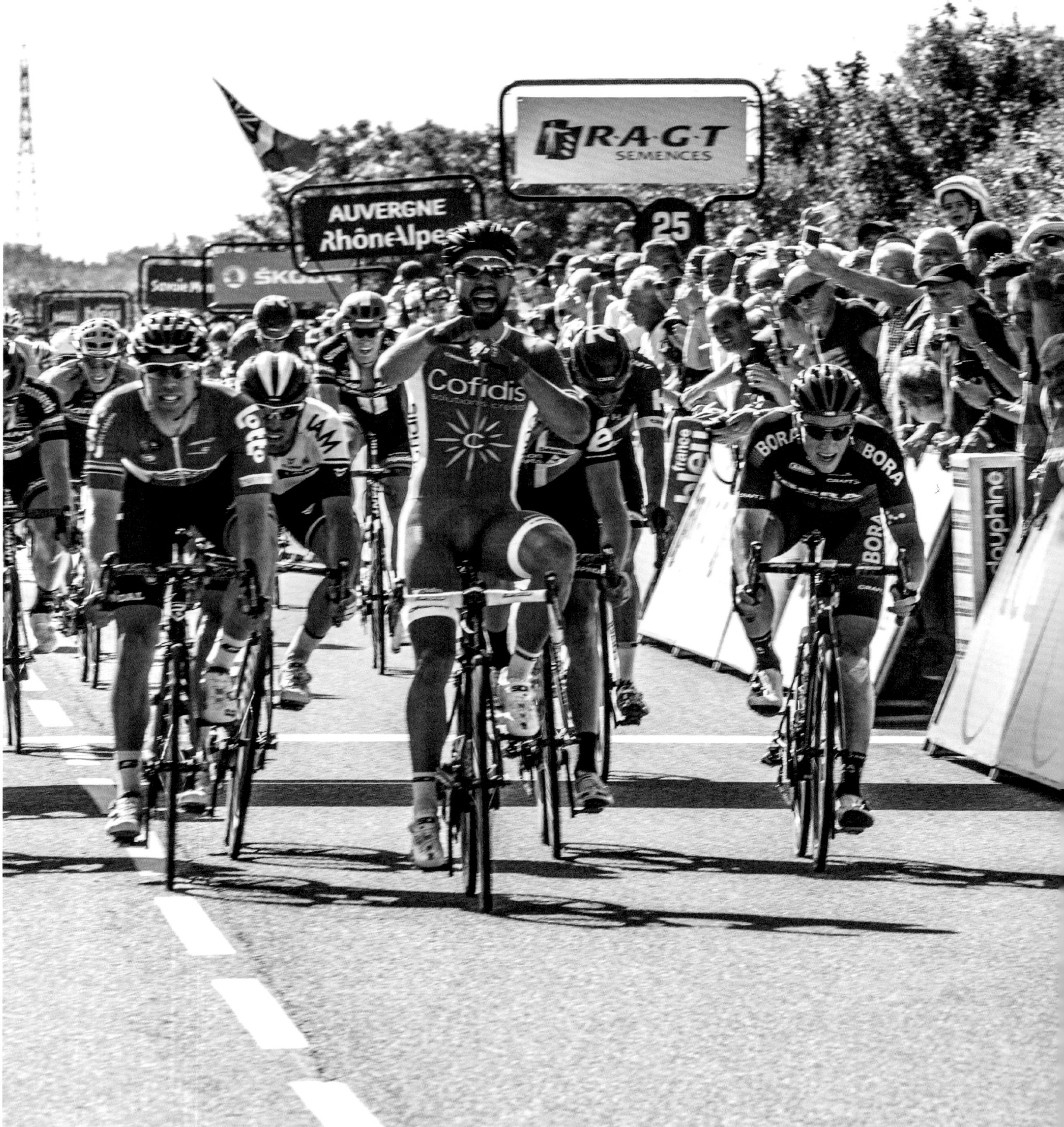
R·A·G·T
SEMENCES
AUVERGNE
25
Cofidis
BORA

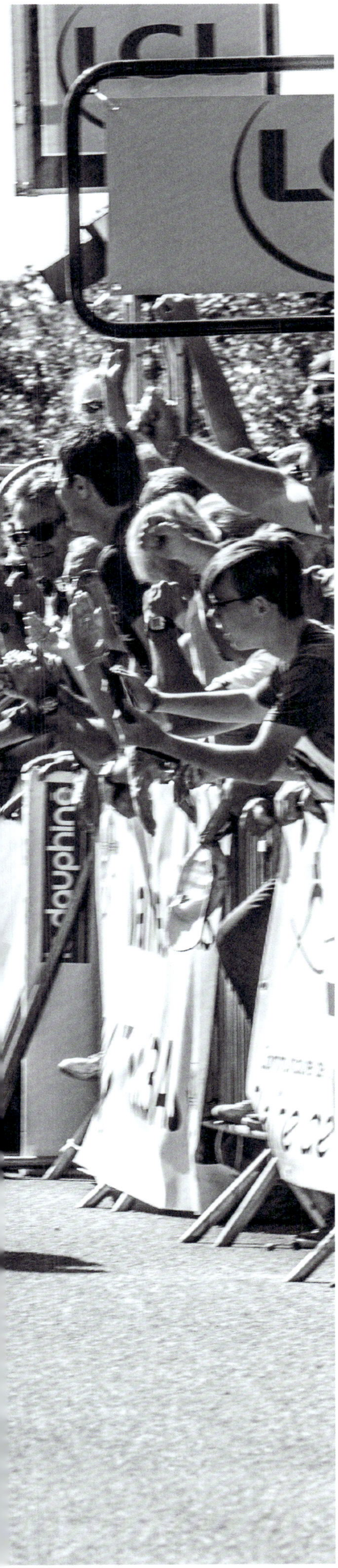

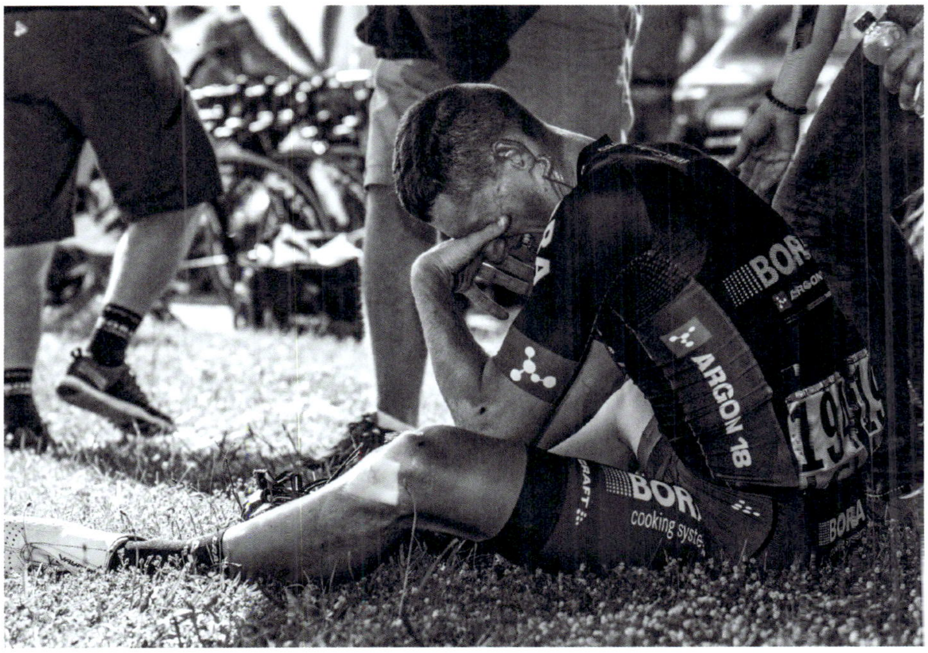

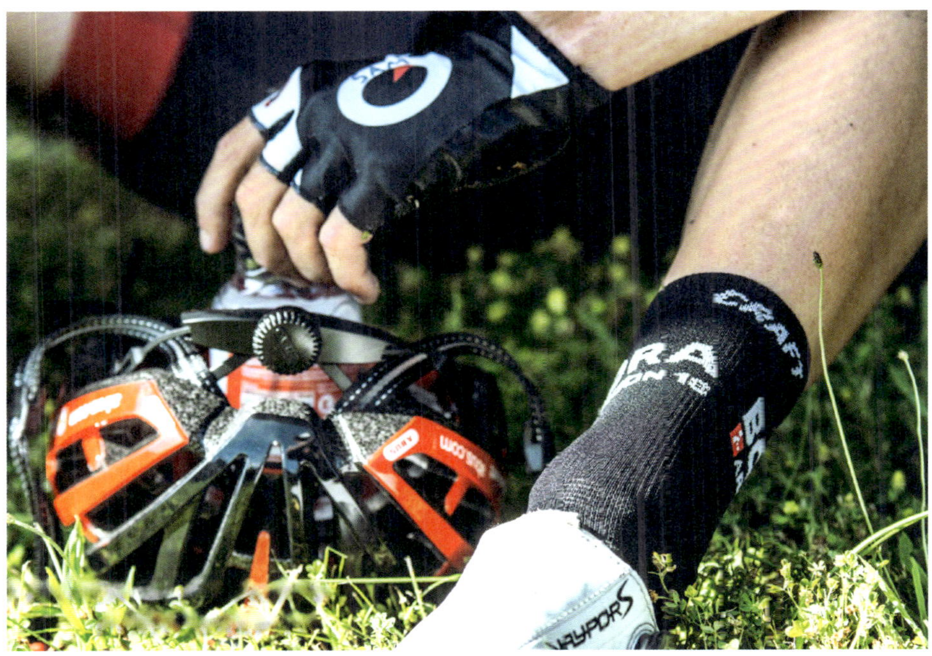

↖ Nacer Bouhanni (Cofidis) gewinnt die 1. Etappe vor Jens Debusschere (Lotto Soudal) und Sam Bennett (BORA - ARGON 18) nach einem hart umkämpften Massensprint. **Nacer Bouhanni (Cofidis) wins the 1st stage ahead of Jens Debusschere (Lotto Soudal) and Sam Bennett (BORA - ARGON 18) after a bitterly contested mass sprint.** *Nacer Bouhanni (Cofidis) remporte la 1re étape devant Jens Debusschere (Lotto Soudal) et Sam Bennett (BORA - ARGON 18) après un sprint final âprement disputé.*

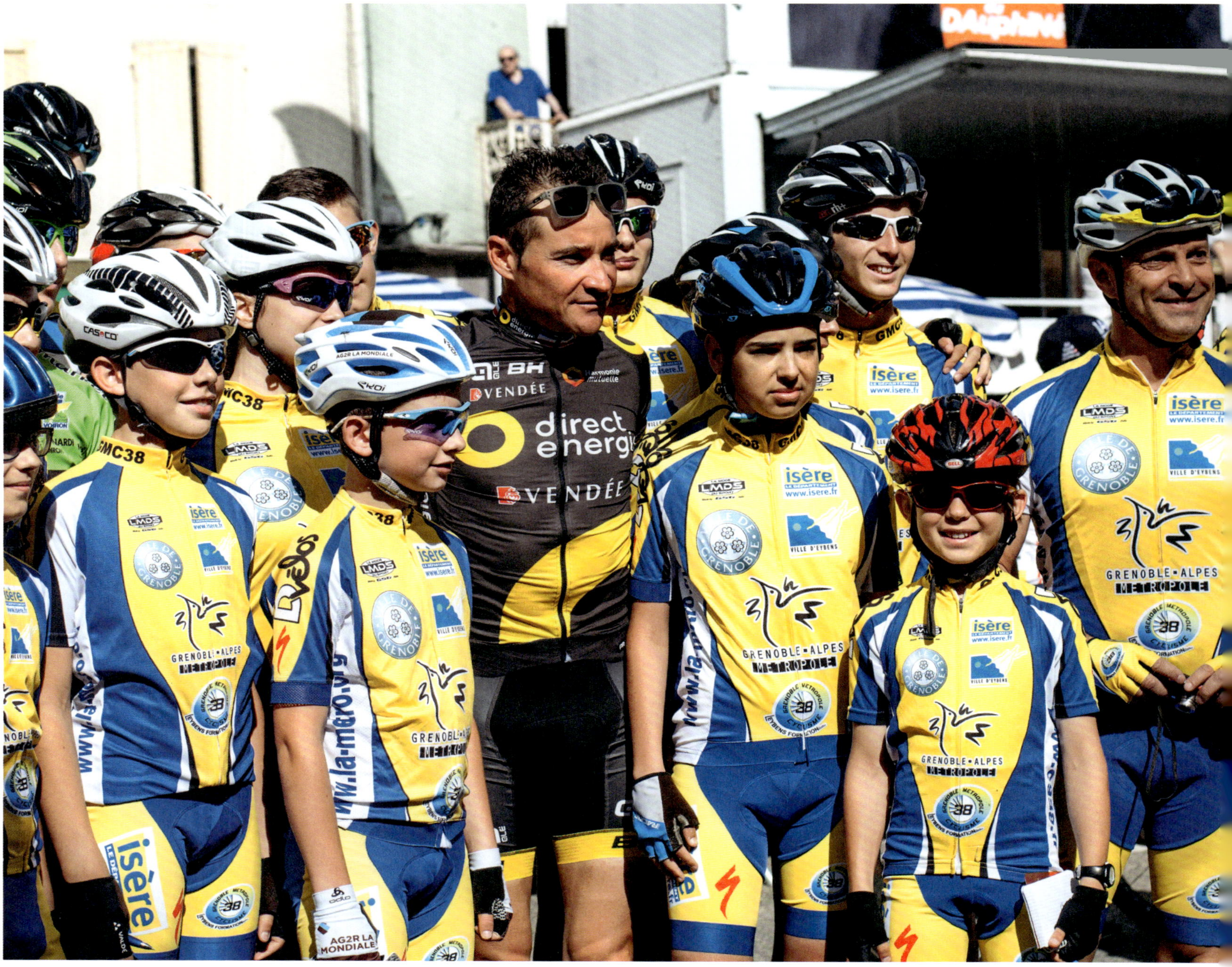

↑ Thomas Voeckler (Direct Énergie) mit seinen Fans. **Thomas Voeckler (Direct Énergie) with his fans.** *Thomas Voeckler (Direct Énergie) avec ses fans.*

↗ Joaquim Rodríguez' Tattoo (Team Katusha). **Joaquim Rodriguez's tattoo (Team Katusha).** *Le tatouage de Joaquim Rodríguez (Team Katusha).*

→ Edvald Boasson Hagen (Dimension Data) auf dem Weg zur Einschreibung. **Edvald Boasson Hagen (Dimension Data) on his way to the signature podium.** *Edvald Boasson Hagen (Dimension Data) en route pour la signature.*

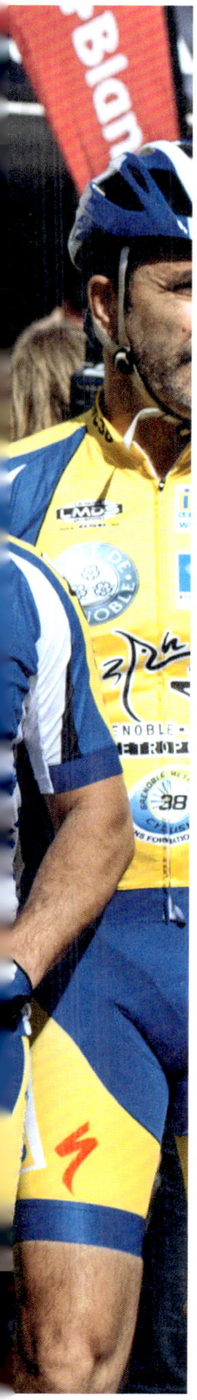

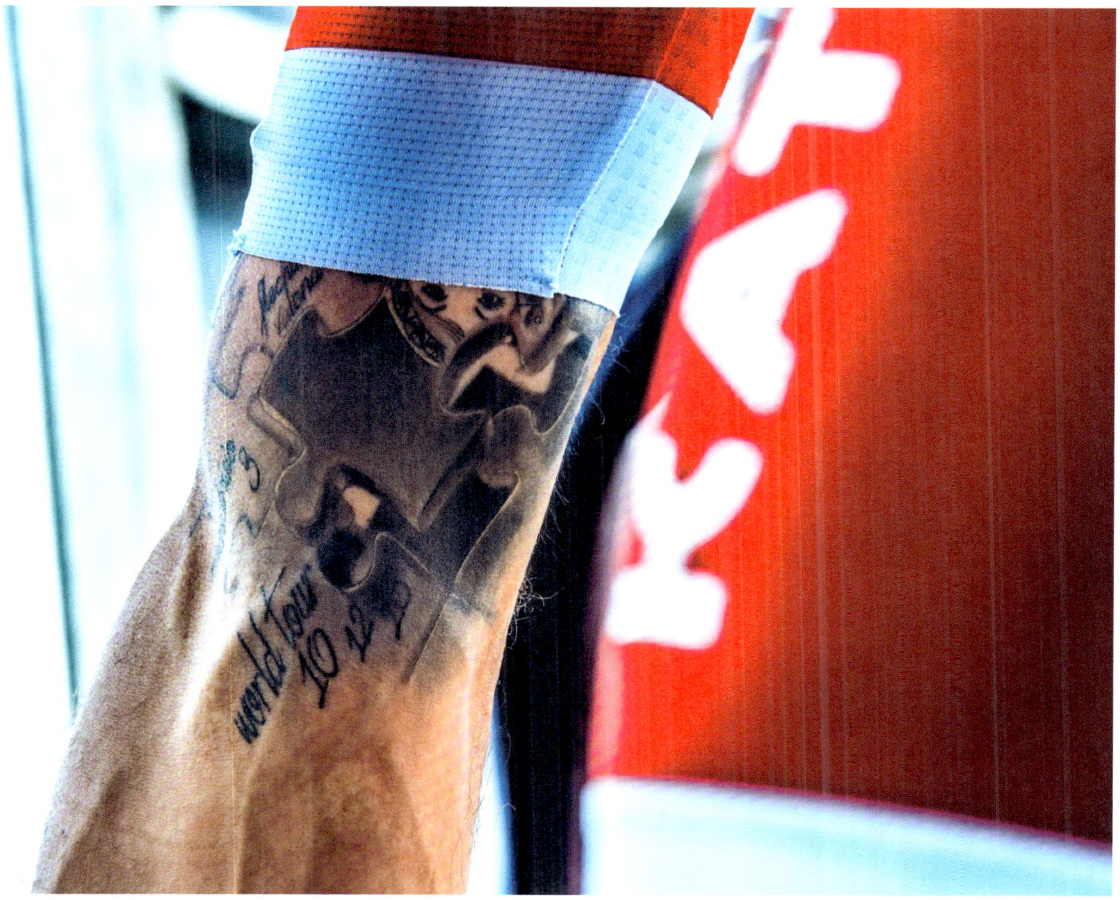

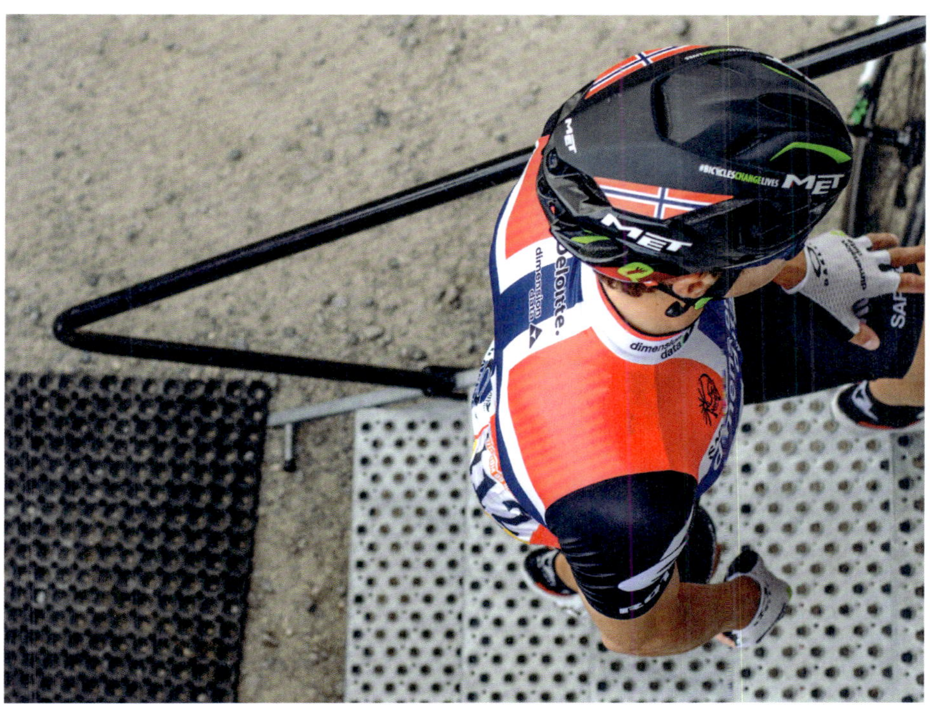
MET

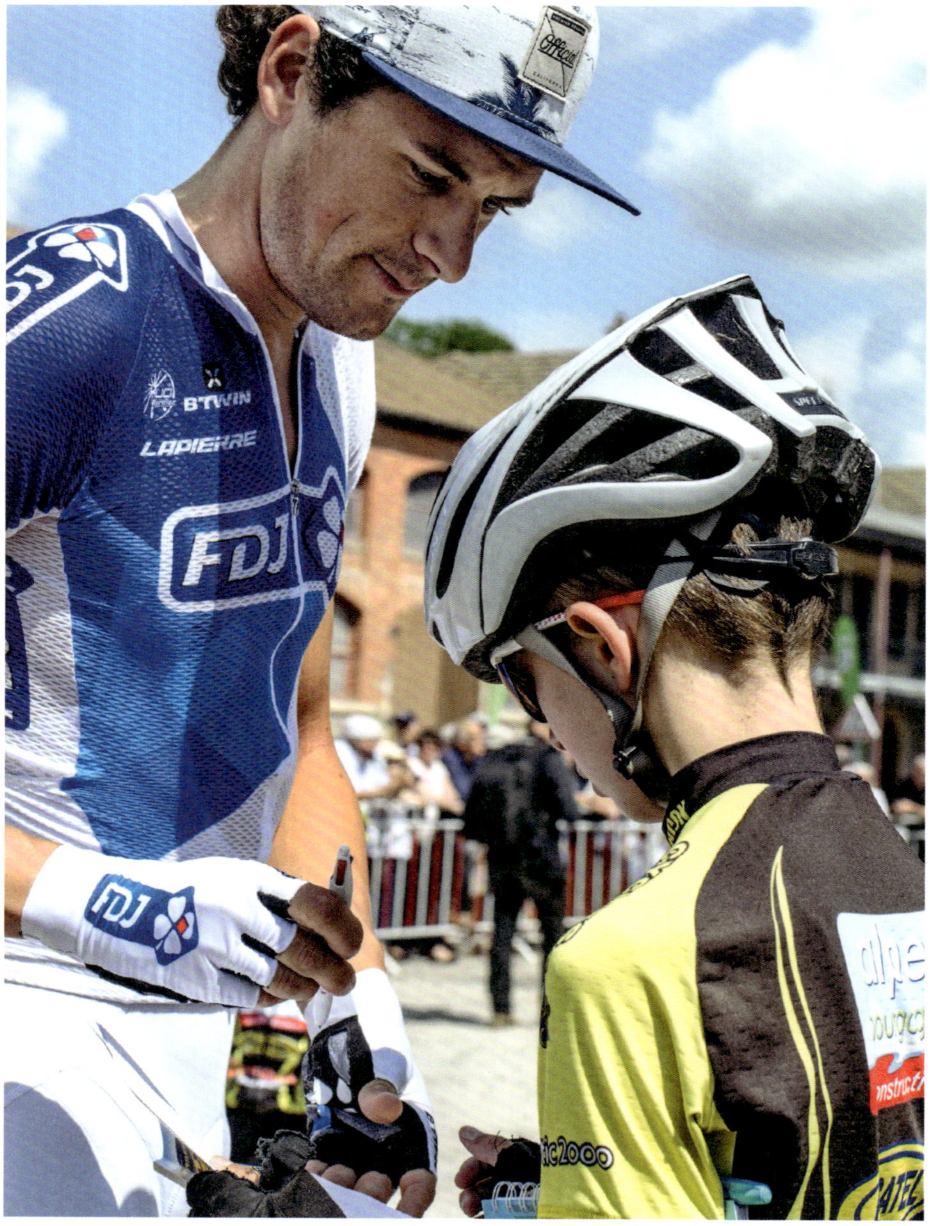
B'TWIN
LAPIERRE
FDJ

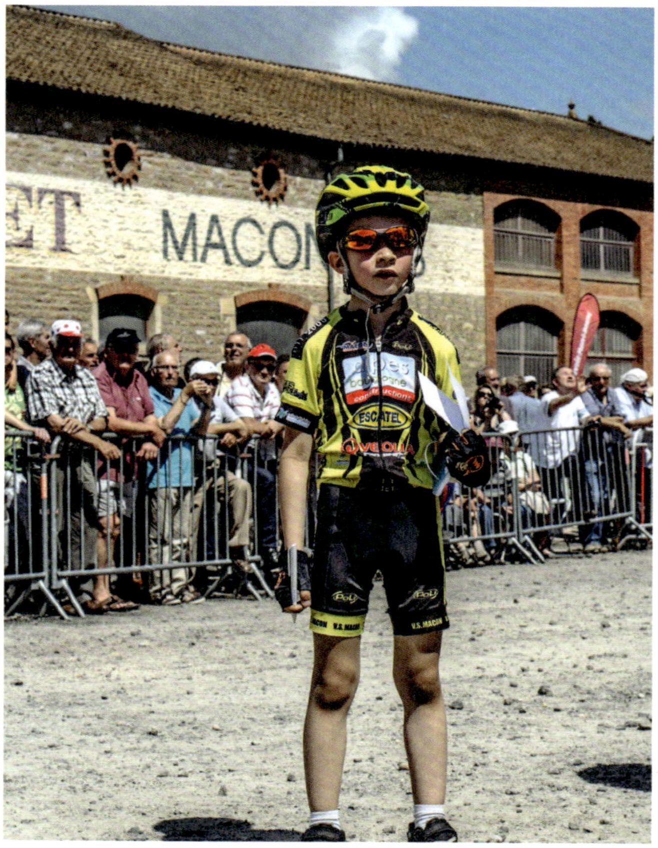
MACON

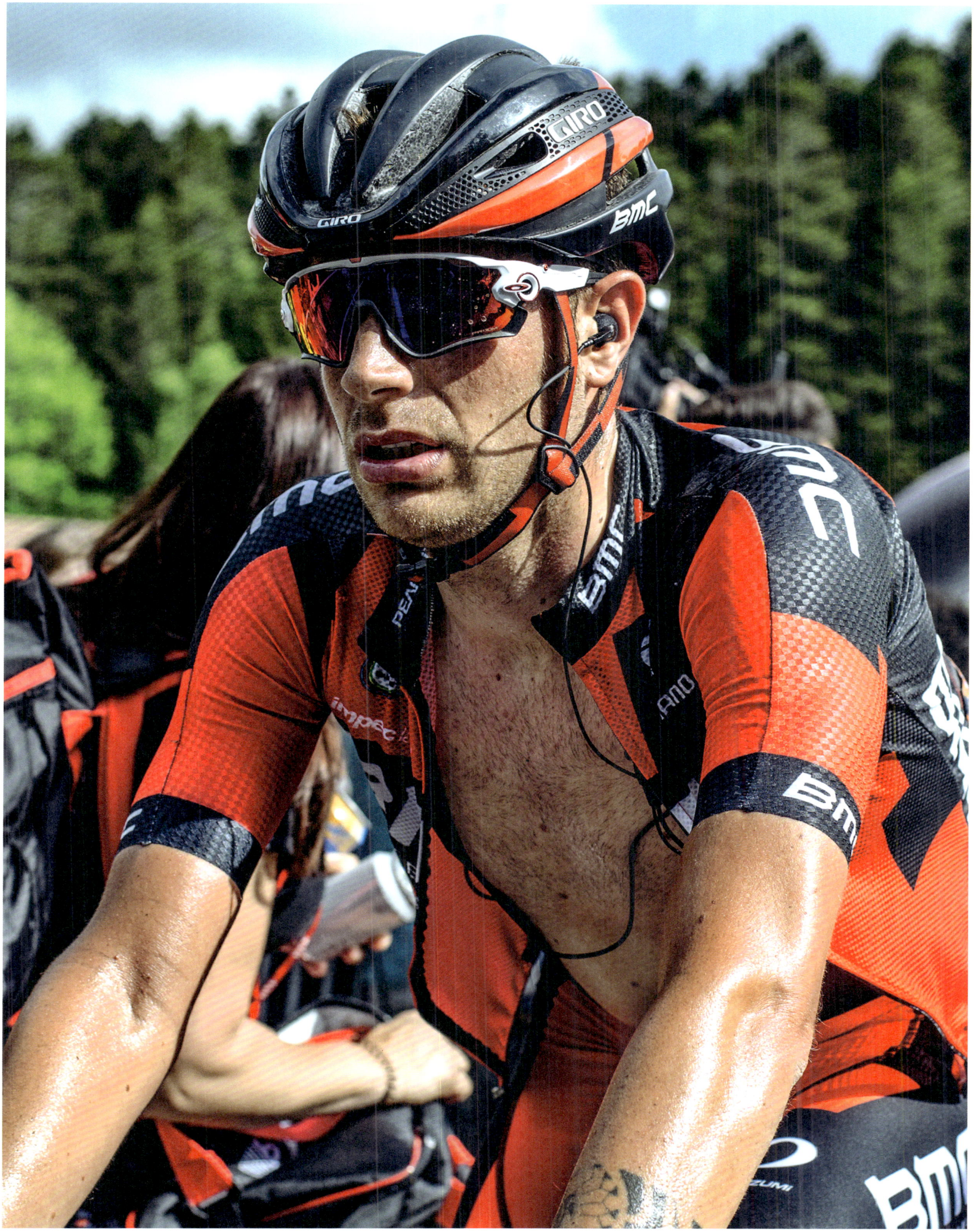

← Autogrammstunde mit Anthony Roux (FDJ). **Autograph session with Anthony Roux (FDJ).** *Séance d'autographes avec Anthony Roux (FDJ).*
↑ Damiano Caruso (BMC Racing Team). **Damiano Caruso (BMC Racing Team).** *Damiano Caruso (BMC Racing Team).*

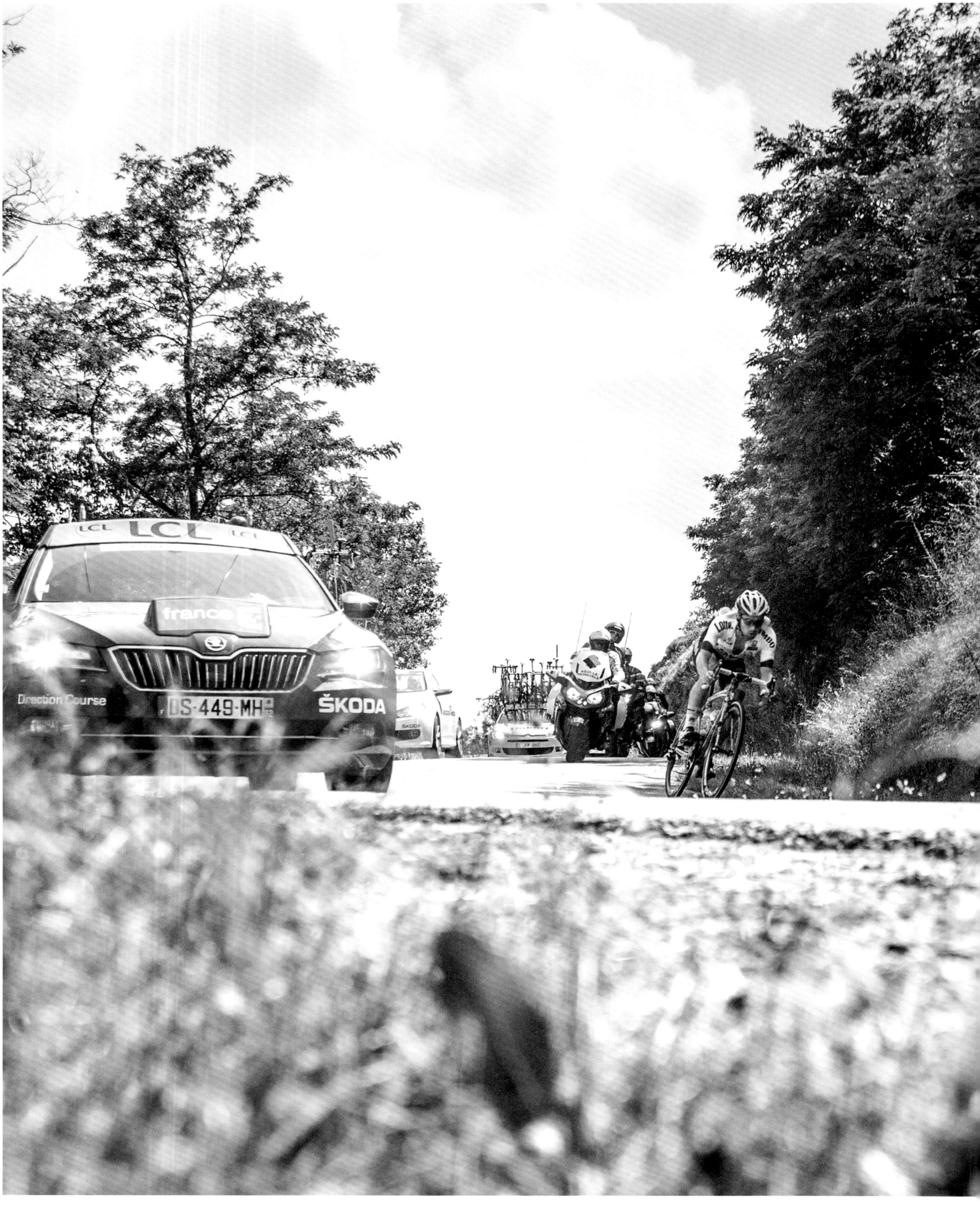
LCL
france
Direction Course
DS-449-MH
ŠKODA

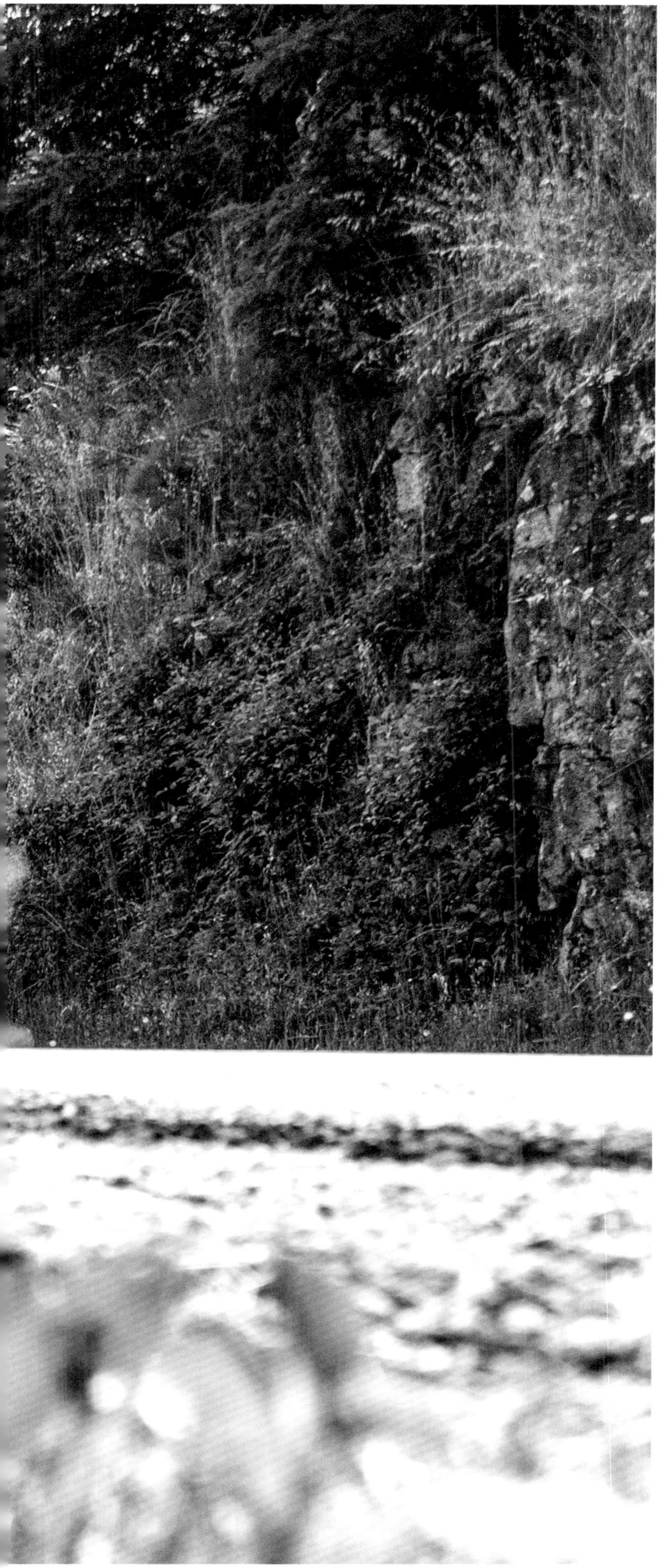

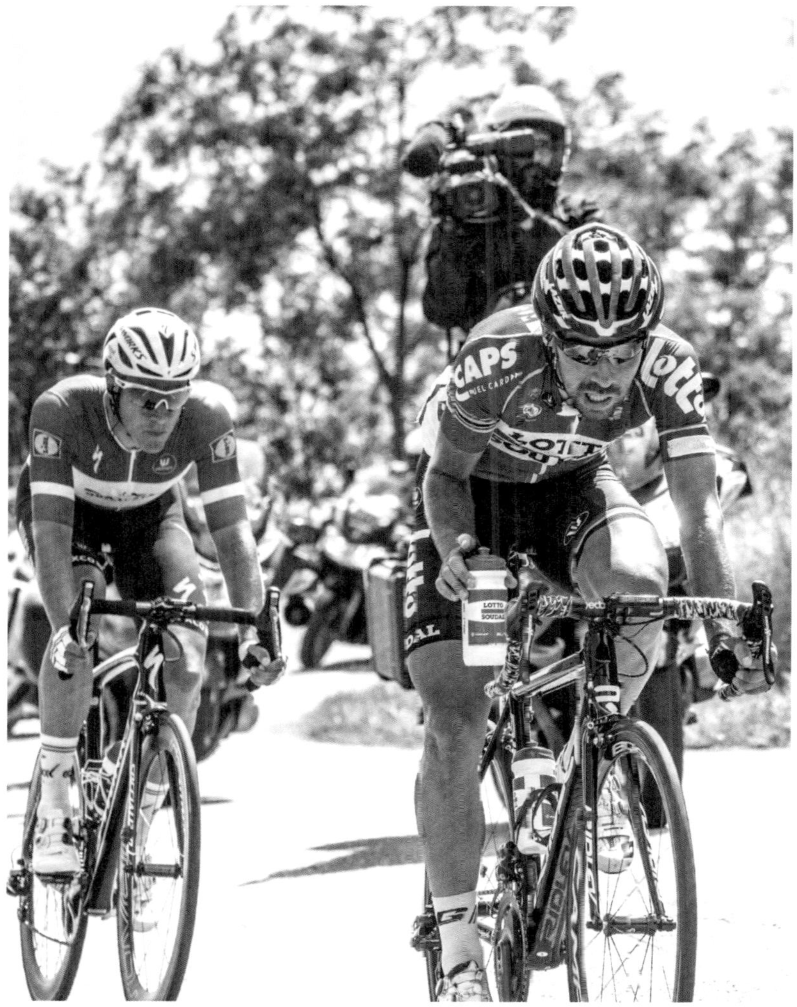

Vor dem Fahrerfeld. **Ahead of the peloton.** *Devant le peloton.*

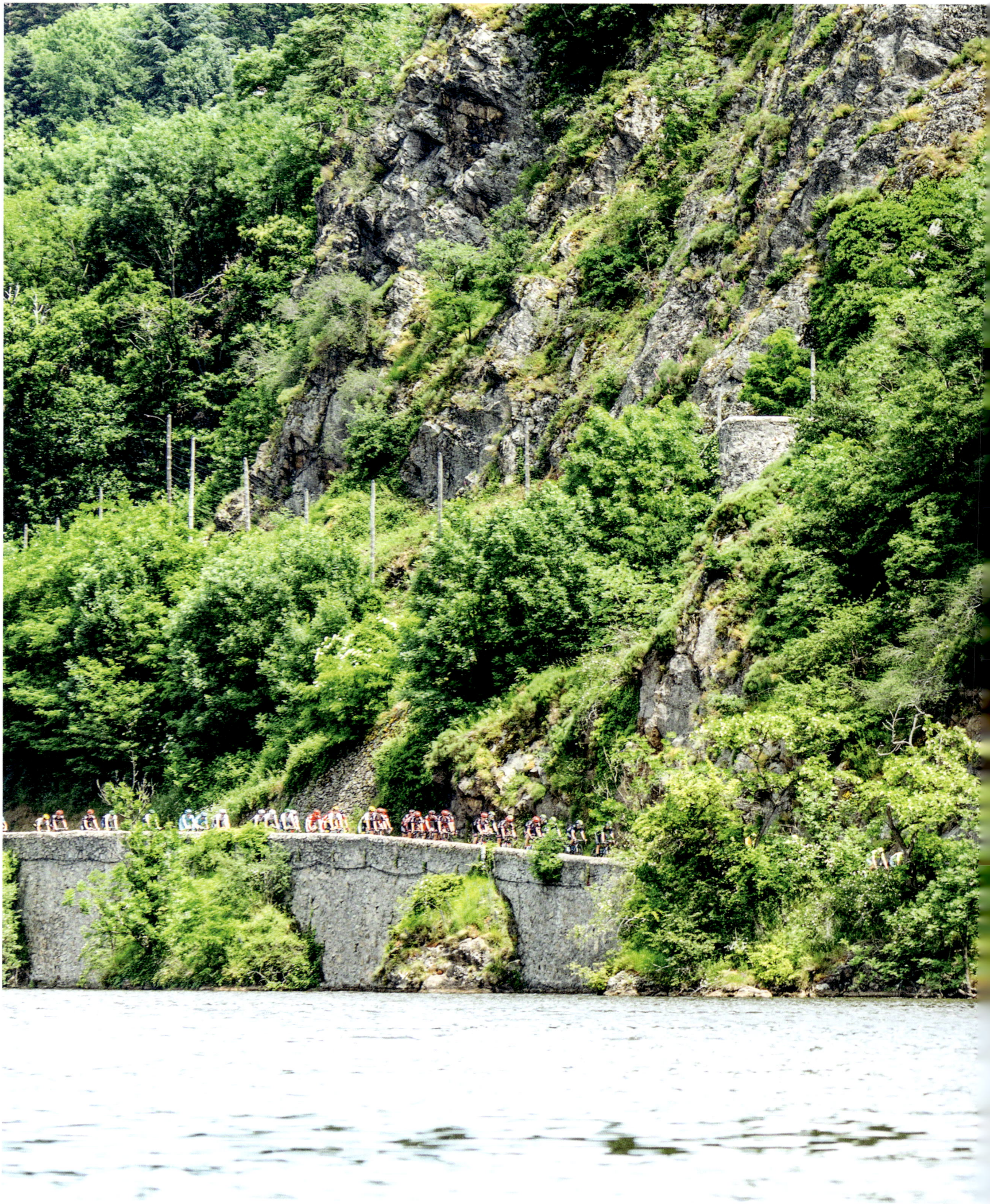

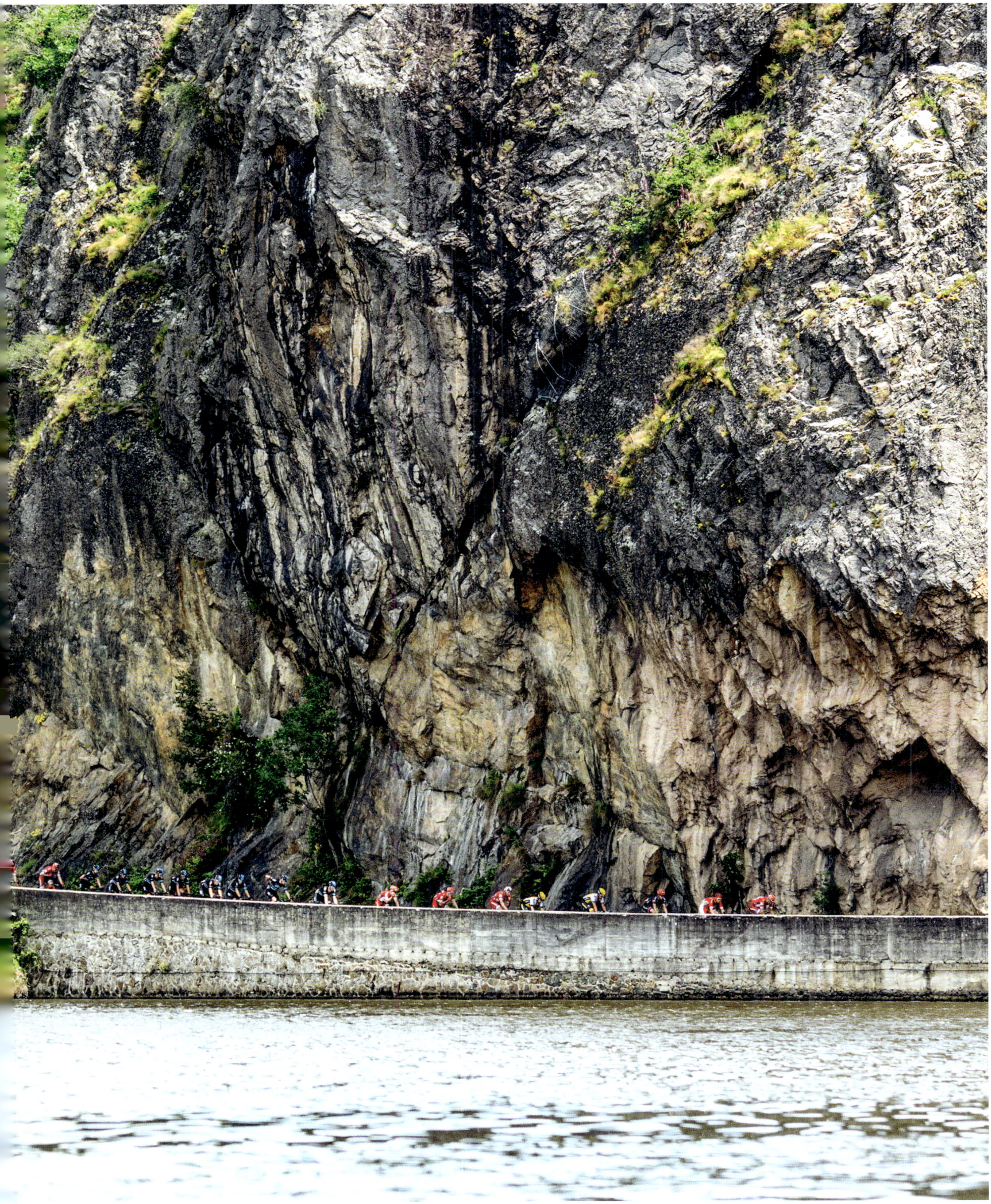

Spektakulär: Szene vor Tournon. **Spectacular: scene before Tournon.** *Scène spectaculaire avant Tournon.*

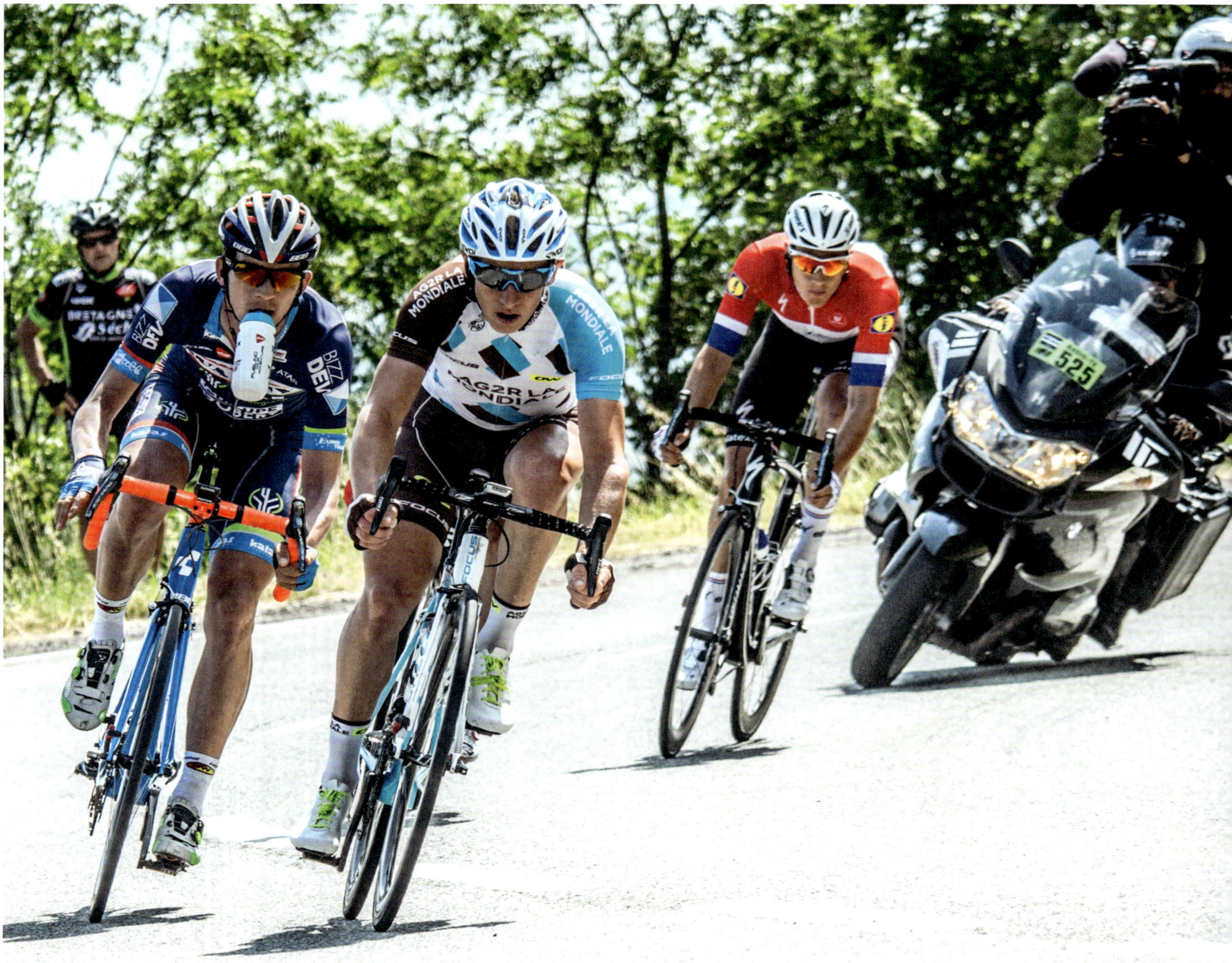

Etappe 3 der Dauphiné. **Stage 3 of the Dauphiné.** *3e étape du Dauphiné.*

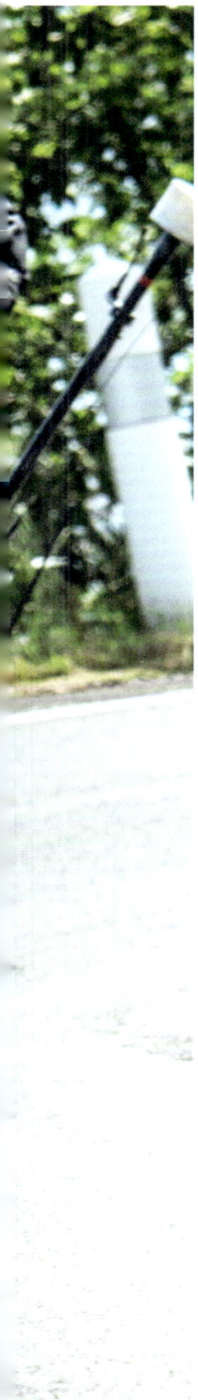

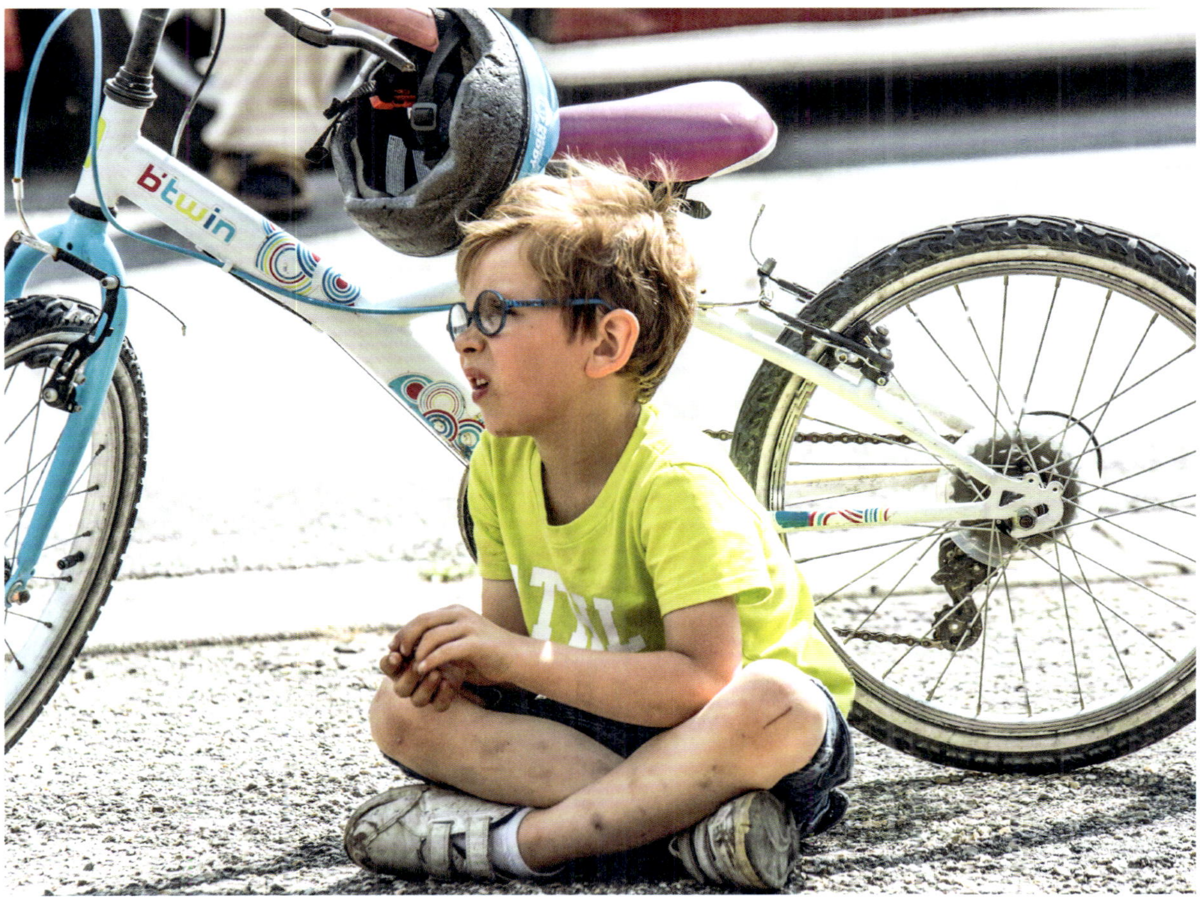

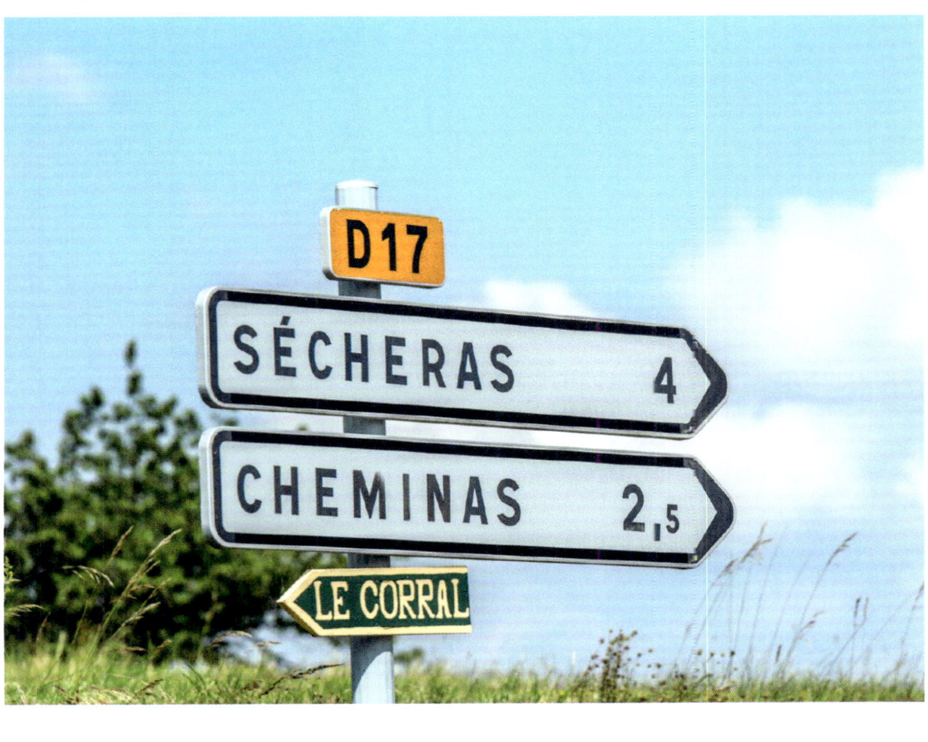
D17
SÉCHERAS 4
CHEMINAS 2,5
LE CORRAL

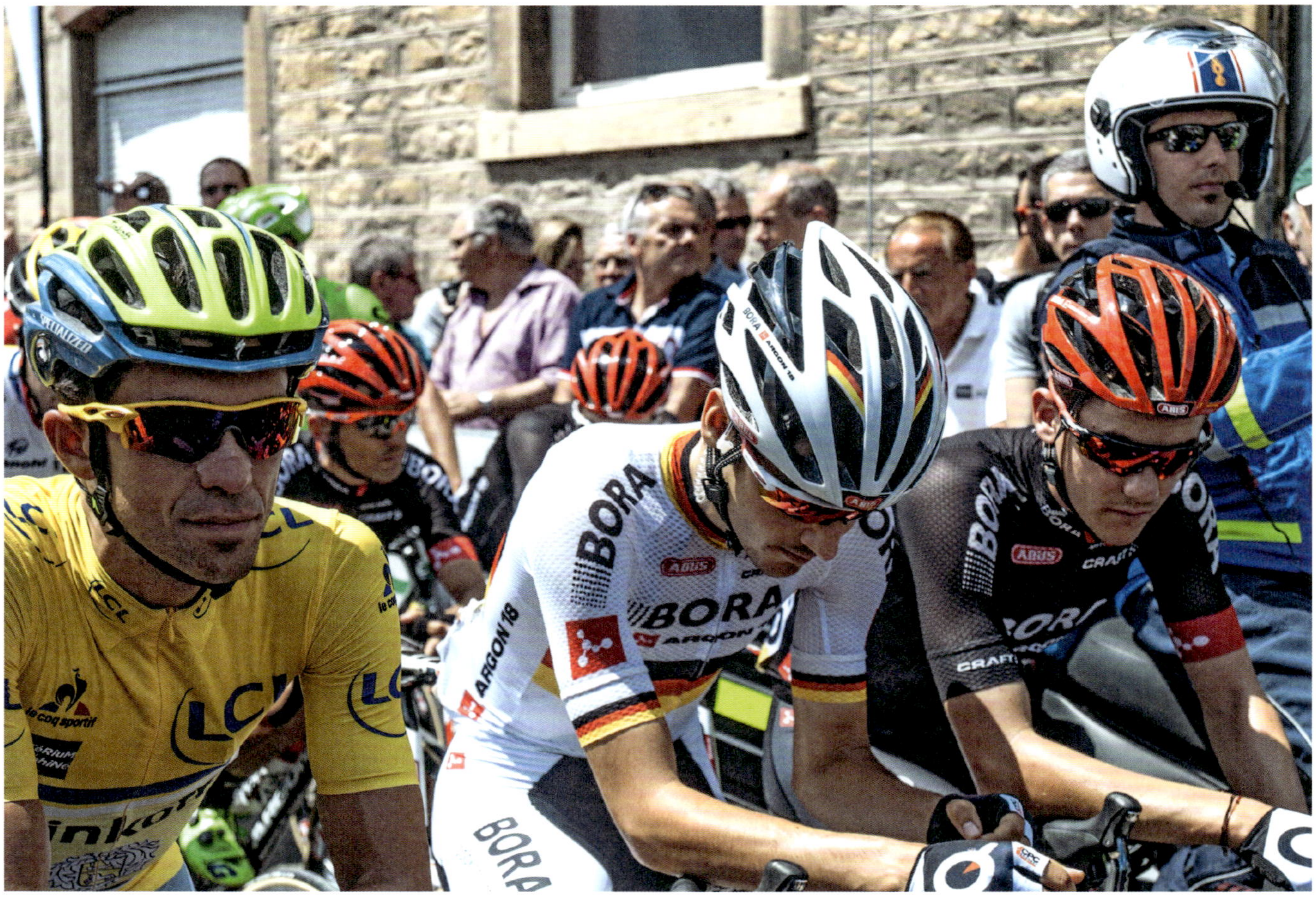

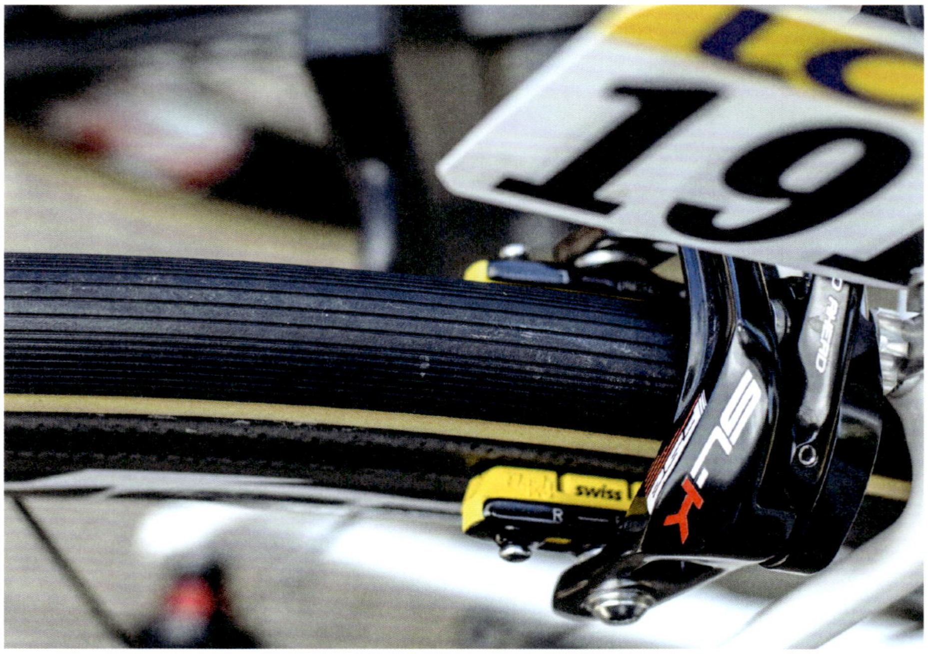

↑ Vor dem Start der 1. Etappe: Alberto Contador (Tinkoff) in Gelb, Emanuel Buchmann und Patrick Konrad (beide BORA - ARGON 18). **Before the start of the 1st stage: Alberto Contador (Tinkoff) in yellow, Emanuel Buchmann and Patrick Konrad (both BORA - ARGON 18).** *Avant le départ de la 1re étape : Alberto Contador (Tinkoff) en jaune, Emanuel Buchmann et Patrick Konrad (tous deux chez BORA - ARGON 18).*

→ George Bennett (Team LottoNL-Jumbo) mit Glücksbringer. **George Bennett (Team LottoNL-Jumbo) with a lucky charm.** *George Bennett (Team LottoNL-Jumbo) avec son porte-bonheur.*

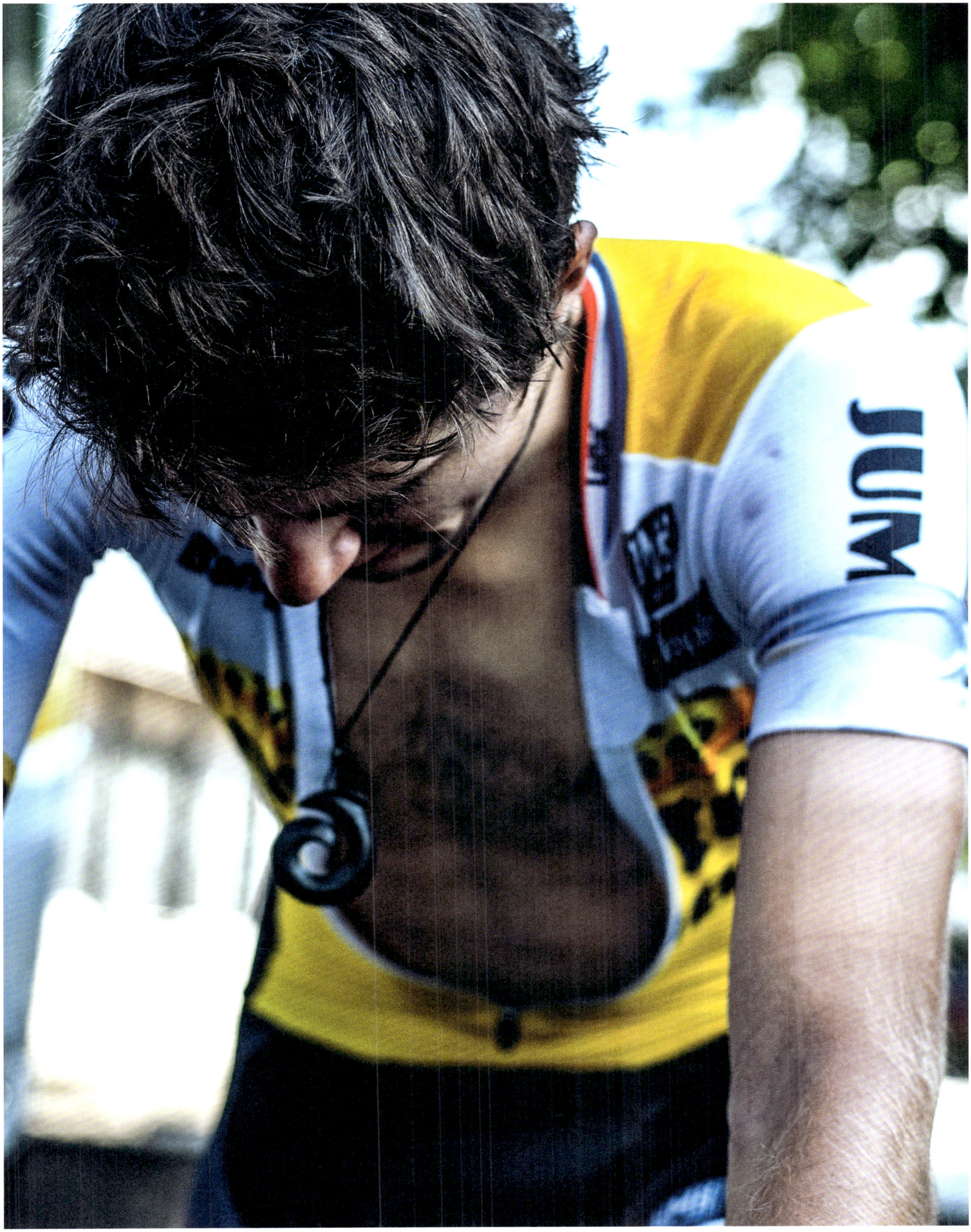

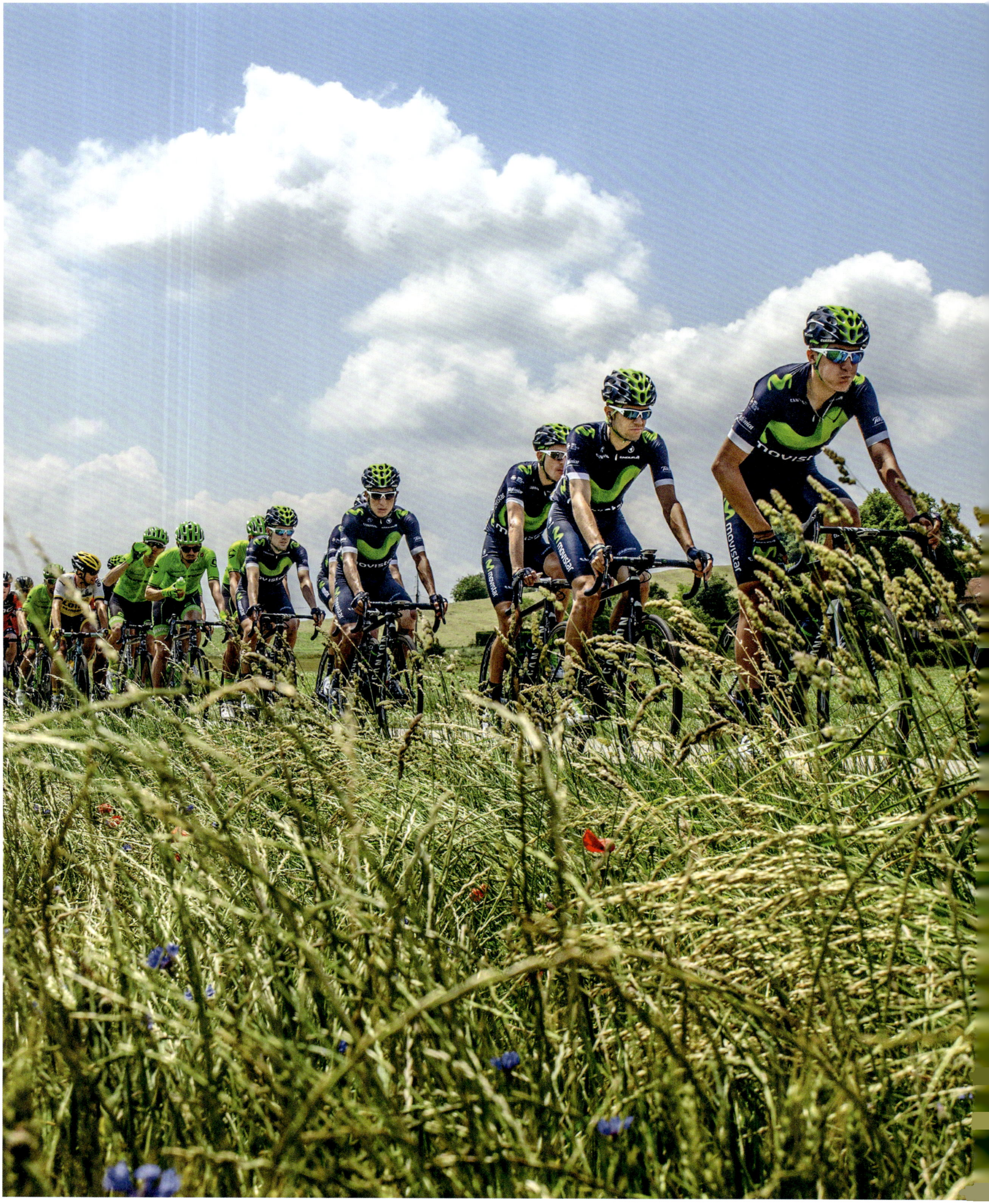
movistar

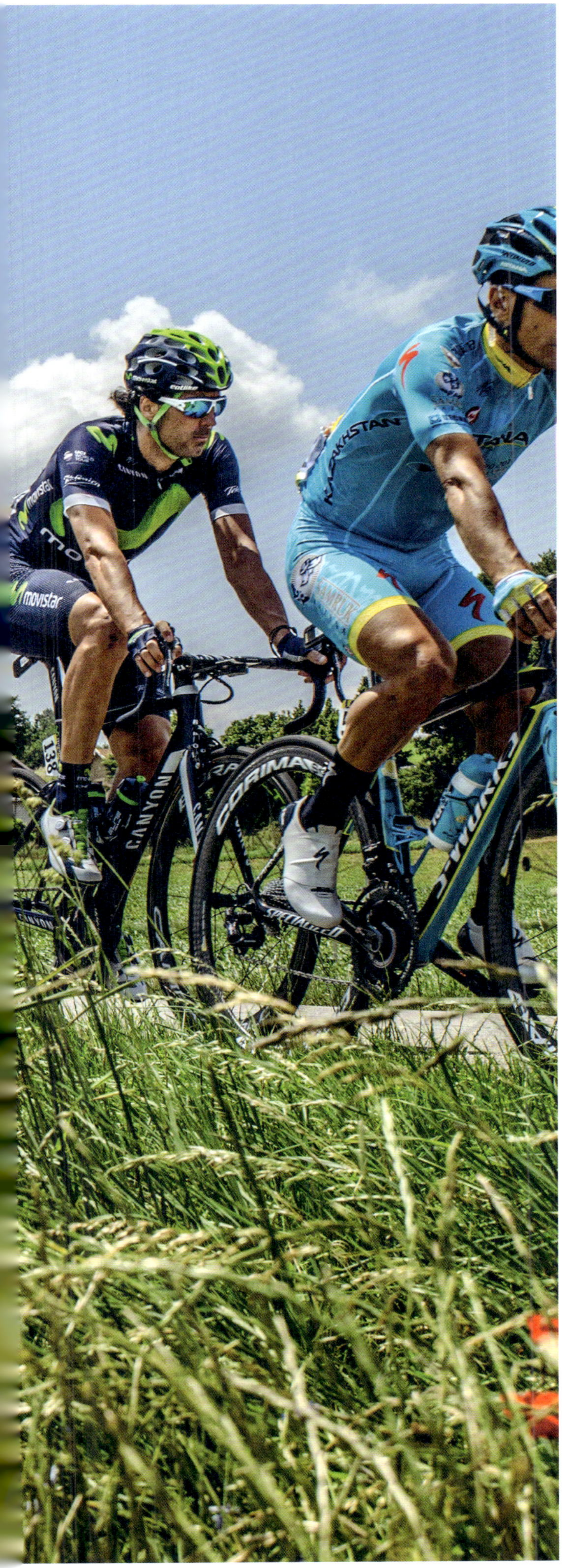

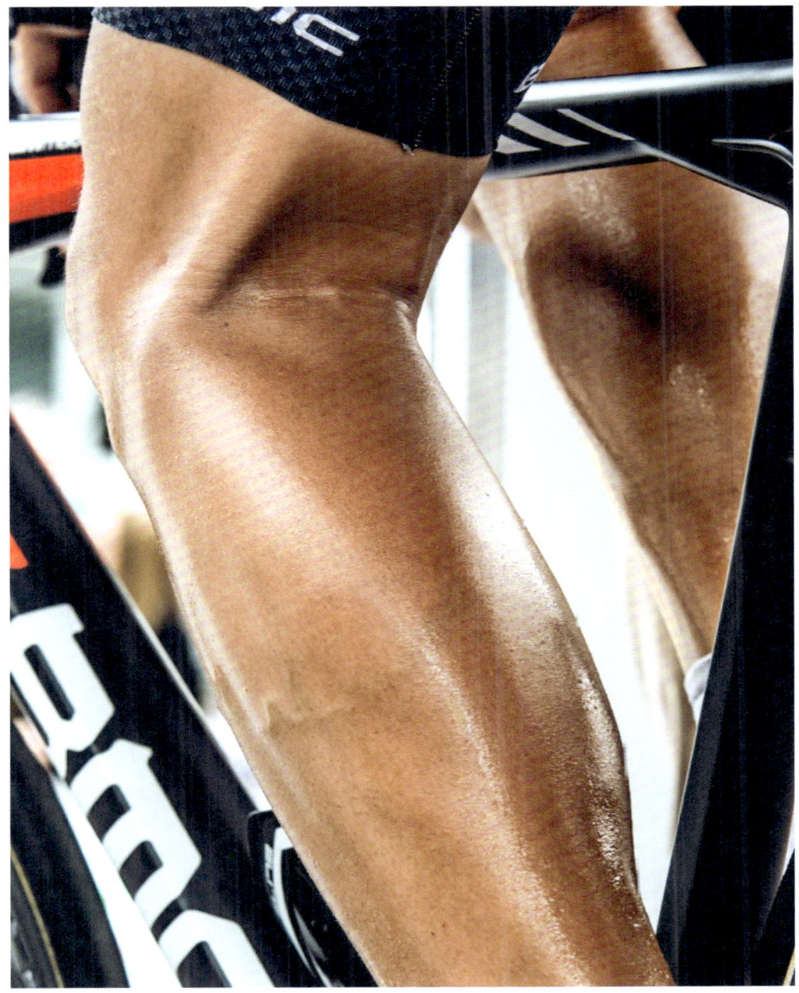

4. Etappe. **4th stage.** *4e étape.*

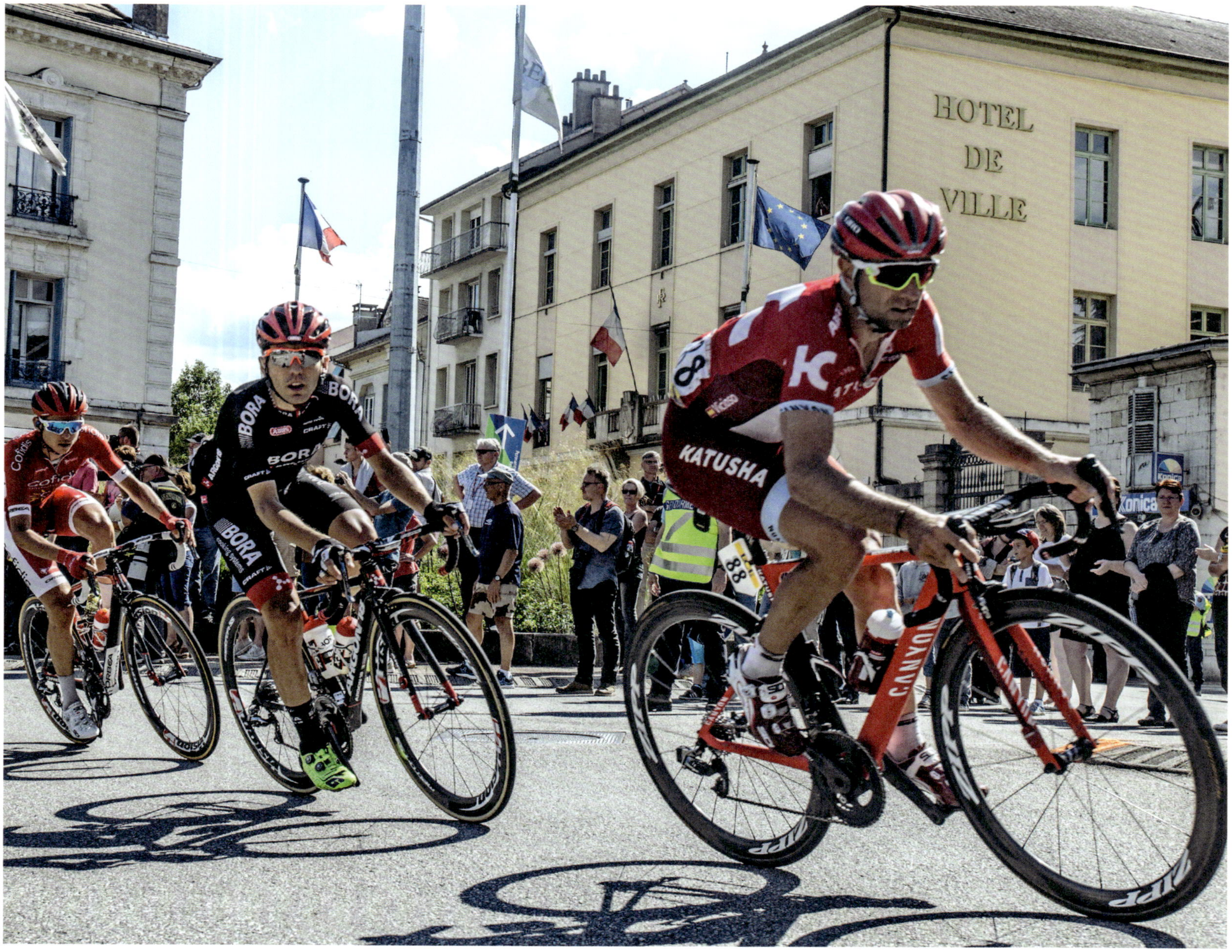

↑ Ángel Vicioso (Team Katusha) vor Cesare Benedetti (BORA - ARGON 18). **Ángel Vicioso (Team Katusha) ahead of Cesare Benedetti (BORA - ARGON 18).**
Ángel Vicioso (Team Katusha) devant Cesare Benedetti (BORA - ARGON 18).

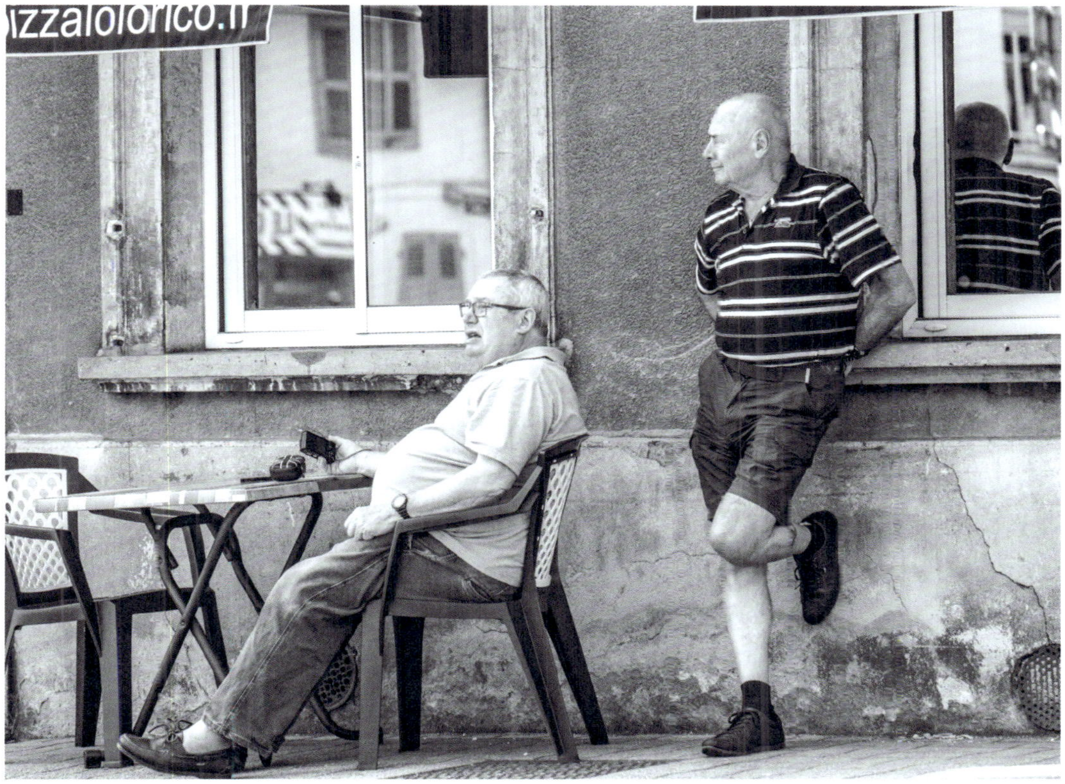

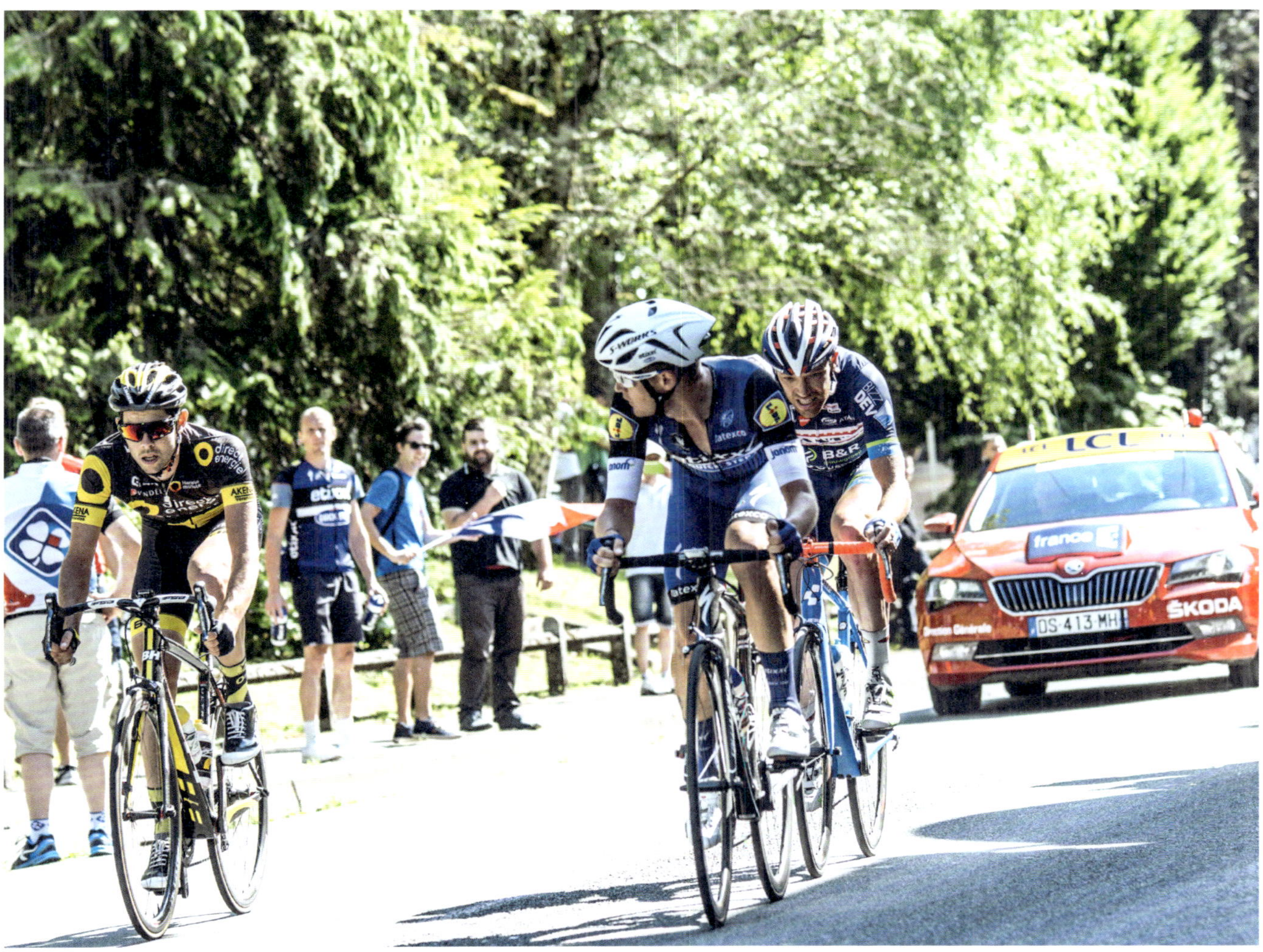
LCL
ŠKODA
DS-413-MH

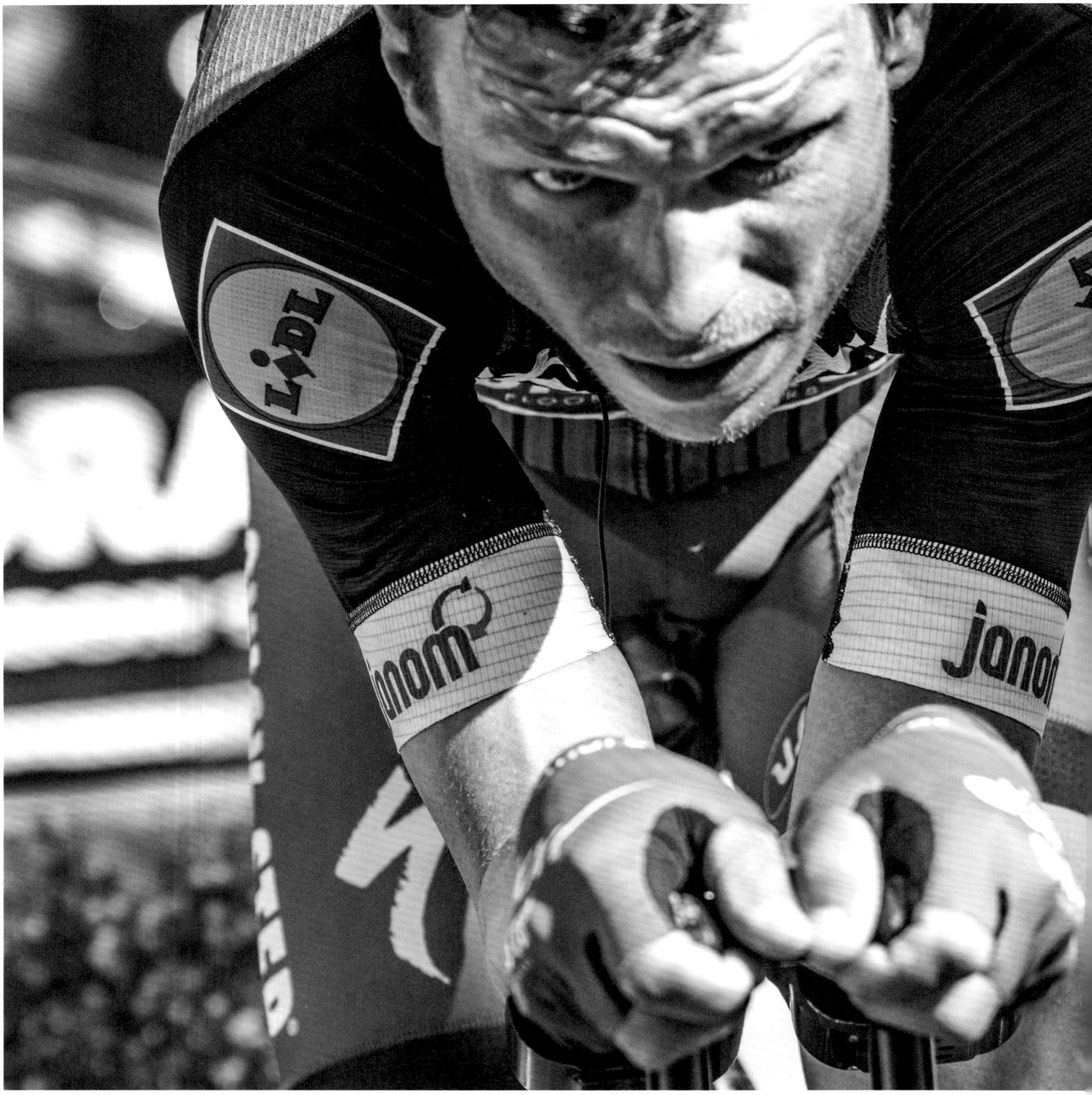

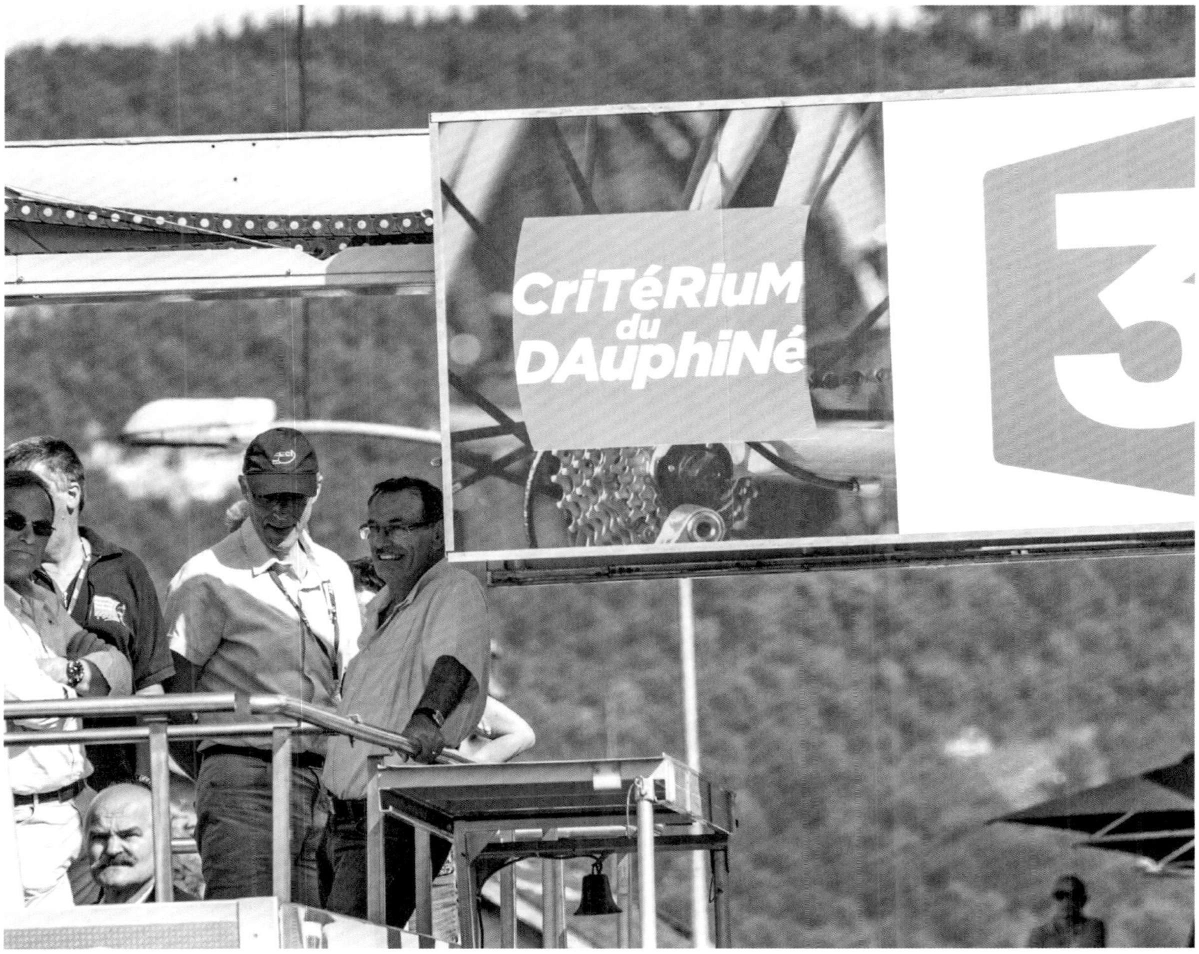

Tony Martin (Etixx – Quick Step) beim Warm-down nach der 4. Etappe. **Tony Martin (Etixx – Quick Step) warming down after the 4th stage.**
Tony Martin (Etixx – Quick Step) lors de la récupération après la 4e étape.

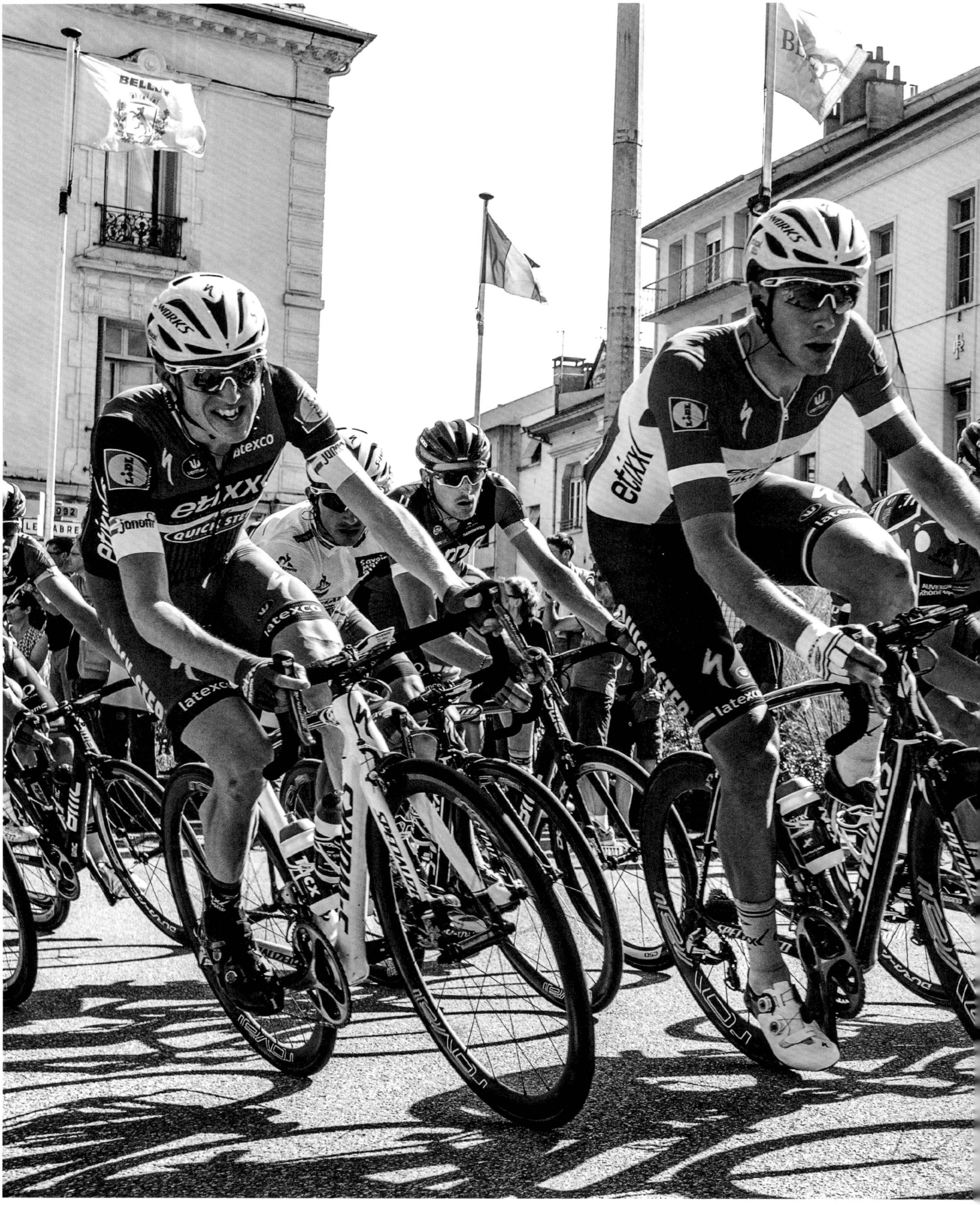
BELLEY
etixx
latexco

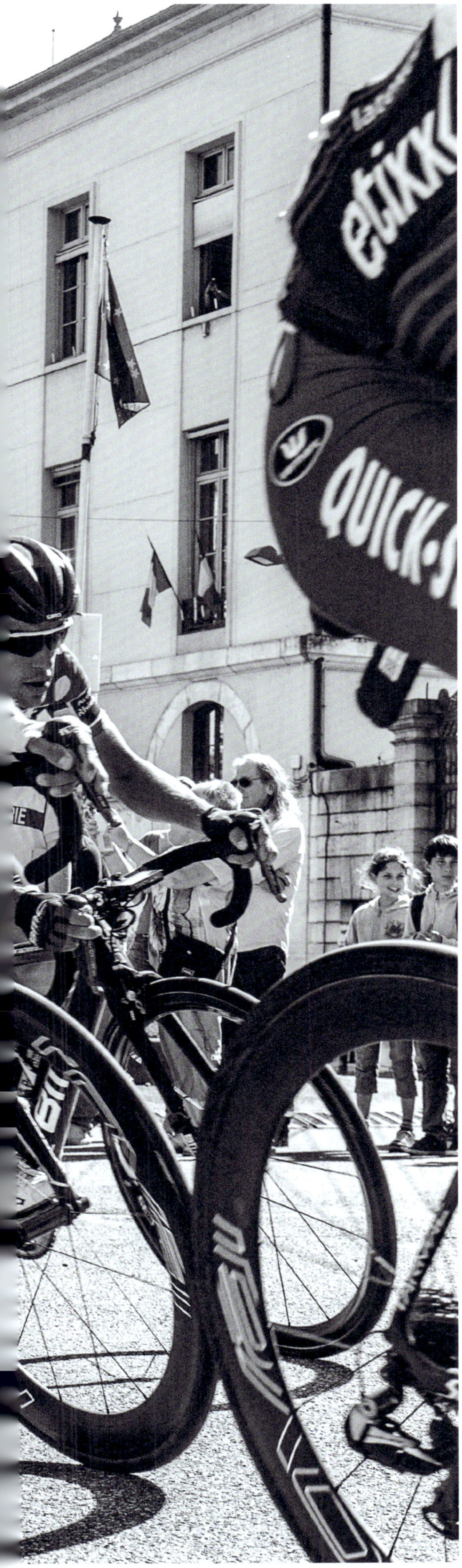

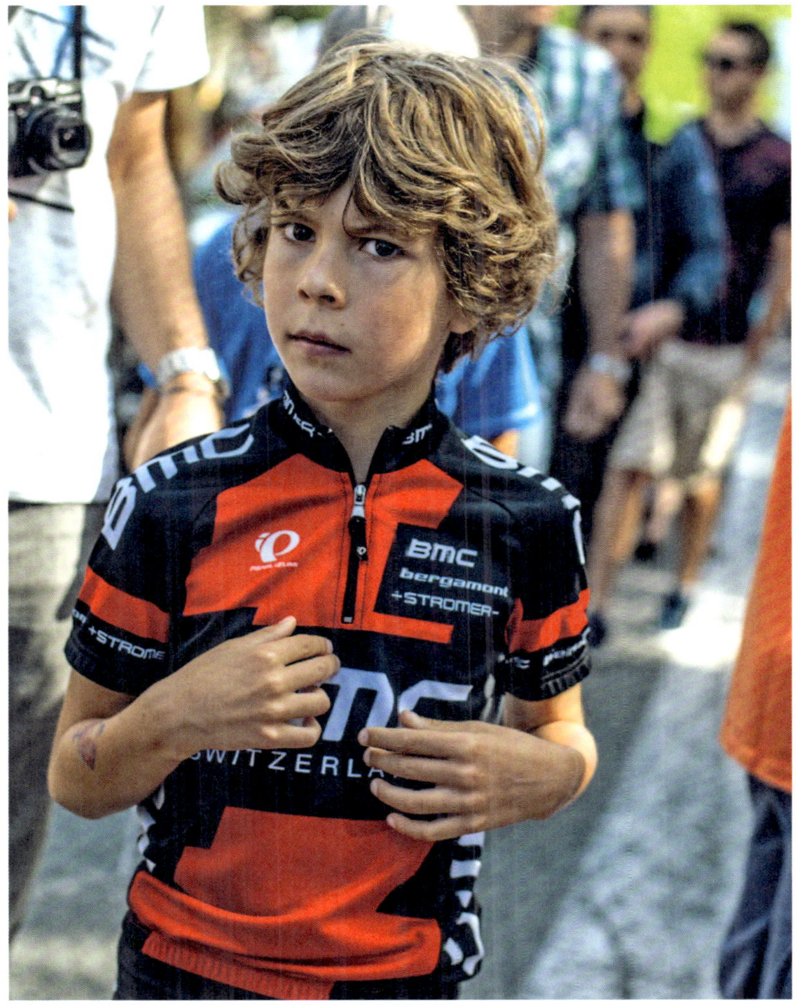

Kurz vor dem Ziel in Belley. **Just shy of the finish line in Belley.** *Juste avant l'arrivée à Belley.*

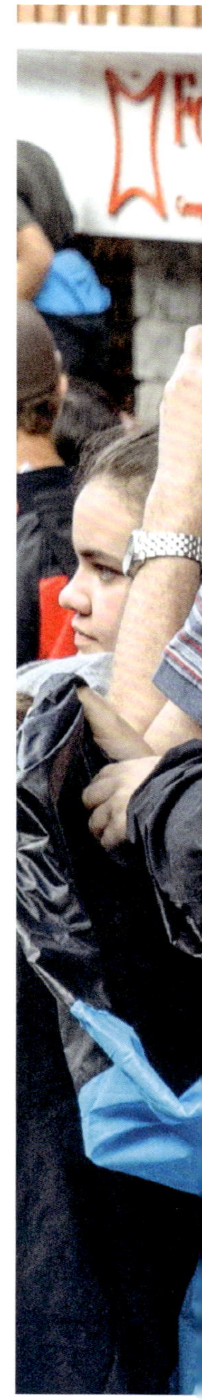

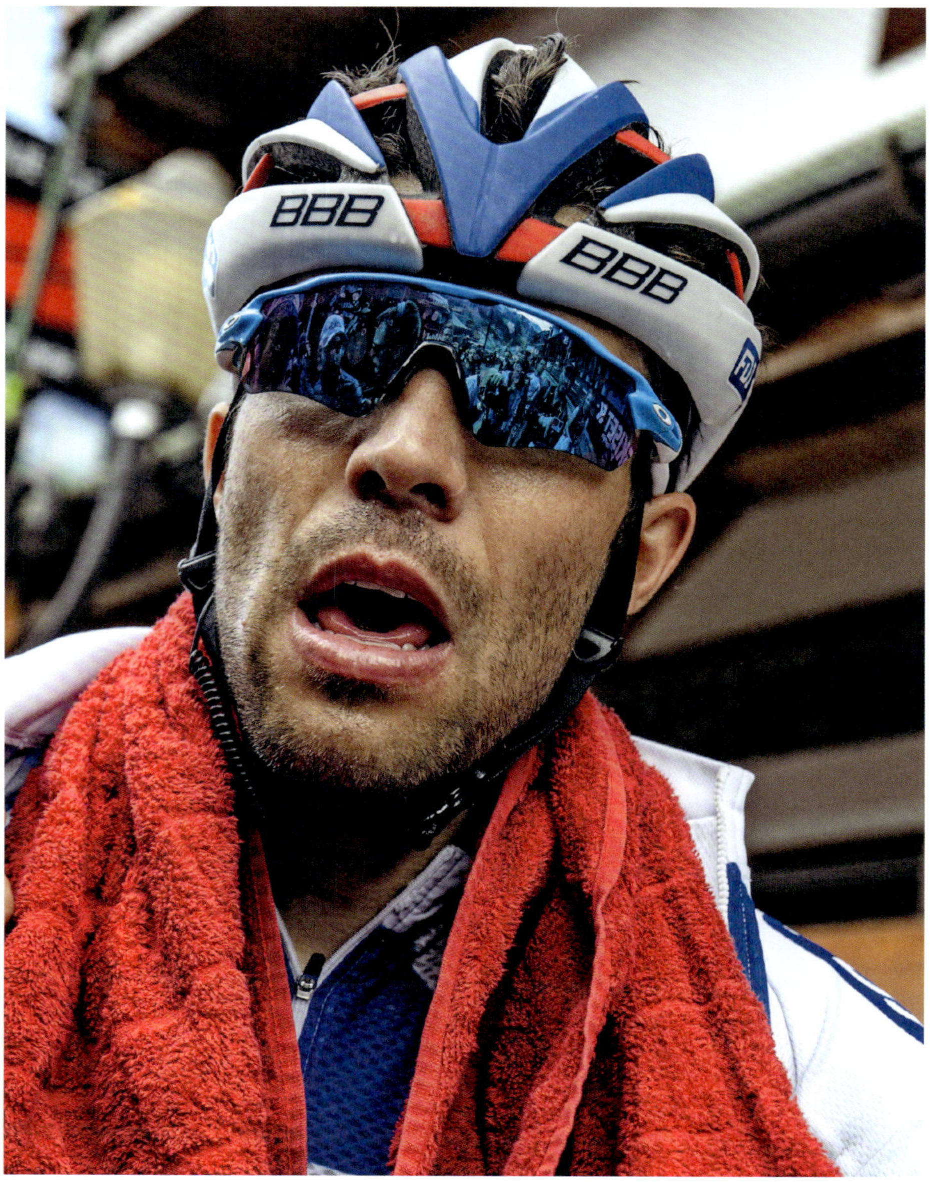
BBB
BBB

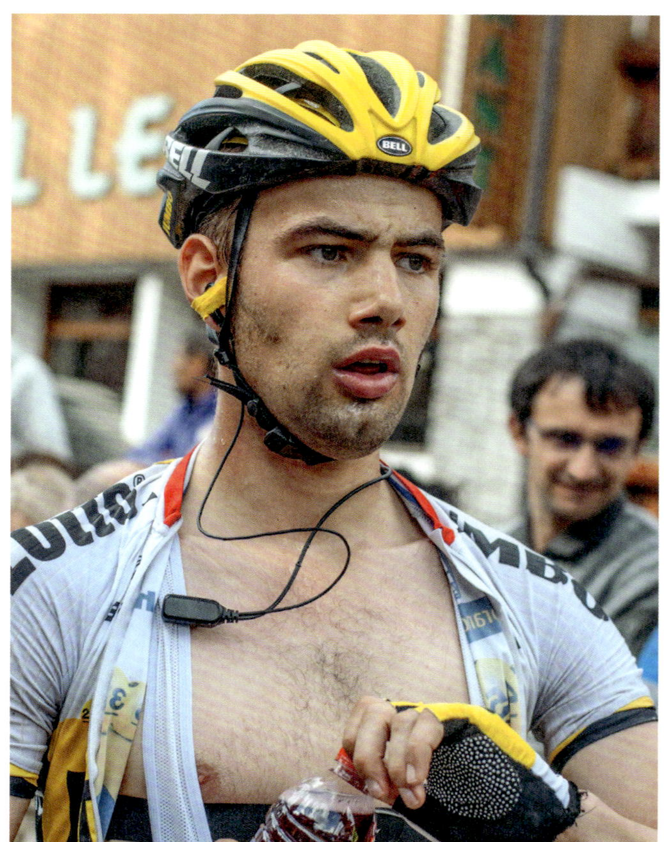

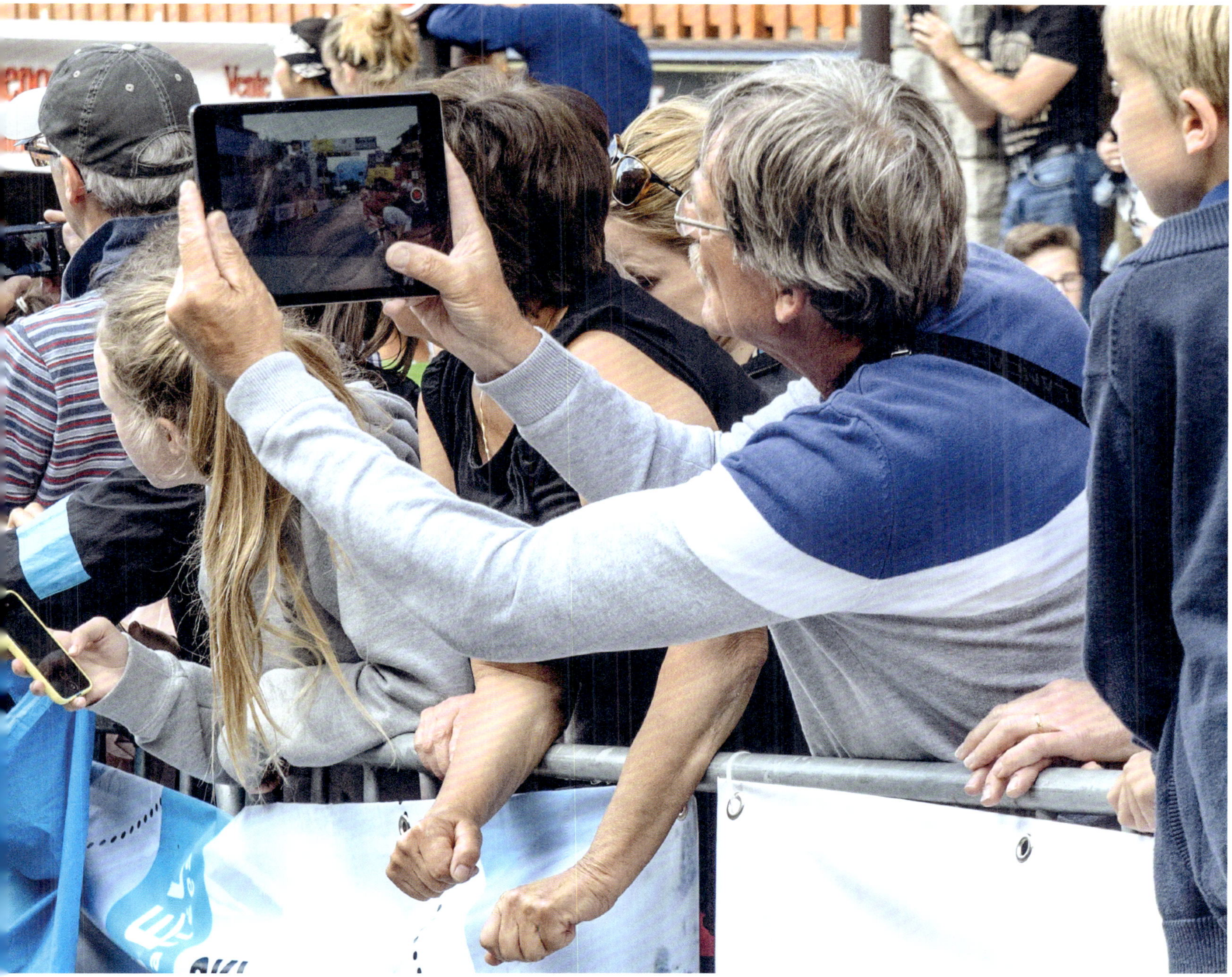

Abgekämpft: Thibaut Pinot (FDJ) und Victor Campenaerts (Team LottoNL-Jumbo). **Exhausted: Thibaut Pinot (FDJ) and Victor Campenaerts (Team LottoNL-Jumbo).** *Épuisés par la bataille : Thibaut Pinot (FDJ) et Victor Campenaerts (Team LottoNL-Jumbo).*

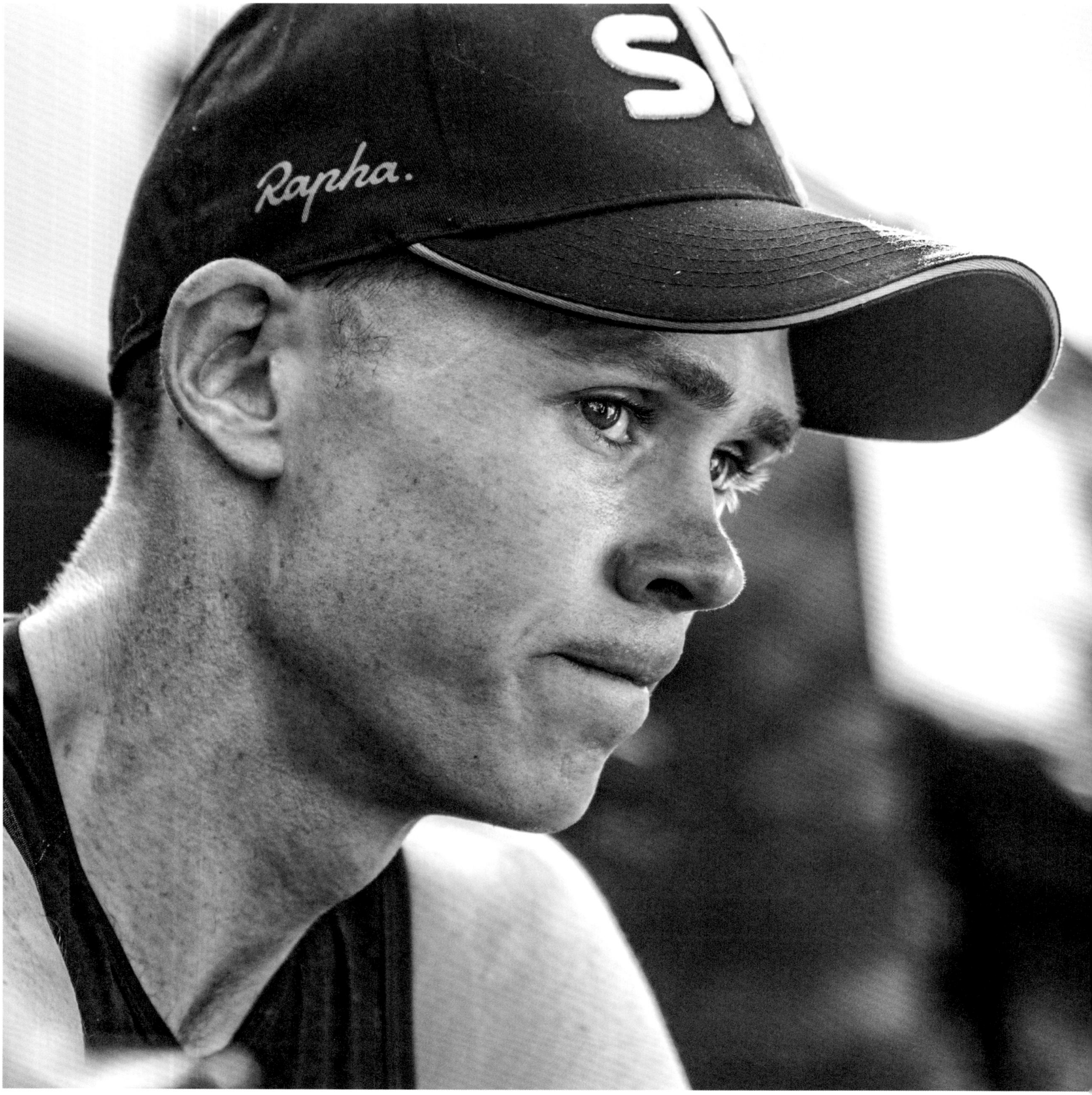

↑ Chris Froome (Team Sky) im Interview nach der 4. Etappe. Im Gesamtklassement ist er nur 4 Sekunden hinter Alberto Contador (Tinkoff). **Chris Froome (Team Sky) in an interview after the 4th stage. In the overall ranking, he trails Alberto Contador (Tinkoff) by a mere 4 seconds.** *Chris Froome (Team Sky) en pleine interview après la 4e étape. Au classement général, il ne se trouve qu'à 4 secondes d'Alberto Contador (Tinkoff).*

→ Marcus Burghardt (BMC Racing Team). **Marcus Burghardt (BMC Racing Team).** *Marcus Burghardt (BMC Racing Team).*

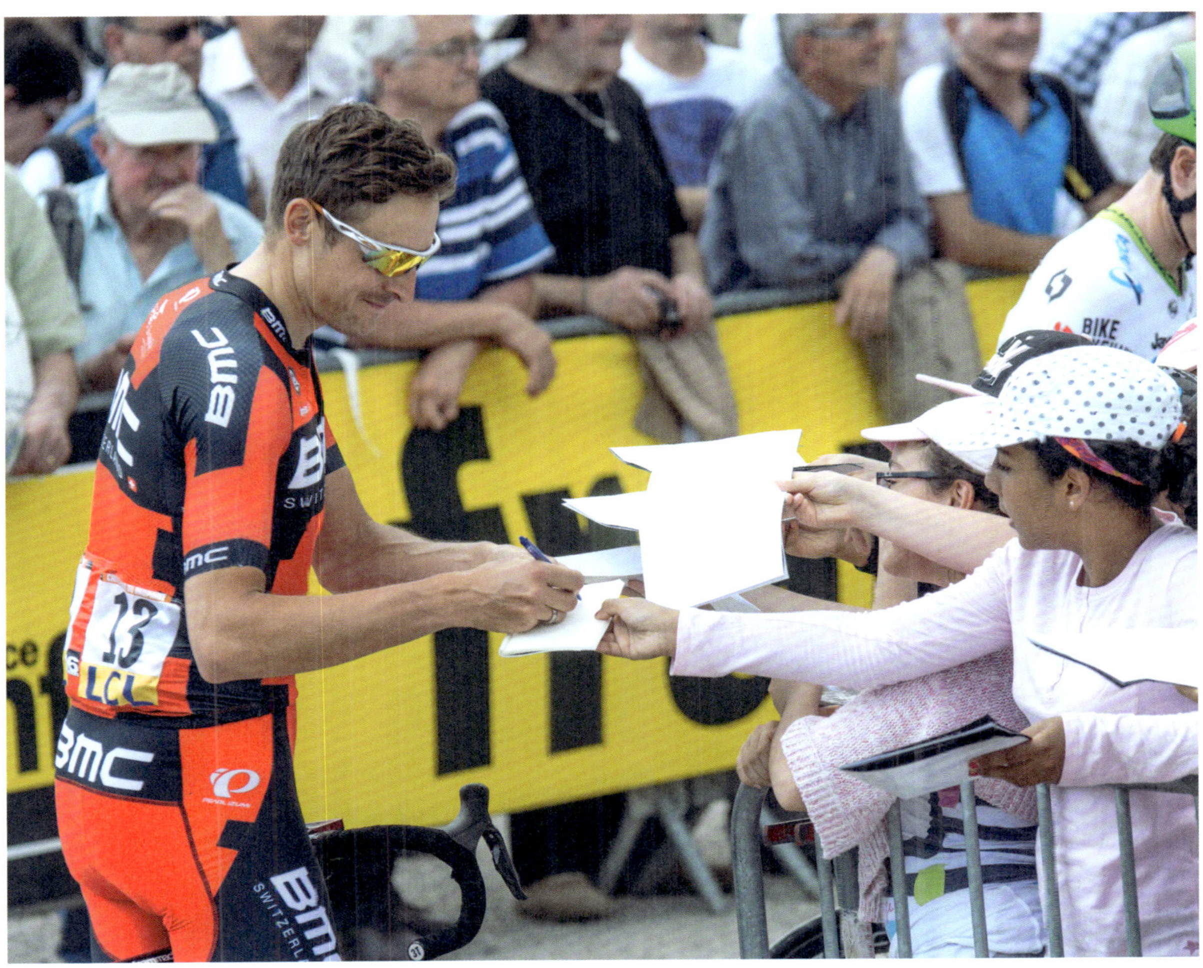
BMC
13
LCL

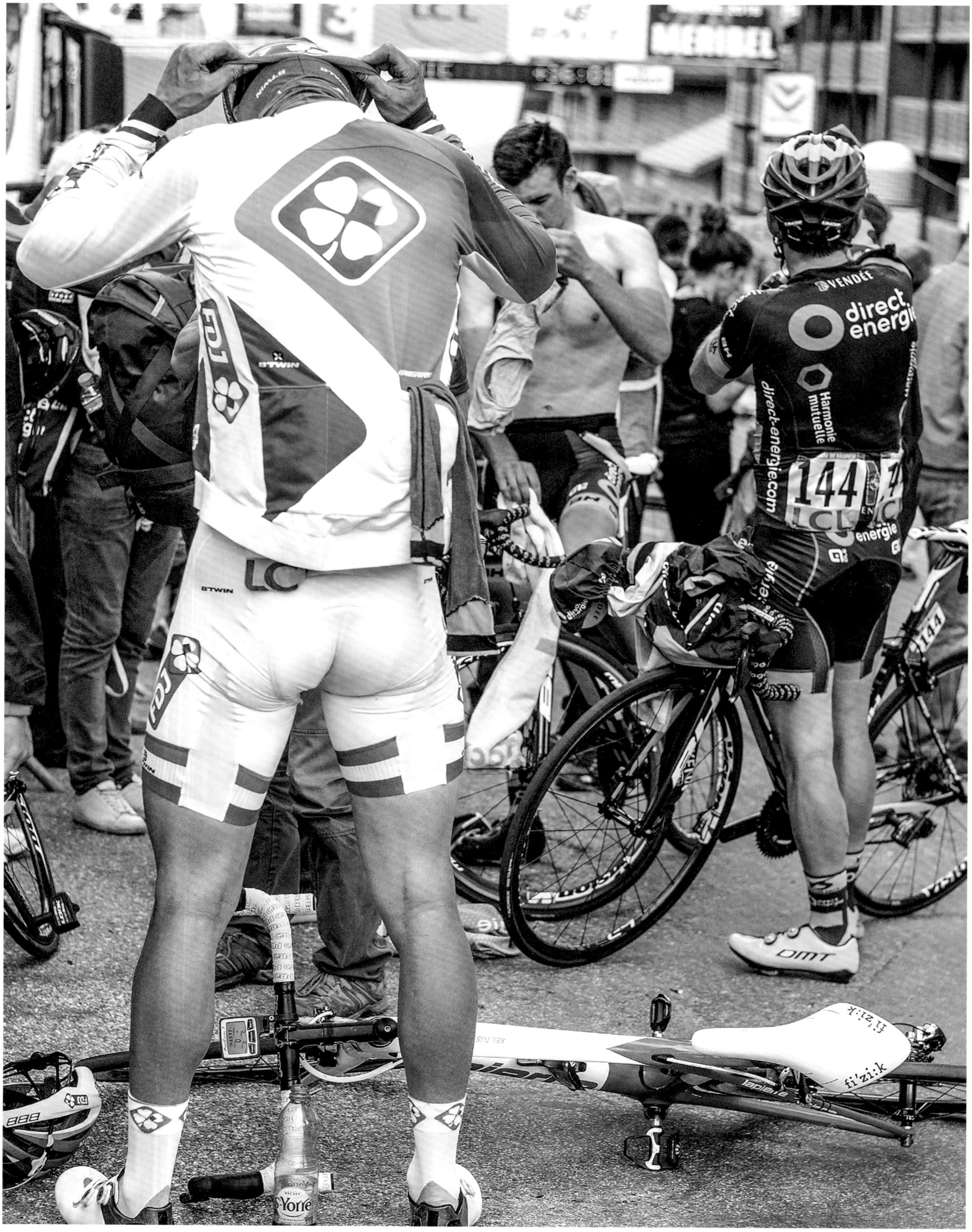

Szenen nach der 5. Etappe in Vaujany. **Scenes after the 5th stage in Vaujany.** *Scènes après la 5e étape à Vaujany.*

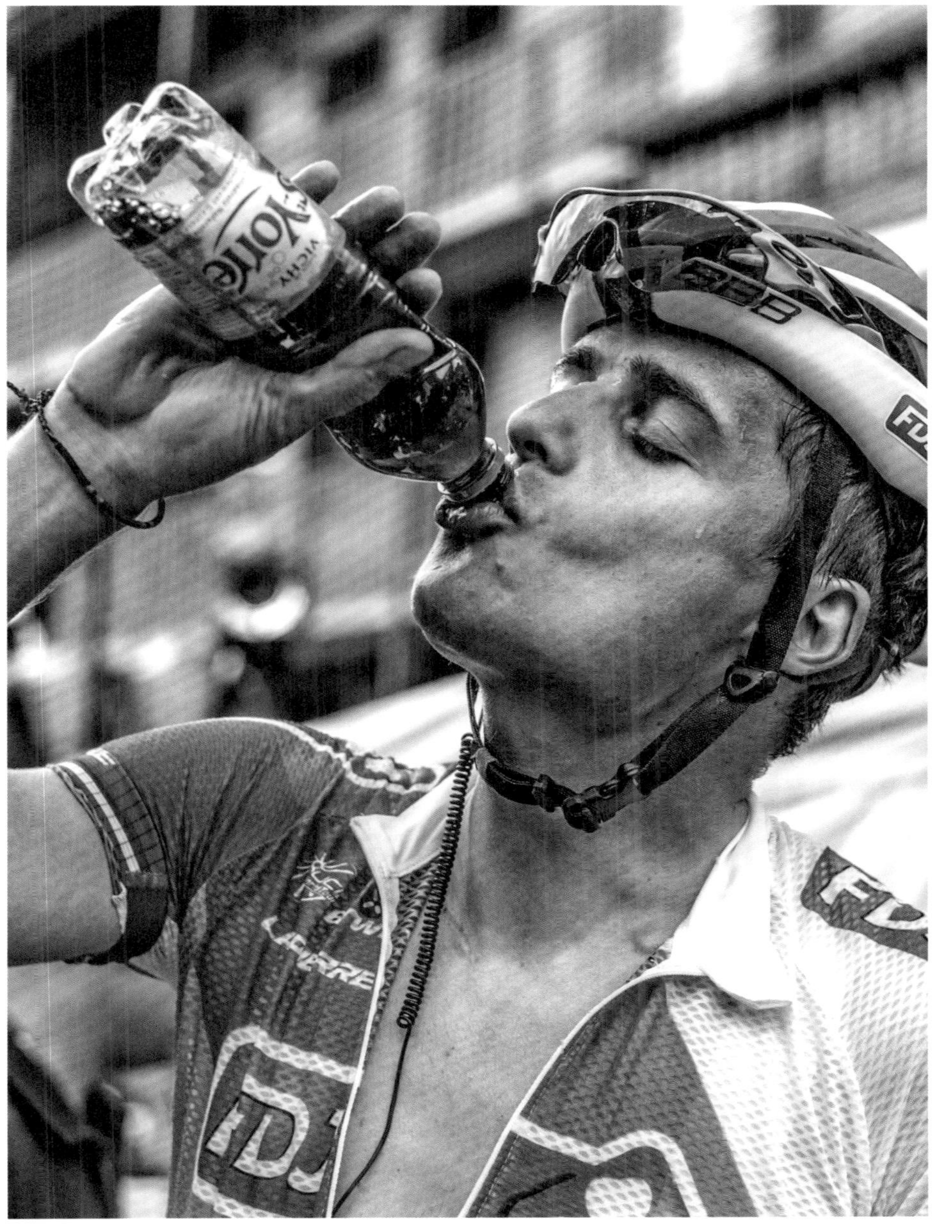
BBB
FDJ

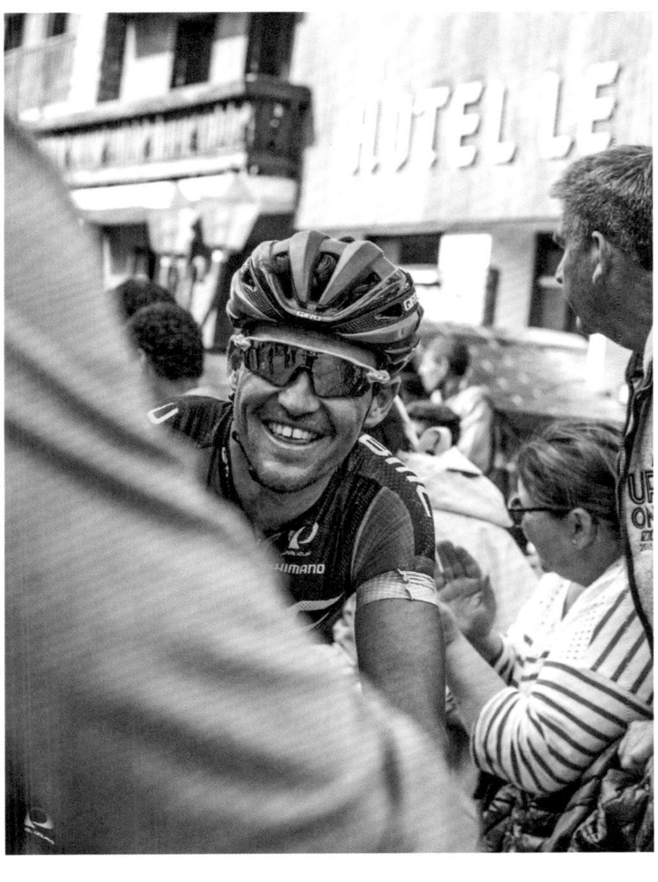
HOTEL LE
SHIMANO

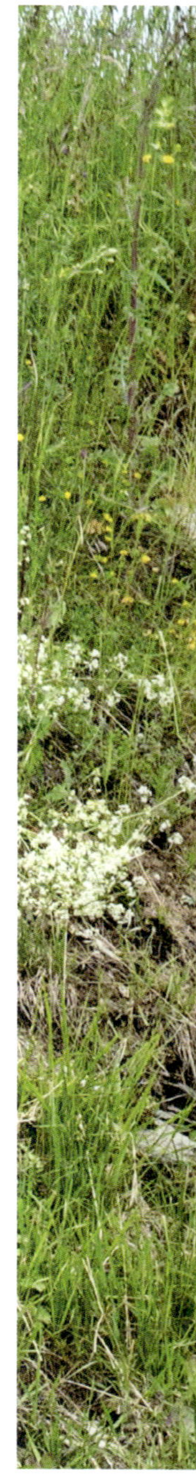

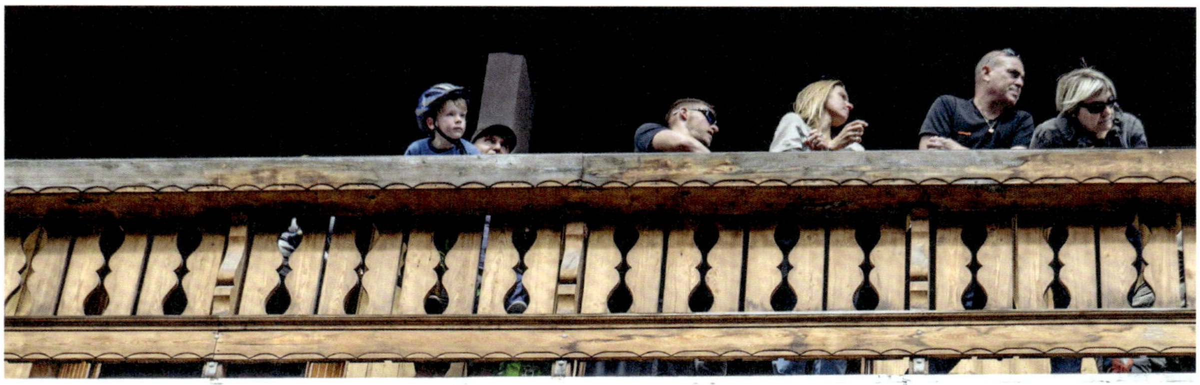

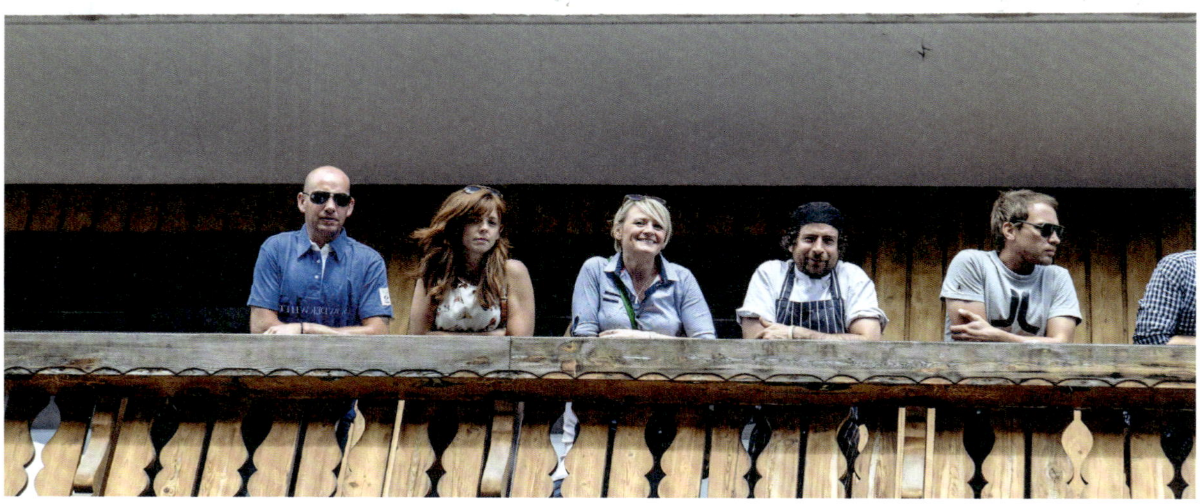

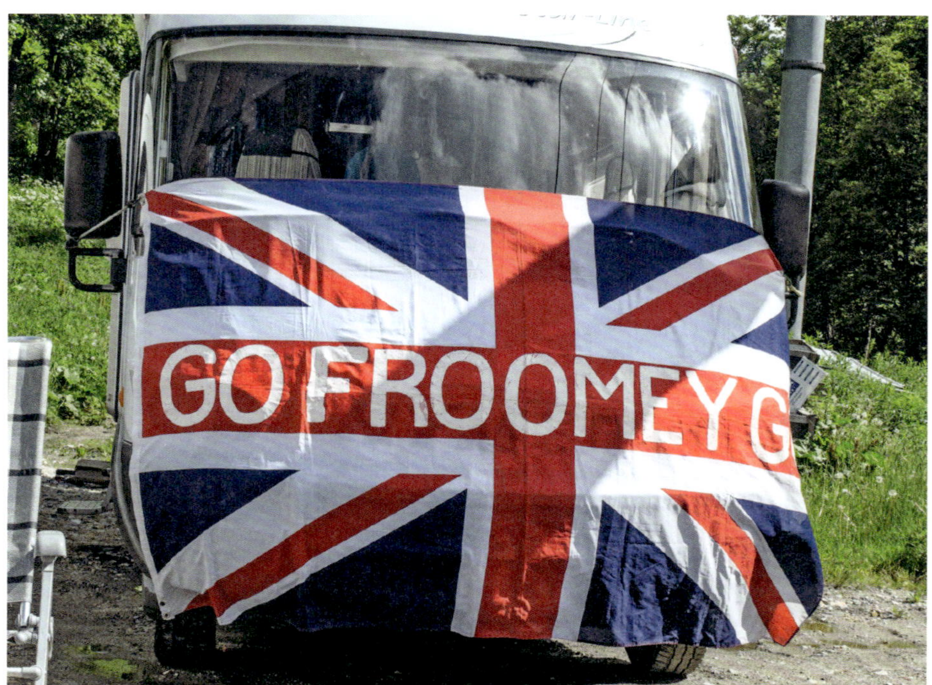
GO FROOMEY G

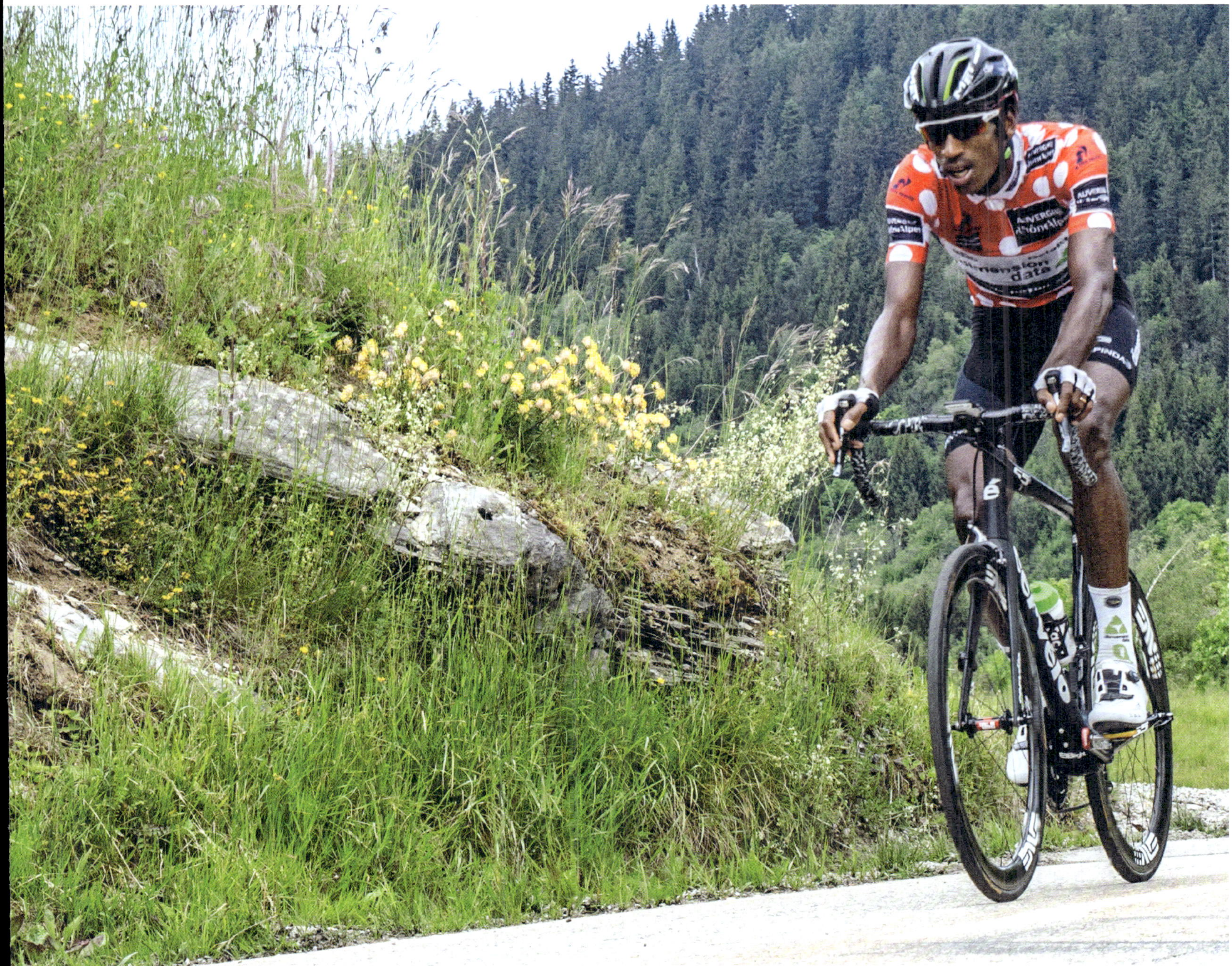

Daniel Teklehaimanot (Dimension Data) im Bergtrikot bei der 5. Etappe. **Daniel Teklehaimanot (Dimension Data) in the polka-dot jersey in the 5th stage.**
Daniel Teklehaimanot (Dimension Data) avec le maillot du meilleur grimpeur lors de la 5e étape.

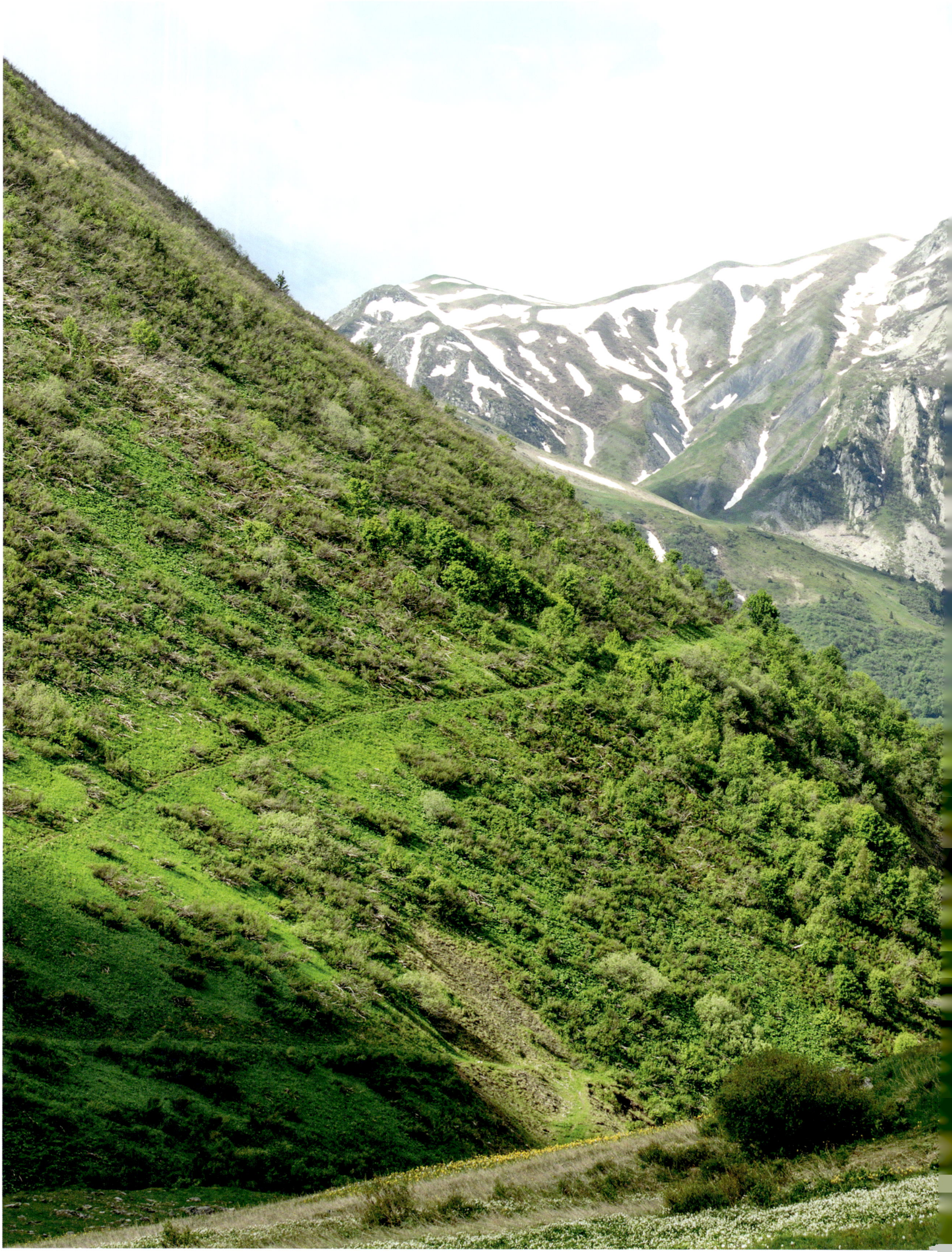

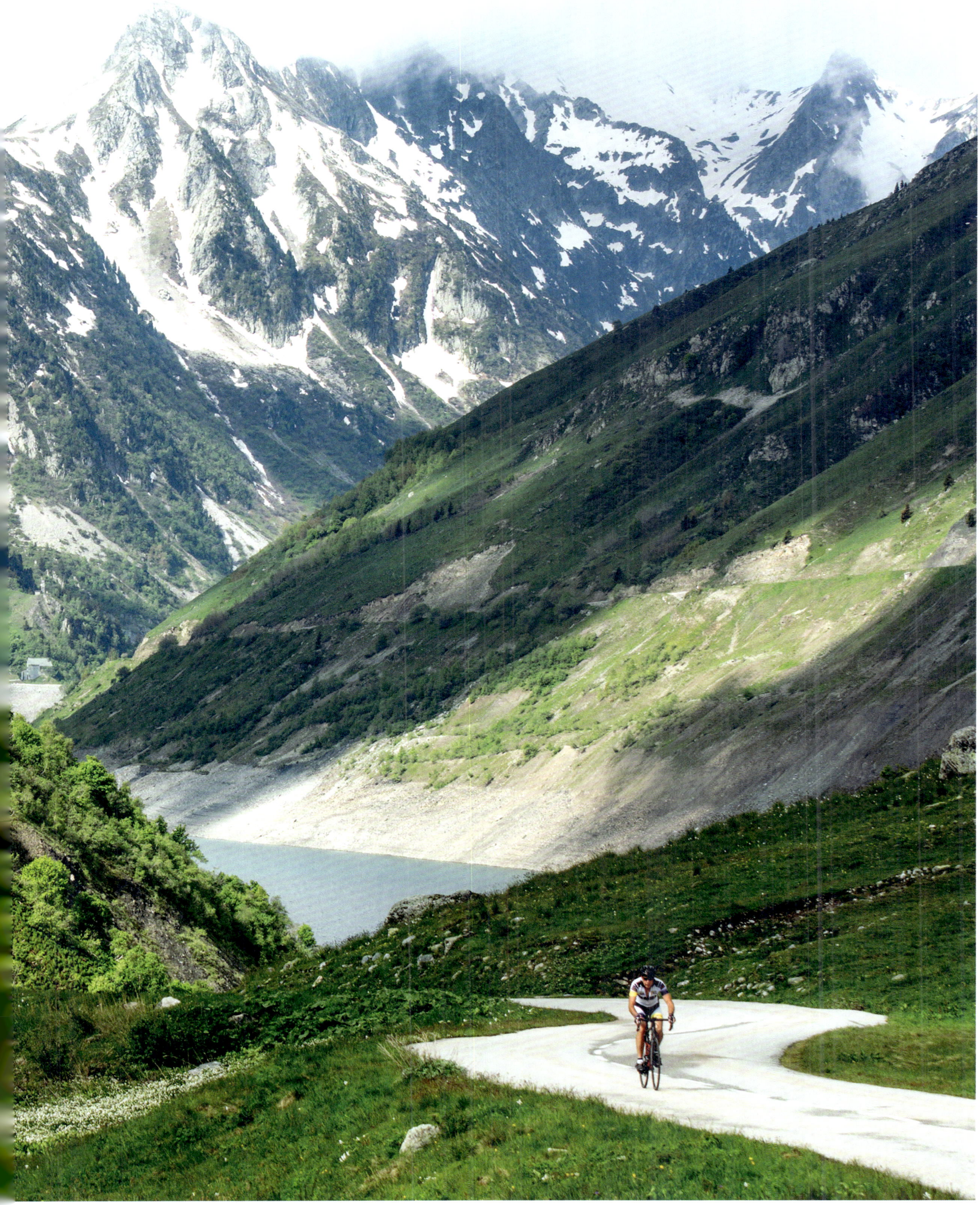

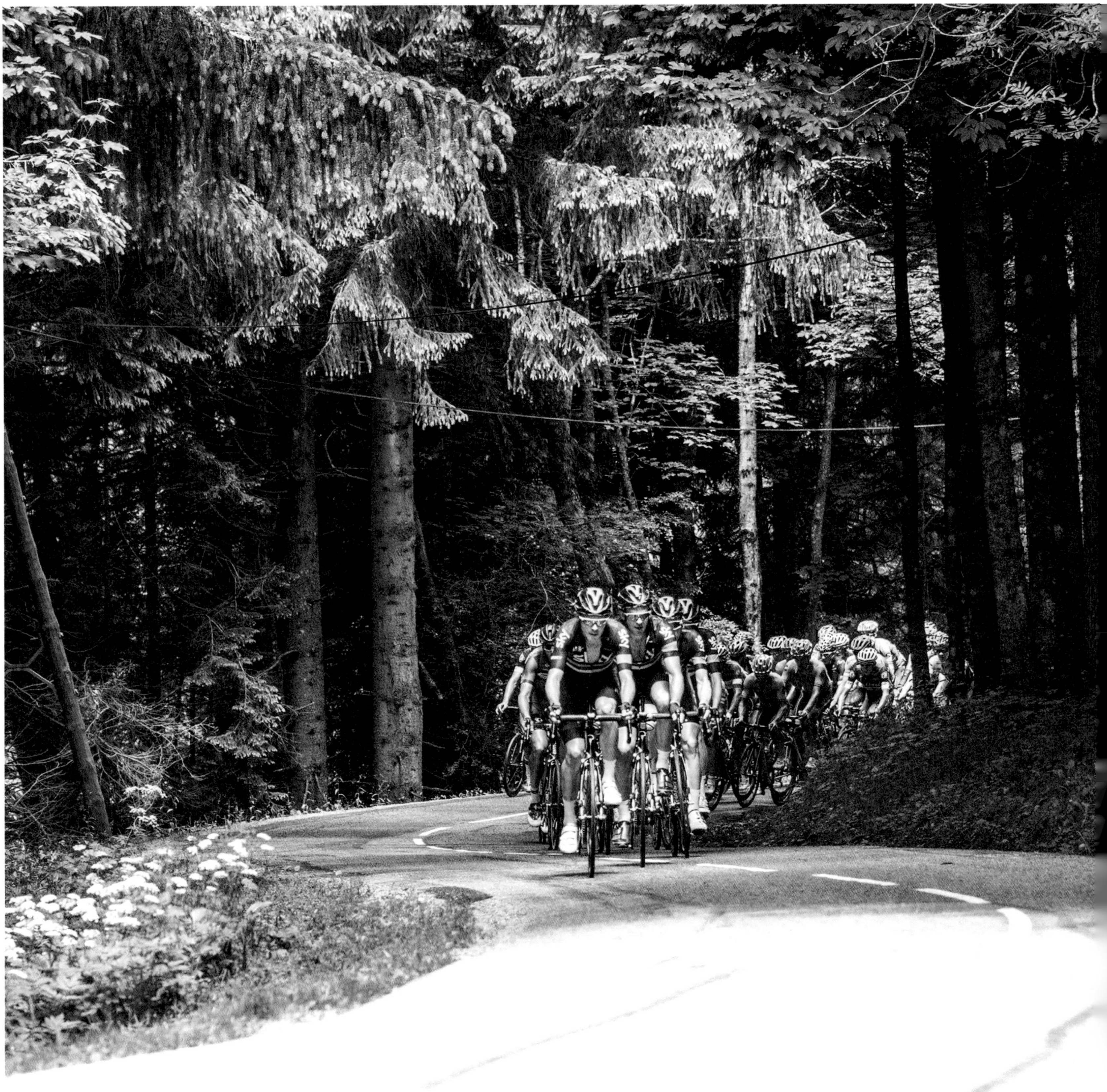

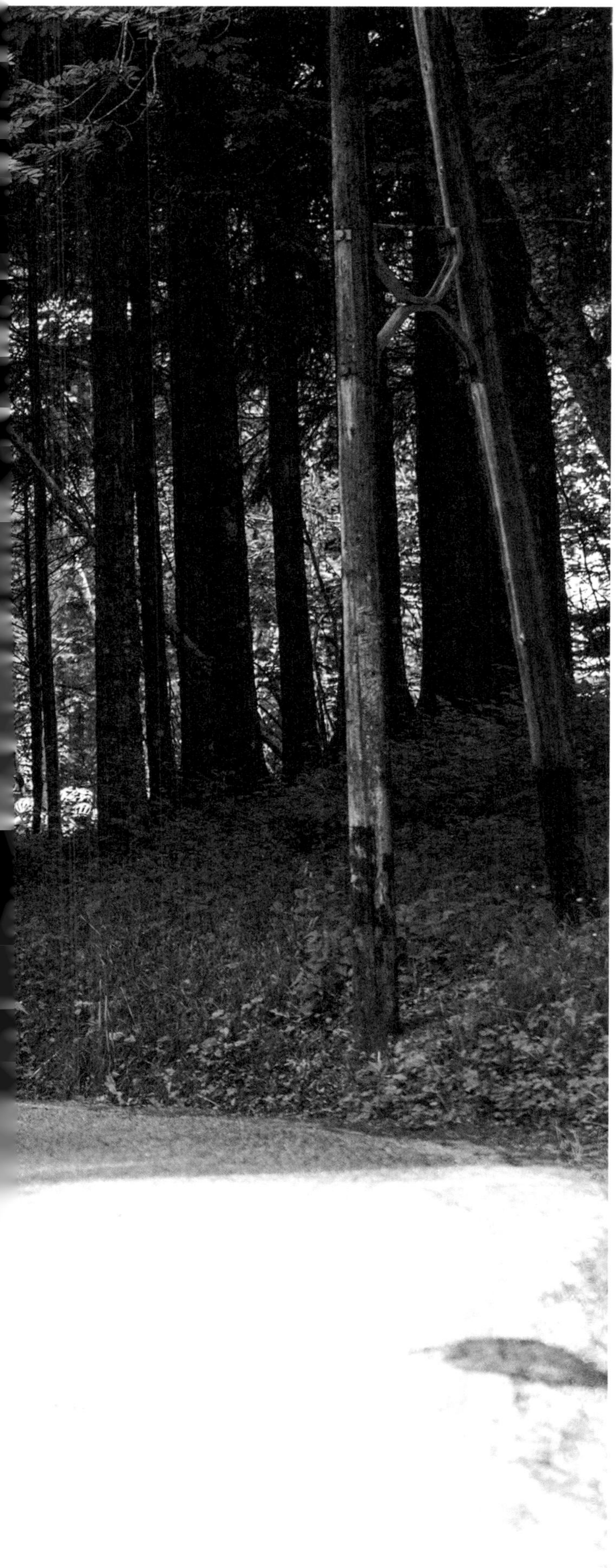

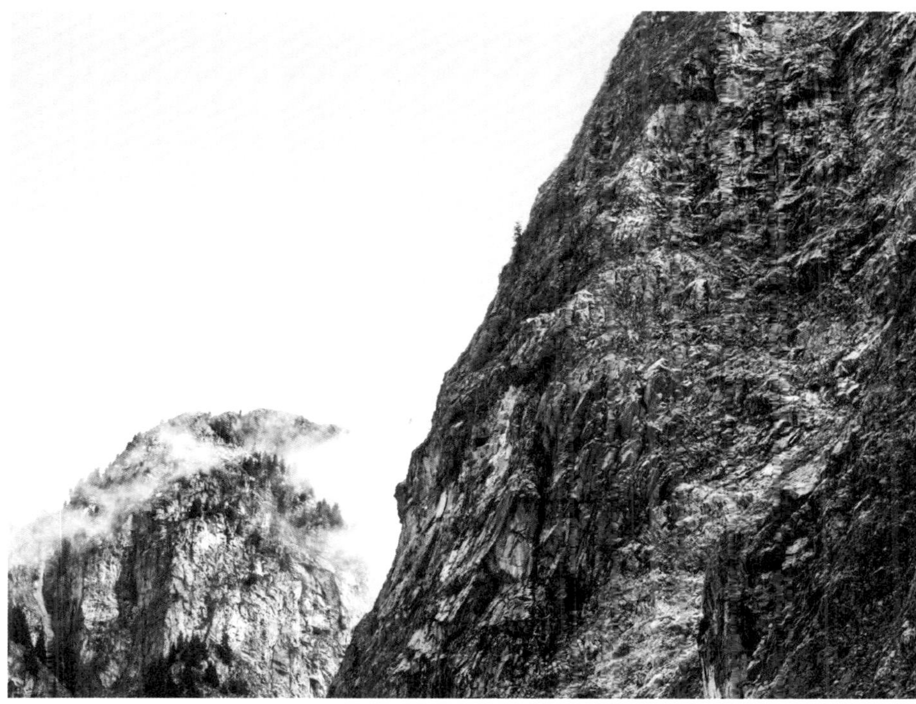

Das Peloton bei der 6. Etappe. **The peloton in the 6th stage.** *Le peloton lors de la 6e étape.*

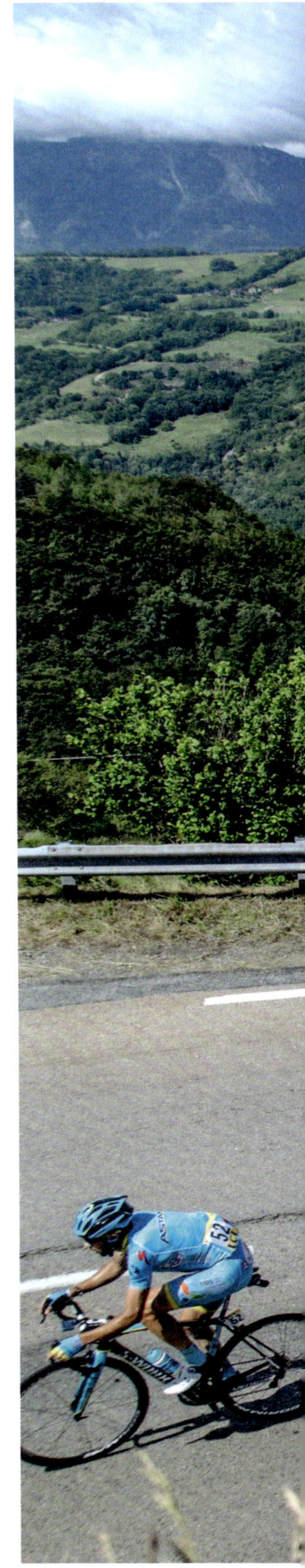
52

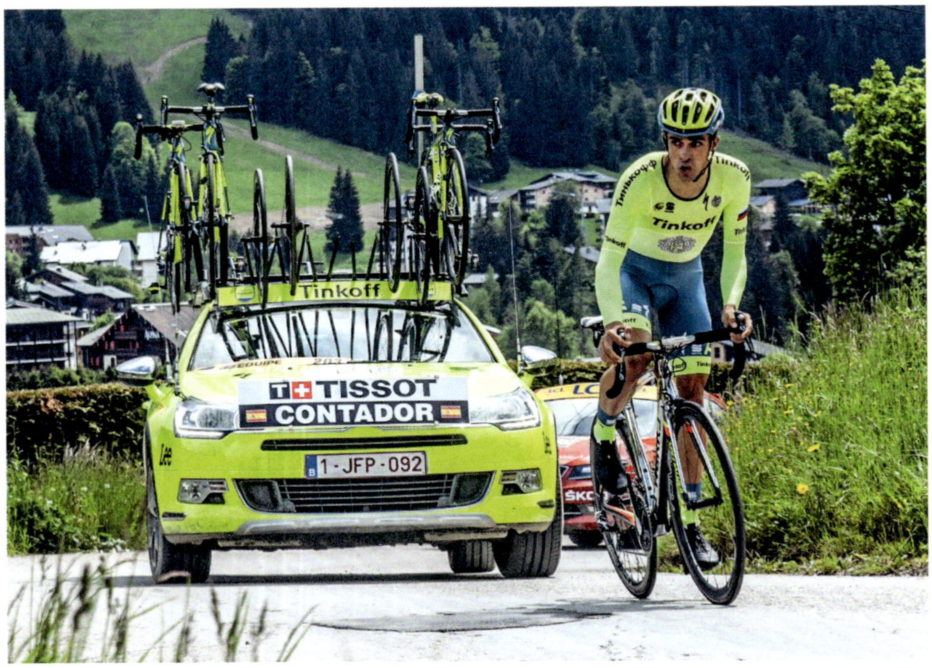
Tinkoff
TISSOT
CONTADOR
1-JFP-092

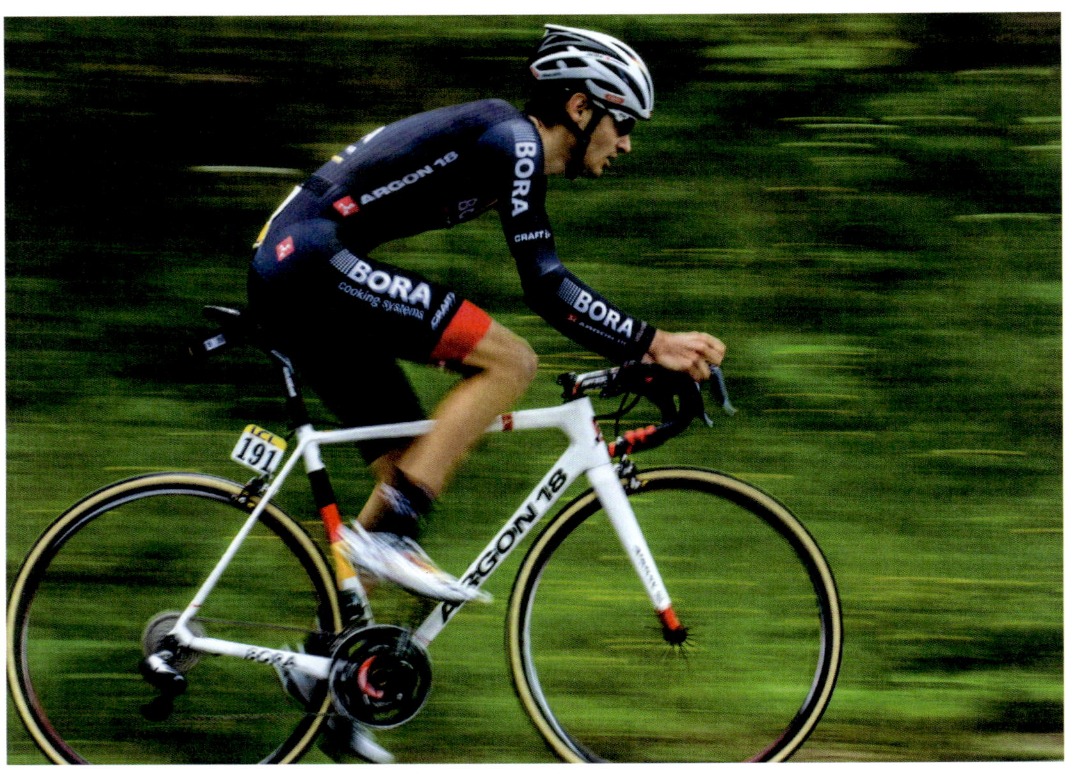
BORA
ARGON 18
BORA
cooking systems
BORA
191
ARGON 18

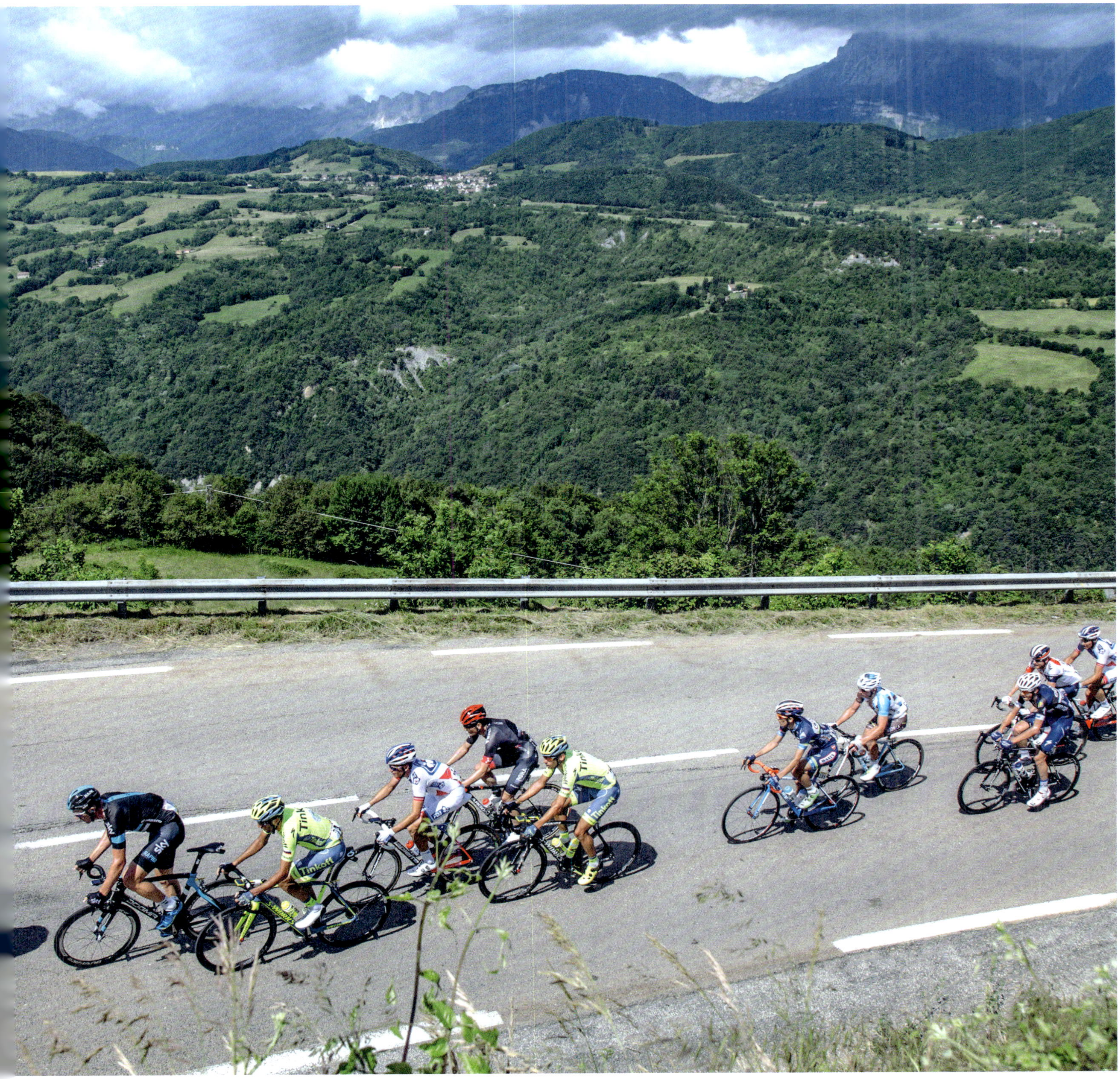

← Alberto Contador (Tinkoff), Emanuel Buchmann (BORA - ARGON 18) alleine gegen die Uhr auf dem Weg zum Mont Chéry. **Alberto Contador (Tinkoff) and Emanuel Buchmann (BORA - ARGON 18) alone against the clock on their way to Mont Chéry.** *Alberto Contador (Tinkoff) et Emanuel Buchmann (BORA - ARGON 18) seuls contre la montre en direction du mont Chéry.*

↑ Anstieg zum Col de Moissière, 7. Etappe. **Ascent to Col de Moissière, 7th stage.** *Ascension du col de Moissière, 7e étape.*

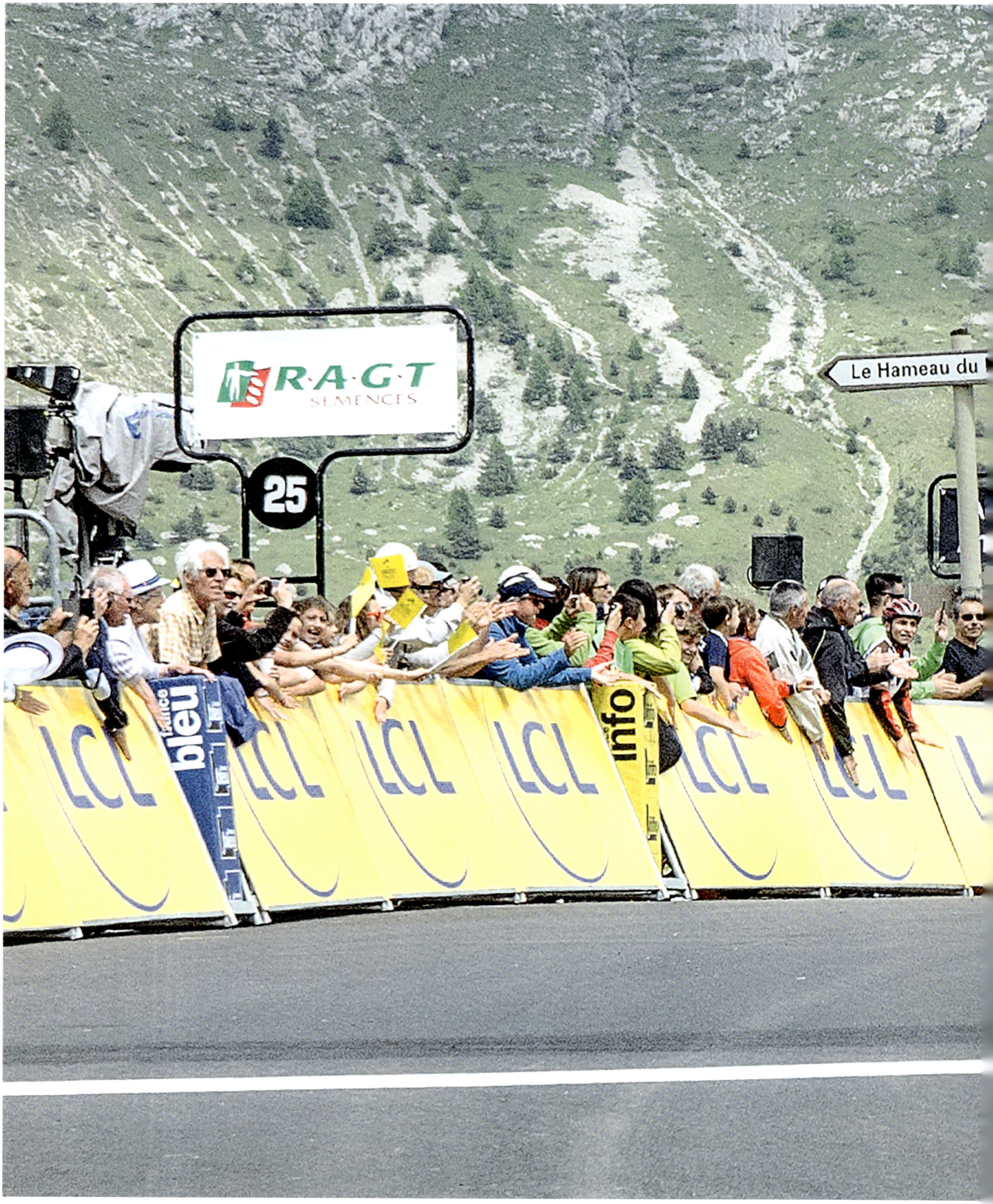
R·A·G·T
SEMENCES
25
Le Hameau du
bleu
info
LCL
LCL
LCL
LCL
LCL
LCL

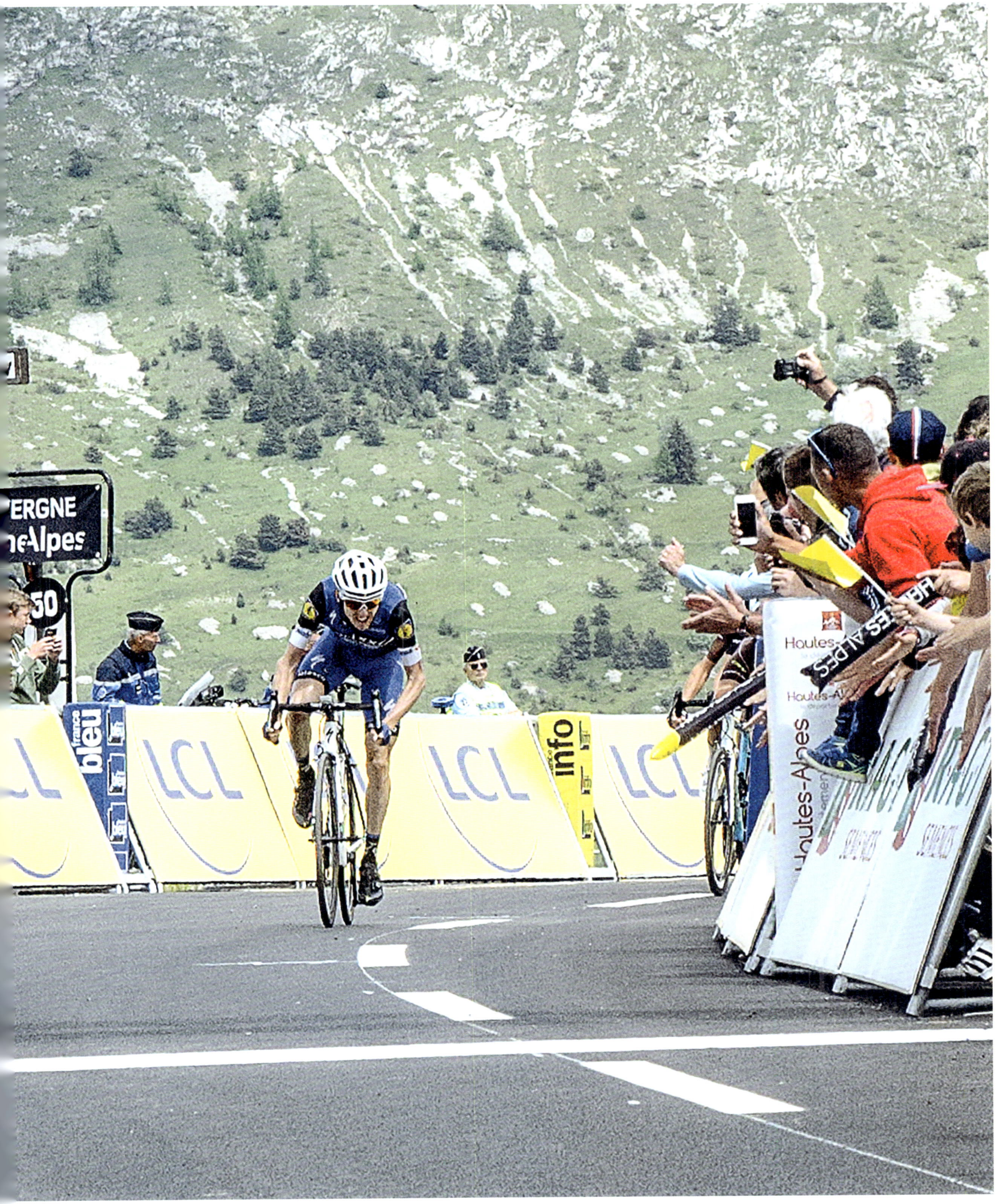

Der Etappenzweite Daniel Martin (Etixx – Quick Step) 25 Meter vor dem Ziel der 7. Etappe in Superdévoluy. **The stage-second Daniel Martin (Etixx – Quick Step) 25 metres before the finish line of the 7th stage in Superdévoluy.** *Daniel Martin (Etixx – Quick Step), deuxième de la 7e étape, 25 mètres avant l'arrivée à Superdévoluy.*

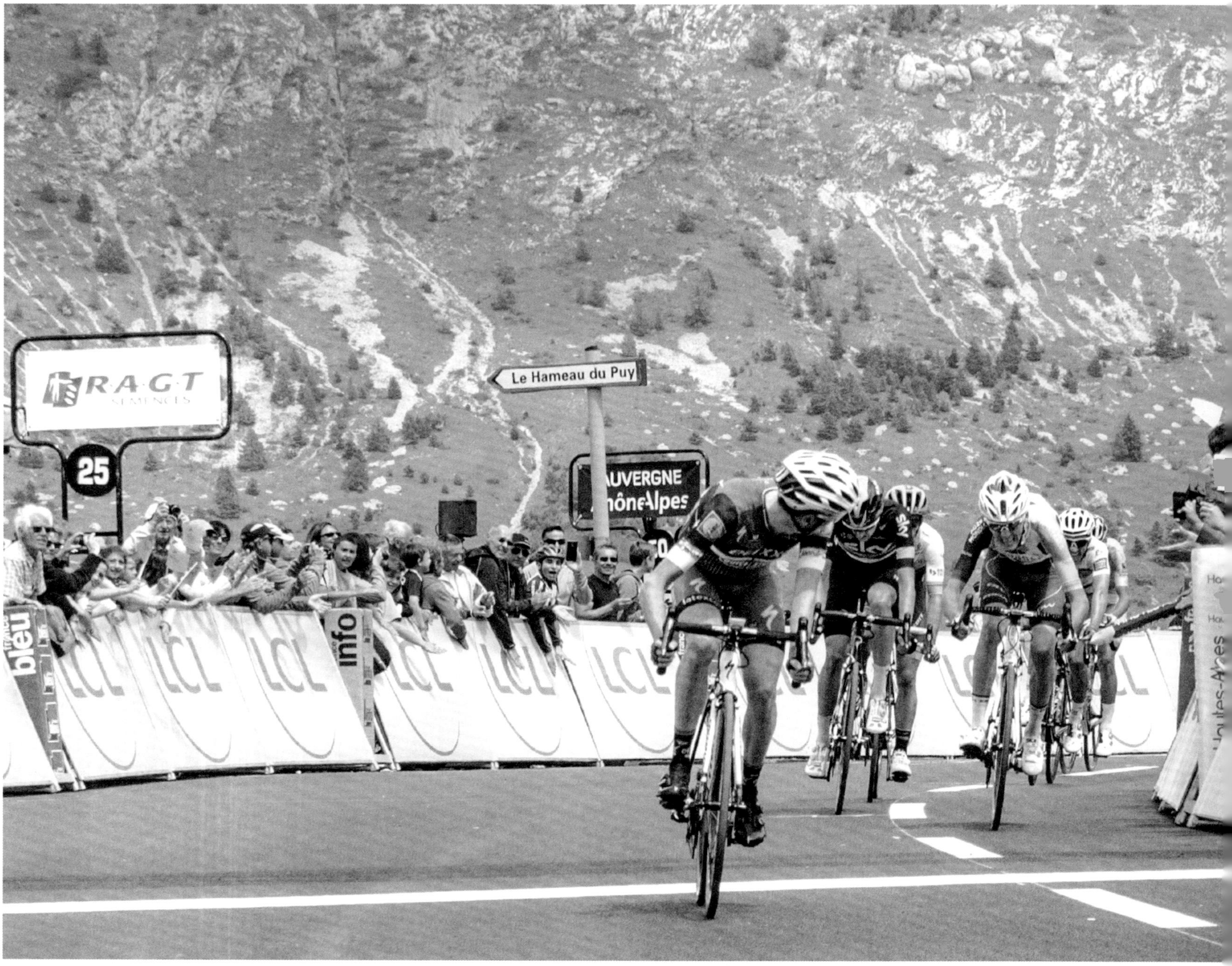
R·A·G·T
SEMENCES
25
Le Hameau du Puy
AUVERGNE
RhôneAlpes
bleu
info
LCL

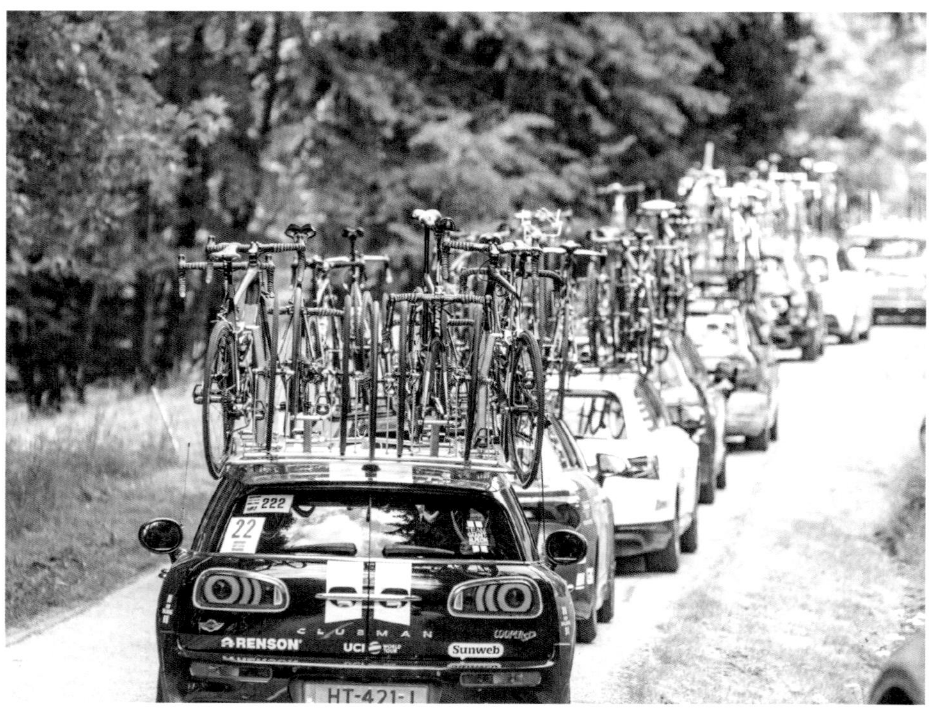
222
22
RENSON
UCI
Sunweb
HT-421-L

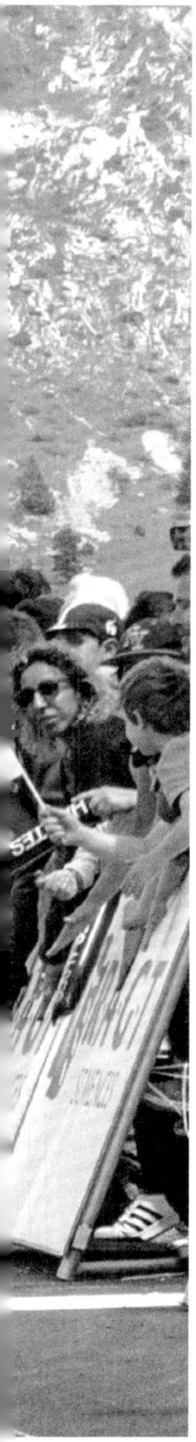

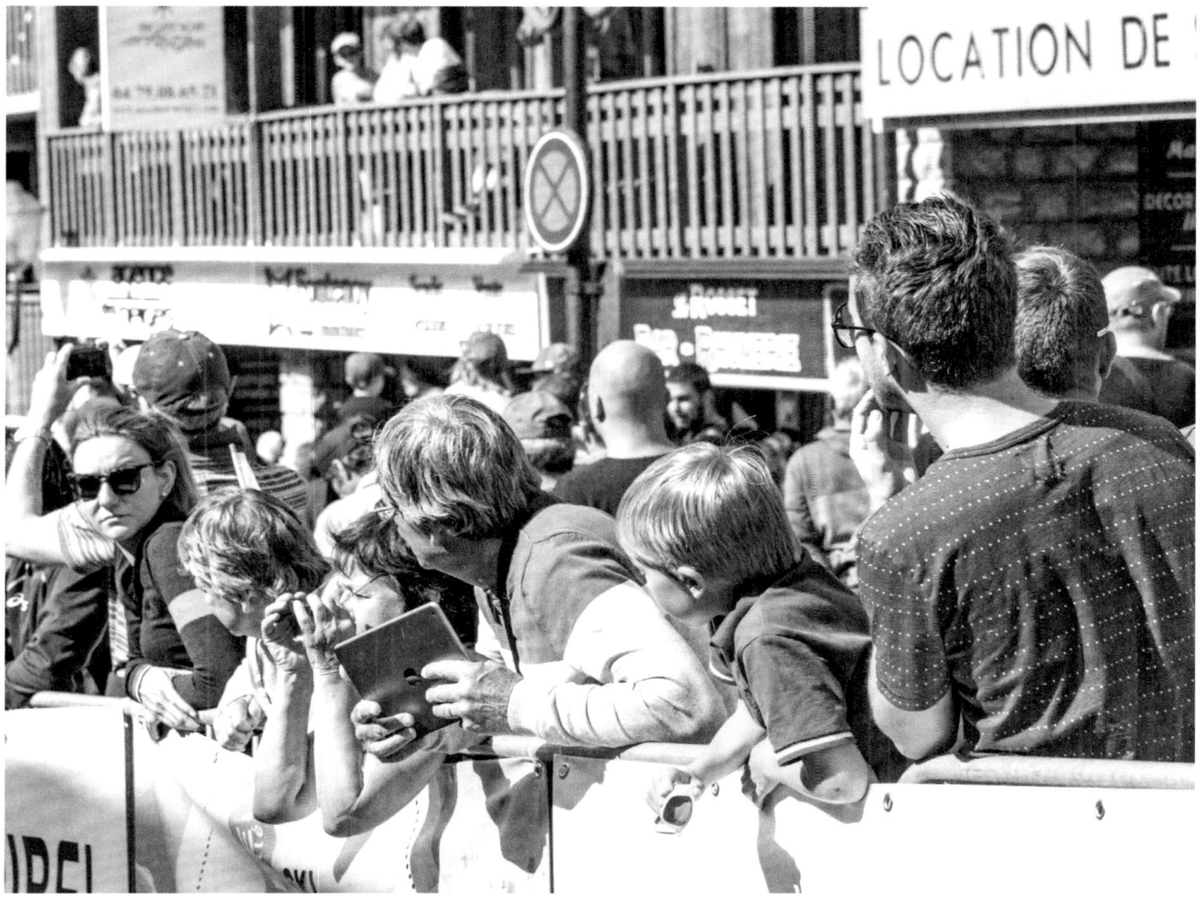

↖ Daniel Martin (Etixx – Quick Step) im Ziel gefolgt von Romain Bardet (FDJ) und Wout Poels (Team Sky). **Daniel Martin (Etixx – Quick Step) crosses the finish line trailed by Romain Bardet (FDJ) and Wout Poels (Team Sky).** *Daniel Martin (Etixx – Quick Step) à l'arrivée, suivi de près par Romain Bardet (FDJ) et Wout Poels (Team Sky).*

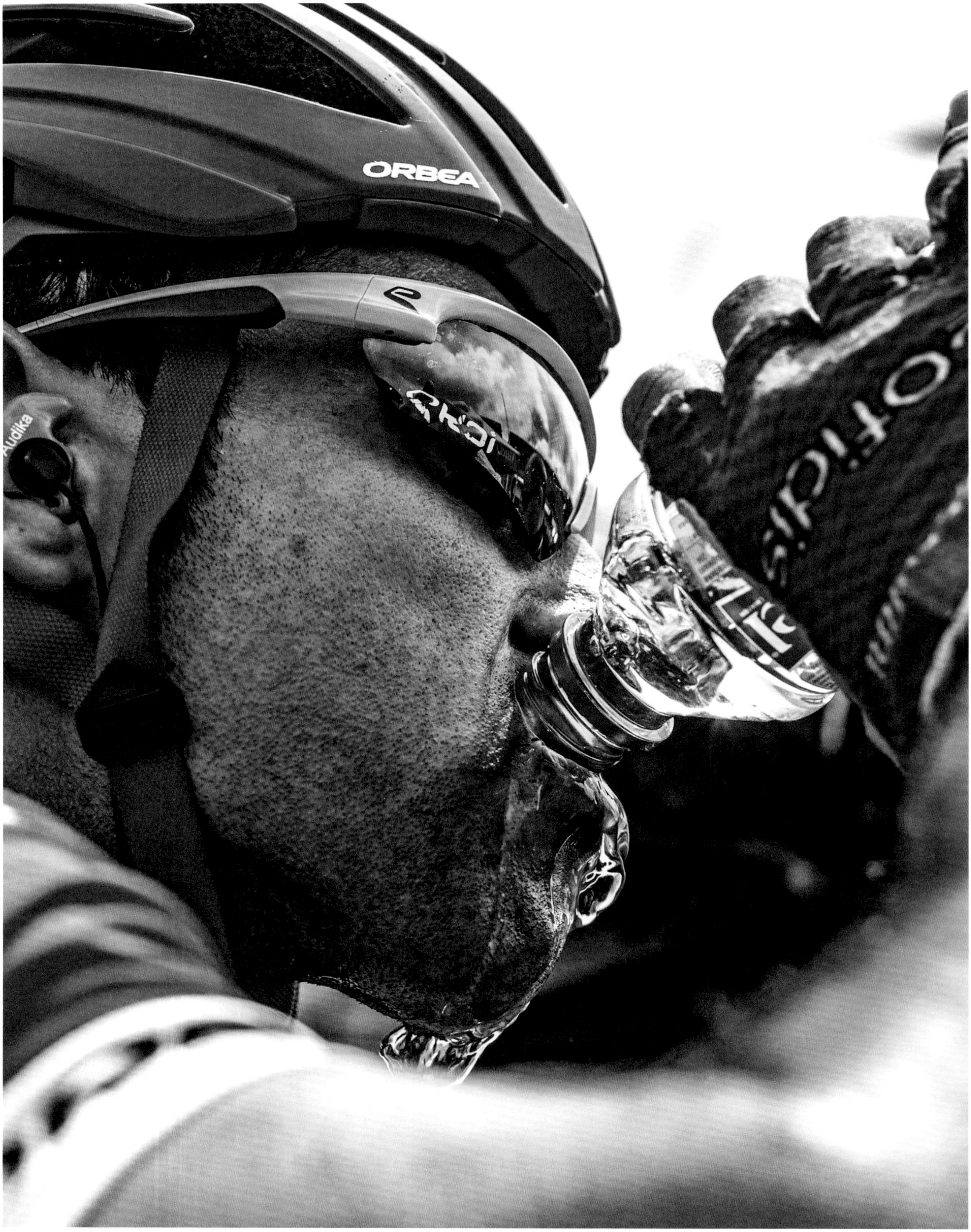

6. Etappe. **6th stage.** *6e étape.*

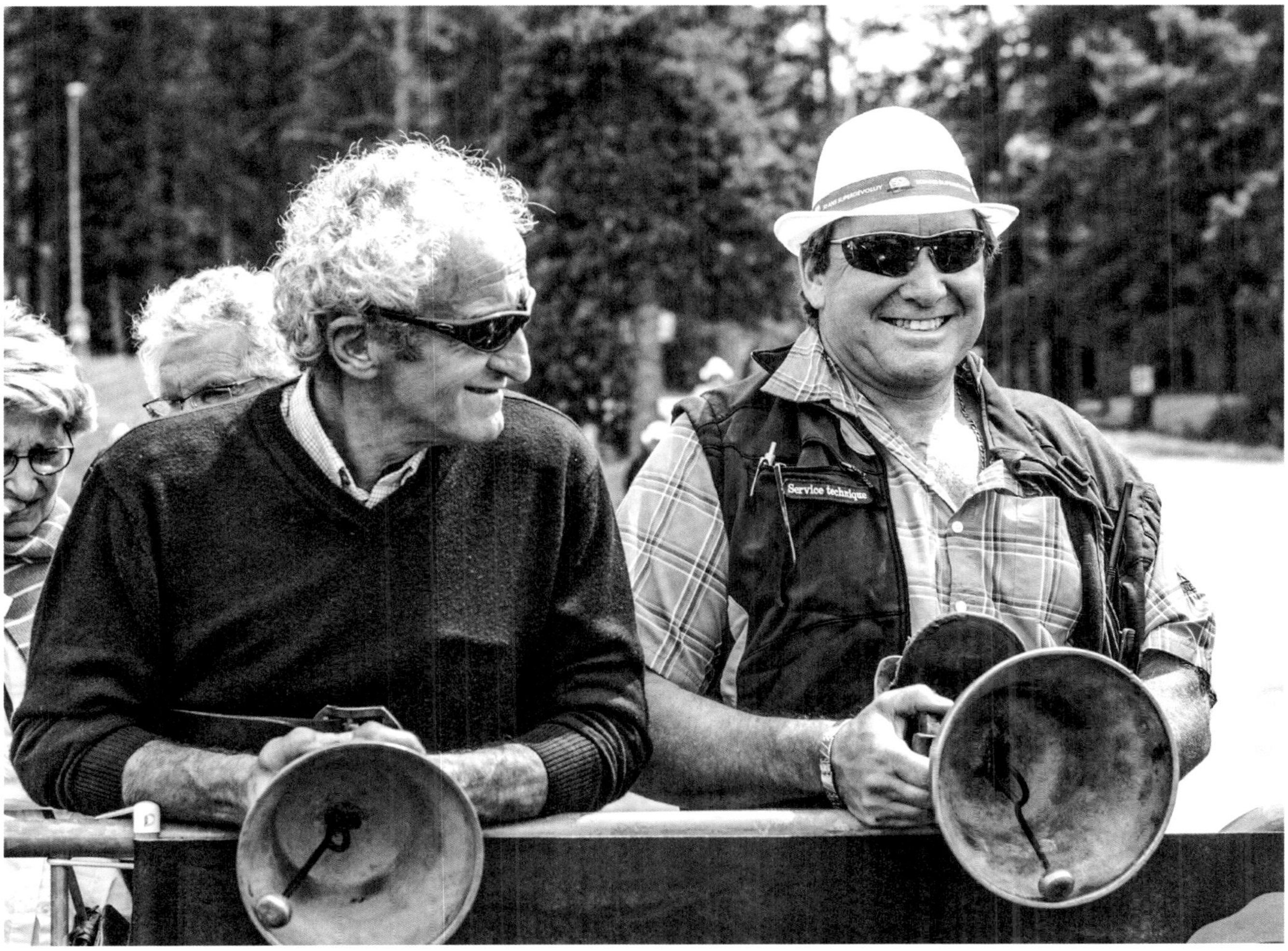
Service technique

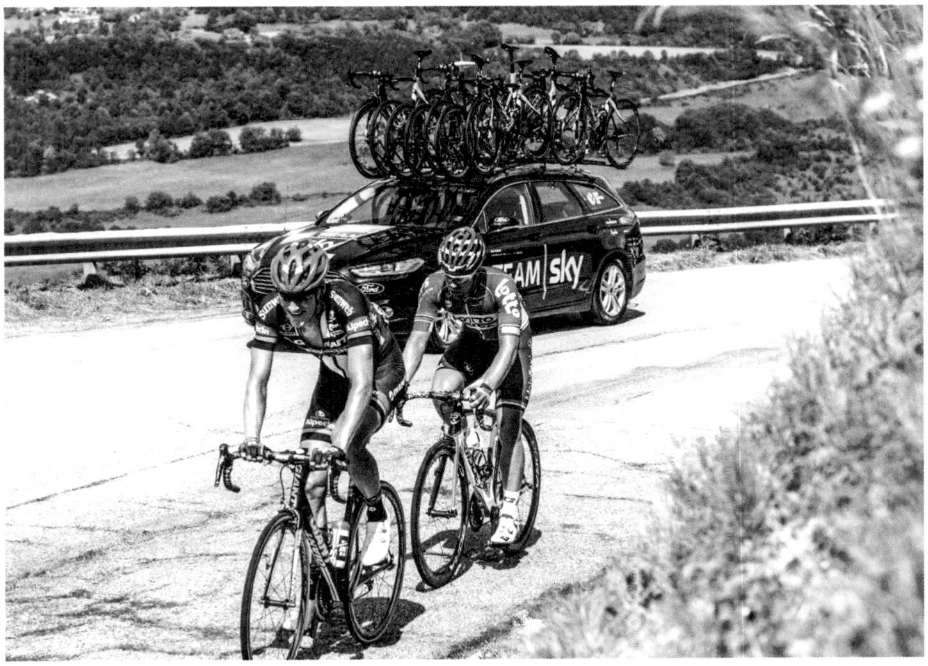
TEAM sky

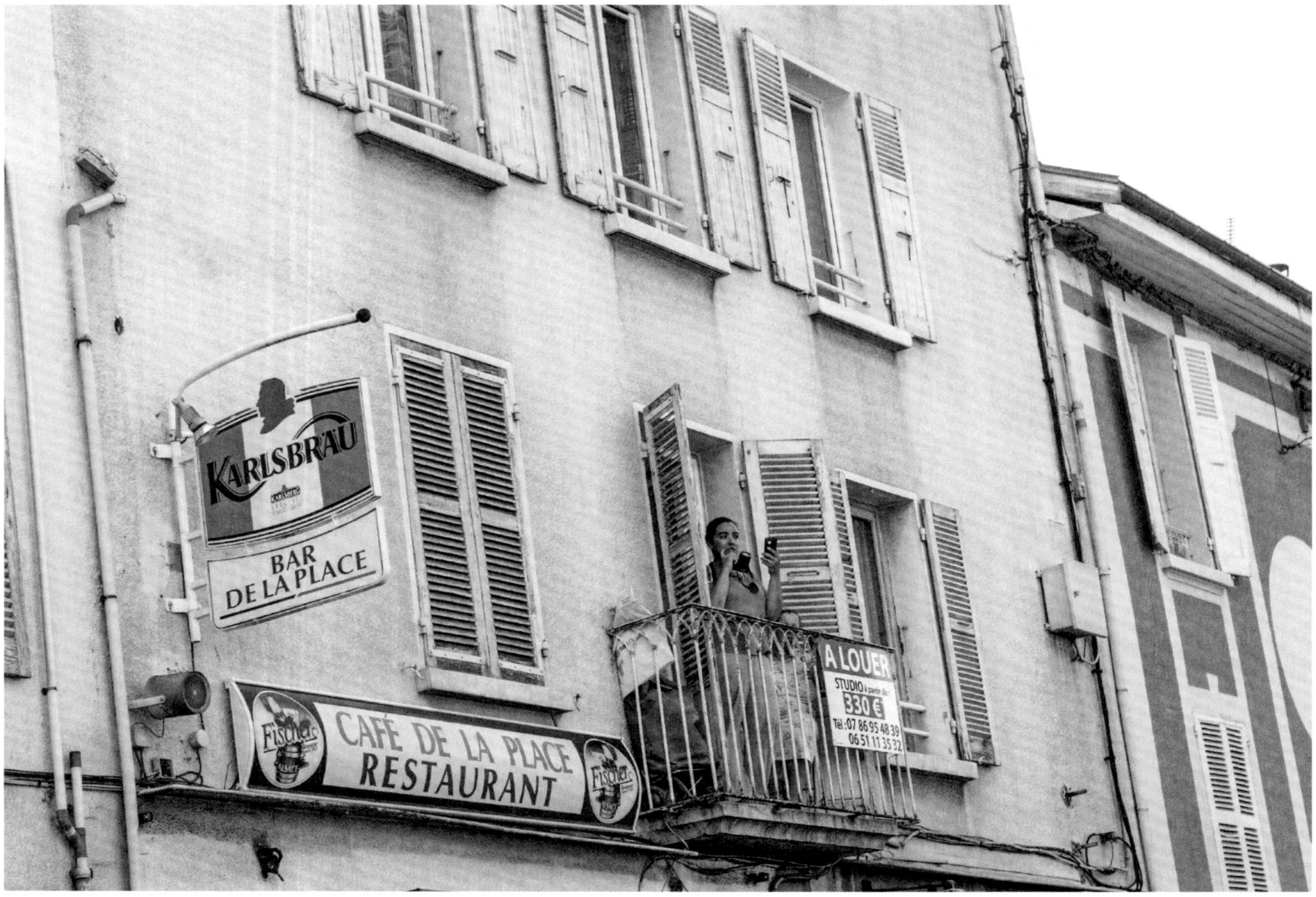
KARLSBRÄU
BAR DE LA PLACE
CAFÉ DE LA PLACE
RESTAURANT
A LOUER
330 €

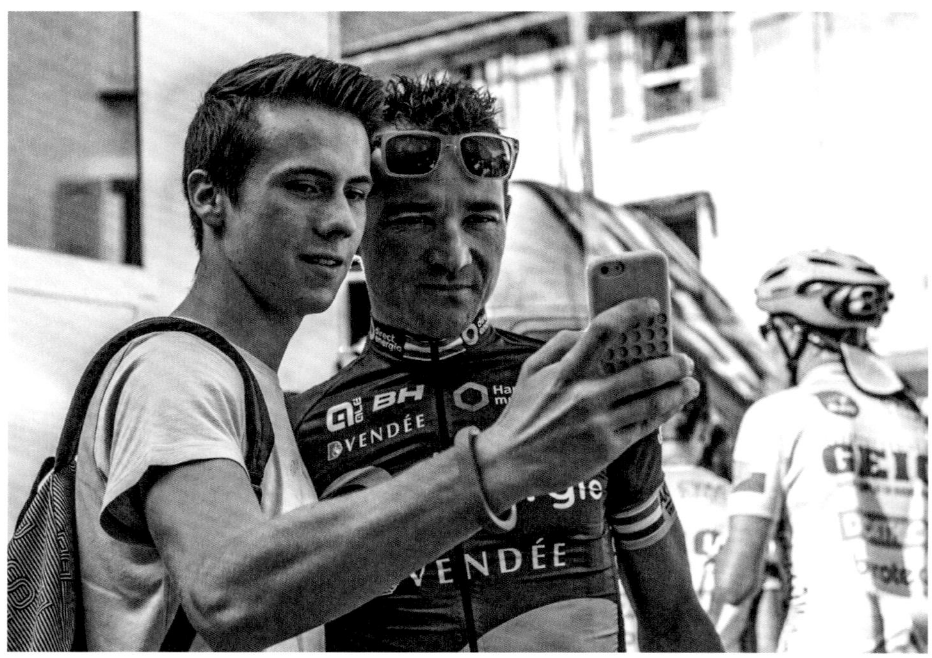
BH
VENDÉE
VENDÉE

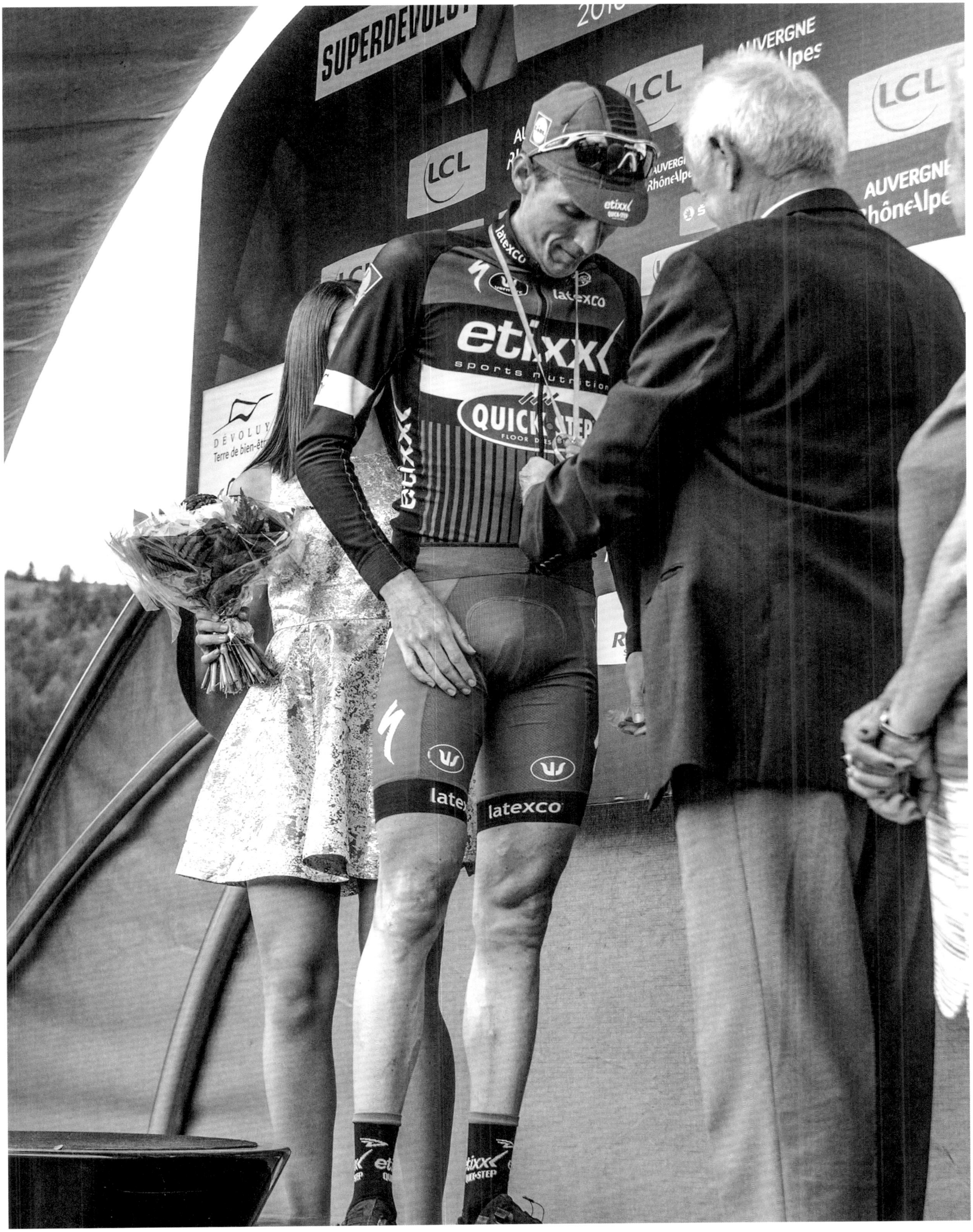

← Selfie mit seinen Fans: Thomas Voeckler (Direct Énergie). **Selfie with his fans: Thomas Voeckler (Direct Énergie).** *Selfies avec ses fans : Thomas Voeckler (Direct Énergie).*

↑ Daniel Martin (Etixx – Quick Step) auf dem Podium der 7. Etappe. **Daniel Martin (Etixx – Quick Step) on the podium of the 7th stage.** *Daniel Martin (Etixx – Quick Step) sur le podium de la 7e étape.*

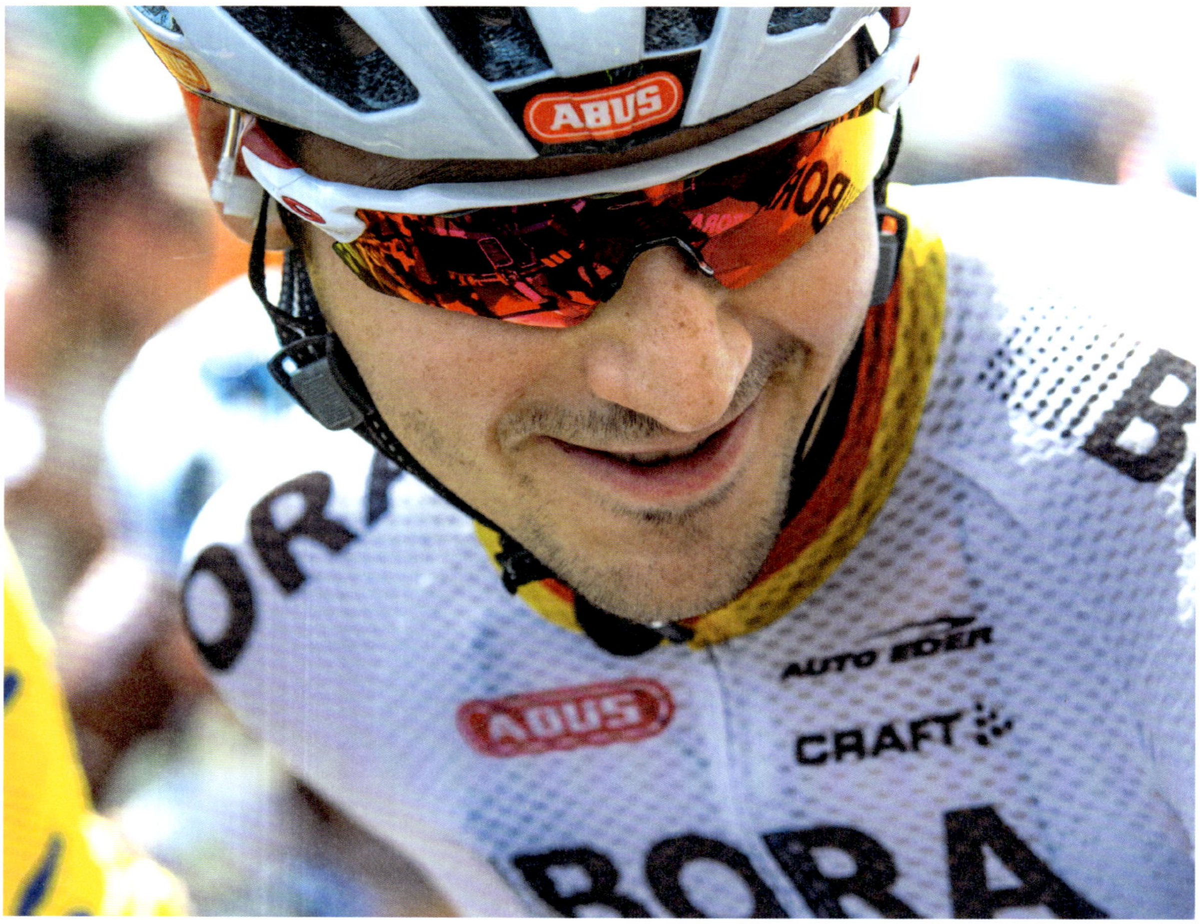

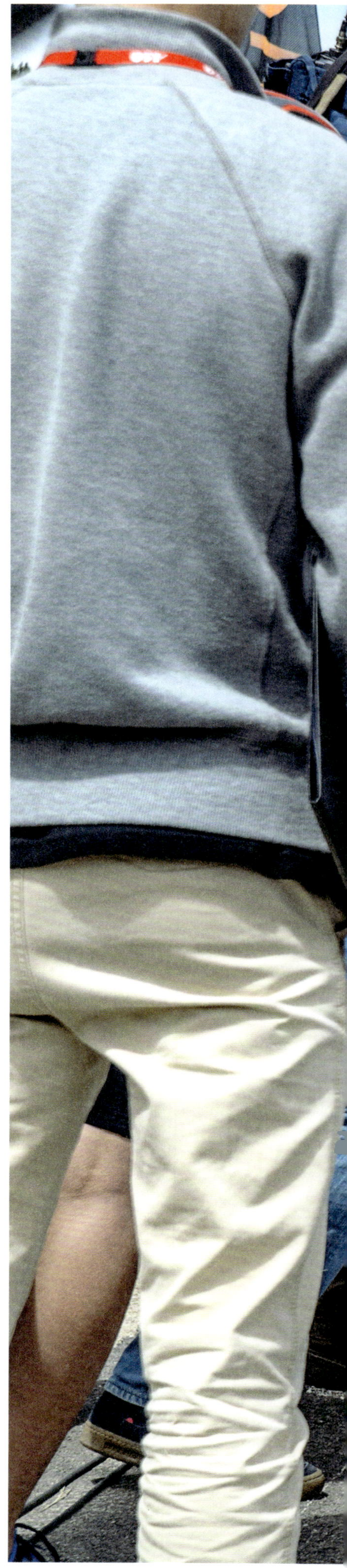

↑ Emanuel Buchmann im Trikot des Deutschen Meisters (BORA - ARGON 18). **Emanuel Buchmann in the German National Road Race Champion jersey (BORA - ARGON 18).** *Emanuel Buchmann avec le maillot de champion d'Allemagne (BORA - ARGON 18).*

→ Julian Alaphilippe (Etixx – Quick Step) im Interview. **Julian Alaphilippe (Etixx – Quick Step) in an interview.** *Julian Alaphilippe (Etixx – Quick Step) en pleine interview.*

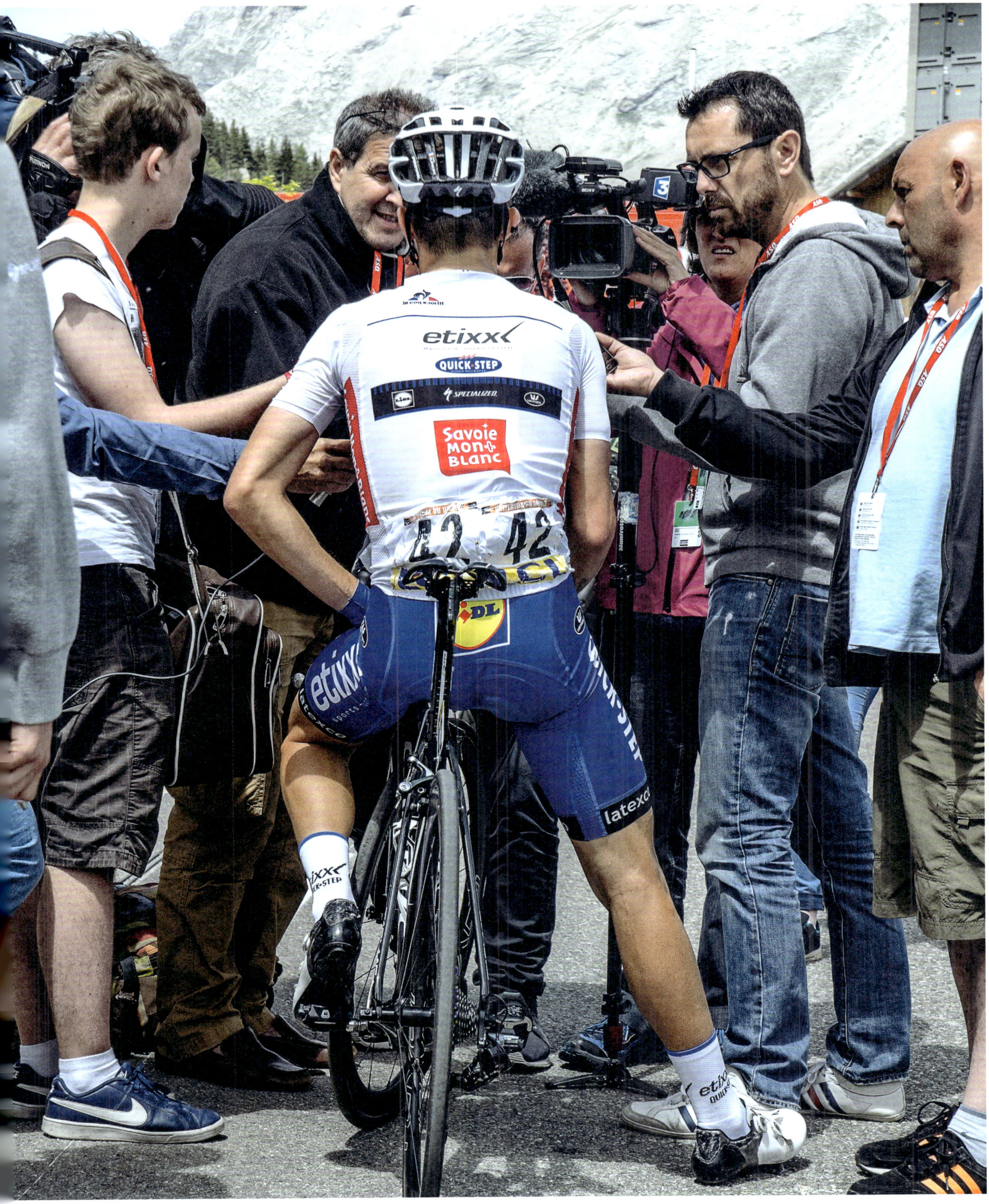
etixx
QUICK-STEP
Savoie
Mont
Blanc
42
latexco

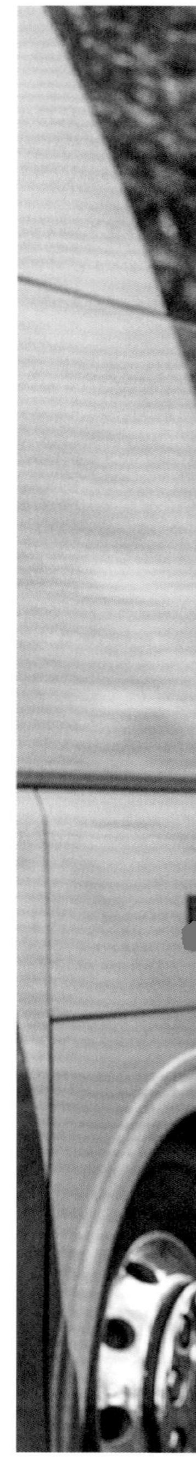

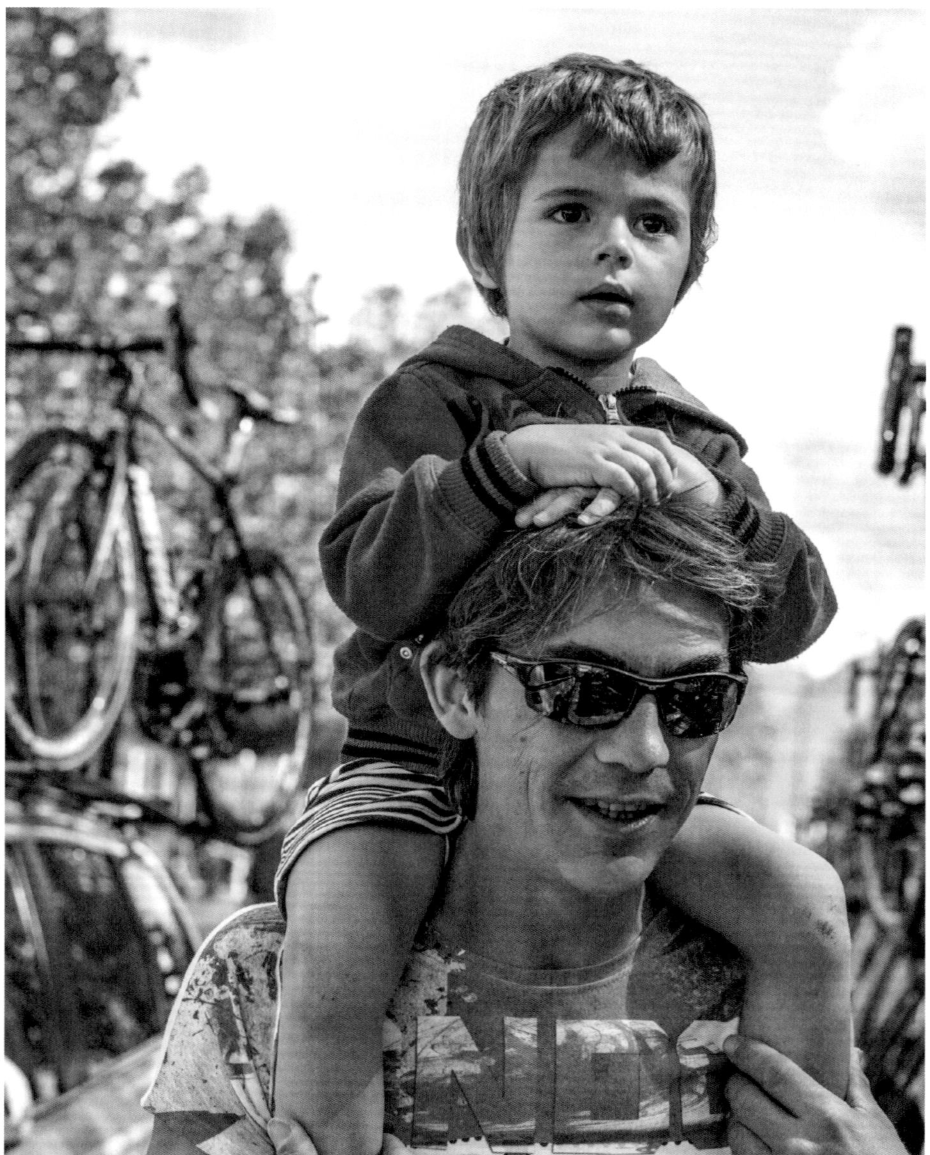

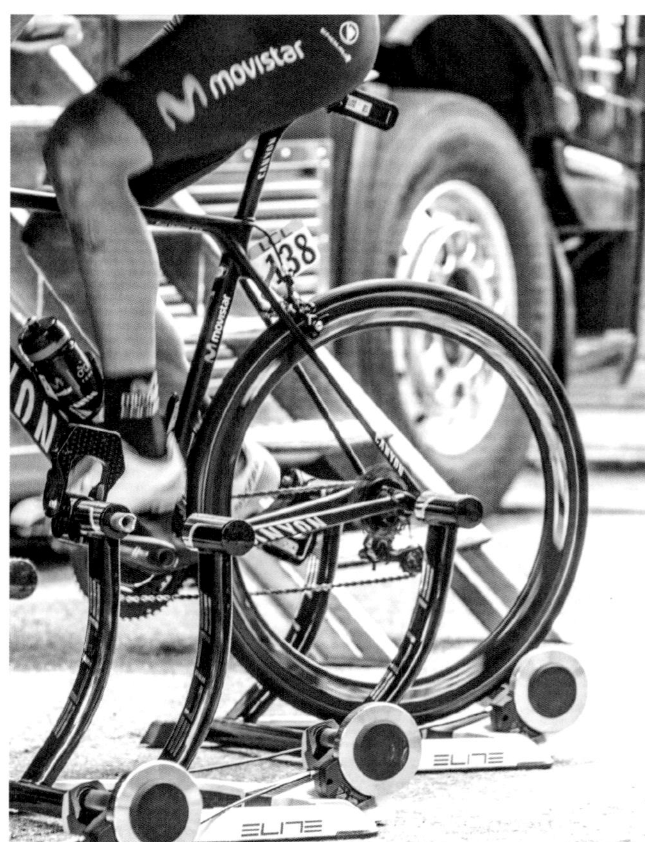
movistar

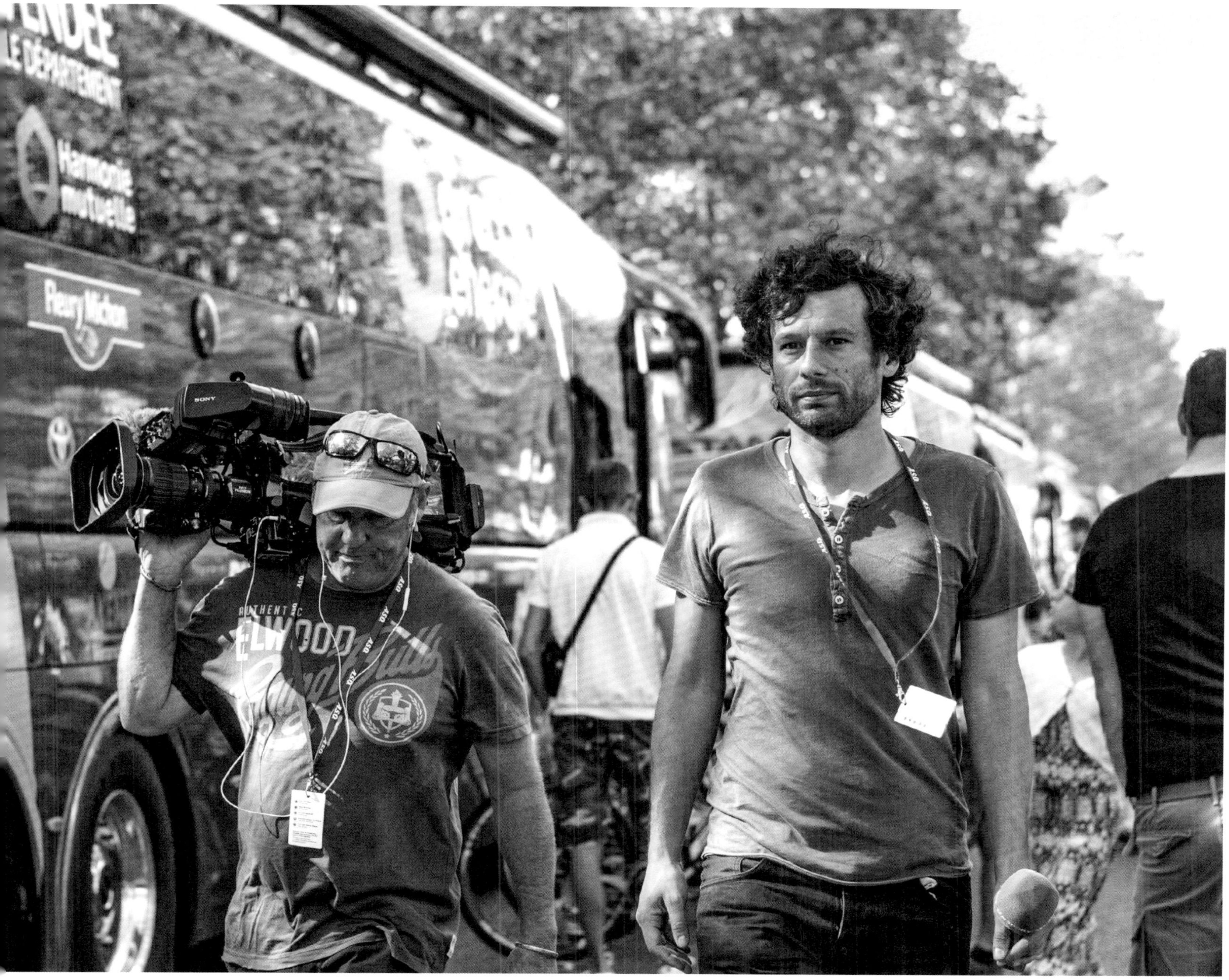

Impressionen rund ums Rennen. **Impressions of the race.** *Impressions sur la course.*

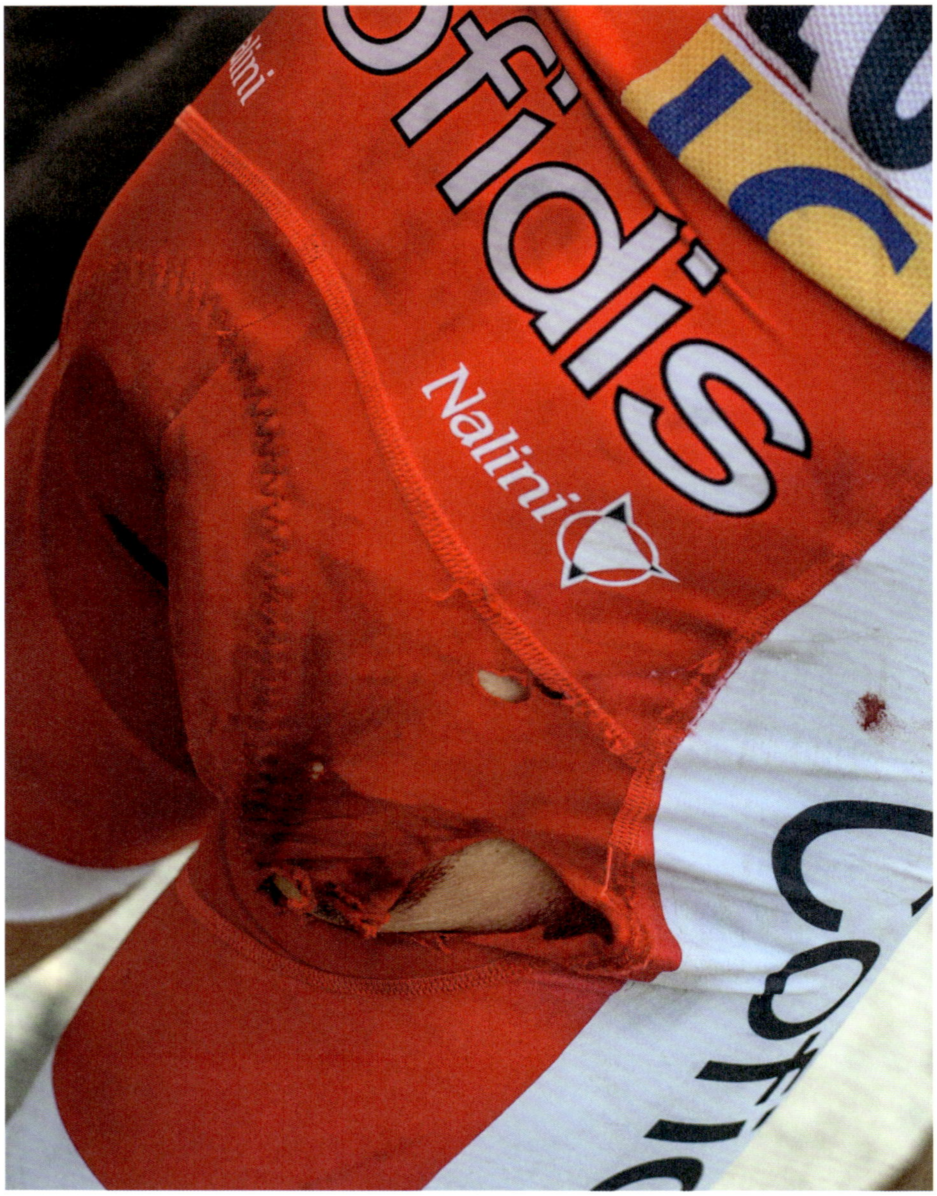

↑ Hart im Nehmen. **Tough.** *Pas question de se laisser abattre.*
→ Internationaler und teamübergreifender Radsport: Shane Archbold (BORA - ARGON 18) mit einem IAM-Fan. **International and cross-team cycling: Shane Archbold (BORA - ARGON 18) with an IAM fan.** *Le cyclisme, un sport international et inter-équipes : Shane Archbold (BORA - ARGON 18) avec un fan d'IAM.*

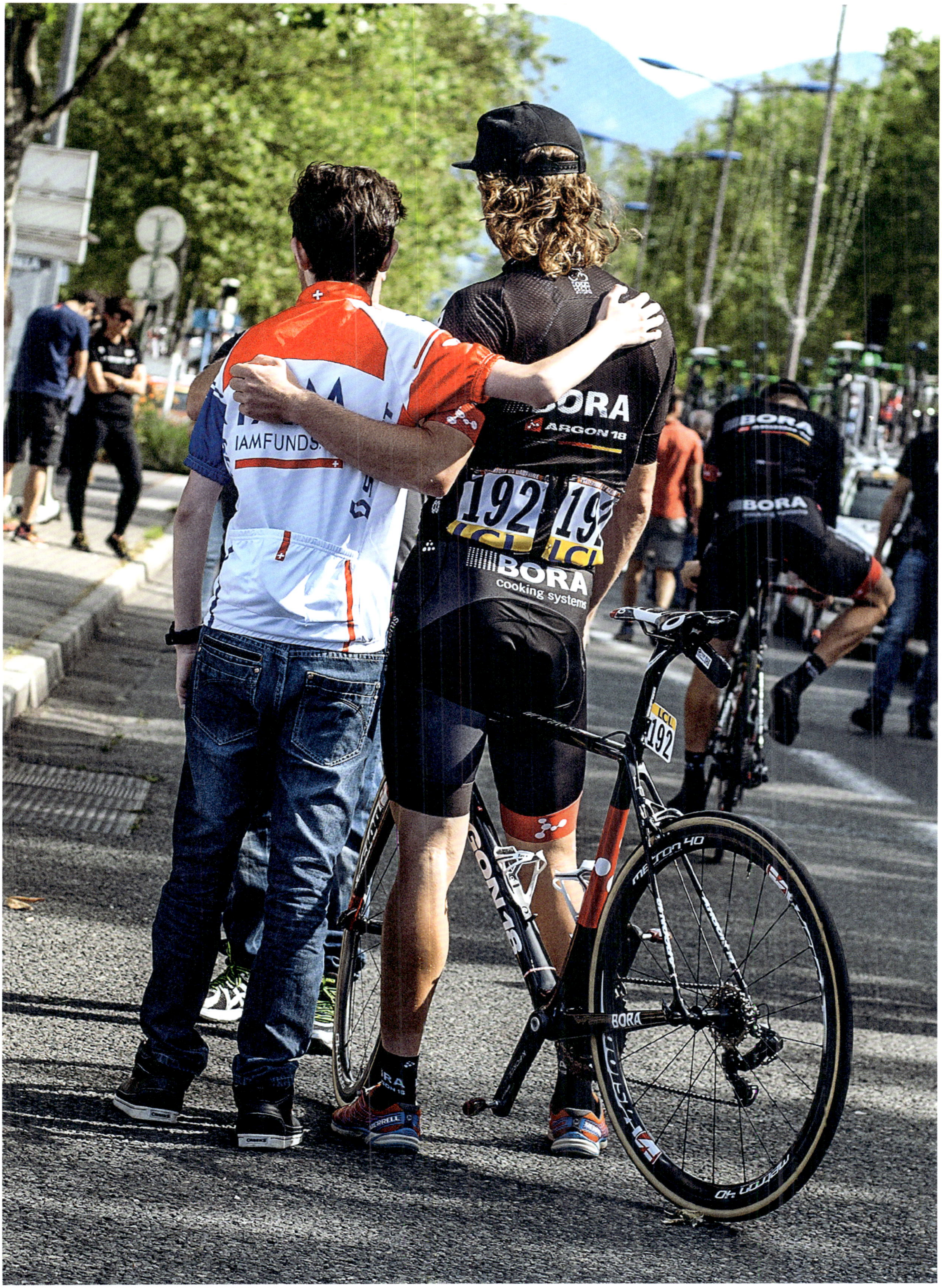
IAMFUNDS
BORA
ARGON 18
192
BORA
cooking systems
BORA
BORA

Tour de France

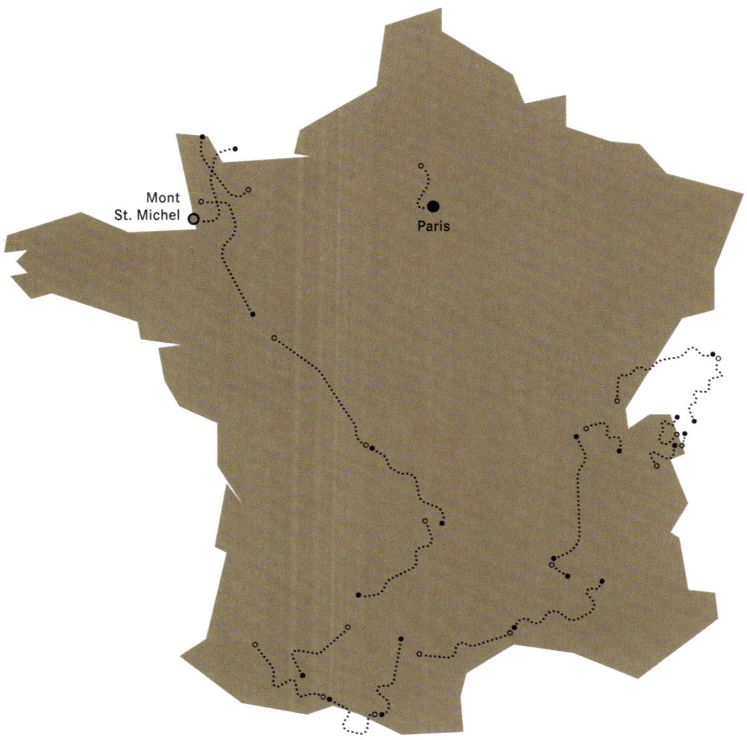

3,535

KILOMETRE

DATE: 2.-24.07.2016

FIRST TOUR: 1903

DURATION: 89:04:48

ALTIMETRE: 47,850 m

39.682

KM/H AVG. SPEED WINNER

„La Grande Boucle“, die Große Schleife durch Frankreich ist eine der drei Grand Tours und das größte jährliche Sportereignis der Welt, das seit 1975 traditionell auf den Champs-Élysées in Paris endet. **'La Grande Boucle', the great loop through France is one of the three Grand Tours and the world's biggest annual sporting event. Since 1975, it has traditionally ended on the Champs-Élysées in Paris.** *La Grande Boucle, à travers la France, est l'un des trois grands Tours et le plus grand événement sportif annuel du monde. Depuis 1975, il se termine traditionnellement sur les Champs-Élysées à Paris.*

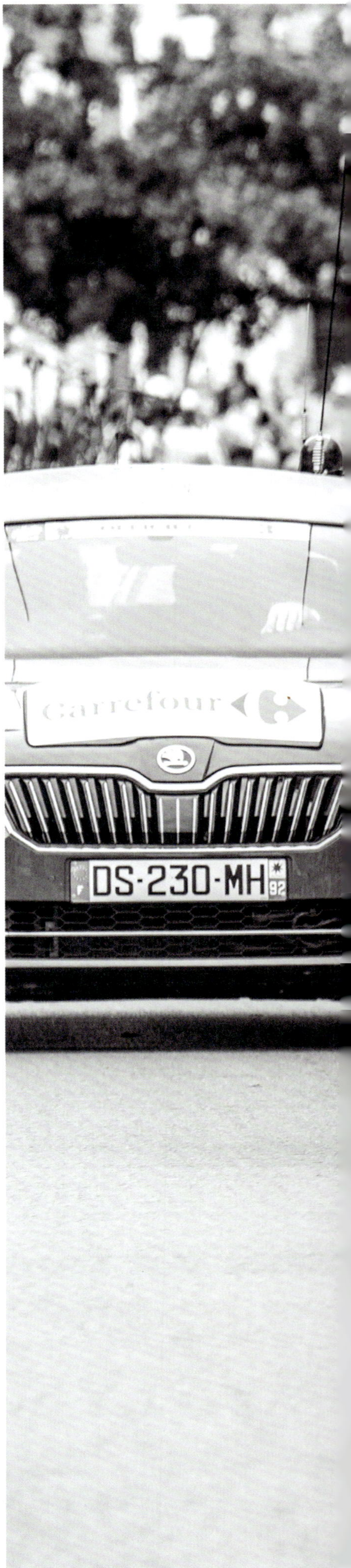

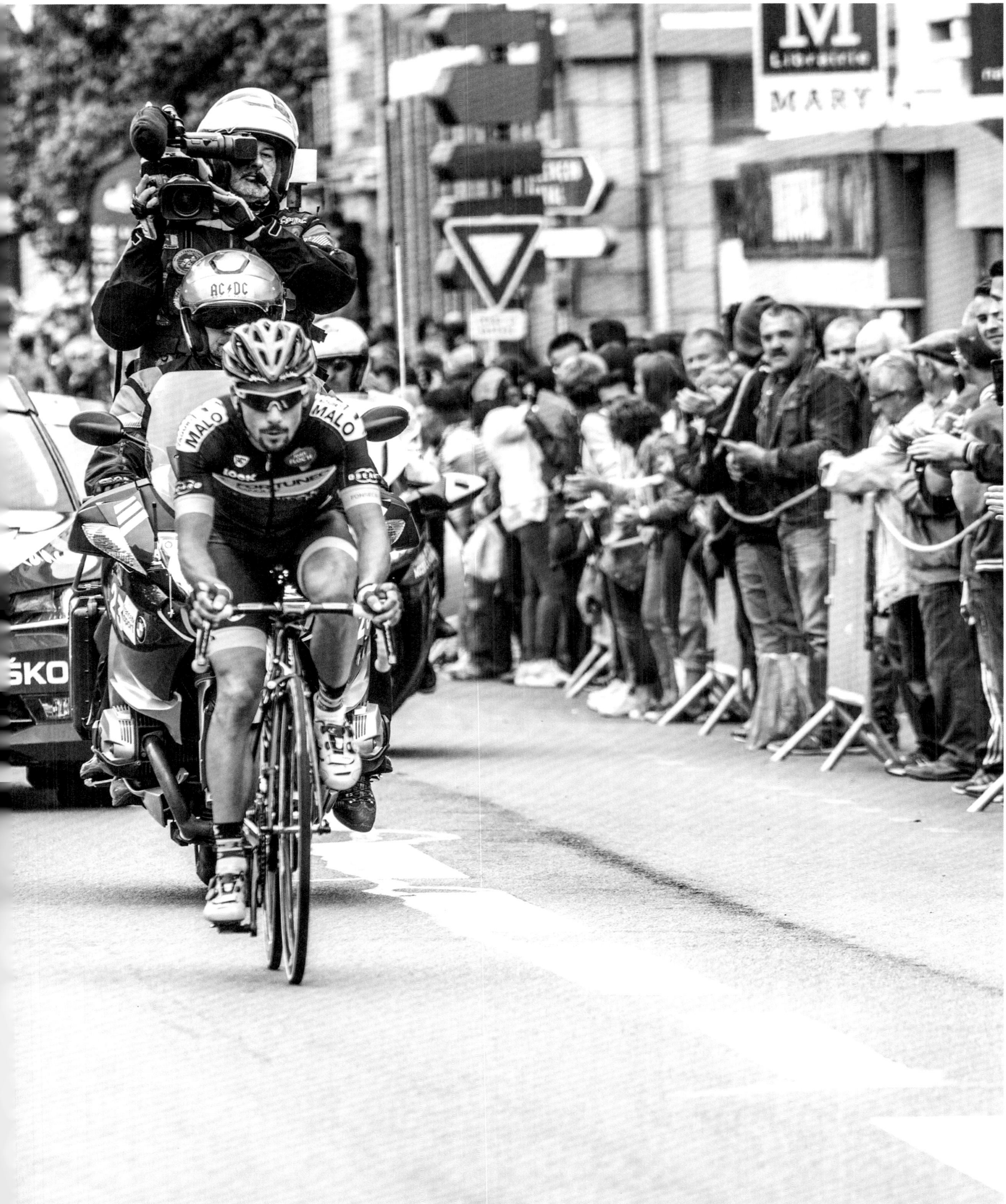

Armindo Fonseca (Fortuneo-Vital Concept) bestreitet die 3. Etappe ab dem Start in Granville im Alleingang und wird erst 8 km vor dem Ziel vom Peloton eingefangen. **Armindo Fonseca (Fortuneo-Vital Concept) made his impression on the 3rd stage with a solo ride from the start in Granville and was only caught by the peloton 8 km before the finish.** *Armindo Fonseca (Fortuneo-Vital Concept) attaque en solitaire dès le départ de la 3e étape, à Granville. Il est rattrapé par le peloton à 8 km de l'arrivée.*

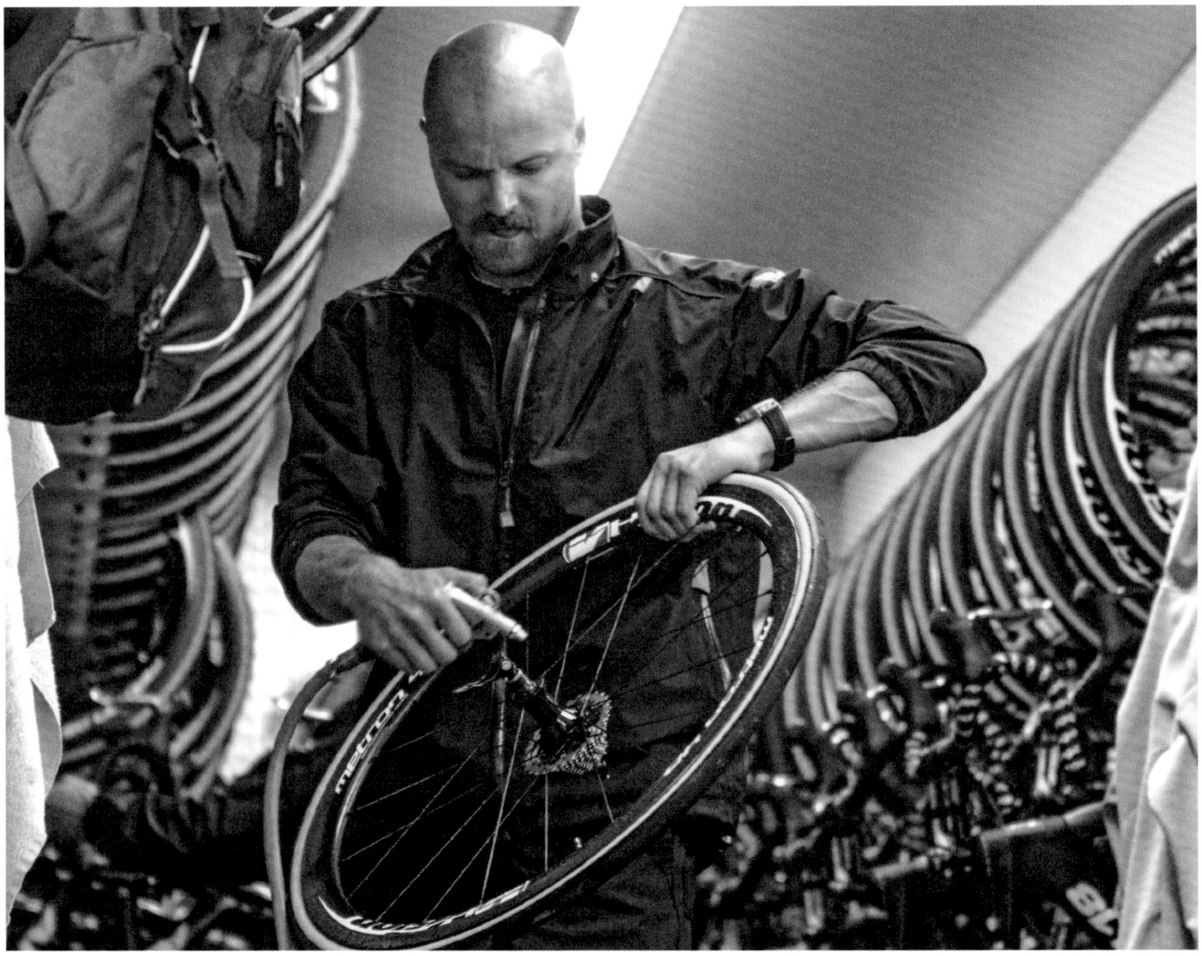

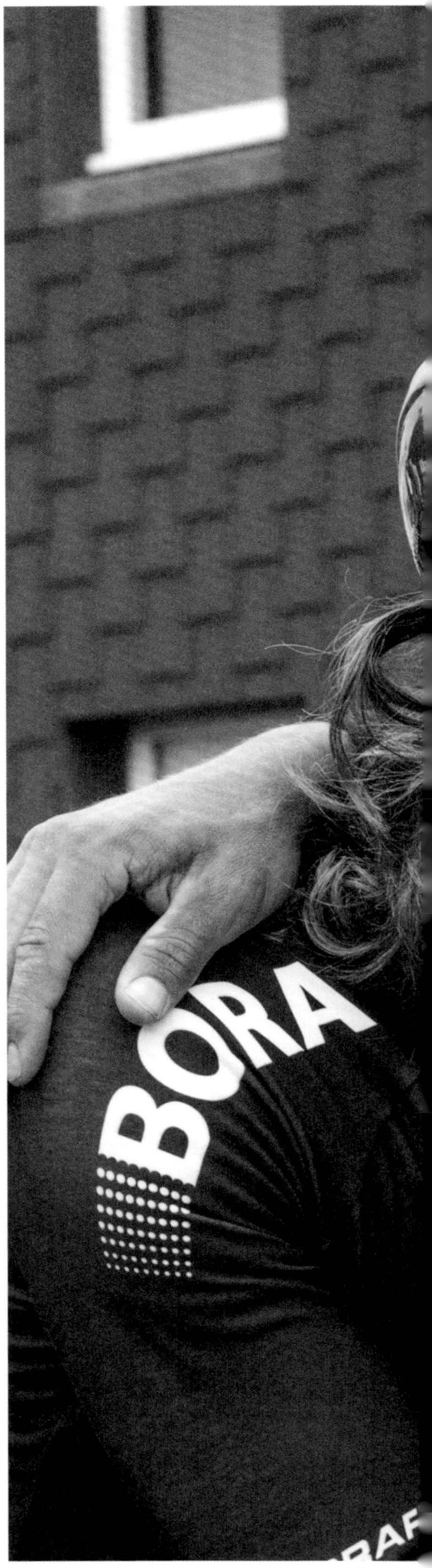
BORA

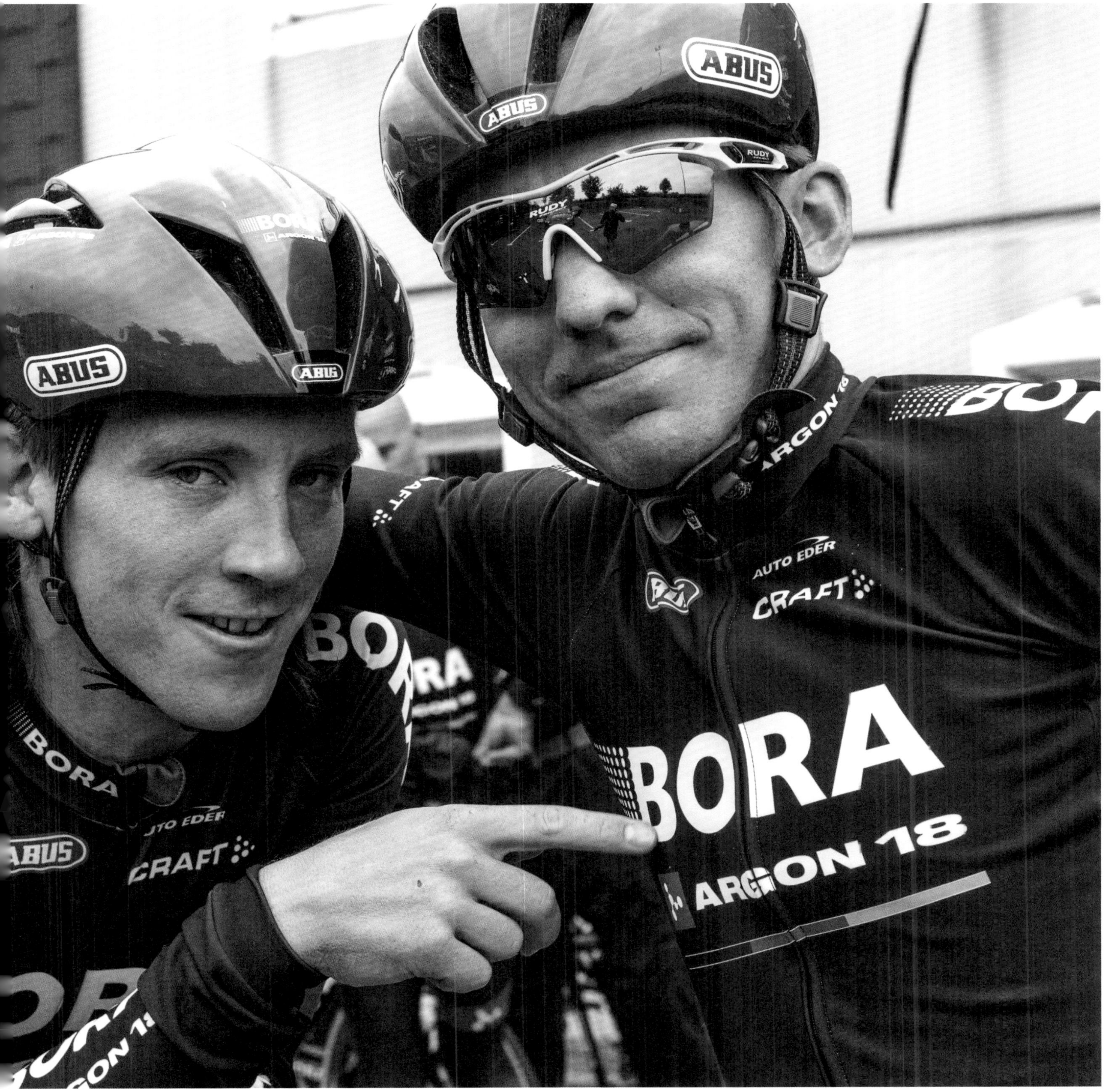

← Risto Usin (Chef-Mechaniker BORA - ARGON 18) hat alles im Griff. **Risto Usin (head mechanic BORA - ARGON 18) has everything under control.** *Risto Usin (mécanicien de l'équipe BORA - ARGON 18) en action.*

↑ Teamkollegen und Freunde: Shane Archbold und Cesare Benedetti (BORA - ARGON 18). **Teammates and friends: Shane Archbold and Cesare Benedetti (BORA - ARGON 18).** *Coéquipiers et amis : Shane Archbold et Cesare Benedetti (BORA - ARGON 18).*

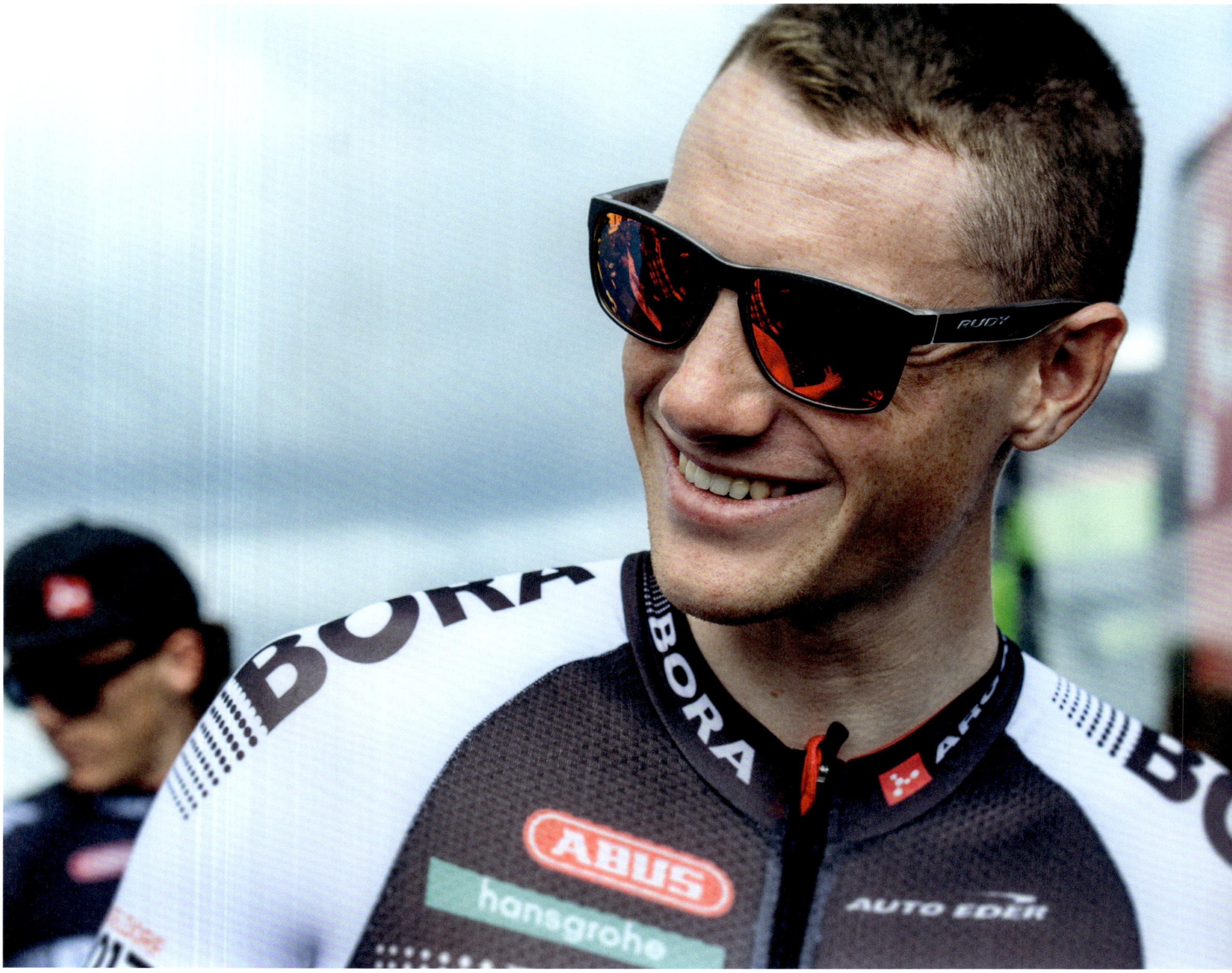

↑ Sam Bennett (BORA - ARGON 18). **Sam Bennett (BORA - ARGON 18).** *Sam Bennett (BORA - ARGON 18).*

↗ Teamköchin und Ernährungsexpertin Jeaun-Mari Breytenbach (BORA - ARGON 18) verpflegt die Fahrer bestens im BORA Küchentruck.
Teamchef and nutristionist Jeaun-Mari Breytenbach (BORA - ARGON 18) inside the BORA kitchen truck taking good care of the riders.
Chef et diététicienne de l'équipe BORA - ARGON 18, Jeaun-Mari Breytenbach, en cuisinant pour les coureurs dans le truck de BORA.

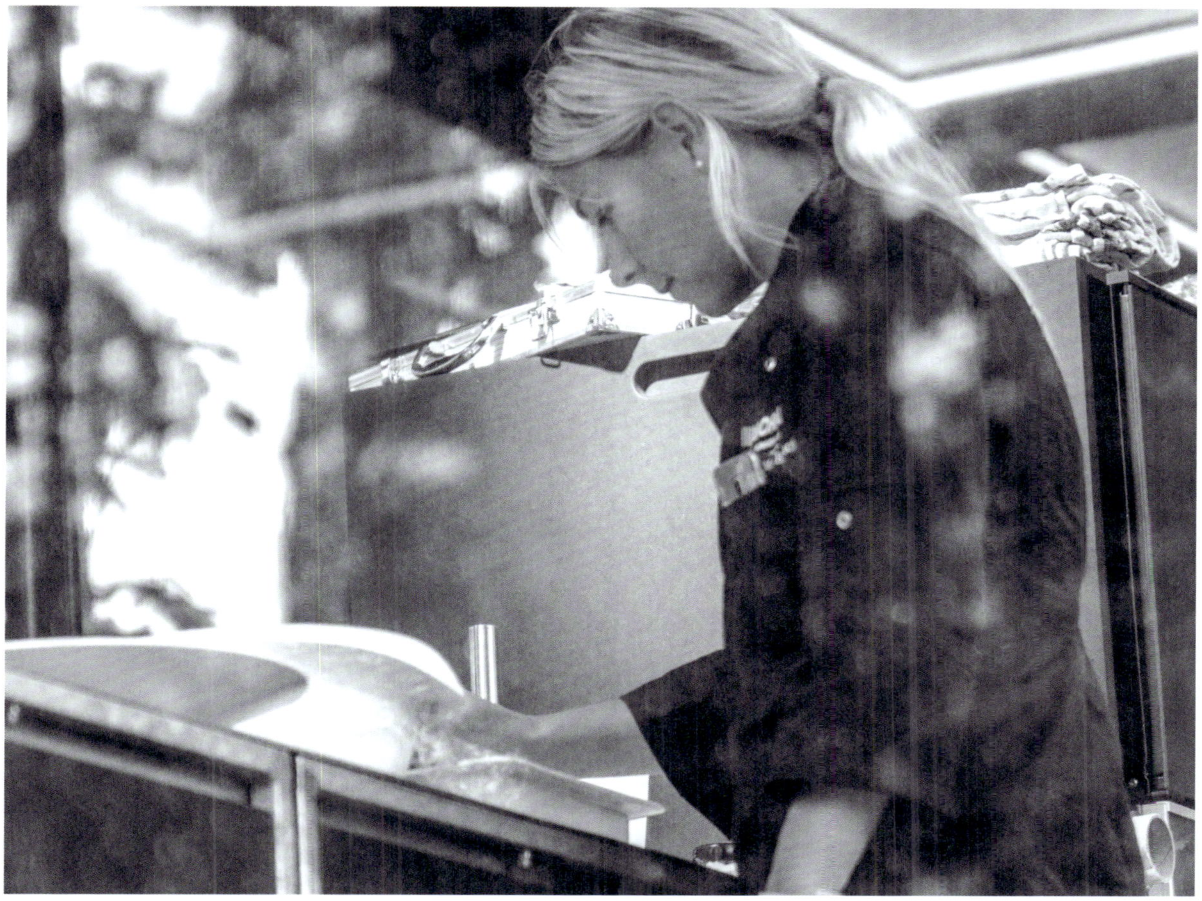

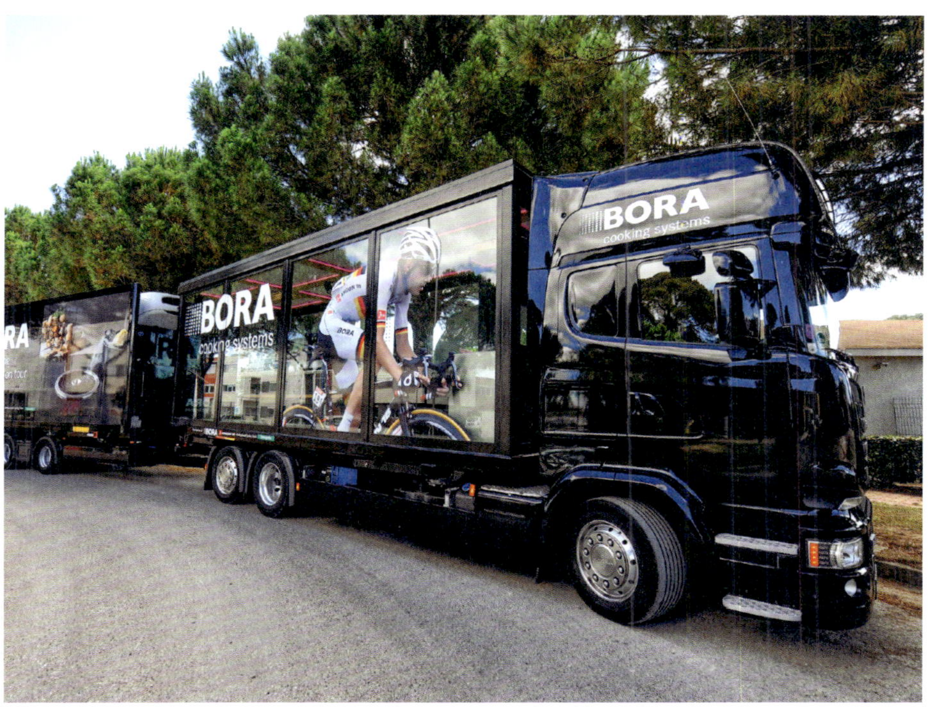
BORA
cooking systems
BORA
cooking systems

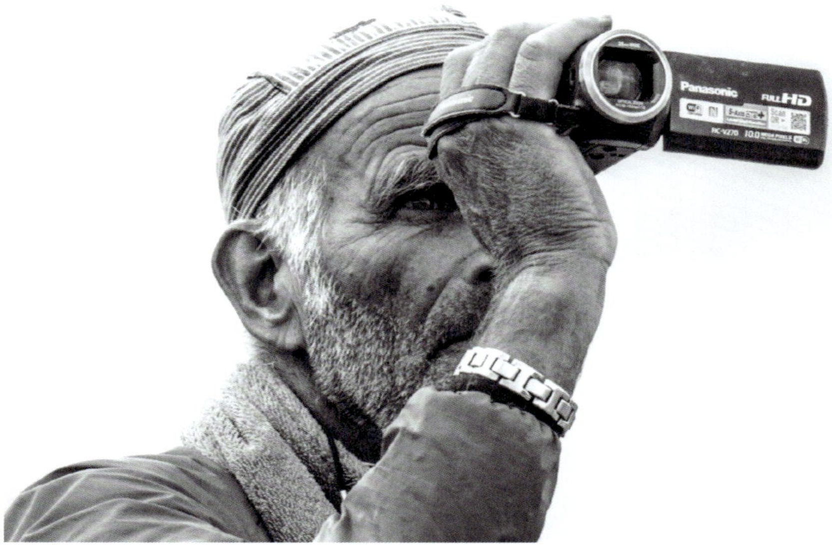

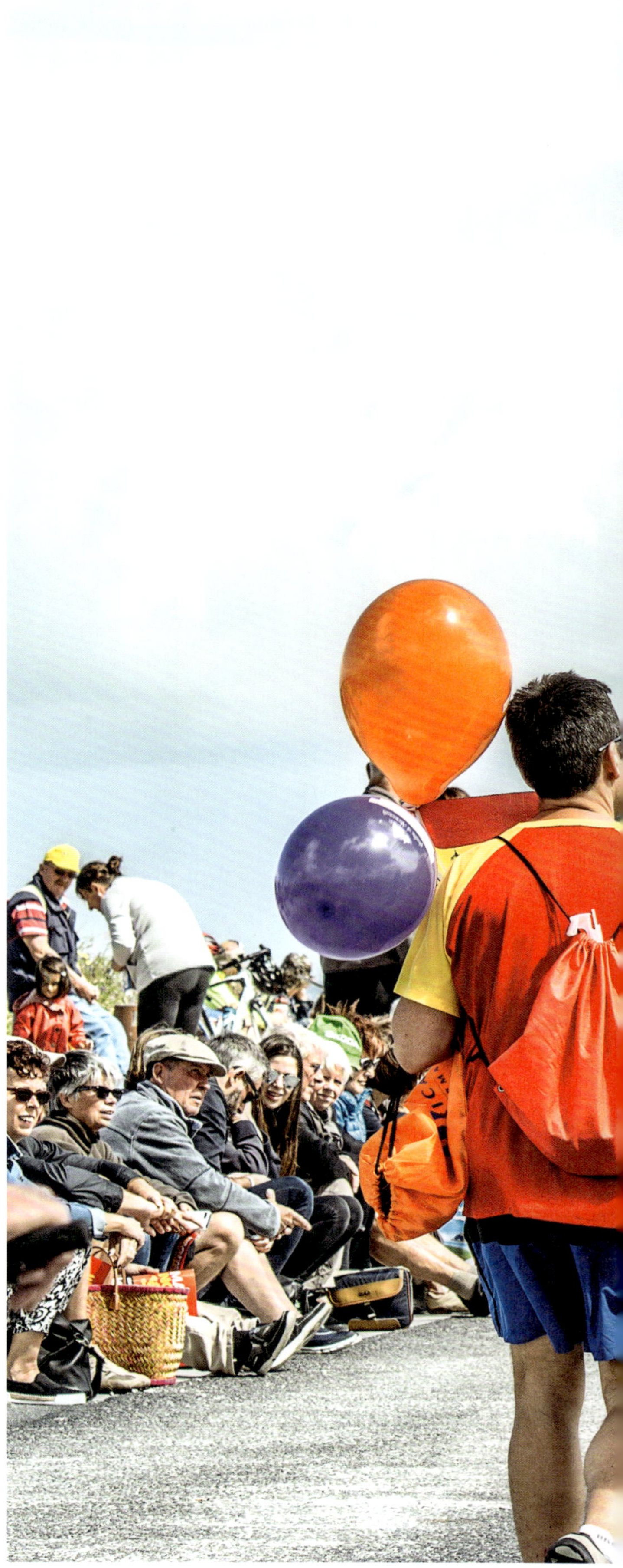

Fans pilgern zum außergewöhnlichen Startort der Tour de France 2016: Mont St. Michel in der Normandie. **Fans on their pilgrimage to the extraordinary starting point of the Tour de France 2016: Mont Saint-Michel in Normandy.** *Les spectateurs en pèlerinage au point de départ exceptionnel du Tour de France 2016 : le Mont-Saint-Michel, en Normandie.*

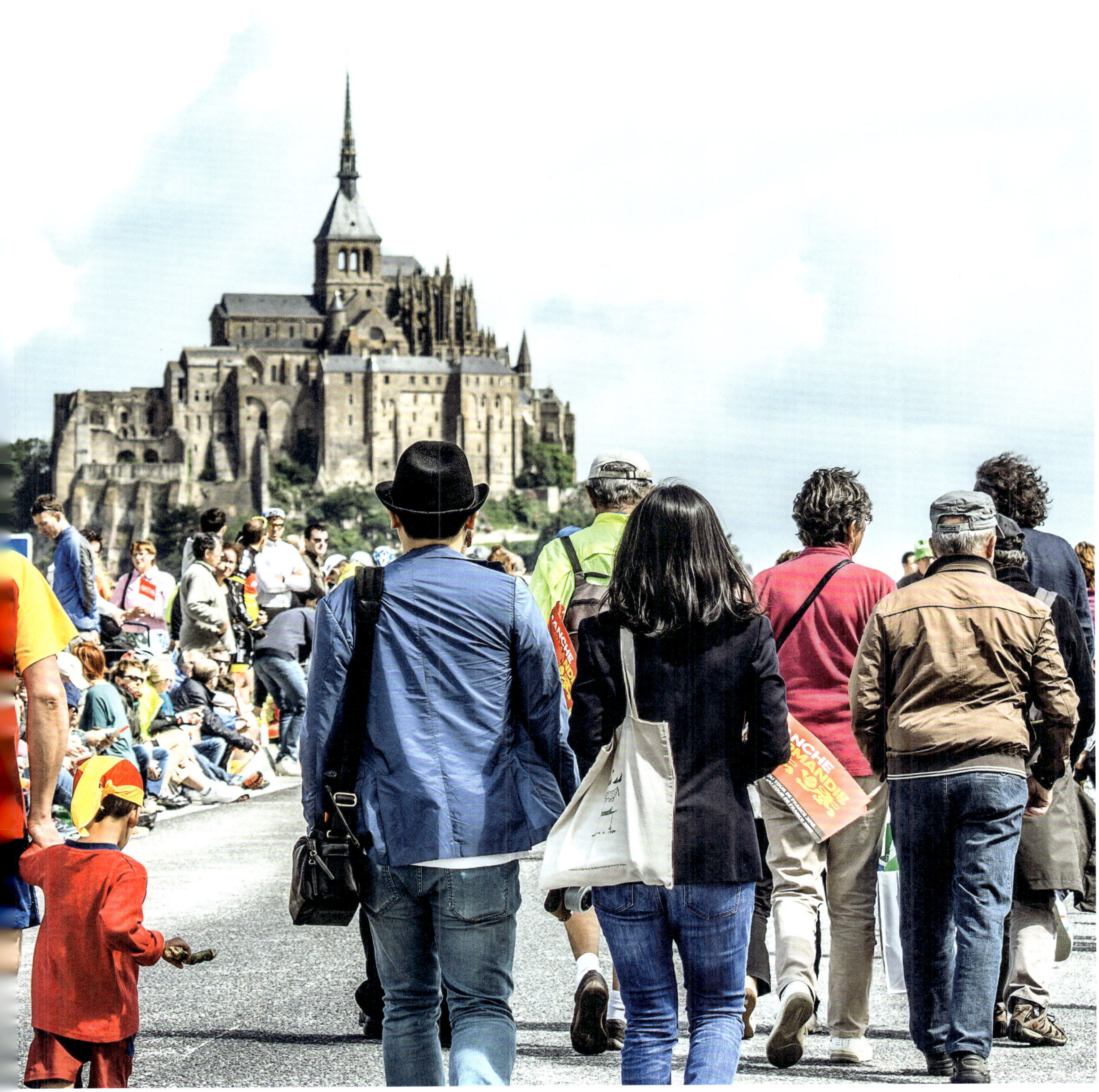

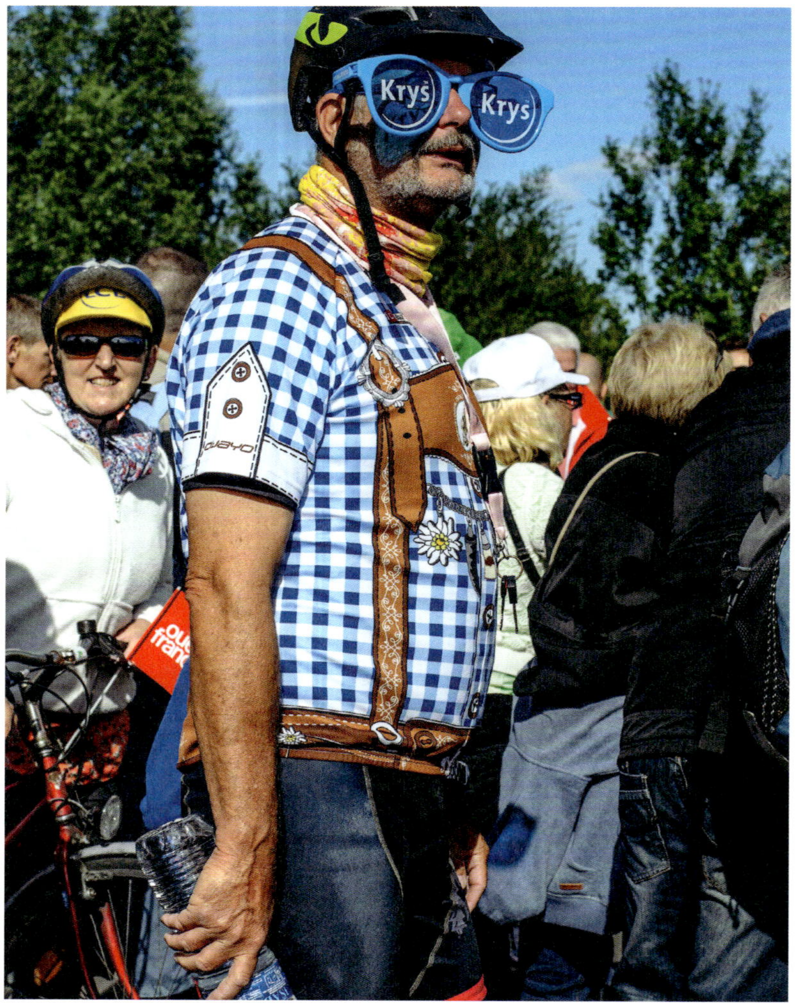
Krys
Krys

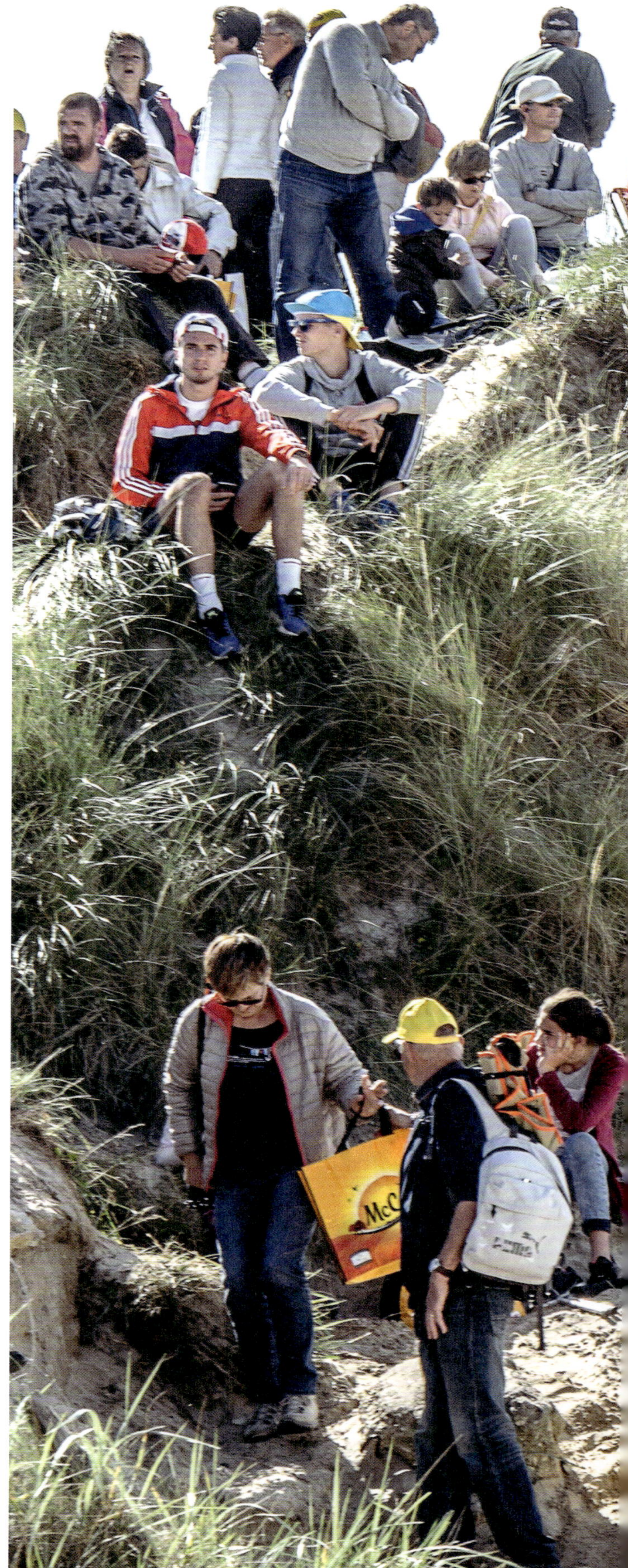

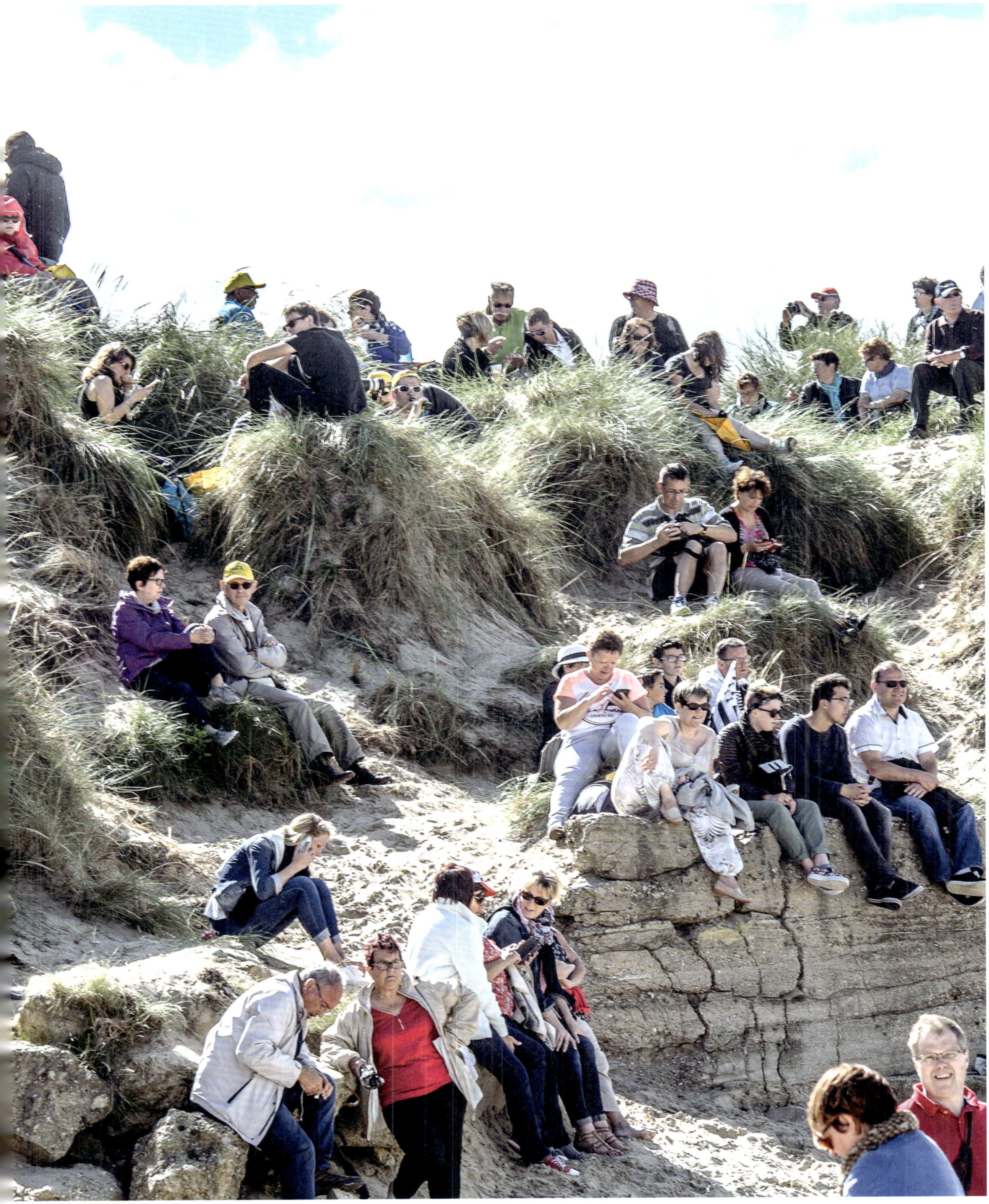

Utah Beach, Ziel der 1. Etappe. **Utah Beach, finish of the 1st stage.** *Utah Beach, arrivée de la 1re étape.*

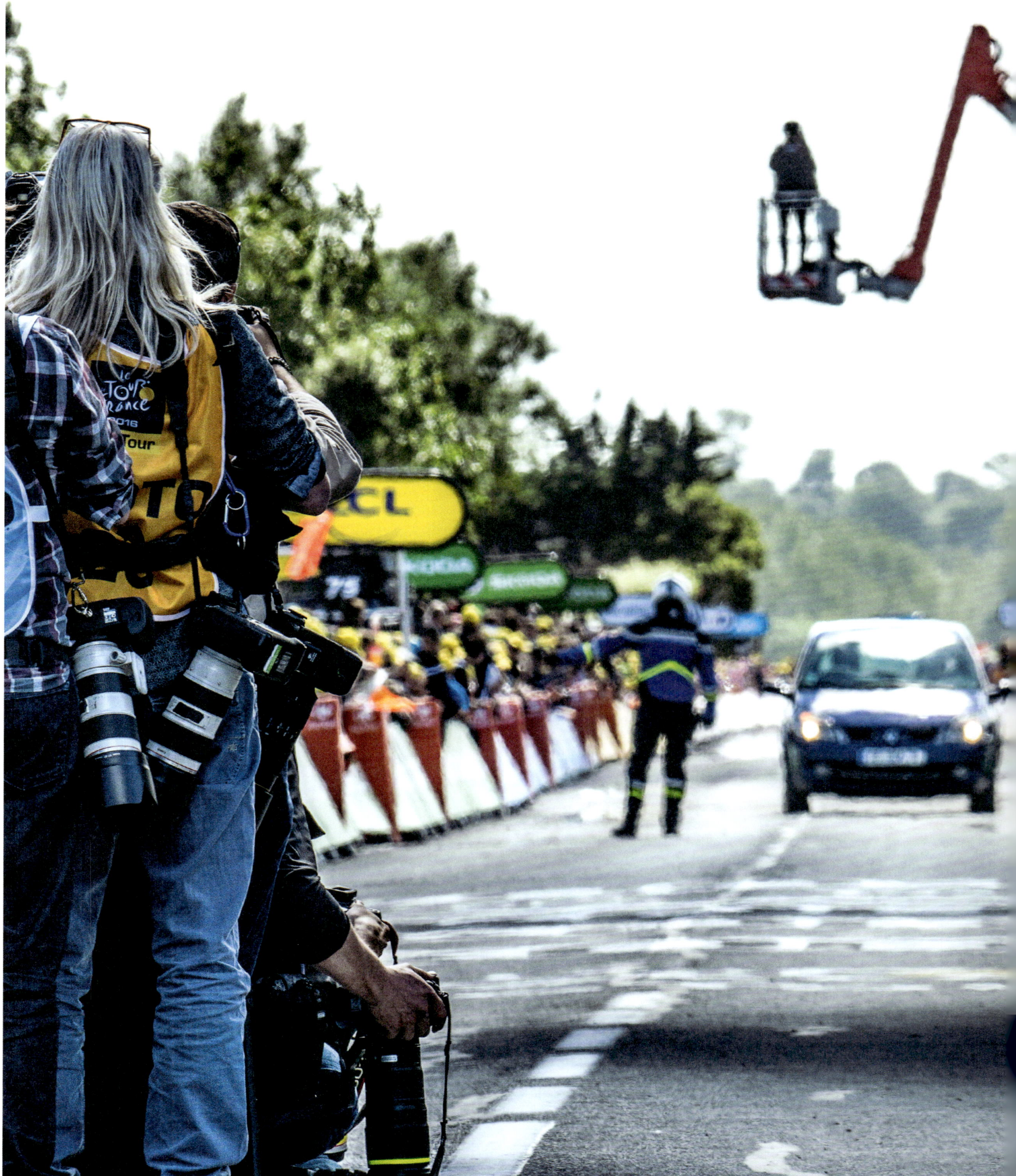

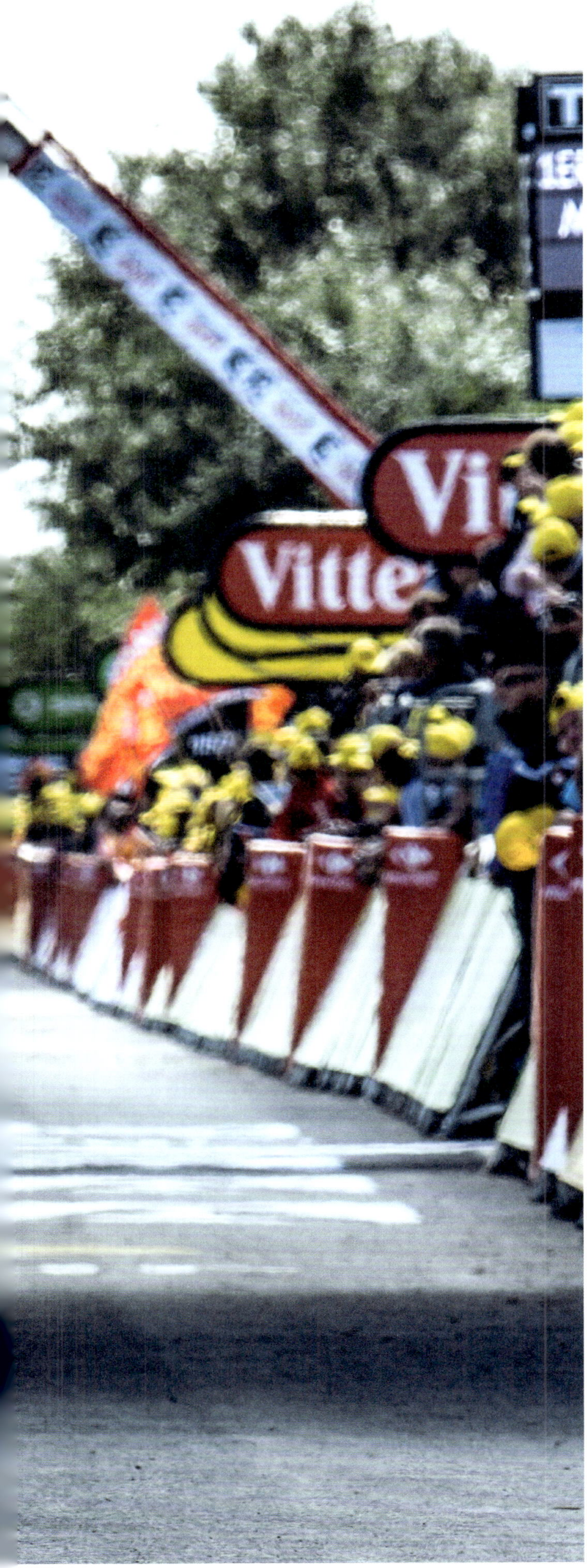

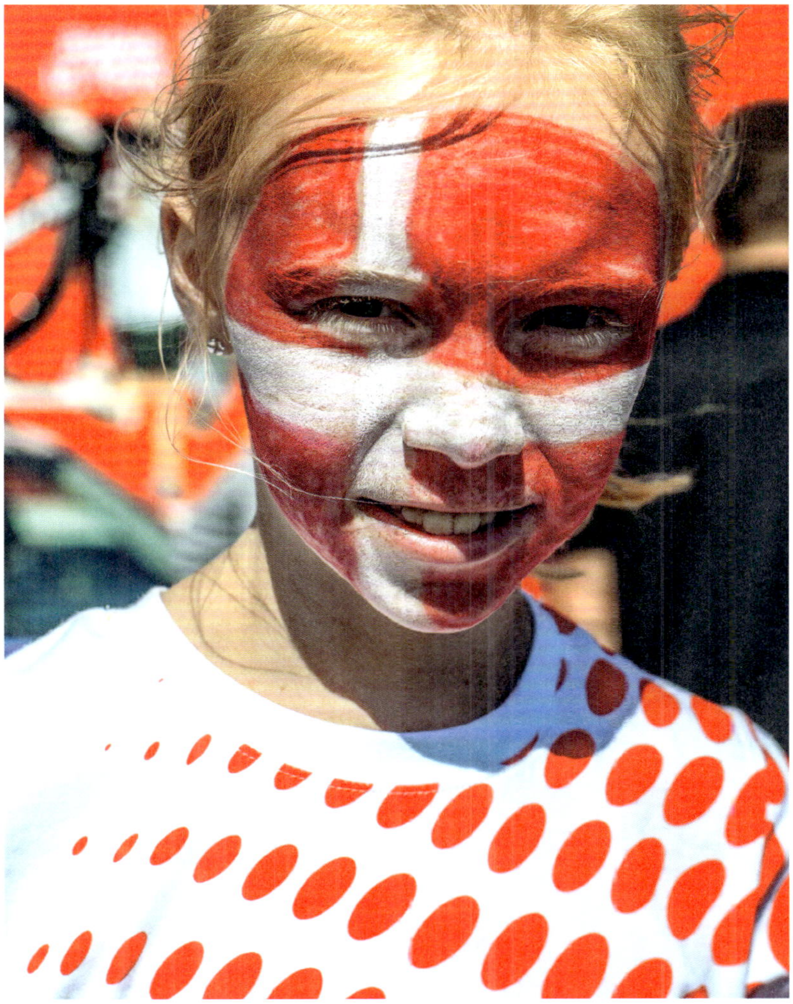

Gespanntes Warten am Ziel. **A tense wait at the finish.** *Dans l'expectative, à l'arrivée.*

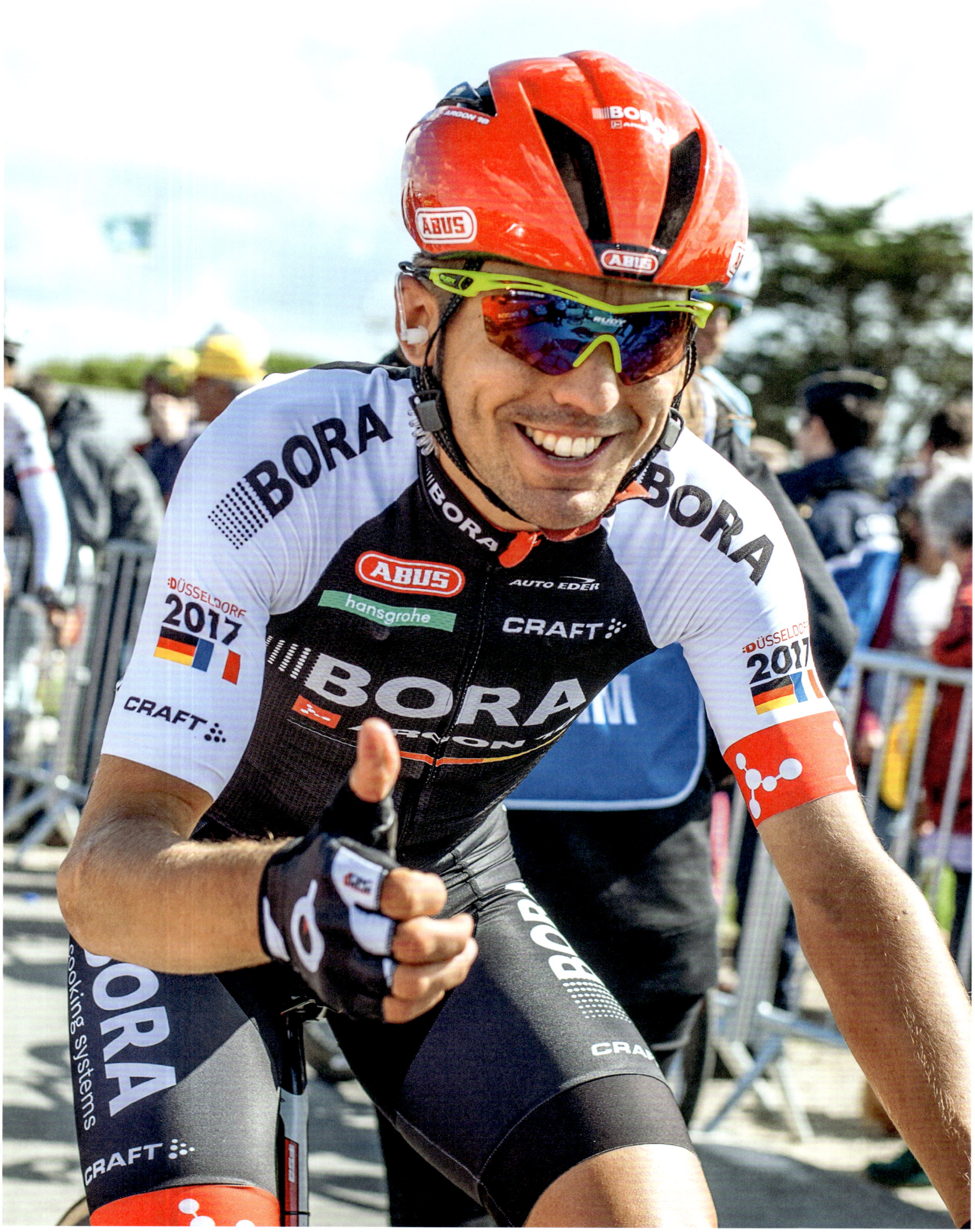

Vor dem Start: gute Laune bei Fans und Fahrern – Cesare Benedetti und Andreas Schillinger (BORA - ARGON 18). **Fans and cyclists in high spirits before the start: Cesare Benedetti and Andreas Schillinger (BORA - ARGON 18).** *Bonne humeur chez les spectateurs comme chez les coureurs au départ : Cesare Benedetti et Andreas Schillinger (BORA - ARGON 18).*

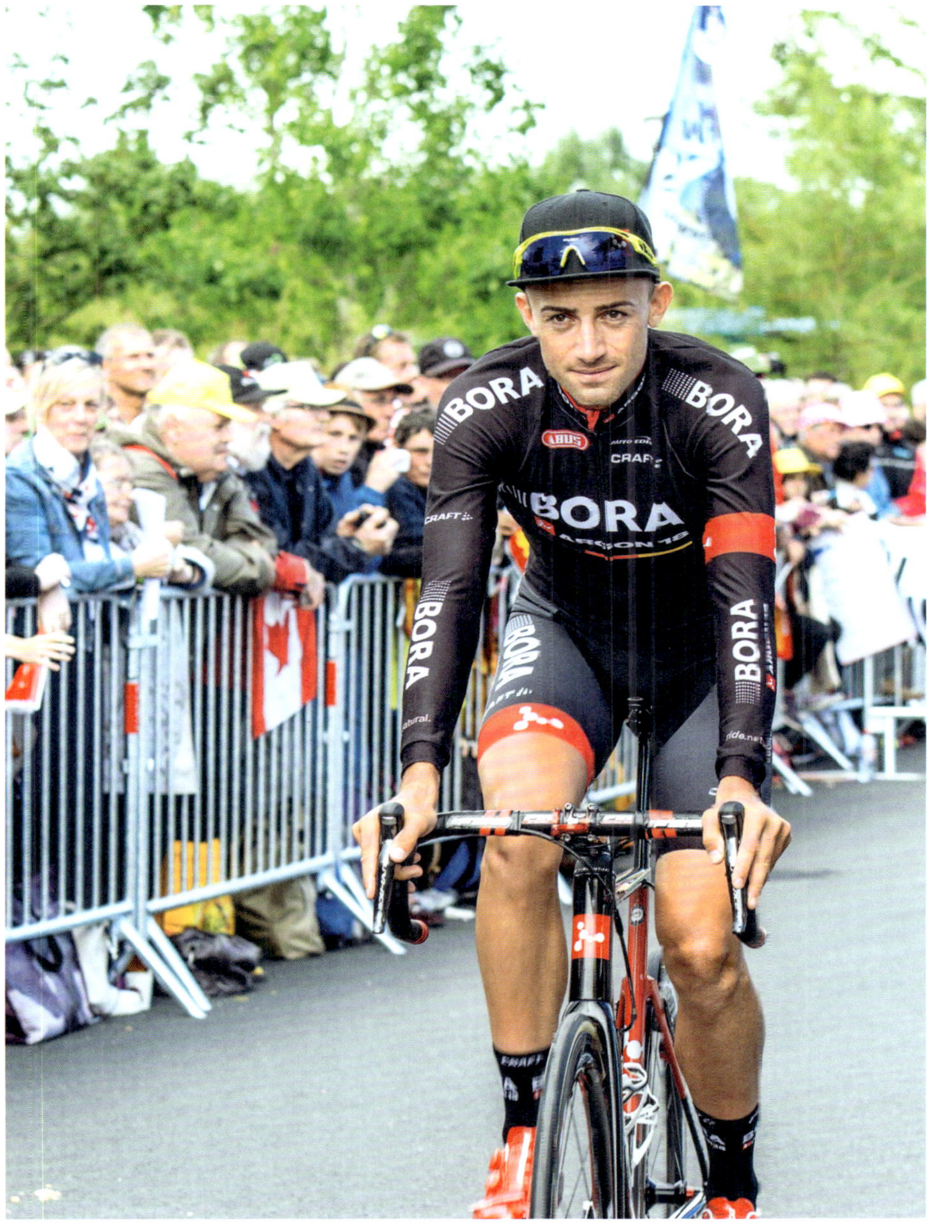
BORA
BORA
BORA
CRAFT
BORA
BORA

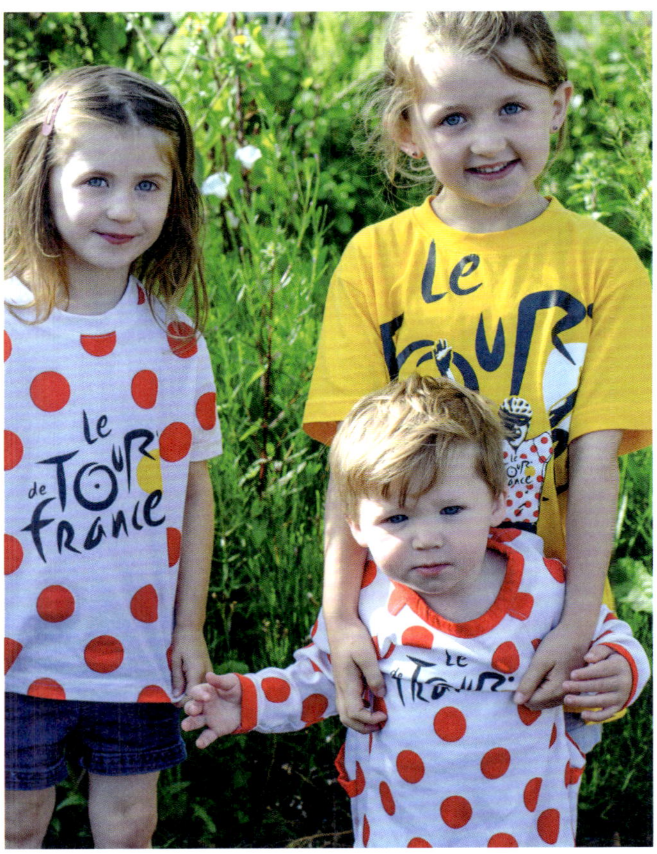
Le TOUR de France
Le TOUR

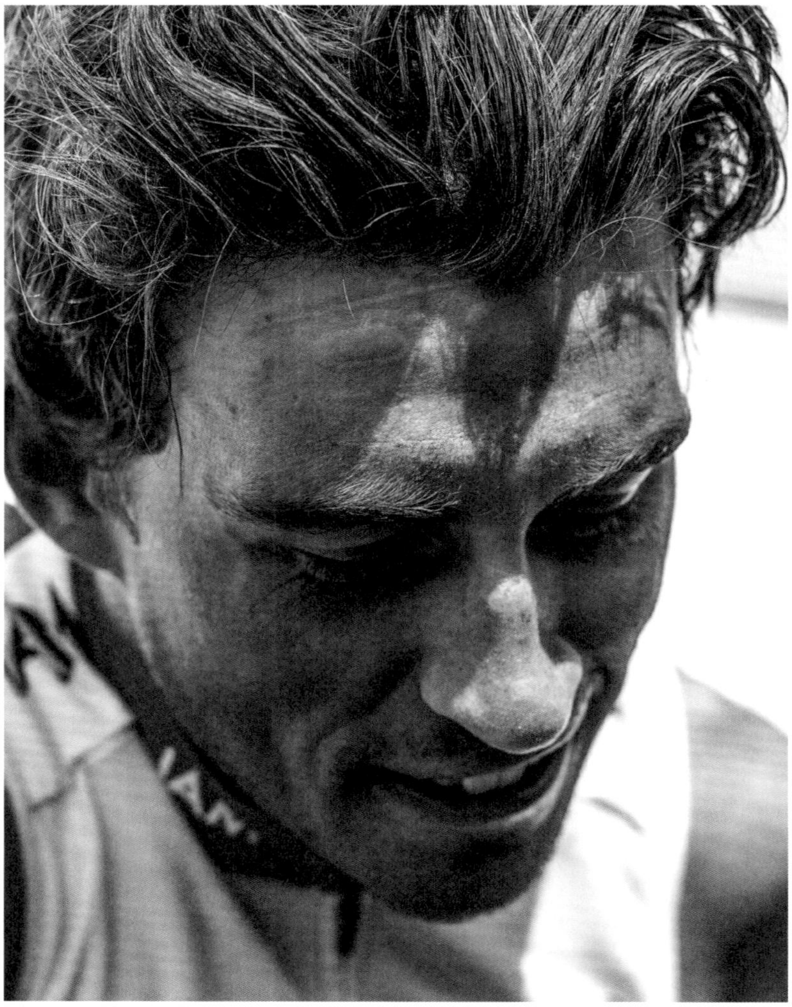

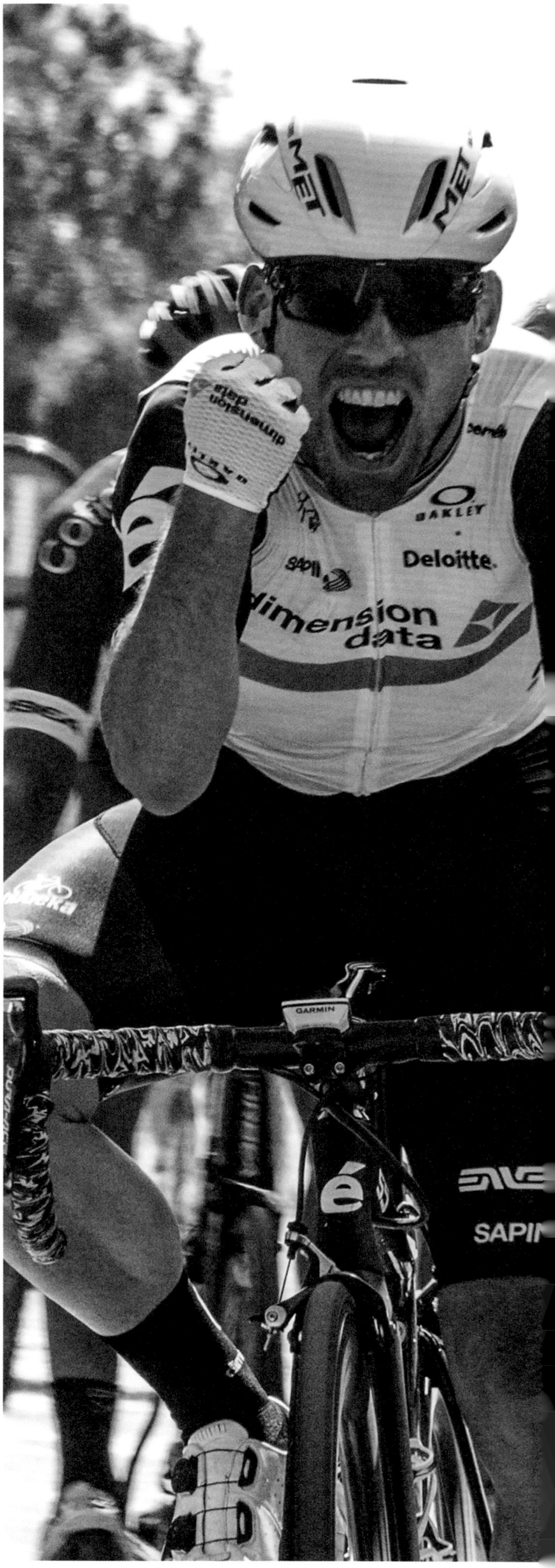

↑ Sondre Holst Enger (IAM Cycling). **Sondre Holst Enger (IAM Cycling).** *Sondre Holst Enger (IAM Cycling).*
→ „The Manx Missile“ Mark Cavendish (Dimension Data) gewinnt die 1. Etappe vor Marcel Kittel (Etixx – Quick Step) und Peter Sagan (Tinkoff). **'The Manx Missile' Mark Cavendish (Dimension Data) wins the first stage ahead of Marcel Kittel (Etixx – Quick Step) and Peter Sagan (Tinkoff).** *The Manx Missile Mark Cavendish (Dimension Data) remporte la 1re étape devant Marcel Kittel (Etixx – Quick Step) et Peter Sagan (Tinkoff).*

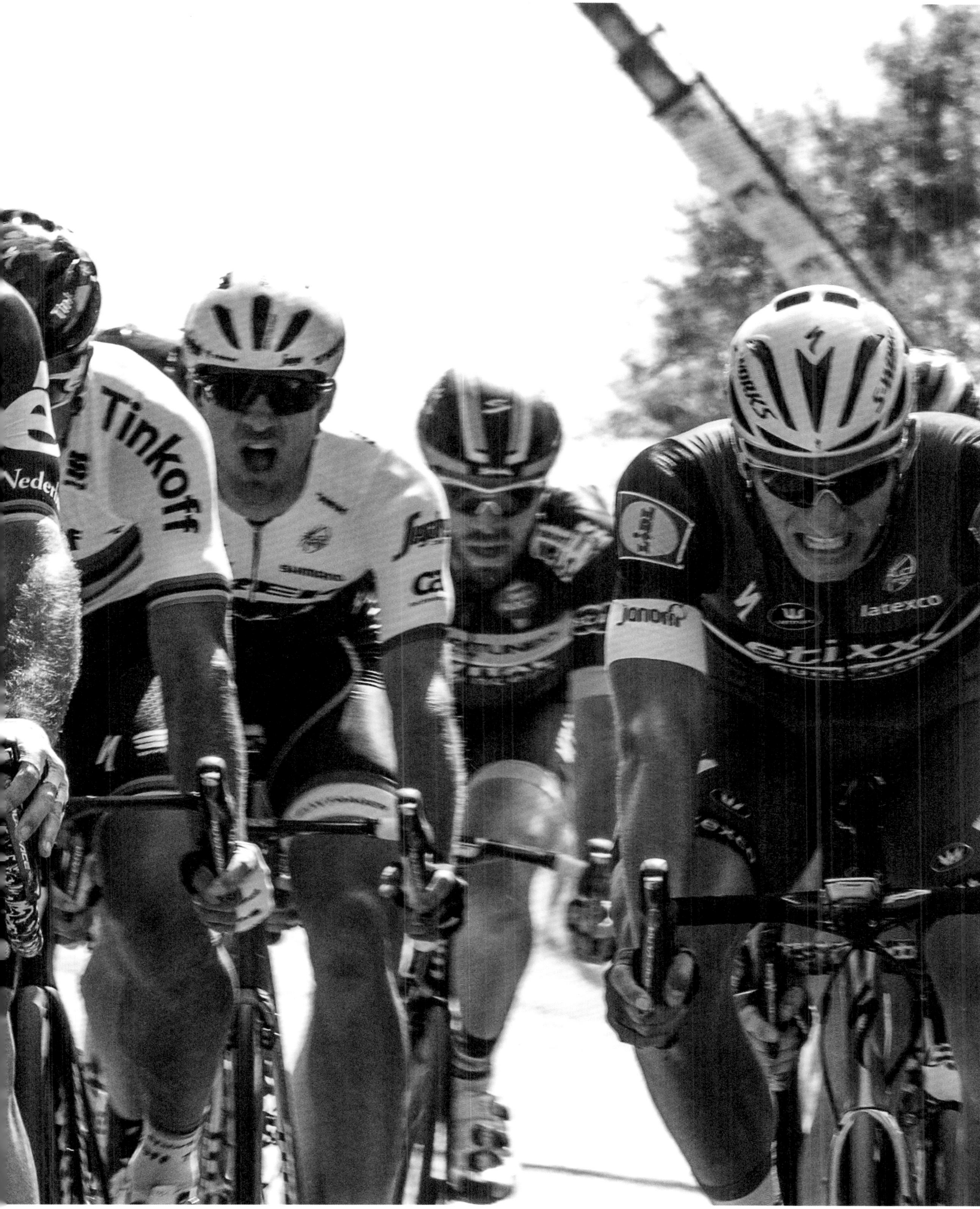
Tinkoff
latexco
etixx

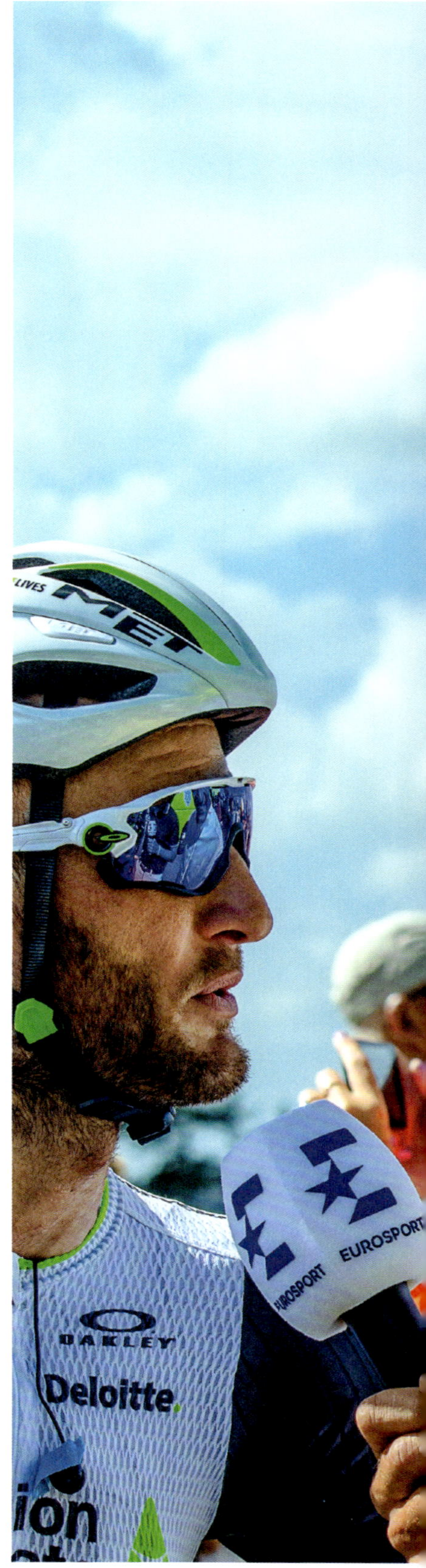
Deloitte.
OAKLEY
EUROSPORT

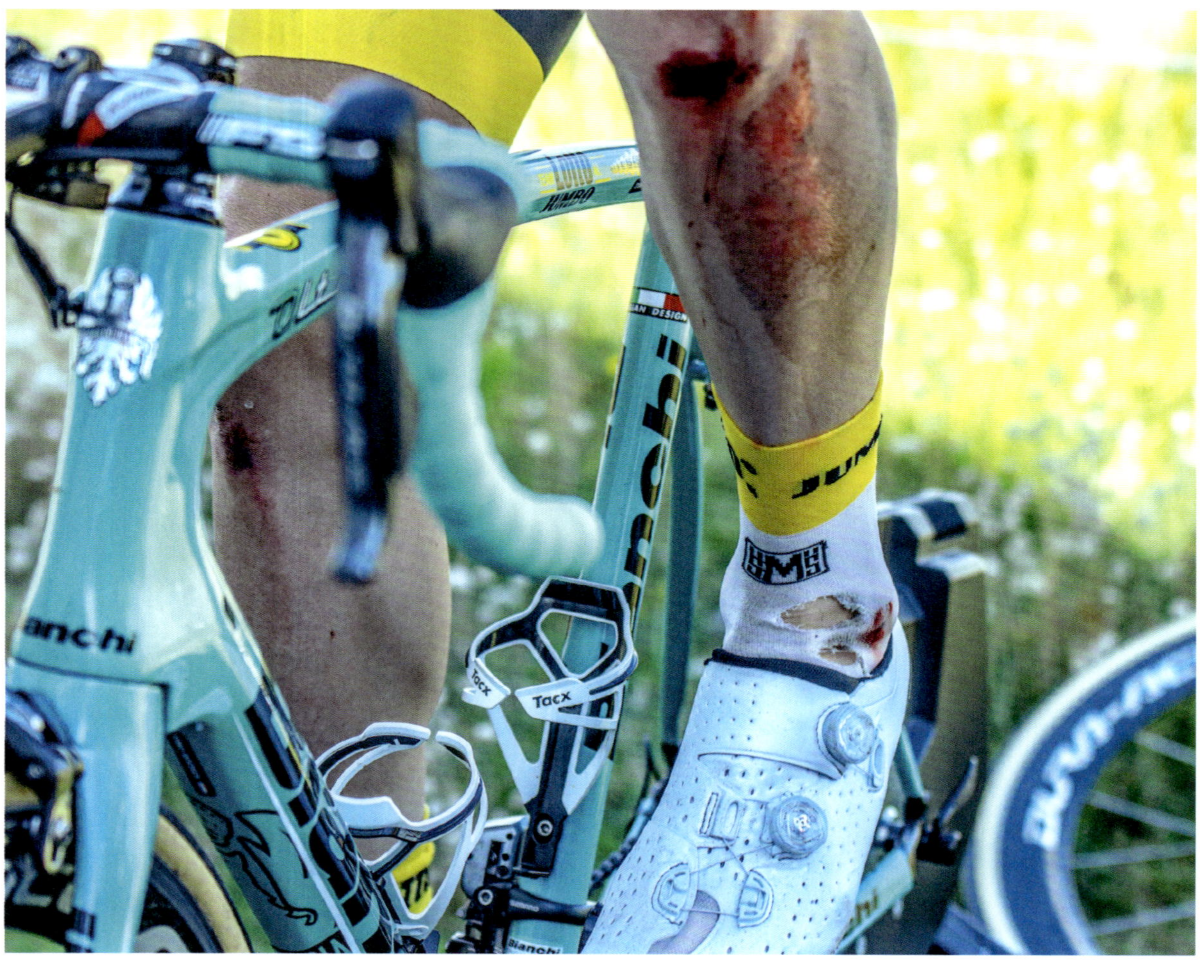
Tacx
Tacx

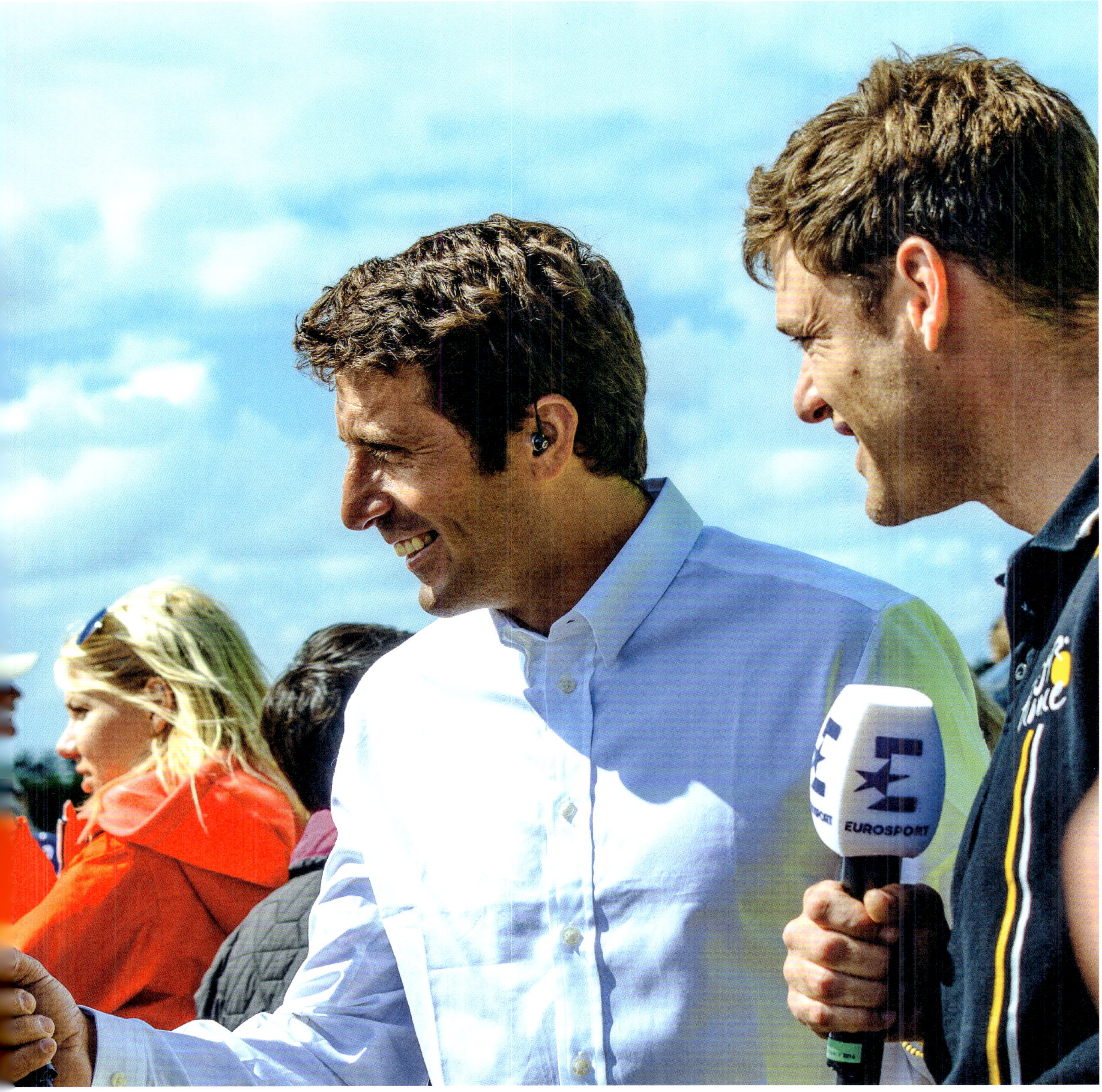

Stephen Cummings (Dimension Data) im Interview mit Legende Juan Antonio Flecha und Ashley House, Eurosport. **Interview with Stephen Cummings (Dimension Data) by the legendary Juan Antonio Flecha and Ashley House, Eurosport.** *Stephen Cummings (Dimension Data) interviewé par le légendaire Juan Antonio Flecha et Ashley House, d'Eurosport.*

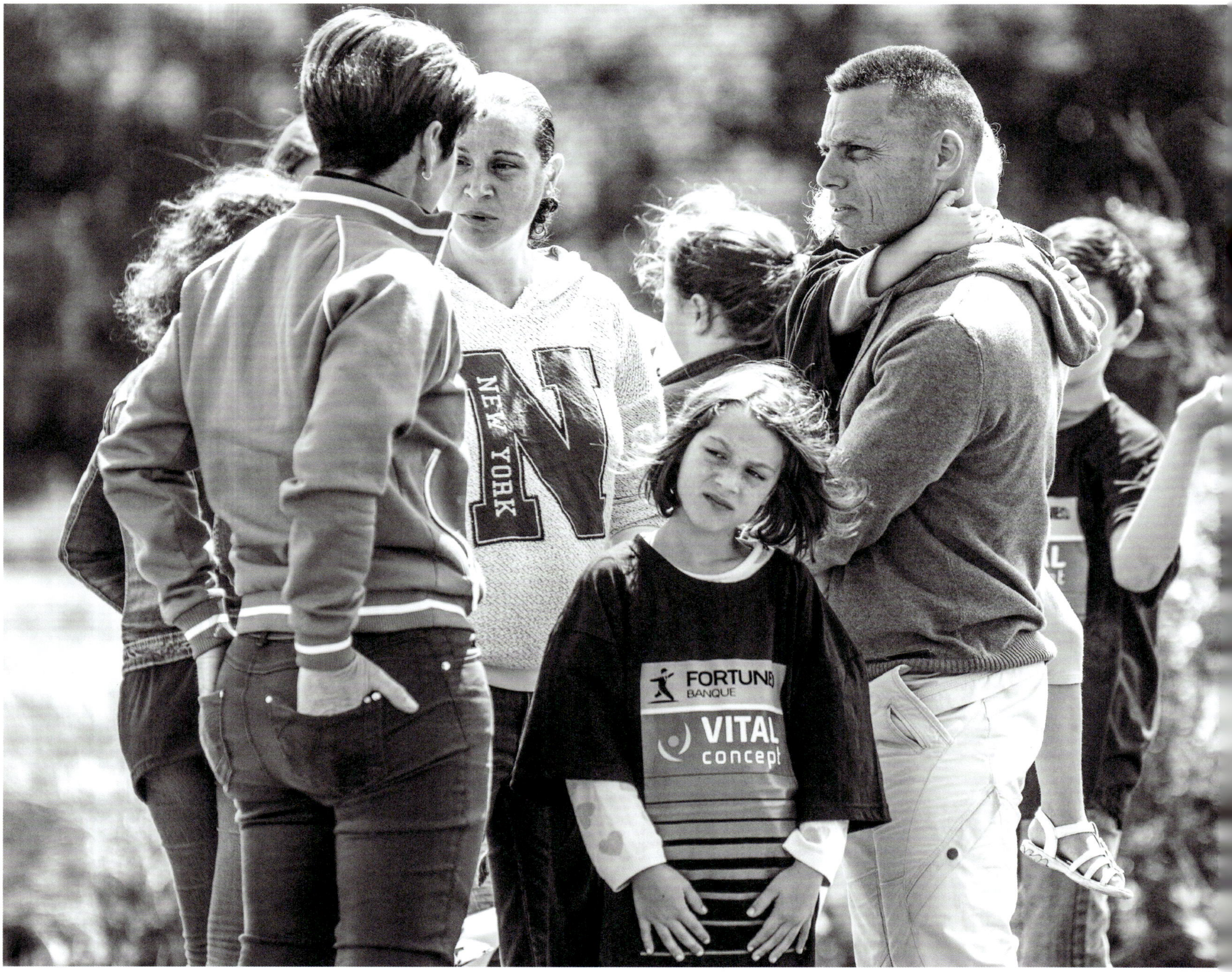
NEW YORK
FORTUNEO
BANQUE
VITAL
concept

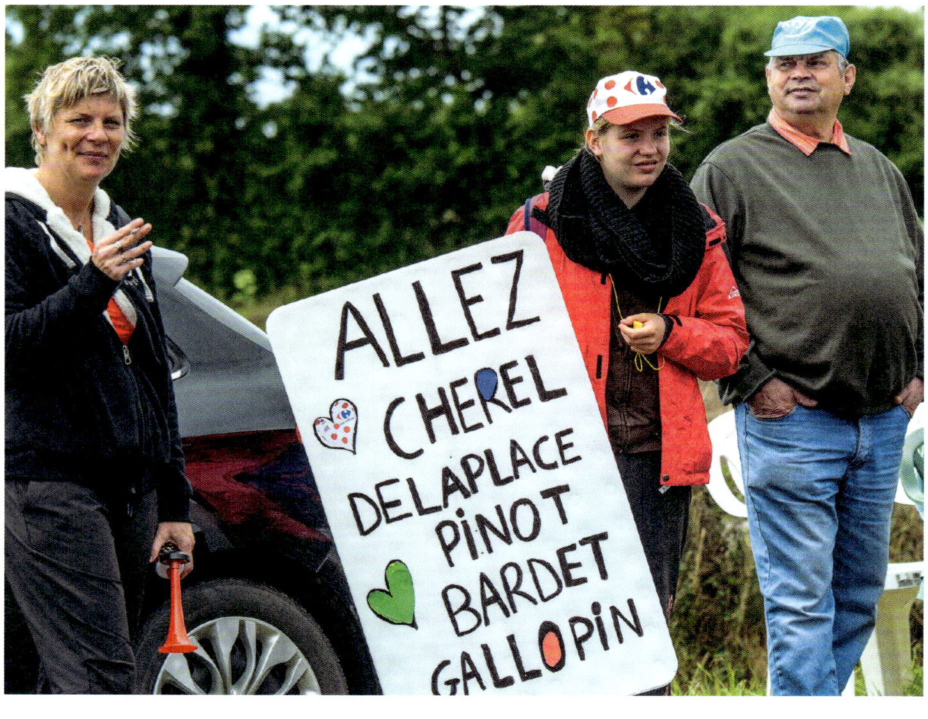
ALLEZ
CHEREL
DELAPLACE
PINOT
BARDET
GALLOPIN

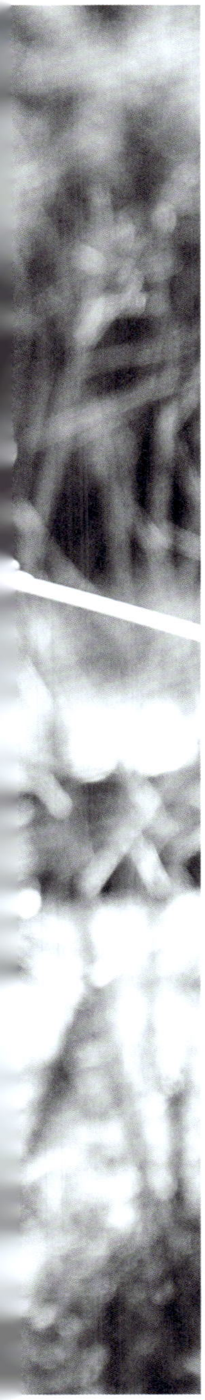

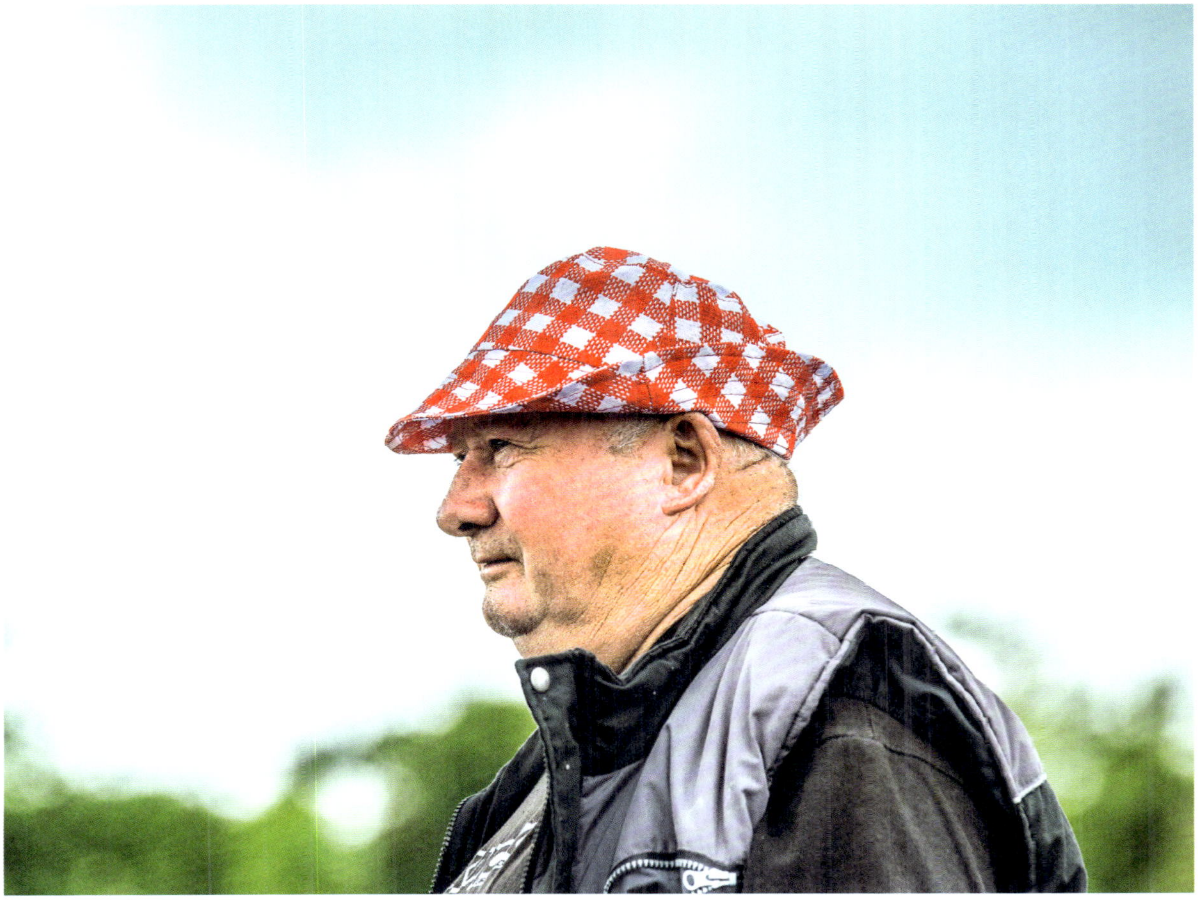

Berufung: Fan. **Vocation: Fan.** *Vocation : spectateur.*

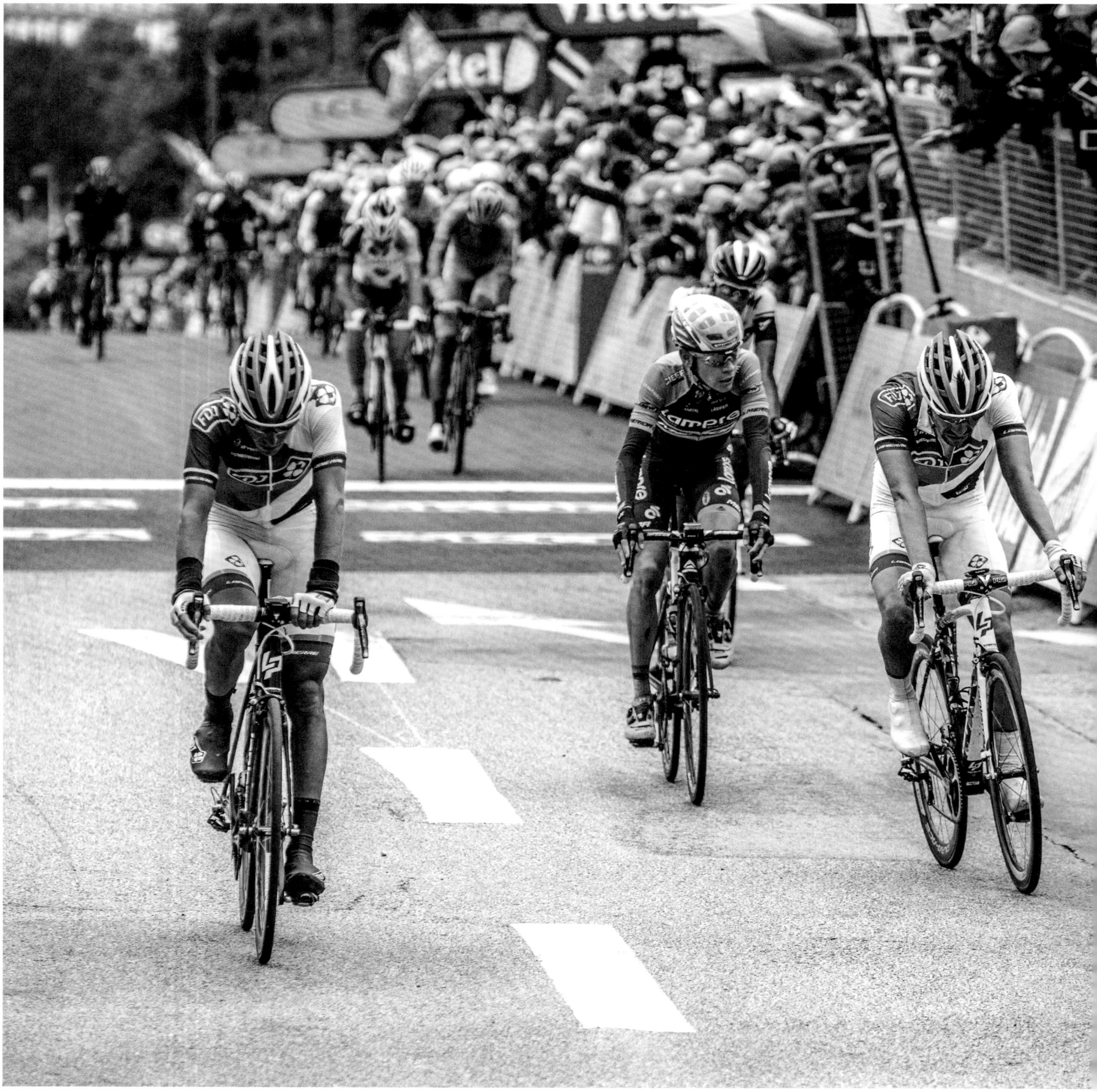

Abgekämpft: Sébastien Reichenbach (FDJ), Louis Meintjes (Lampre-Merida), Thibaut Pinot (FDJ), Vincenzo Nibali (Astana).

Done and dusted: Sébastien Reichenbach (FDJ), Louis Meintjes (Lampre-Merida), Thibaut Pinot (FDJ), Vincenzo Nibali (Astana).

Epuisés: Sébastien Reichenbach (FDJ), Louis Meintjes (Lampre-Merida), Thibaut Pinot (FDJ), Vincenzo Nibali (Astana).

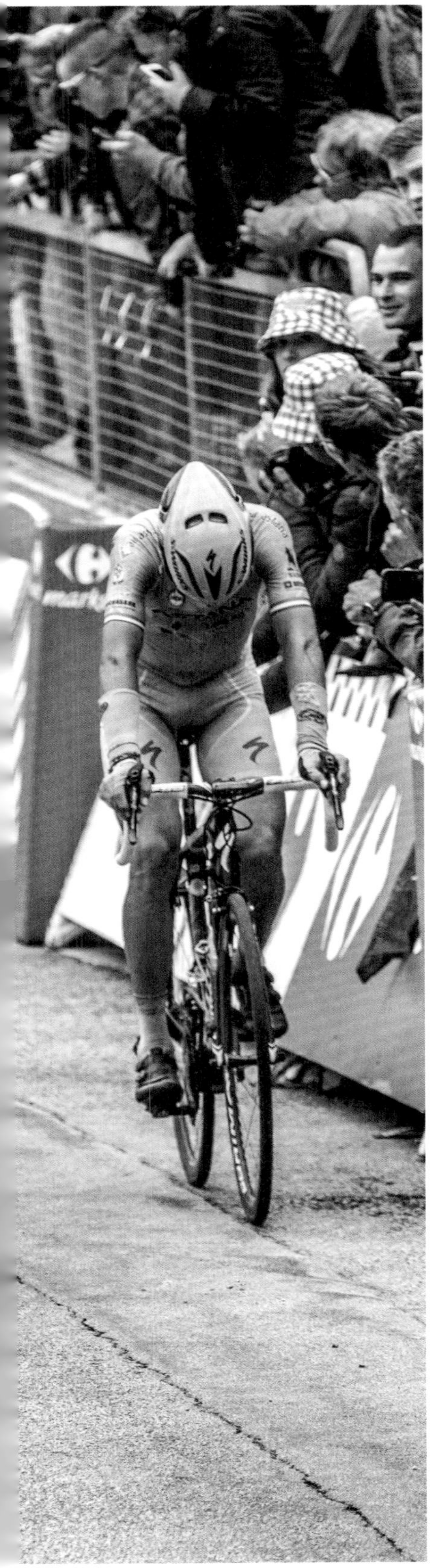

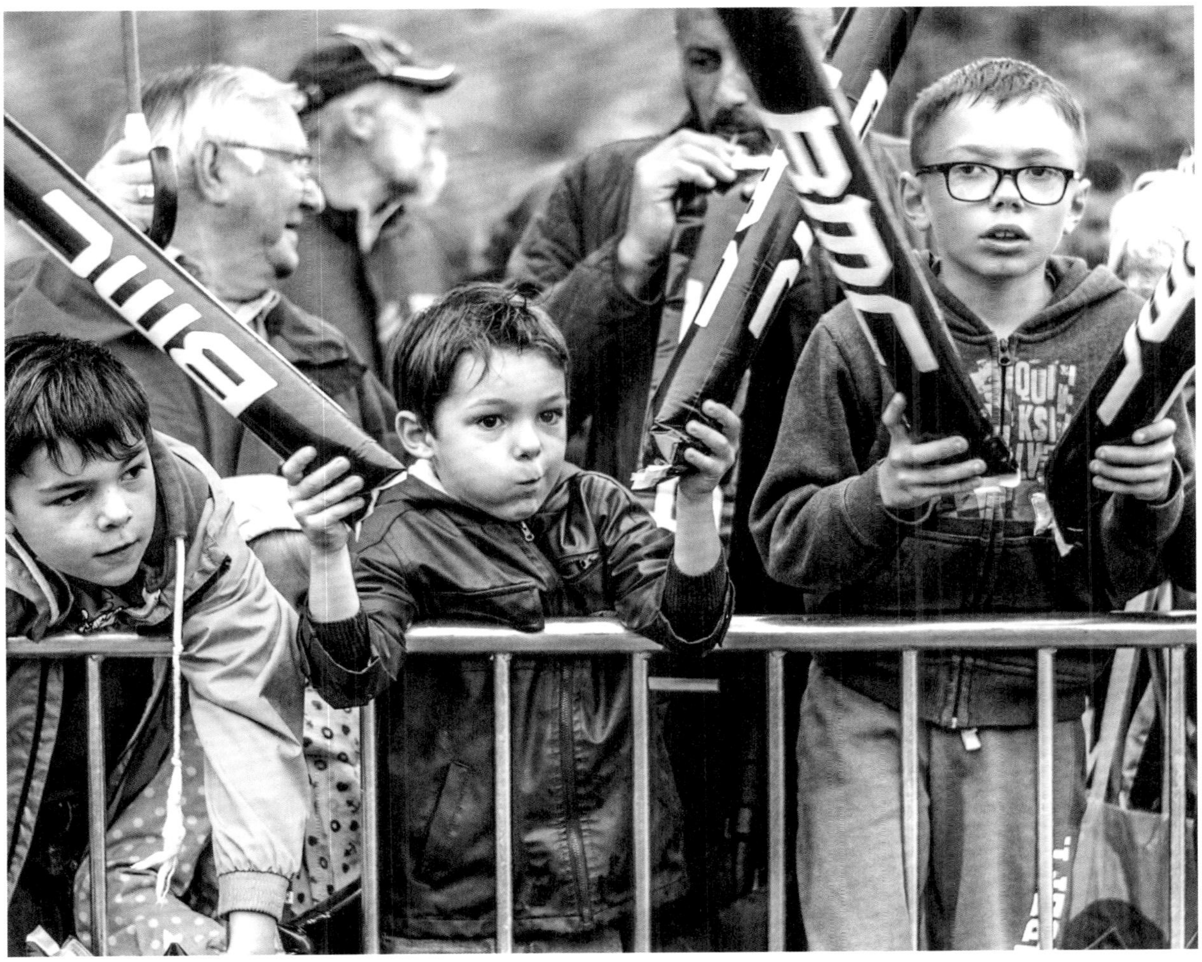

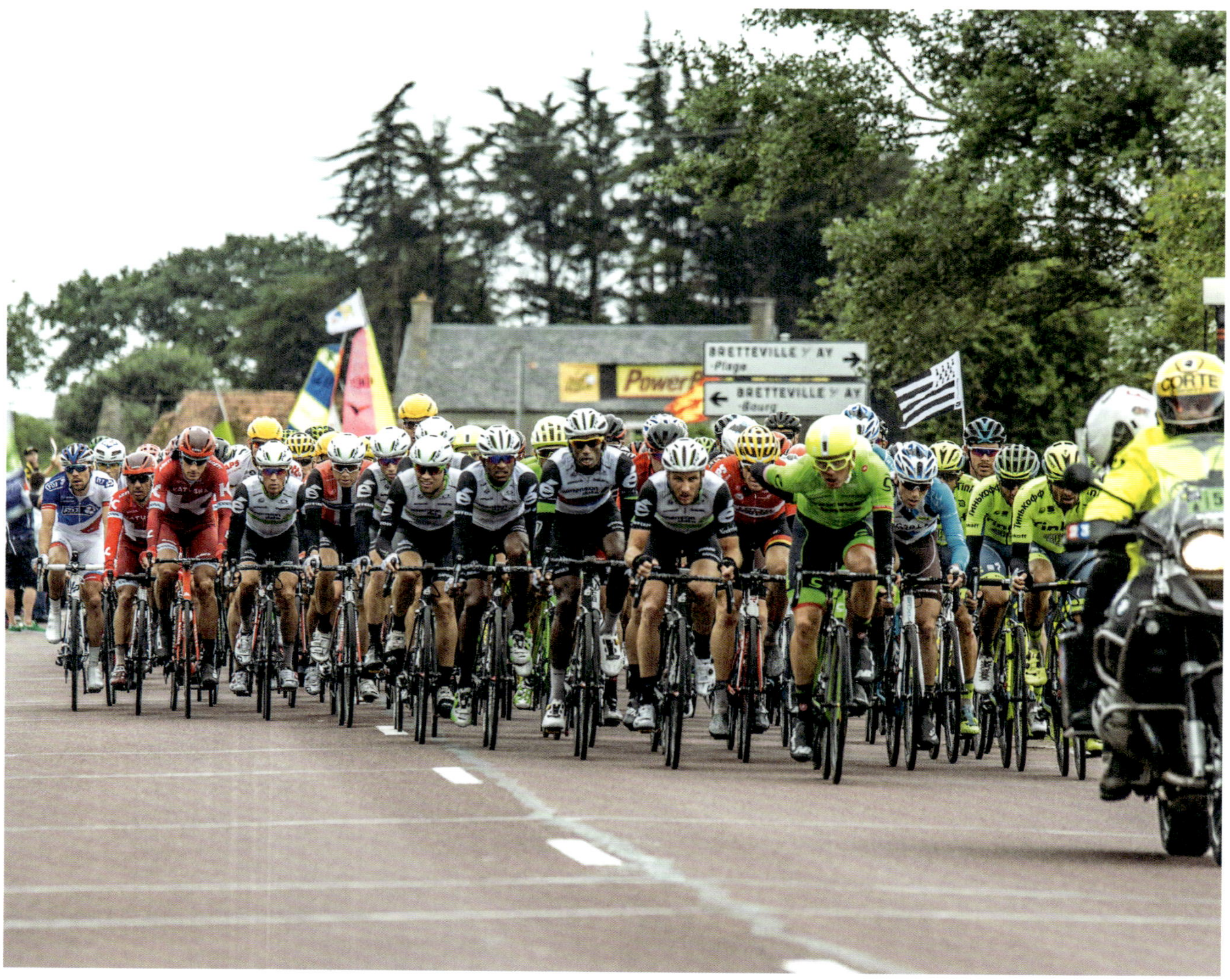
BRETTEVILLE s/ AY
-Plage
BRETTEVILLE s/ AY
-Bourg

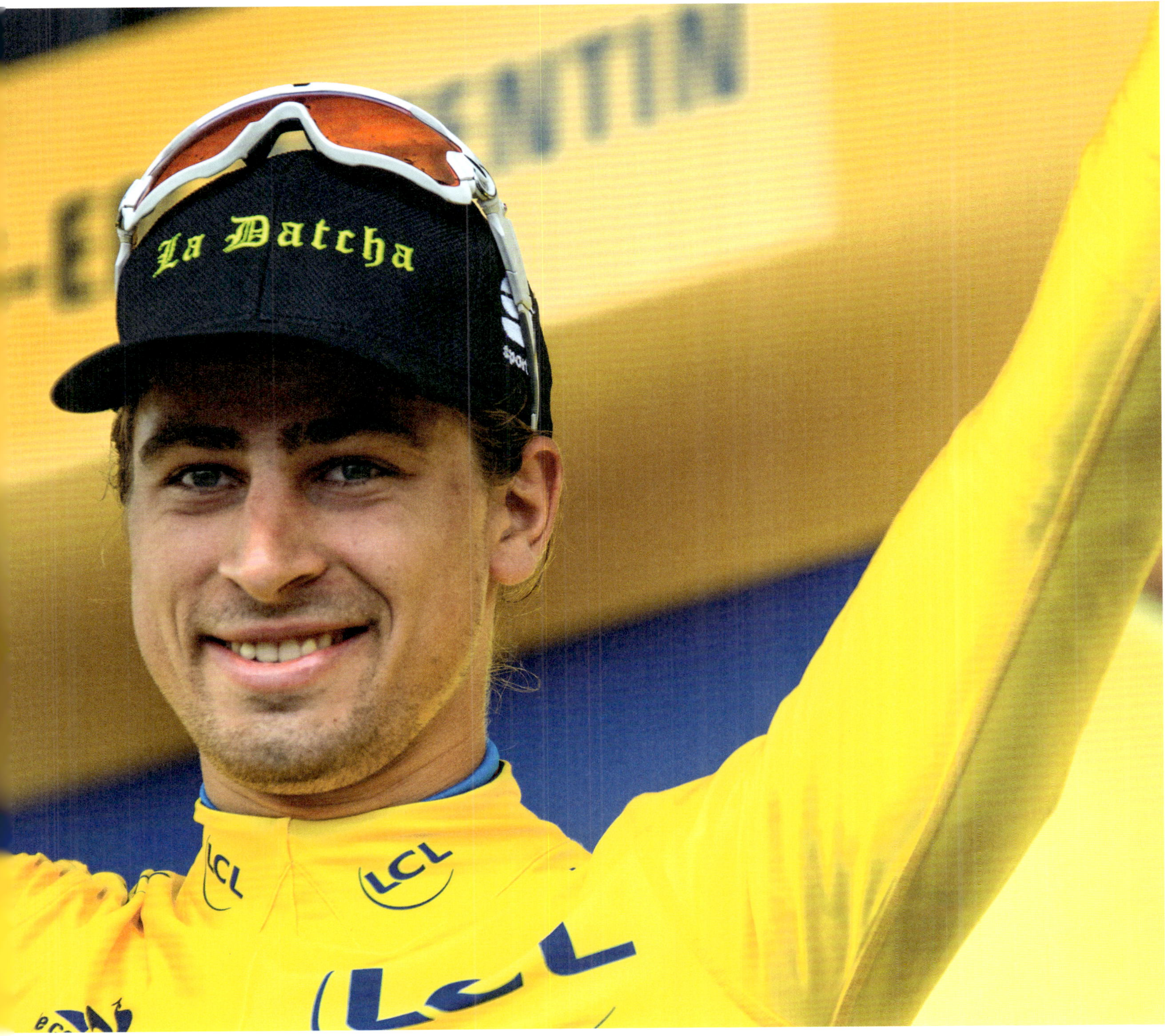

2. Etappe: Etappensieg und Gelbes Trikot für Peter Sagan (Tinkoff). **2nd stage: stage win and the yellow jersey for Peter Sagan (Tinkoff).**
2e étape : victoire et maillot jaune pour Peter Sagan (Tinkoff).

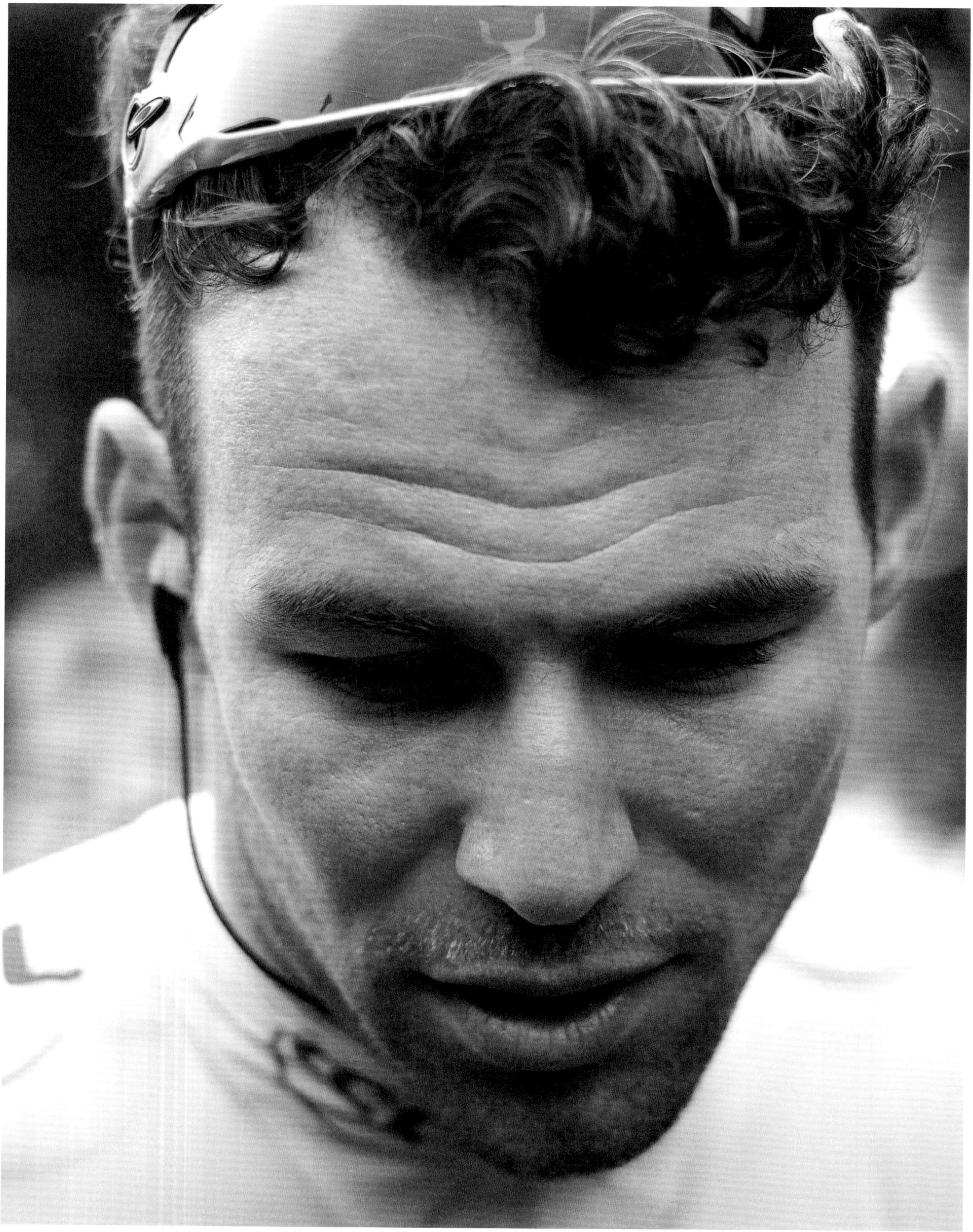

↑ Powerhouse Mark Cavendish (Dimension Data). **Powerhouse Mark Cavendish (Dimension Data).** *Powerhouse Mark Cavendish (Dimension Data).*
→ Family-Time im Ziel: Cyril Lemoine (Cofidis). **Family time at the finish: Cyril Lemoine (Cofidis).** *Rencontre de famille à l'arrivée : Cyril Lemoine (Cofidis).*
↗ Der Superfan. **The super fan.** *Superfan.*

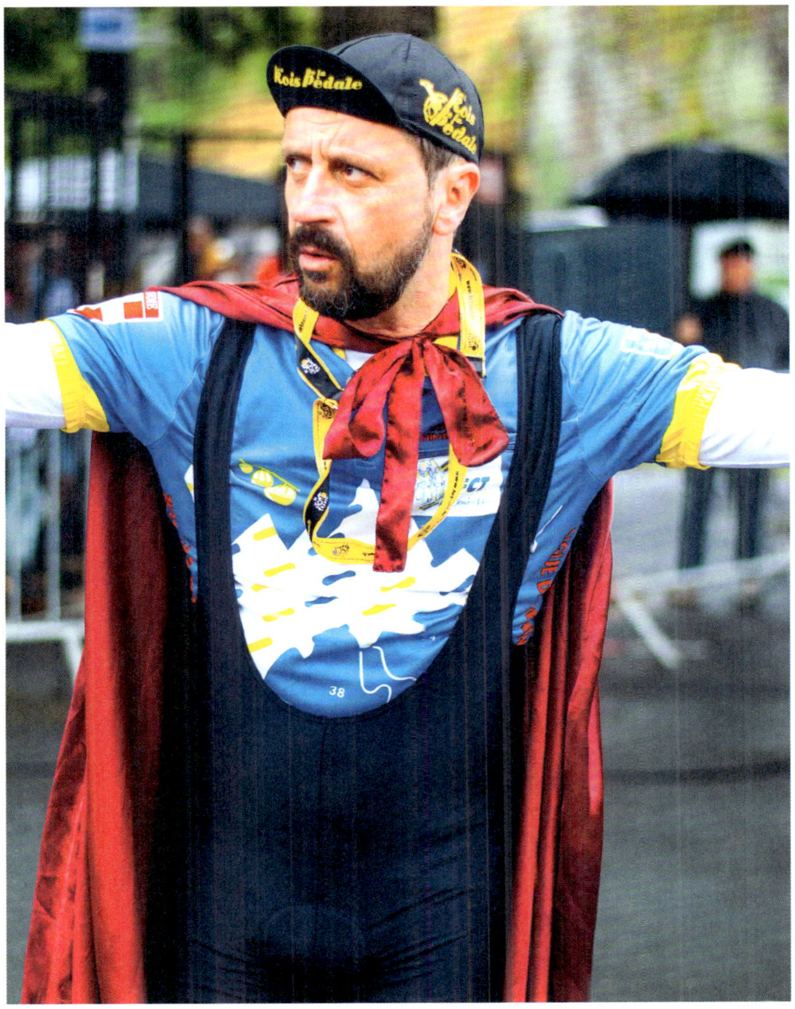
Rois Pédale

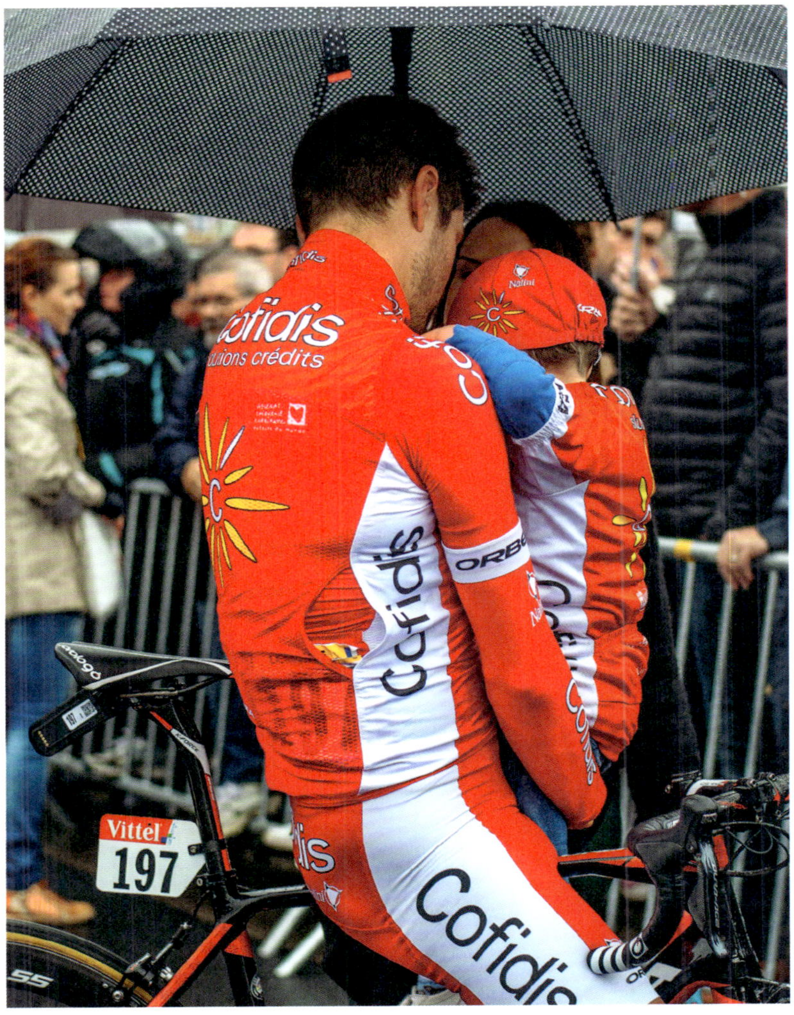
Cofidis
Vittel
197

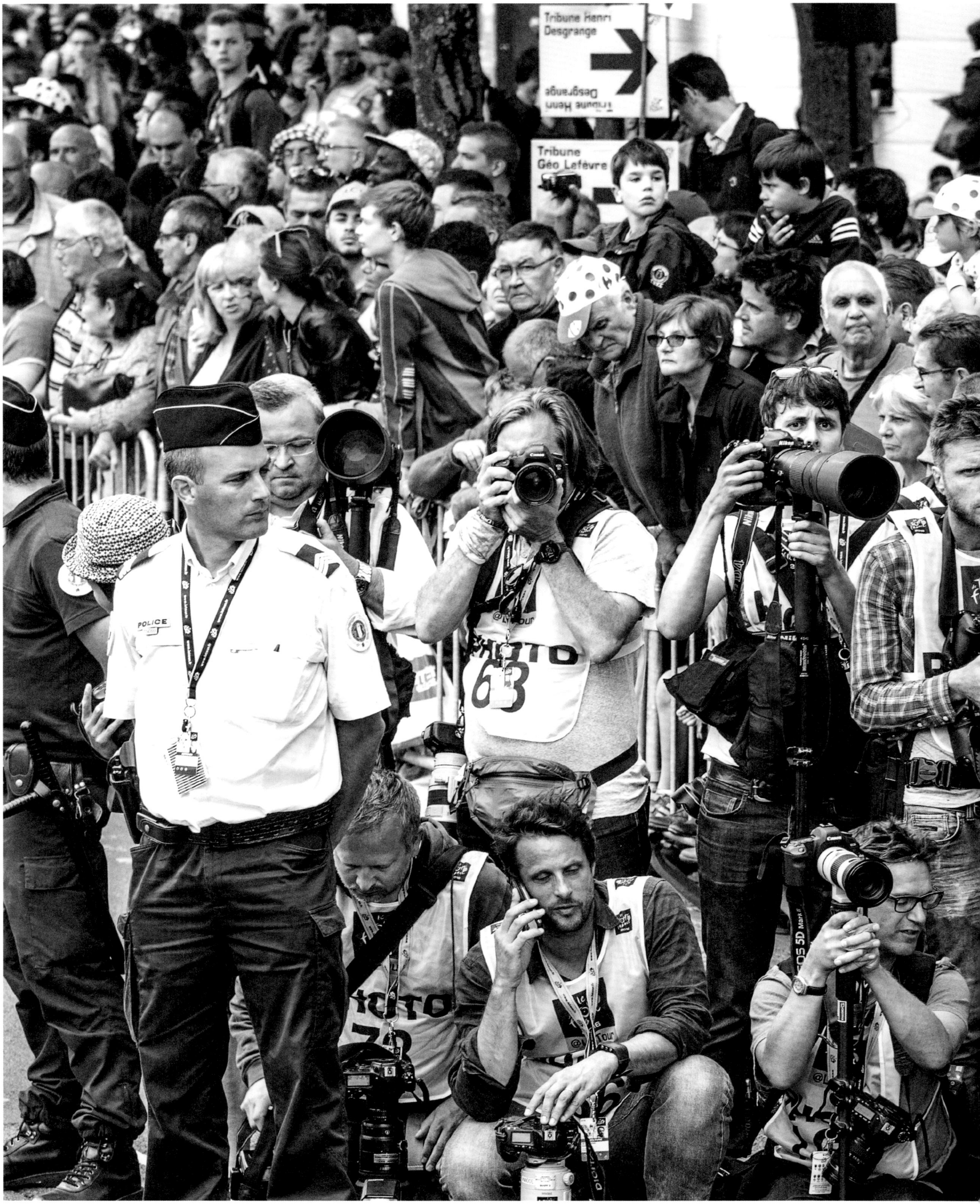
Tribune Henri Desgrange
Tribune Géo Lefèvre
POLICE

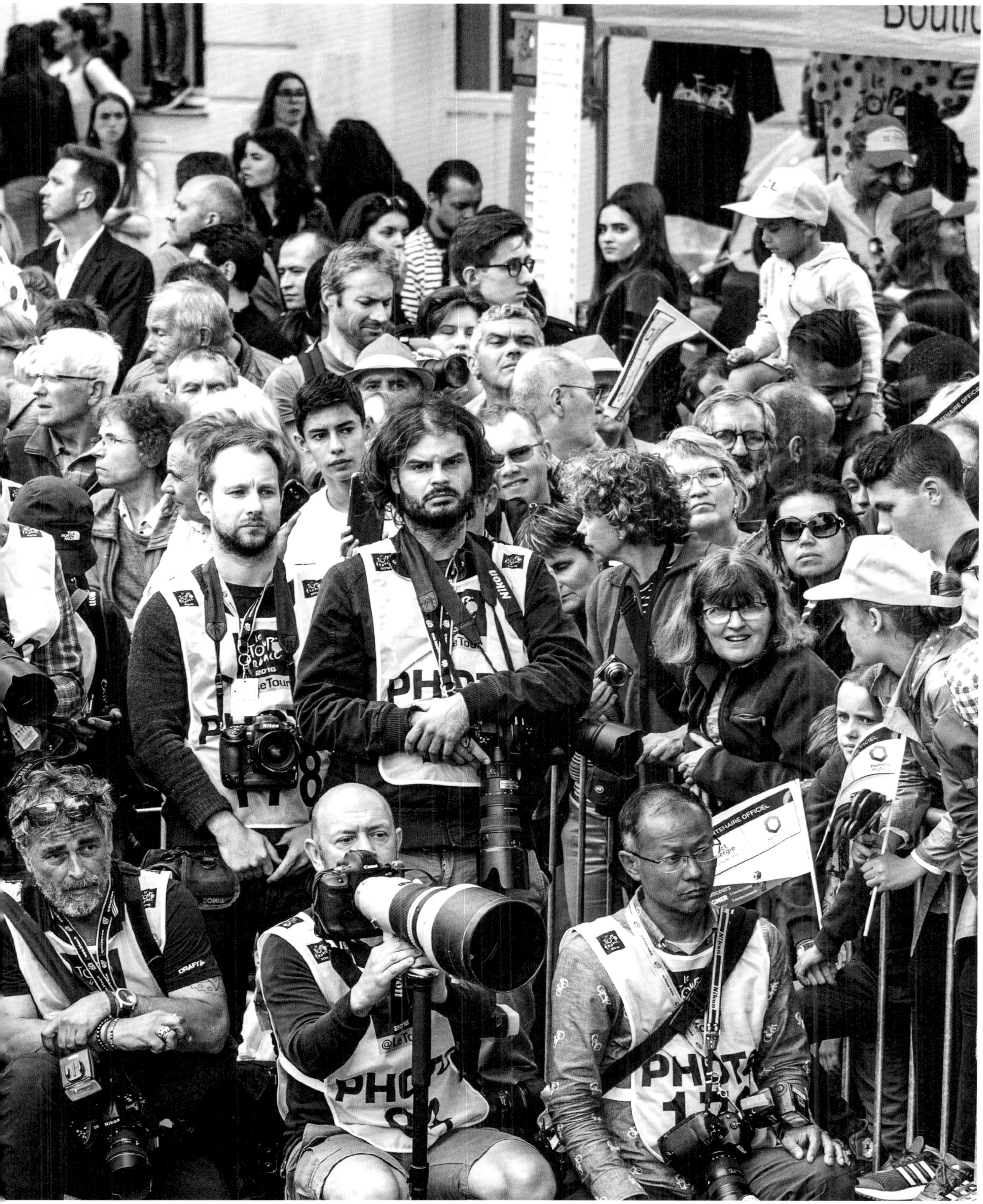

Ein Meer aus Fotografen und Fans am Ziel der 3. Etappe. **A sea of photographers and fans at the finish of the 3rd stage.** *Une marée de photographes et de spectateurs à l'arrivée de la 3e étape.*

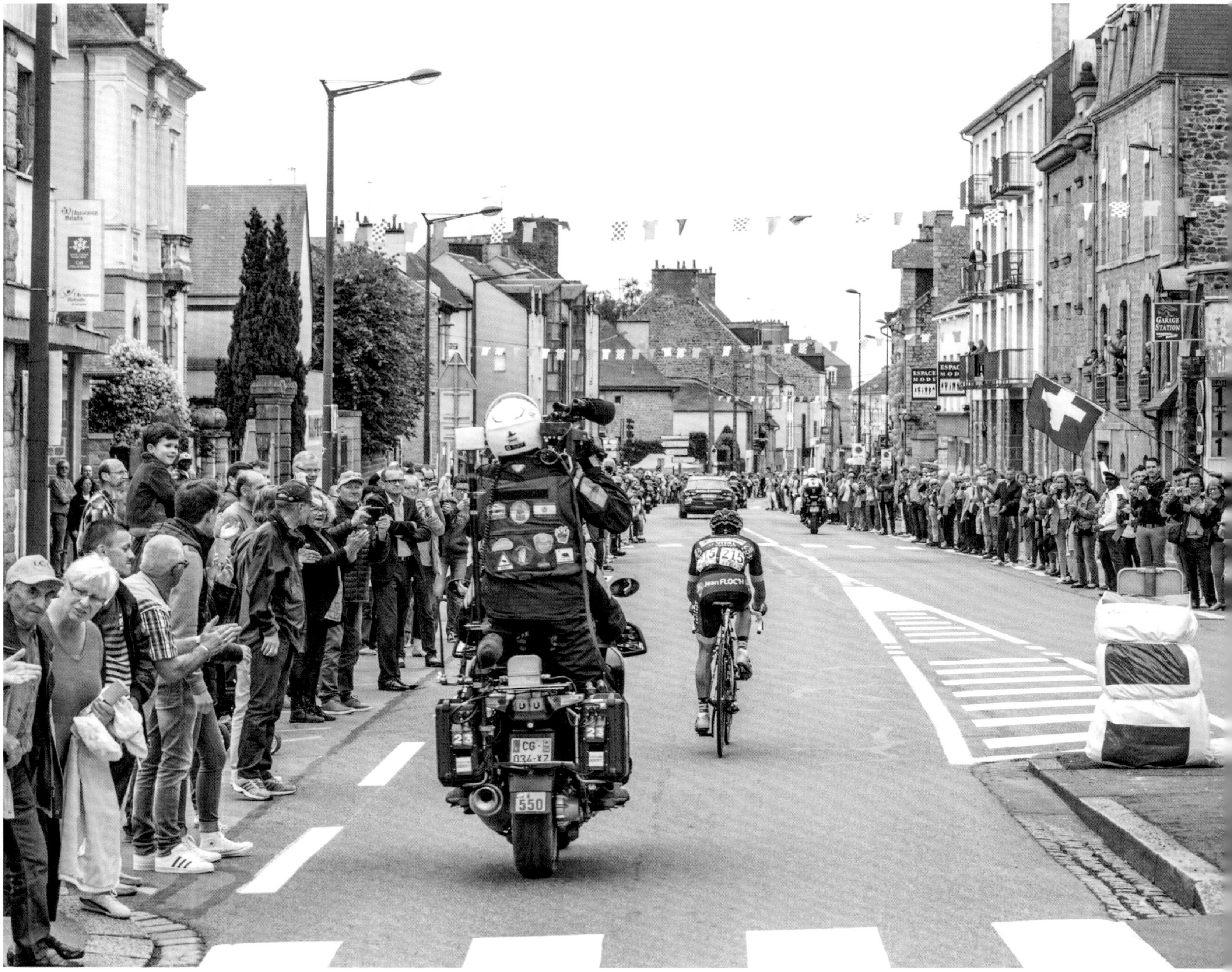

↑ Armindo Fonseca (Fortuneo-Vital Concept) im Alleingang. **Armindo Fonseca (Fortuneo-Vital Concept) going it alone.**
Armindo Fonseca (Fortuneo-Vital Concept) en solitaire.
↗ Die Verfolger mit Alberto Contador (Tinkoff, 3. v. l.). **The chase group with Alberto Contador (Tinkoff, 3rd from left).**
Les poursuivants avec Alberto Contador (Tinkoff, 3e à p. de la g.).

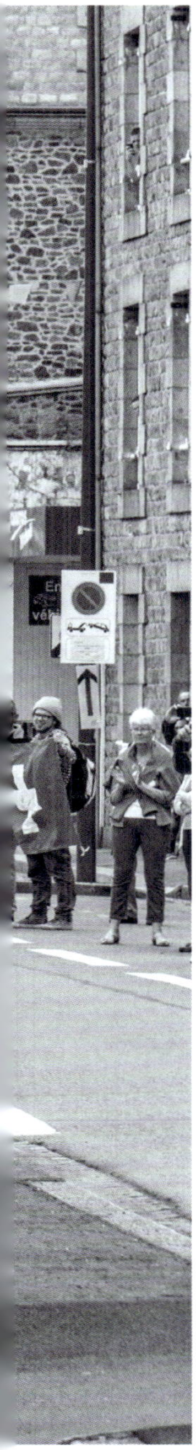

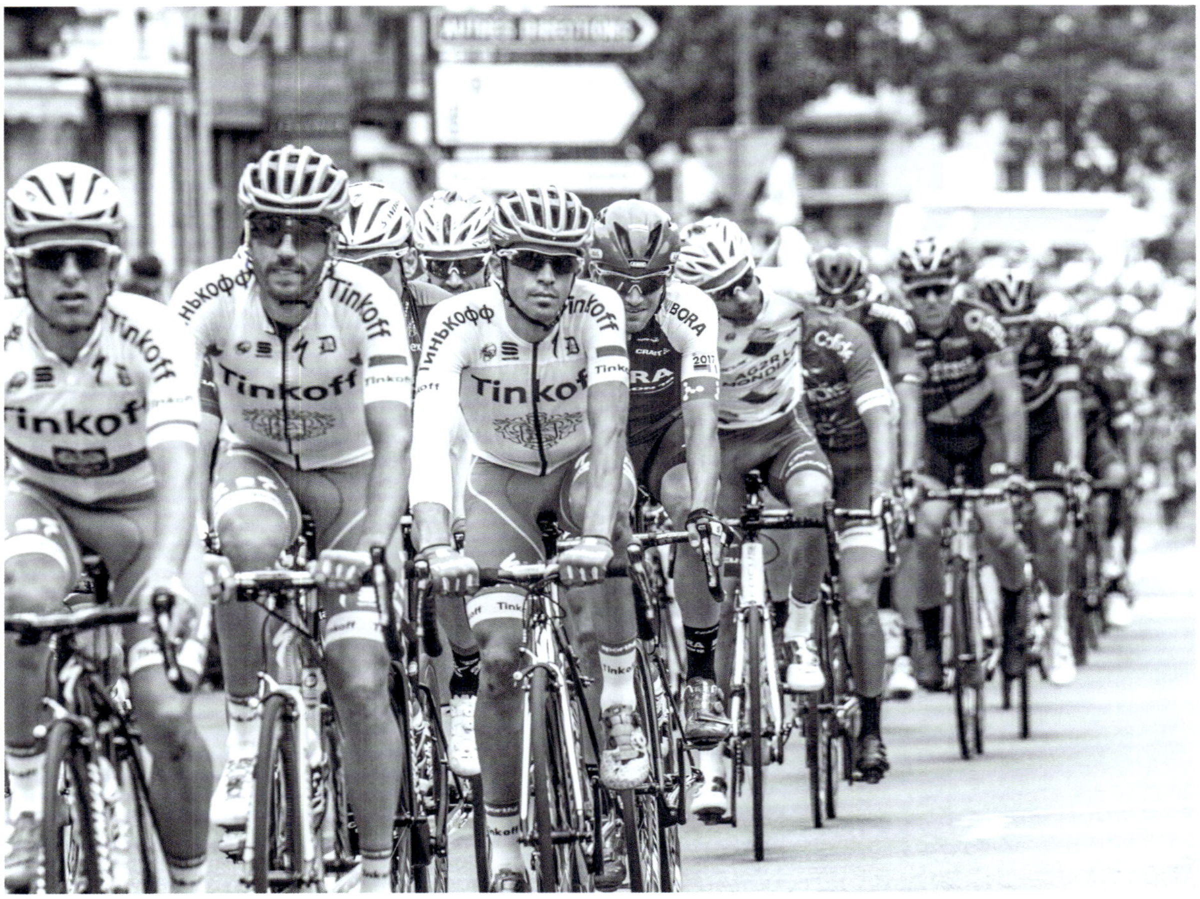
Tinkoff

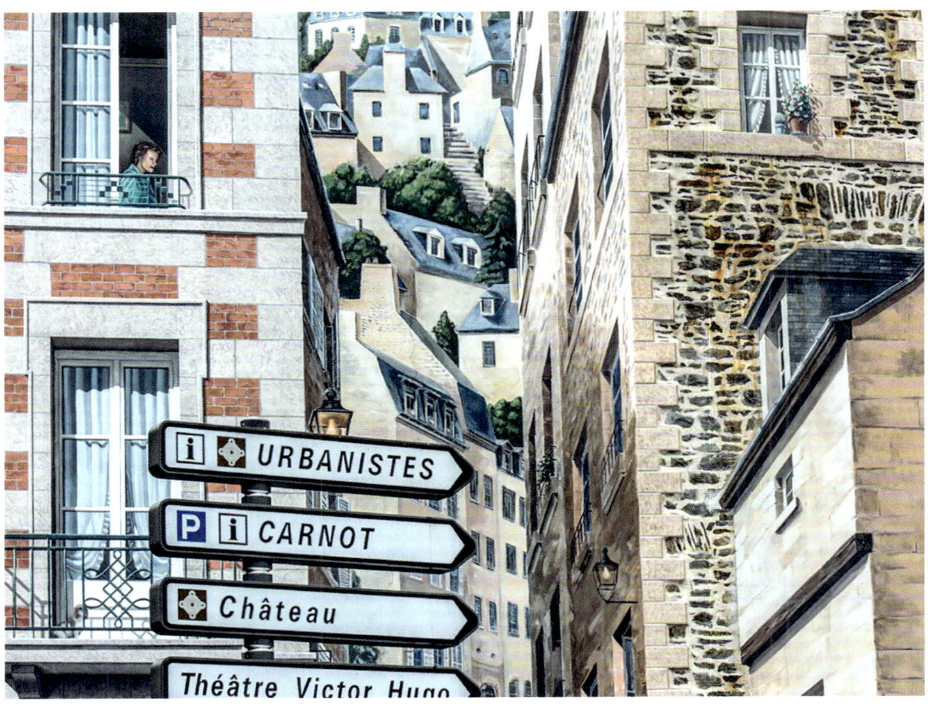
URBANISTES
P CARNOT
Château
Théâtre Victor Hugo

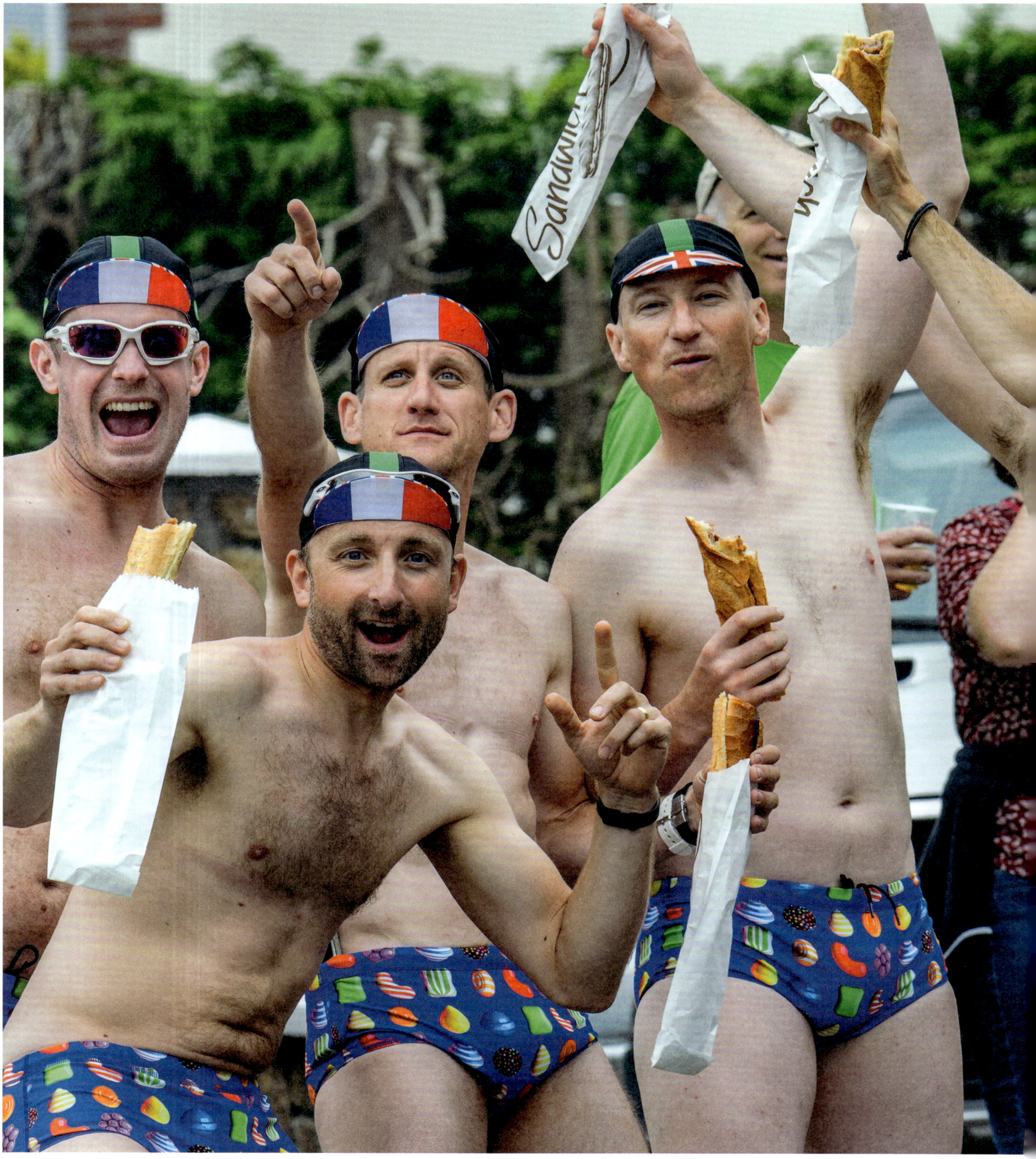
Sandwich

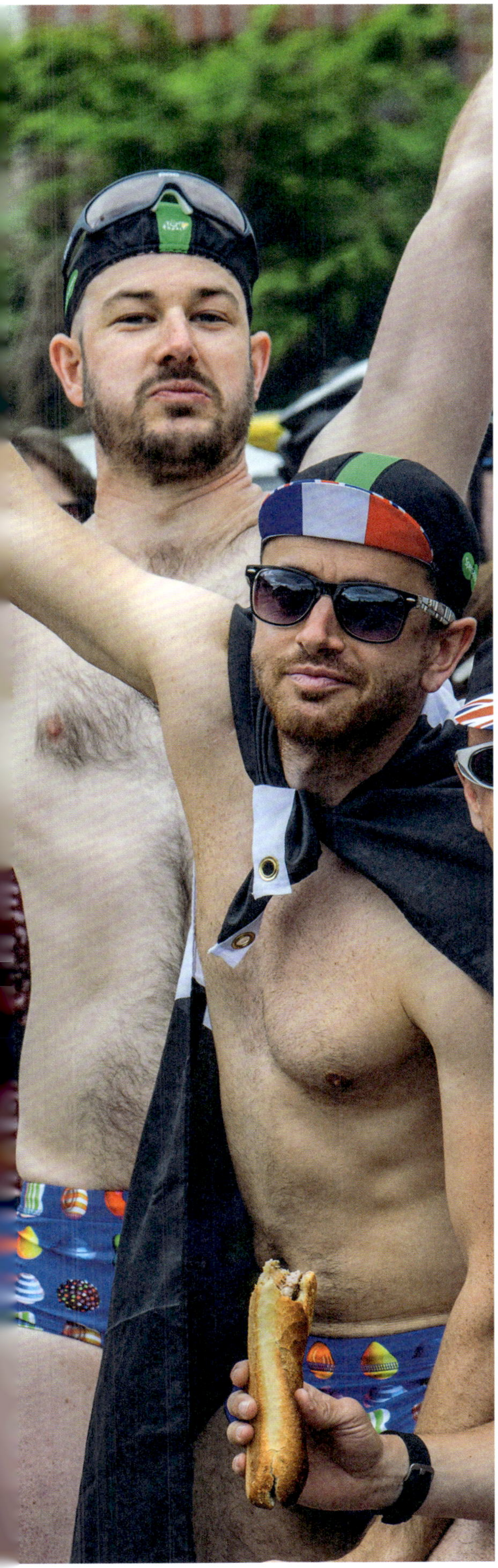

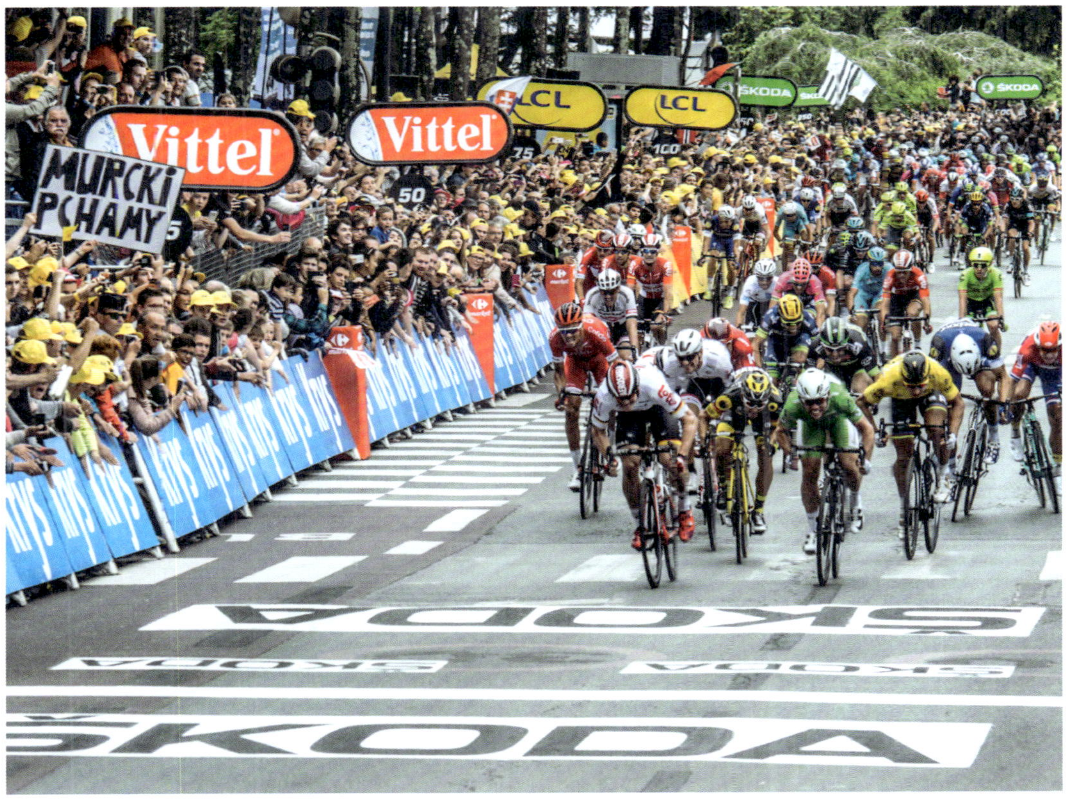

↖ Mit Herzblut und Badehose dabei. **With passion and swimming trunks**. *Enthousiasme et maillots de bain.*

↗ Mark Cavendish (Dimension Data) vor seinem zweiten Etappensieg in Angers (3. Etappe), vor André Greipel (Lotto Soudal) und Bryan Coquard (Direct Énergie). **Mark Cavendish (Dimension Data) before his second stage victory in Angers (3rd stage), followed by André Greipel (Lotto Soudal) and Bryan Coquard (Direct Énergie).** *Mark Cavendish (Dimension Data) avant sa seconde victoire à Angers (3eme étape), devant André Greipel (Lotto Soudal) et Bryan Coquard (Direct Énergie).*

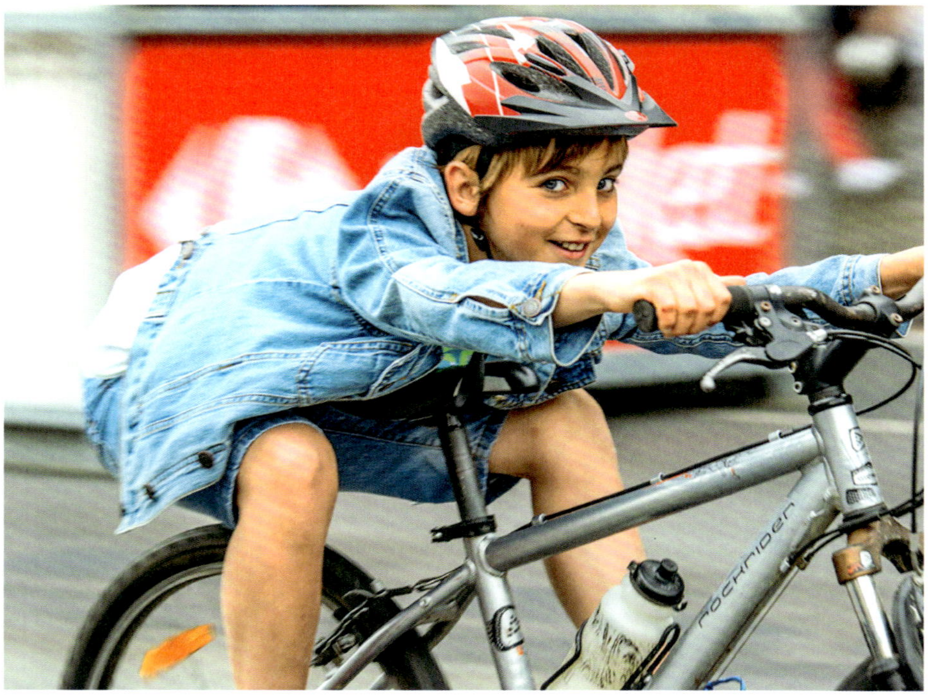

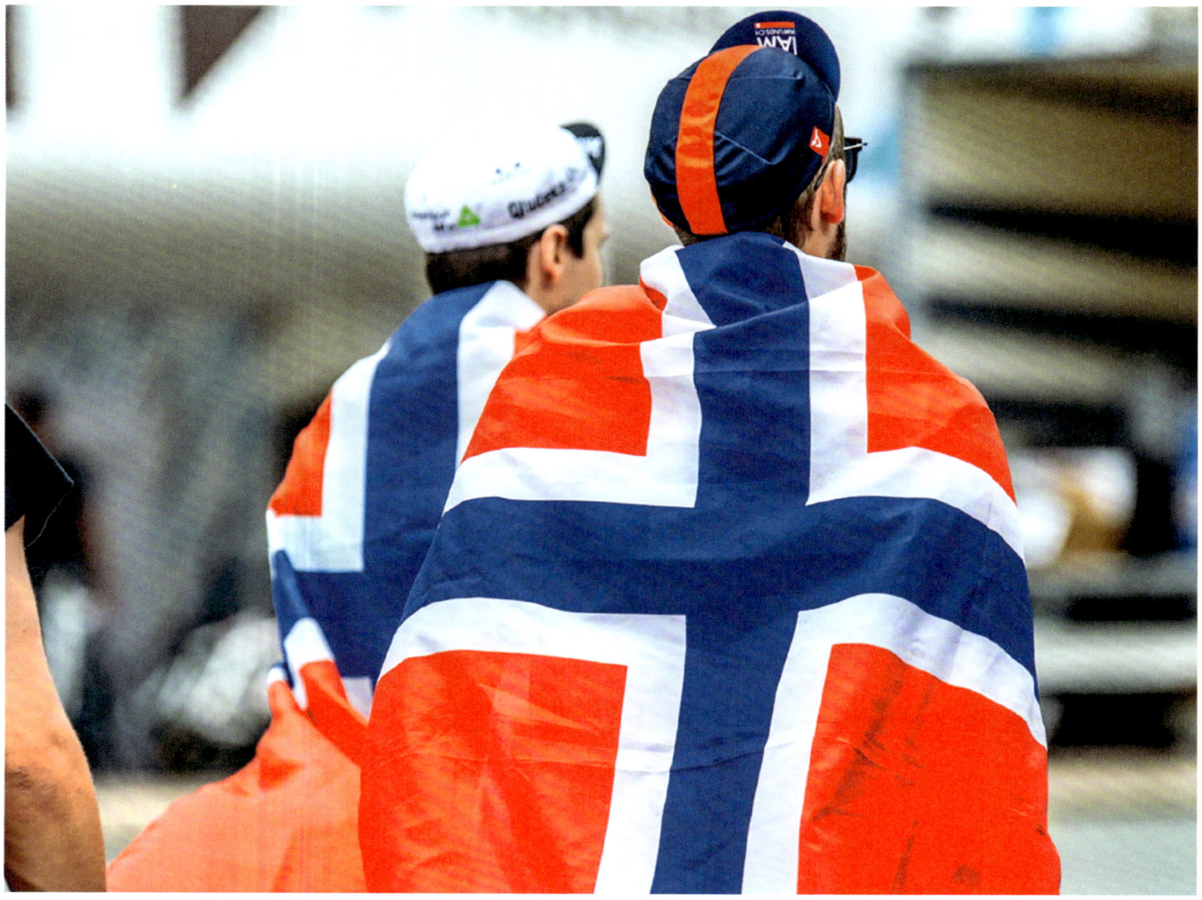

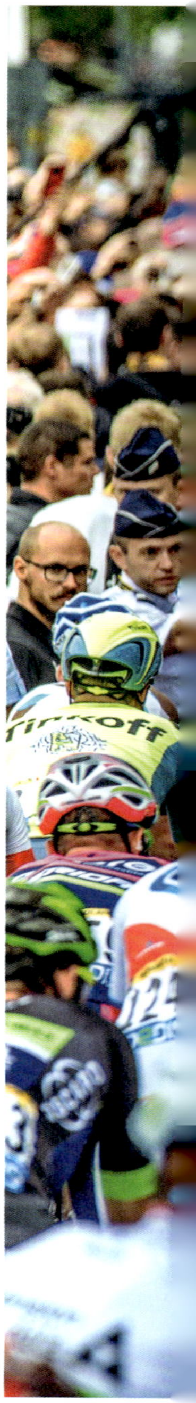

Das Peloton am Start. **The peloton ready to start.** *Le peloton au départ.*

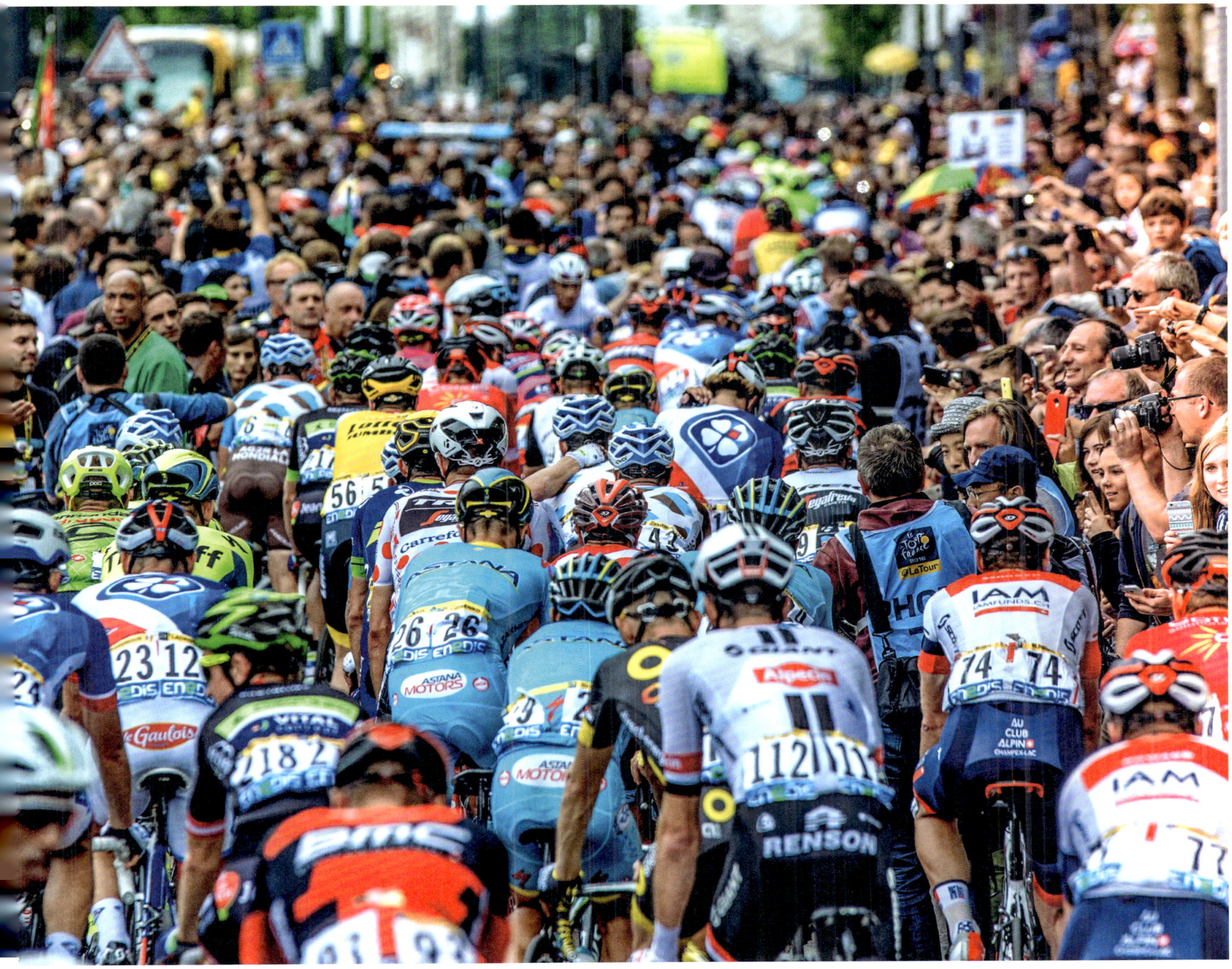
IAM
ASTANA MOTORS
GIANT
Alpecin
RENSON
LeGaulois
AU CLUB ALPIN

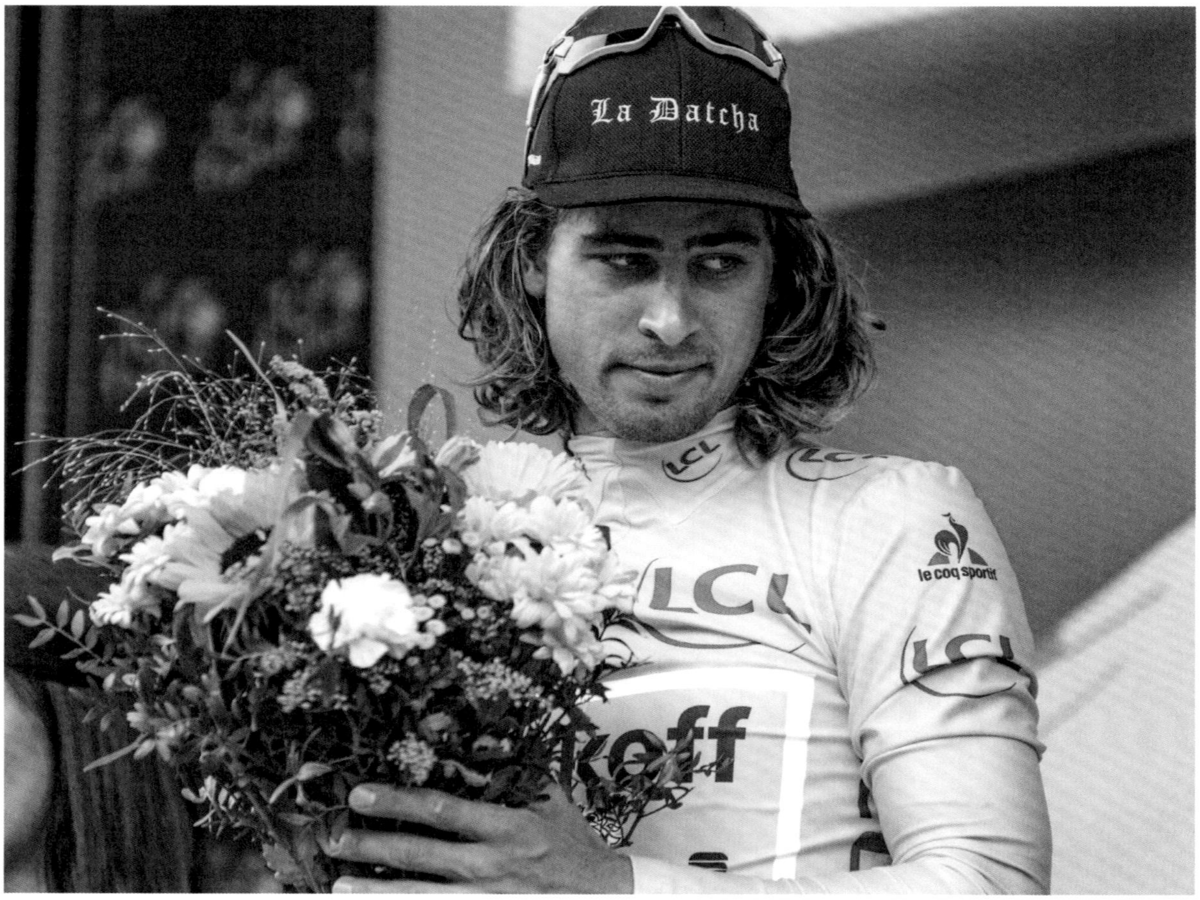

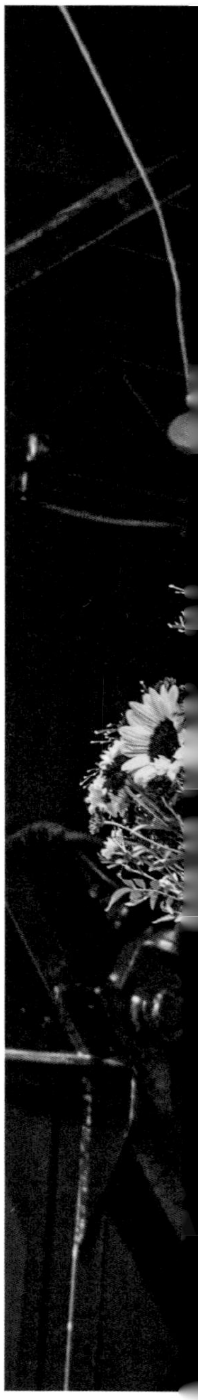

↑ Peter Sagan (Tinkoff) noch immer in Gelb. **Peter Sagan (Tinkoff) still in yellow.** *Peter Sagan (Tinkoff) toujours en jaune.*

↗ Mark Cavendish (Dimension Data) feiert den Etappensieg auf dem Podium mit seinen Kindern. **Mark Cavendish (Dimension Data) celebrates the stage victory on the podium with his children.** *Mark Cavendish (Dimension Data) célèbre sa victoire avec ses enfants sur le podium.*

→ Thomas Voeckler (Direct Énergie) gewinnt den „Prix de la Combativité" und wird kämpferischster Fahrer der 3. Etappe. **Thomas Voeckler (Direct Énergie) wins the 'Prix de la combativité' and becomes the most aggressive rider of the 3rd stage.** *Thomas Voeckler (Direct Énergie) remporte le prix de la Combativité de la 3eme étape.*

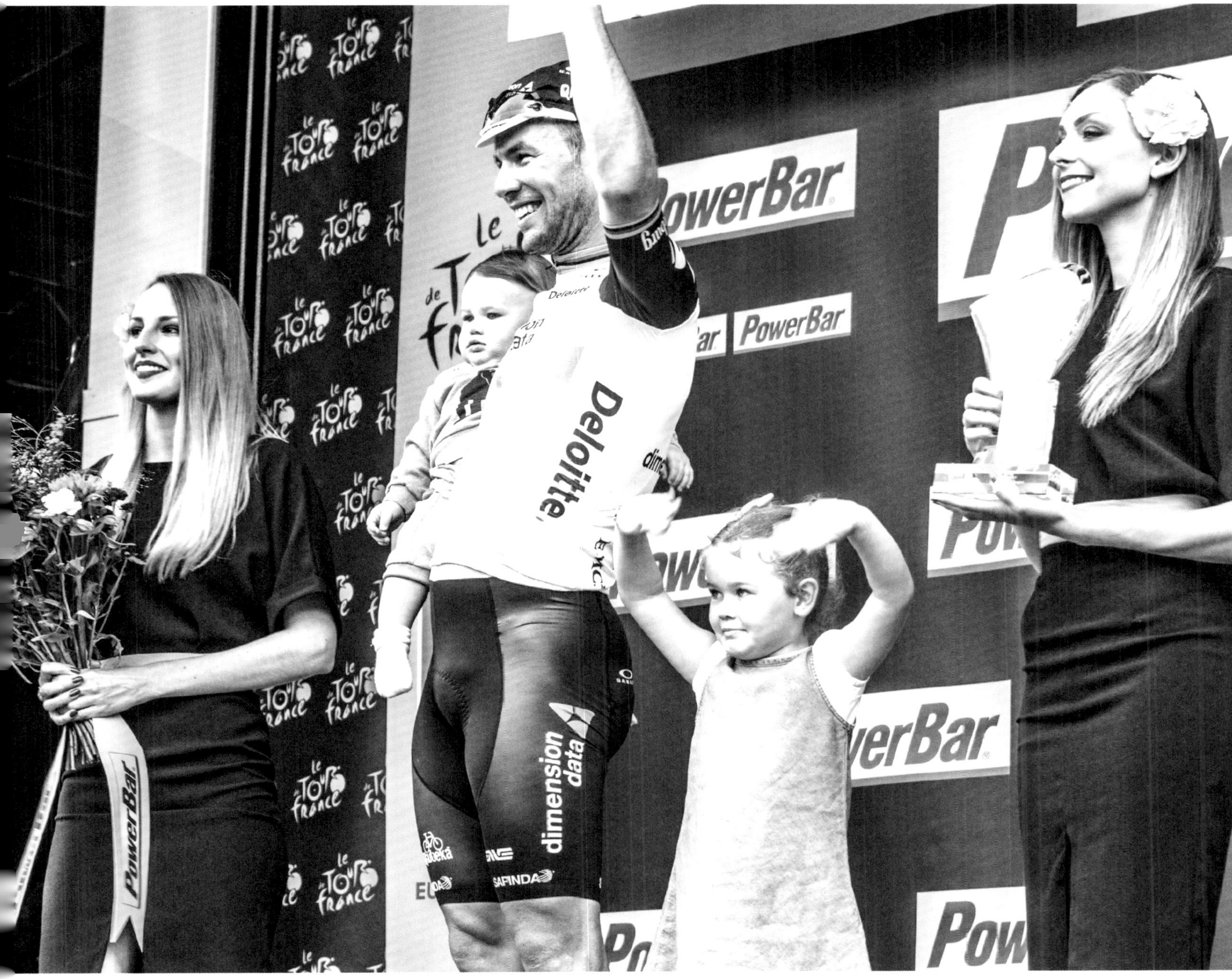
PowerBar
PowerBar
PowerBar
Deloitte.
dimension data
PowerBar

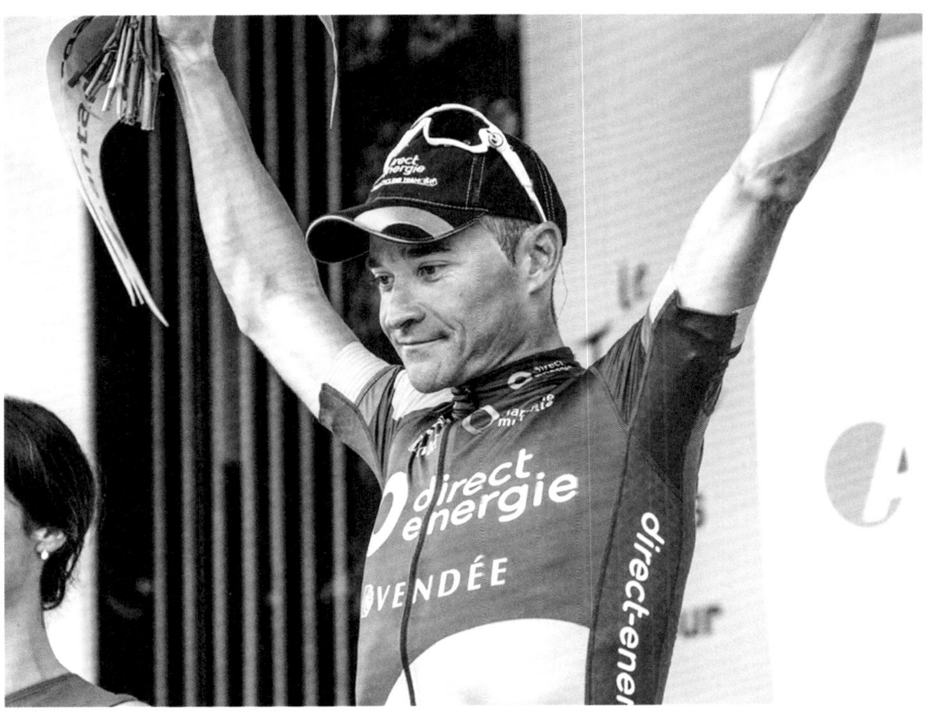
direct energie
VENDÉE
direct-ener

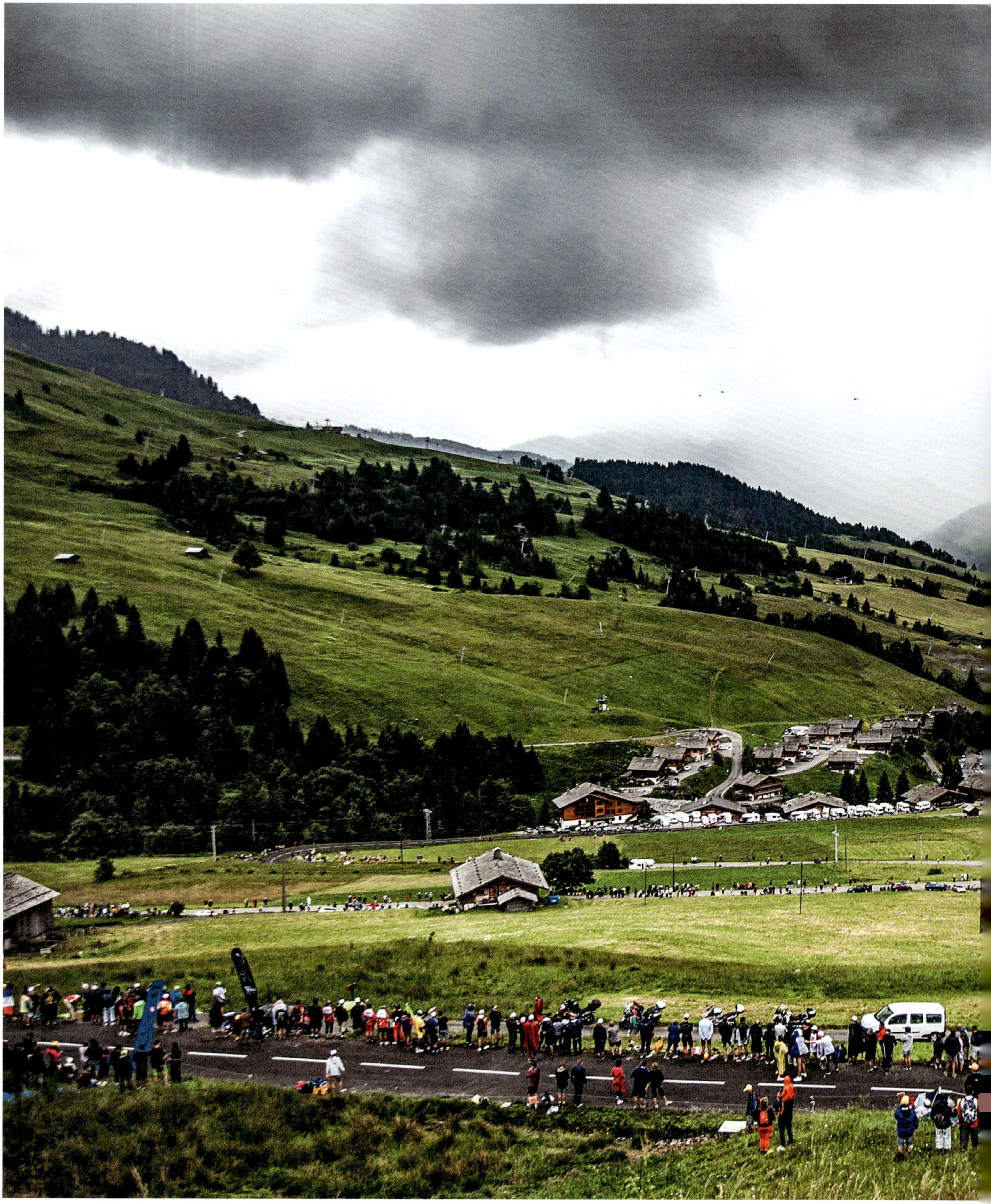

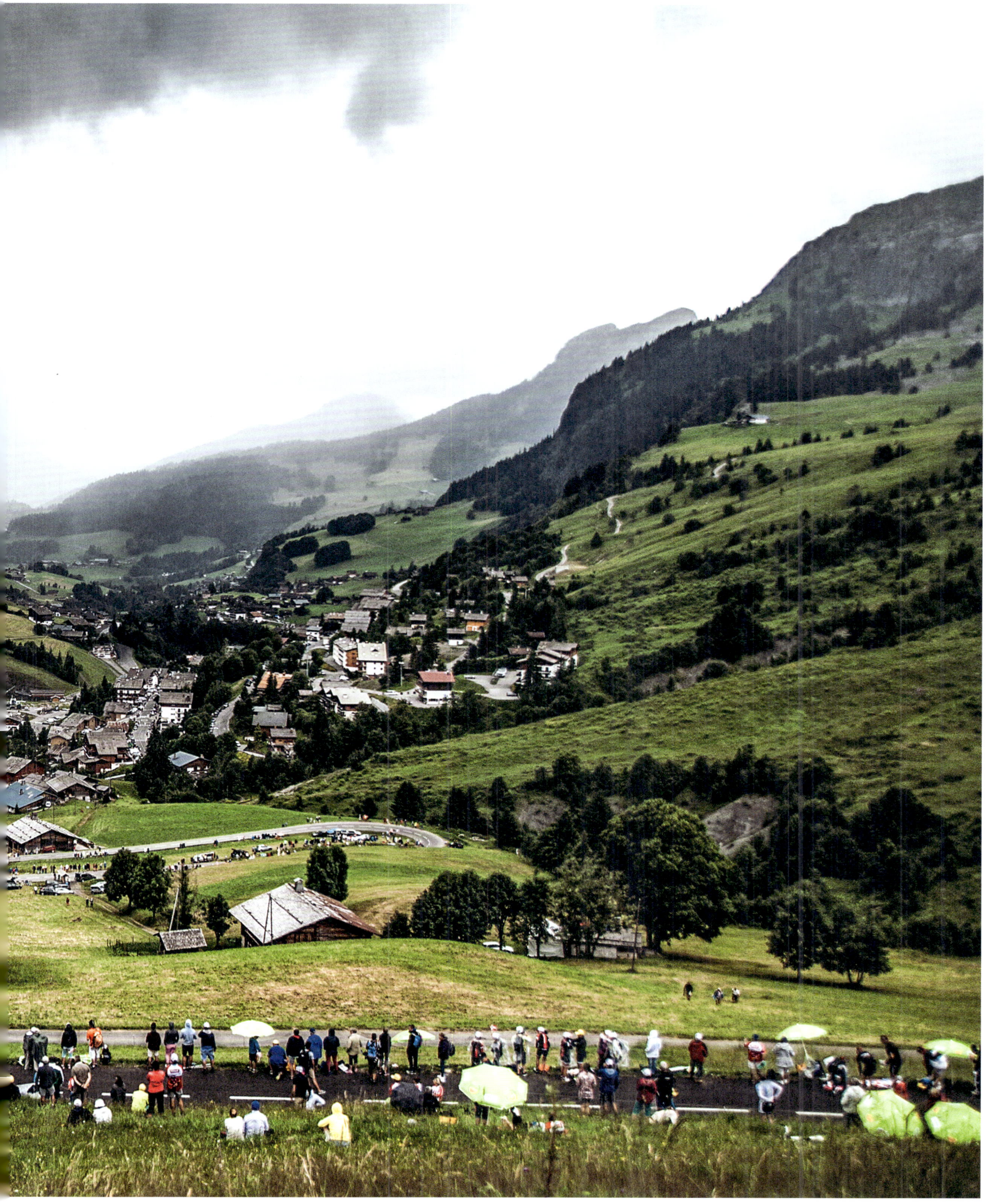

Auf dem Weg Richtung Pyrenäen. **On the way to the Pyrenees.** *En route vers les Pyrénées.*

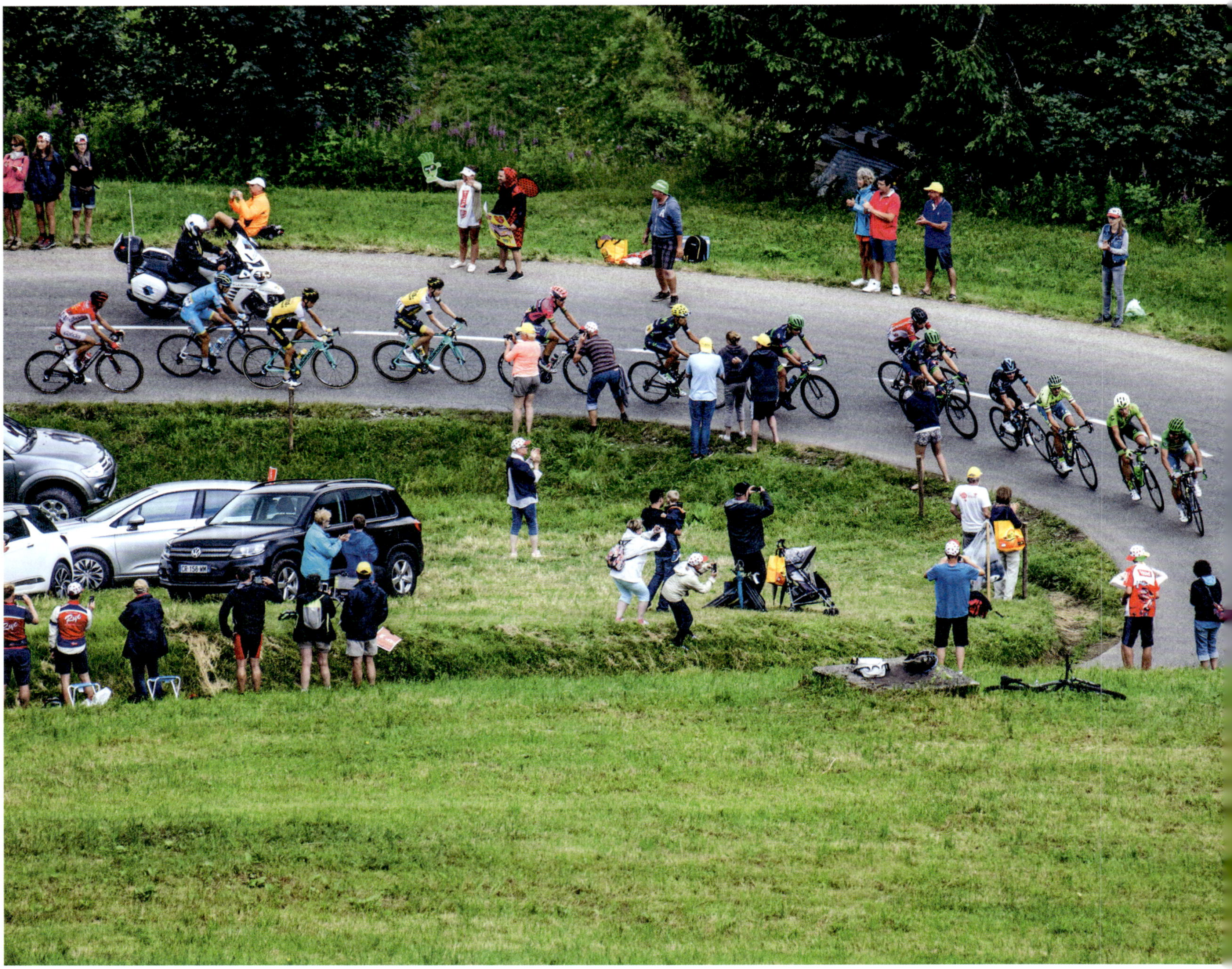

 Begeisterung und Unterstützung überall. **Enthusiasm and support everywhere.** *Enthousiasme et sont de mise pour encourager les coureurs.*

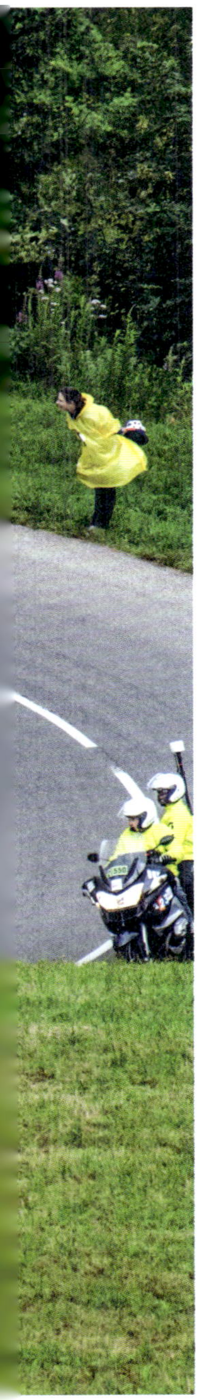

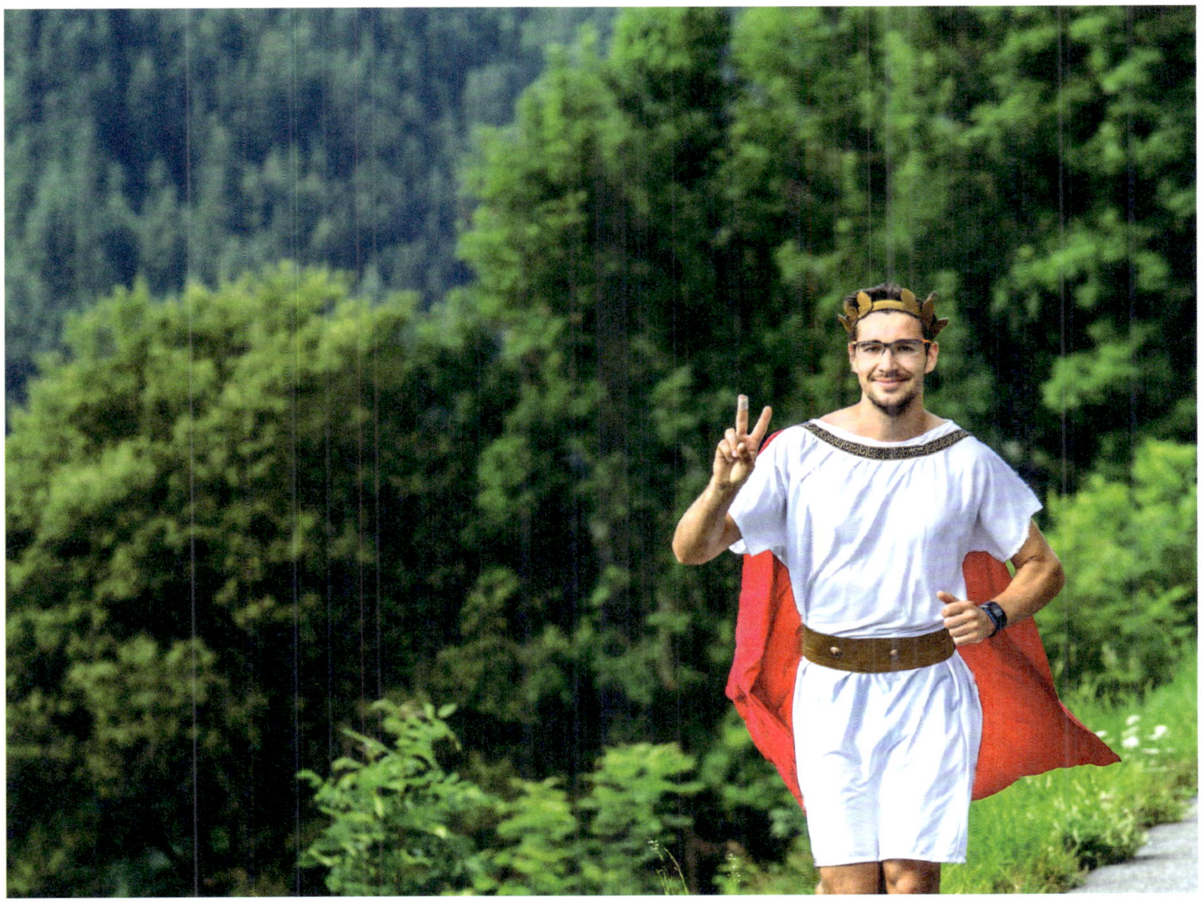

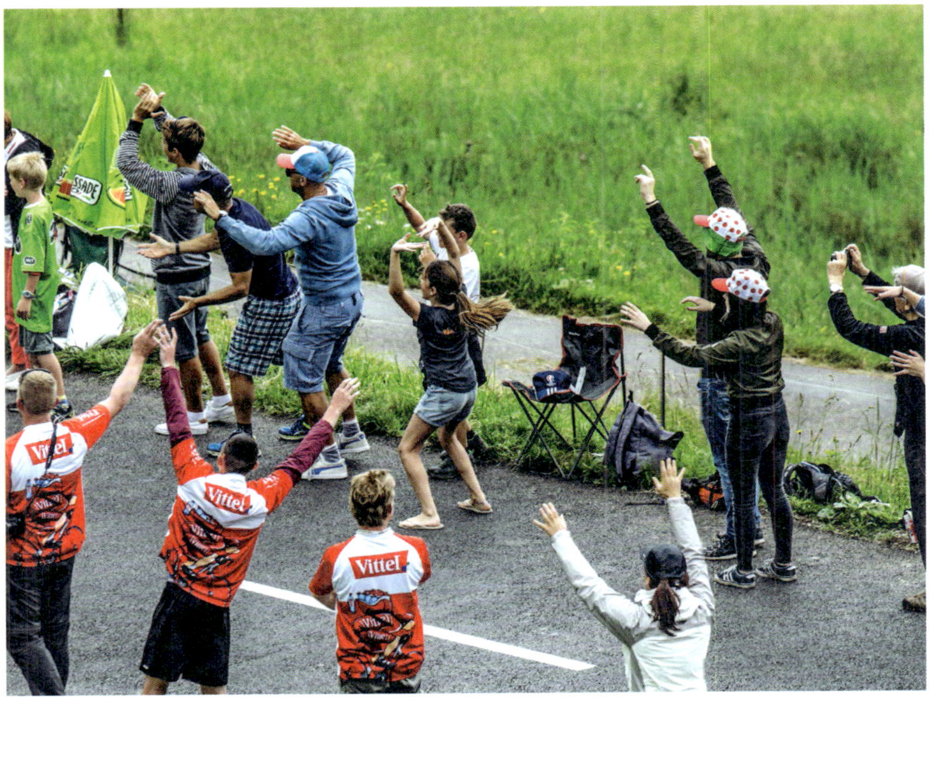
Vittel

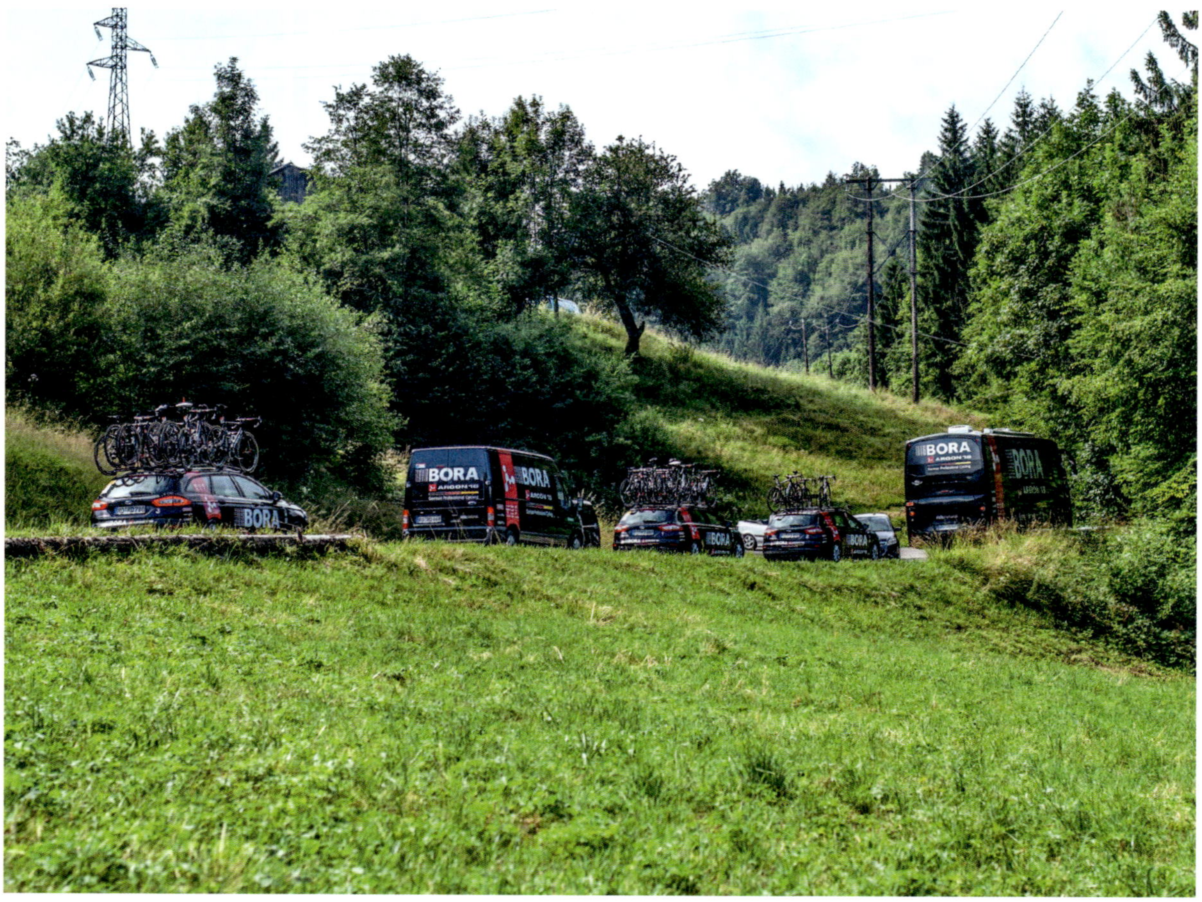

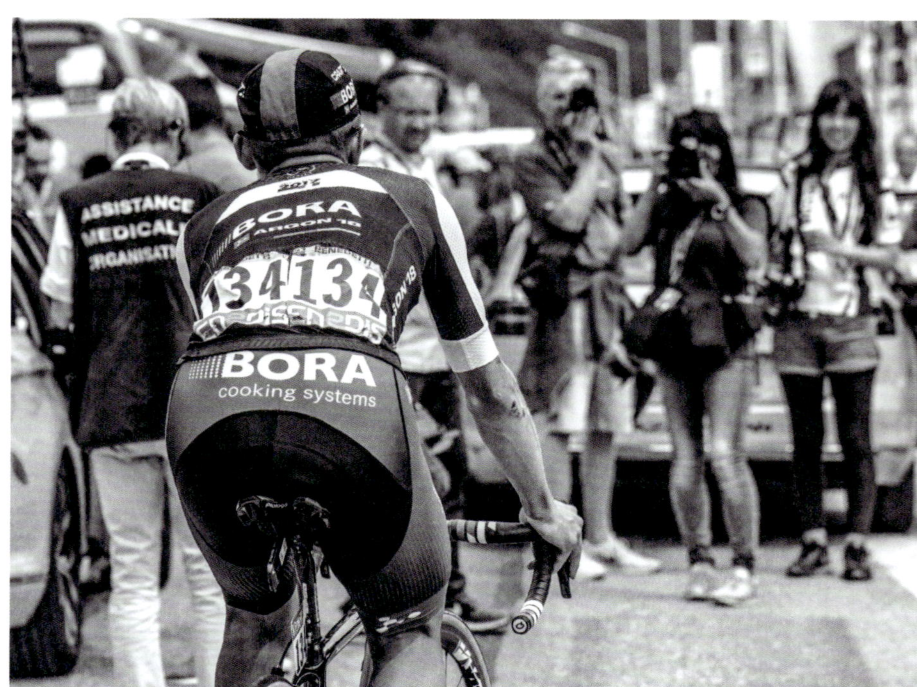
ASSISTANCE
BORA
cooking systems

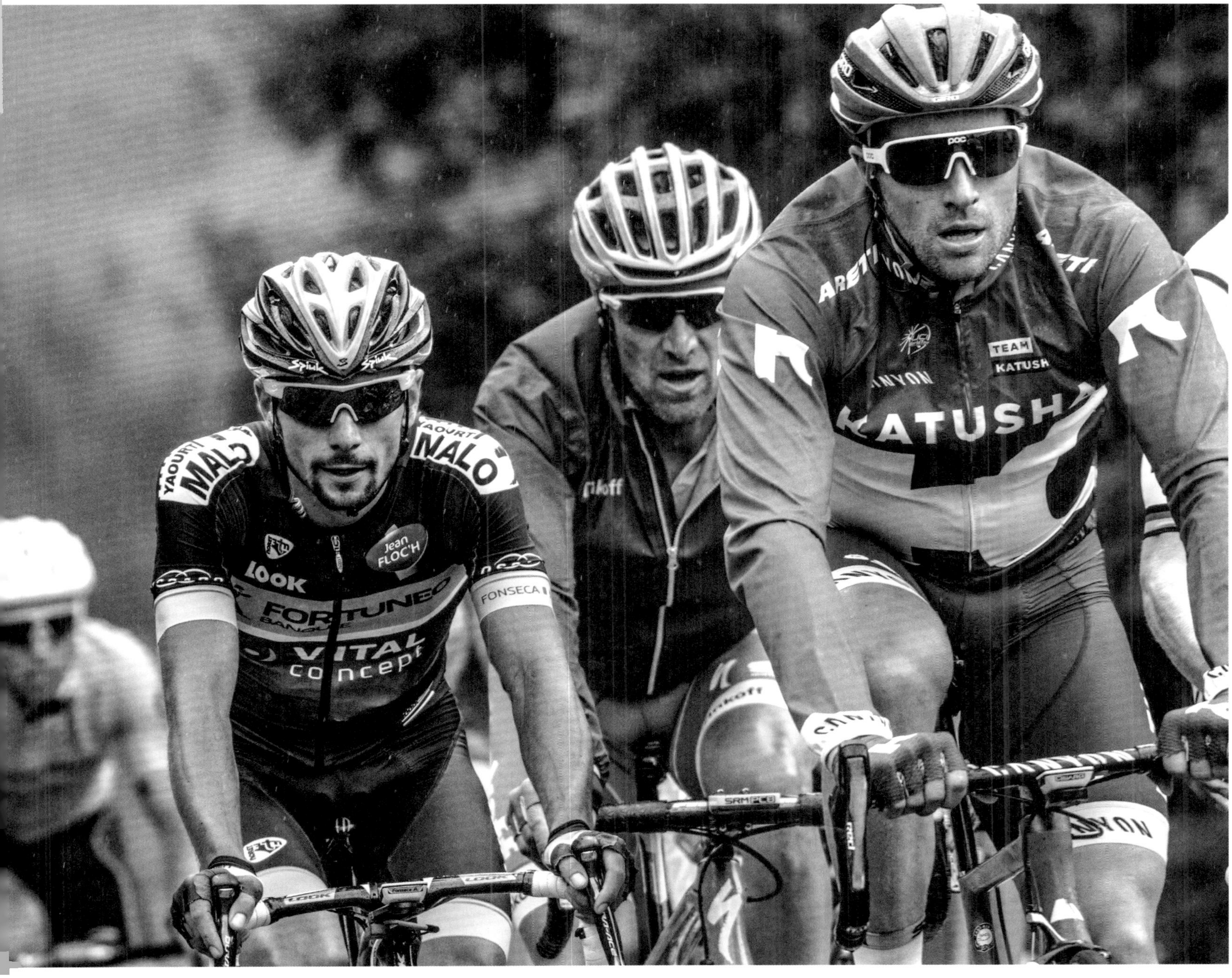

Der Tour-Tross. **The tour entourage.** *Dans la caravane du Tour.*

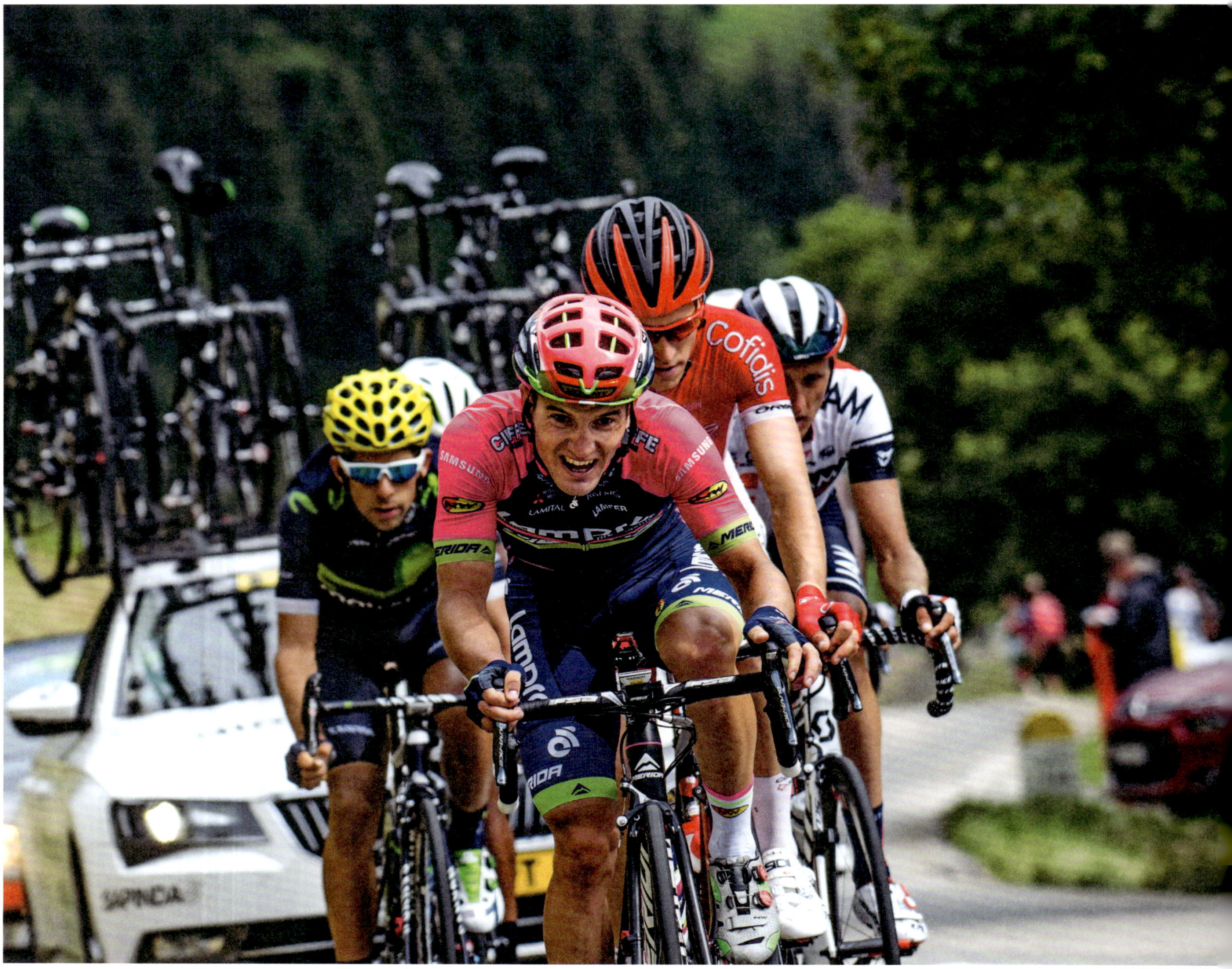

↑ Alles geben. **Give everything.** *Tout donner.*
→ Fanimpressionen. **Fan impressions.** *Images de spectateurs.*

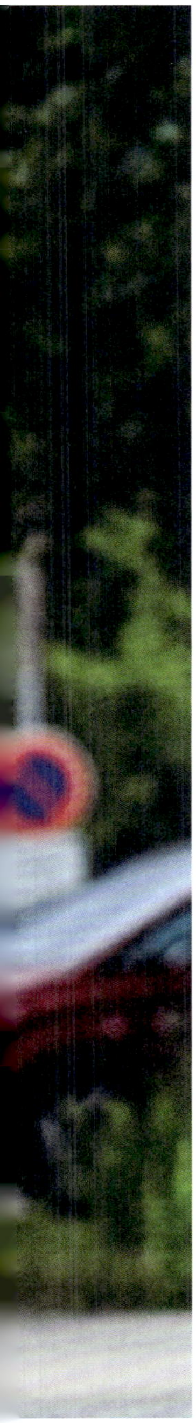

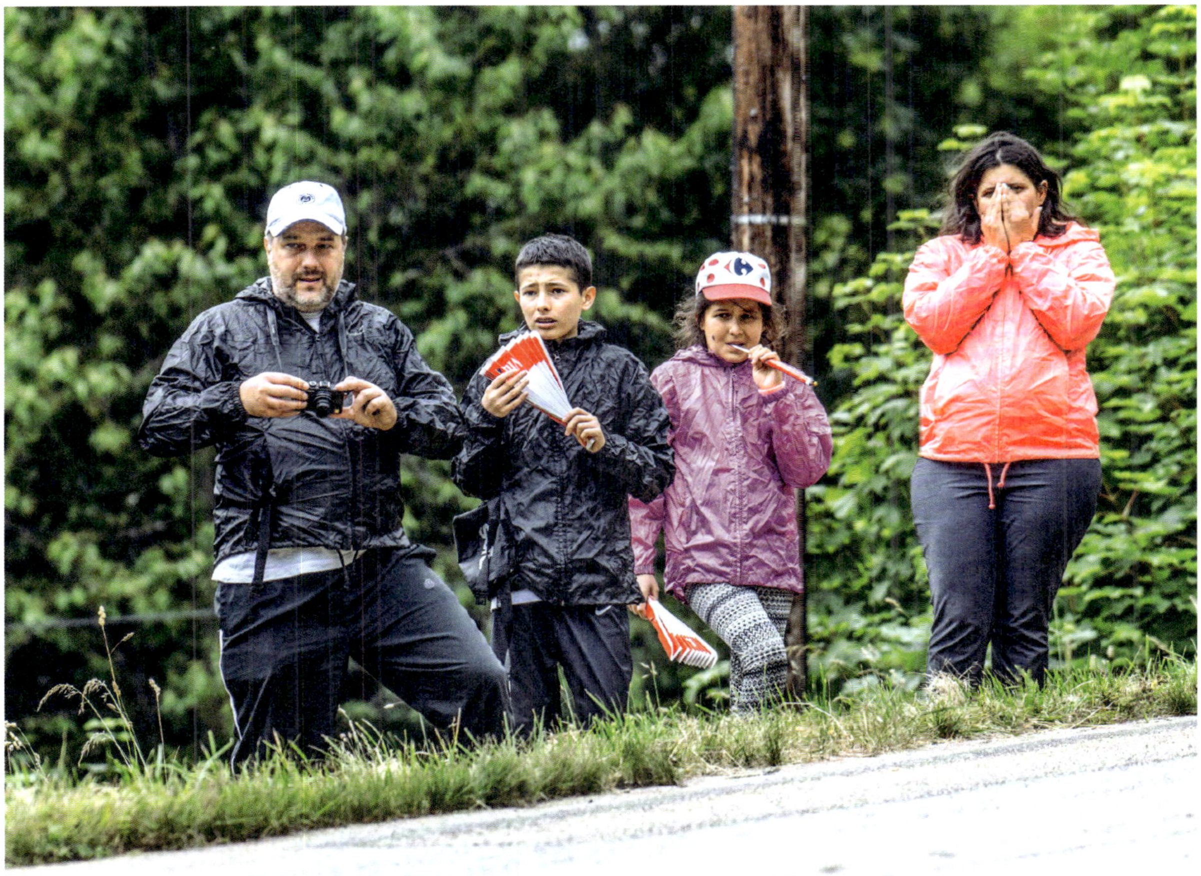

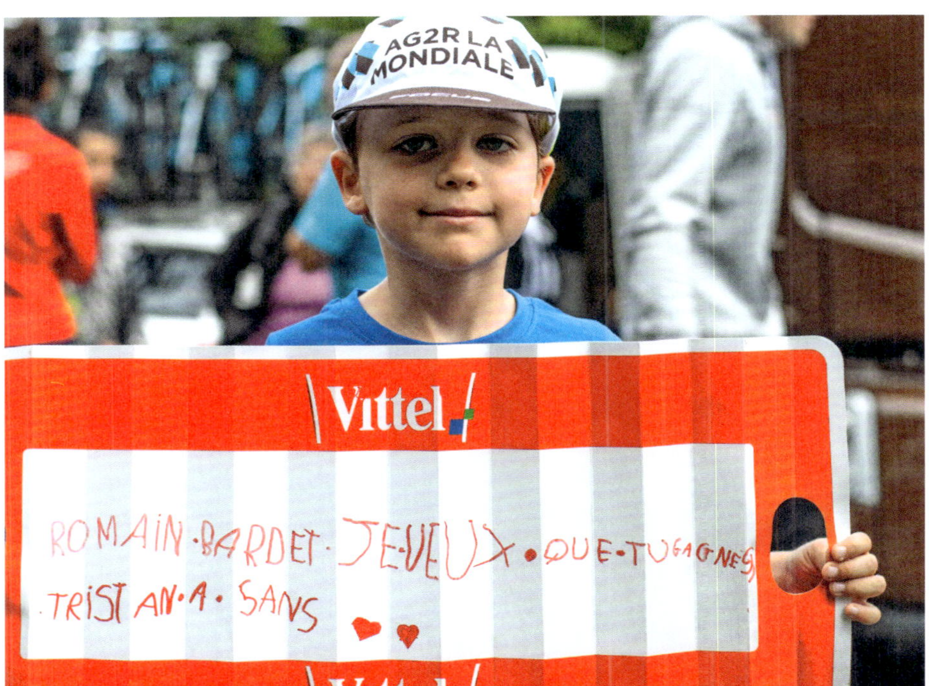
AG2R LA MONDIALE
Vittel
ROMAIN·BARDET·JE·VEUX·QUE·TU GAGNES
TRISTAN·A·SANS
Vittel

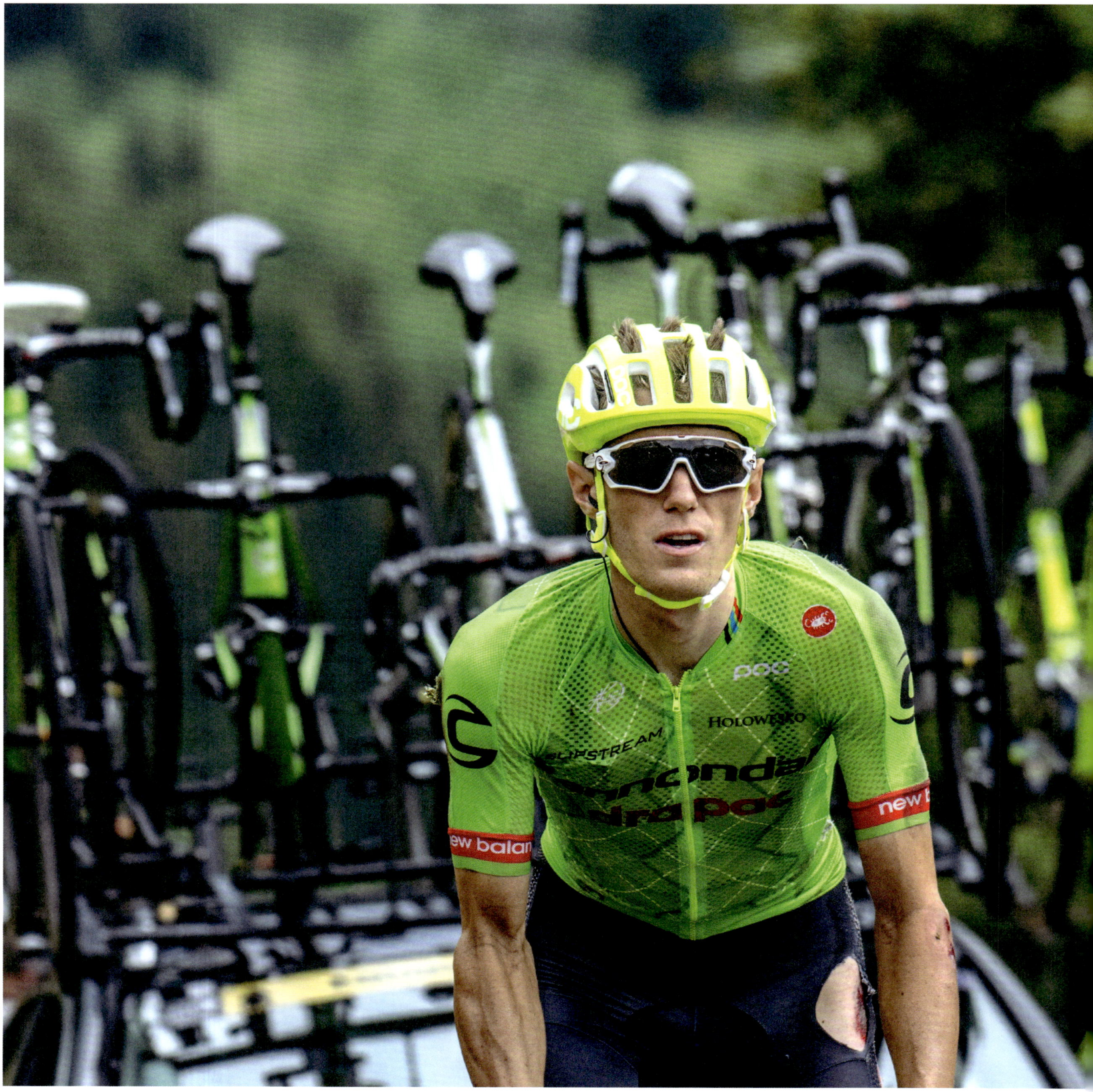
poc
HOLOWESKO

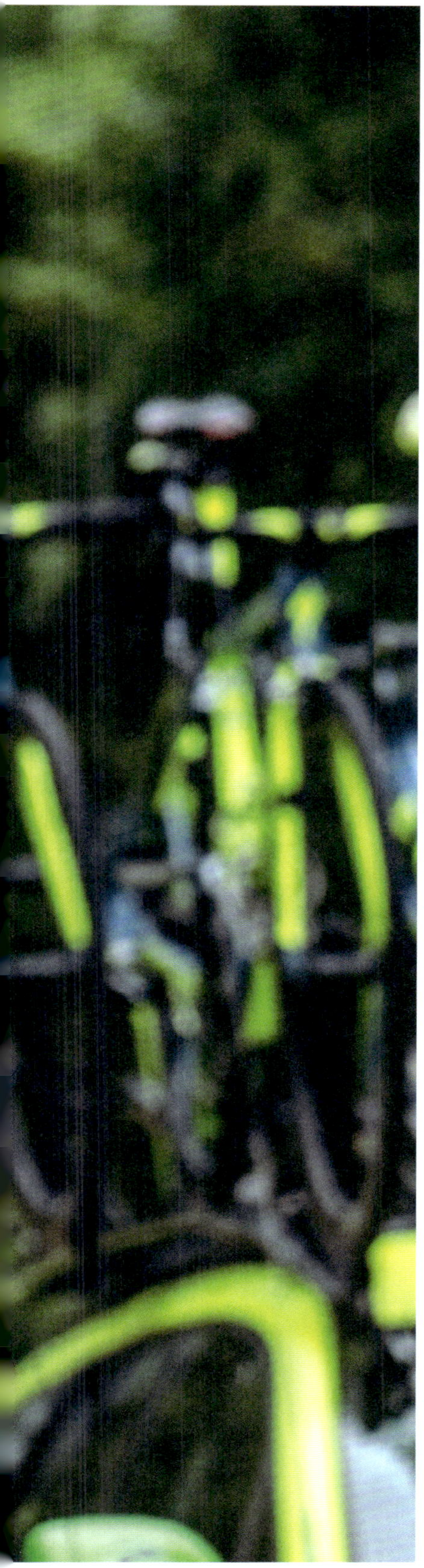

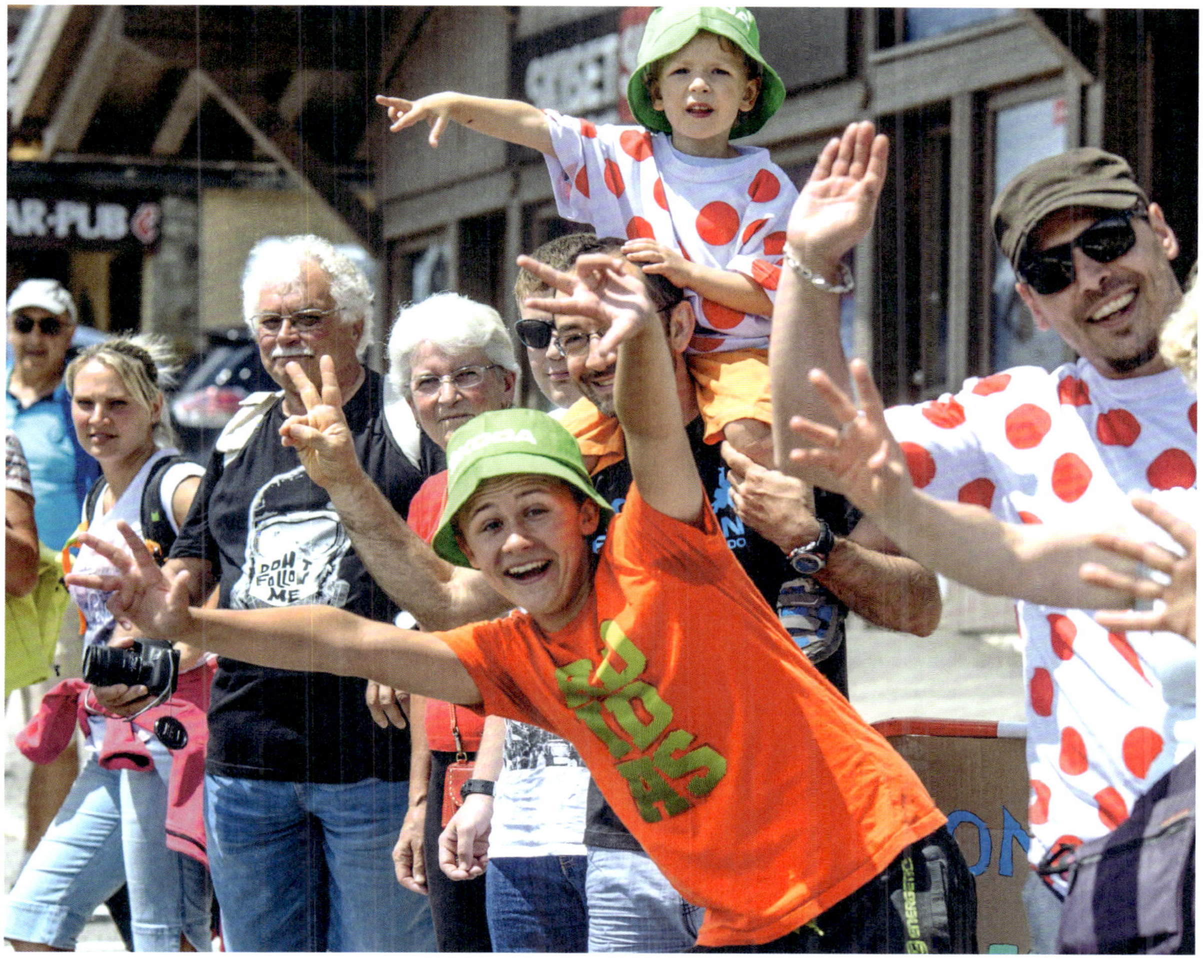

Pierre Rolland (Cannondale-Drapac Pro Cycling Team) nach seinem Sturz bei der 19. Etappe. **Pierre Rolland (Cannondale-Drapac Pro Cycling Team) after his fall during the 19th stage.** *Pierre Rolland (Cannondale-Drapac Pro Cycling Team) après sa chute dans la 19e étape.*

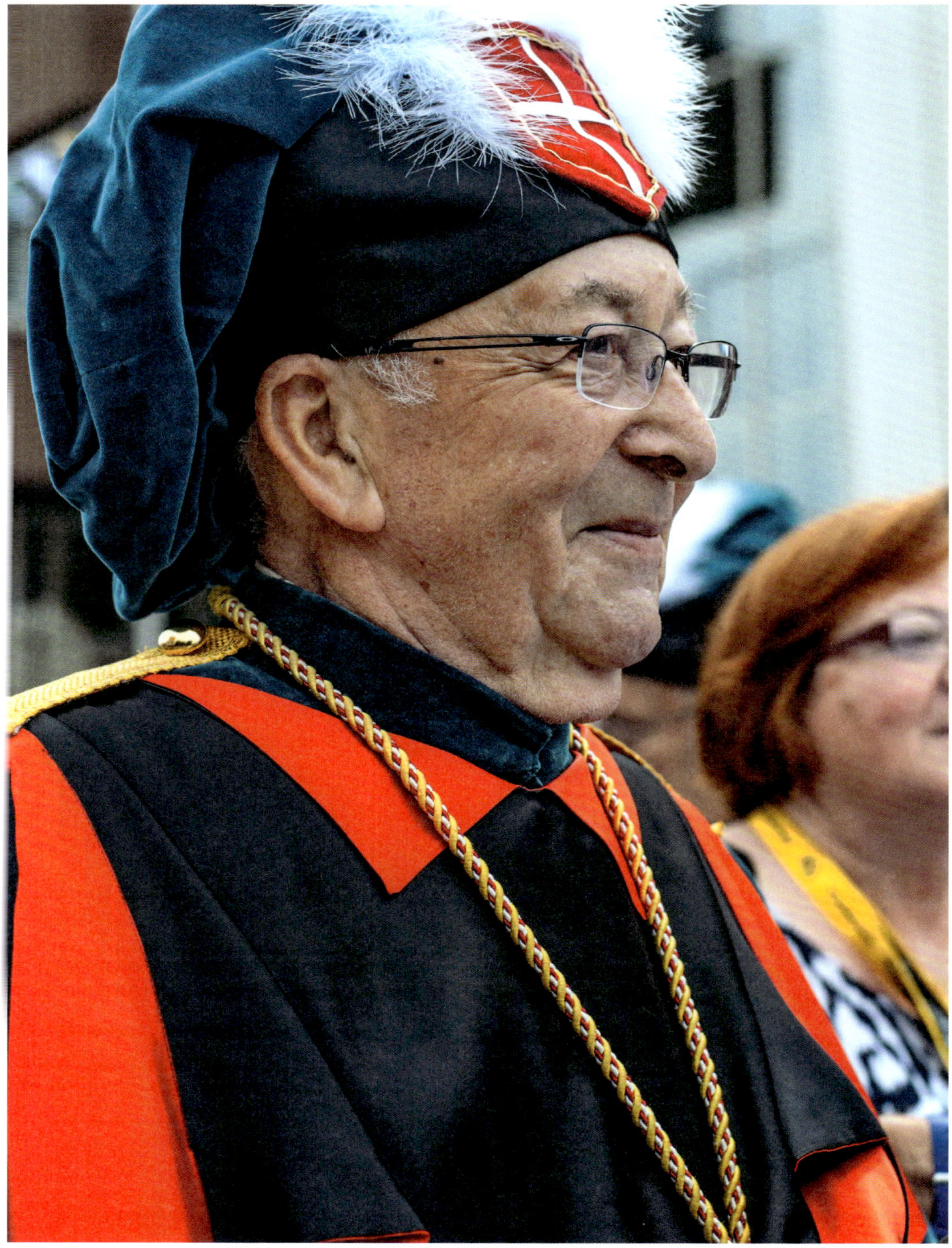

Honoratioren beehren die Tour. **Notables honour the tour.** *Des notables honorent le Tour de leur présence.*

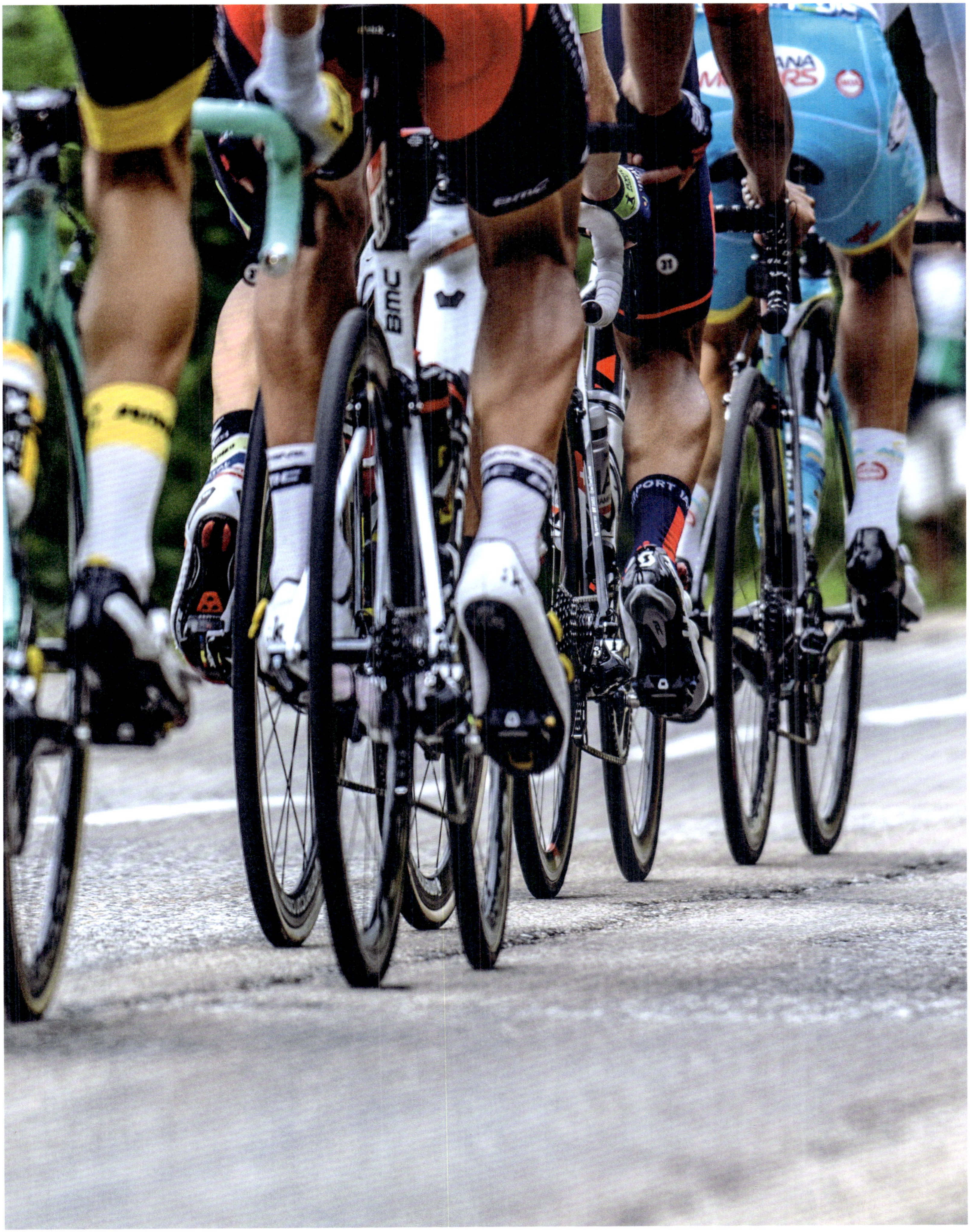
BMC

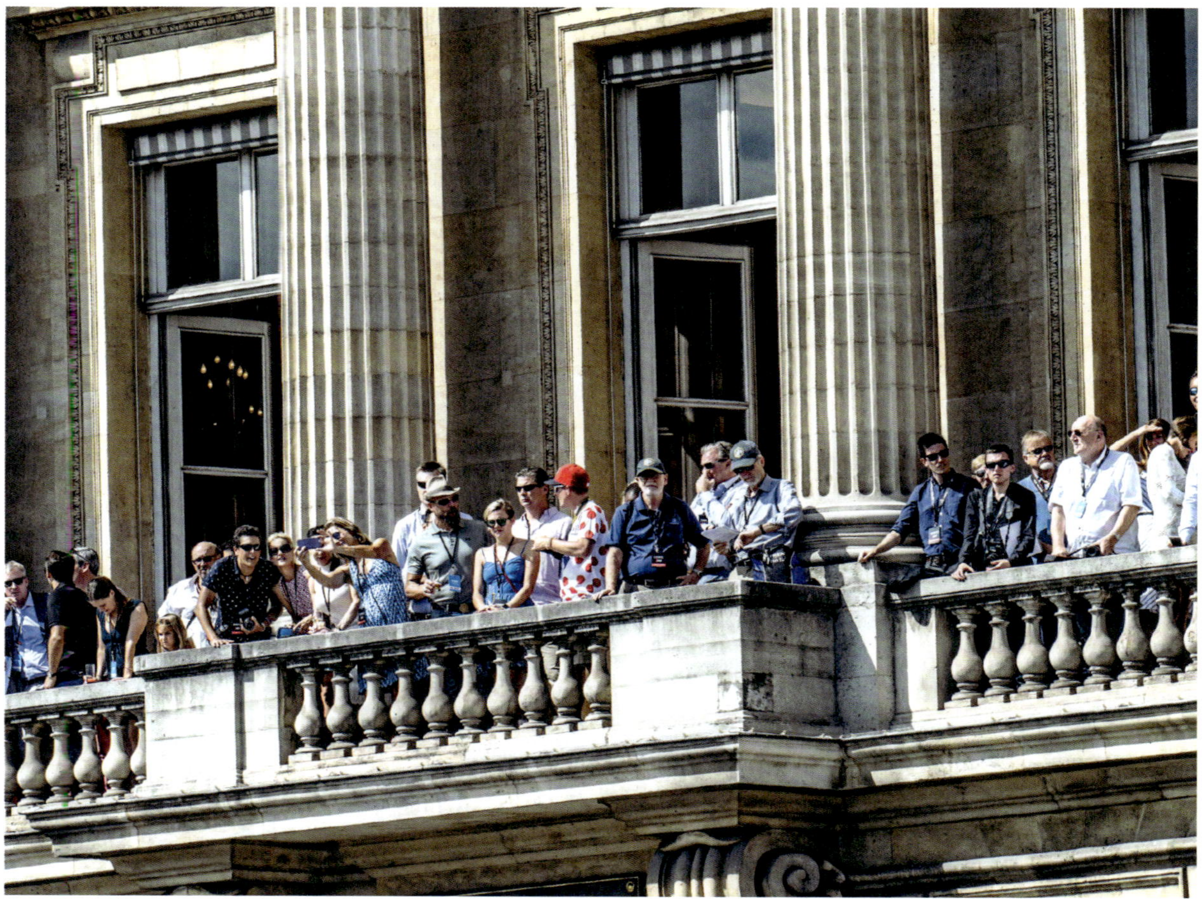

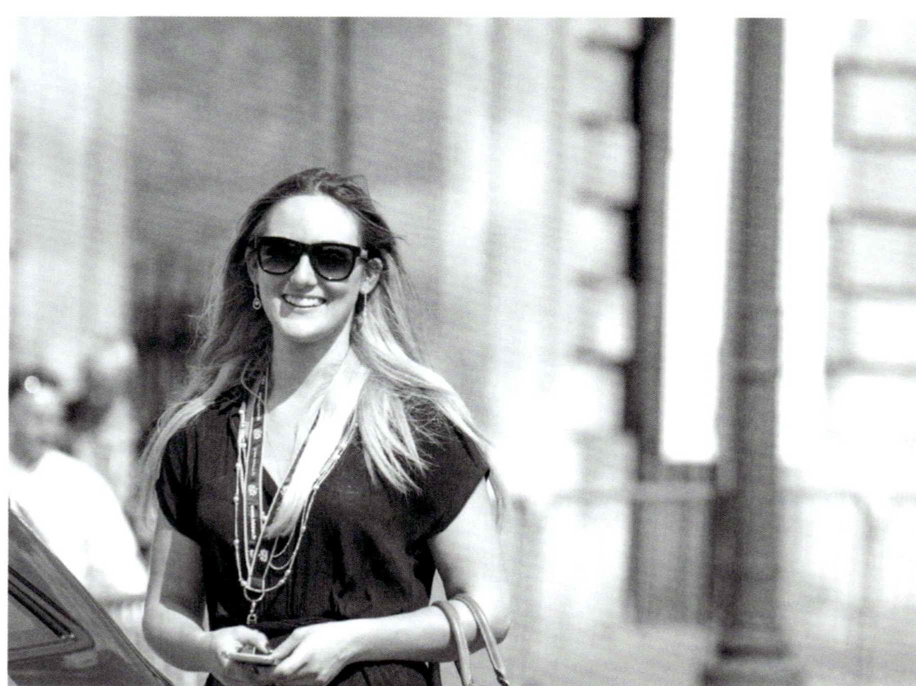

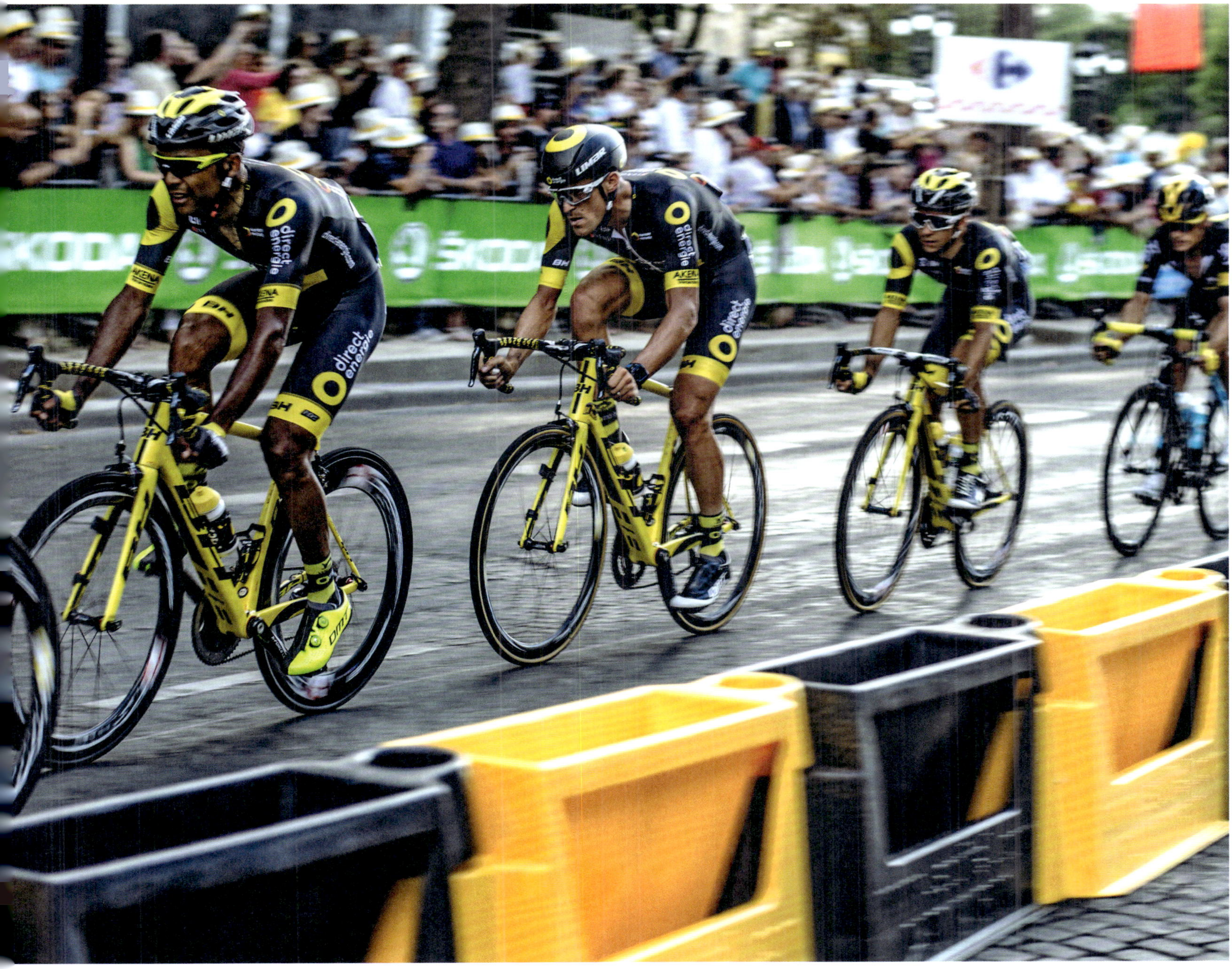

← Paris. Fans und Fahrerfamilien erwarten das Peloton auf den Champs-Élysées. **Paris: fans and family await the peloton on the Champs-Élysées.**
Paris. Spectateurs et familles des coureurs attendent le peloton sur les Champs-Élysées.

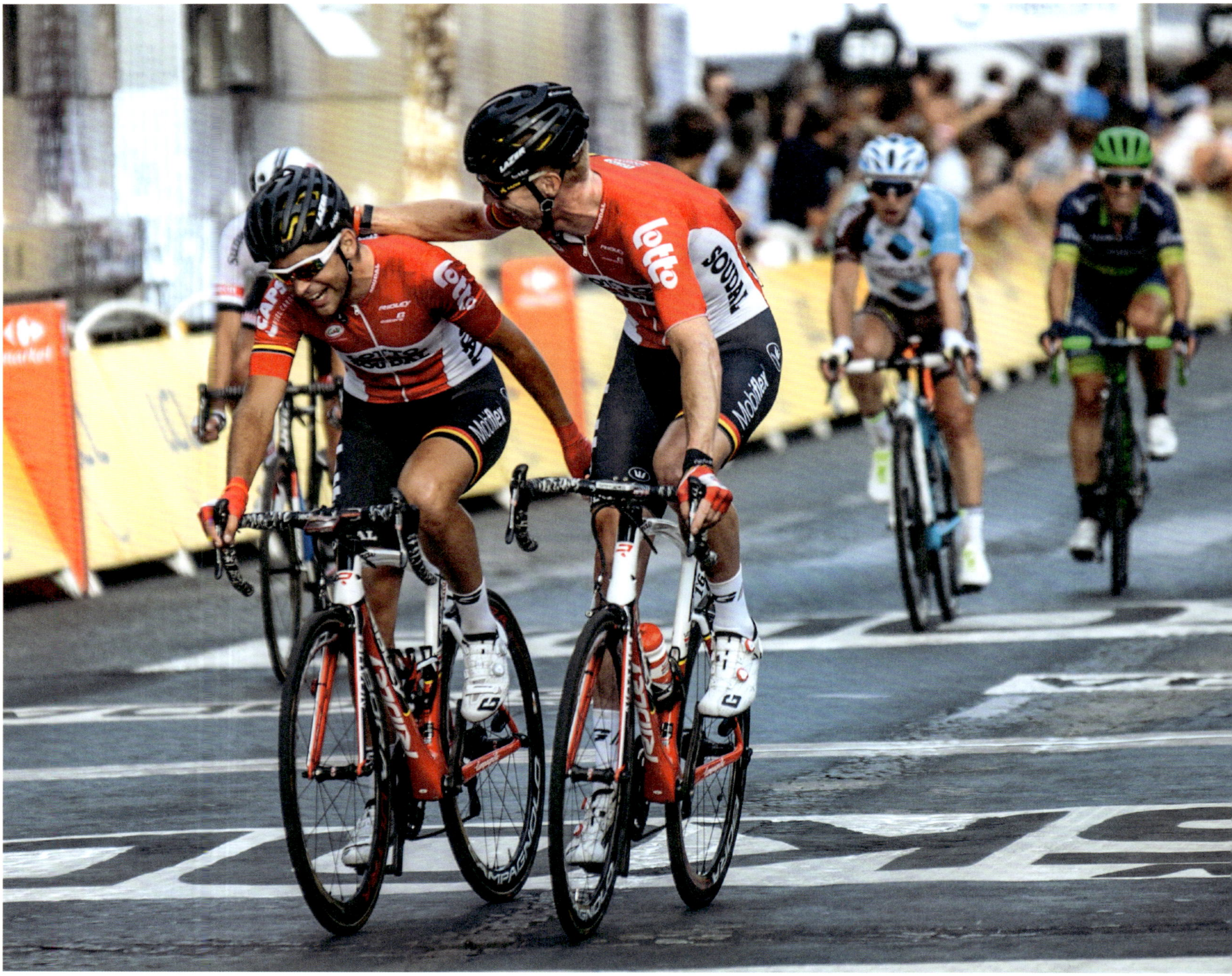

↑ Marcel Sieberg und Tony Gallopin können es kaum fassen, dass ihr Kapitän André Greipel zum zweiten Mal in Folge den Zielsprint auf den Champs-Élysées für sich entscheiden konnte. **Marcel Sieberg and Tony Gallopin are overwhelmed by their teammate André Greipel winning the sprint finish on the Champs-Élysées for the second time in a row.** *Marcel Sieberg et Tony Gallopin réalisent à peine la deuxième victoire consécutive de leur coéquipier André Greipel sure les Champs-Élysées.*

↗ Team Sky mit dem Gesamtsieger Chris Froome in Gelb auf der Ziellinie der Champs-Élysées. **Team Sky with the overall winner, Chris Froome, in yellow on the finish line on the Champs-Élysées.** *La Team Sky avec Chris Froome, vainqueur du Tour, en jaune, sur la ligne d'arrivée aux Champs-Élysées.*

→ Nairo Quintana (Movistar), immer umringt von kolumbianischen Fans. **Nairo Quintana (Movistar) always surrounded by Columbian fans.** *Nairo Quintana (Movistar) toujours entouré de fans colombiens.*

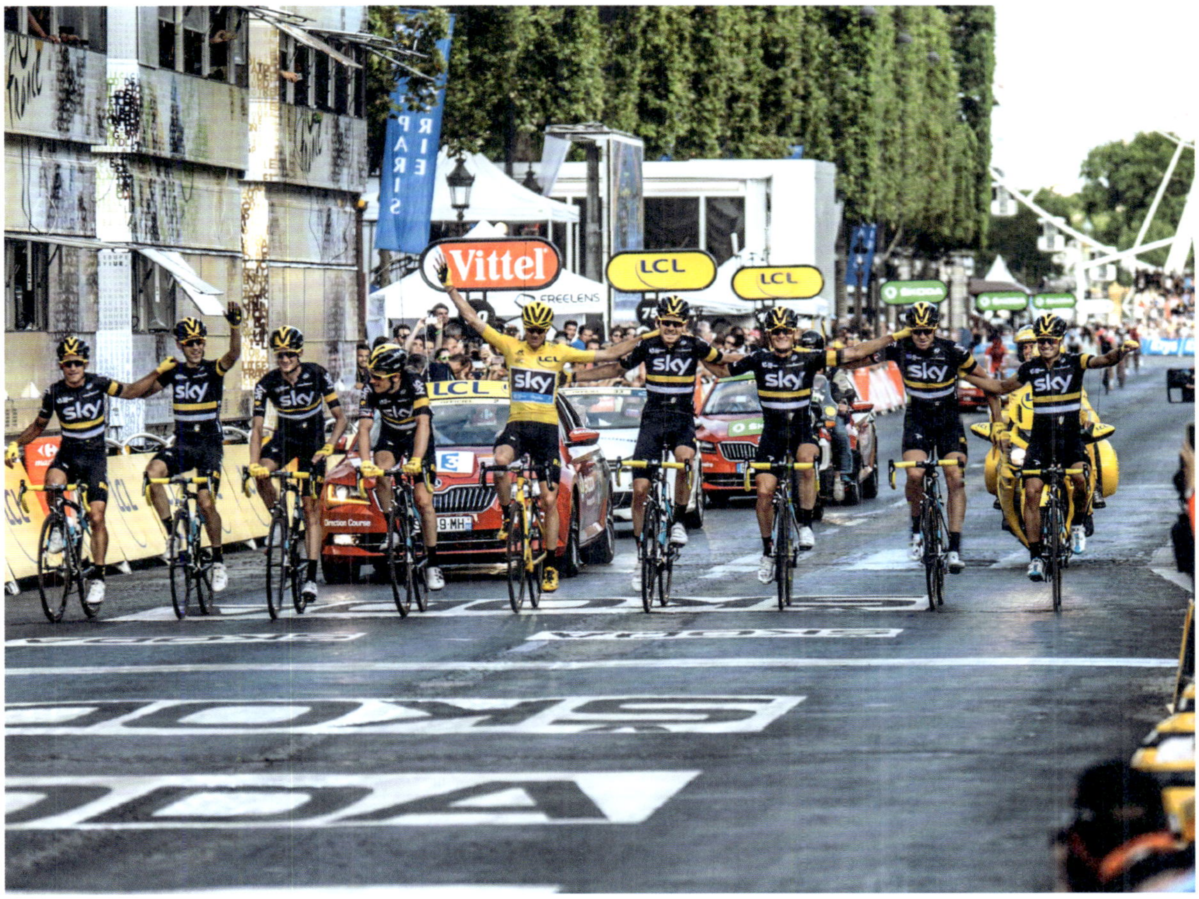
PARIS
Vittel
LCL
LCL
sky

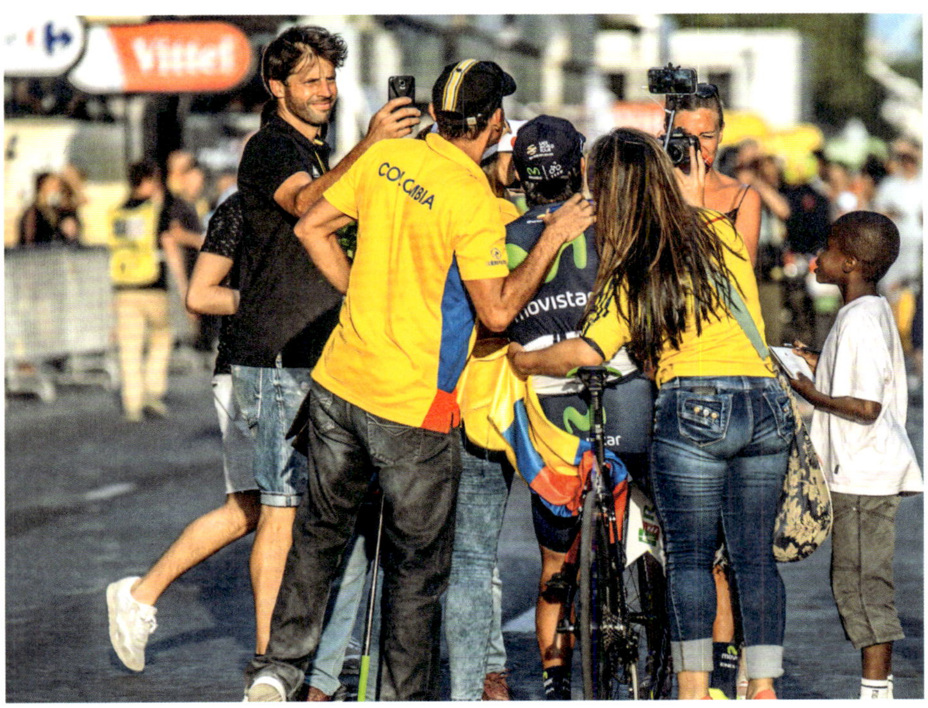
Vittel

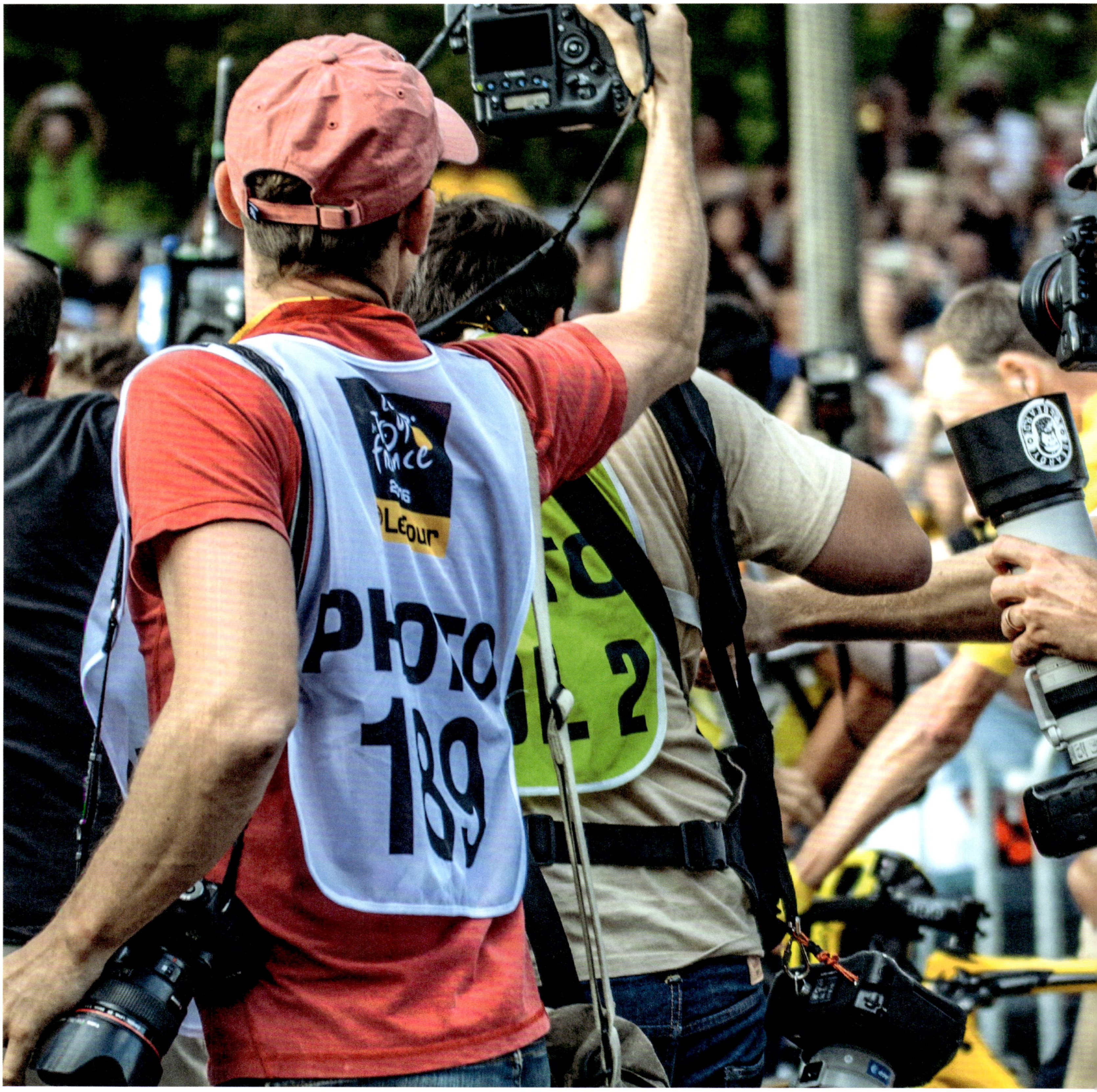

↑ Hinter den Fotografen kaum zu erkennen: Chris Froome (Team Sky), Sieger der Tour de France 2016. **Hardly recognisable behind the photographers: Chris Froome (Team Sky), winner of the Tour de France 2016.** *À peine reconnaissable derrière les photographes : Chris Froome (Team Sky), vainqueur du Tour de France 2016.*

→ Joaquim Rodríguez (Team Katusha). **Joaquim Rodríguez (Team Katusha).** *Joaquim Rodríguez (Team Katusha).*

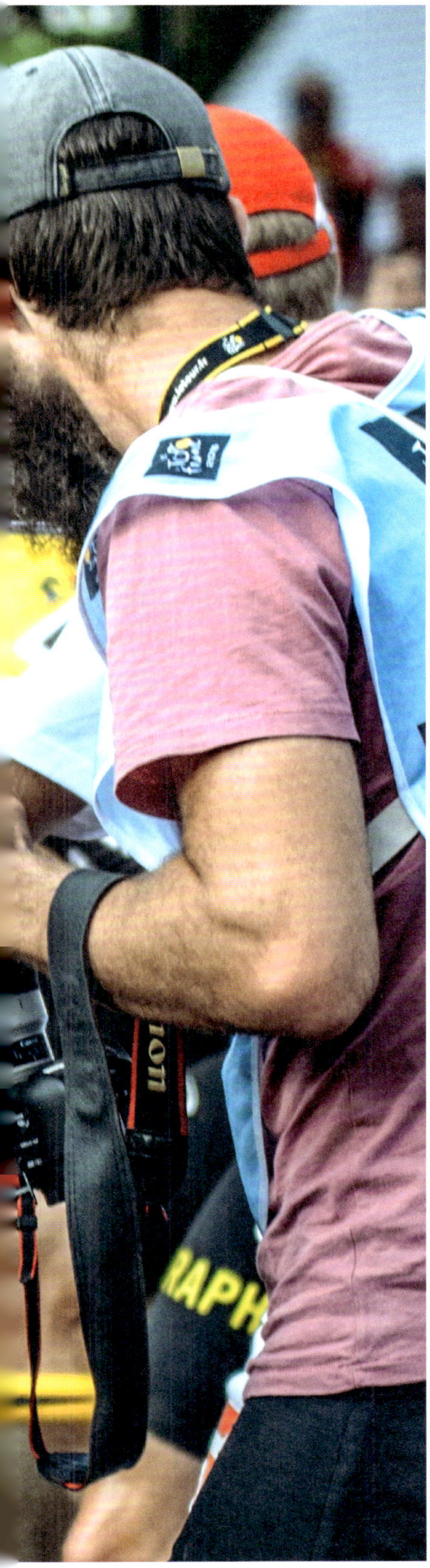

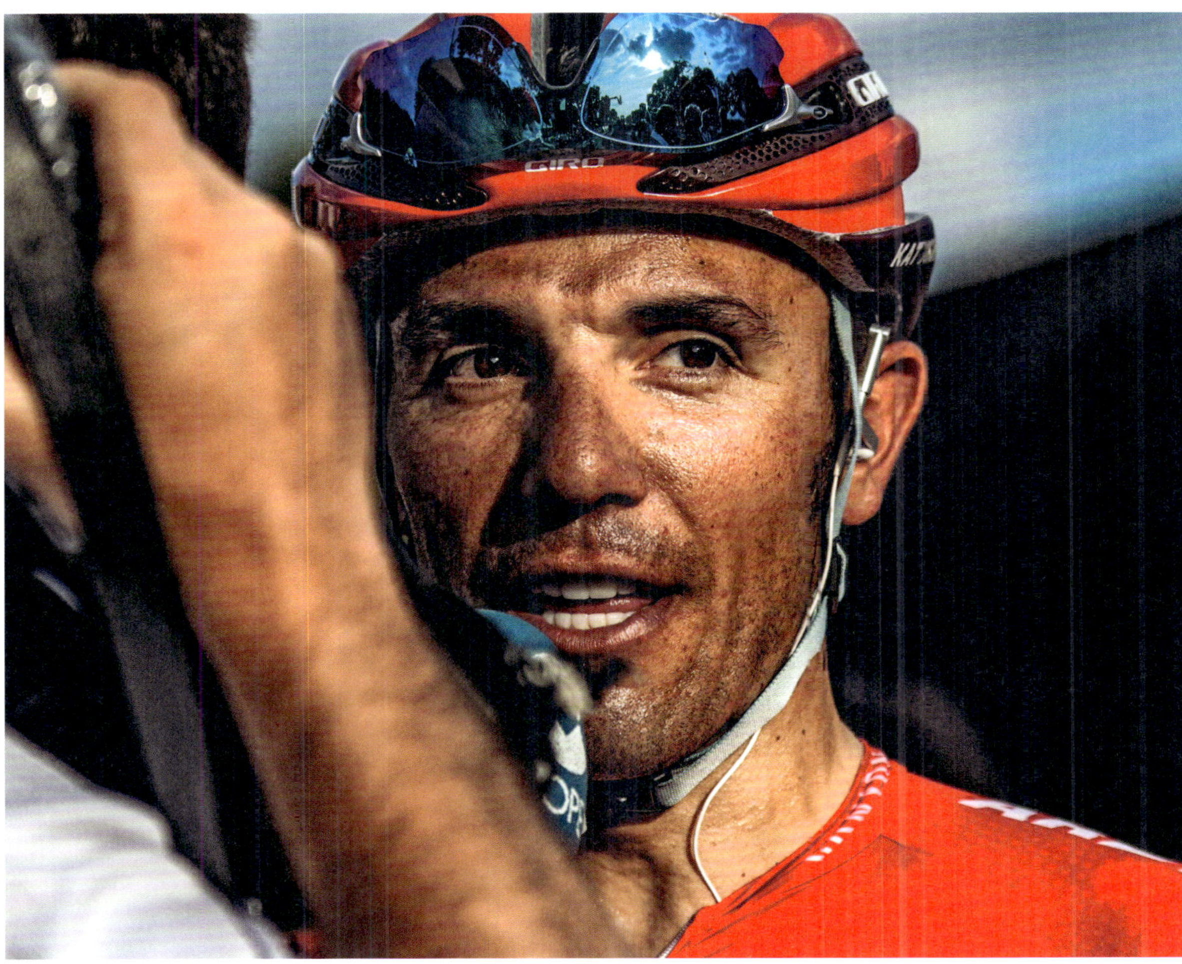
GIRO

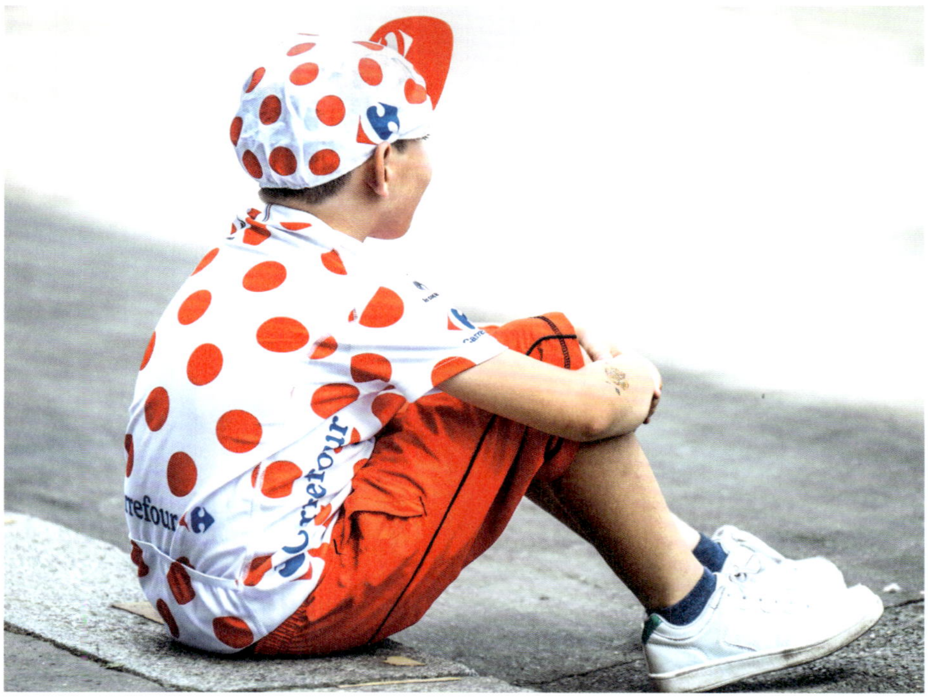

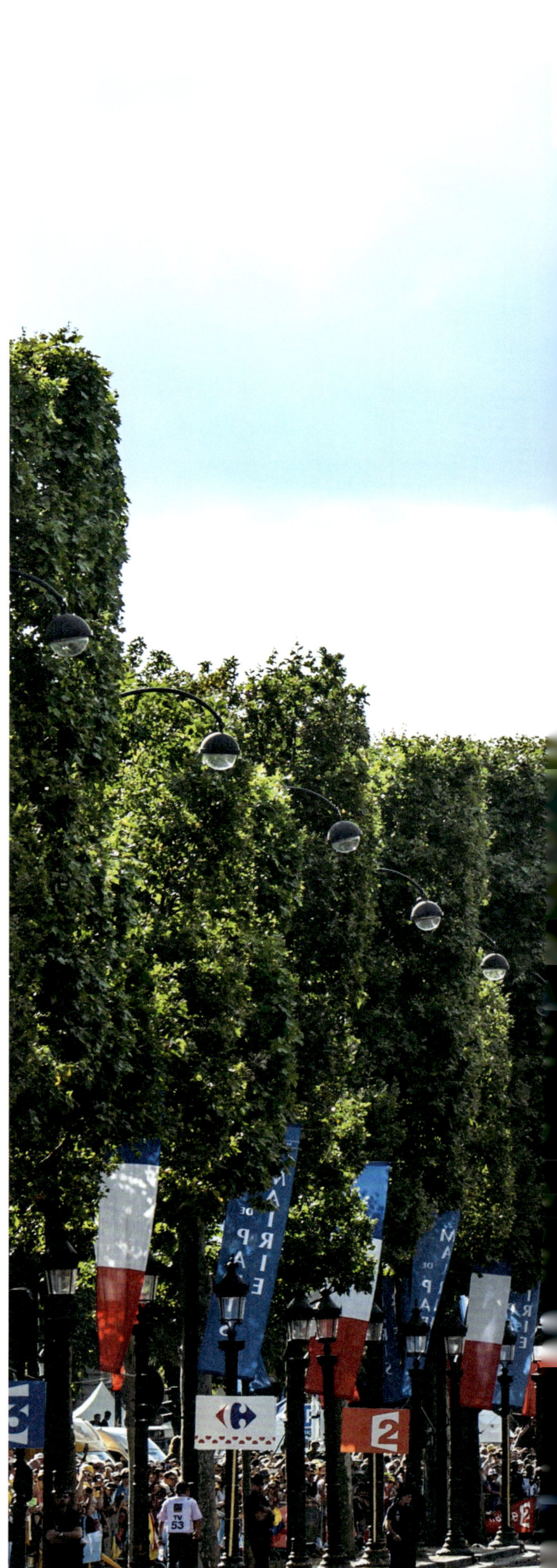

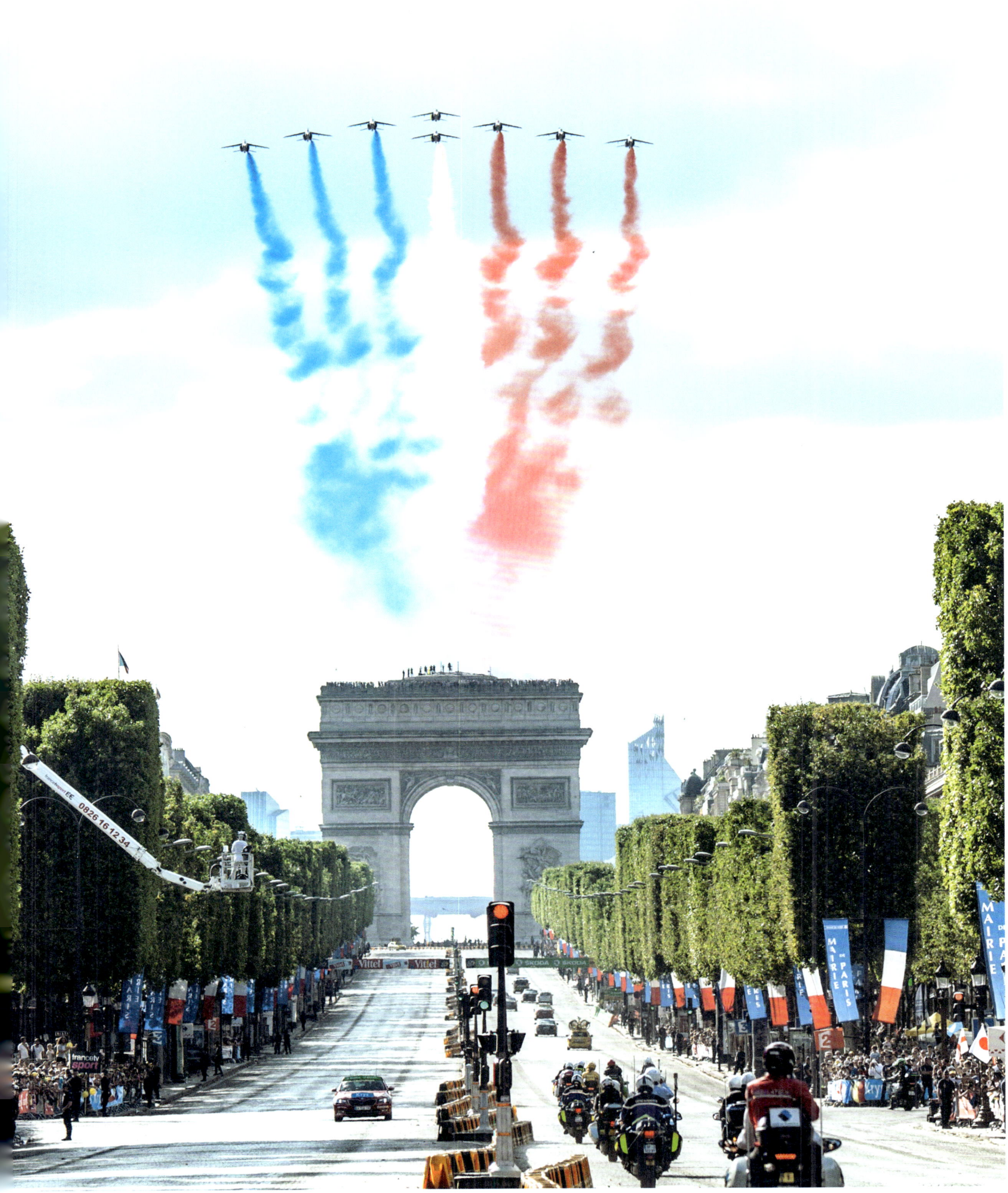

Die Flugstaffel malt die Trikolore in den Himmel. Au revoir, Tour de France! **The squadron paints the tricolour in the sky. Au revoir, Tour de France!**
L'escadrille dessine le drapeau tricolore dans le ciel. Au revoir, le Tour !

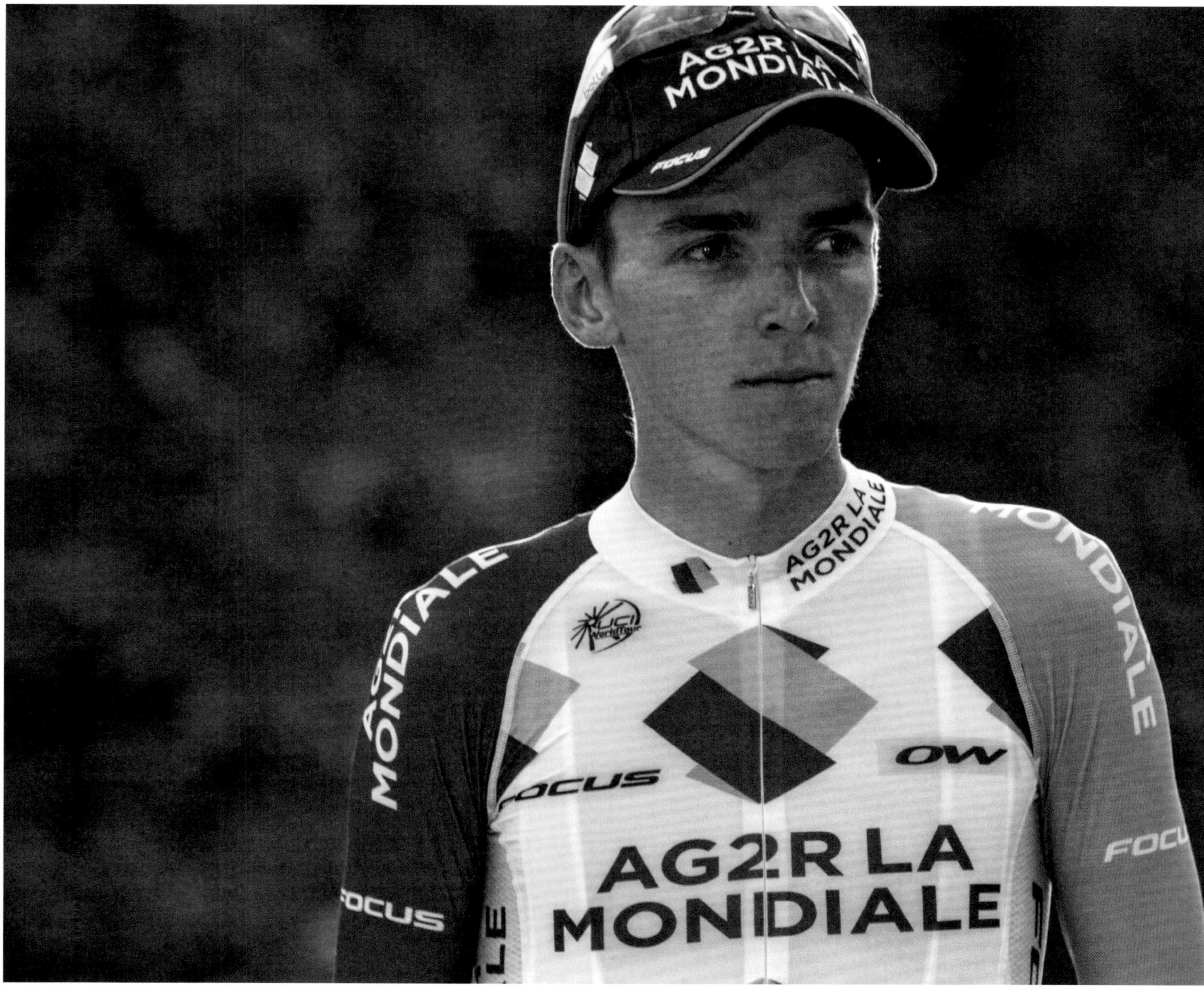

↑ Romain Bardet (AG2R La Mondiale) wird zweiter im Gesamtklassement hinter Chris Froome. **Romain Bardet (AG2R La Mondiale) is second in the GC behind Chris Froome.** *Romain Bardet (AG2R La Mondiale), deuxième au classement général derrière Chris Froome.*

→ Der Deutsche Meister André Greipel wird für seinen Etappensieg geehrt. **André Greipel, the German champion, is honoured for his stage victory.** *Le champion allemand André Greipel récompensé pour sa victoire d'étape.*

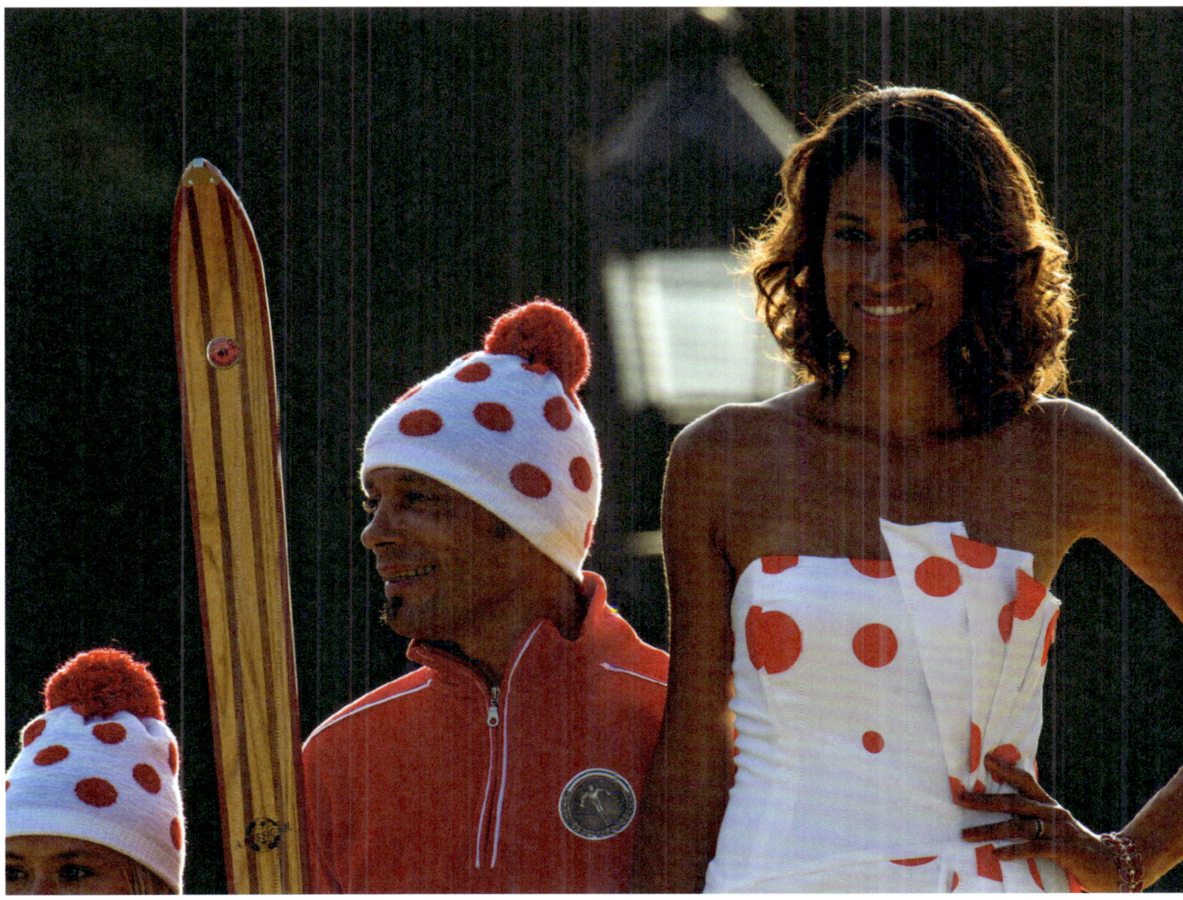

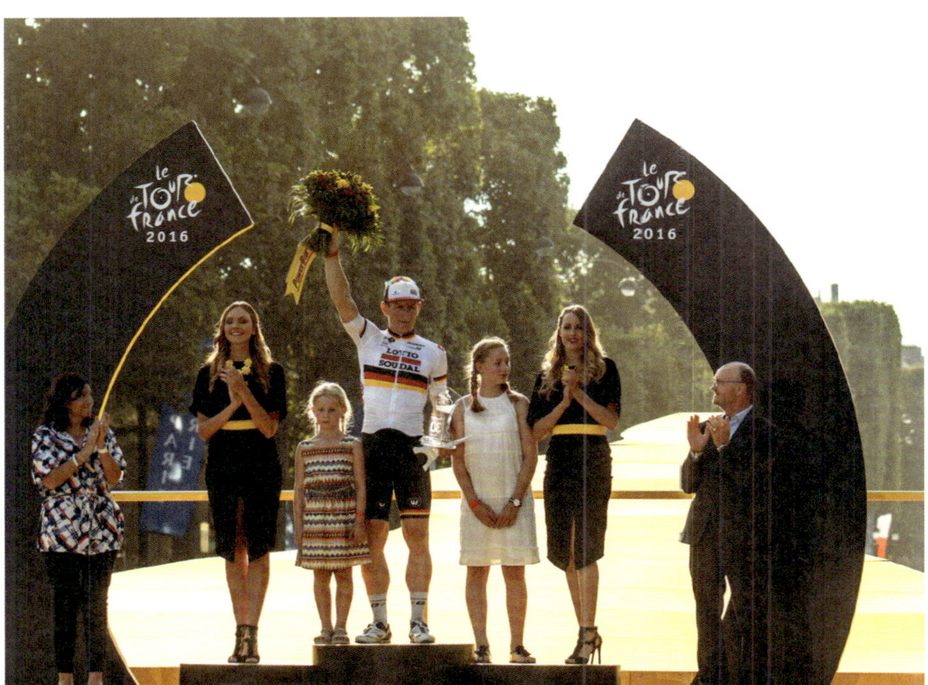
2016
2016
LOTTO SOUDAL

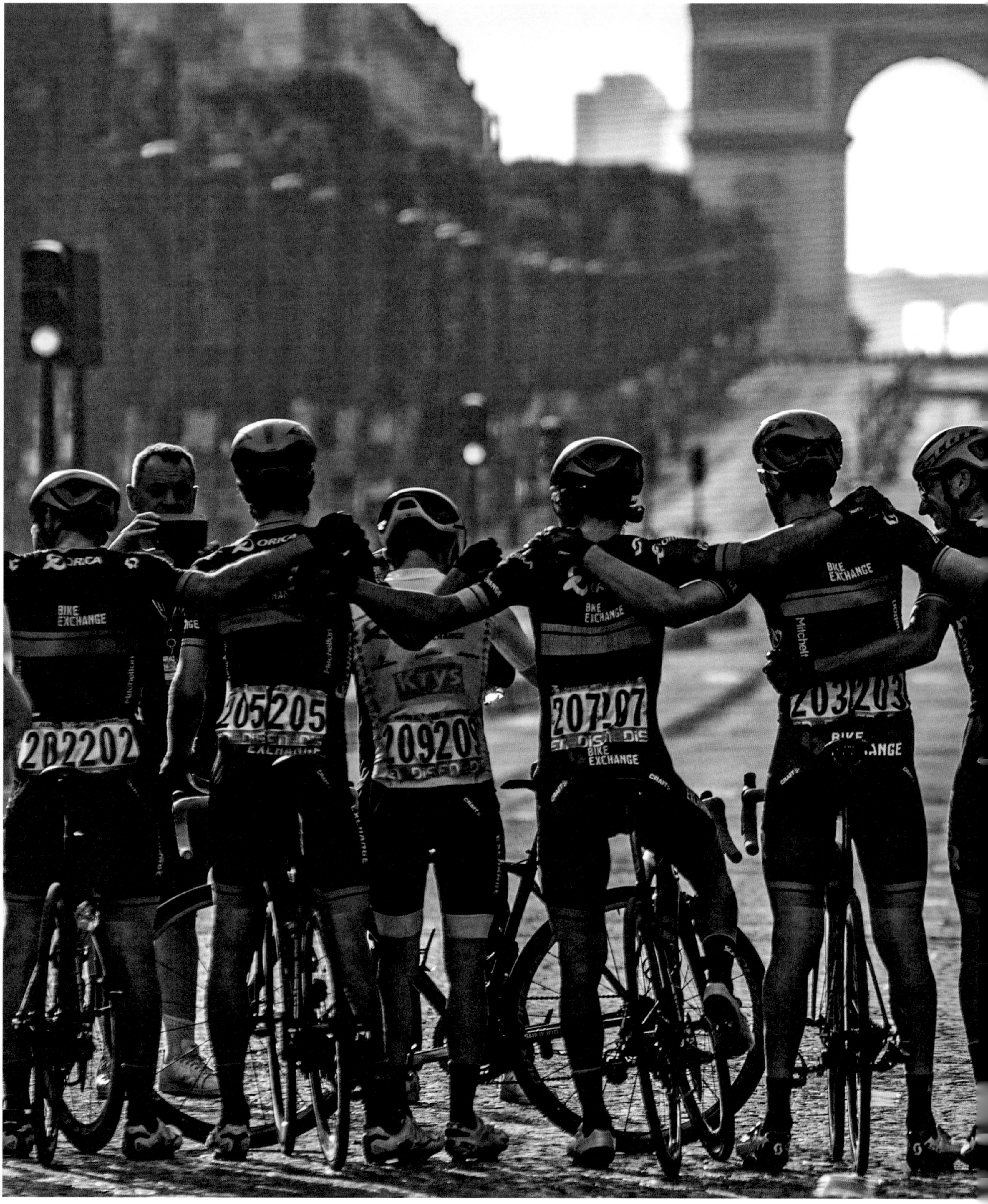
ORICA
BIKE EXCHANGE
205 205
Krys
203 203

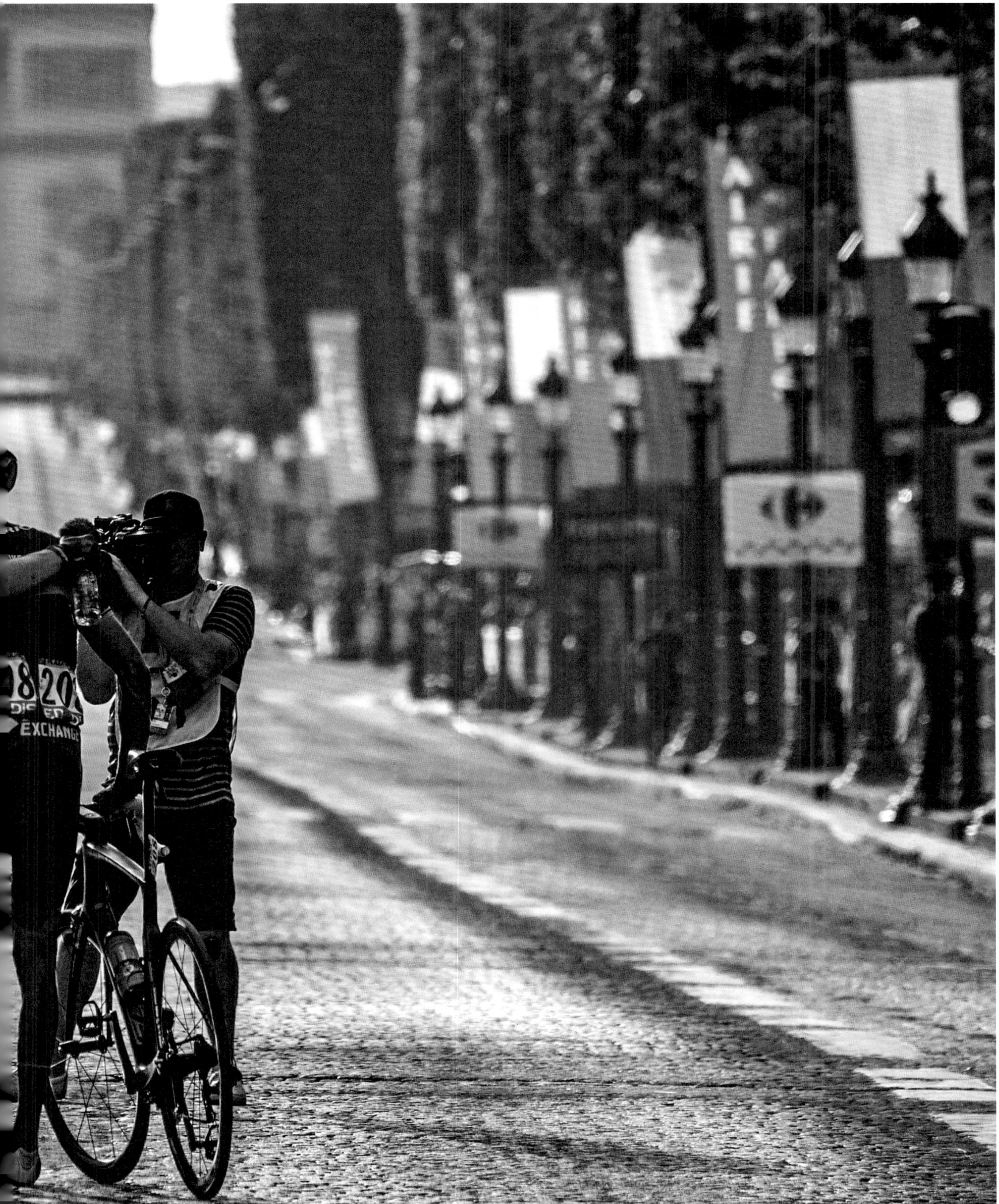

Geschafft! Teambild ORICA-BikeExchange auf der Prachtmeile. **Done! Team picture of ORICA-BikeExchange on the golden boulevard.** *Ils l'ont fait ! Photo de l'équipe ORICA-BikeExchange sur l'Avenue.*

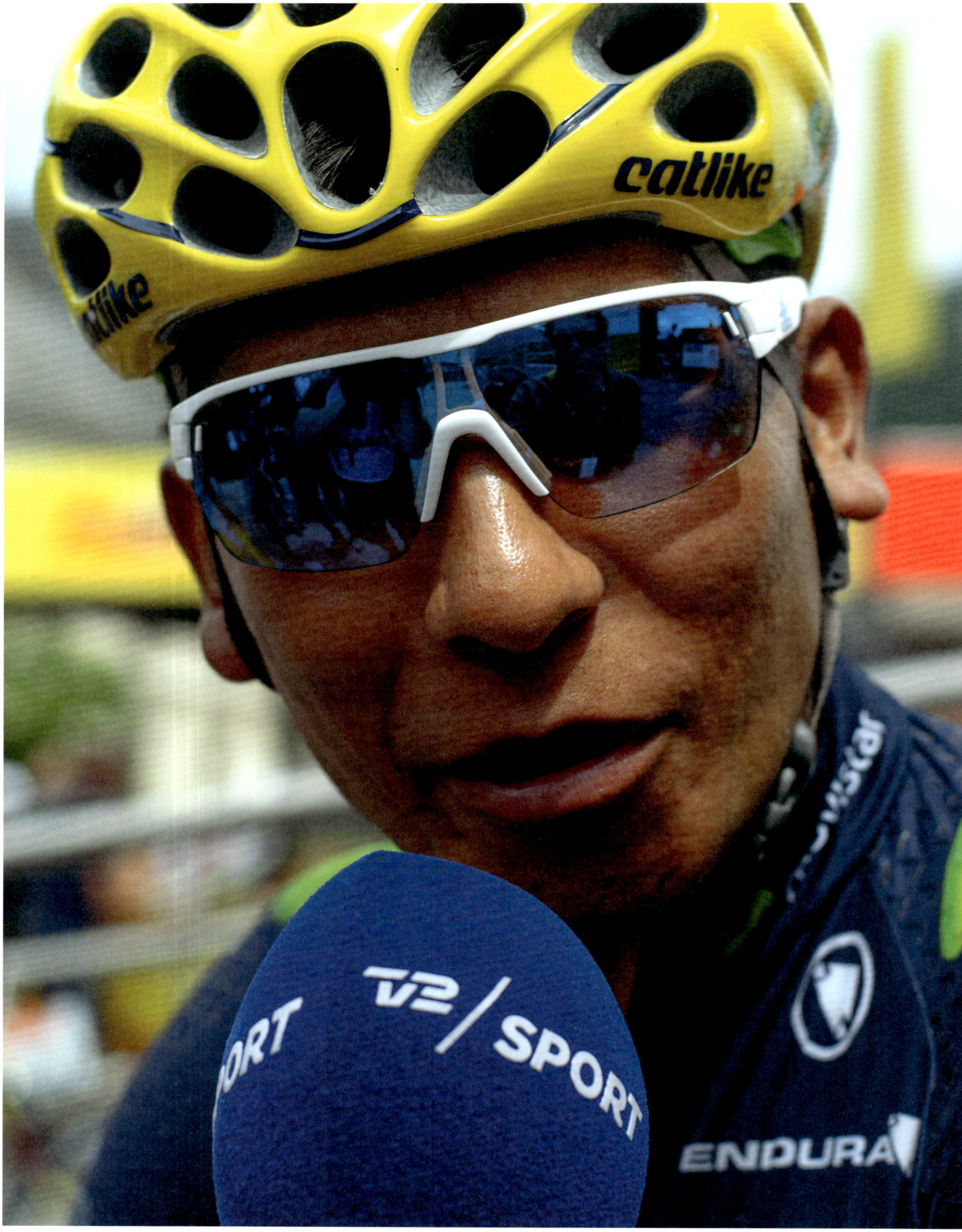
catlike
TV2 / SPORT
ENDURA

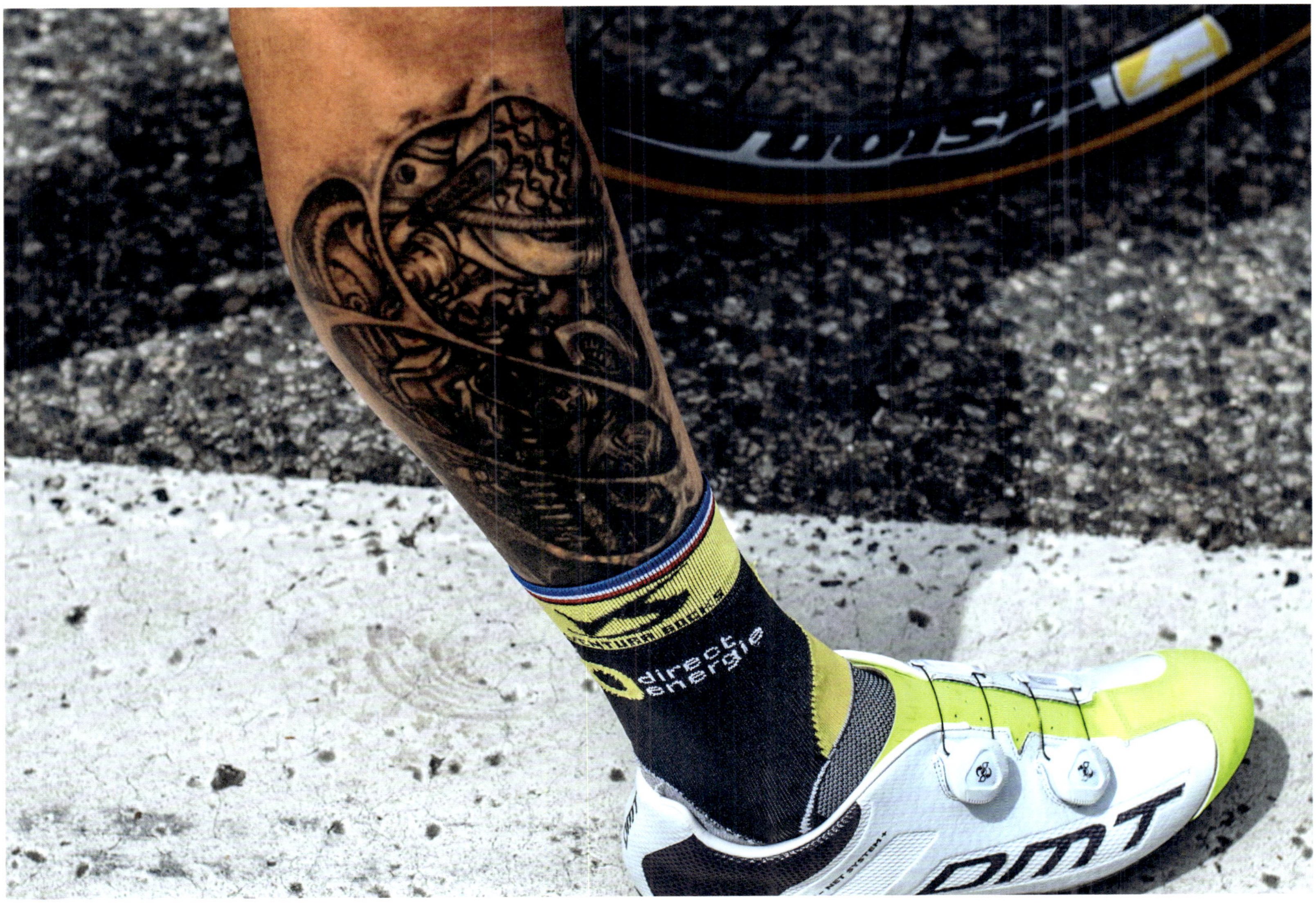

← Nairo Quintana (Movistar) im Interview. **Interview with Nairo Quintana (Movistar).** *Nairo Quintana (Movistar) interviewé.*

↑ Tattoo-Art am Bein von Sylvain Chavanel (Direct Énergie). **Sylvain Chavanel (Direct Énergie) and his leg tattoo.** *Tatouage à la jambe de Sylvain Chavanel (Direct Énergie).*

EuroEyes Cyclassics Hamburg

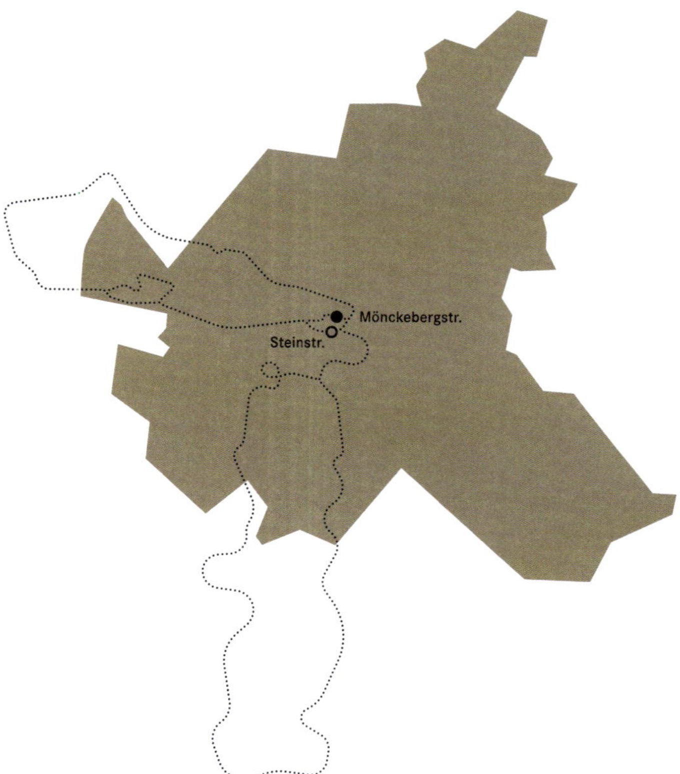

217.7

KILOMETRE

DATE: 21.08.2016

FIRST TOUR: 1996

DURATION: 04:54:26

Die Hamburg „Cyclassics", der „Klassiker" im Norden Deutschlands, ging in 2016 in die 21. Runde. Mit dem am gleichen Tag stattfindenden Jedermannrennen ist es das größte Radrennen Europas. **The Hamburg 'Cyclassics', the north German 'classic', was held for the 21st time in 2016. Together with the Cyclassics Sportive which takes place on the same day, they form the biggest cycle race in Europe.** *La Cyclassics de Hambourg, la classique du Nord de l'Allemagne, en est en 2016 à sa 21e édition. Avec la cyclosportive – ouverte à tous – c'est la plus importante course cycliste d'Europe.*

44.363

KM/H AVG. SPEED WINNER

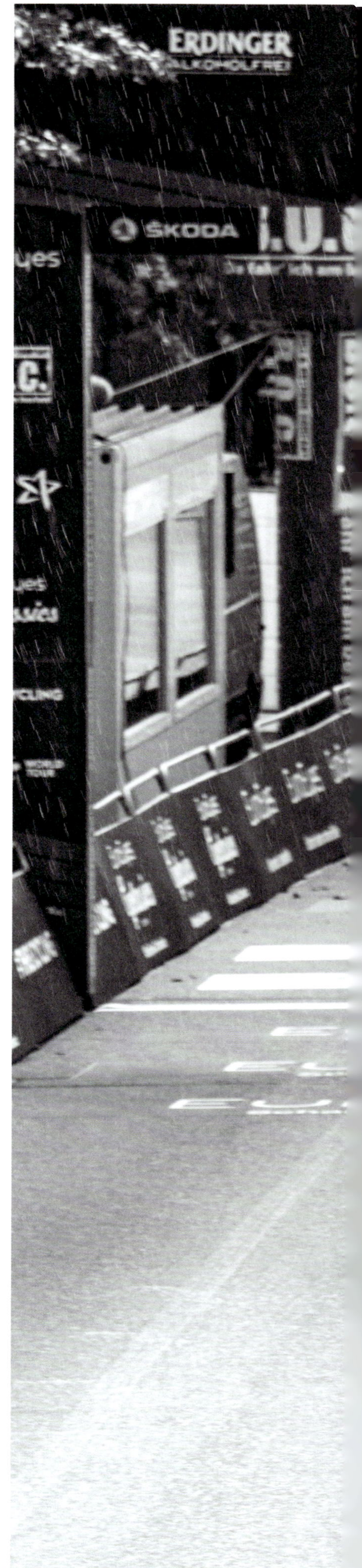

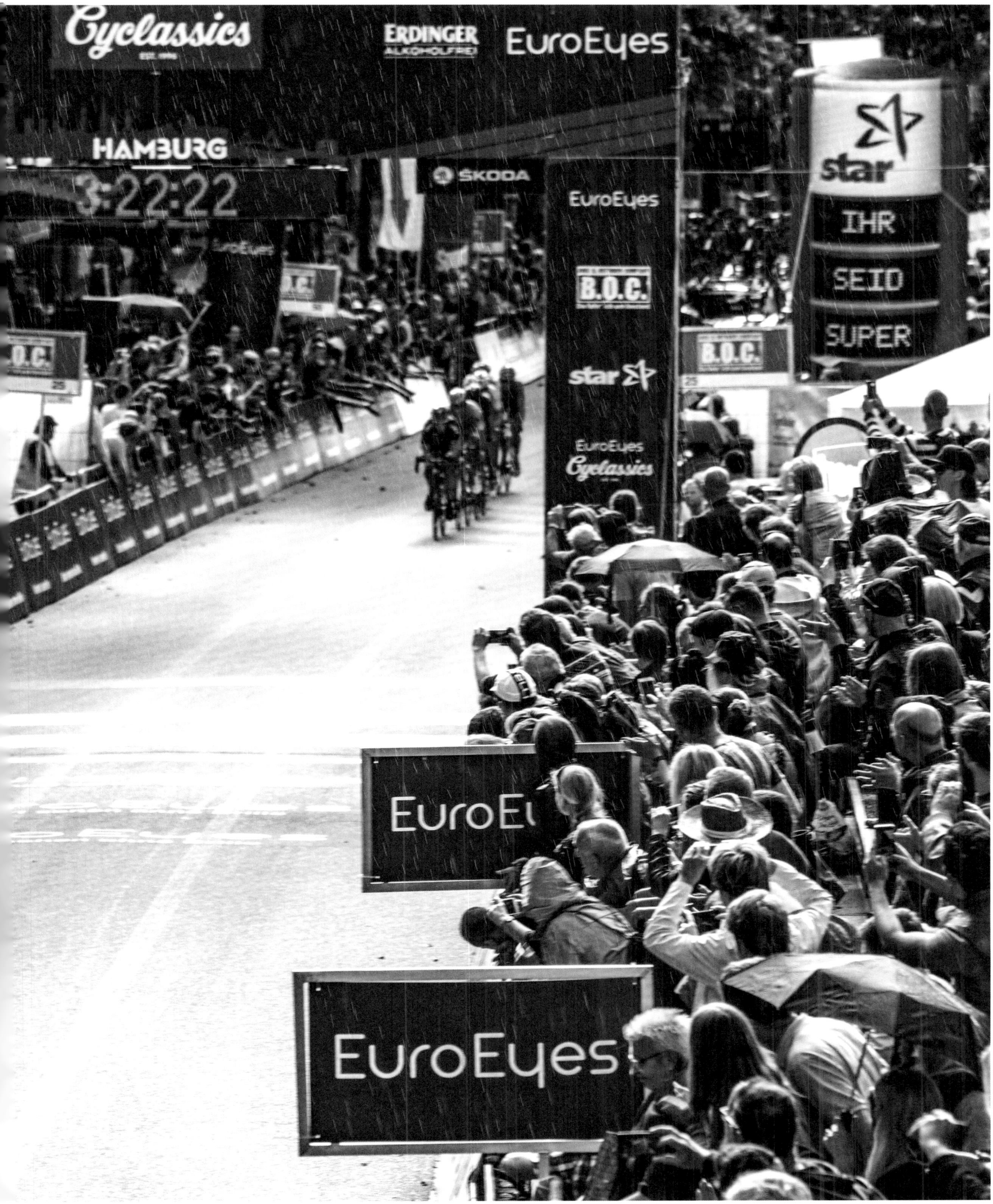

Strömender Regen mitten in der Stadt: Lukas Pöstlberger (BORA - ARGON 18) führt die Ausreißergruppe auf der Mönckebergstraße an. **Pouring rain in the heart of the city: Lukas Pöstlberger (BORA - ARGON 18) leads the breakaway group on Mönckebergstrasse.** *Une course sous des pluies torrentielles en plein cœur de la ville : Lukas Pöstlberger (BORA - ARGON 18) est en tête de l'échappée sur la Mönckebergstraße.*

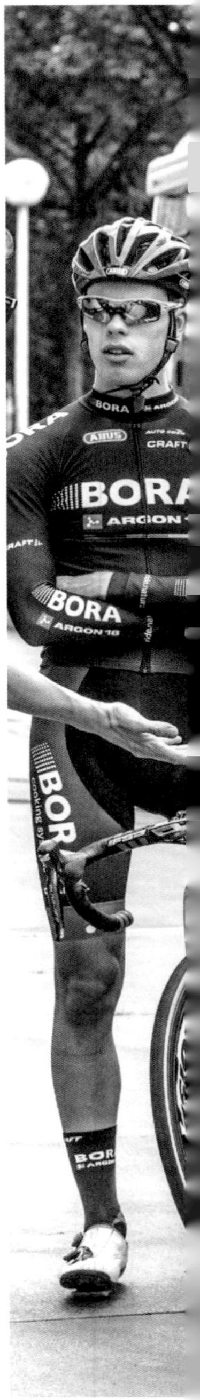
BORA
ARGON 18
CRAFT
ABUS

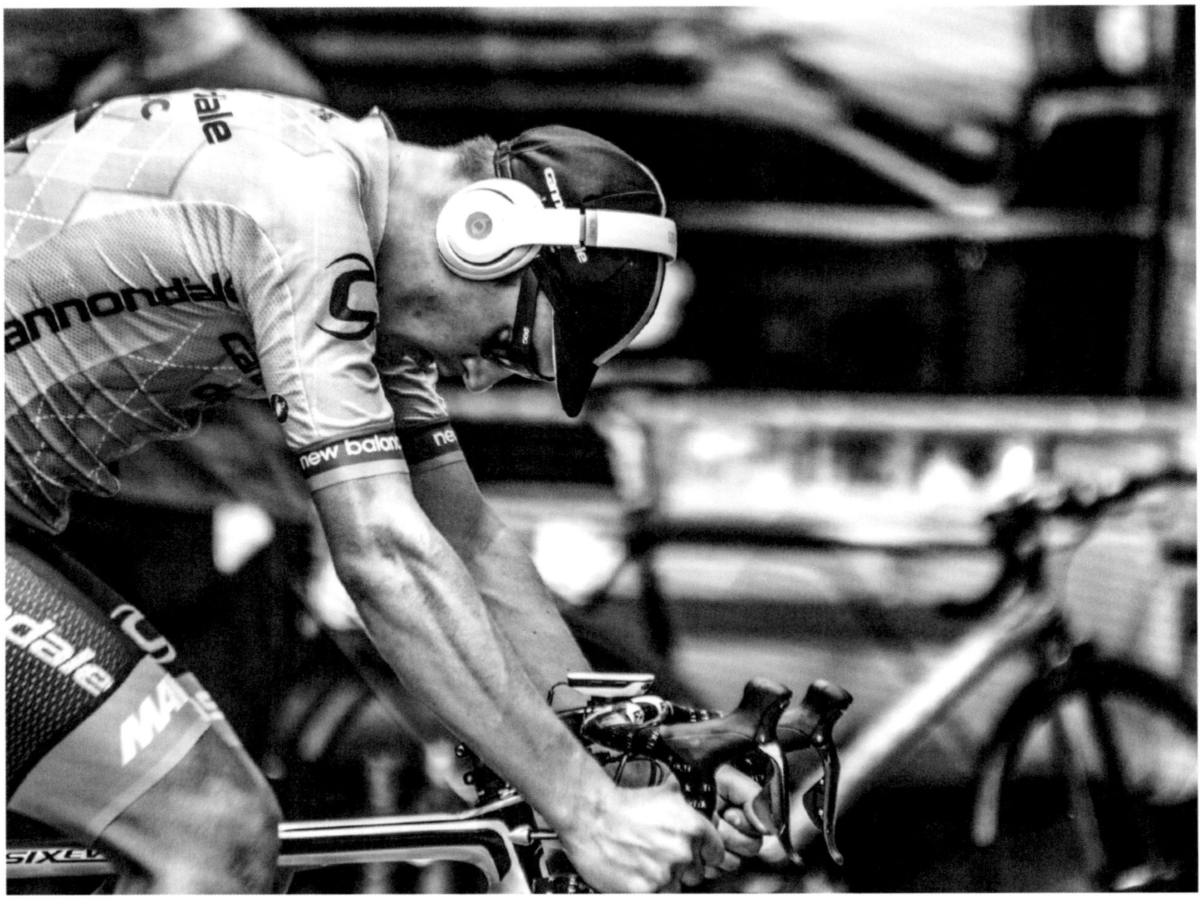
cannondale
new balance

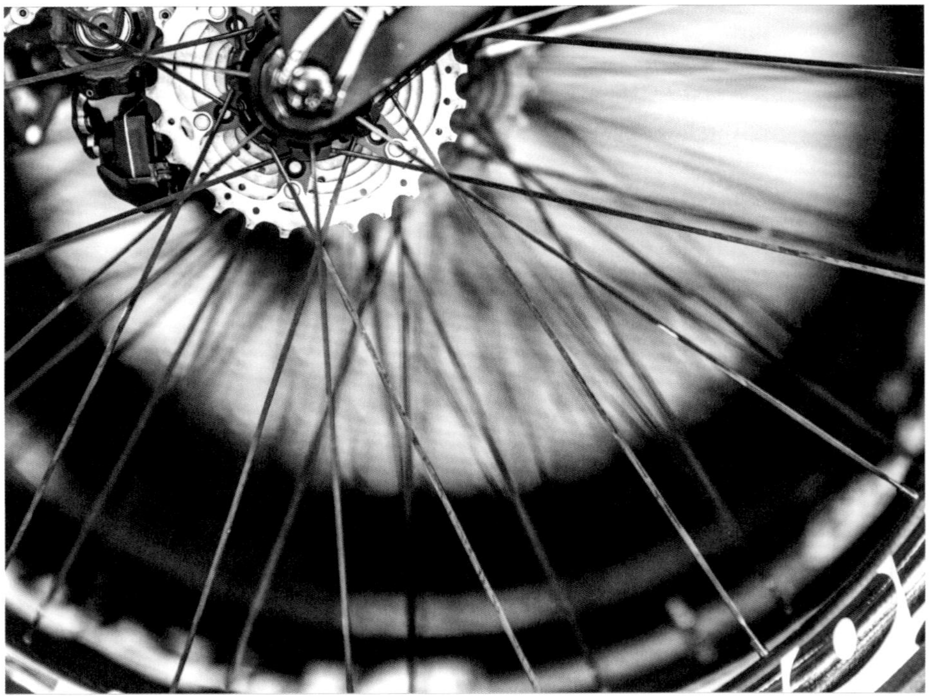

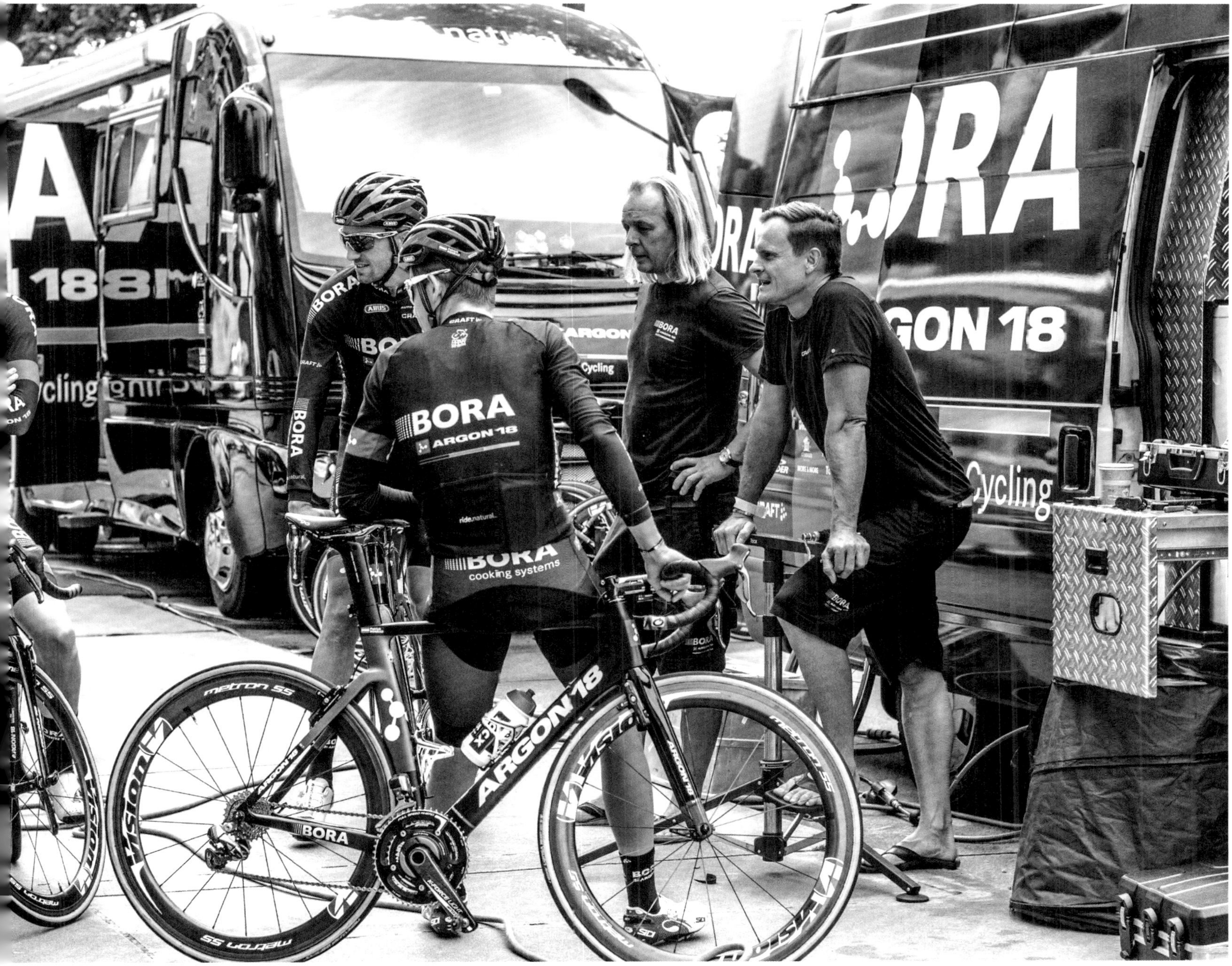

Team und Mechaniker nach dem Rennen am Teambus von BORA - ARGON 18. **Team and mechanics at the team bus of BORA - ARGON 18 right after the race.** *Équipe et mécaniciens devant le bus de BORA - ARGON 18 après la course.*

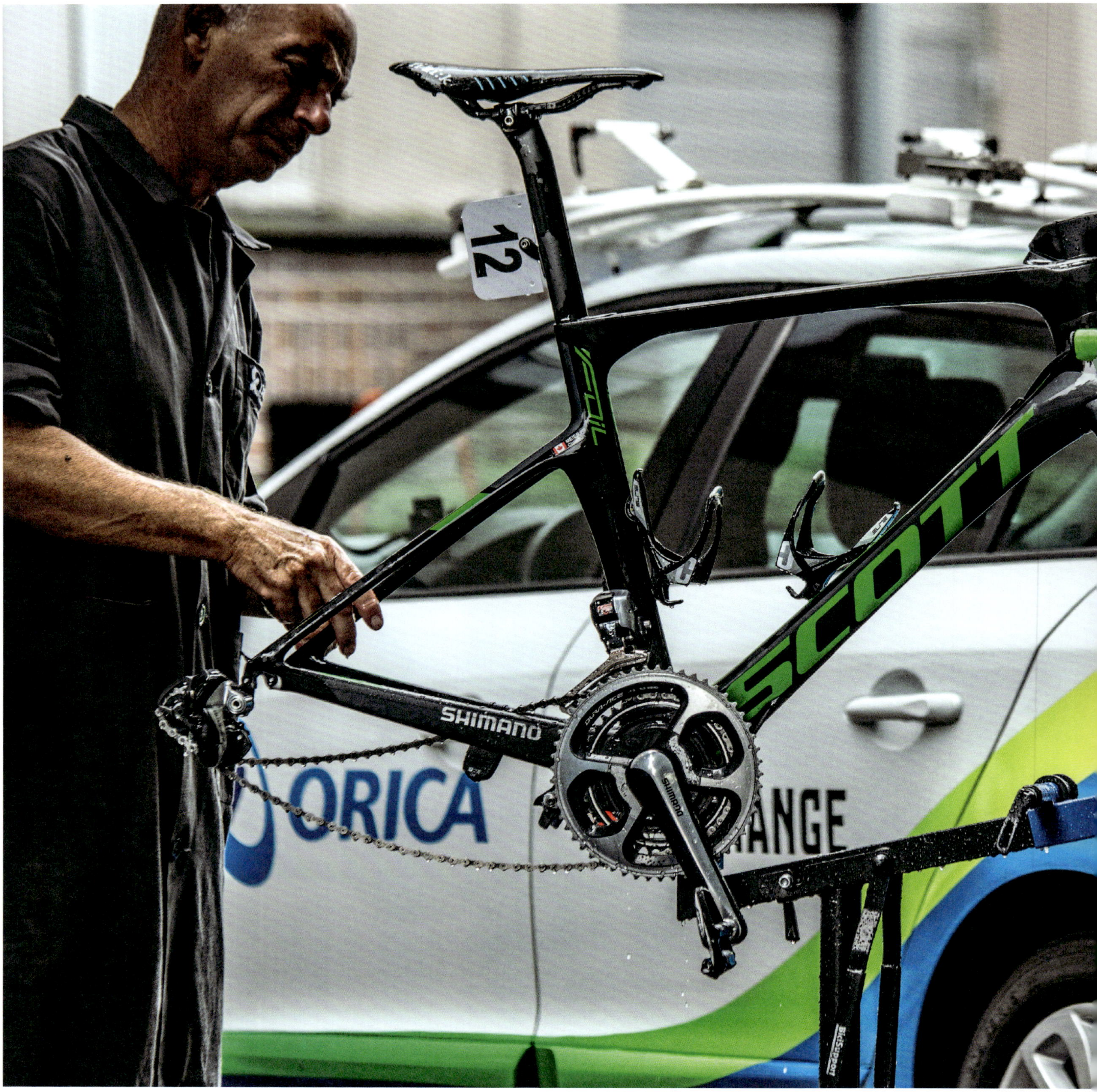

 Präzision und Liebe zum Detail. **Precision and attention to detail.** *Précision et amour du détail.*

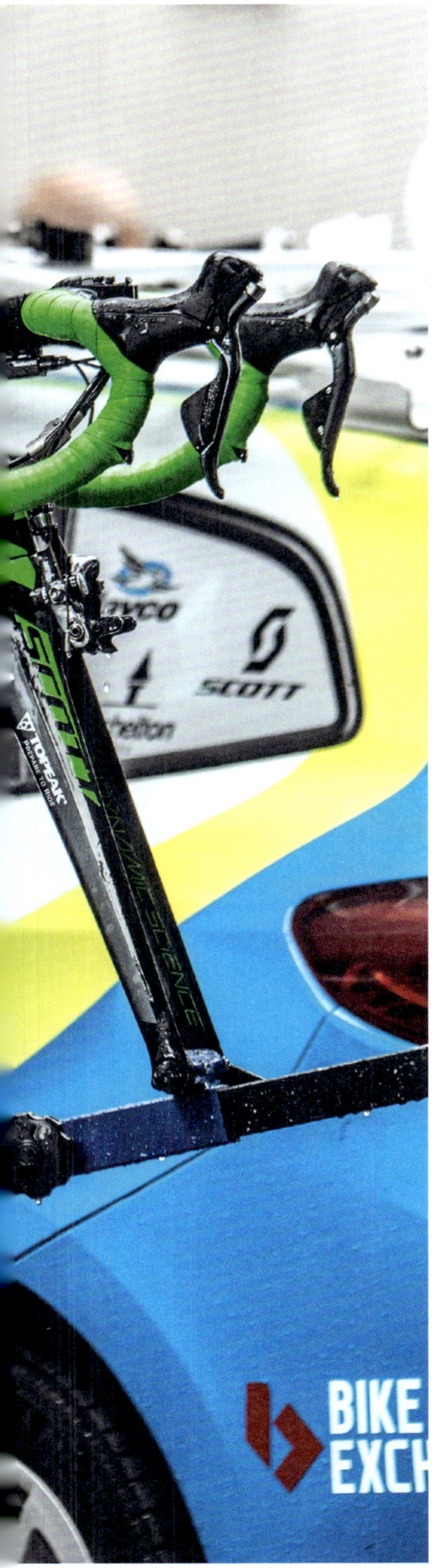
SCOTT
BIKE

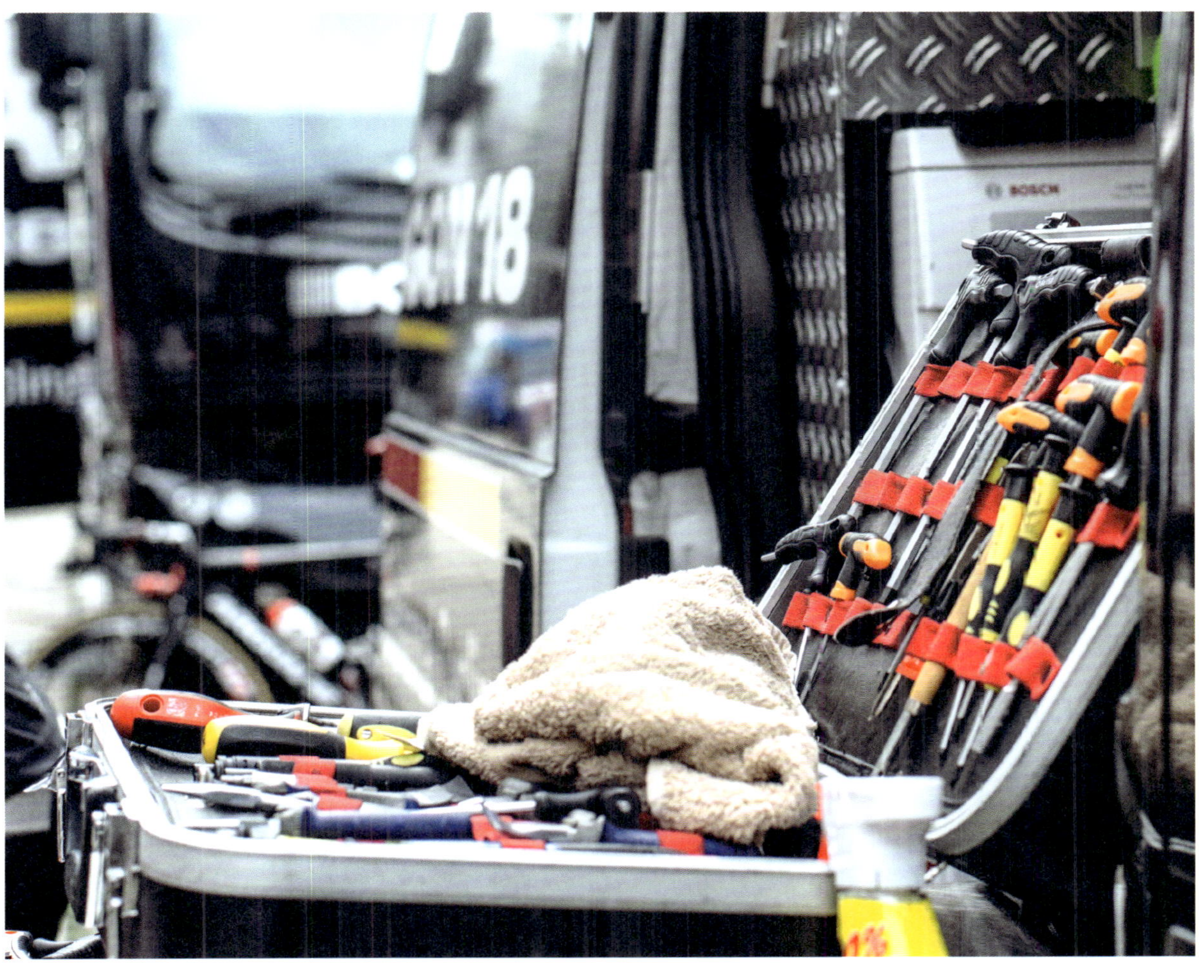

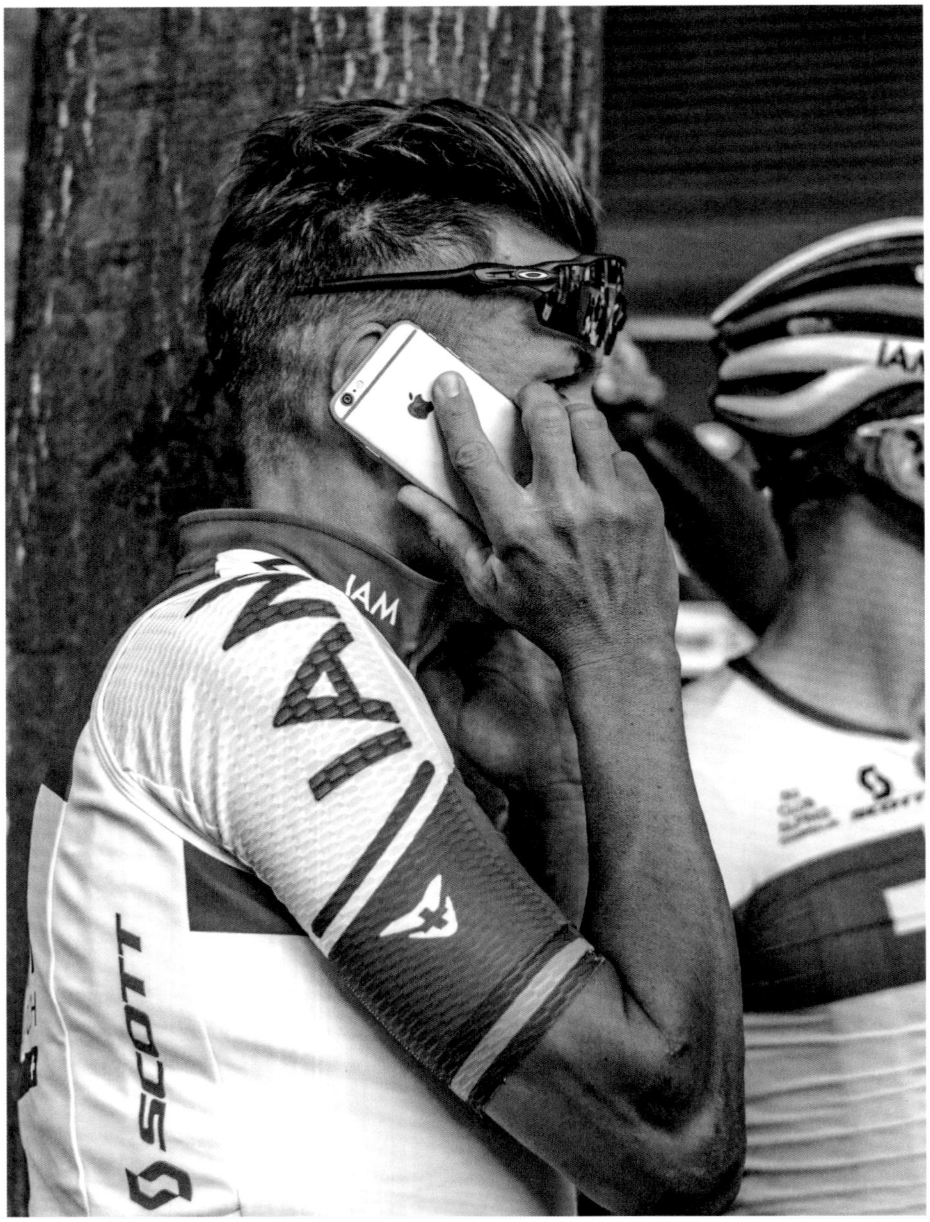
IAM
IAM
SCOTT

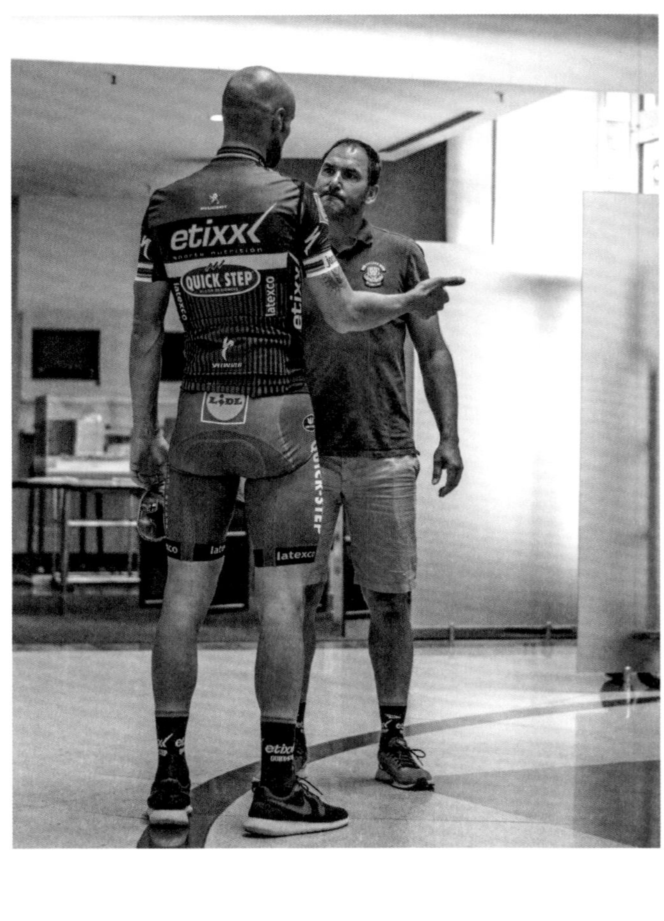
etixx
QUICK STEP
latexco
LIDL

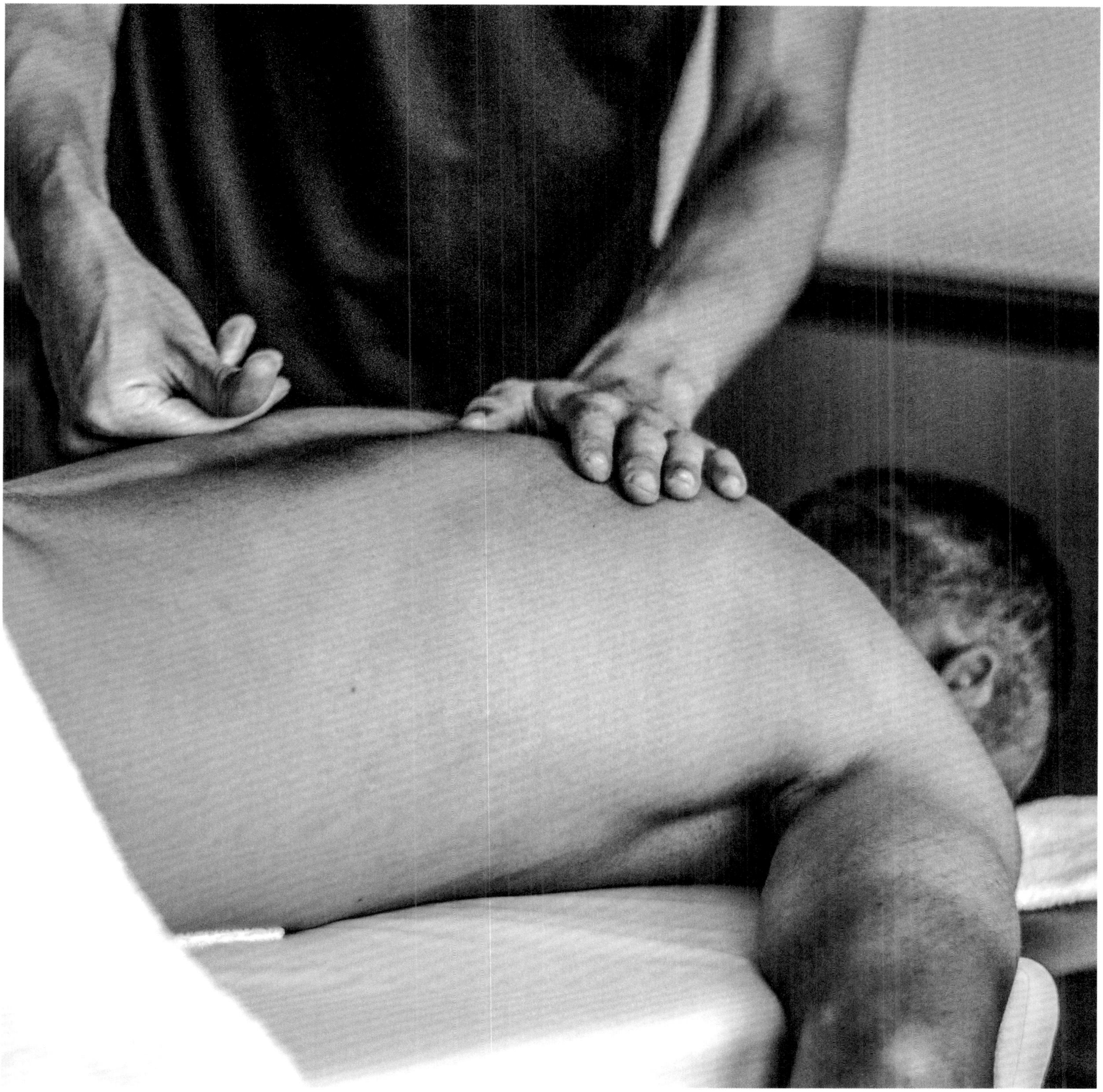

↖ Heinrich Haussler (IAM Cycling) am Telefon. **Heinrich Haussler (IAM Cycling) on the phone.** *Heinrich Haussler (IAM Cycling) au téléphone.*
← Tom Boonen (Etixx – Quick Step) im Gespräch mit dem Mechaniker. **Tom Boonen (Etixx – Quick Step) talking to the mechanic.** *Tom Boonen (Etixx – Quick Step) en pleine discussion avec le mécanicien.*
↑ Entspannung für Körper und Geist. **Relaxation for body and mind.** *Détente pour le corps et l'esprit.*

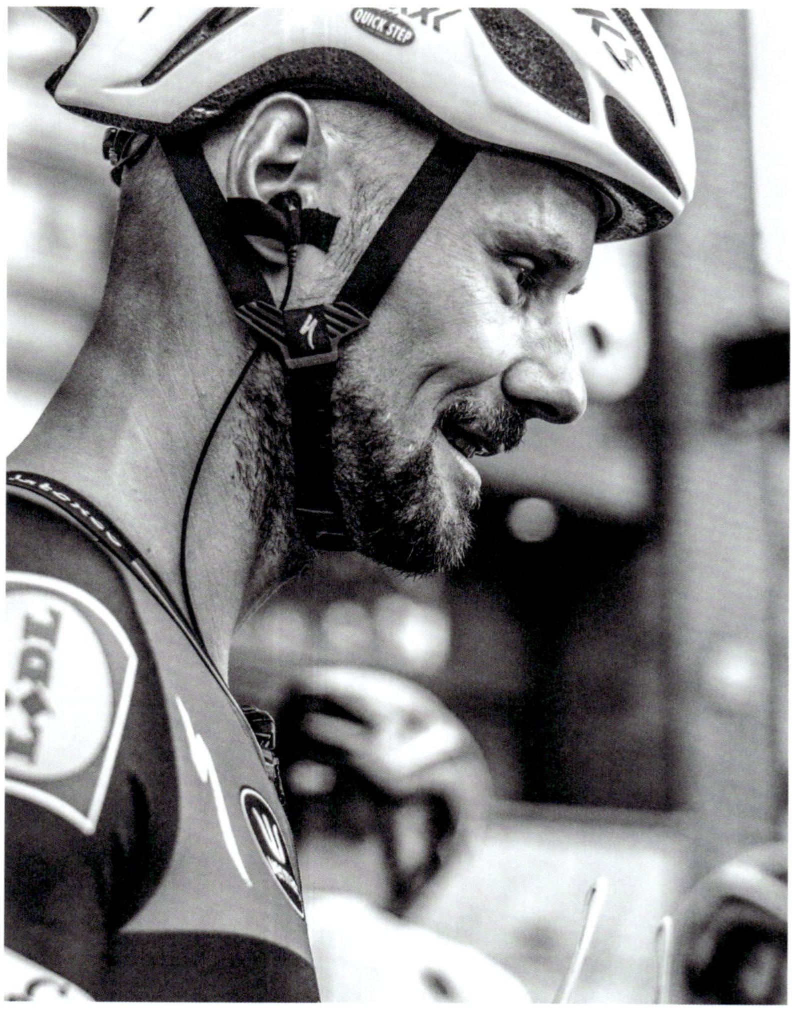

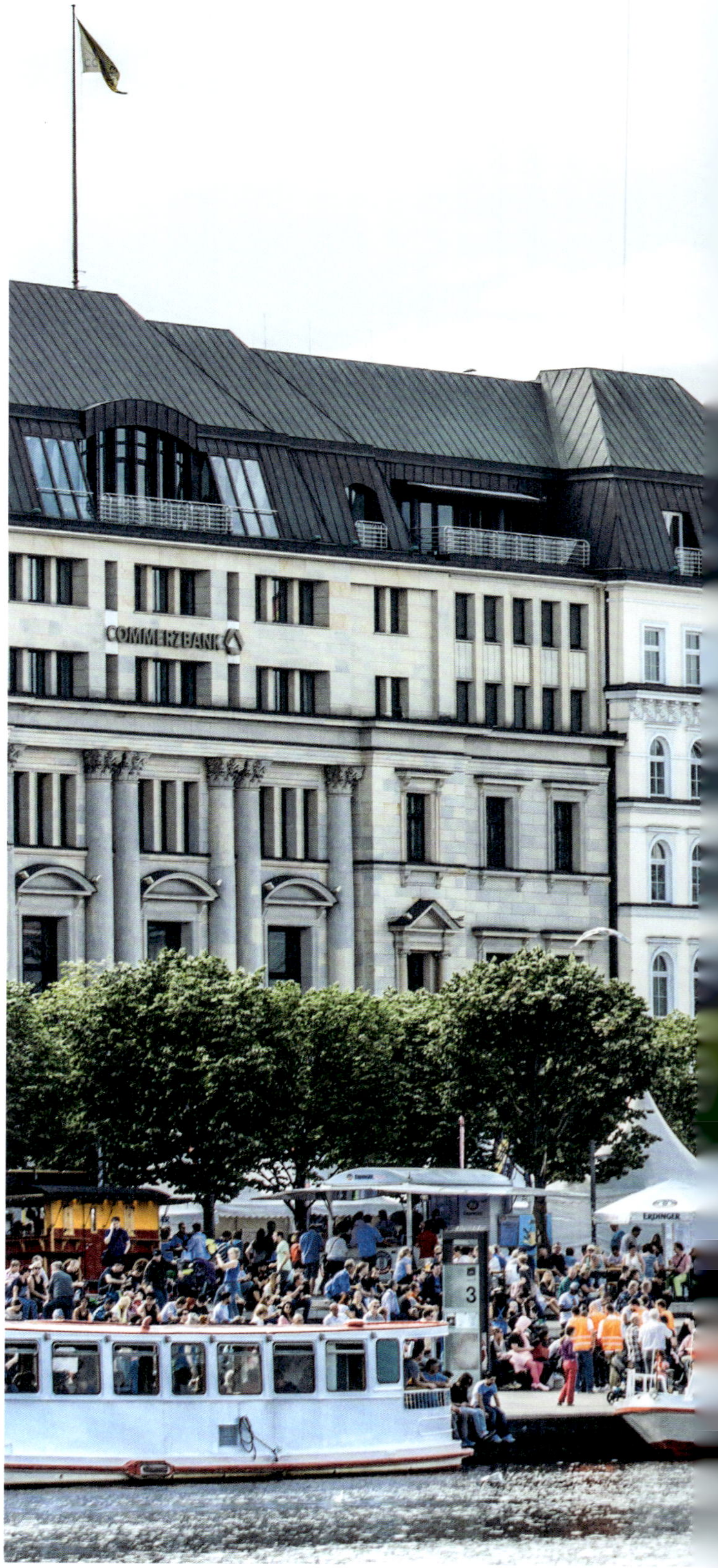

↑ Tom Boonen (Etixx – Quick Step) bei der Team-Präsentation. **Tom Boonen (Etixx – Quick Step) at the team presentation.** *Tom Boonen (Etixx – Quick Step) lors de la présentation des équipes.*

→ Seit über 20 Jahren ein Publikumsmagnet: Cyclassics an der Binnenalster. **A major attraction for more than 20 years: Cyclassics at the Binnenalster.** *Un événement apprécié du grand public depuis plus de 20 ans : la Cyclassics dans la Binnenalster.*

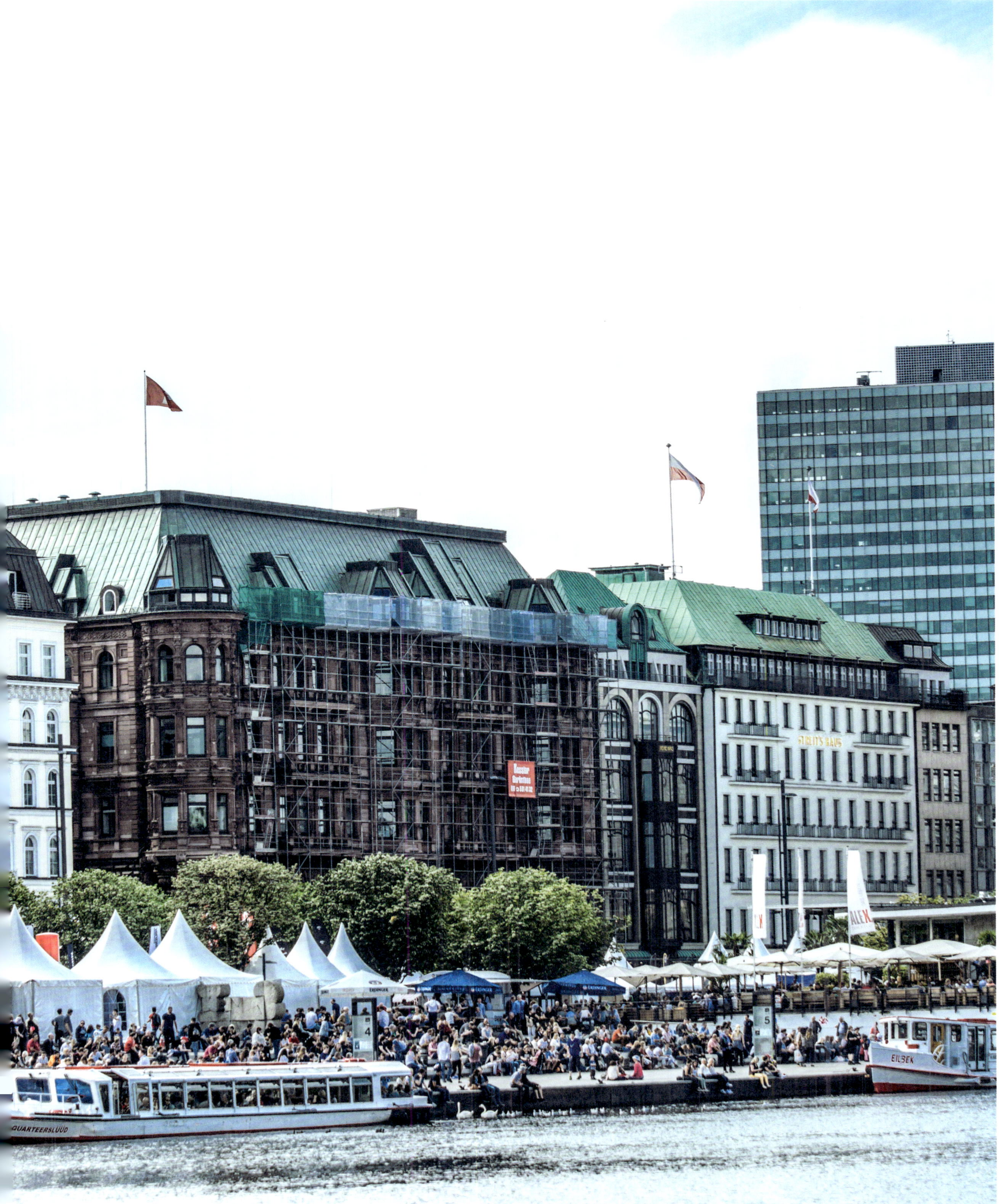
ALEX
EILBEK

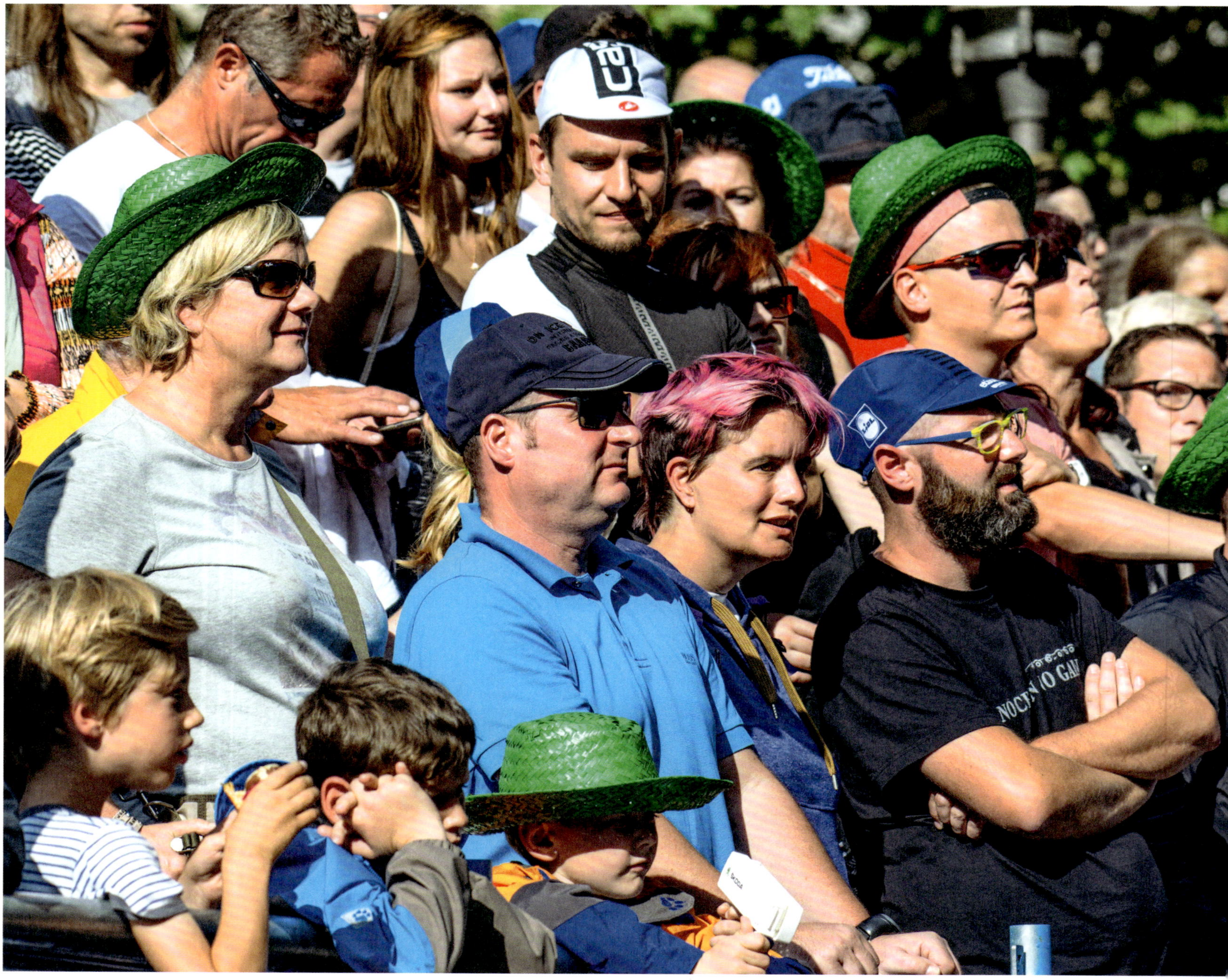

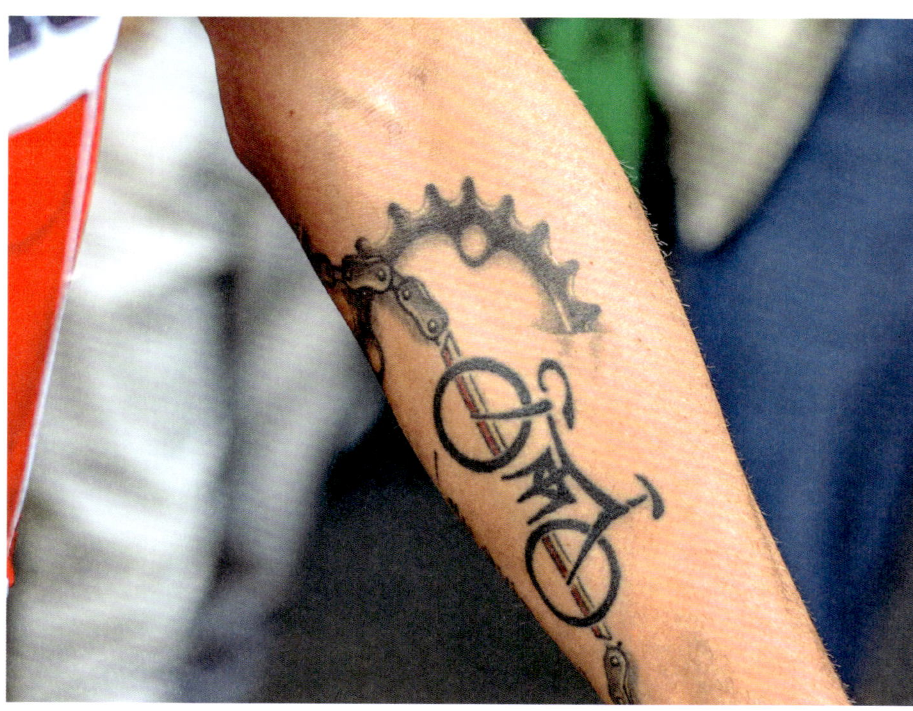

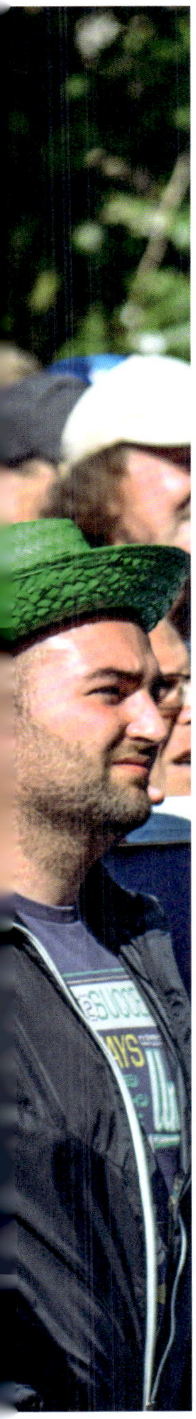

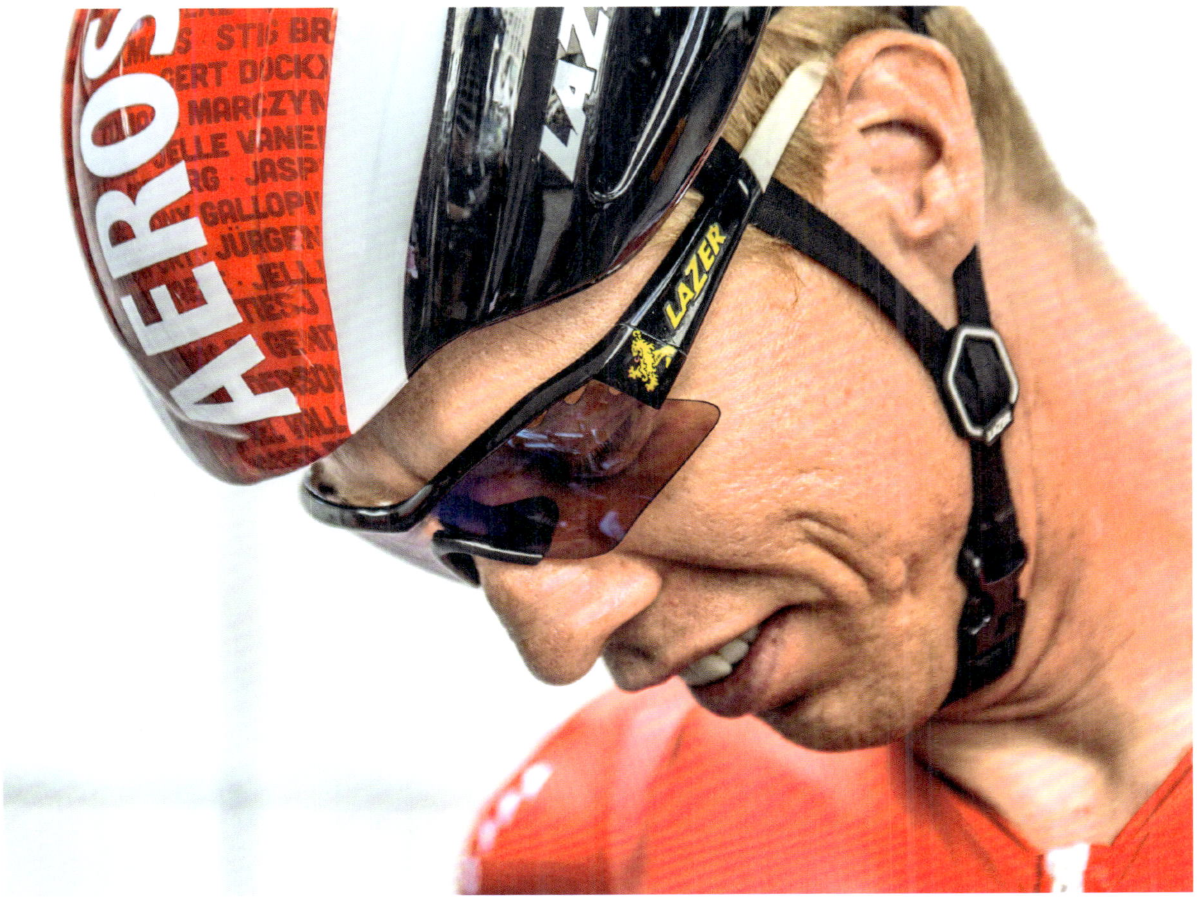

Marcel Sieberg (Lotto Soudal). **Marcel Sieberg (Lotto Soudal).** *Marcel Sieberg (Lotto Soudal).*

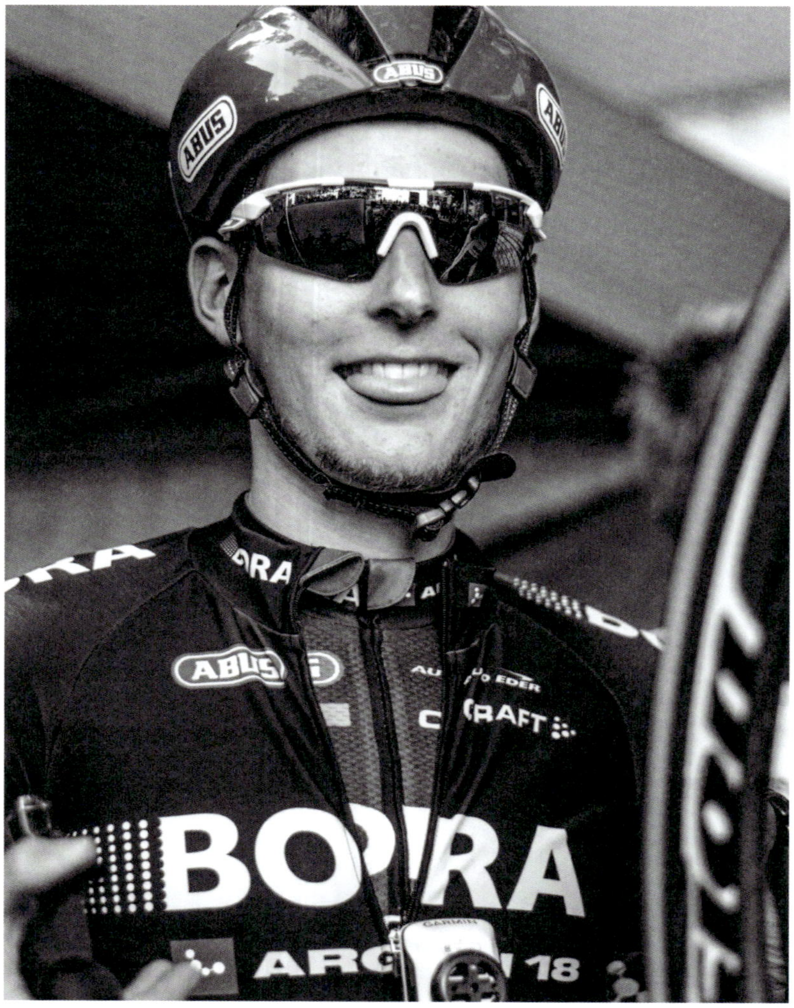

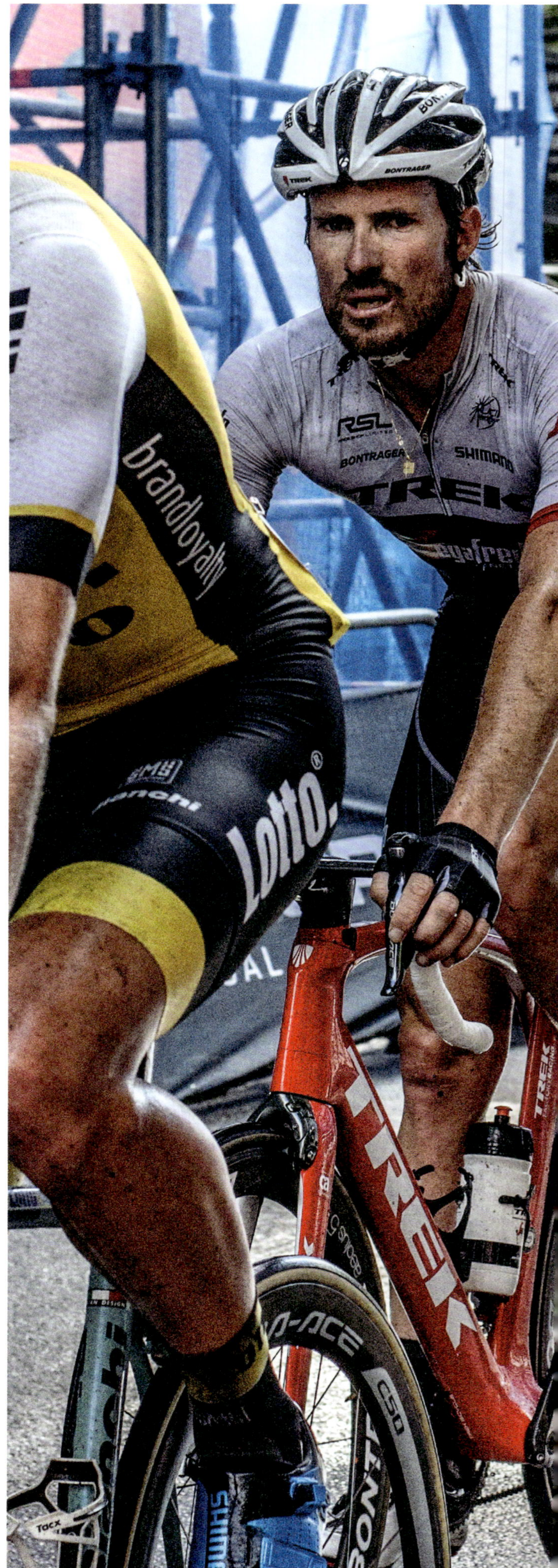

↑ Guter Stimmung vor dem Start: Lukas Pöstlberger (BORA - ARGON 18). **High spirits before the start: Lukas Pöstlberger (BORA - ARGON 18).** *Bonne ambiance avant le départ : Lukas Pöstlberger (BORA - ARGON 18).*

→ Nach 217,7 km im Ziel. **Crossing the finish line after 217.7 km.** *Toucher au but après 217,7 km.*

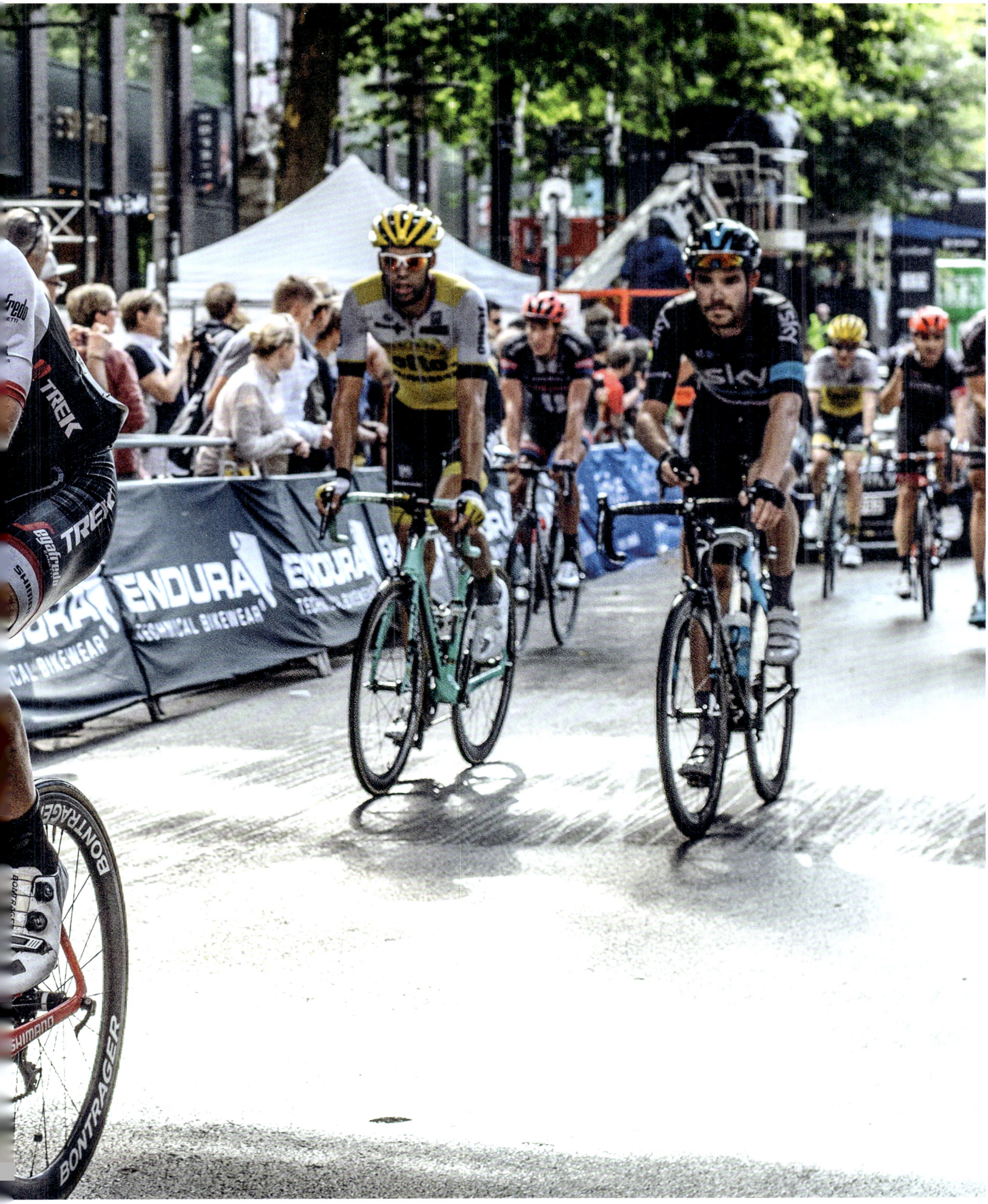
ENDURA
TREK
SKY
BONTRAGER
SHIMANO

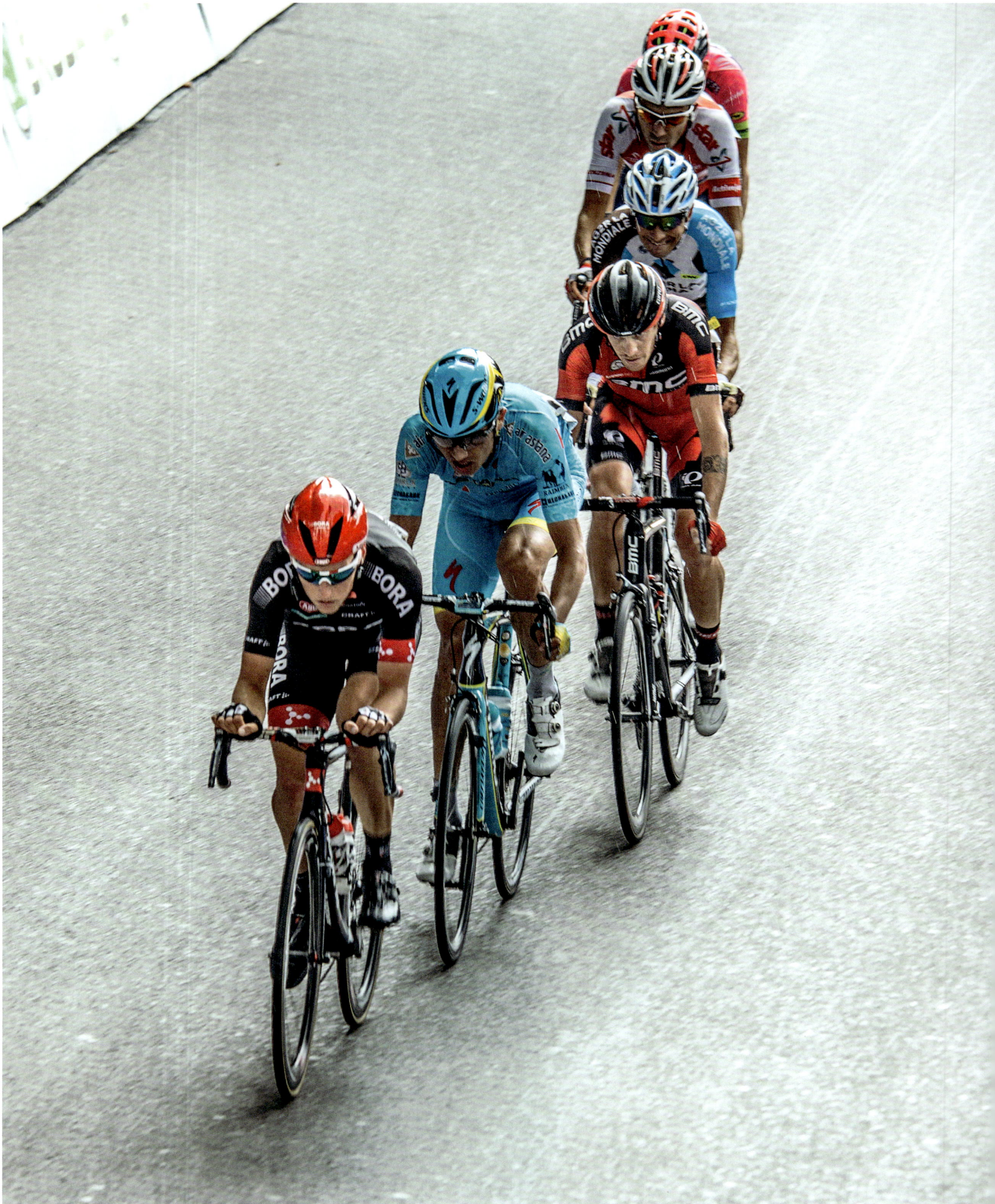
BORA
BMC

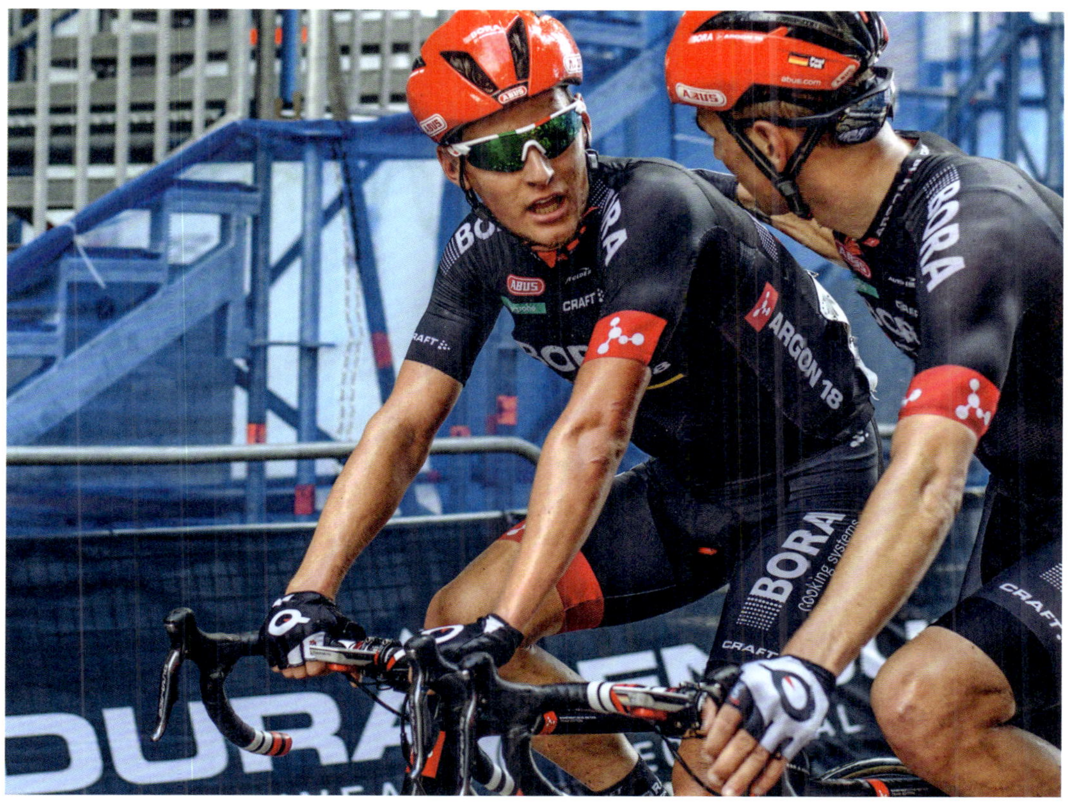

↖ Lukas Pöstlberger (BORA - ARGON 18) führt über lange Strecken die Ausreißergruppe an, die erst kurz vor der Ziellinie eingefangen wird. **Lukas Pöstlberger (BORA - ARGON 18) leads the breakaway group over long stretches. The field only caught up shortly before the finish line.** *Lukas Pöstlberger (BORA - ARGON 18) est resté à la tête du peloton sur de nombreux kilomètres avant d'être rattrapé juste avant la ligne d'arrivée.*

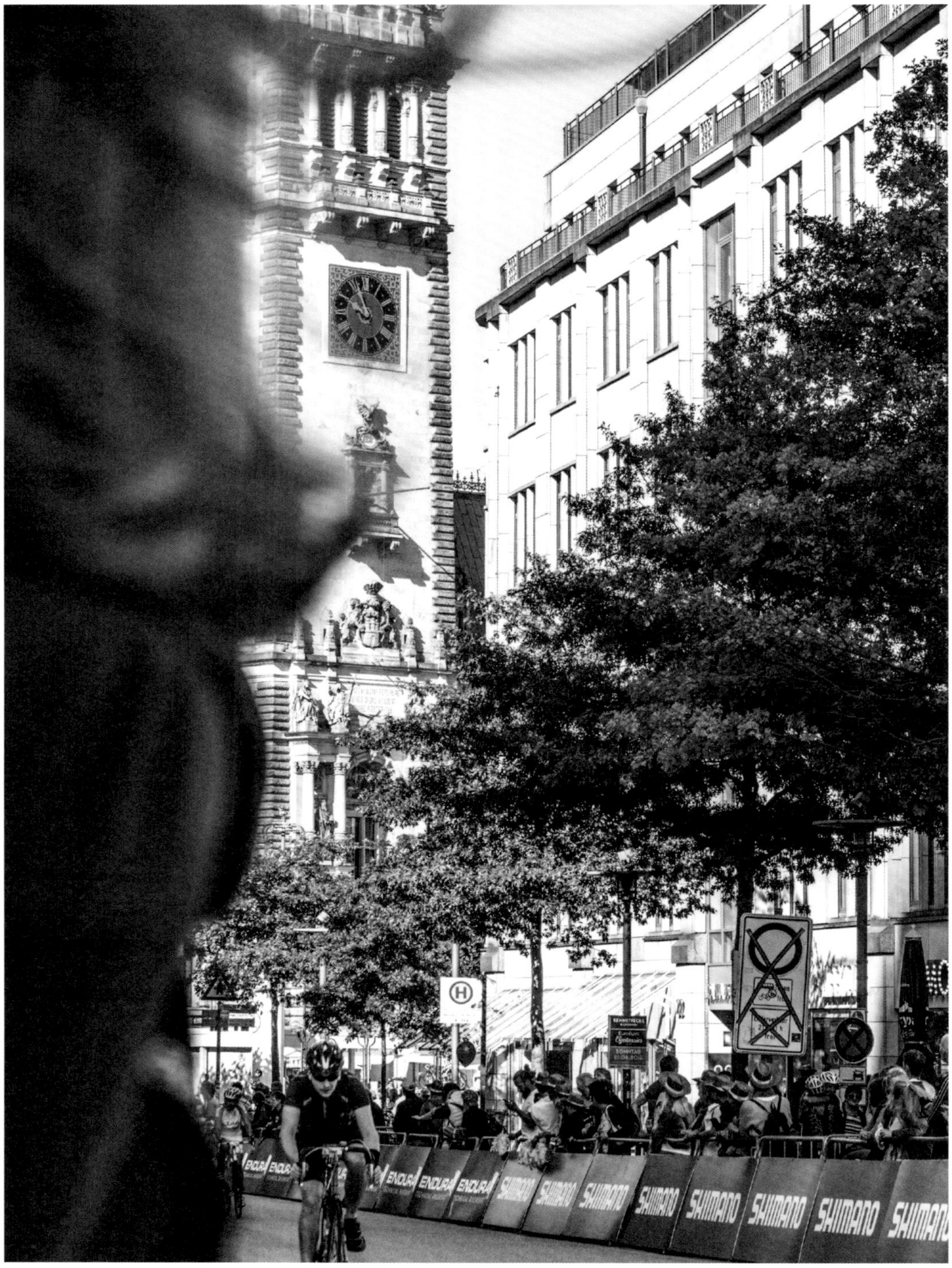
ENDURA
SHIMANO

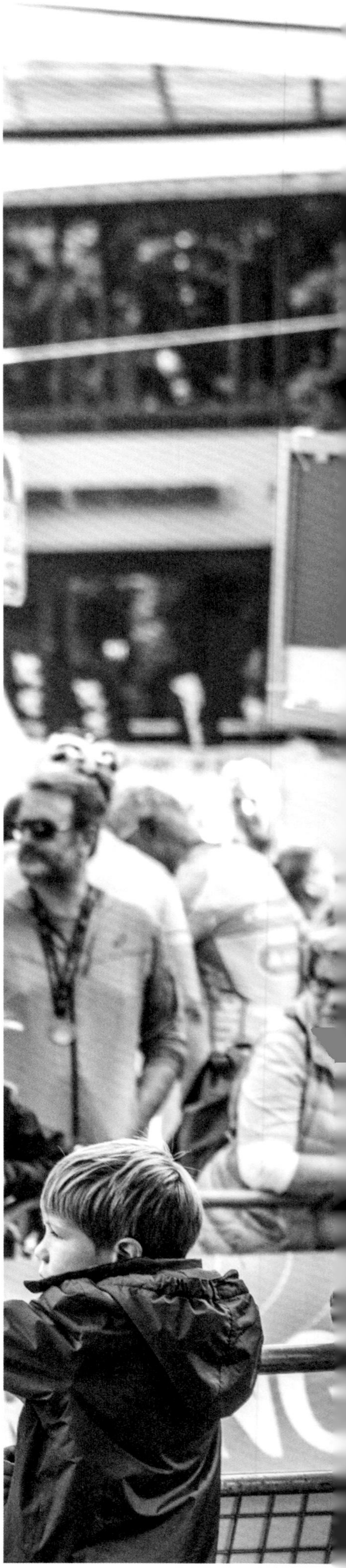

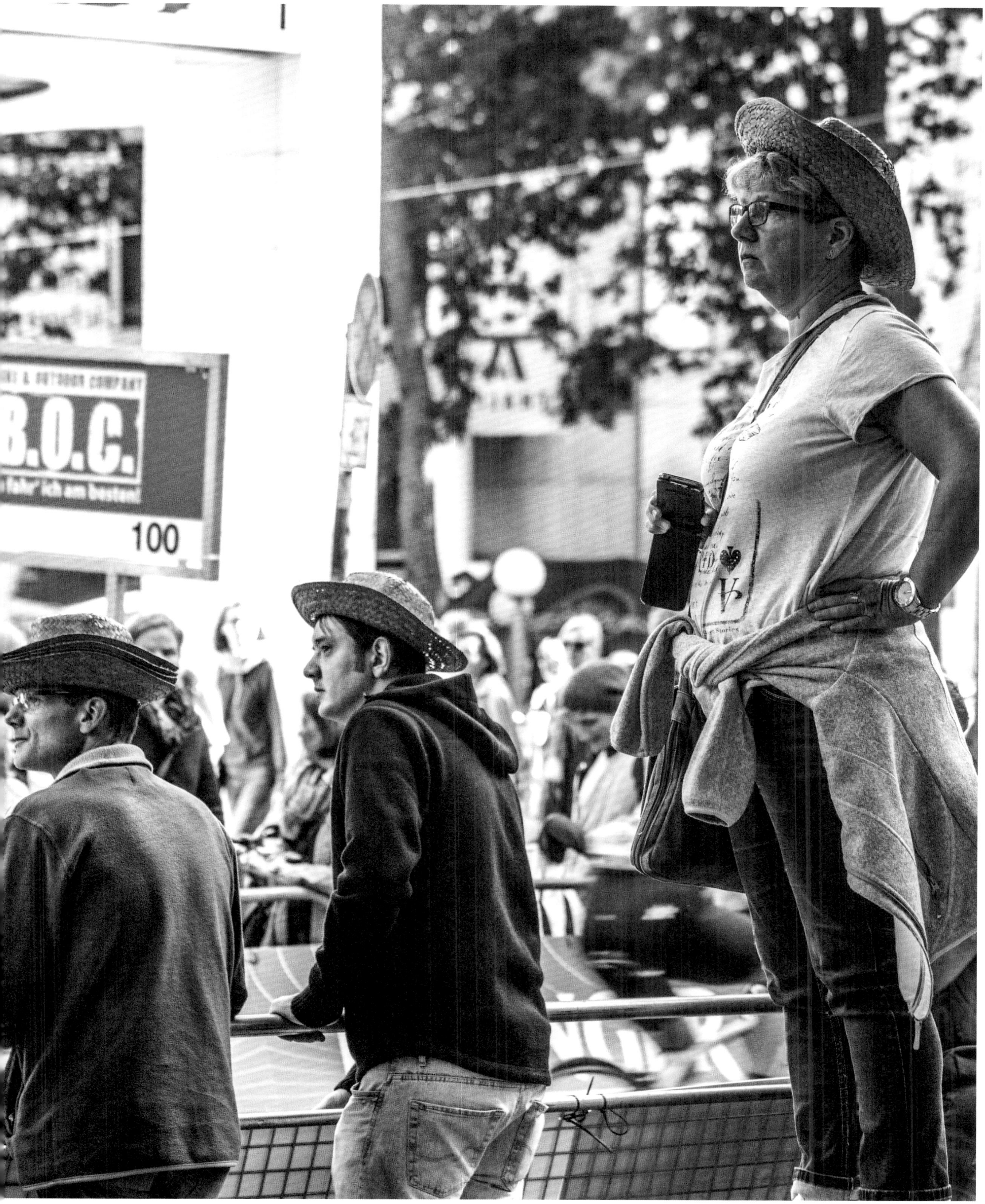

Gut behütet. **Well protected.** *Bien protégés.*

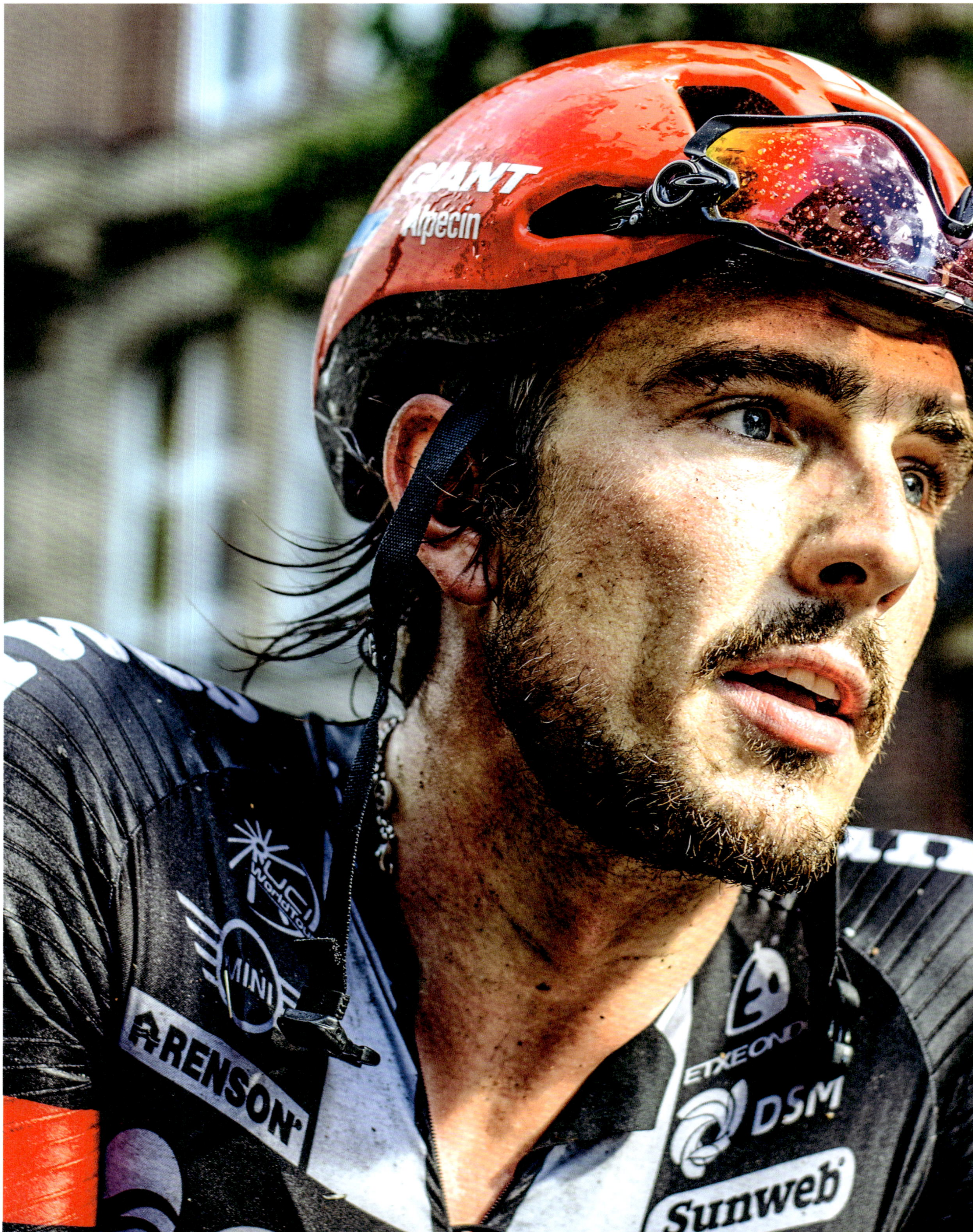
GIANT
Alpecin
MINI
RENSON
DSM
Sunweb

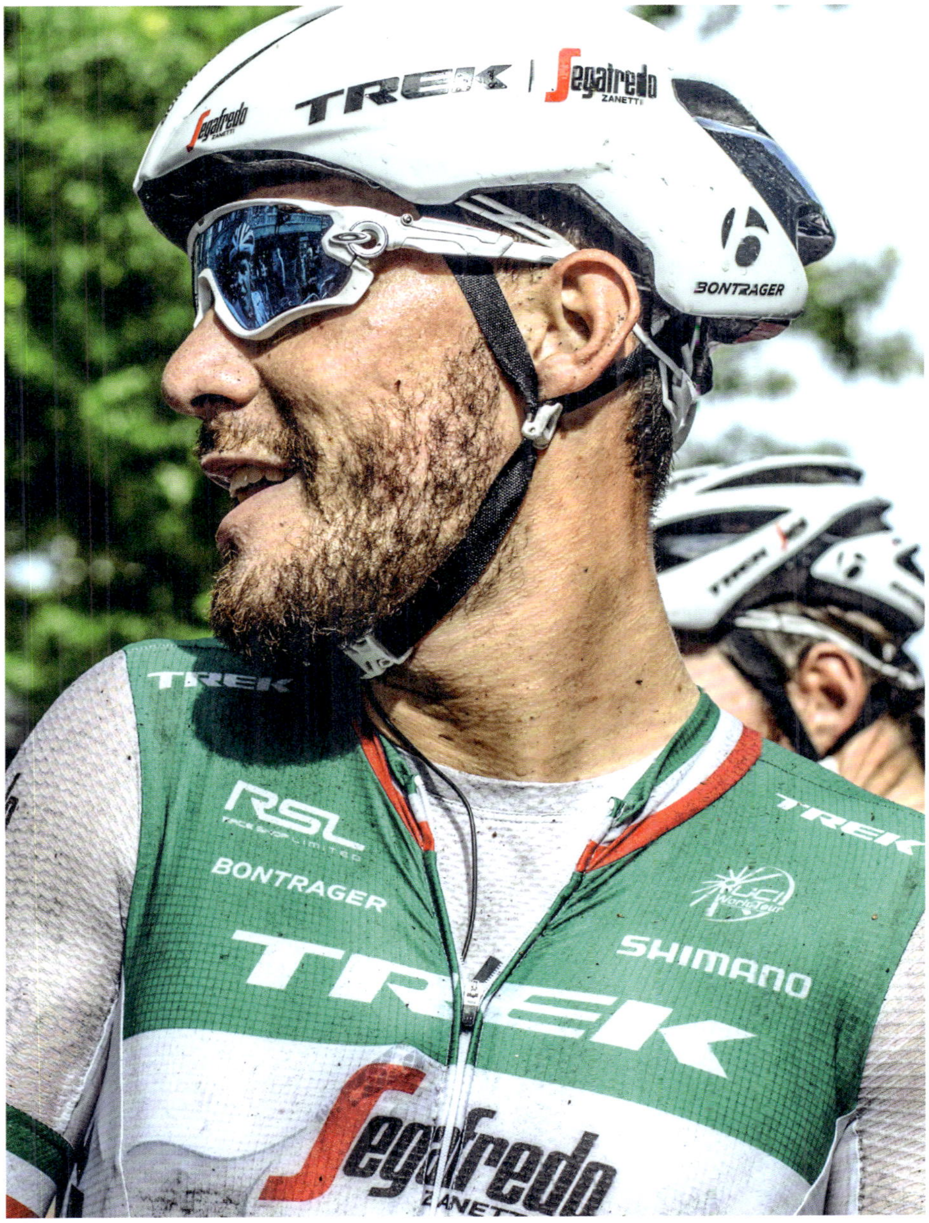

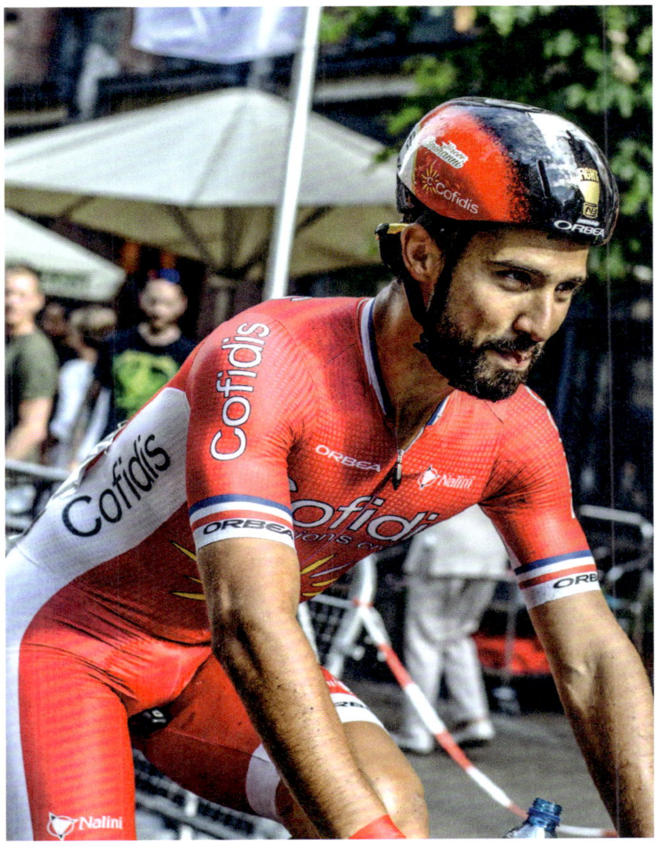

← John Degenkolb (Team Giant-Alpecin), Gesamtzweiter. **John Degenkolb (Team Giant-Alpecin), second place in the overall rankings.** *John Degenkolb (Team Giant-Alpecin), deuxième du classement général.*

↑ Nacer Bouhanni (Cofidis) fährt als Erster durchs Ziel, wird jedoch wegen eines unerlaubten Schlenkers im Zielspurt disqualifiziert, Caleb Ewan (ORICA-BikeExchange) rückt nach. Giacomo Nizzolo (Trek-Segafredo) fährt auf Rang drei. **Nacer Bouhanni (Cofidis) crosses the finish line first but is disqualified for not holding the line in the final sprint. Caleb Ewan (ORICA-BikeExchange) moves up. Giacomo Nizzolo (Trek-Segafredo) comes in third.** *Nacer Bouhanni (Cofidis) arrive en première position à destination, mais a finalement été disqualifié à cause d'un mouvement non autorisé. Caleb Ewan (ORICA-BikeExchange) arrive juste derrière. Giacomo Nizzolo (Trek-Segafredo) termine à la troisième place.*

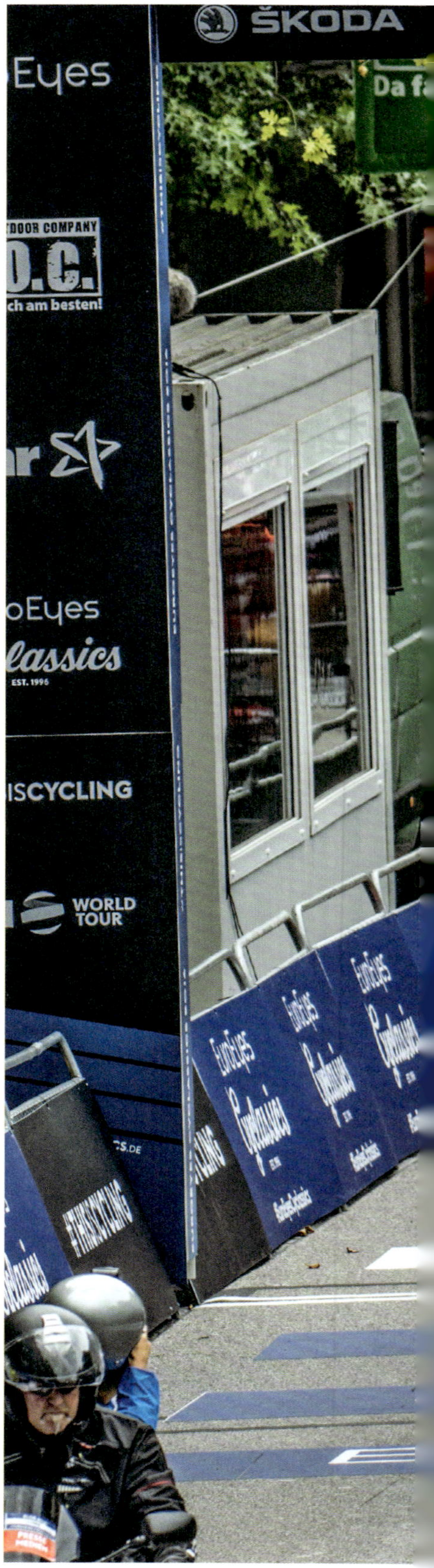
ŠKODA
Eyes
ISCYCLING
WORLD TOUR

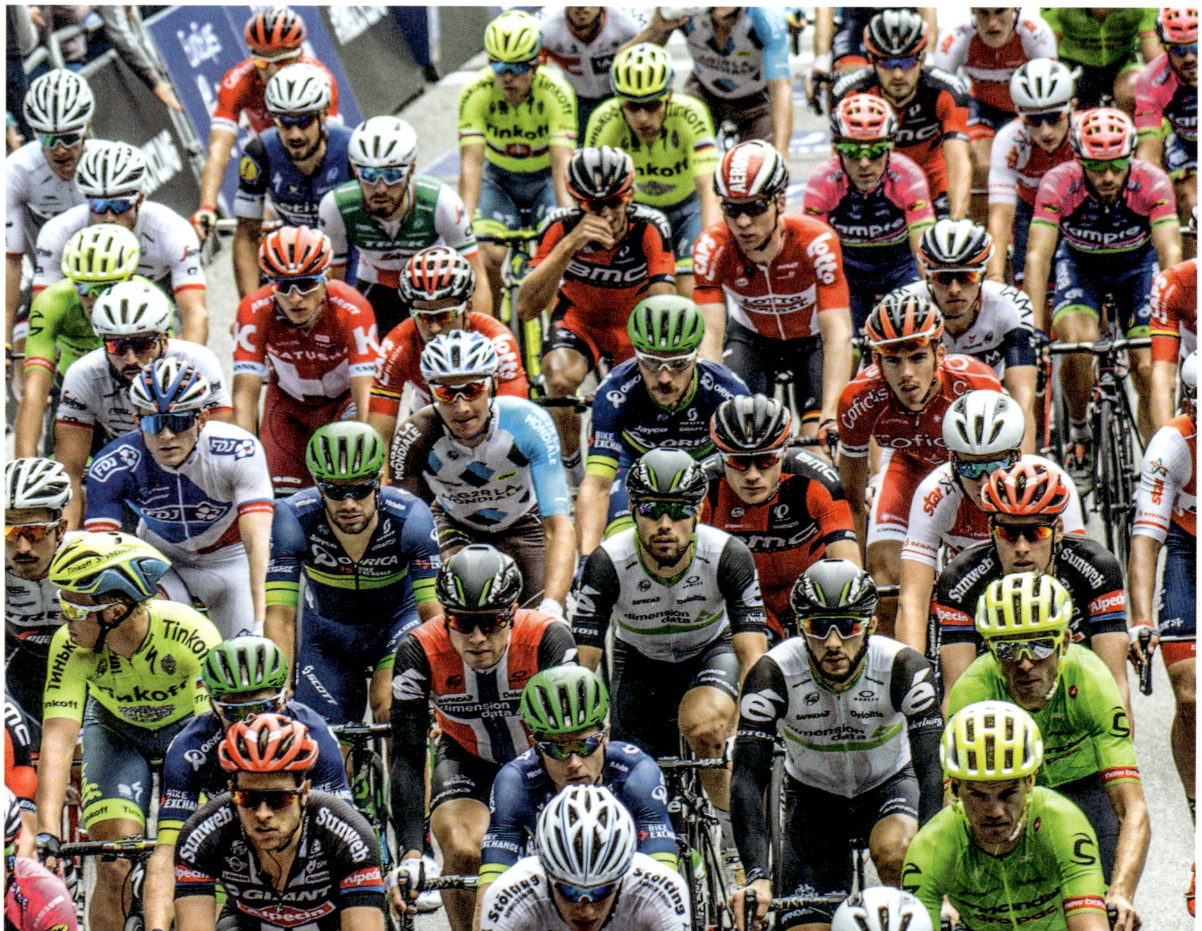

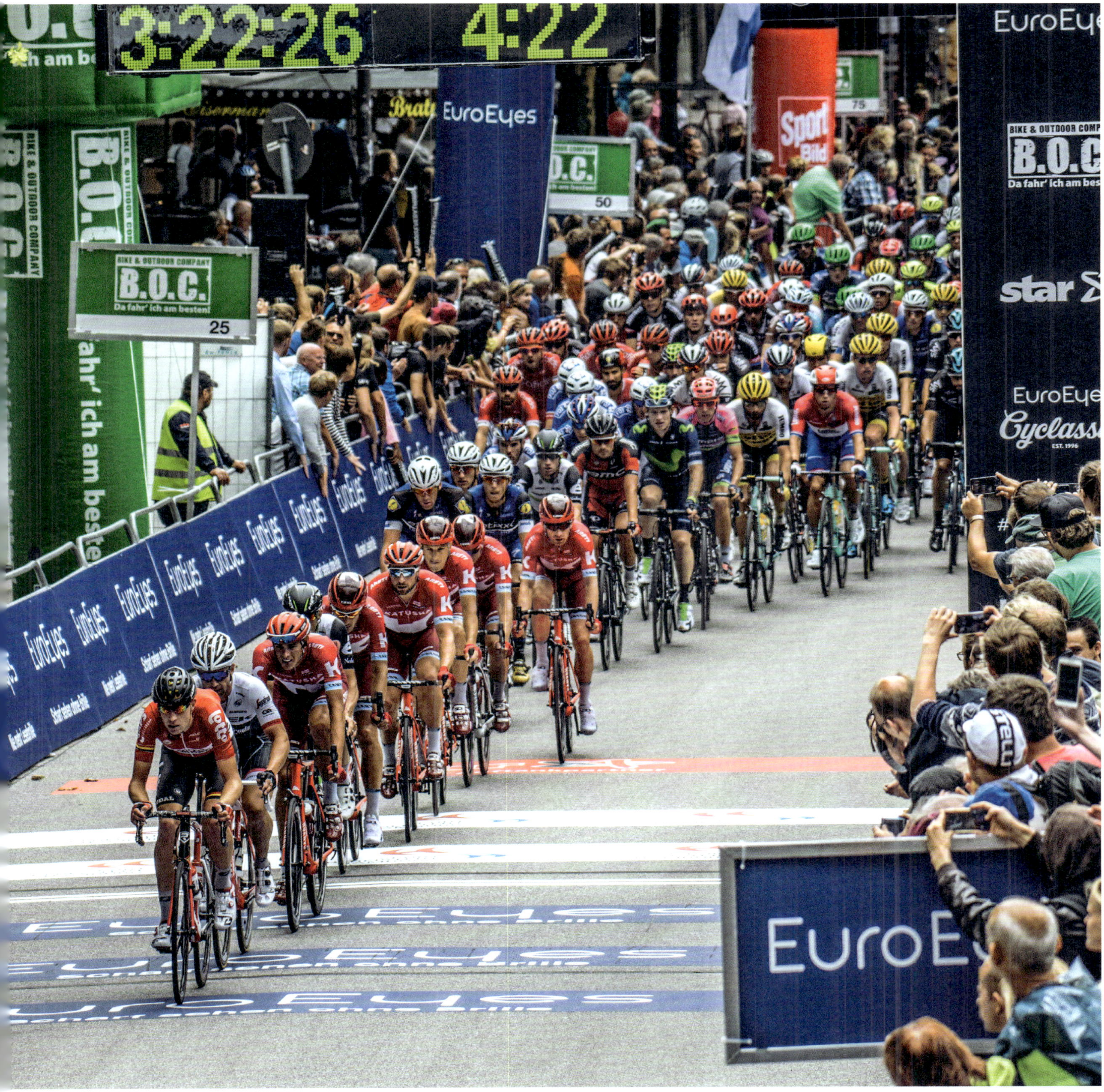

Schlussrunden auf der Mönckebergstraße. **Final laps on Mönckebergstrasse.** *Derniers tours de course sur la Mönckebergstraße.*

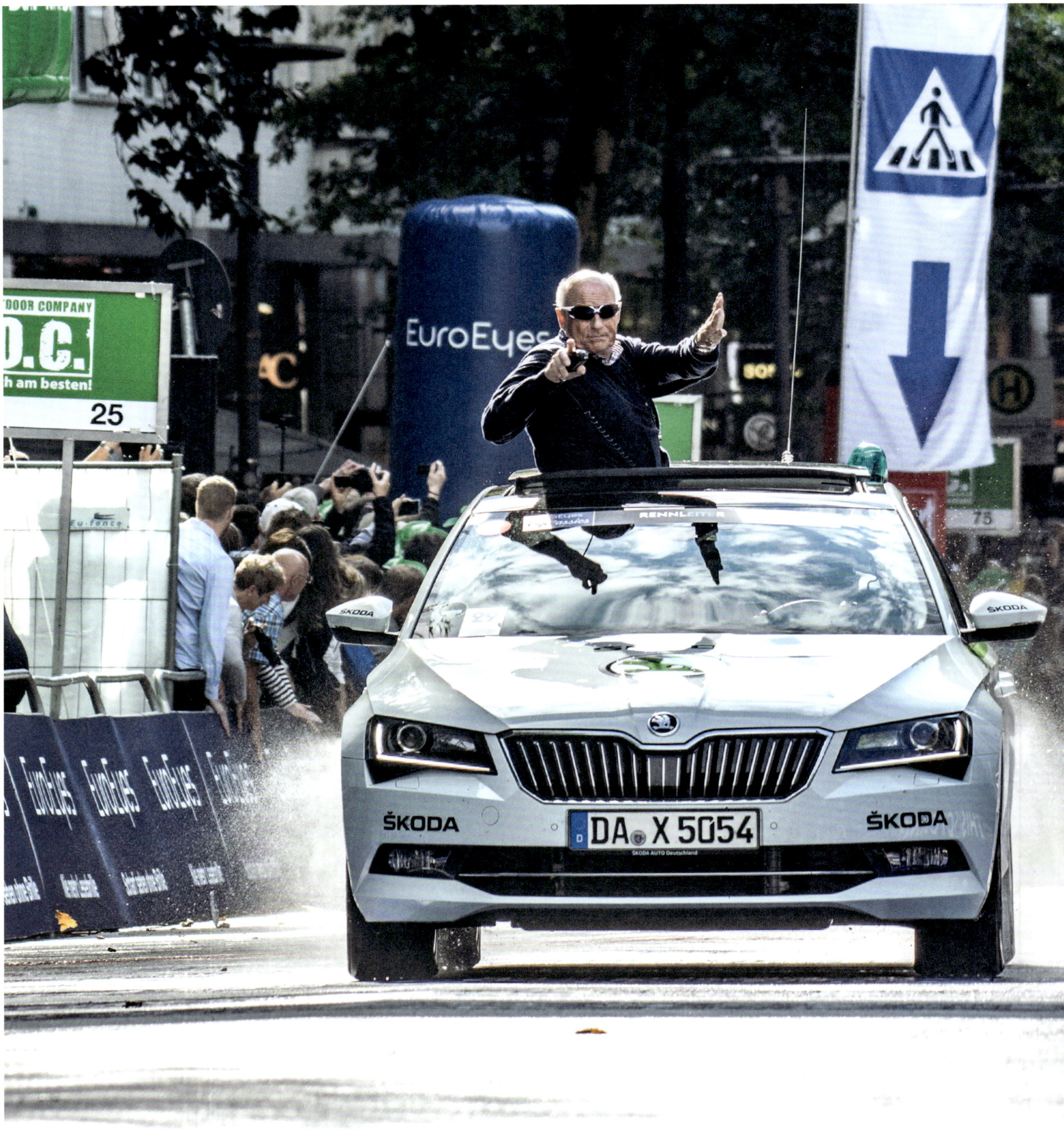
EuroEyes
25
RENNLEITER
ŠKODA
DA X 5054
ŠKODA
75

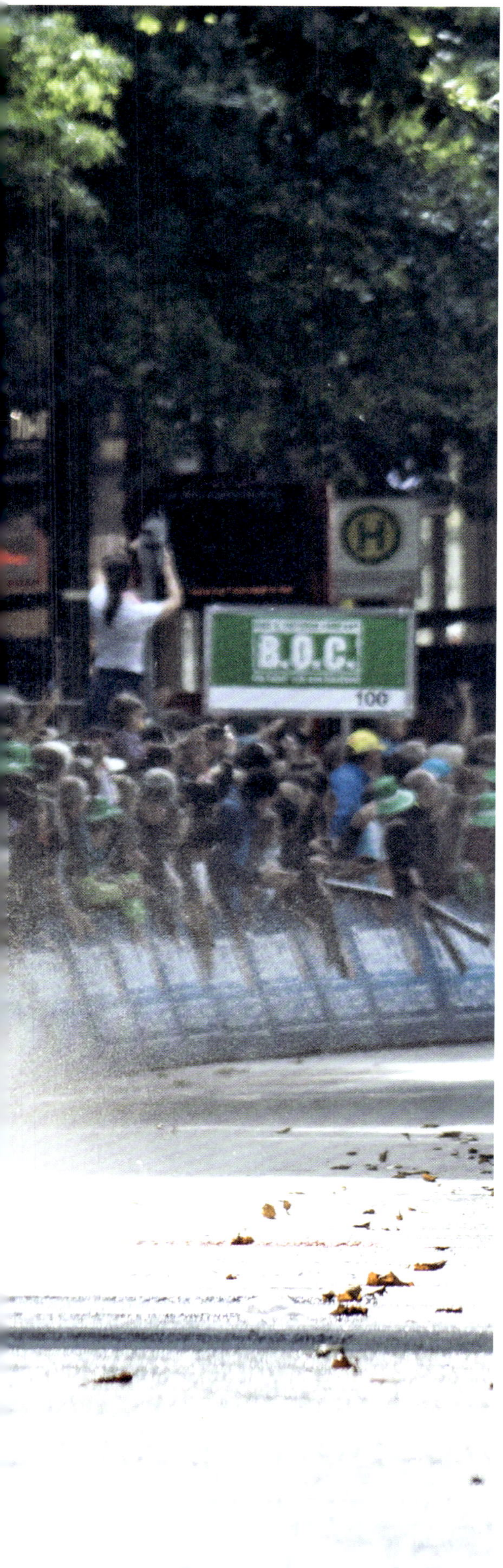

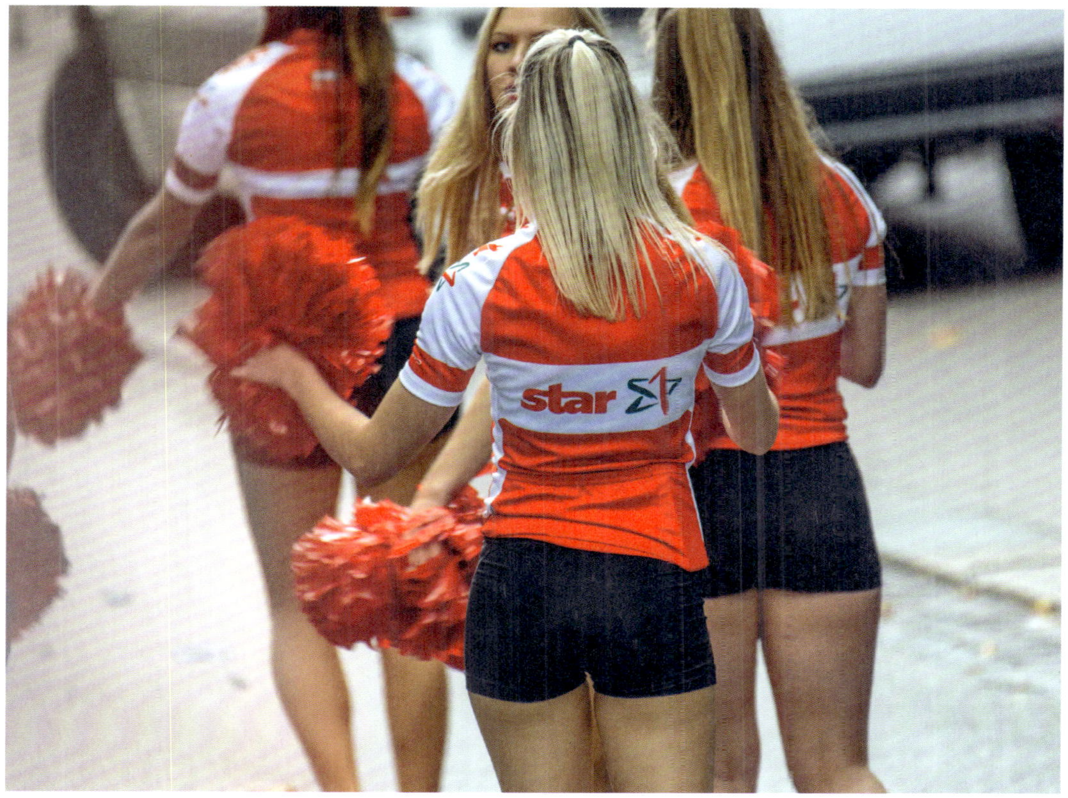

Rund um das Rennen. **Around the race.** *Autour de la course.*

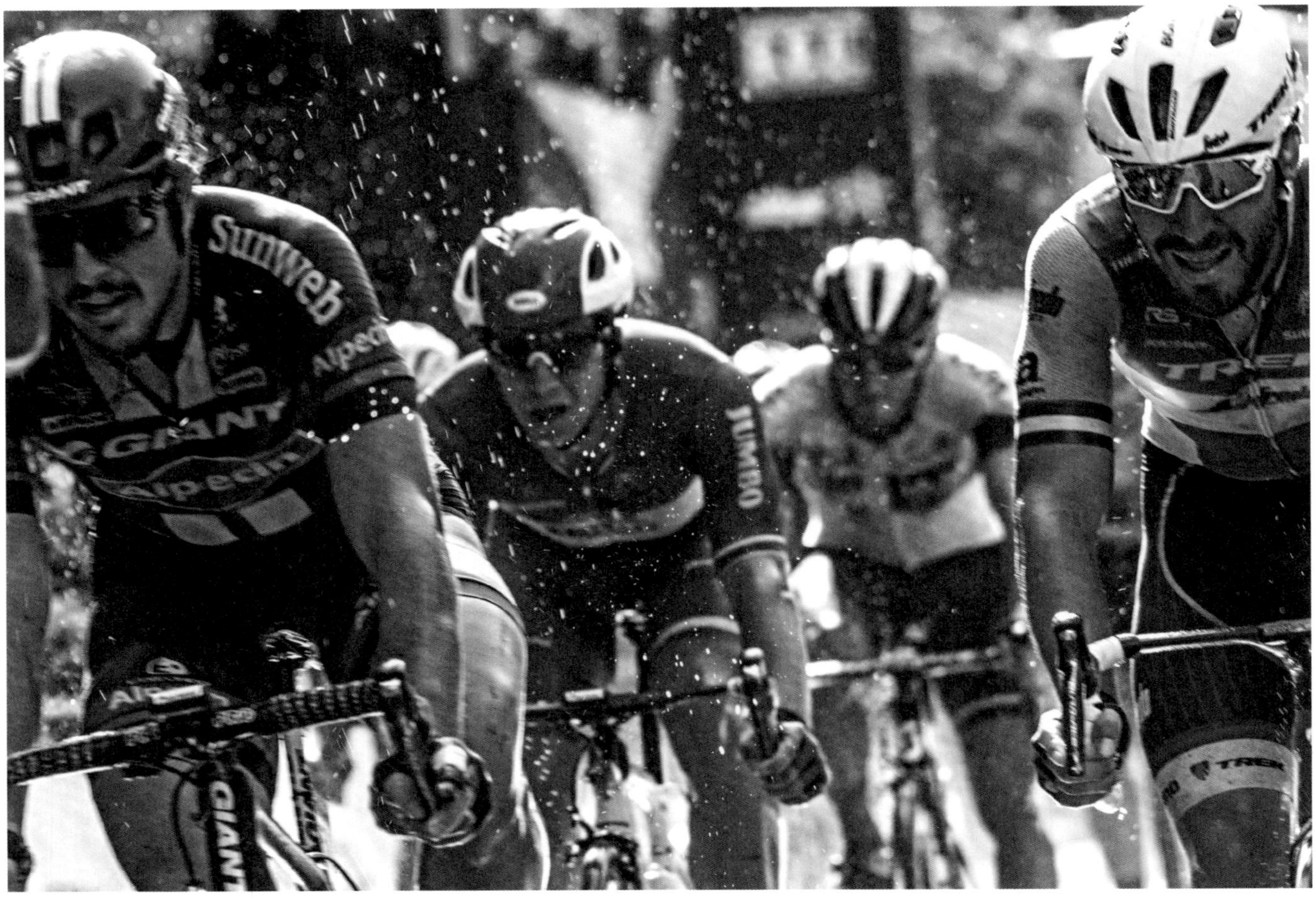

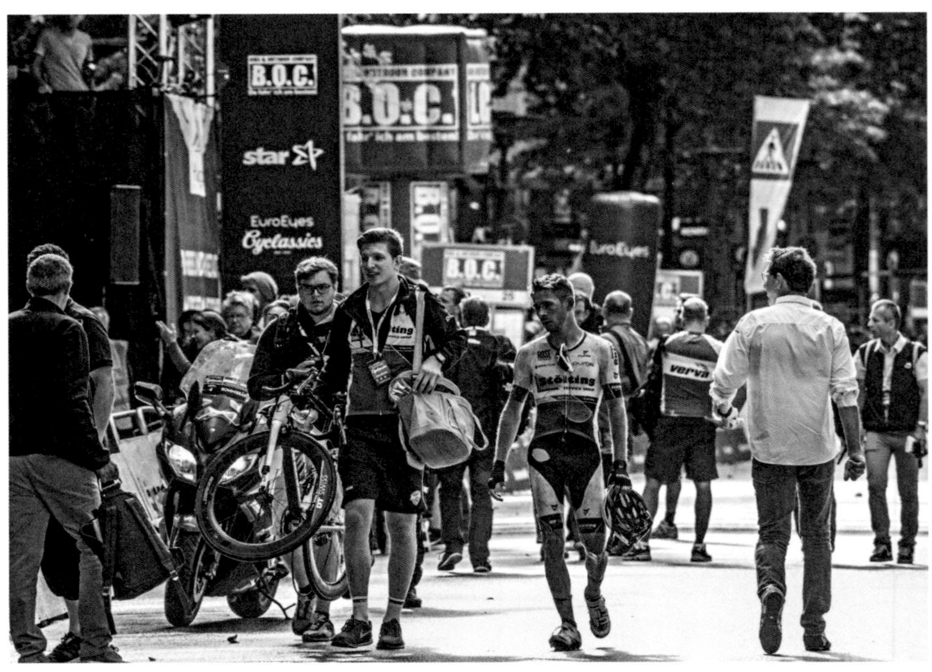

↑ Zweiter und Dritter: John Degenkolb (Team Giant-Alpecin, links) und Giacomo Nizzolo (Trek – Segafredo, rechts). **Second and third: John Degenkolb (Team Giant-Alpecin, left) and Giacomo Nizzolo (Trek – Segafredo, right).** *Deuxième et troisième place : John Degenkolb (Team Giant-Alpecin, à gauche) et Giacomo Nizzolo (Trek – Segafredo, à droite).*

→ Turbulenter Schlusssprint. **Frantic finish line sprint.** *Un sprint final très disputé.*

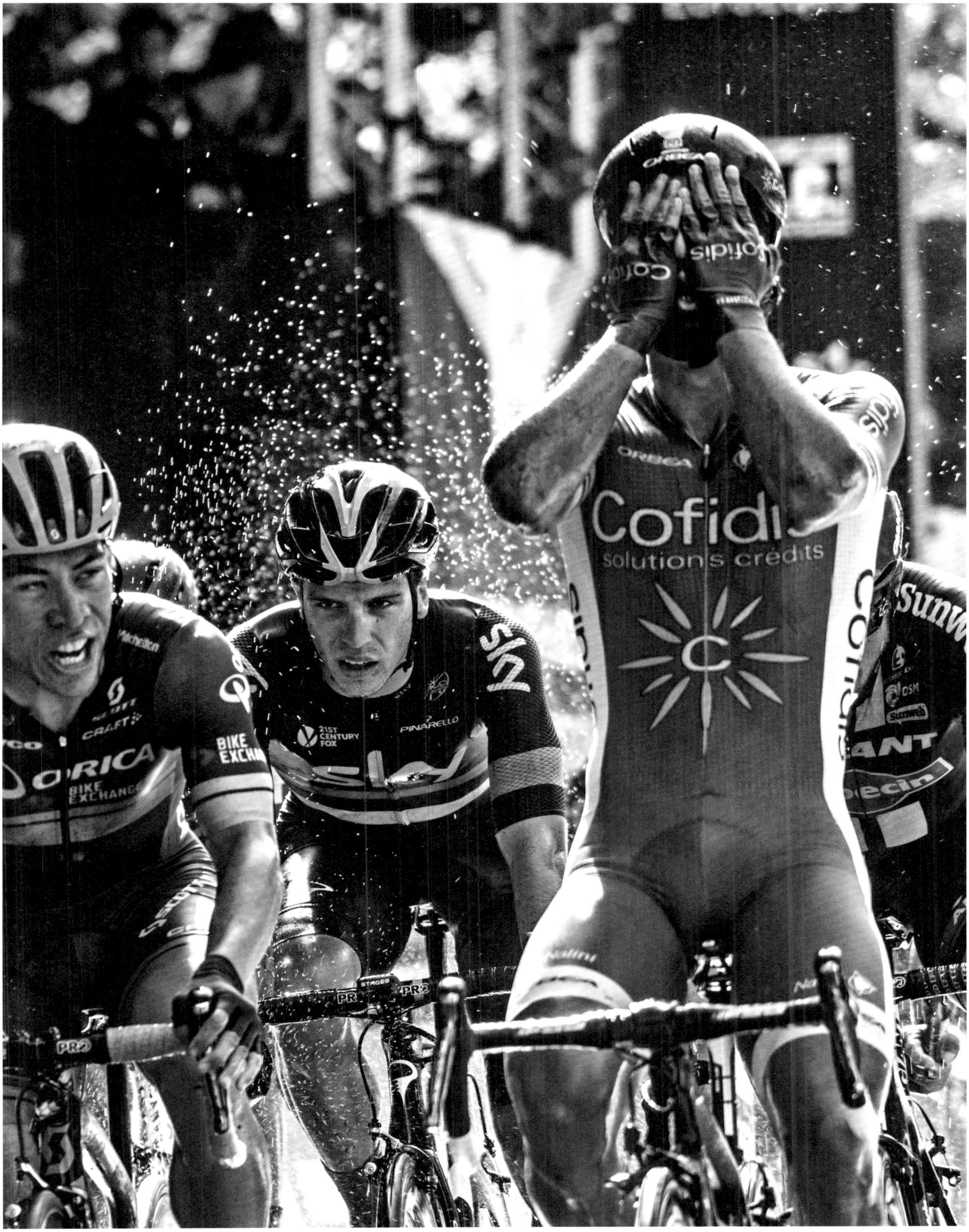
Cofidis
solutions crédits
cofidis
ORICA
ORICA
BIKE EXCHANGE
BIKE EXCHANGE
SCOTT
CRAFT
21ST CENTURY FOX
PINARELLO
Sunweb

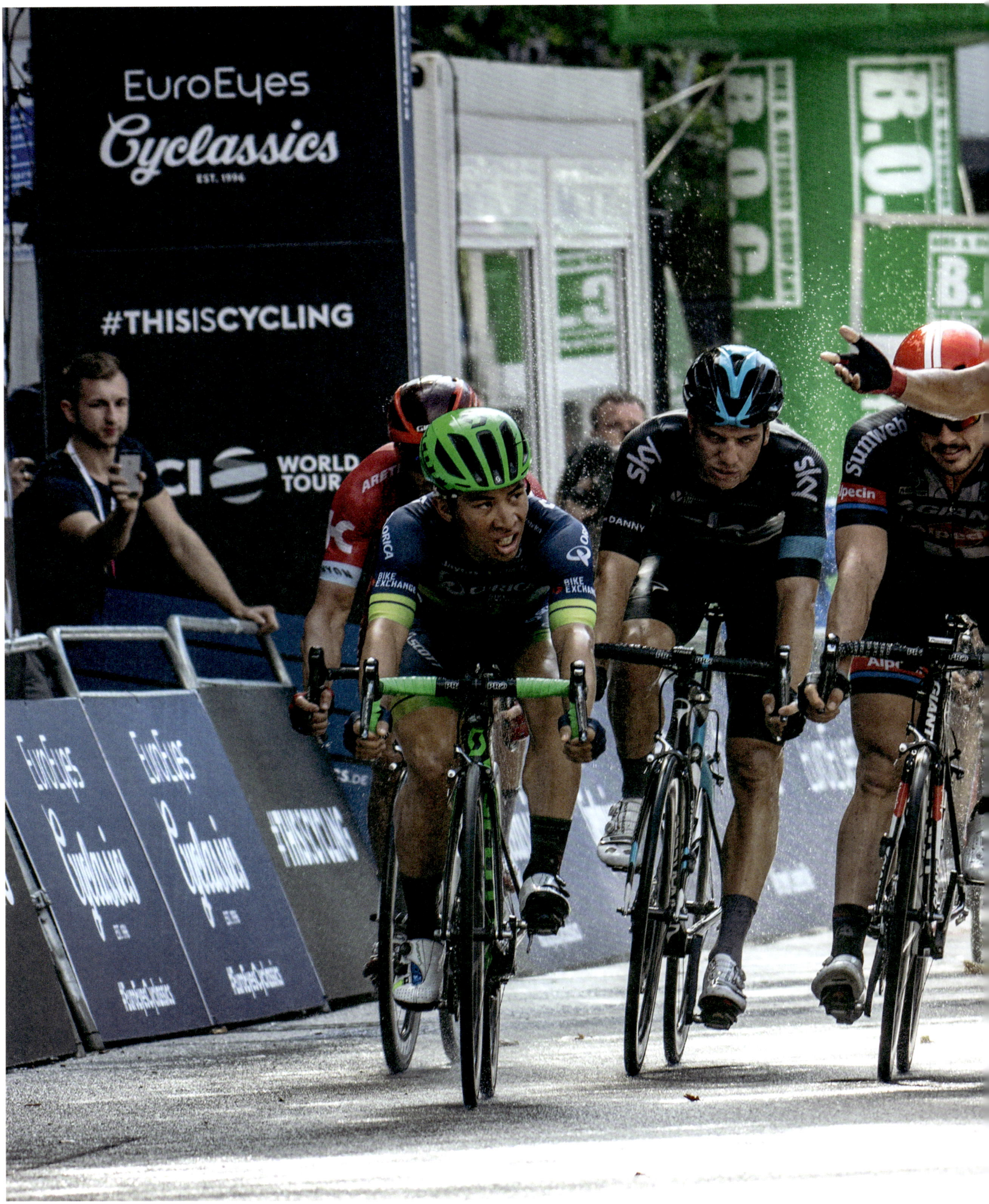
EuroEyes
Cyclassics
EST. 1996
#THISISCYCLING
WORLD TOUR

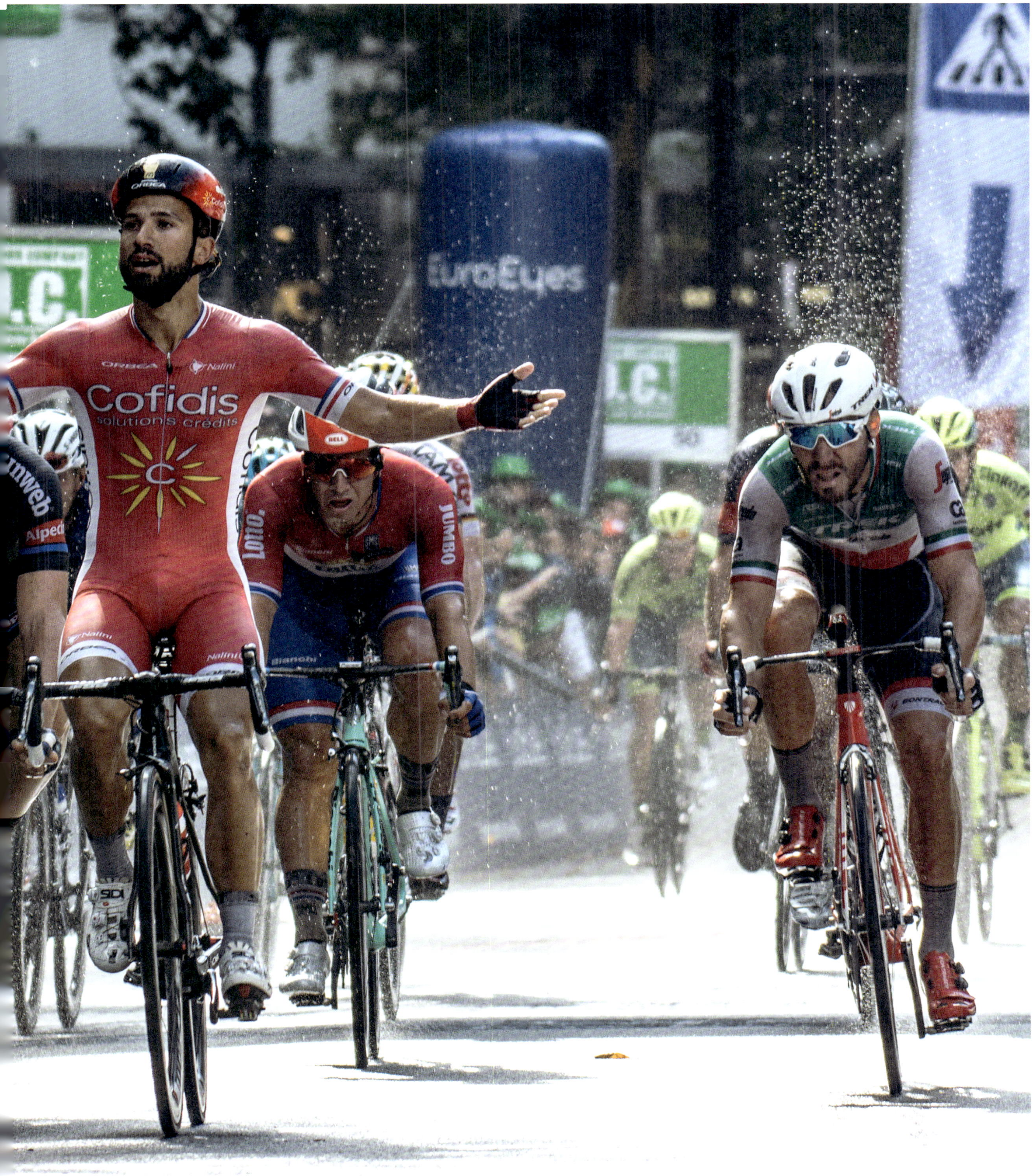

Caleb Ewan fährt als Zweiter durchs Ziel, wütend auf den Sieger Nacer Bouhanni (Cofidis), der ihn im Schlusssprint behindert hat und später disqualifiziert wird. Caleb Ewan wird schließlich Sieger der EuroEyes Cyclassics 2016. **Caleb Ewan crosses the finish line second, angered by winner Nacer Bouhanni (Cofidis) obstructing him during the finish line sprint which eventually led to Bouhanni's disqualification. Caleb Ewan is ultimately named winner of the EuroEyes Cyclassics 2016.** *Caleb Ewan arrive en deuxième position à destination, fâché après le vainqueur Nacer Bouhanni (Cofidis) qui l'a gêné pendant le sprint et a finalement été disqualifié. Caleb Ewan termine donc en grand vainqueur de l'EuroEyes Cyclassics 2016.*

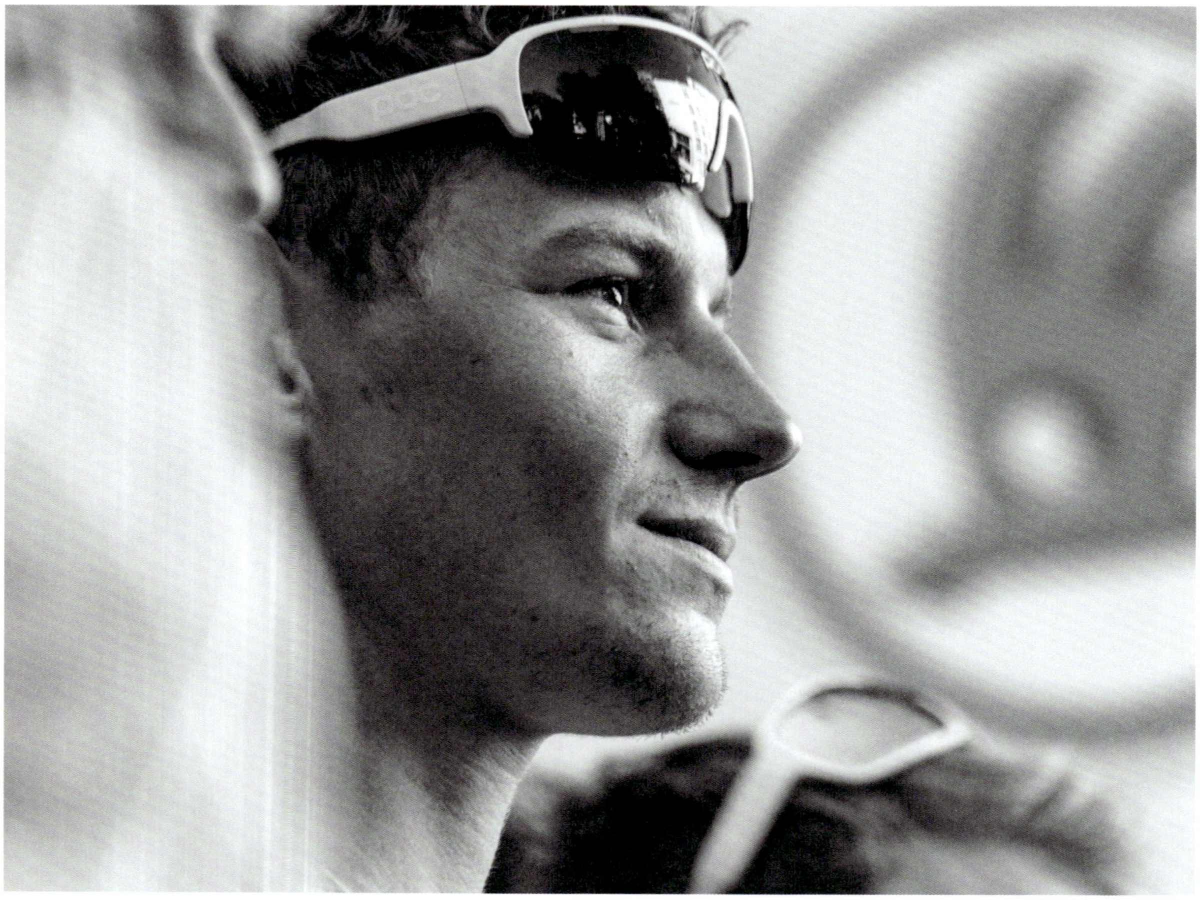

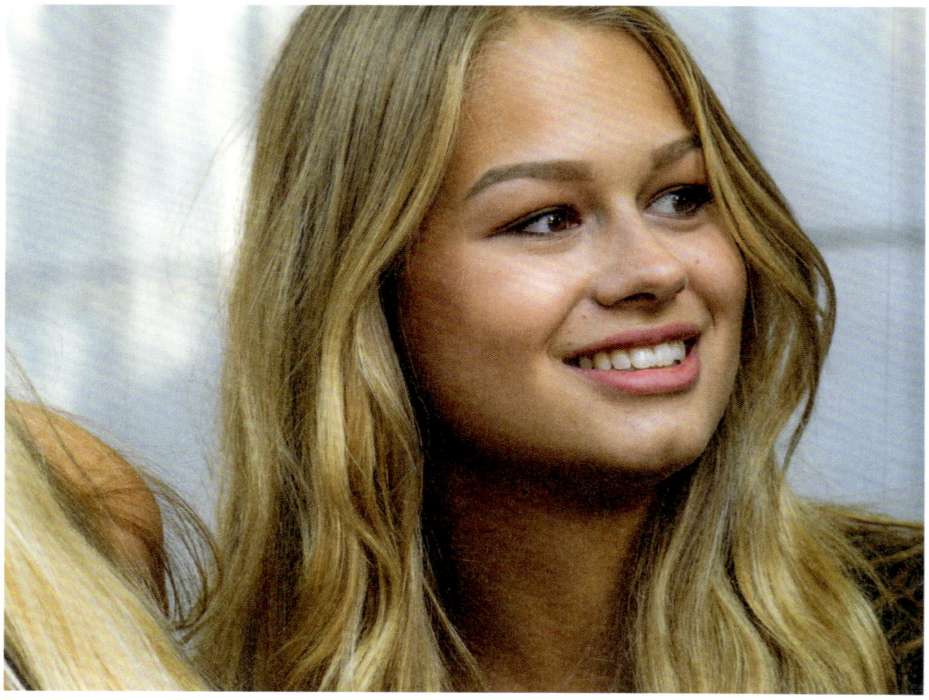

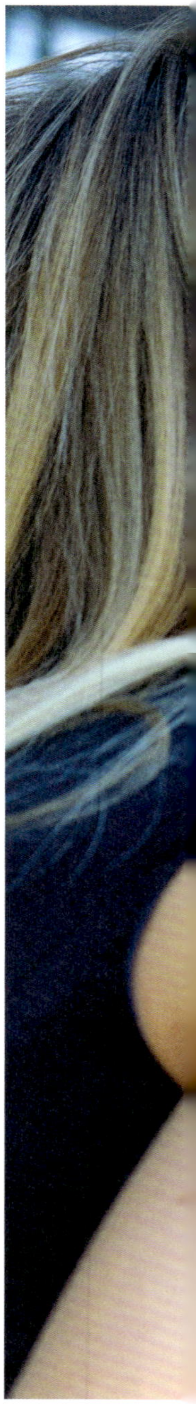

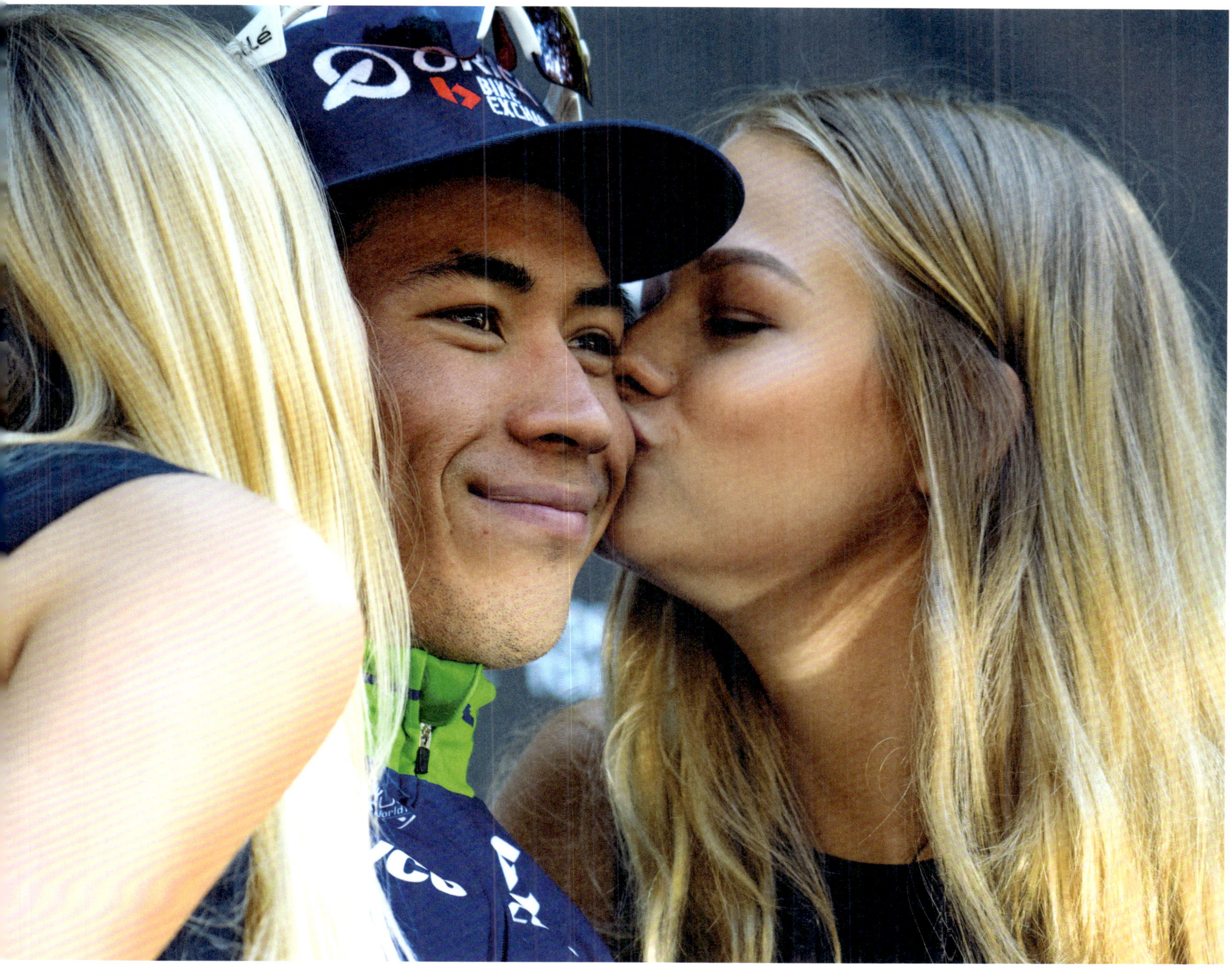

The winner takes it all: Caleb Ewan (ORICA-BikeExchange) als glücklicher Gewinner auf dem Podium. **The winner takes it all: Caleb Ewan (ORICA-BikeExchange) is the elated winner on the podium.** *« The winner takes it all » : Caleb Ewan (ORICA-BikeExchange) en tant que vainqueur heureux sur le podium.*

Vuelta a España

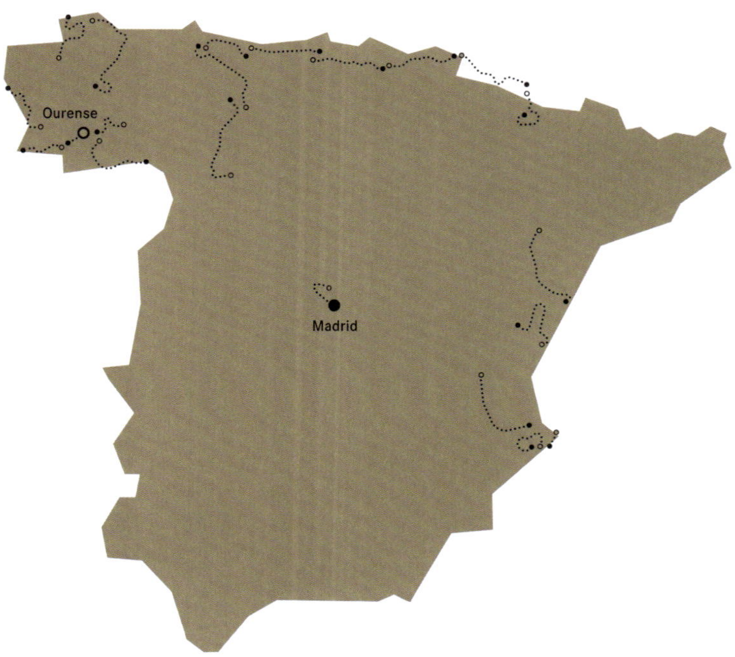

3,315.4

KILOMETRE

DATE: 20.8.-11.9.-2016

FIRST TOUR: 1996

DURATION: 83:31:28

Die Spanien-Rundfahrt ist die dritte Grand Tour im Radsportkalender. Steile Anstiege und große Hitze sind die größten Herausforderungen, mit denen die Aspiranten aufs Rote Trikot zu kämpfen haben. **'La Vuelta a España', the Tour of Spain, is the third Grand Tour in the race calendar. Steep climbs and fierce heat are the biggest challenges facing those who aspire to wear the red jersey.** *Le Tour d'Espagne est le troisième grand Tour dans le calendrier du cyclisme. Des montées raides et une forte chaleur sont les plus grandes difficultés que les candidats au maillot rouge ont à affronter.*

39.694

KM/H AVG. SPEED WINNER

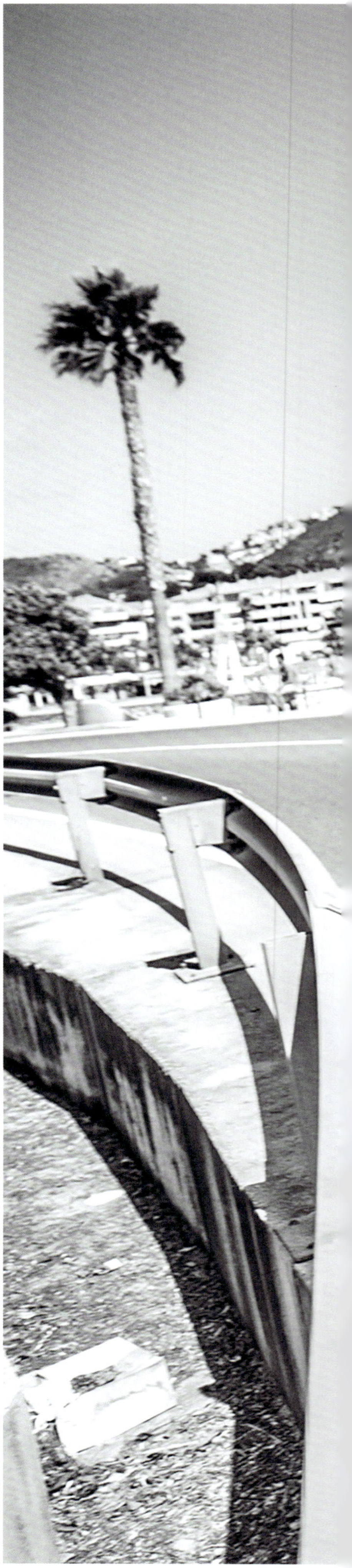

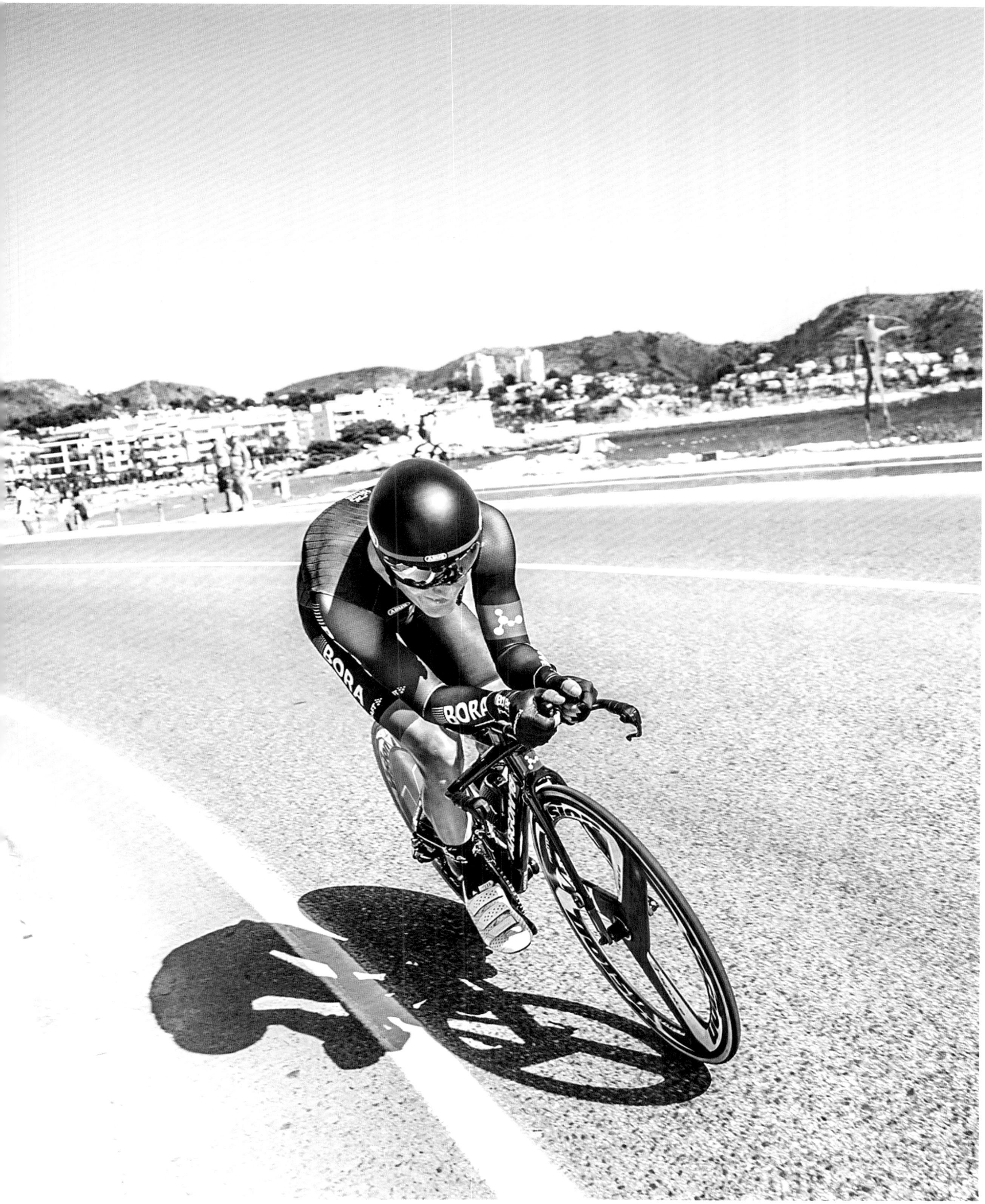

Tempo, Tempo: Scott Thwaites (BORA - ARGON 18) beim Zeitfahren. **Faster, faster: Scott Thwaites (BORA - ARGON 18) in the time trial.** *Tempo, Tempo : Scott Thwaites (BORA - ARGON 18) lors du contre-la-montre.*

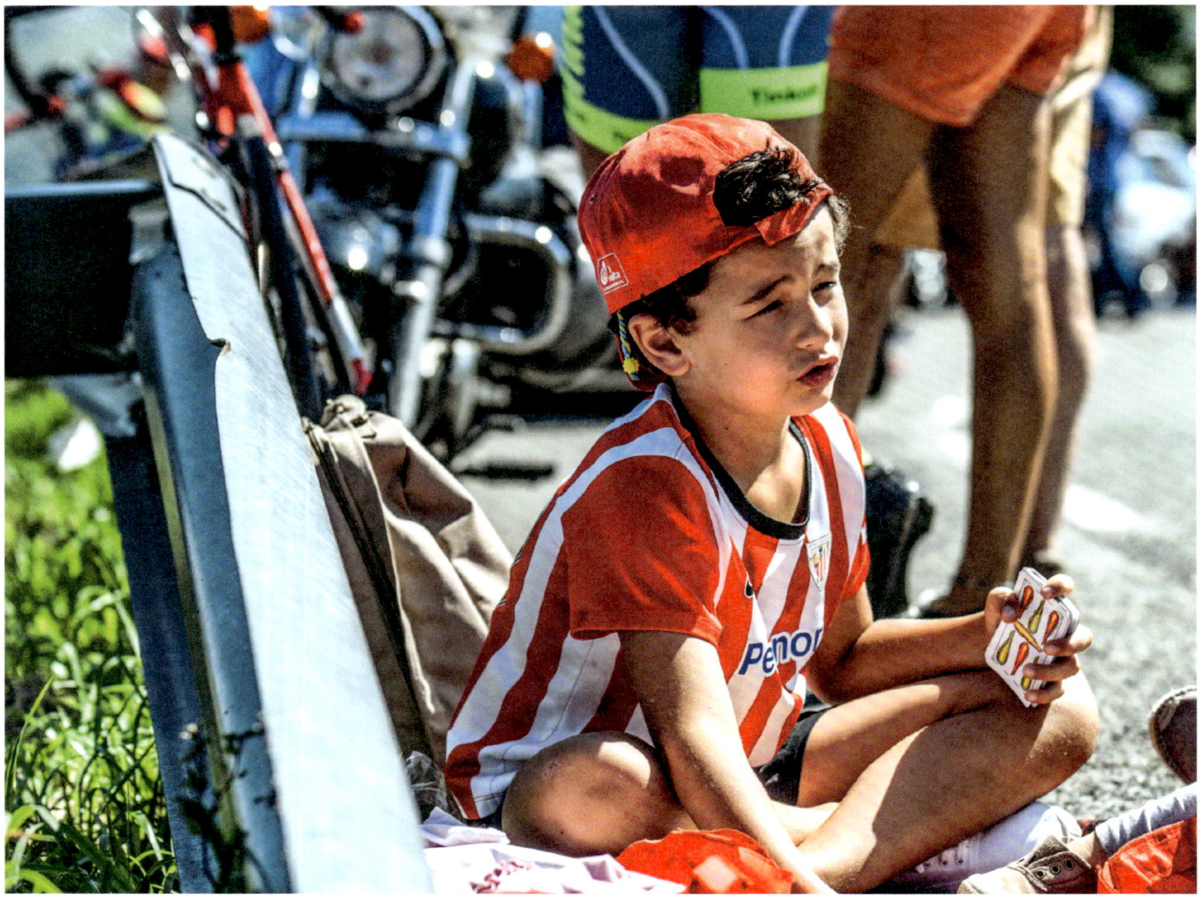

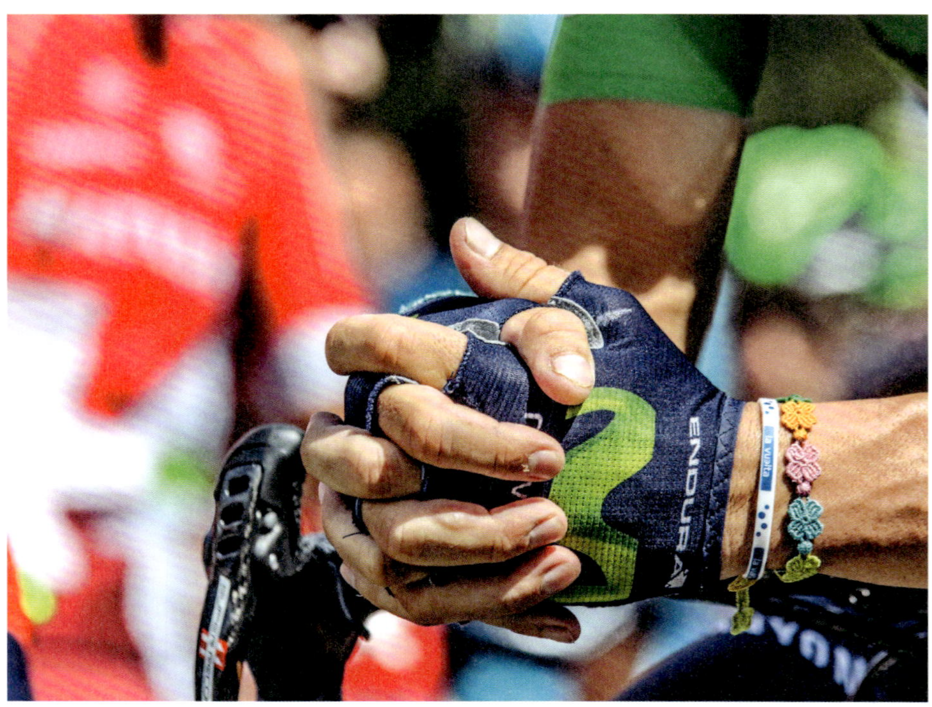
ENDURA

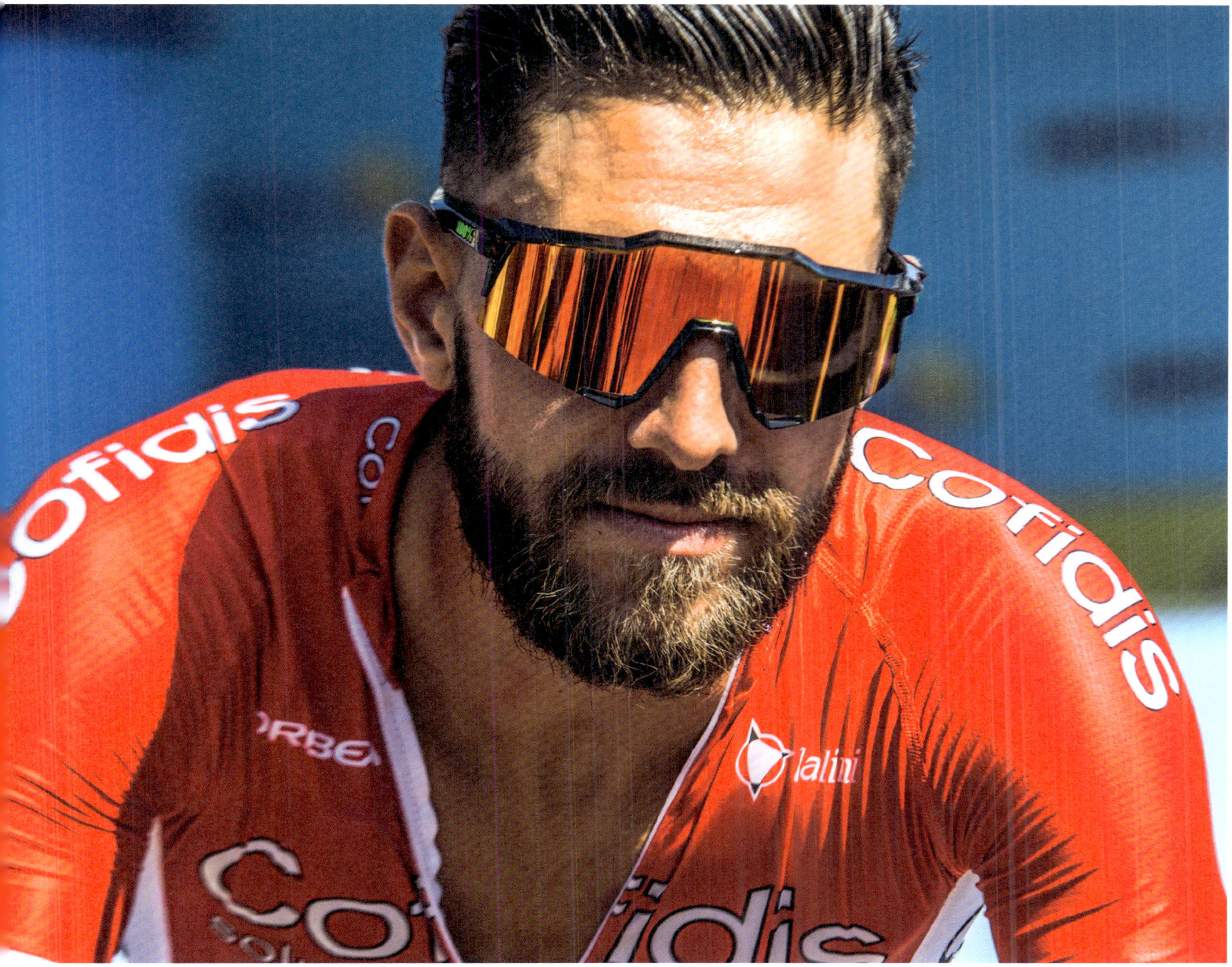

Loïc Chetout (Cofidis). **Loïc Chetout (Cofidis).** *Loïc Chetout (Cofidis).*

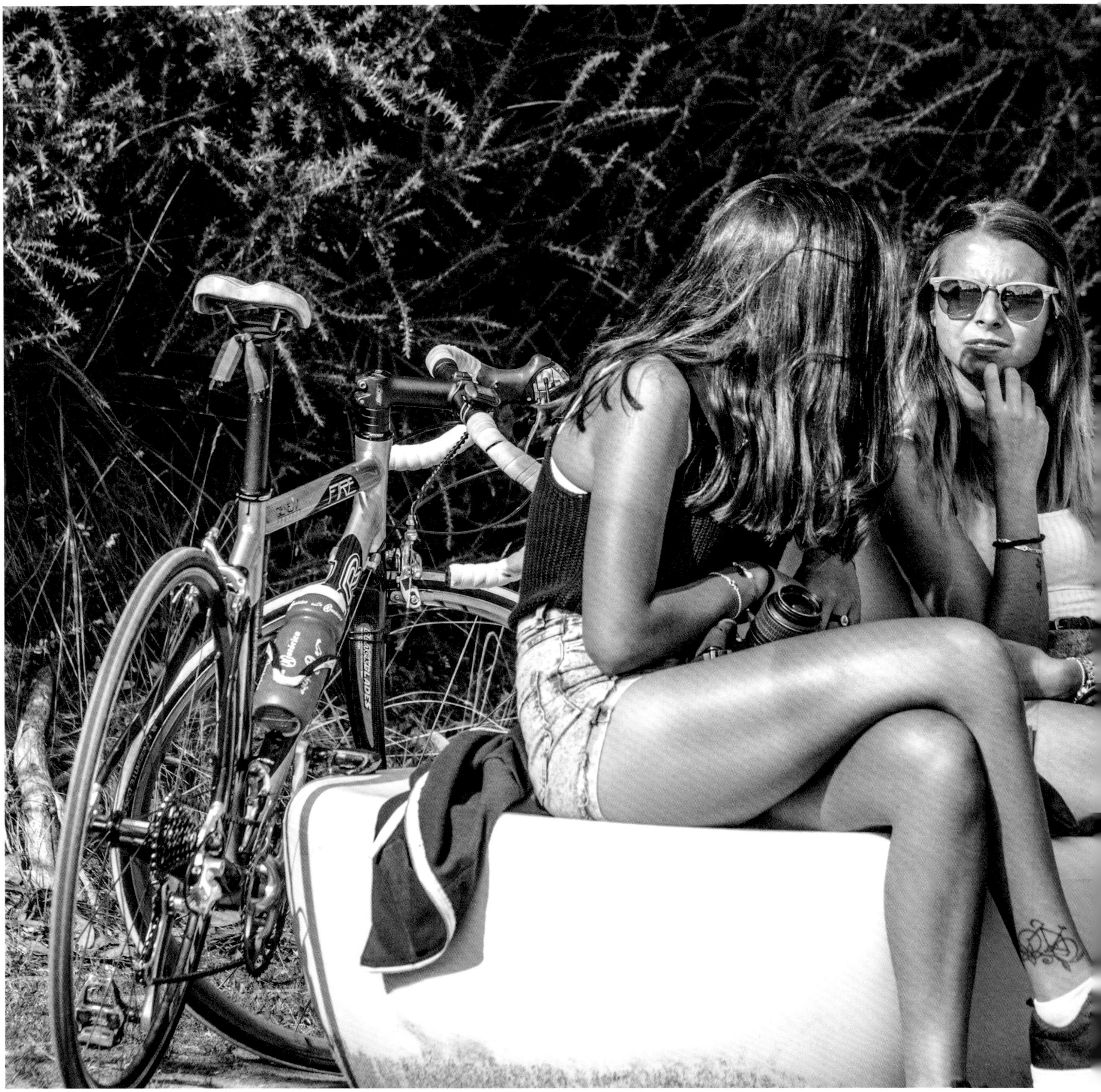

↑ Echte Radsportfans mit Radtattoos. **Real cycling fans with bike tattoos.** *Les fans les plus fervent ont des tatouages de vélos.*
→ Alejandro Valverde (Team Movistar) im Trikot des Punktbesten. **Alejandro Valverde (Team Movistar) in the green jersey.** *Alejandro Valverde (Team Movistar) avec le maillot du classement par points.*

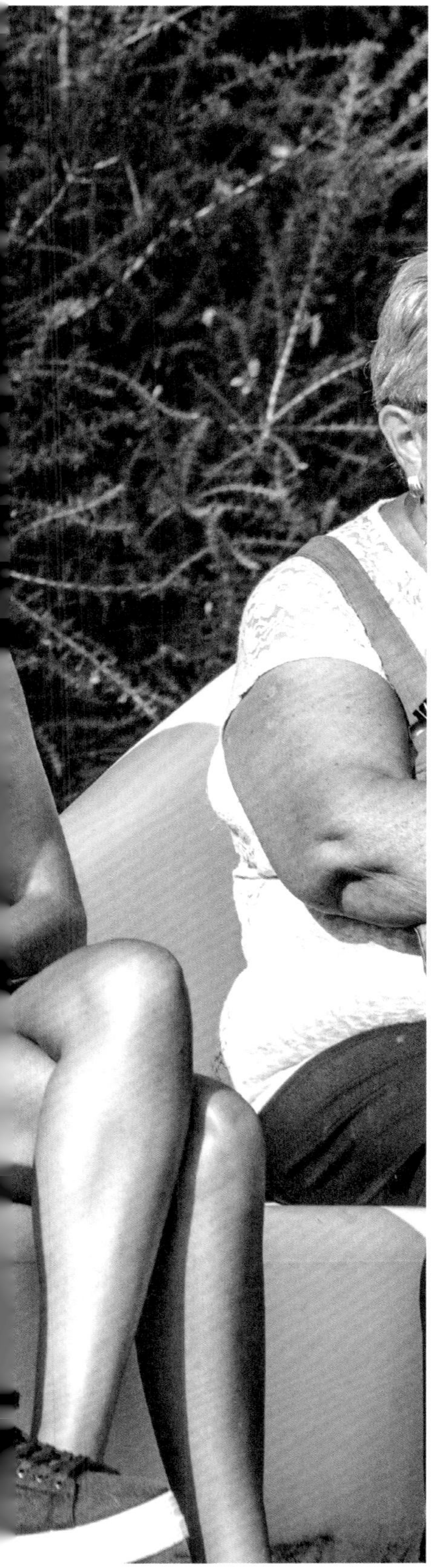

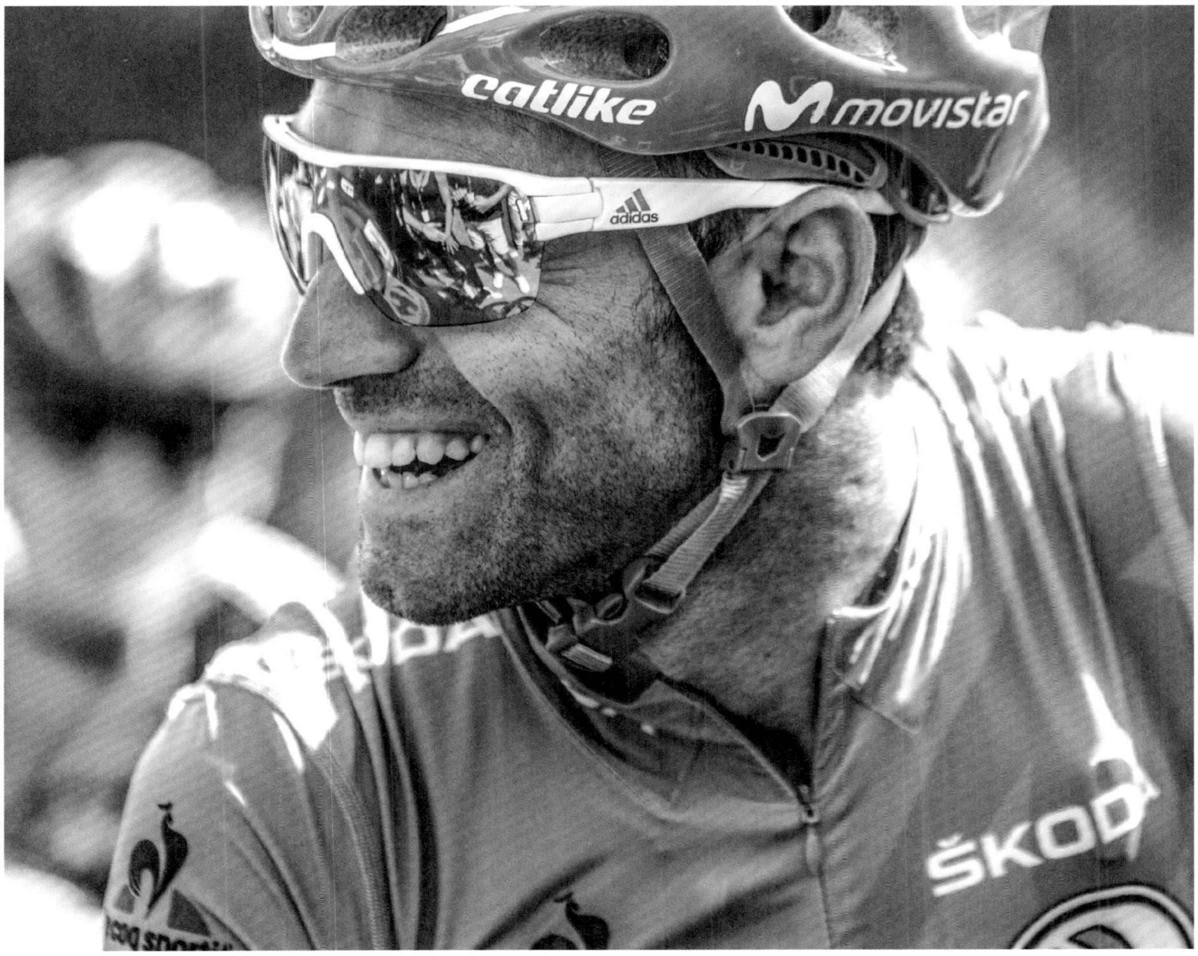
catlike
movistar
adidas
ŠKOD

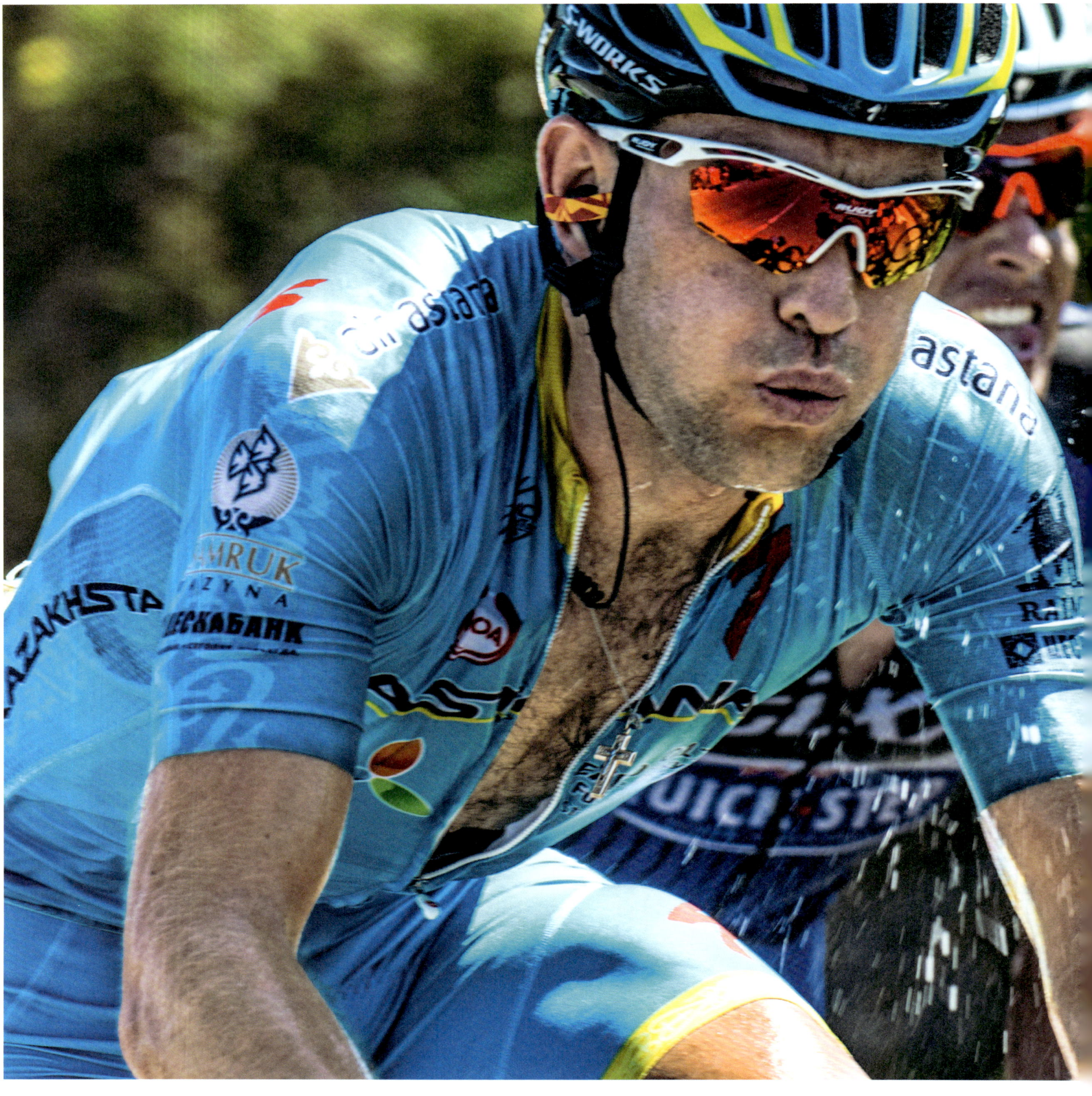
S-WORKS
astana

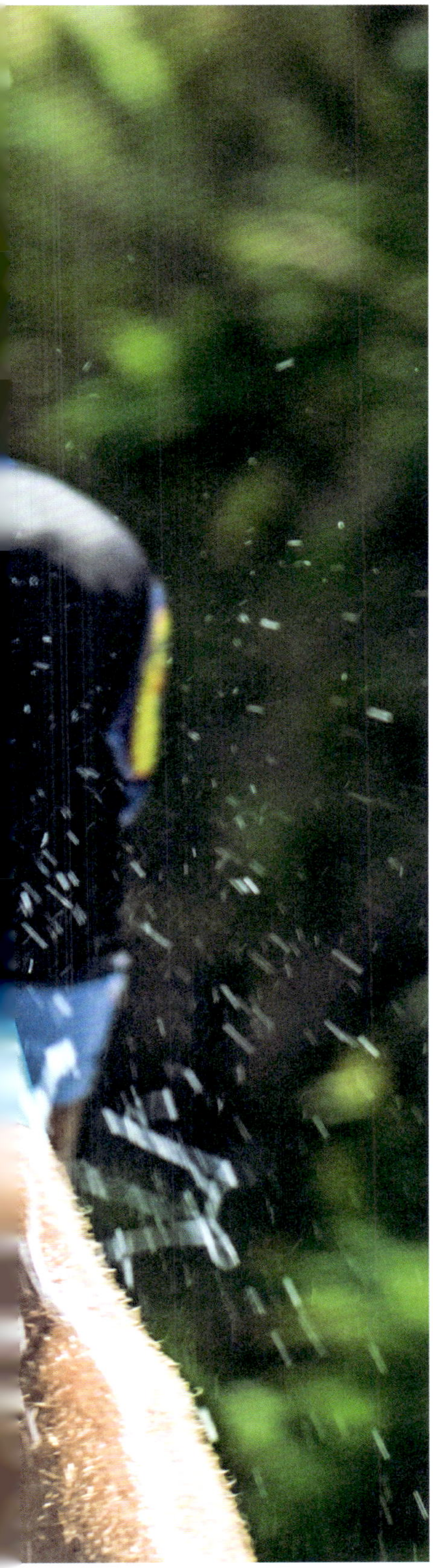

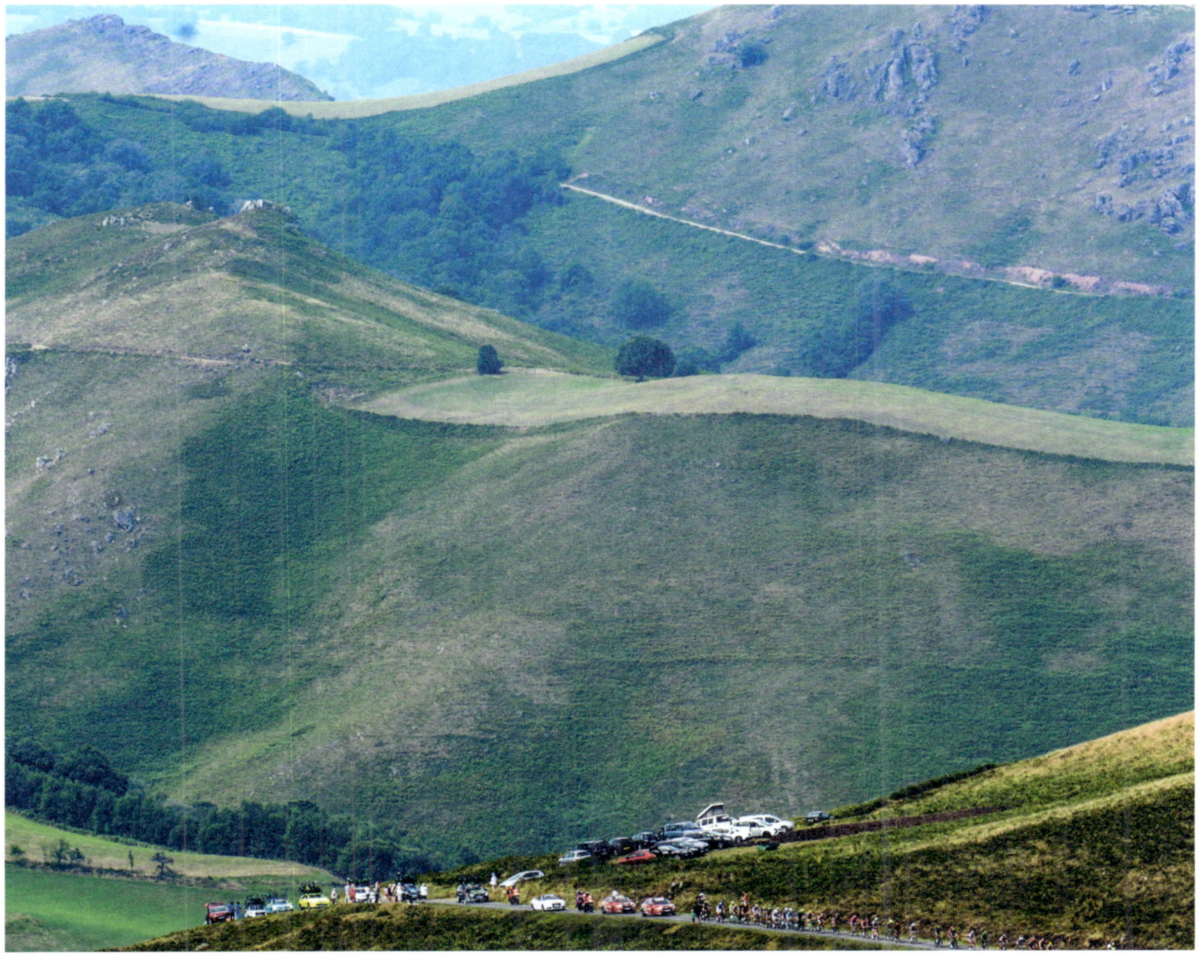

↖ Dmitriy Gruzdev (Astana Pro Team). **Dmitriy Gruzdev (Astana Pro Team).** *Dmitriy Gruzdev (Astana Pro Team).*

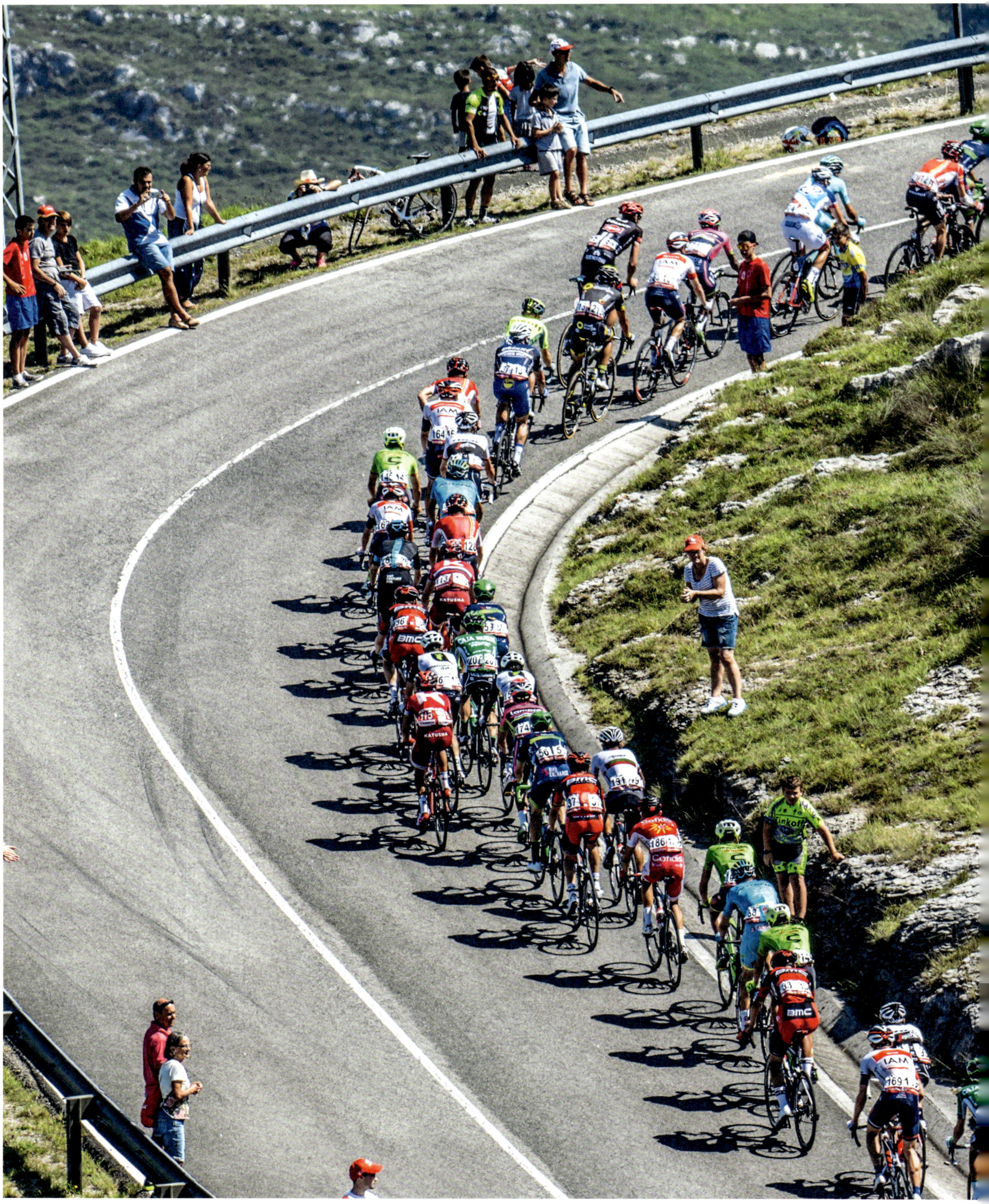

 Anstieg bei Etappe 11. **Climb at stage 11.** *Montée lors de la 11e étape.*

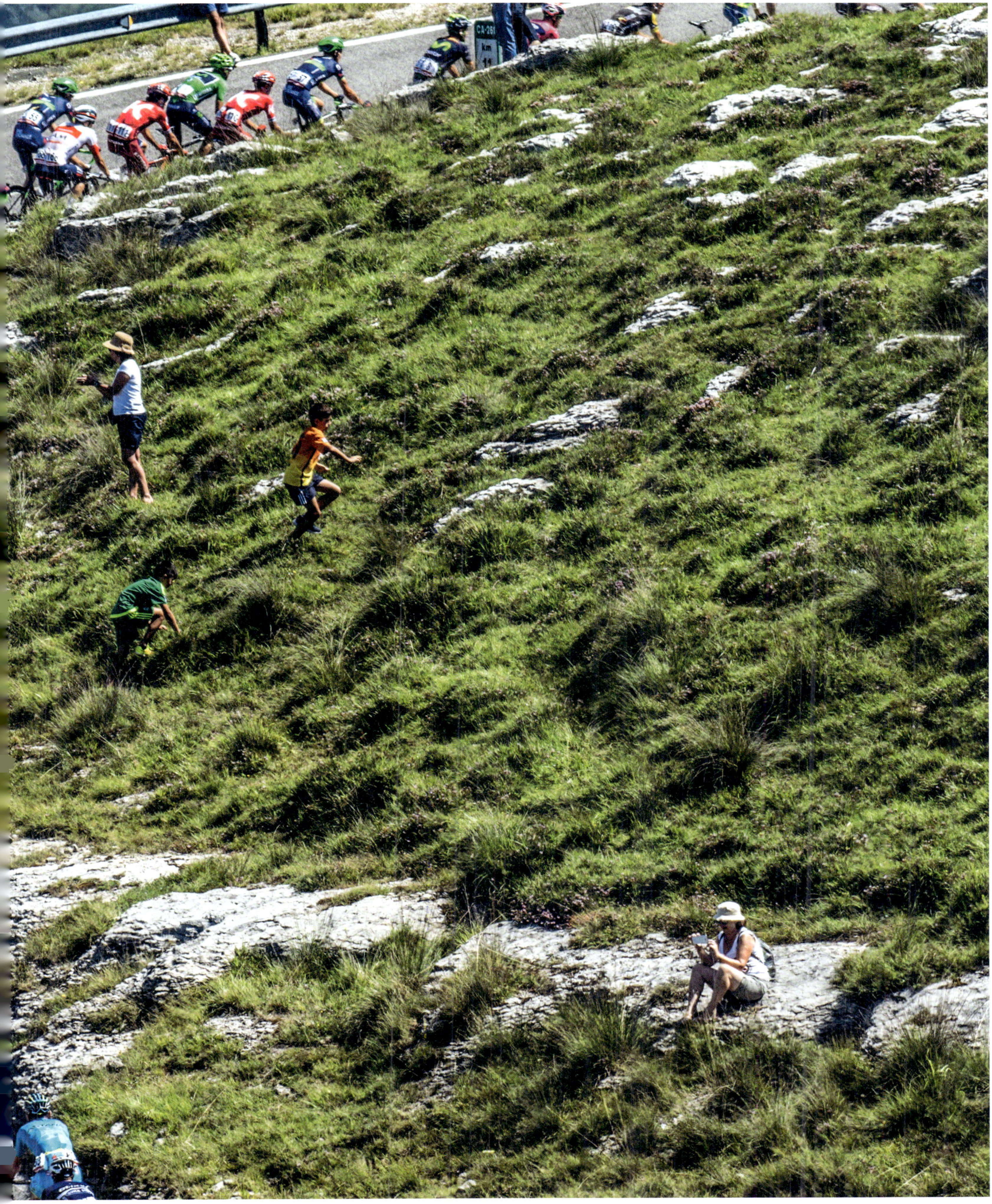

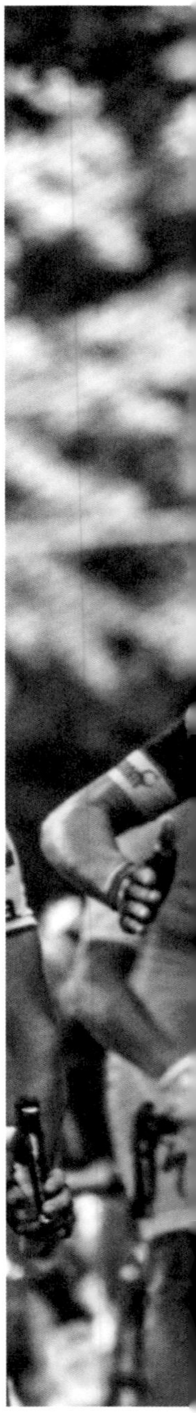

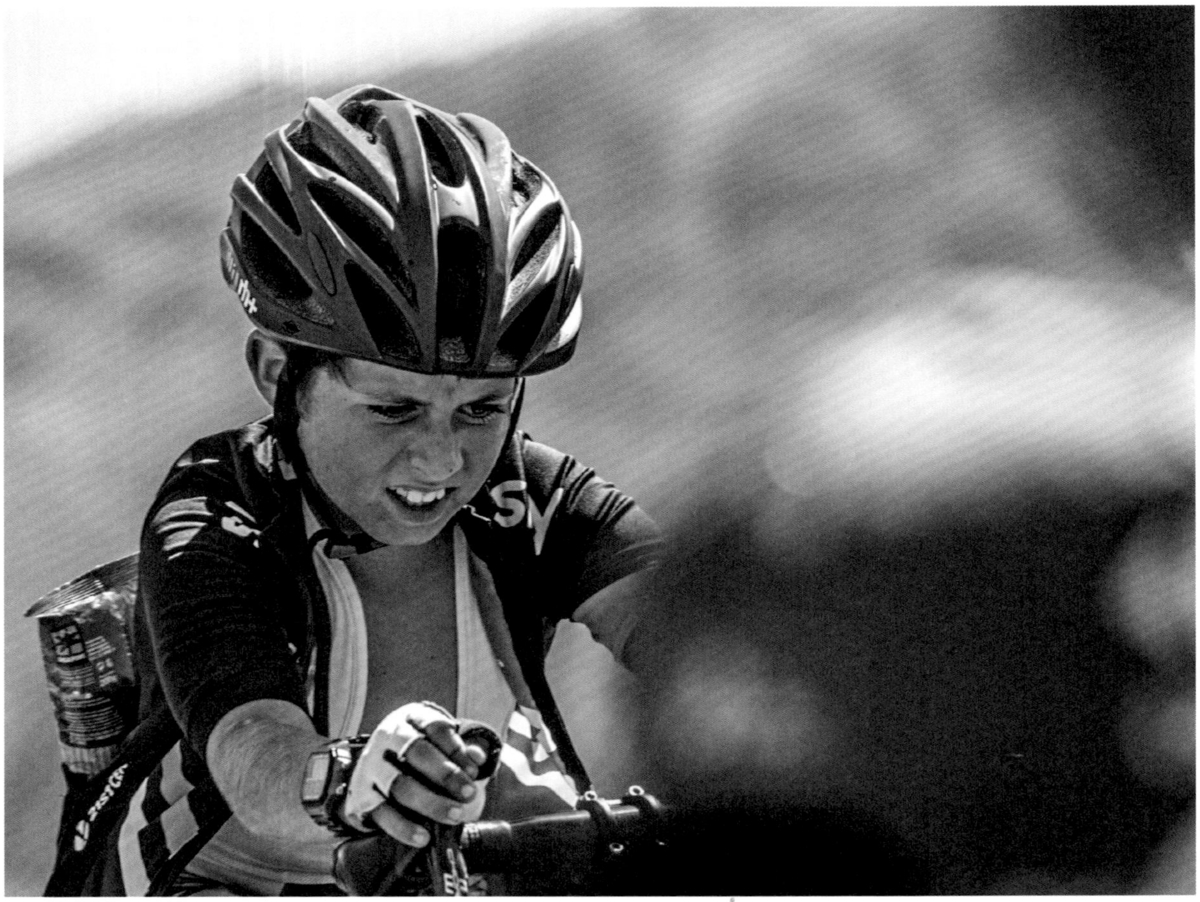

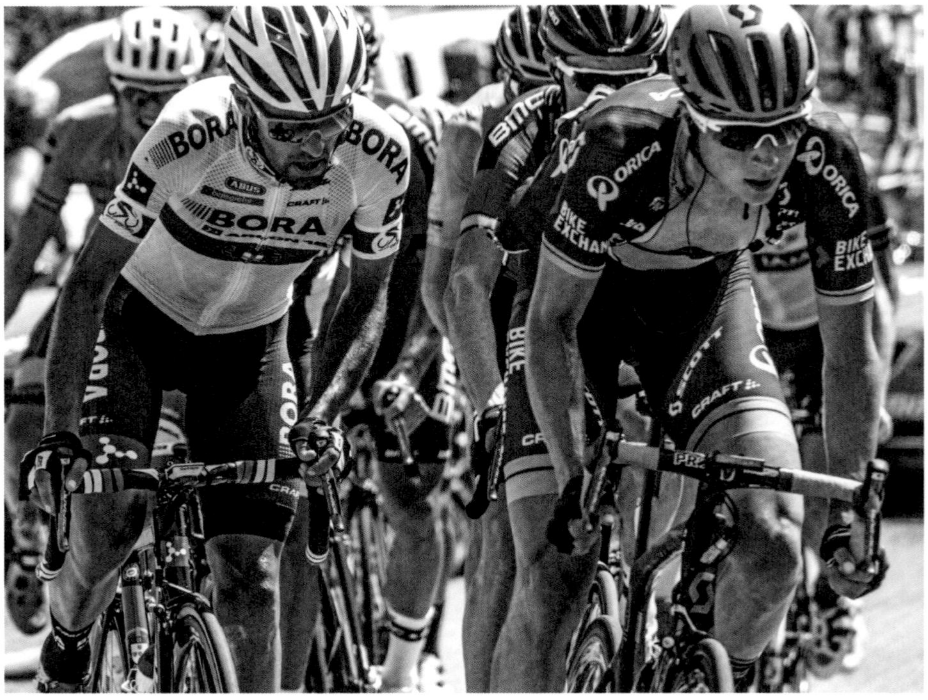
BORA
BORA
BORA
ORICA
ORICA

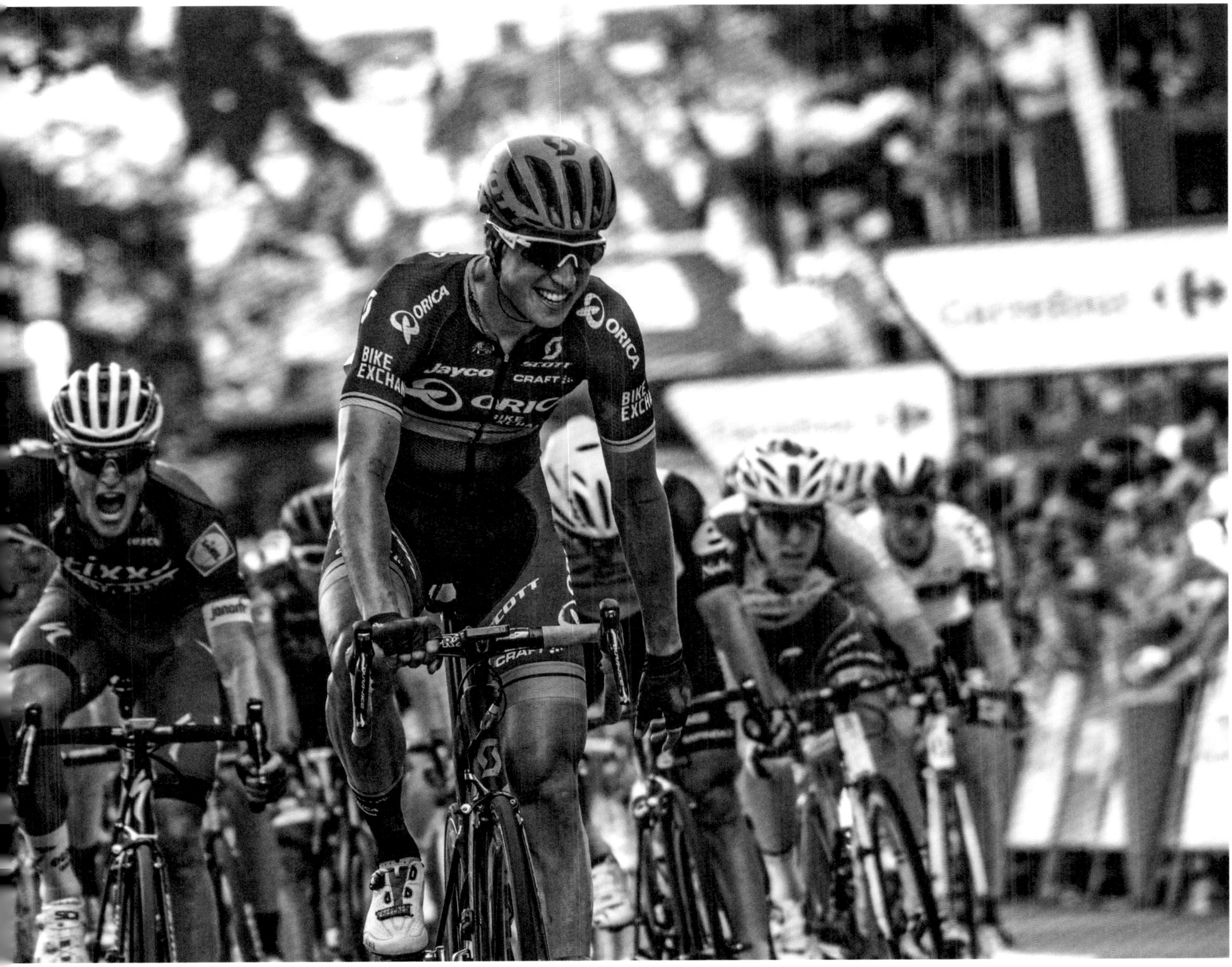

↖ Mini-Team Sky. **Mini-Team Sky.** *Mini-Team Sky.*

← Der portugiesische Meister José Mendes (BORA - ARGON 18, links) und Jens Keukeleire (ORICA - BikeExchange). **The Portuguese champion José Mendes (BORA - ARGON 18, left) and Jens Keukeleire (ORICA - BikeExchange).** *Le champion portugais José Mendes (BORA - ARGON 18, à gauche) et Jens Keukeleire (ORICA - BikeExchange).*

↑ Jens Keukeleire (ORICA-BikeExchange) gewinnt die 12. Etappe in Bilbao vor Maxime Bouet (Etixx - Quick Step, links). **Jens Keukeleire (ORICA-BikeExchange) wins the 12th stage in Bilbao ahead of Maxime Bouet (Etixx - Quick Step, left).** *Jens Keukeleire (ORICA-BikeExchange) remporte la 12e étape à Bilbao devant Maxime Bouet (Etixx - Quick Step, à gauche).*

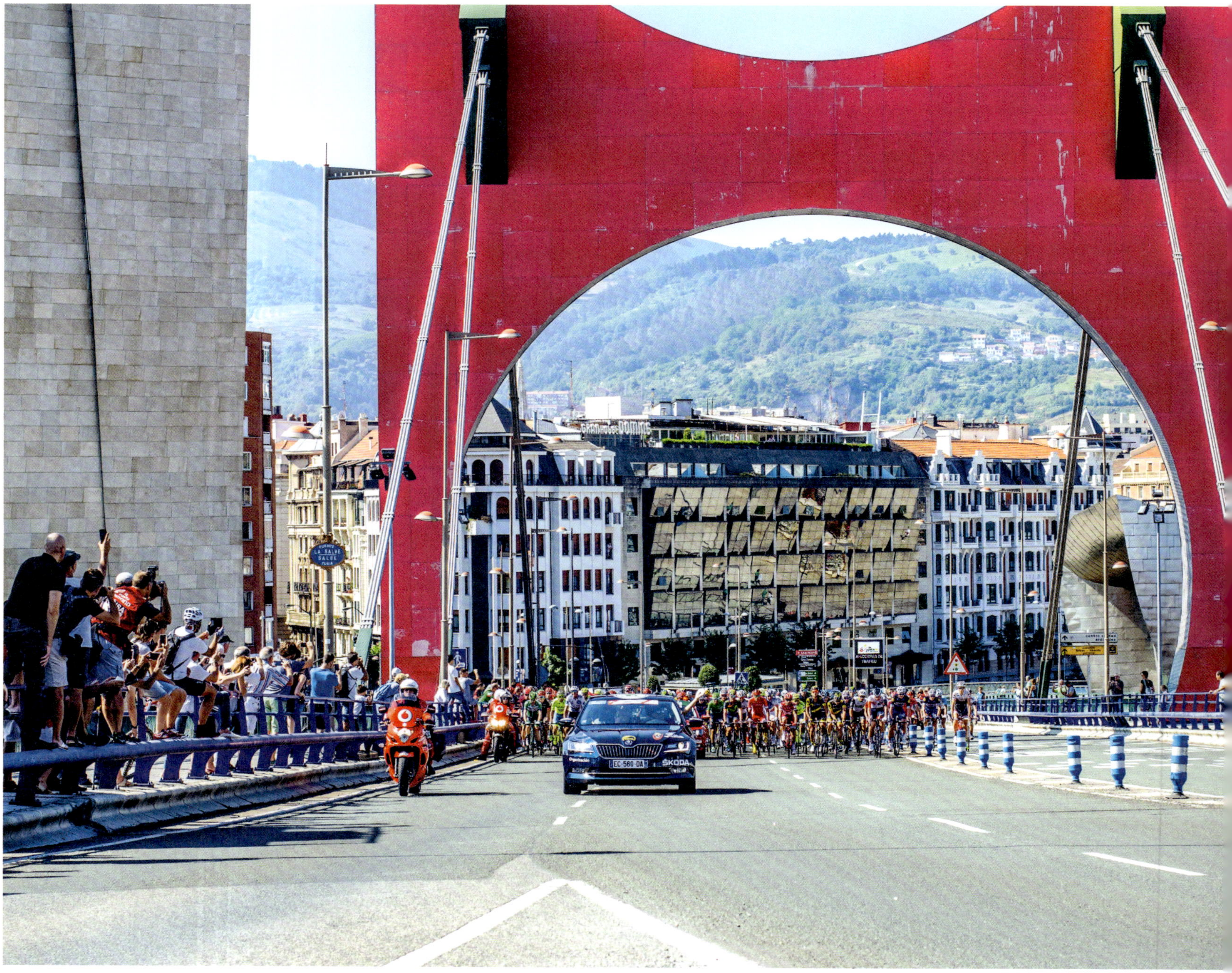
PUENTE
LA SALVE
SALBE
ZUBIA
EC-560-DA
ŠKODA

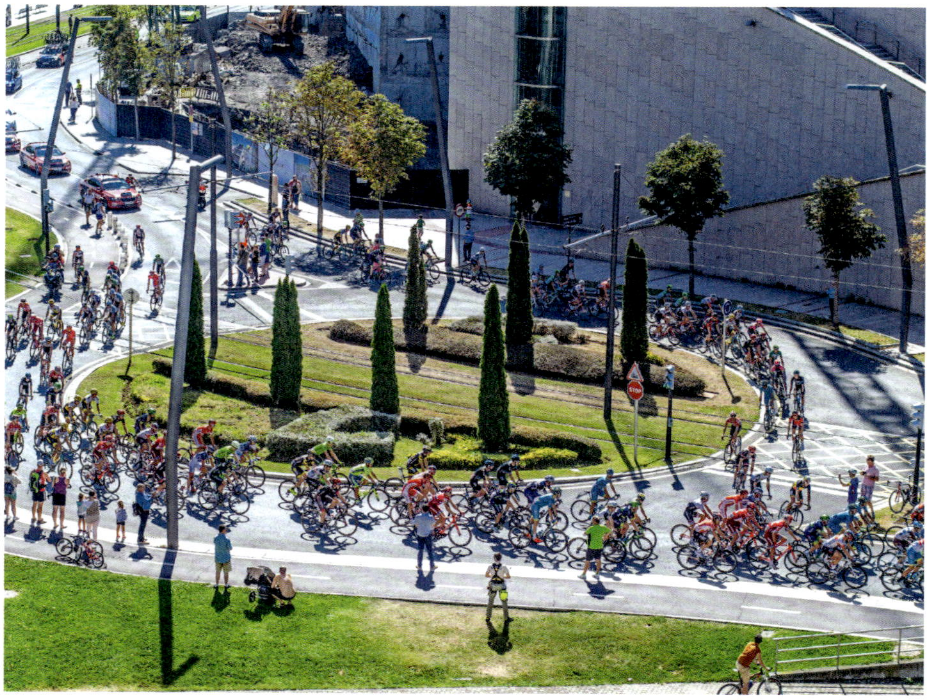

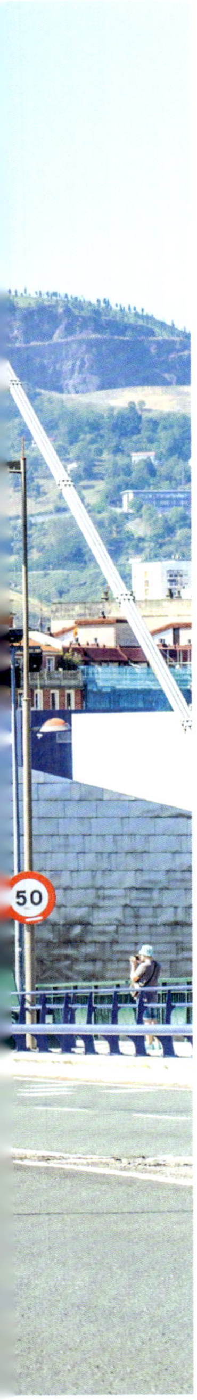

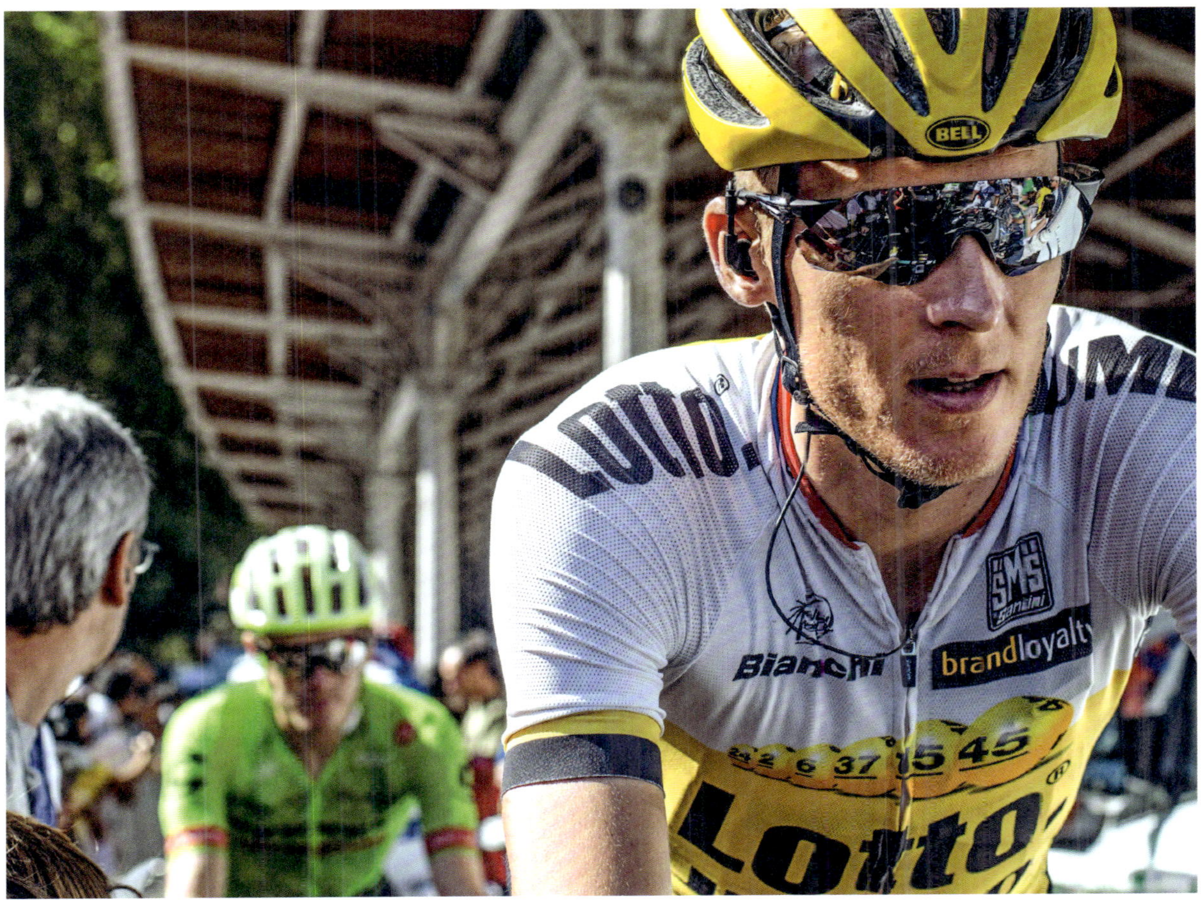

↖ Start der 13. Etappe in Bilbao. **Start of the 13th stage in Bilbao.** *Départ de la 13e étape à Bilbao.*

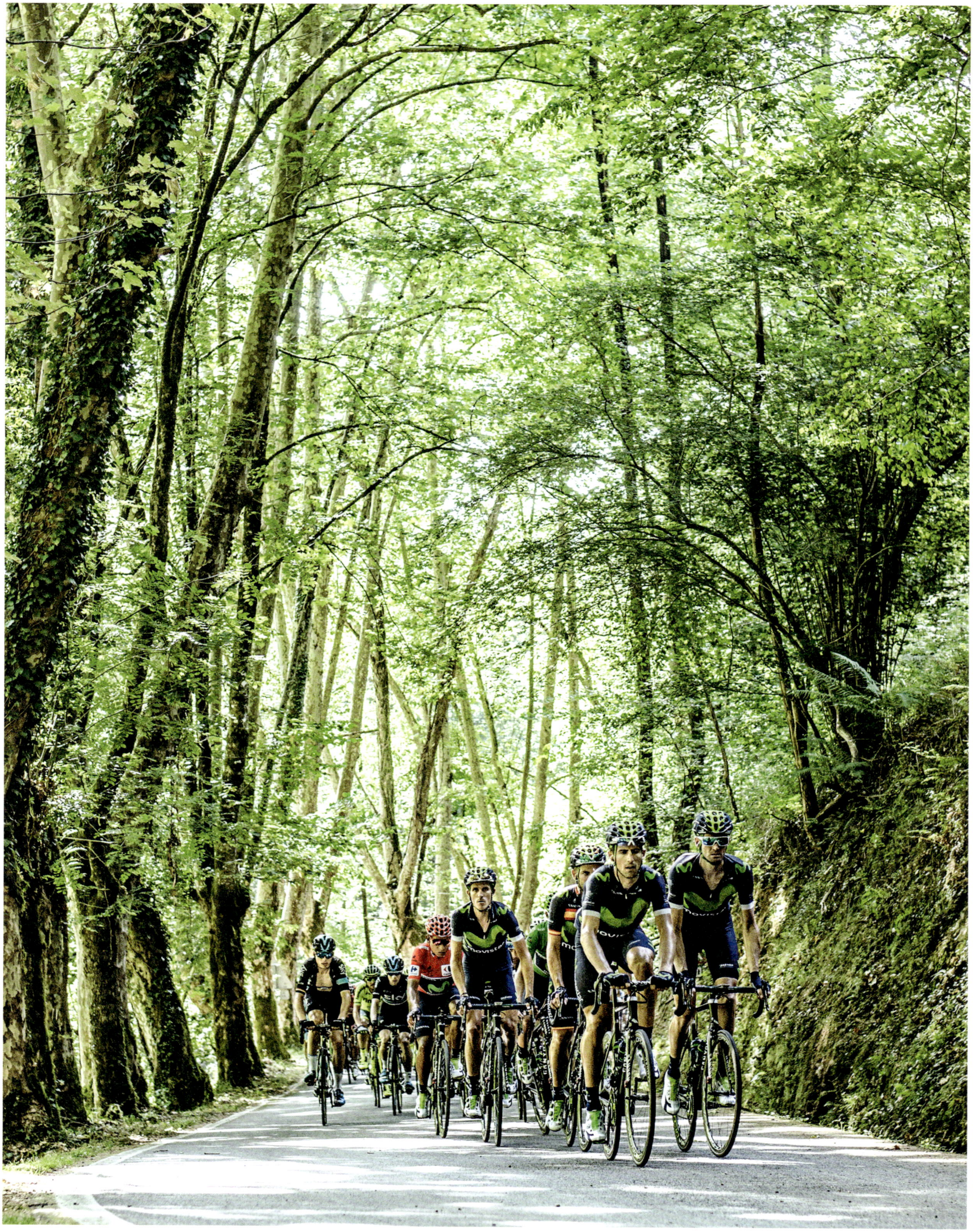

↑ Movistar führt das Peloton an. **Movistar leads the peloton.** *Movistar mène le peloton.*
↗ Erfrischung für José Mendes (BORA - ARGON 18). **Refreshment for José Mendes (BORA - ARGON 18).** *Rafraîchissement pour José Mendes (BORA - ARGON 18).*
→ Luis Ángel Maté (Cofidis). **Luis Ángel Maté (Cofidis).** *Luis Ángel Maté (Cofidis).*

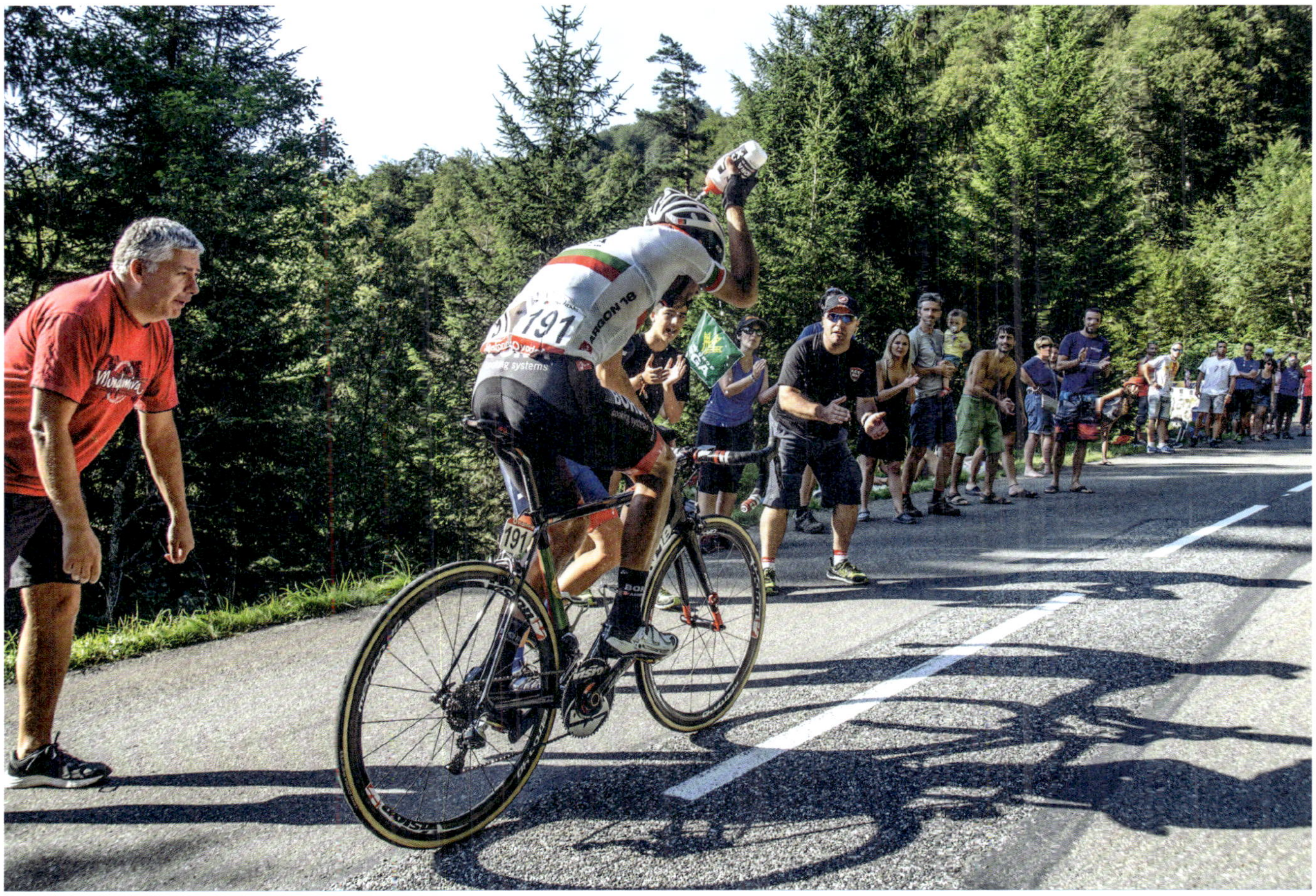
191

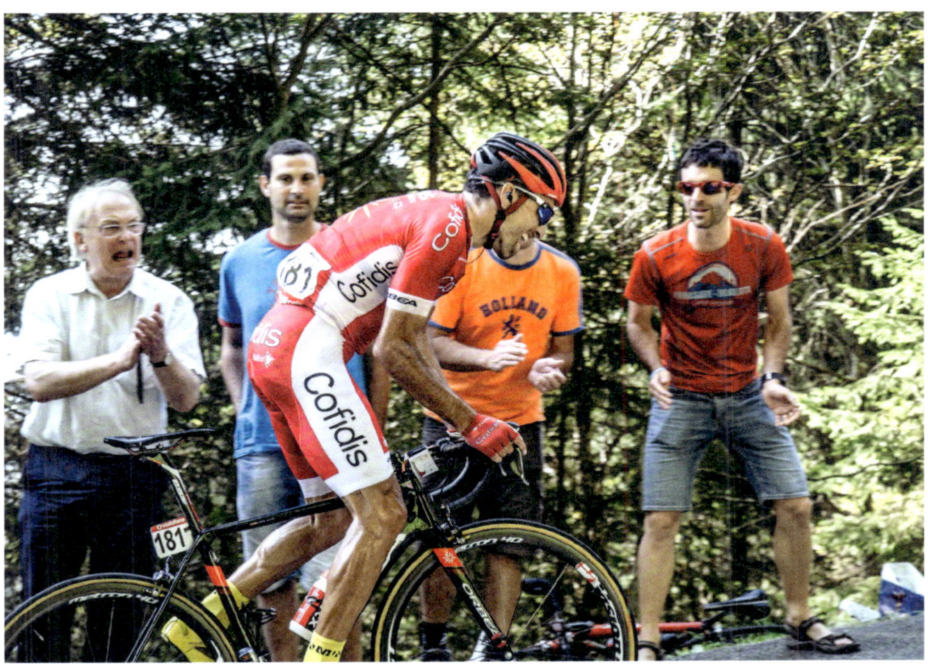
Cofidis
HOLLAND
181

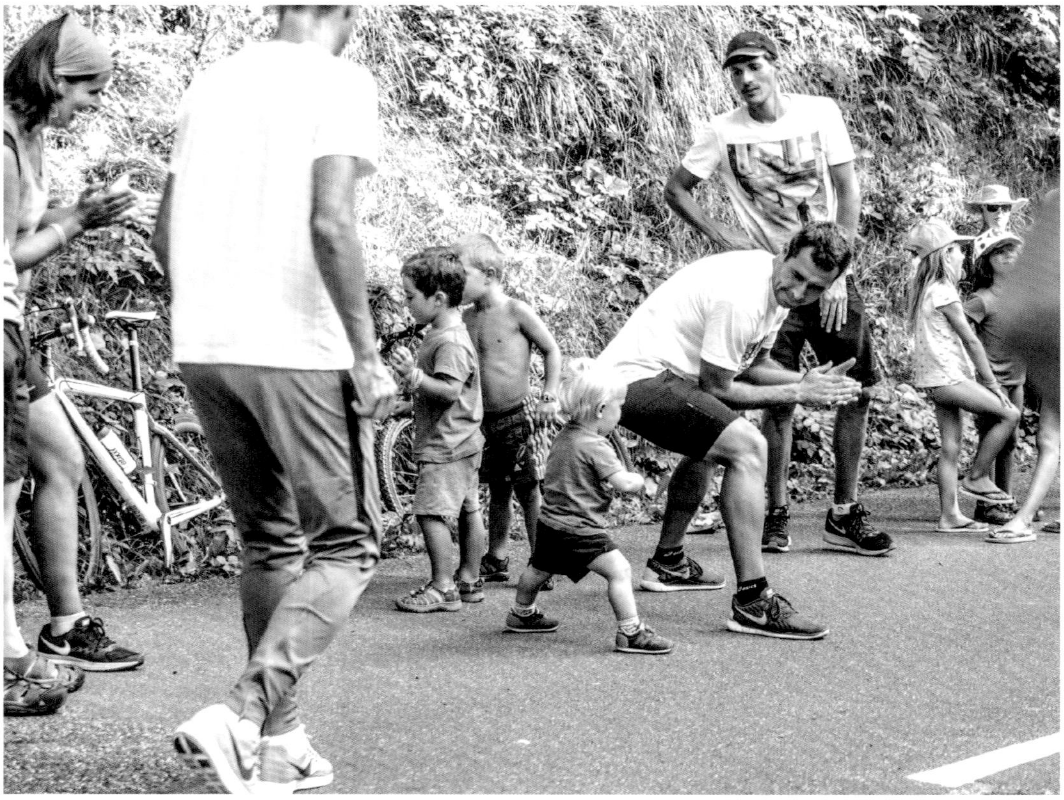

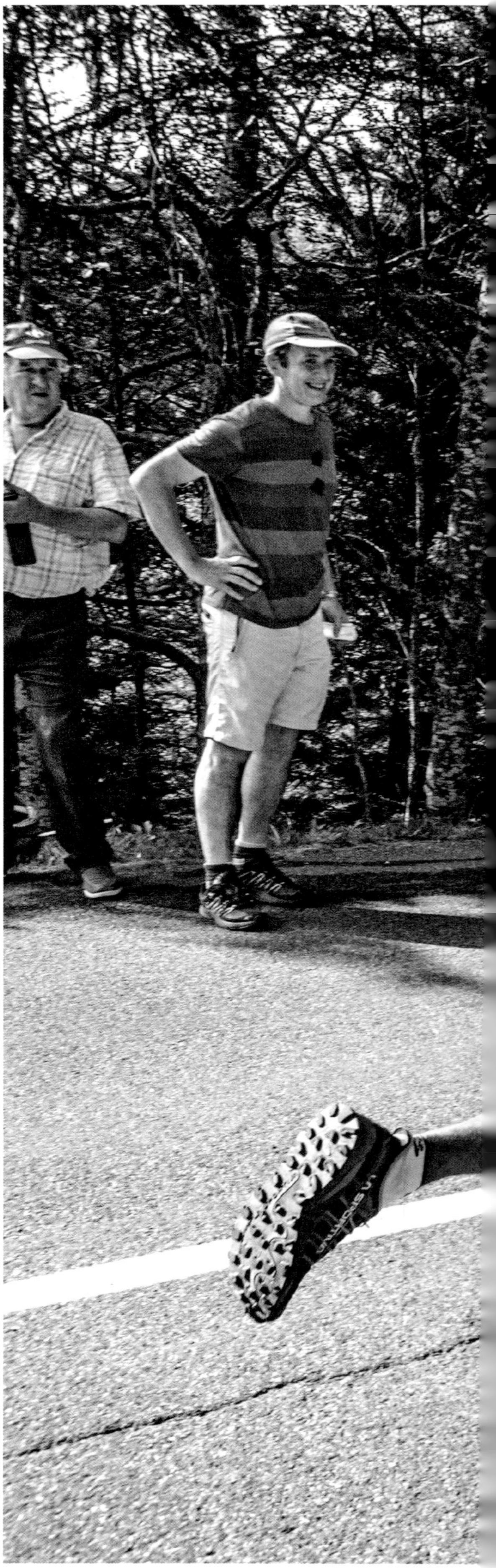

↑ Unterstützung von Groß und Klein. **Support from young and old alike.** *Soutien des grands et des petits.*
→ Michael Gogl (Tinkoff). **Michael Gogl (Tinkoff).** *Michael Gogl (Tinkoff).*

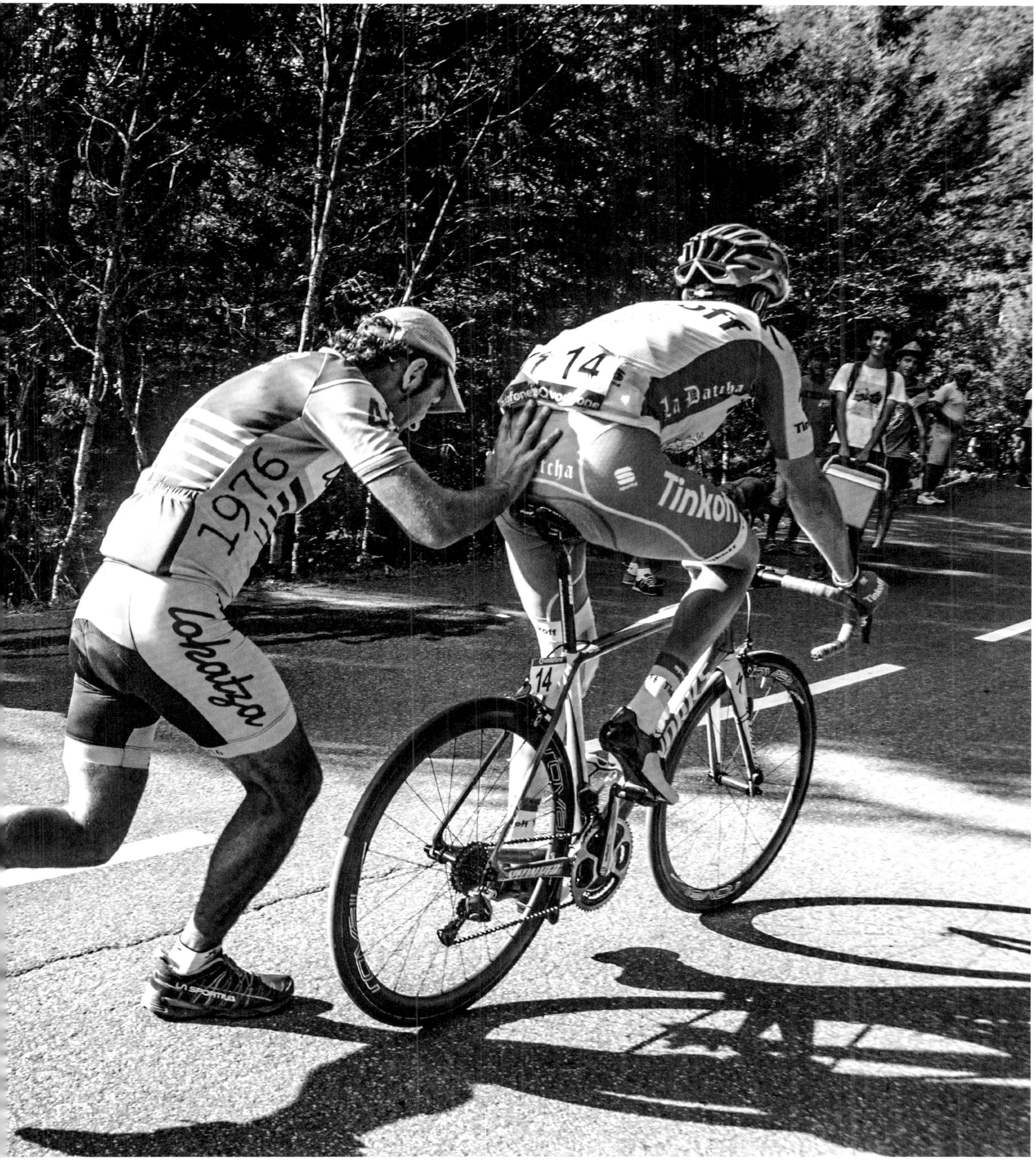
14
1976
La Datcha
Tinkoff

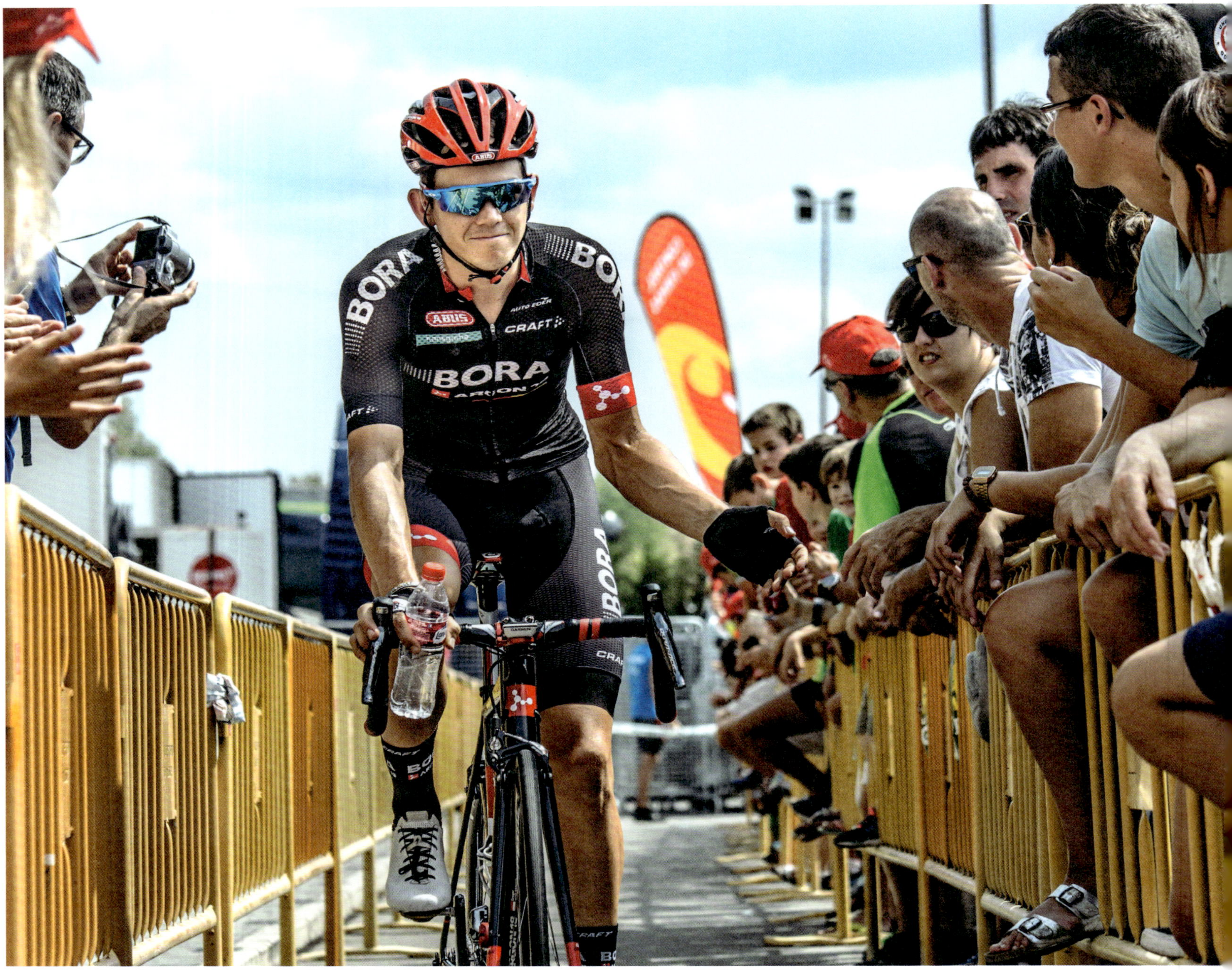

↑ Gregor Mühlberger (BORA - ARGON 18) bei der 15. Etappe. **Gregor Mühlberger (BORA - ARGON 18) at the 15th stage.**
Gregor Mühlberger (BORA - ARGON 18) lors de la 15e étape.

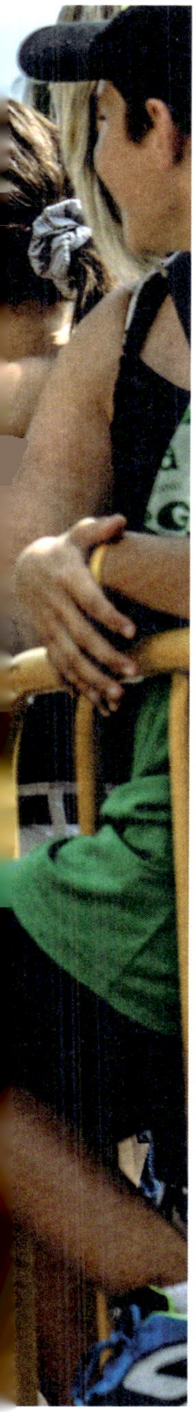

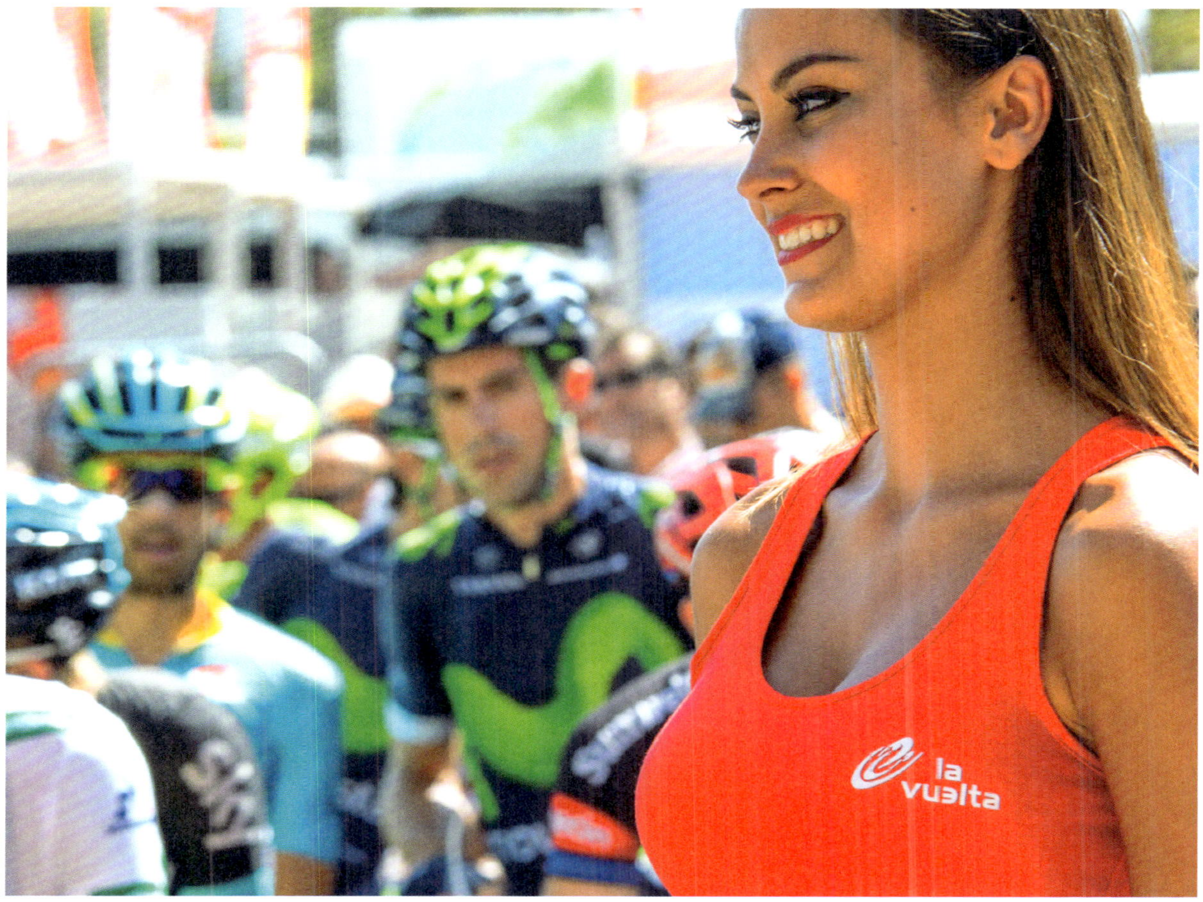
la
vuelta

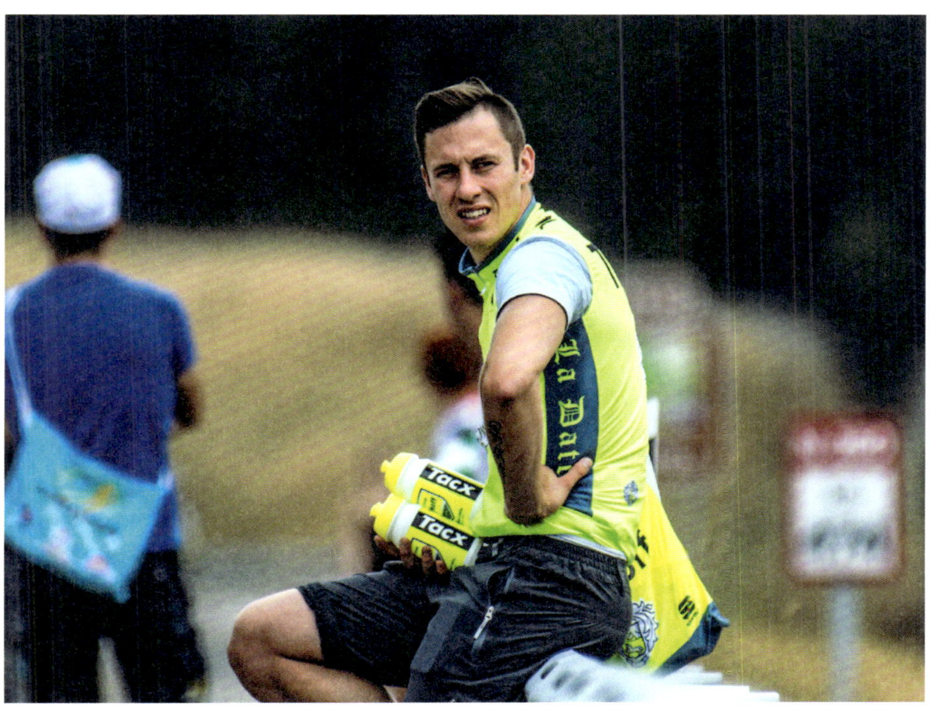
Tacx
Tacx

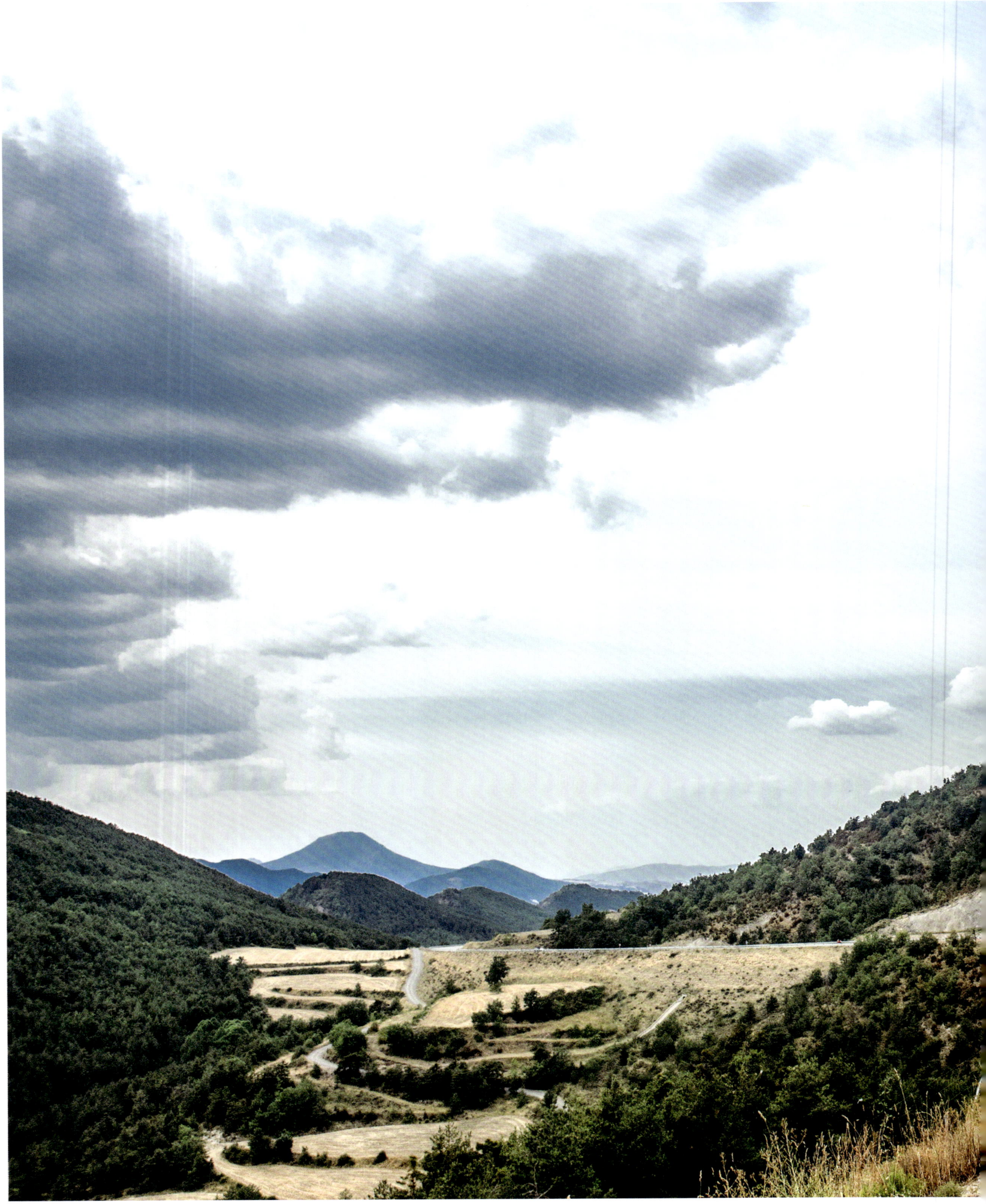

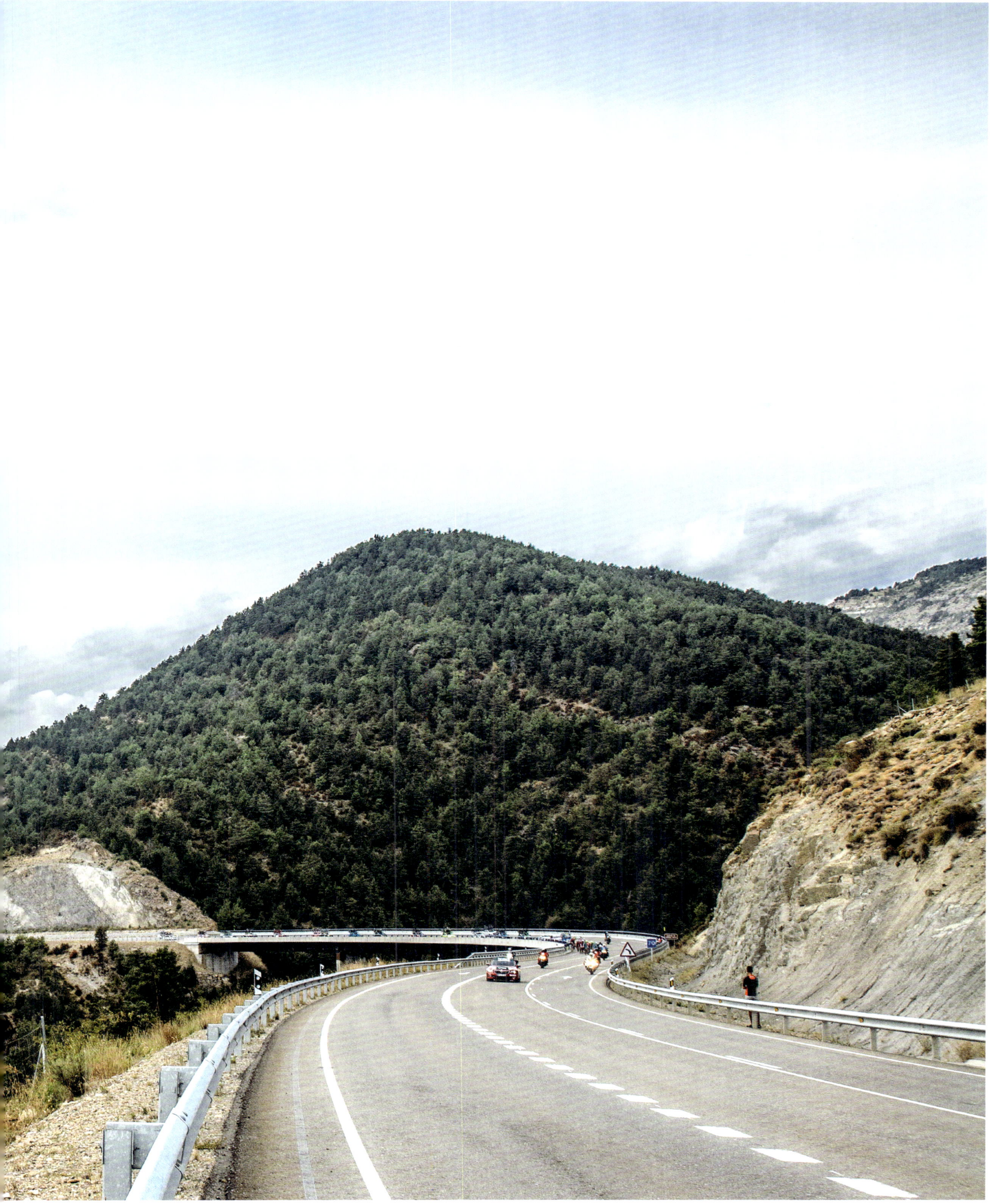

15. Etappe: Das Peloton nähert sich. **15th stage: the peloton approaches.** *15e étape : le peloton se rapproche.*

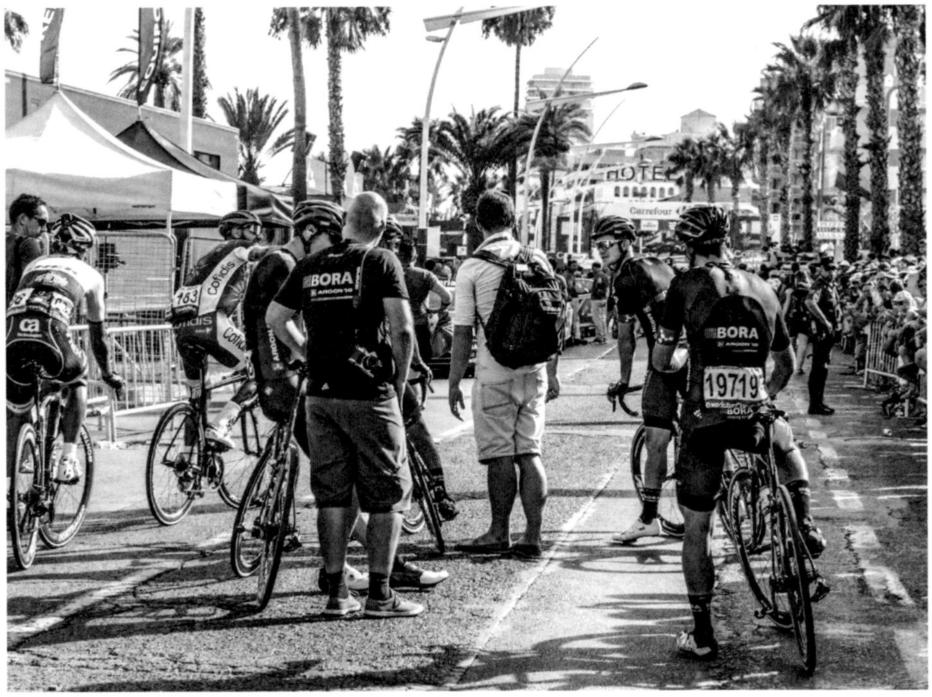
BORA
ARGON 18
19719

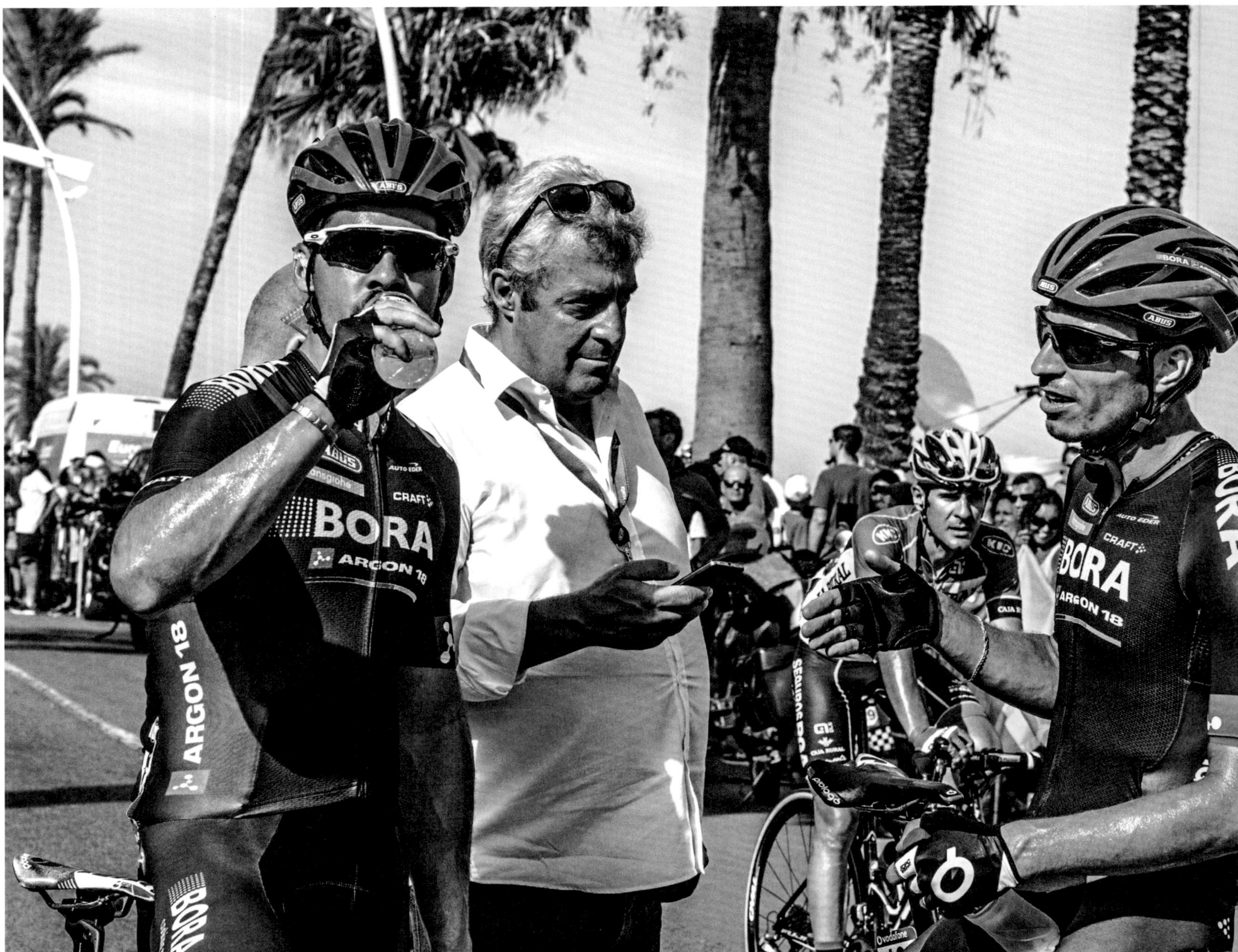
ABUS
AUTO EDER
CRAFT
BORA
ARGON 18

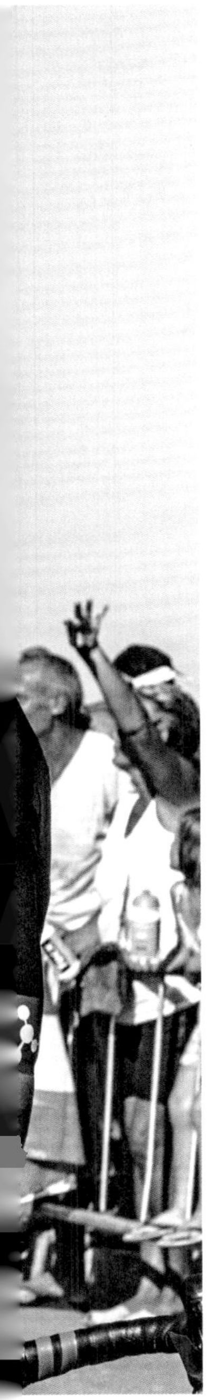

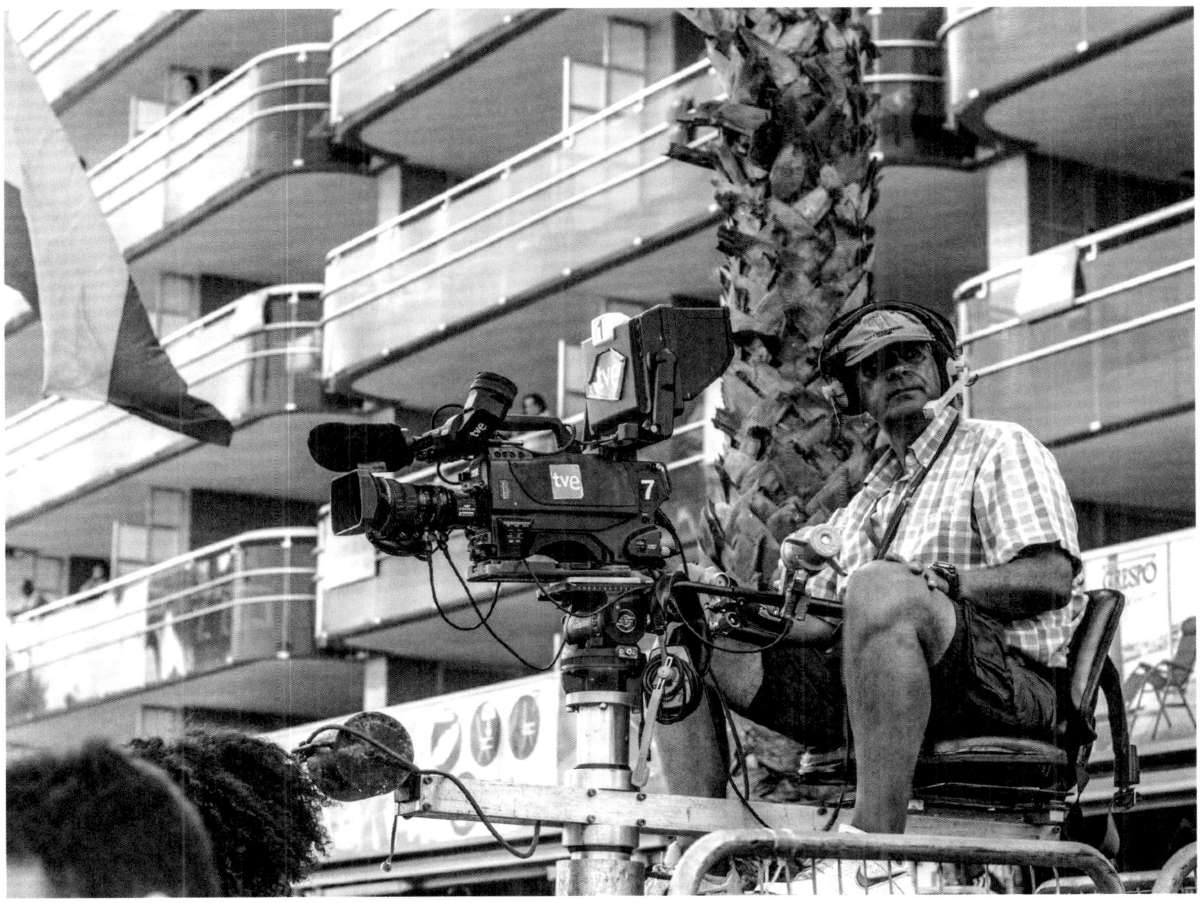

← Michael Schwarzmann und Rüdiger Selig (BORA - ARGON 18) im Interview. **Michael Schwarzmann and Rüdiger Selig (BORA - ARGON 18) in an interview.**
Interview de Michael Schwarzmann et Rüdiger Selig (BORA - ARGON 18).

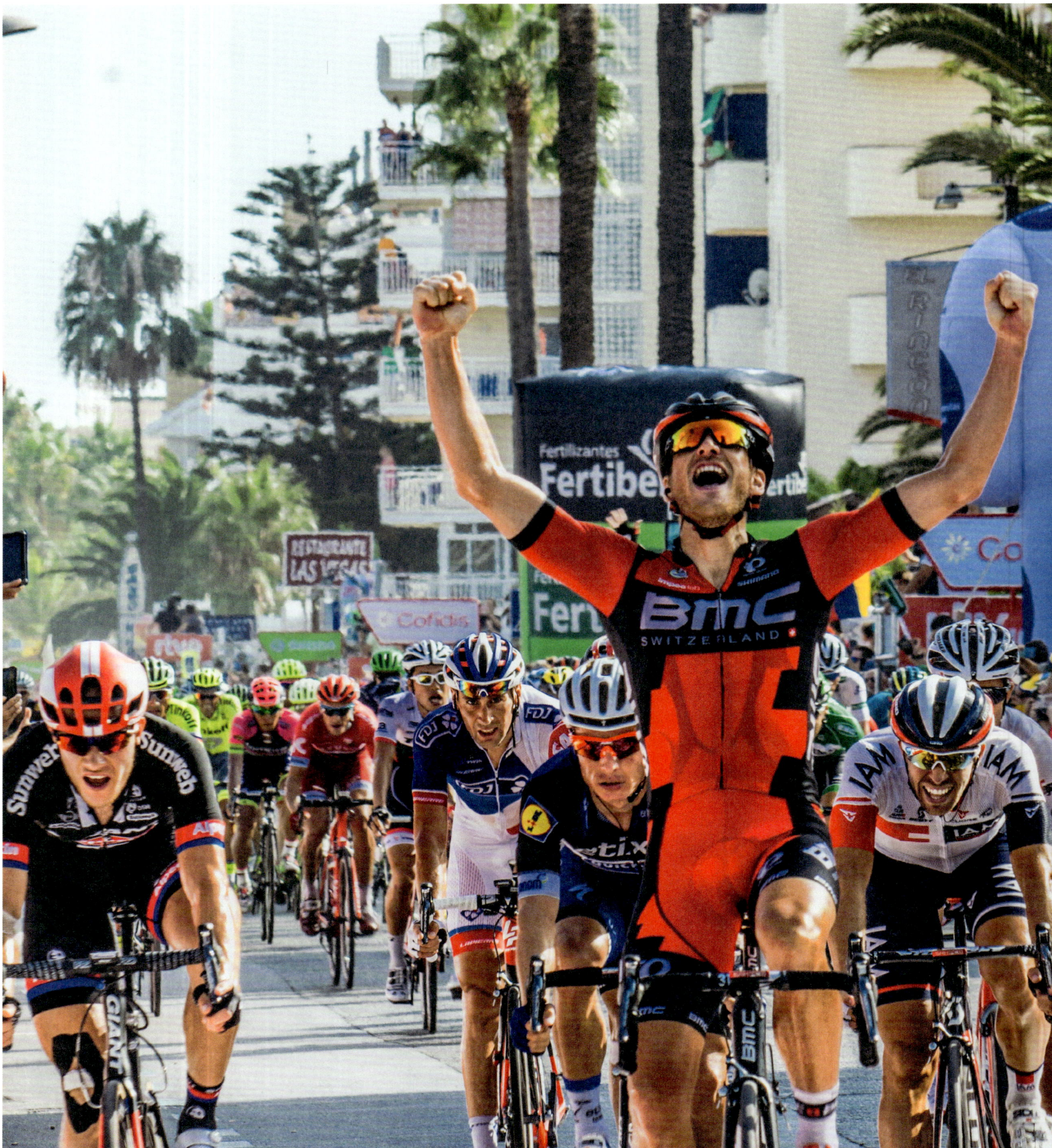
Fertilizantes
Fertibe
BMC
SWITZERLAND
Sunweb
RESTAURANTE
LAS VEGAS
Cofidis
FDJ
IAM
GIANT

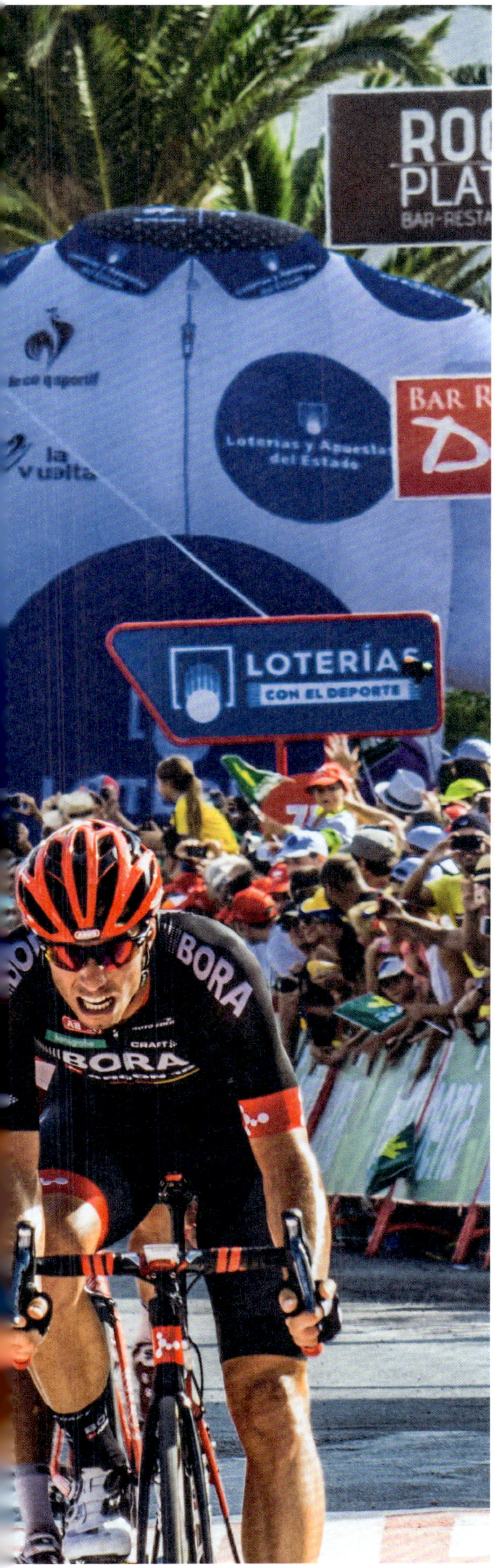

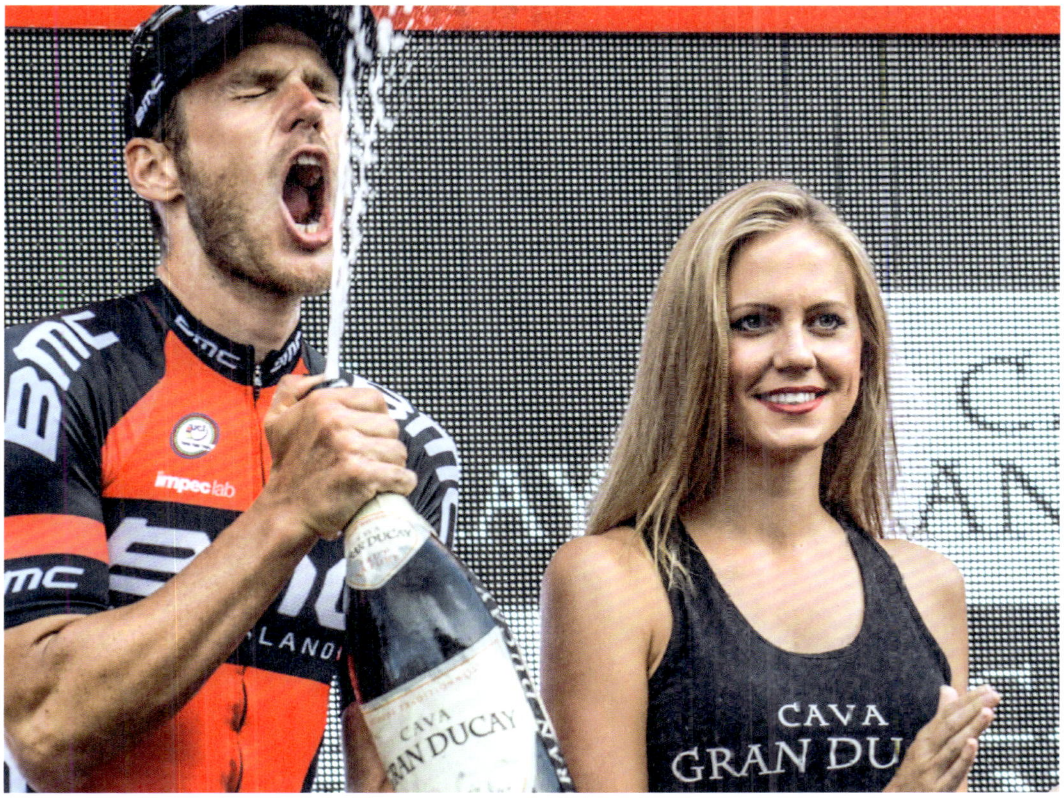

← Jean-Pierre Drucker (BMC Racing Team) entscheidet die 16. Etappe im Sprint für sich. Rüdiger Selig (BORA - ARGON 18, rechts) wird Zweiter vor Nikias Arndt (Team Giant-Alpecin, links). **Jean-Pierre Drucker (BMC Racing Team) wins the 16th stage during the sprint. Rüdiger Selig (BORA - ARGON 18, right) takes second place ahead of Nikias Arndt (Team Giant-Alpecin, left).** *Jean-Pierre Drucker (BMC Racing Team) remporte la 16e étape au sprint Rüdiger Selig (BORA - ARGON 18, à droite) termine à la deuxième place devant Nikias Arndt (Team Giant-Alpecin, à gauche).*

↗ Verdiente Champagnerdusche für Drucker (BMC Racing Team). **A well deserved champagne shower for Drucker (BMC Racing Team).** *Une douche de champagne bien méritée pour Drucker (BMC Racing Team).*

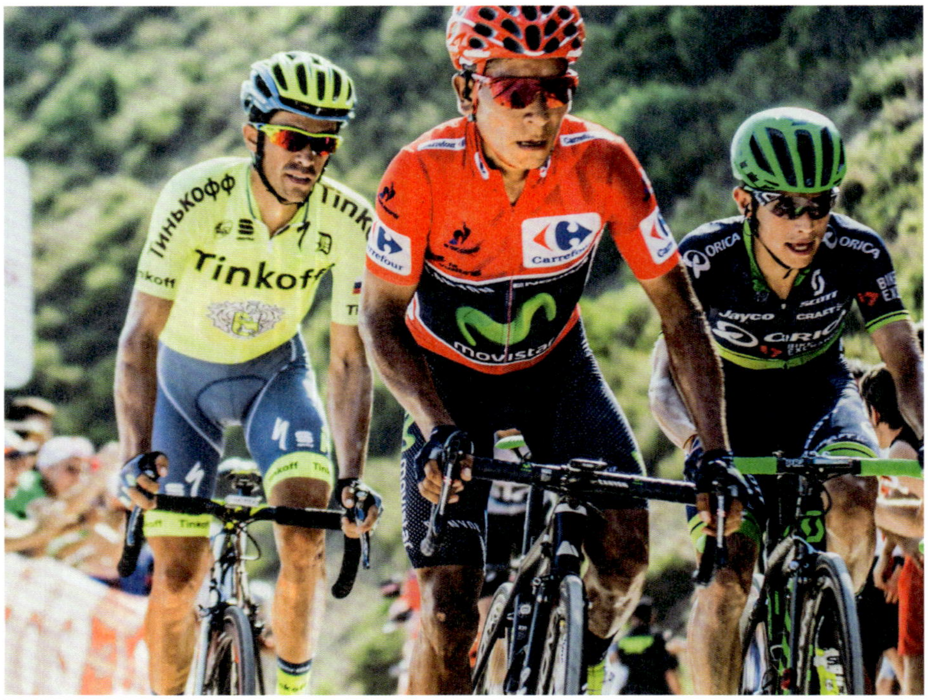

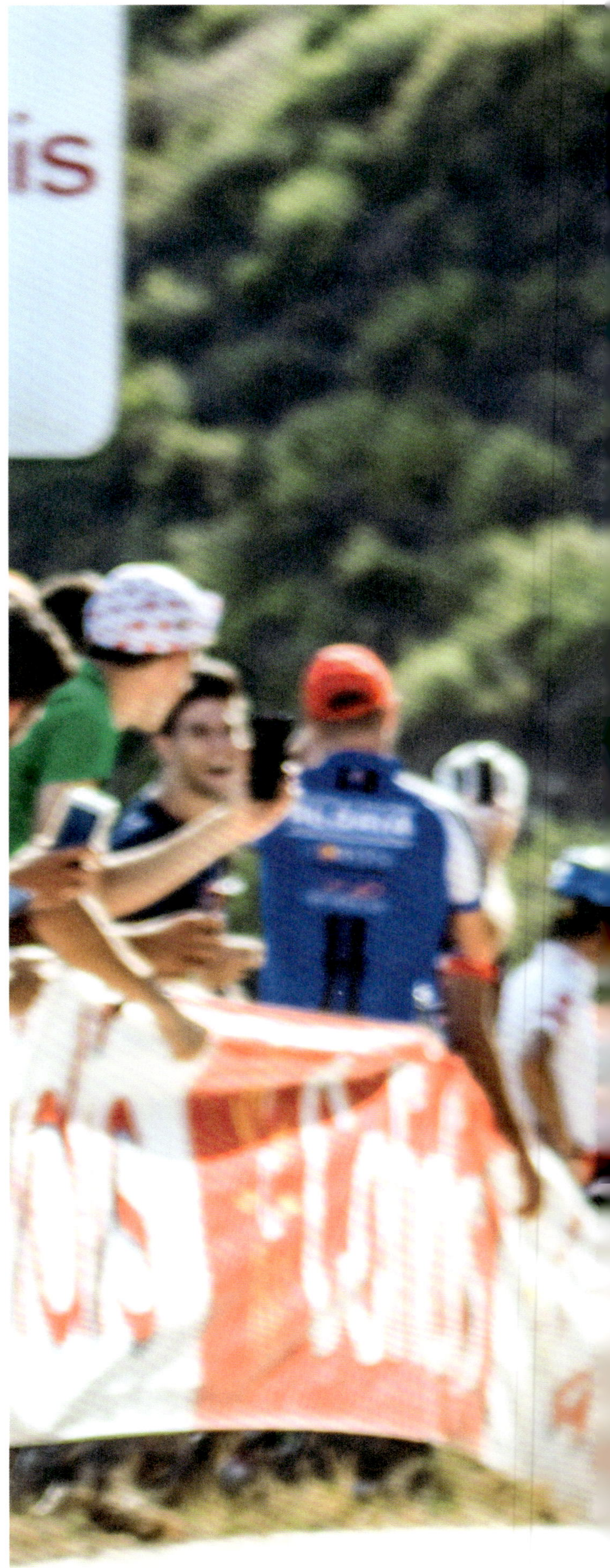

↑ Alberto Contador (Tinkoff), Nairo Quintana (Movistar) in Rot und Esteban Chaves (ORICA-BikeExchange). **Alberto Contador (Tinkoff), Nairo Quintana (Movistar) in red and Esteban Chaves (ORICA-BikeExchange).** *Alberto Contador (Tinkoff), Nairo Quintana (Movistar) en rouge et Esteban Chaves (ORICA-BikeExchange).*
→ Pavel Kochetkov (Katusha) am Schlussanstieg der 17. Etappe. **Pavel Kochetkov (Katusha) on the final climb of the 17th stage.** *Pavel Kochetkov (Katusha) lors de l'ascension finale de la 17e étape.*

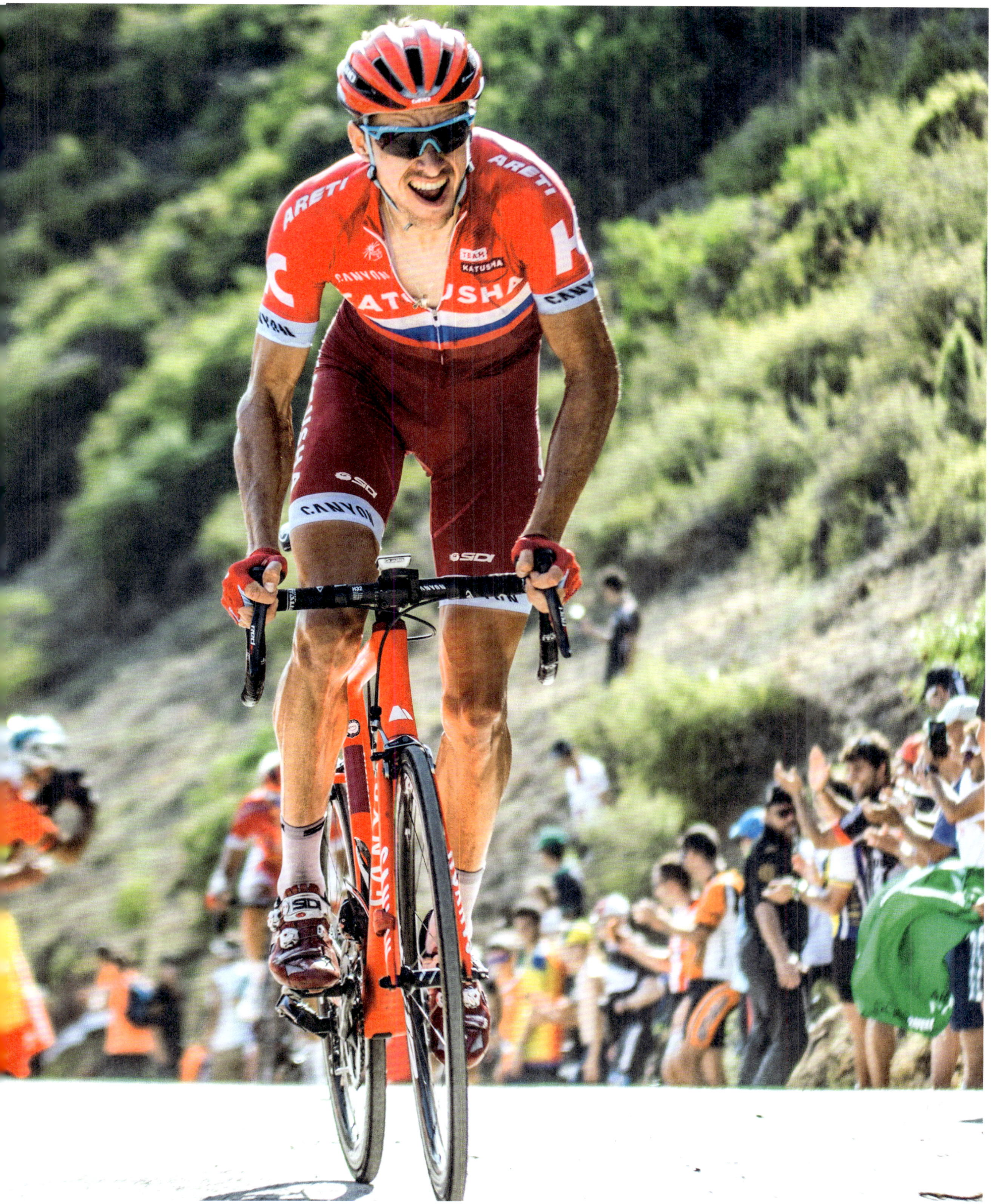
ARETI
ARETI
CANYON
SIDI

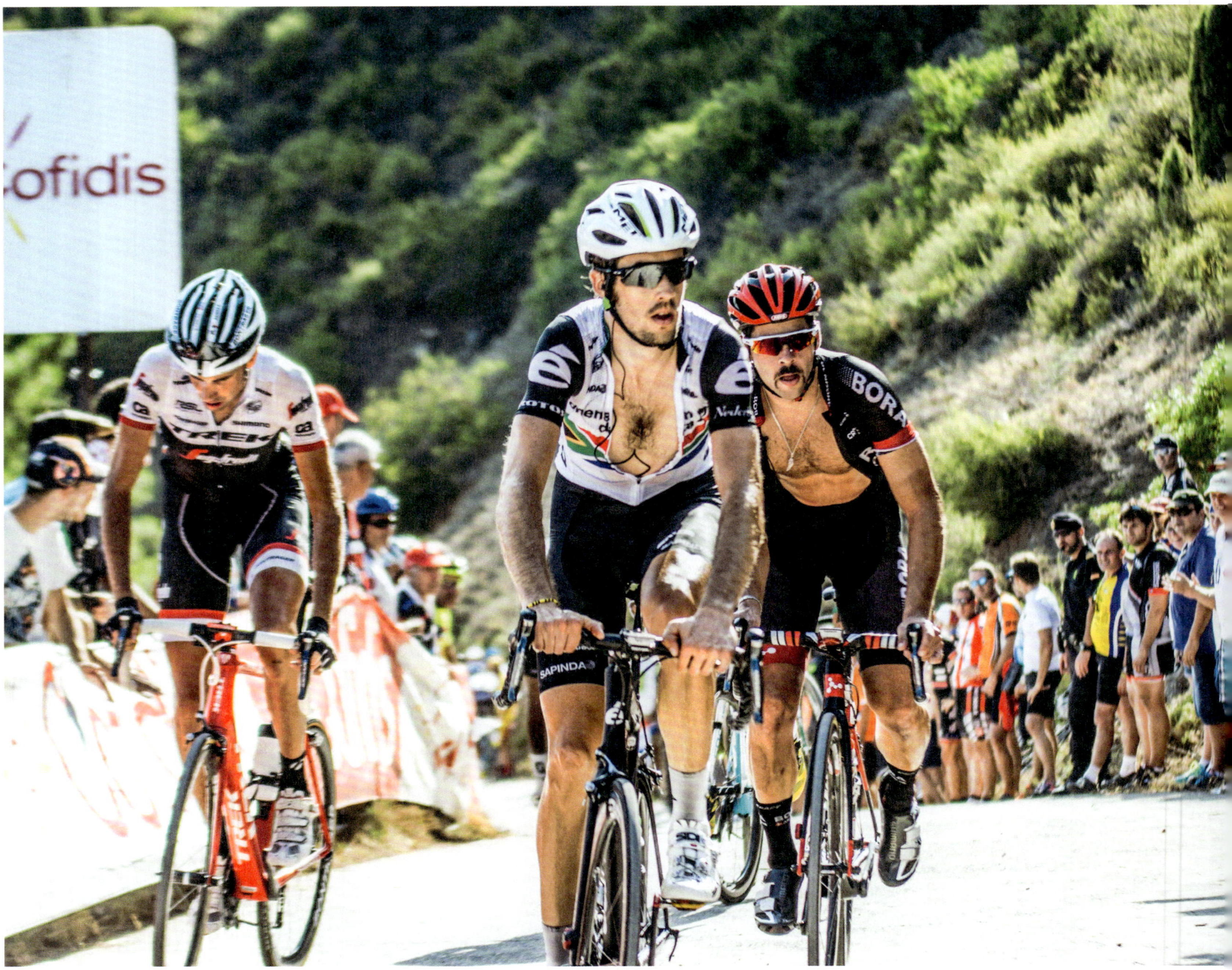

↑ Jaco Venter (Dimension Data) und Michael Schwarzmann alias „Moustache Carlos" (BORA - ARGON 18) am Schlussanstieg. **Jaco Venter (Dimension Data) and Michael Schwarzmann a.k.a 'Moustache Carlos' (BORA - ARGON 18) on the final climb.** *Jaco Venter (Dimension Data) et Michael Schwarzmann alias Moustache Carlos (BORA - ARGON 18) lors de l'ascension finale.*

↗ Alejandro Valverde (Movistar) gibt Autogramme. **Alejandro Valverde (Movistar) signing autographs.** *Alejandro Valverde (Movistar) signe quelques autographes.*

→ Die kolumbianische Fangemeinde reist mit. **The Colombian fan community comes along too.** *La communauté des fans colombiens est aussi du voyage.*

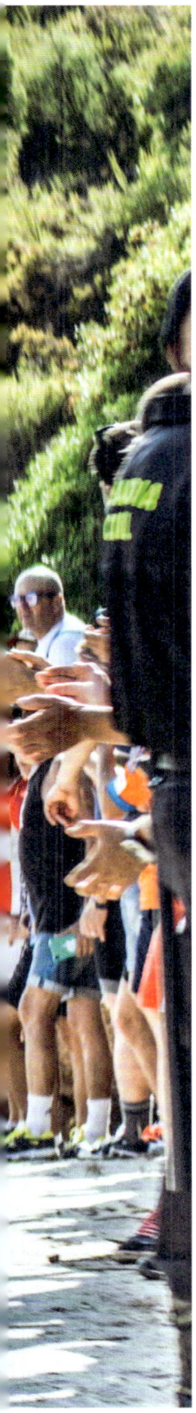

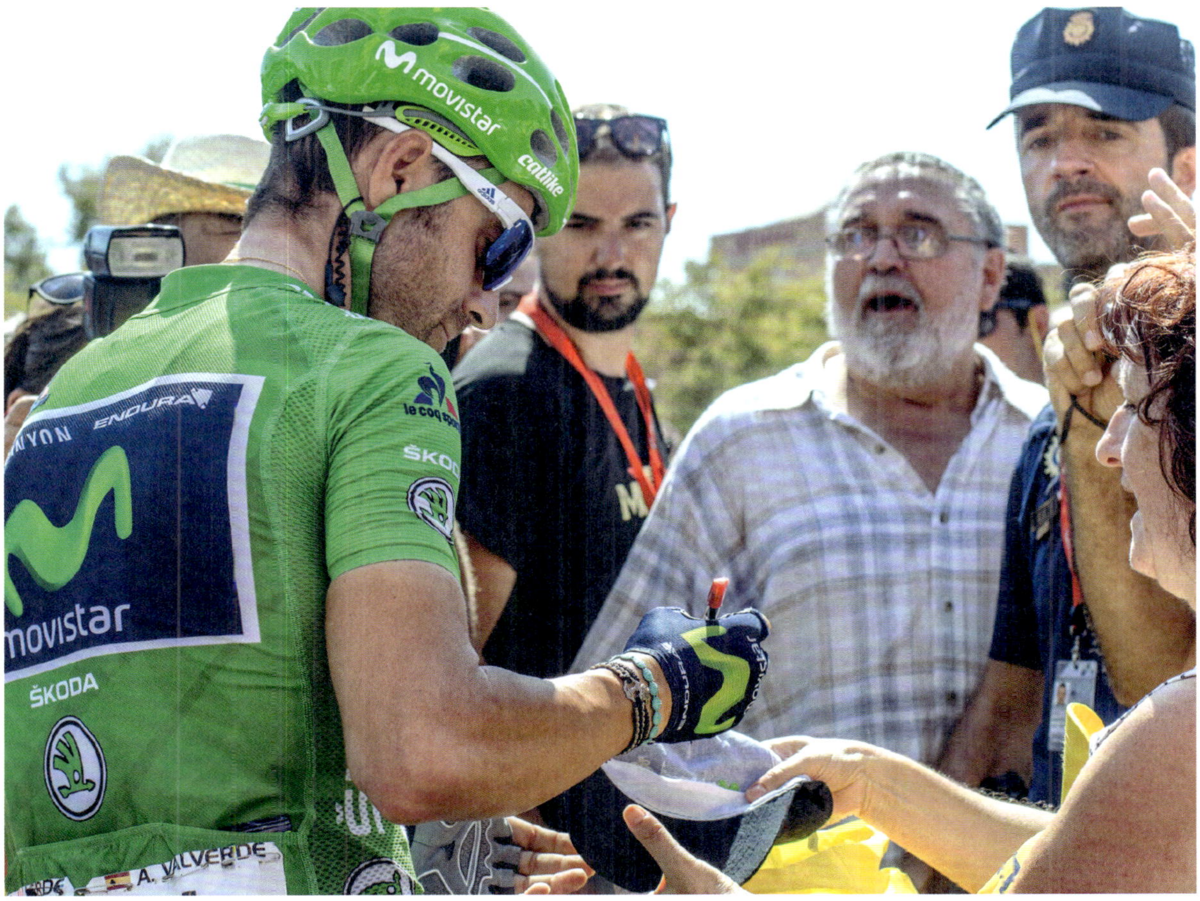
movistar
catlike
ENDURA
movistar
ŠKODA
ŠKODA
A. VALVERDE

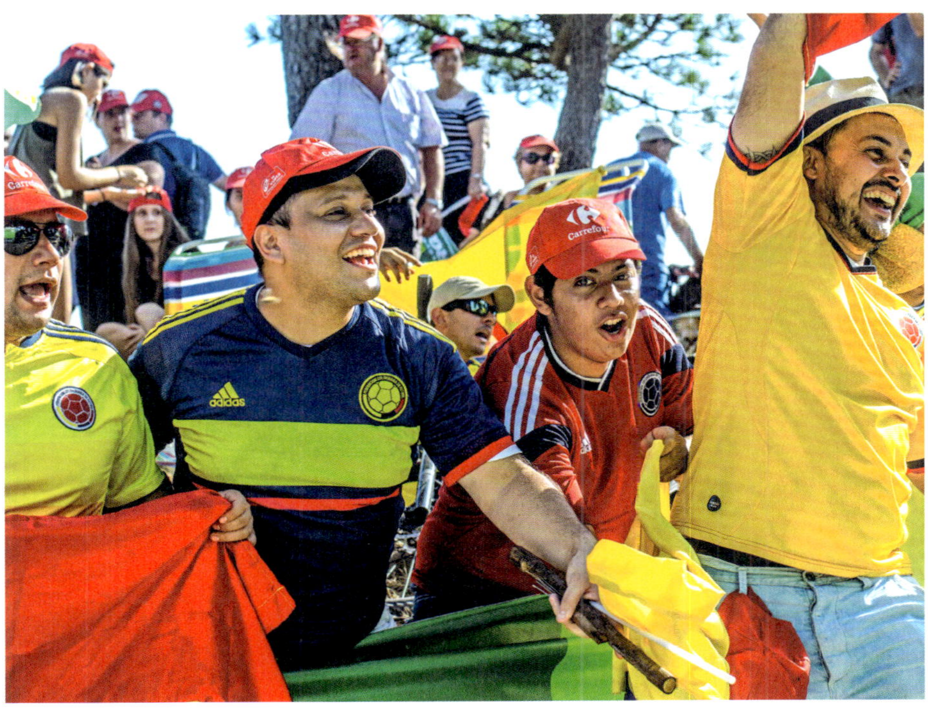
adidas

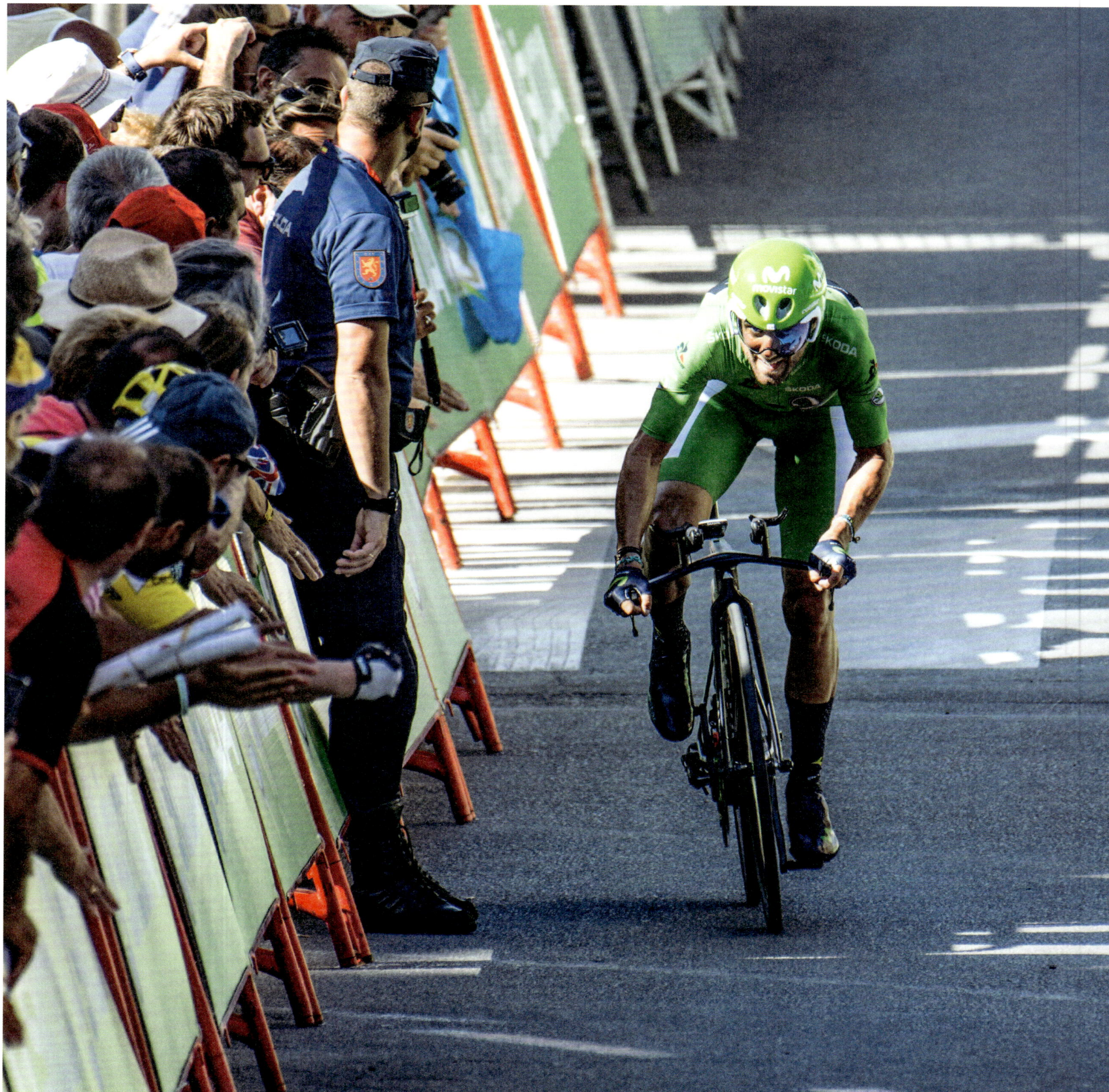

↑ Zeitfahren von Xábia nach Calp: Alejandro Valverde (Movistar). **Time-trial from Xábia to Calp: Alejandro Valverde (Movistar).** *Contre-la-montre entre Xábia et Calp : Alejandro Valverde (Movistar).*

→ Start in Xábia. **Start in Xábia.** *Départ de Xábia.*

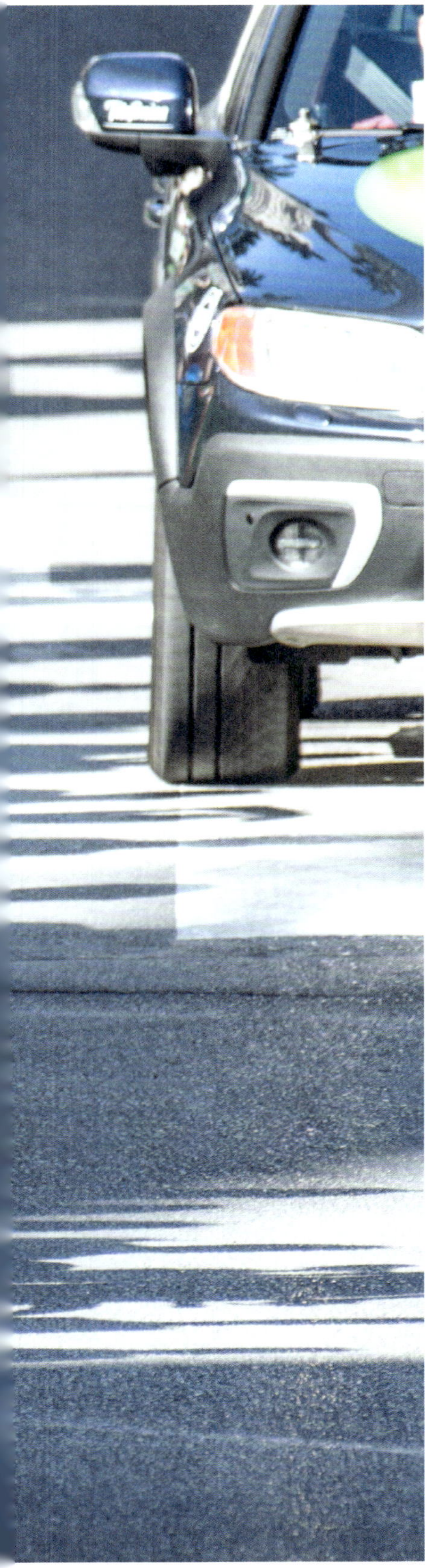

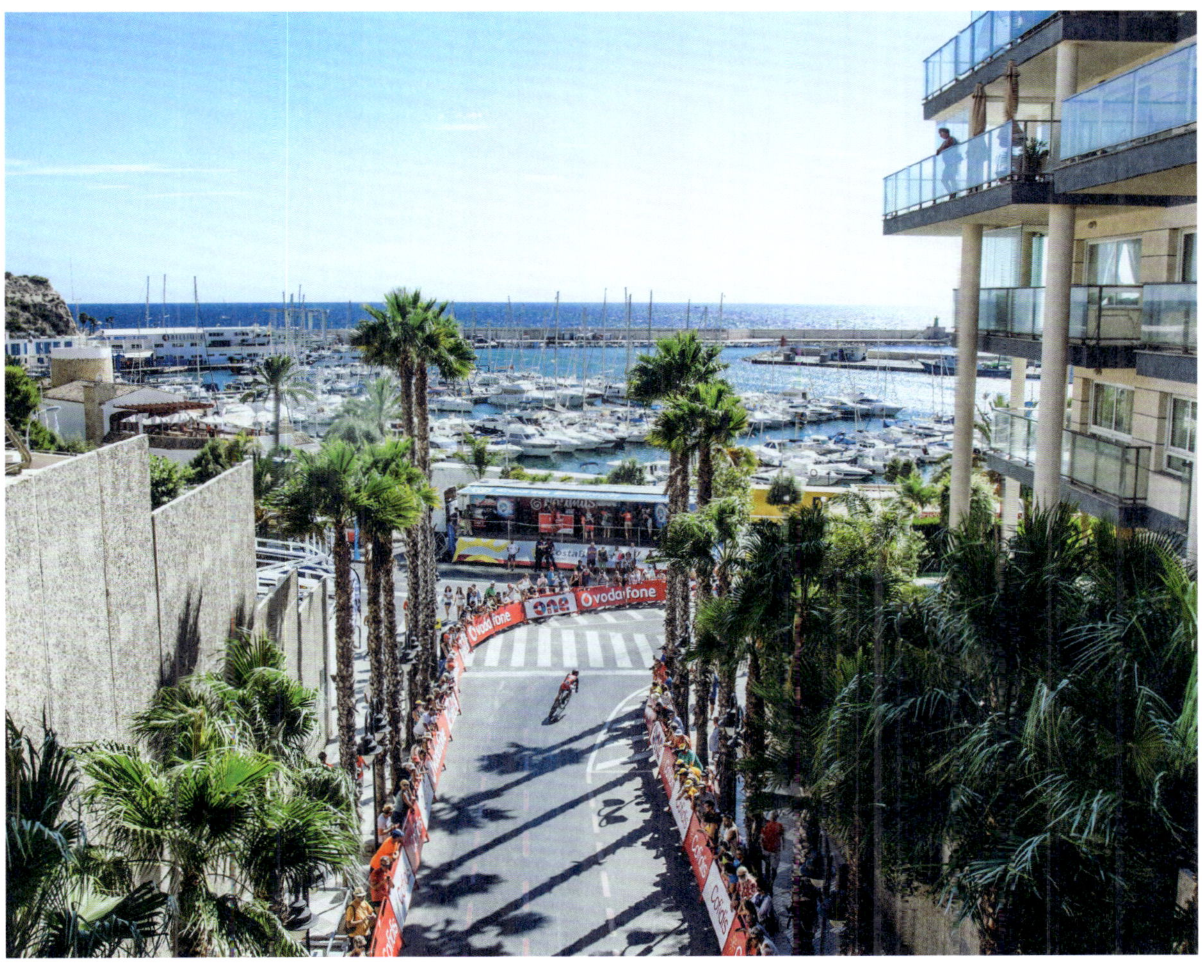
vodafone

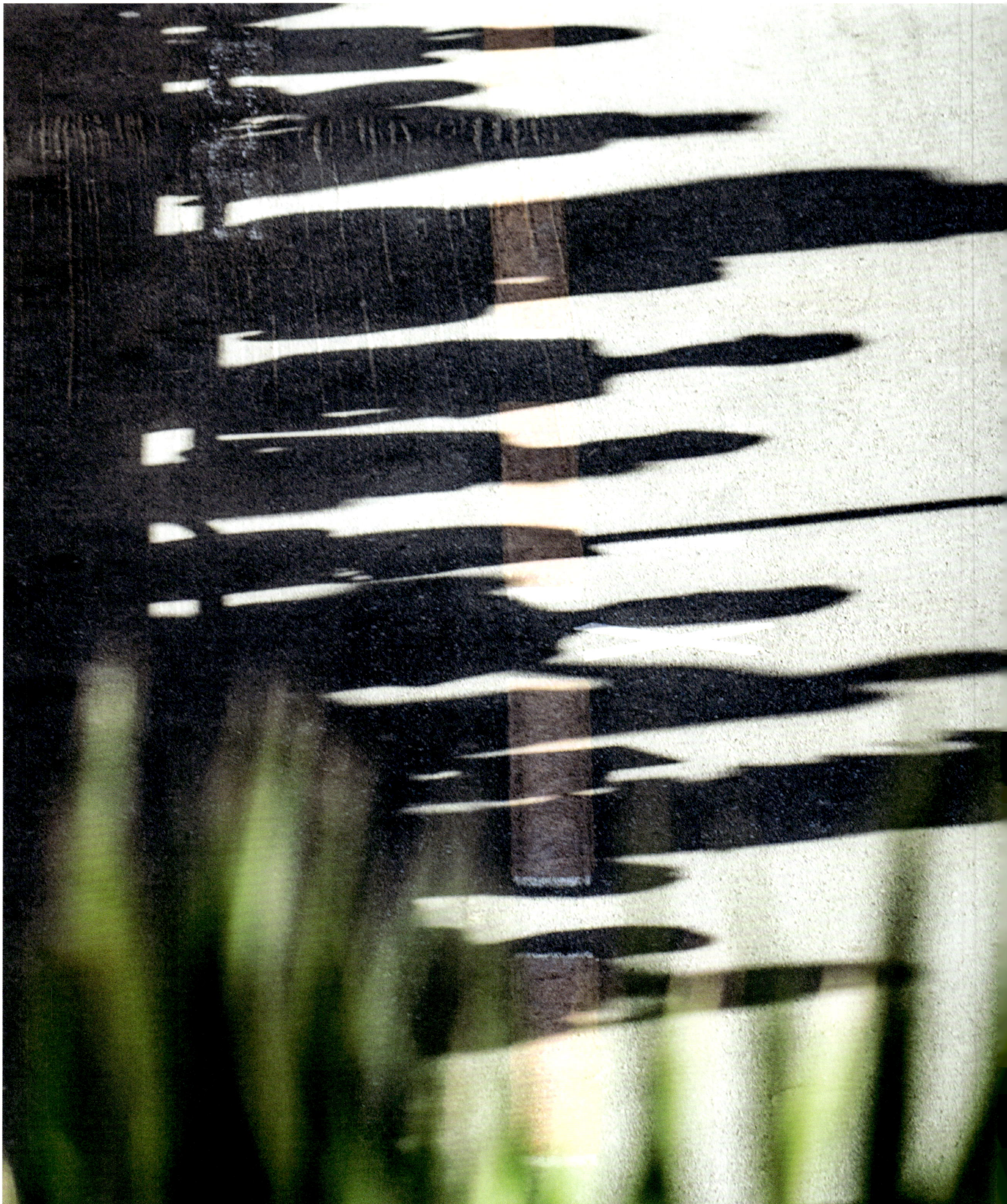

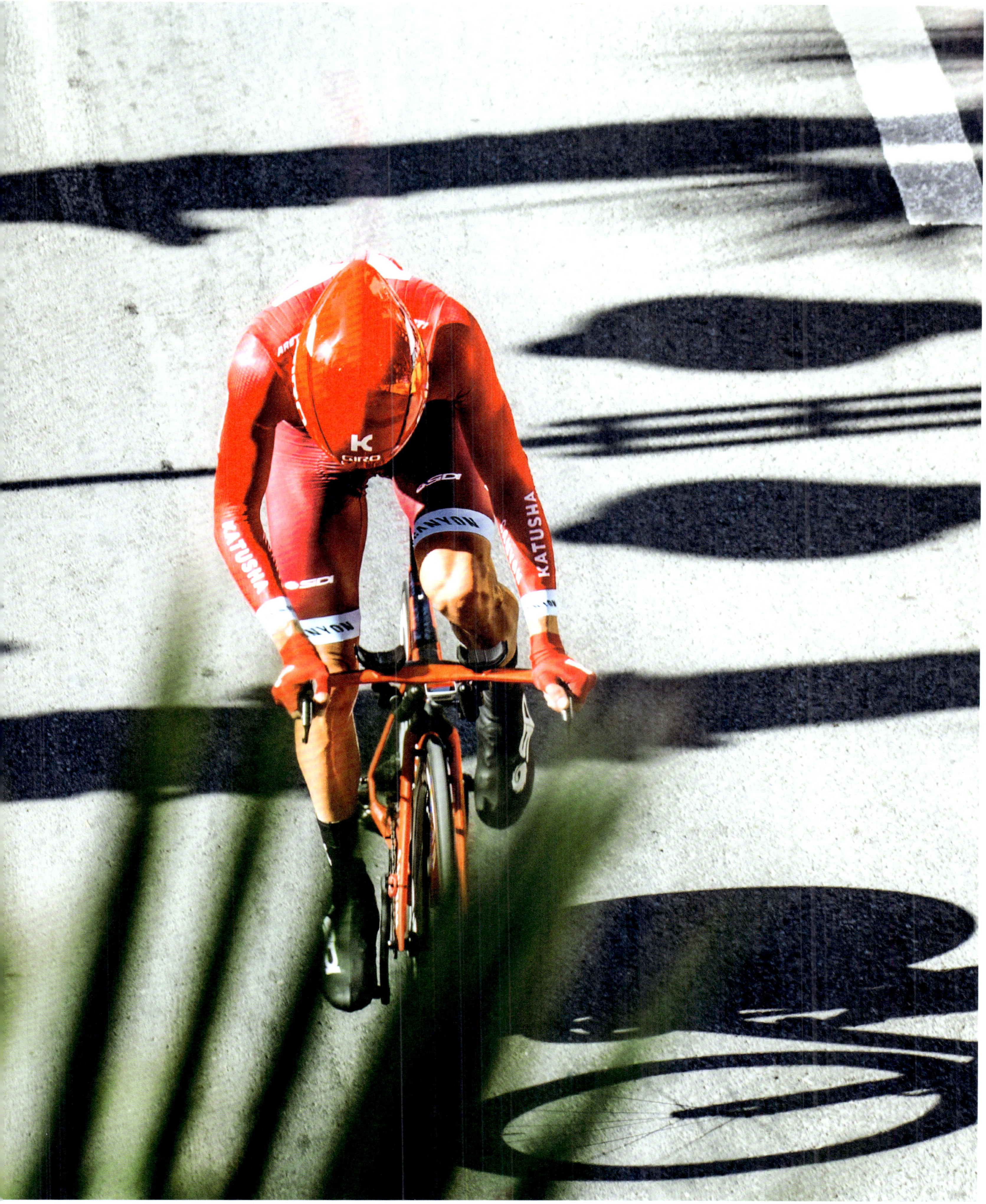

19. Etappe, Einzelzeitfahren. **19th stage, individual time trials.** *19e étape : contre-la-montre individuel.*

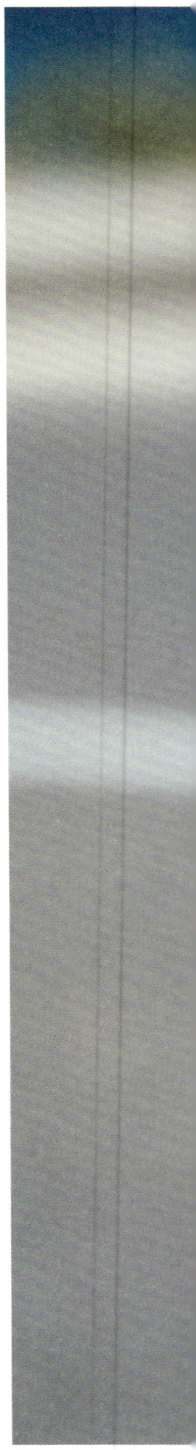

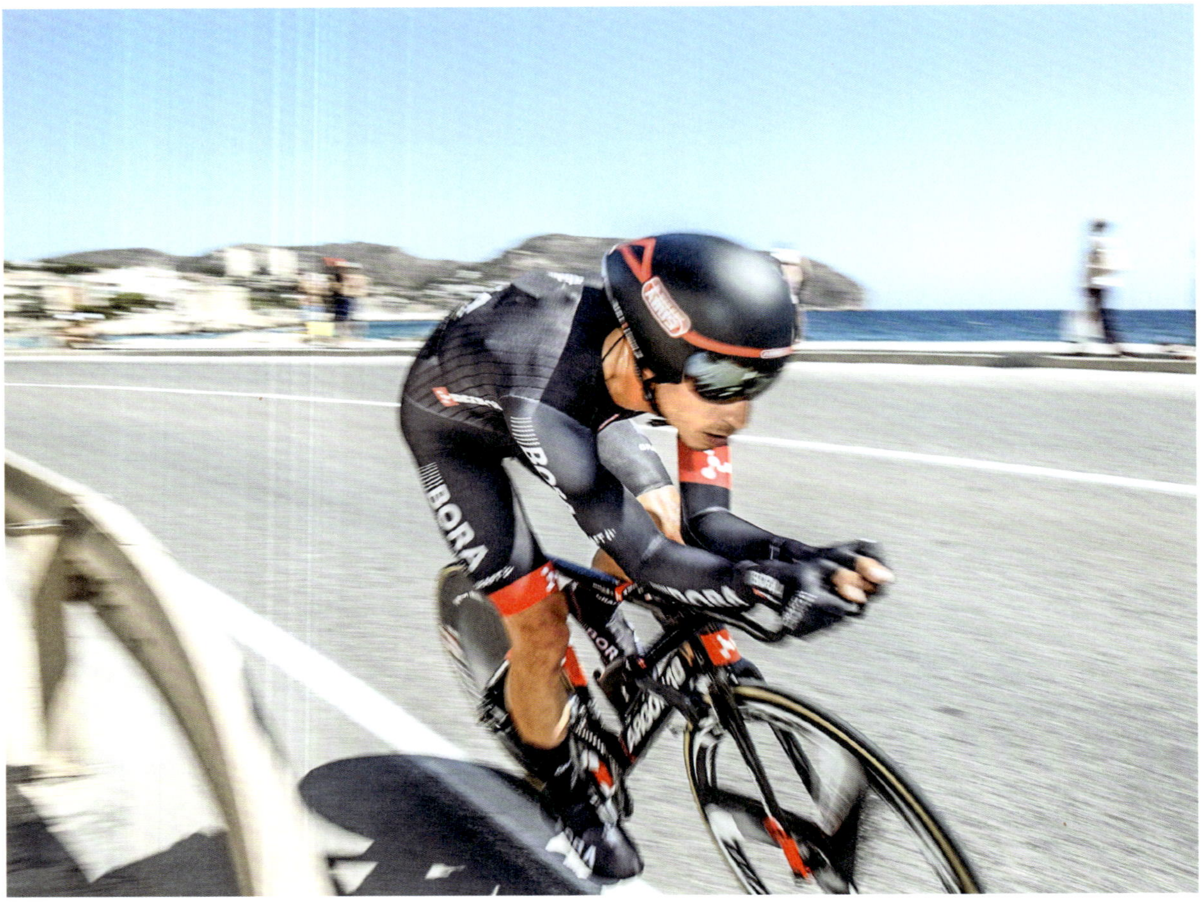
BORA

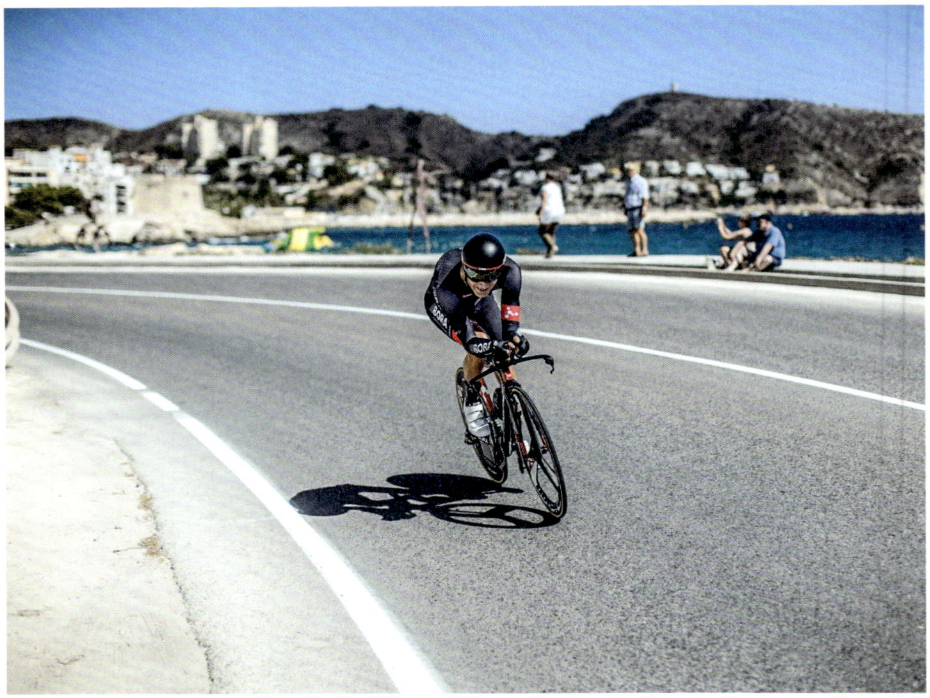

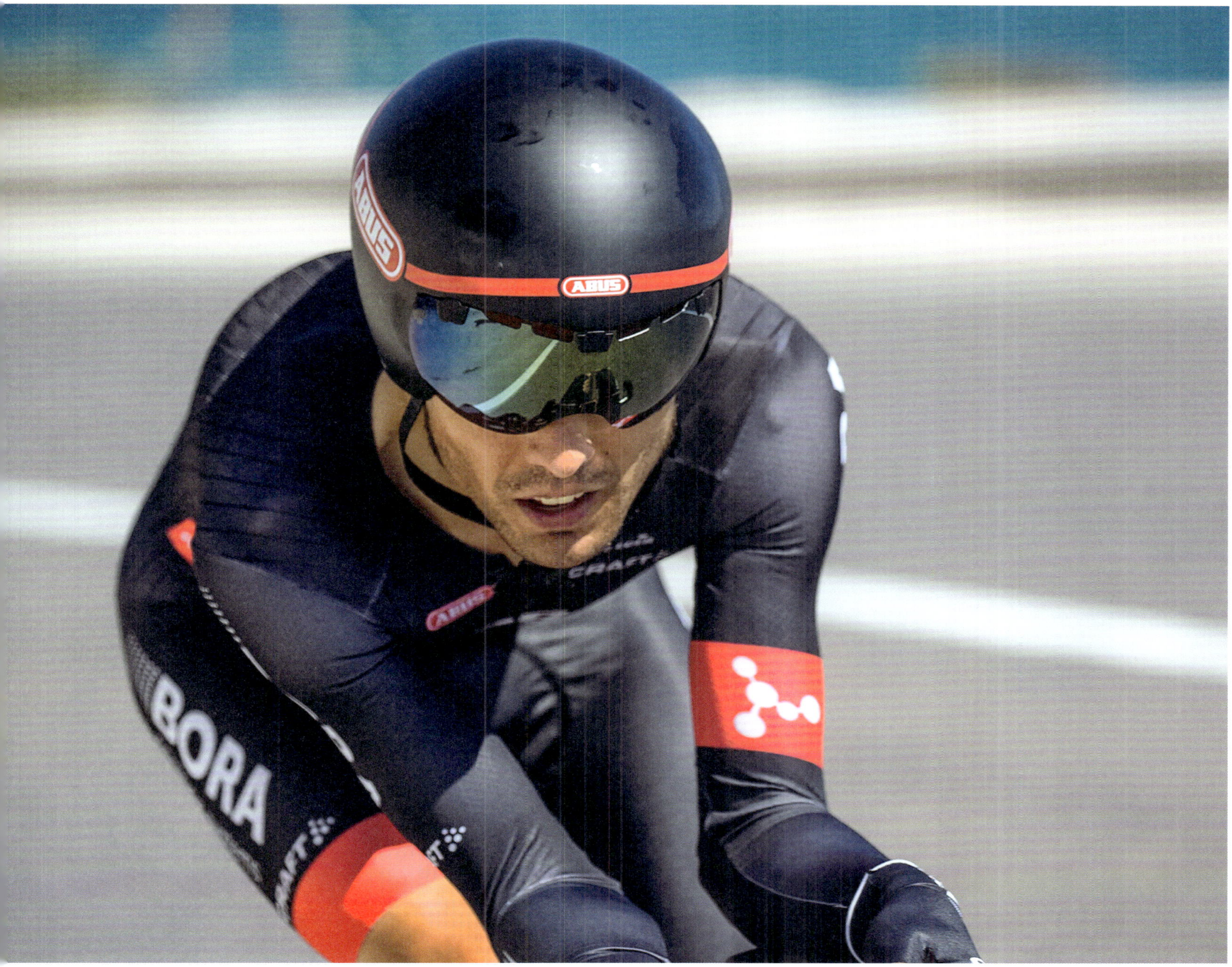

Rüdiger Selig, Scott Thwaites und Cesare Benedetti (alle BORA - ARGON 18), allein gegen die Uhr. **Rüdiger Selig, Scott Thwaites and Cesare Benedetti (all BORA - ARGON 18), alone against the clock.** *Rüdiger Selig, Scott Thwaites et Cesare Benedetti (tous BORA - ARGON 18), seuls contre la montre.*

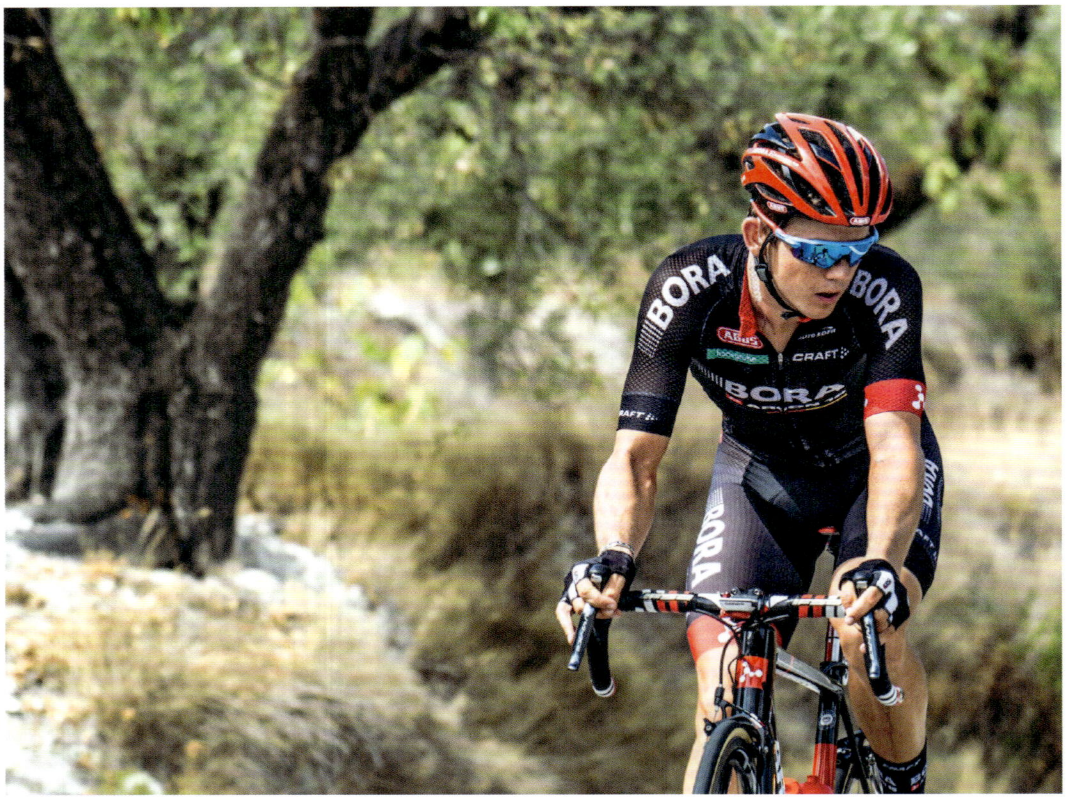

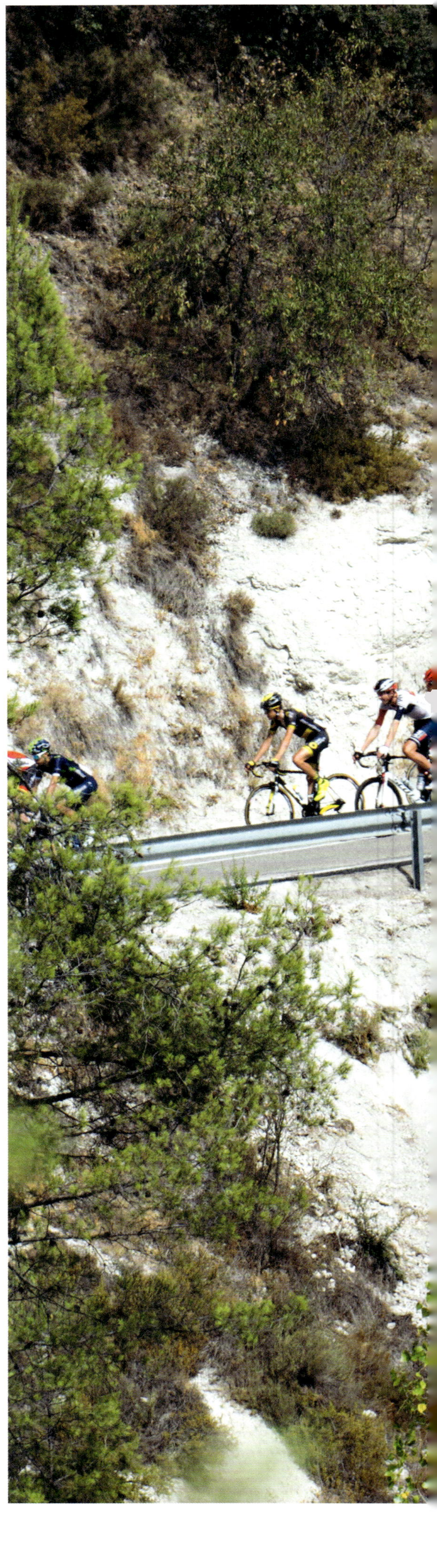

↑ Gregor Mühlberger (BORA - ARGON 18). **Gregor Mühlberger (BORA - ARGON 18).** *Gregor Mühlberger (BORA - ARGON 18).*

→ 20. Etappe. **20th stage.** *20e étape.*

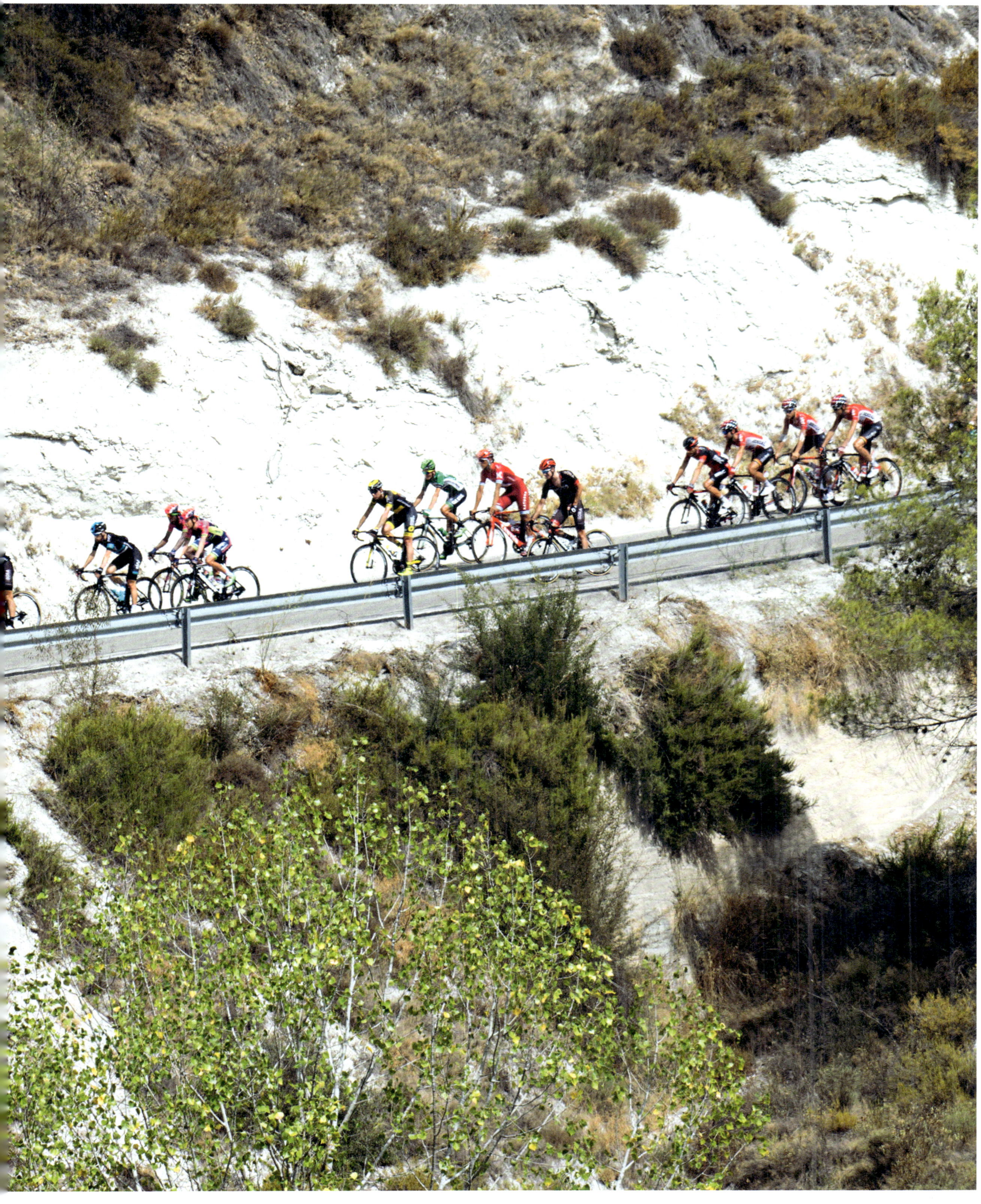

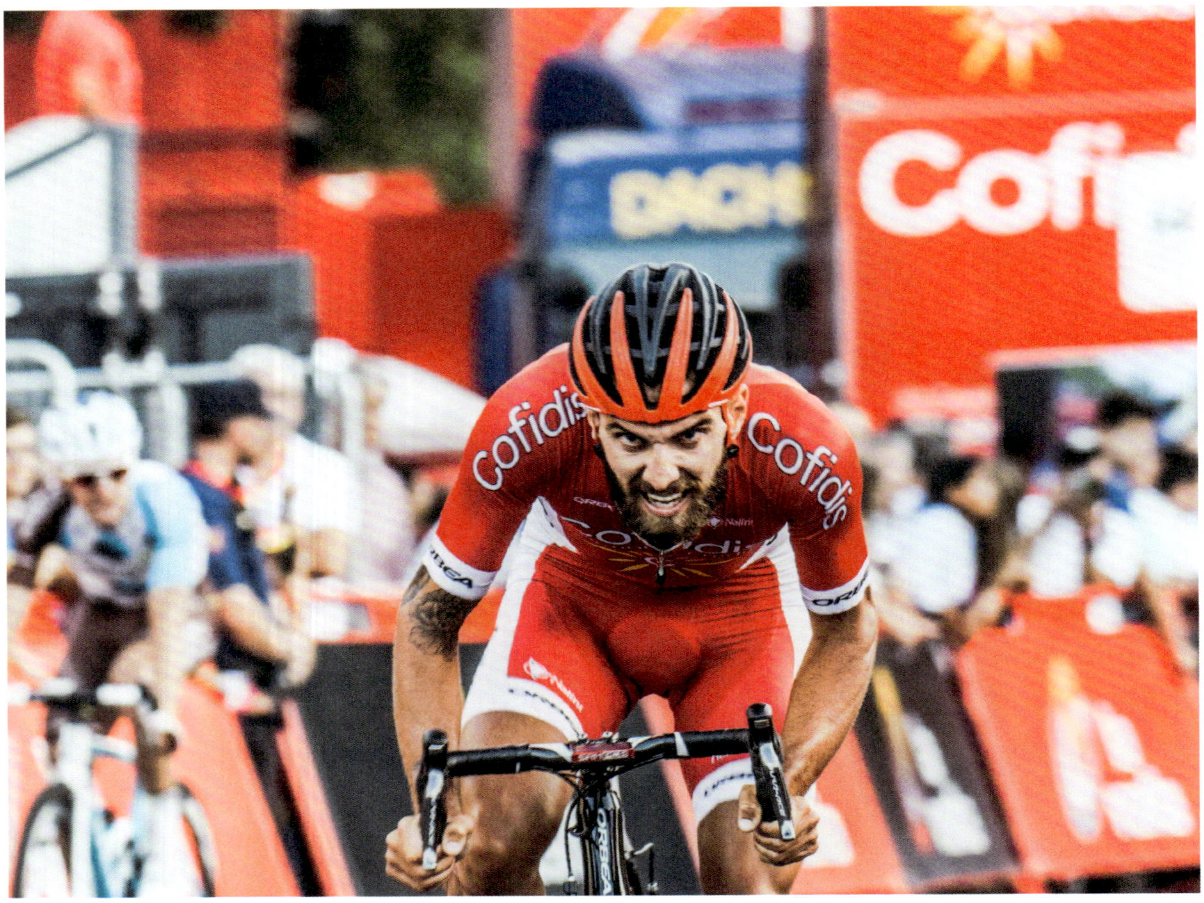

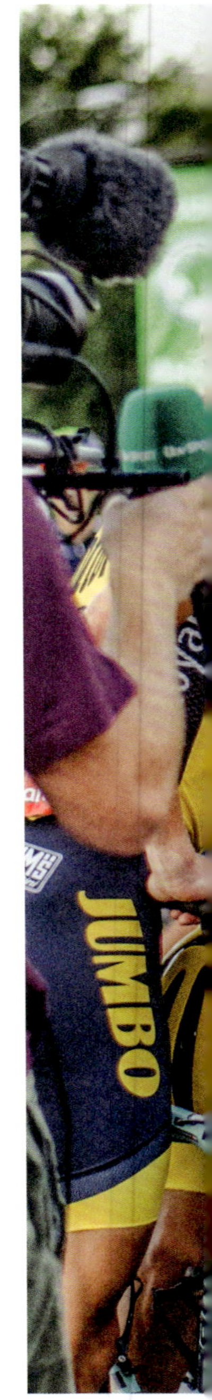

↑ Loïc Chetout (Cofidis) am Ziel in Madrid. **Loïc Chetout (Cofidis) at the finish line in Madrid.** *Loïc Chetout (Cofidis) à l'arrivée à Madrid.*

↗ Die Vuelta 2016 beendet: Selfie-Time für Team LottoNL-Jumbo. **La Vuelta 2016 concluded: selfie-time for Team LottoNL-Jumbo.** *La Vuelta 2016 se termine : c'est l'heure des selfies pour la Team LottoNL-Jumbo.*

→ Alles gegeben: Rüdiger Selig (BORA - ARGON 18). **He gave it his best: Rüdiger Selig (BORA - ARGON 18).** *Exténué : Rüdiger Selig (BORA - ARGON 18).*

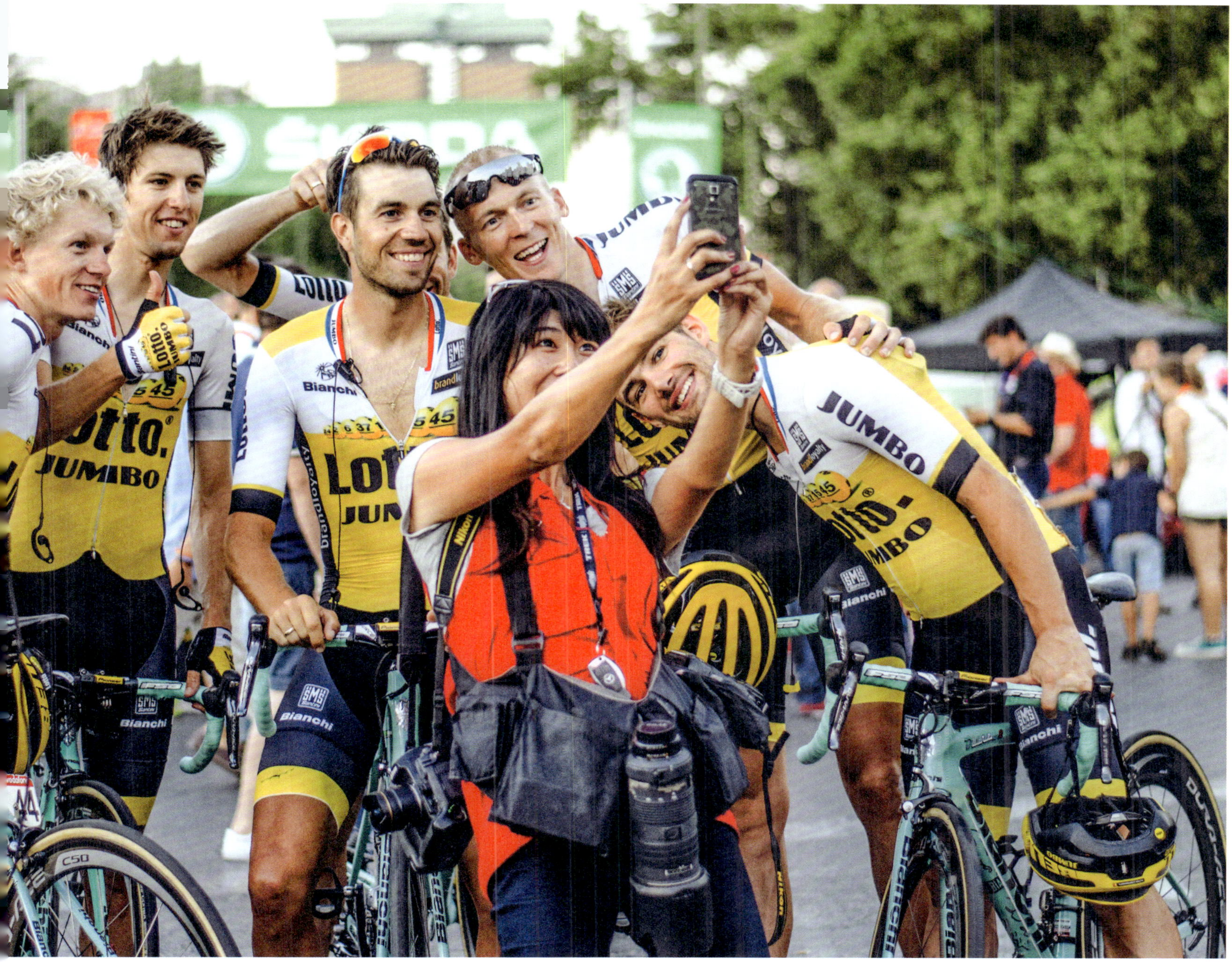
ŠKODA
Lotto. JUMBO
JUMBO
Bianchi
brandloyalty
Nikon

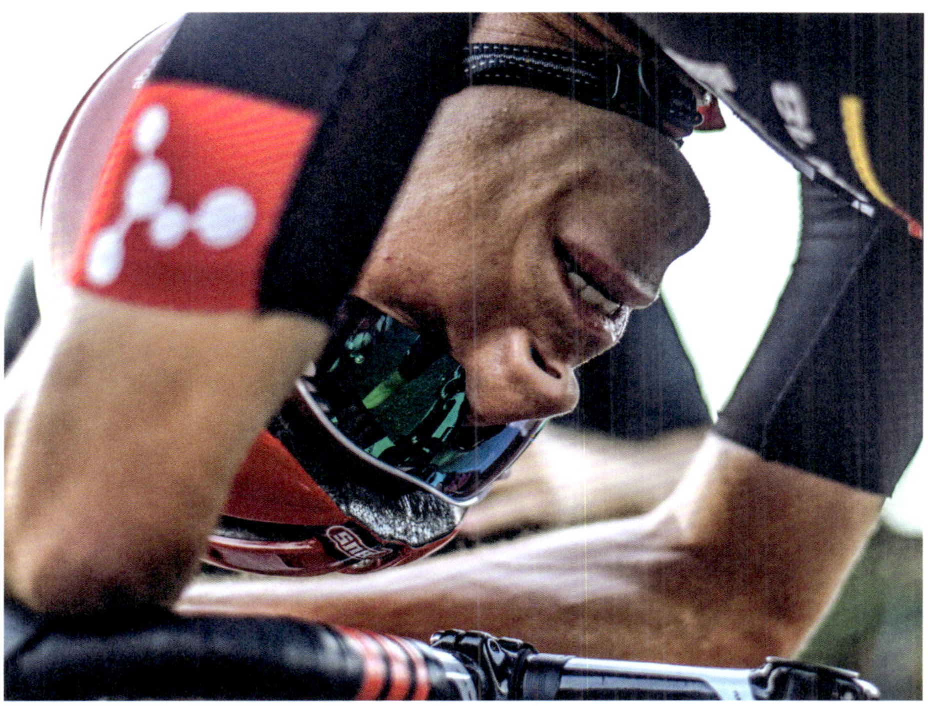

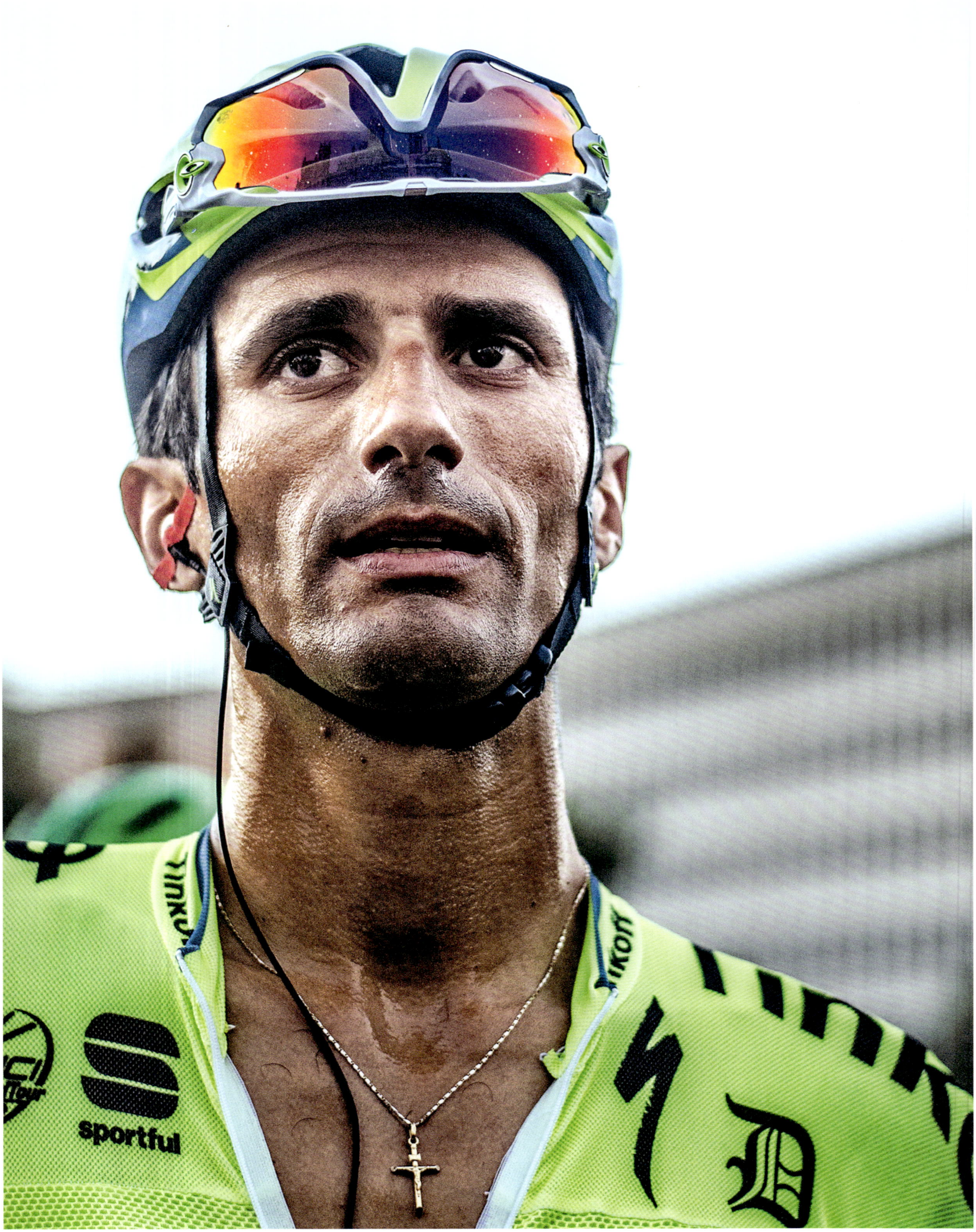

↑ Daniele Bennati (Tinkoff), Zweiter der Schlussetappe nach Madrid. **Daniele Bennati (Tinkoff), second place on the final stage to Madrid.**
Daniele Bennati (Tinkoff), deuxième de l'étape finale vers Madrid.

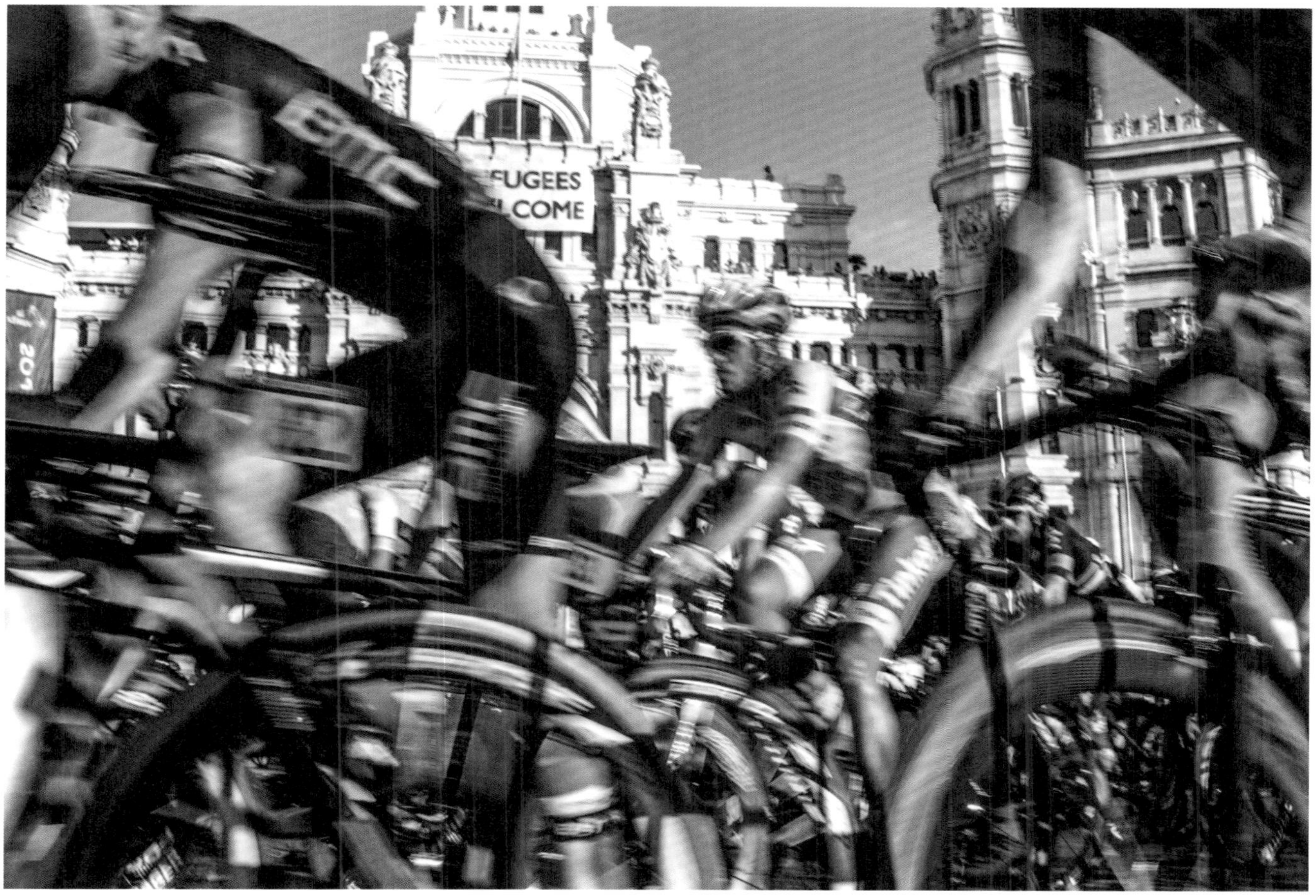
BMC

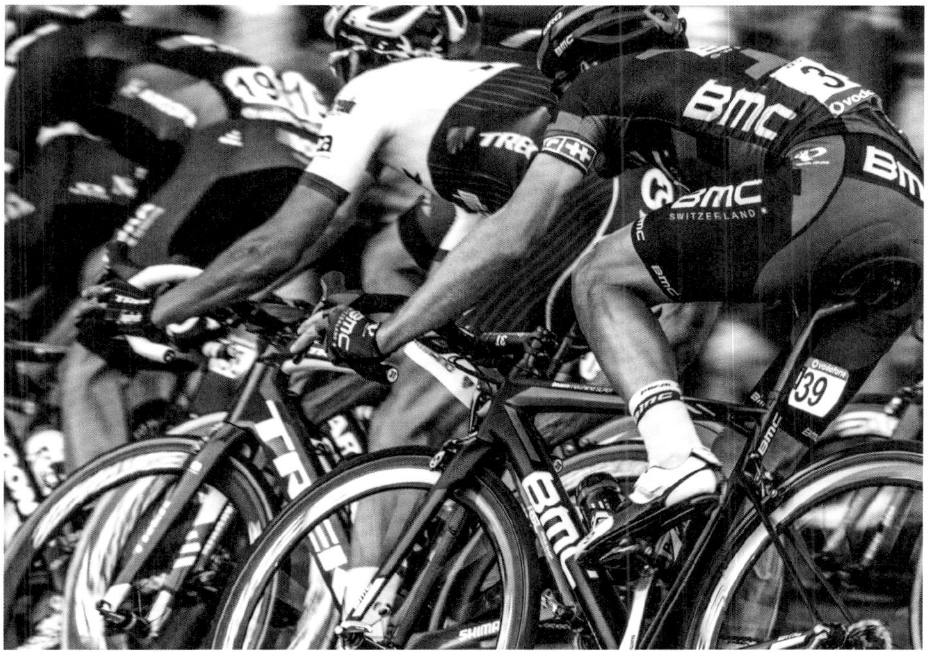
BMC
BMC
SWITZERLAND
39

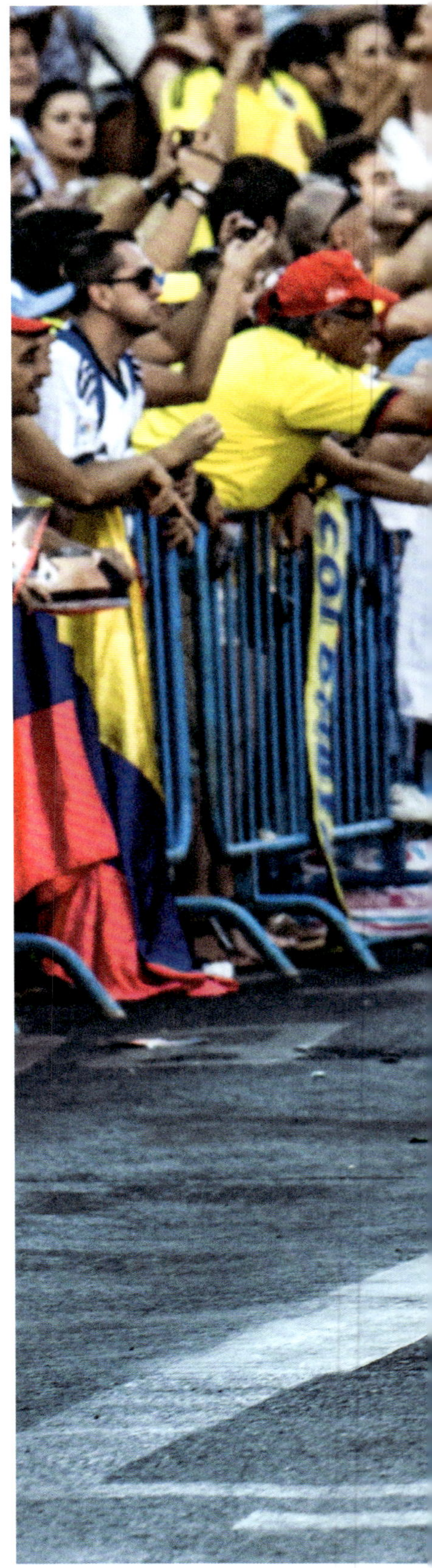

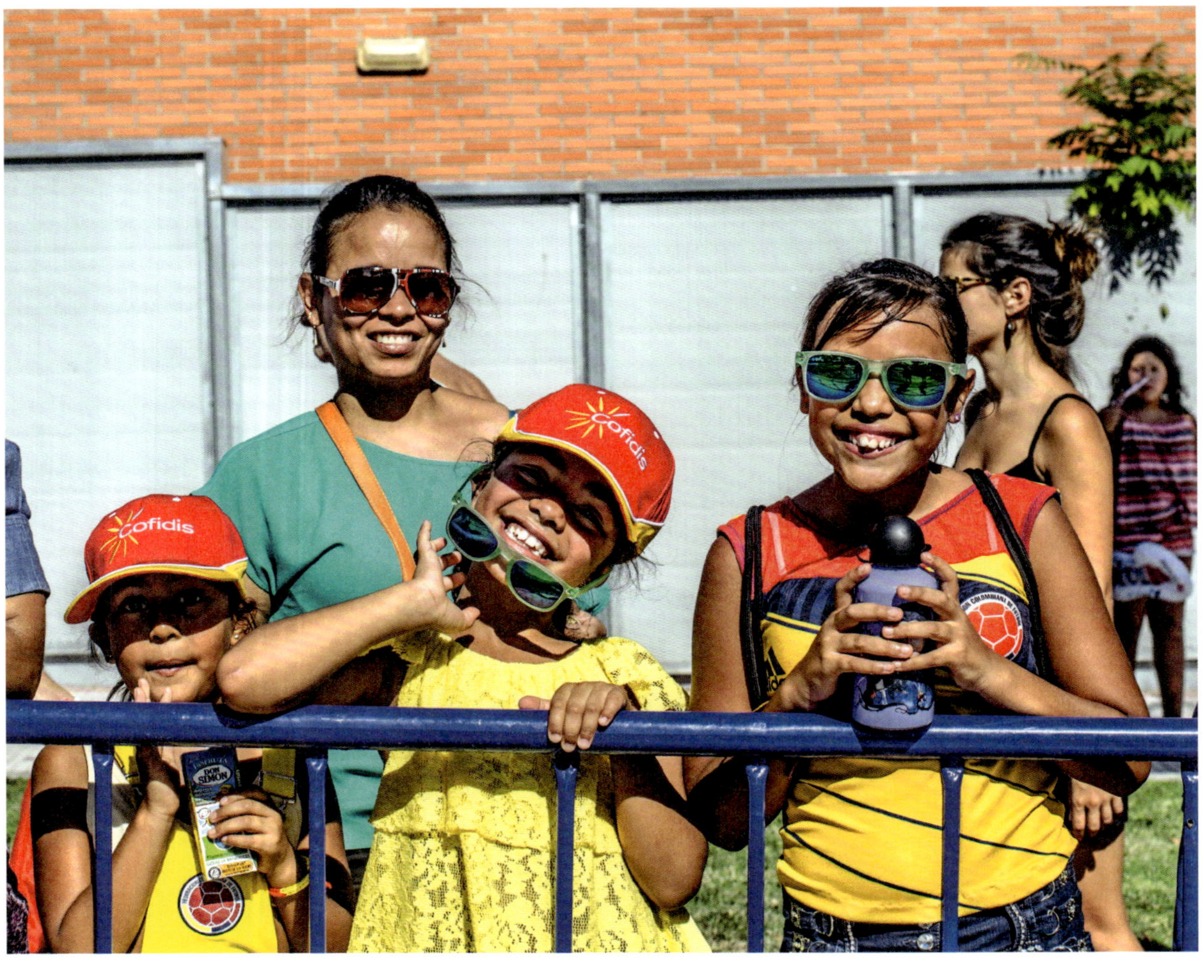
Cofidis
Cofidis

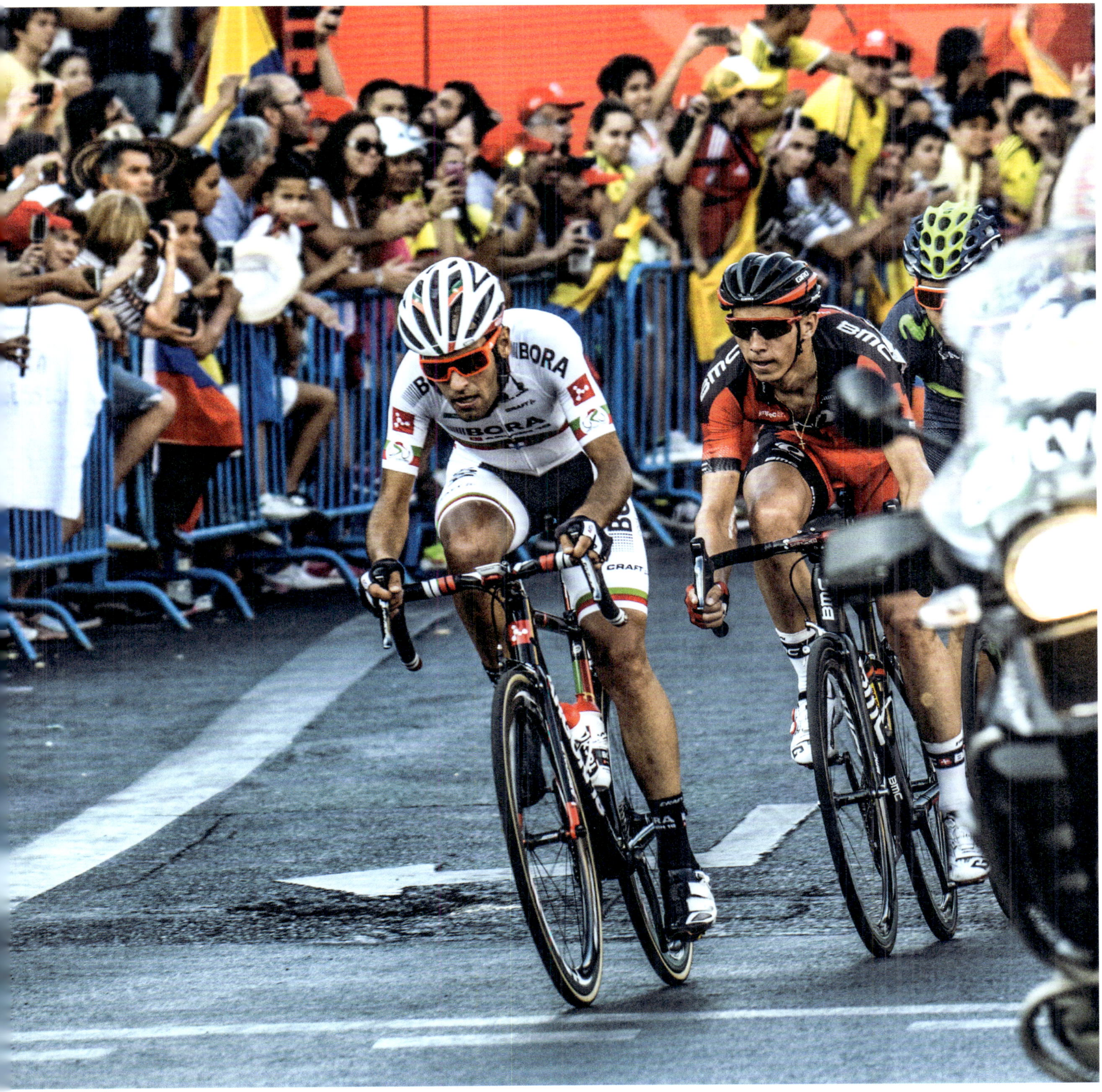

↑ José Mendes (BORA - ARGON 18) und Dylan Teuns (BMC Racing Team). **José Mendes (BORA - ARGON 18) and Dylan Teuns (BMC Racing Team).**
José Mendes (BORA - ARGON 18) et Dylan Teuns (BMC Racing Team).

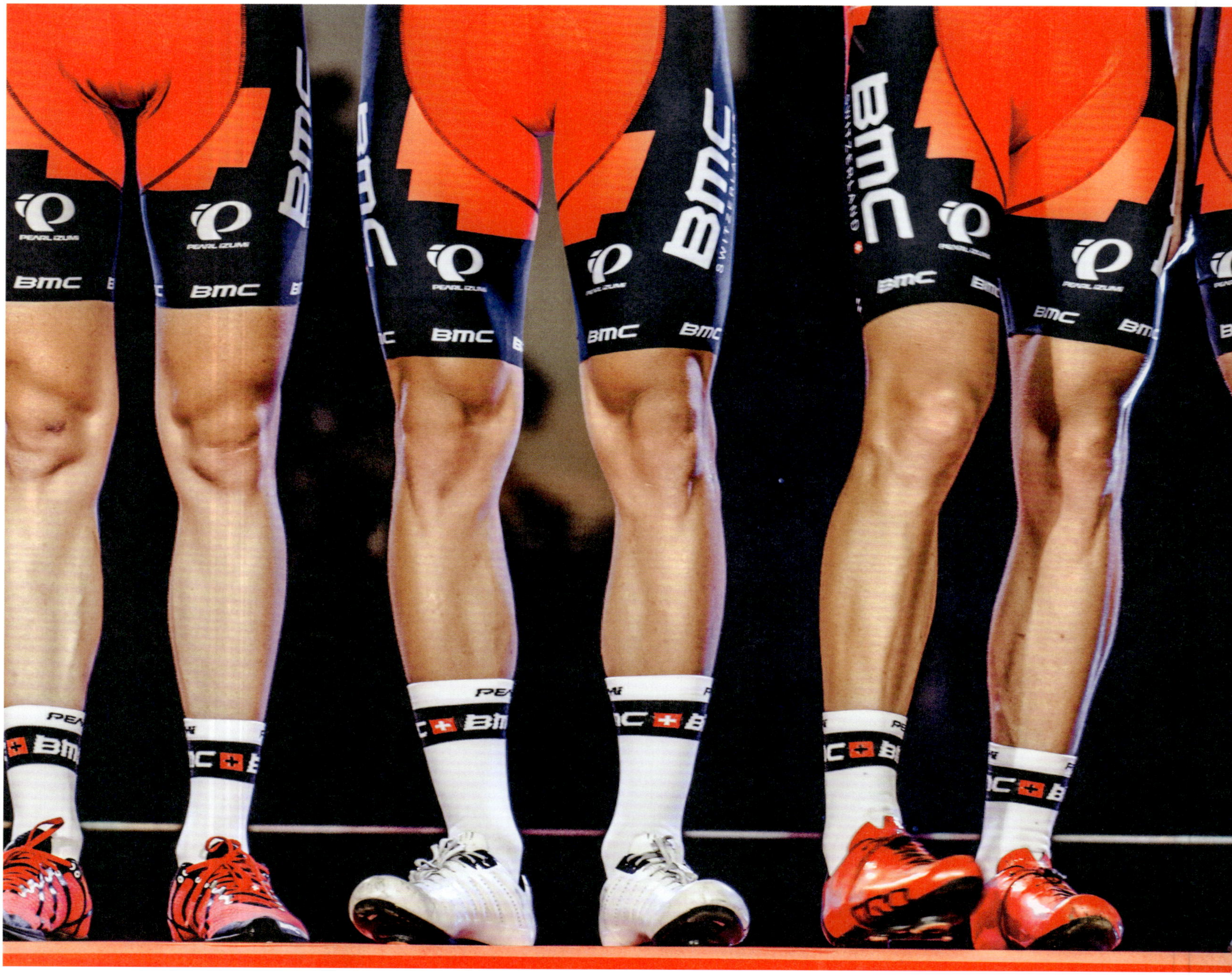

↑ Die stärksten Beine der Vuelta 2016: Das BMC Racing gewinnt die Teamwertung. **The most powerful legs of La Vuelta 2016: BMC Racing wins the team classification.** *Les jambes les plus vigoureuses de la Vuelta 2016 : le BMC Racing remporte le classement par équipes.*

↗ Champagnerdusche auf dem Podium: Nairo Quintana (Movistar) gewinnt seine zweite Grand Tour vor Chris Froome (Team Sky) und Esteban Chaves (ORICA-BikeExchange). Kolumbien ist somit doppelt vertreten. **Champagne shower on the podium: Nairo Quintana (Movistar) wins his second Grand Tour ahead of Chris Froome (Team Sky) and Esteban Chaves (ORICA-BikeExchange). Columbia is therefore represented twice.** *Le champagne coule à flot sur le podium : Nairo Quintana (Movistar) remporte son deuxième Grand Tour devant Chris Froome (Team Sky) et Esteban Chaves (ORICA-BikeExchange). La Colombie compte deux représentants sur le podium.*

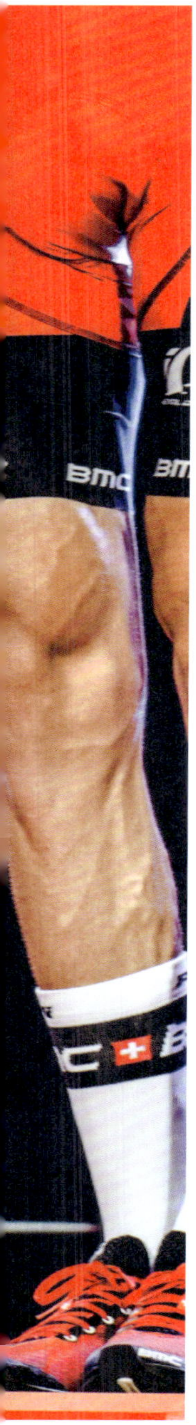
BMC

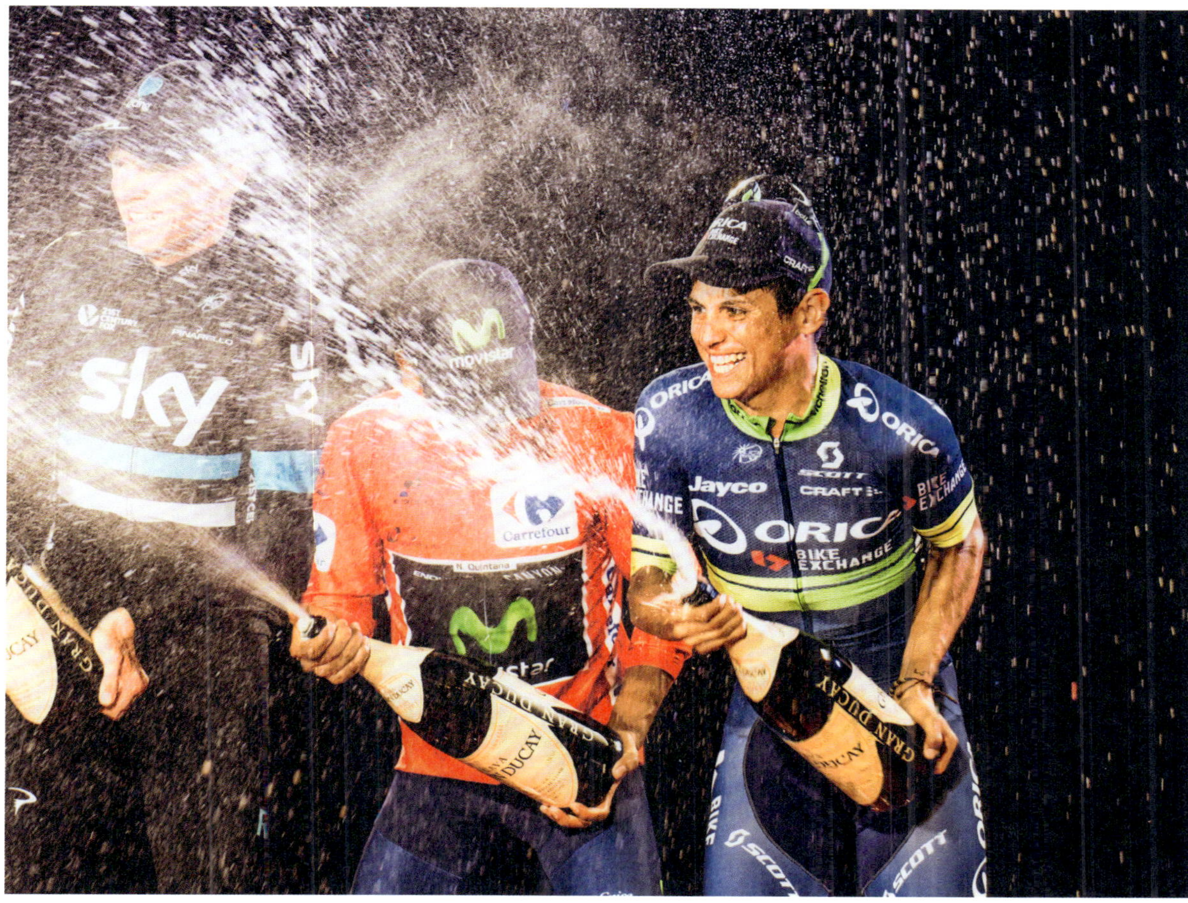
sky
movistar
Carrefour
Jayco
ORICA
BIKE EXCHANGE
SCOTT
CRAFT
GRAN DUCAY

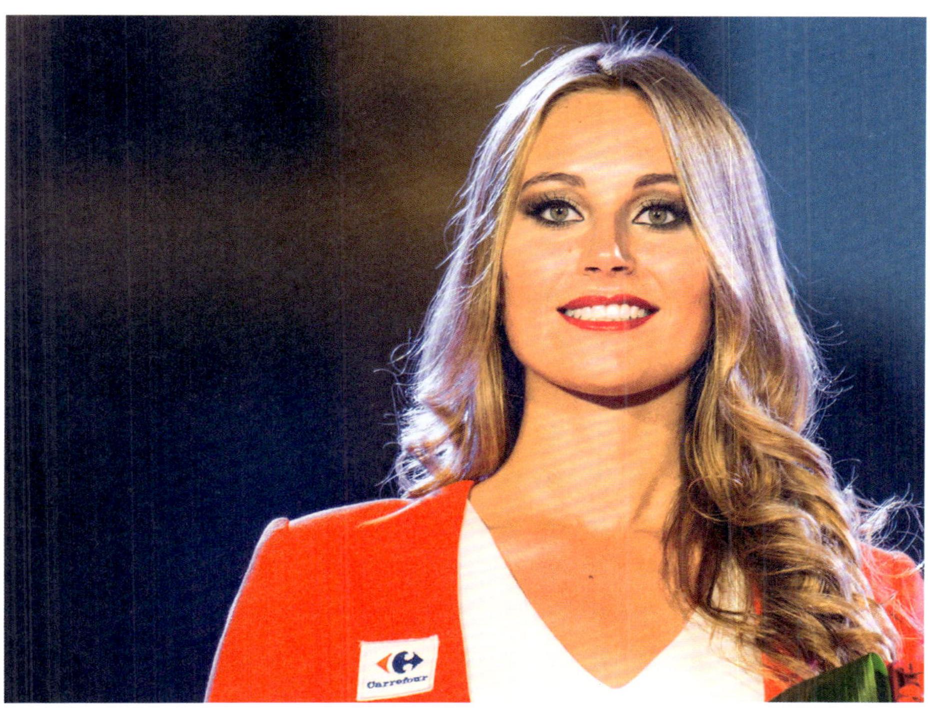
Carrefour

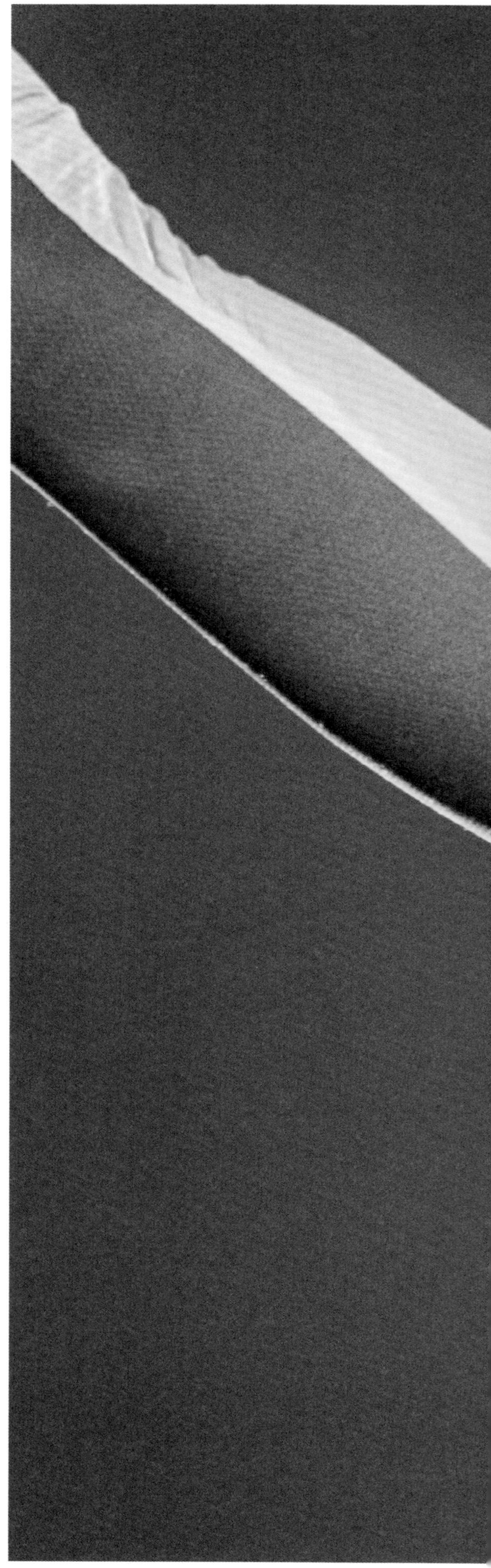

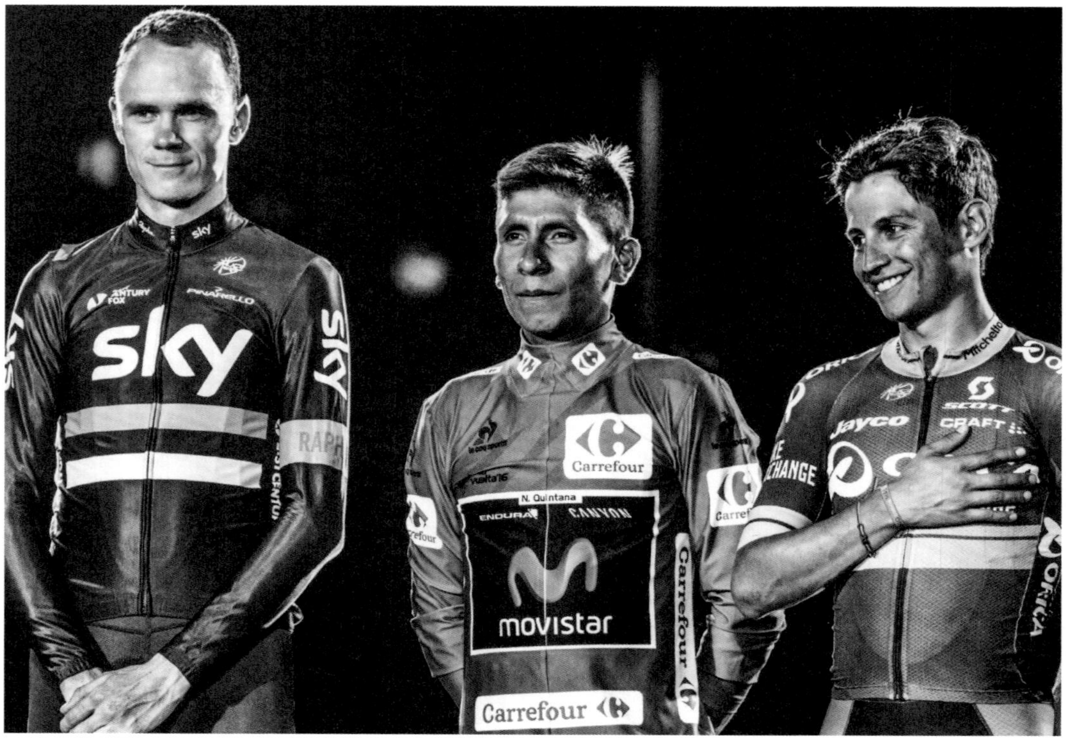

↑ Zufrieden, stolz und glücklich: Chris Froome (Team Sky), Nairo Quintana (Movistar) und Esteban Chaves (ORICA-BikeExchange, v. l. n. r.). **Content, proud and happy: Chris Froome (Team Sky), Nairo Quintana (Movistar) and Esteban Chaves (ORICA-BikeExchange, from left to right)** *Satisfaits, fiers et heureux : Chris Froome (Team Sky), Nairo Quintana (Movistar) et Esteban Chaves (ORICA-BikeExchange, de gauche à droite).*

→ Alberto Contador (Tinkoff) wird kämpferischster Fahrer der Vuelta 2016. **Alberto Contador (Tinkoff) named most aggressive rider at La Vuelta 2016.** *Alberto Contador (Tinkoff) remporte le prix de la Combativité de la Vuelta 2016.*

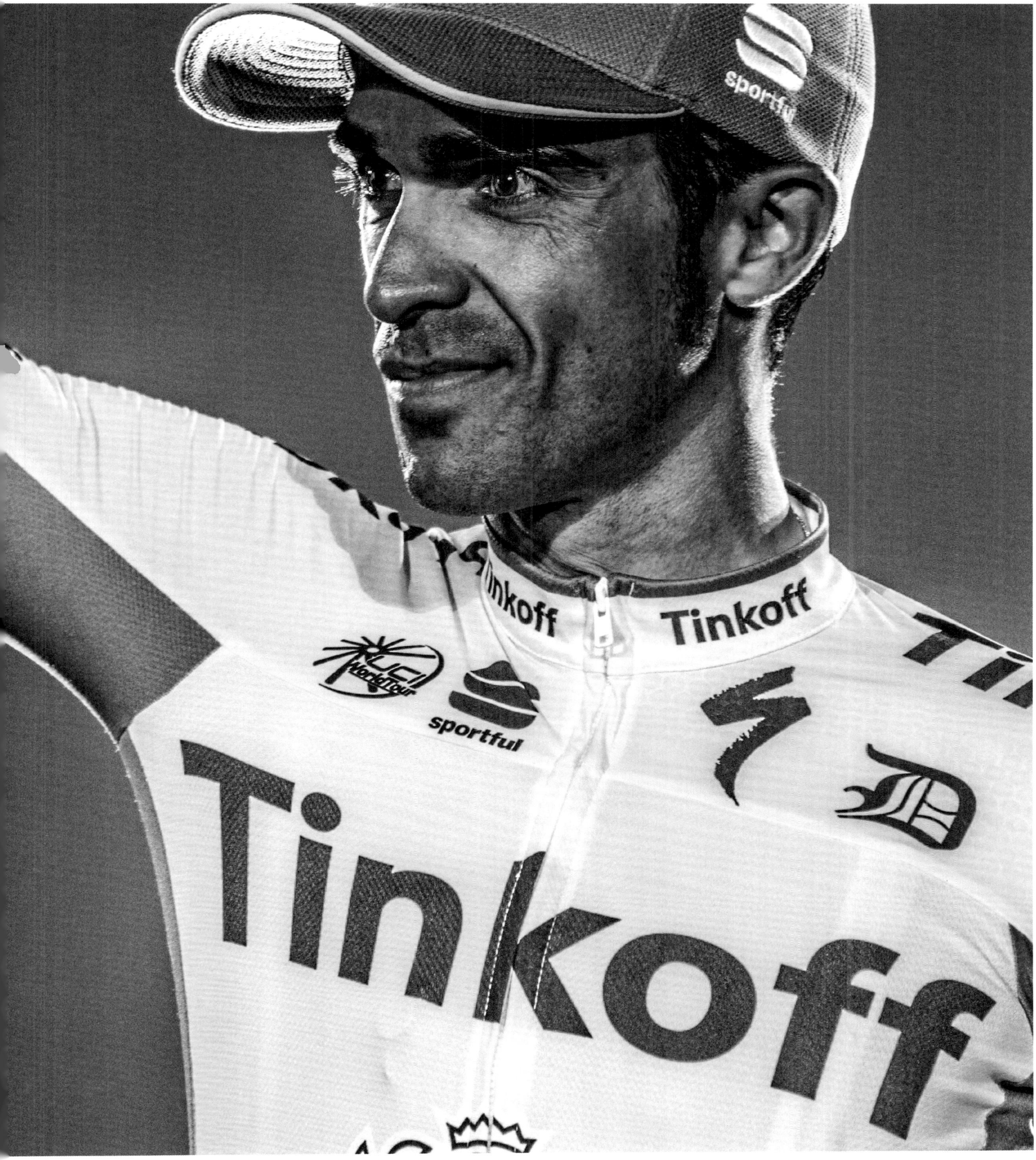
sportful
Tinkoff
Tinkoff
sportful
Tinkoff

Impressum

Herausgeber: Willi Bruckbauer
BORA Holding GmbH
Prof.-Dr.-Anton-Kathrein-Straße 3
A-6342 Niederndorf
Österreich
www.bora.com

elegant
eine Marke der Edel Germany GmbH

Neumühlen 17, 22763 Hamburg
www.edel.com
www.elegant.edel.com

Konzept und Redaktion: derks brand management consultants,
Strähuberstraße 18, 81479 München
Text: Heide Sahl, Klaudia Meinert
Layout und Gestaltung: Johanna Höflich
Projektkoordination: Guido Neuhaus
Übersetzung: Lykkebo Gruppe UG
Umschlagfotos: Karen Edwards
Fotos Innenteil: Karen Edwards
Fotos Tour de France: Karen Edwards, Brian Hodes
Lithografie: Alphabeta GmbH,
Hammerbrookstraße 93, 20097 Hamburg
Druck und Bindung: optimal media GmbH,
Glienholzweg 7, 17207 Röbel / Müritz

Printed in Germany

ISBN: 978-3-8419-0513-0

ELEGANT